S0-CFO-550

THE NEW
AUSTRALIA

THE NEW AUSTRALIA

Other books by Colin Simpson

GREECE: The Unclouded Eye

KATMANDU

THE VIKING CIRCLE
(Denmark, Norway, Sweden, Finland, Iceland, Greenland)

TAKE ME TO RUSSIA (U.K. ed.: *This is Russia*)

TAKE ME TO SPAIN

WAKE UP IN EUROPE

THE COUNTRY UPSTAIRS
(U.K. ed.: *Picture of Japan*; U.S. ed.: *Japan, An Intimate View*)

ASIA'S BRIGHT BALCONIES (*Hong Kong: Macao: Philippines*)

ADAM IN OCHRE (*Inside Aboriginal Australia*)

ADAM WITH ARROWS (*Inside New Guinea*)

ADAM IN PLUMES (*New Guinea*)

ISLANDS OF MEN (*Inside Melanesia*)

PLUMES AND ARROWS (*Inside New Guinea, a combination*)

SHOW ME A MOUNTAIN (*the Ampol story*)

COME AWAY PEARLER (*a novel*)

Colin Simpson

THE NEW
AUSTRALIA

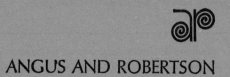

ANGUS AND ROBERTSON

First published in 1971 by

ANGUS AND ROBERTSON (PUBLISHERS) PTY LTD

221 George Street, Sydney
2 Fisher Street, London
107 Elizabeth Street, Melbourne
111-13 Adelaide Street, Brisbane
89 Anson Road, Singapore

Second edition 1971

National Library of Australia
card number and ISBN 0 207 12252 0

Registered in Australia for transmission by post as a book

PRINTED IN AUSTRALIA BY HALSTEAD PRESS, SYDNEY

To CLAIRE,

my wife

CONTENTS

1/NEW AUSTRALIA *Great Hall of the Victorian Arts Centre, Melbourne. Steel columns taper to a magnificent ceiling of stained glass by Leonard French. The hall is sometimes used for formal dinners. The fine new gallery opened in 1968. The Centre is due to be completed in 1975.*   OVERLEAF SPREAD ▶

2/*Blasting iron ore from Mt Whaleback's vast, high-grade lode at Newman in Western Australia.*

3/New, too, is the wider concern of Australians and overseas tourists with what there is for the traveller to enjoy in Australia—such as this peaceful tropical beach at Dunk Isle on the Great Barrier Reef. BELOW: The great monolith of Ayers Rock in the Red Centre glows in the setting sun.

Author's Note

I DON'T MUCH LIKE prefaces, but perhaps a few words are called for about this book's size.

It might be said to be two books in one: a book about Australia's rediscovery in terms of its mineral wealth, and a travel book about this very big country. Although it is primarily an informational book, it does contain comment as well as description and background.

The book could have been more compact if it had been set in smaller type. However, I feel that most readers will welcome the 11-on-12-point text that is easy to read.

ILLUSTRATIONS

Colourplates are listed under *States* and by *plate numbers*, which usually signify a colour page with more than one picture. The 104 colour photographs are located in relation to the nearest text pages. (A), for acknowledgment, indicates that the photograph is not one of the 75 that were taken by the Author. *Acknowledgments* are made on the page following the list of illustrations.

MAPS are by *Josephine Mayo*

Detailed maps begin each State section and some others are on text pages.

Drawing of Barrier Reef marine-life forms, page 46, is by *Claire Simpson*.

Acknowledgments—Illustrations

The colourplates marked (A) are listed by number (and, where there is more than one to a page, by subject). The author and the publishers gratefully acknowledge that these were provided by the following: AUSTRALIAN TOURIST COMMISSION, 1, 7 (coral viewing and tropical fish), 14 (opals), 15 (skiing), 20 (kangaroo), 31 (Ayers Rock from the air); MOUNT NEWMAN MINING—B.H.P., 2; QUEENSLAND DIRECTOR GENERAL OF TOURIST SERVICES, 3 (Dunk Isle), 6 (Hayman Island), 13 (koalas); COMALCO, 4 (Weipa red cliffs); QUEENSLAND ALUMINA, 4 (bauxite stockpile); MACKAY SHIRE COUNCIL, 5 (burning cane); JOHN HARDING, 7 (Crown of Thorns starfish); OLIVE ASHWORTH, 9 (felling hoop-pine); CURRUMBIN BIRD SANCTUARY, 11; LONE PINE SANCTUARY, 14 (tourist with koala); N.S.W. DEPARTMENT OF TOURISM, 17; C.S.I.R.O., 28 (radio telescope); DEPARTMENT OF TRADE AND INDUSTRY, 20 (Canberra aerial), 21, 27 (Hobart bridge), 43 (grape harvest); B.H.P., 25; NABALCO, 37, 38 (alumina plant construction); DR R. K. WARNER, Atomic Energy Commission, 38 (Nabarlek); SOUTH AUSTRALIAN GOVERNMENT TOURIST BUREAU, 40 (Blue Lake).

For special assistance in making it possible to include 56 pages of colour illustrations in the book, the author and his publishers would like to thank, particularly, the Australian Tourist Commission, the Department of Trade and Industry, and the Queensland Director General of Tourist Services (Mr J. Wilson).

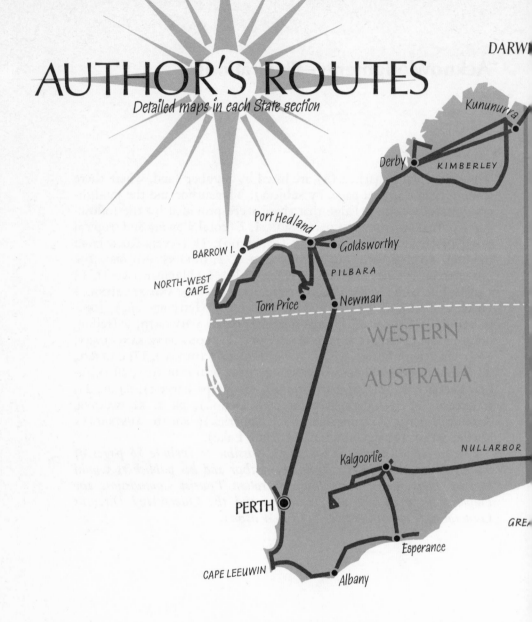

AUTHOR'S ROUTES
Detailed maps in each State section

DARWI

Kununurra

Derby   KIMBERLEY

Port Hedland

BARROW I.   Goldsworthy

NORTH-WEST   PILBARA
CAPE

Tom Price   Newman

WESTERN

AUSTRALIA

NULLARBOR

Kalgoorlie

PERTH

Esperance

CAPE LEEUWIN   GREA

Albany

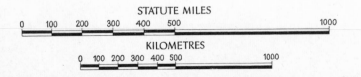

STATUTE MILES

0   100   200   300   400   500   1000

KILOMETRES

0   100 200 300 400 500   1000

THURSDAY I.

CAPE YORK

Gove

Weipa

GROOTE
EYLANDT

GULF OF CARPENTARIA

NORTHERN

TERRITORY

Mount Isa

QUEENSLAND

Cairns

THE GREAT BARRIER REEF

HAYMAN I.

Mackay

Alice Springs

TROPIC OF CAPRICORN

HERON I.

RS
K

SOUTH AUSTRALIA

Wilpena
Pound

Broken
Hill

NEW SOUTH

Lightning Ridge

BRISBANE

WALES

LIAN

Port Lincoln

KANGAROO I.

ADELAIDE

SYDNEY

CANBERRA

Mount Gambier

VIC.

Lakes Entrance

MELBOURNE

BASS STRAIT

Queenstown

TAS.

HOBART

PROLOGUE

The Discovery of What

"THIS IS AN ODD PLACE to begin a book," I thought as I scrambled overside from the big fibreglass launch and into the dinghy. "Nobody comes to Possession Island."

As the Torres Strait Islander rowed for the shore I reminded myself that the book would not be only for travellers in Australia, and that I had what I thought was a good reason for starting it at this island.

It is the island where Cook took possession of the whole of the eastern part of Australia, which he was to call New South Wales, in the name of His Majesty King George III on 22nd August 1770. Possession Island, as he called it, lies off the tip top of the continent. Close to Cape York and south-east of Thursday Island, where I had come to a ten-dollar agreement with Pop Thorpe, who was white-haired and wind-bitten and seventy-four. Pop, who ran the mailboat to the mainland, would veer from his weekly course in the *Mary Elton* and drop me off on uninhabited Possession.

"How long do you want to stay there? Half an hour do you? There's nothing to see except the monument."

In fact, there was something else. The mine I had read about should be close to the monument. I told Pop Thorpe half an hour would do.

And here we were, making for the rocky little point where the obelisk stood. Cook would, surely, have landed on the adjacent beach. But an eminence is a better place for a monument, and it had been placed up above the coralled rocks we landed on, in a calm sea as blue as the eye of heaven.

We scrambled up—a young entomologist named Geoff Monteith who had come aboard at Bamaga and Dick the Torres Strait Islander. Sunburnt grass grew tall and wild round the base of an obelisk that was painfully plain, with just a square bronze plate of lettering that began: LIEUTENANT JAMES COOK, R.N., OF THE ENDEAVOUR. . . . He is written of, even by some historians, as CAPTAIN Cook, but he wasn't, then, in rank, though he captained the *Endeavour*. You could almost hear them gruffing happily at the Admiralty on his return: "Demmed capable feller, Cook. Farm labourer's son, wasn't he? Used to be in colliers. *Have* to give him a captaincy after this voyage."

B

I looked down on the empty beach that made a scallop of white sand near the north end of a bigger island than I had imagined Possession would be, and tried to see Cook—with the *Endeavour* standing off about where Pop Thorpe was hove to and the Redcoats with their muskets for the volley when the flag was raised—landing. The clothes I had seen Cook pictured wearing were much too hot. Knee-breeches and shirtsleeves for the Great Navigator? Great he was. Torres Strait is a labyrinth of reefs, as I knew from sailing it on the old missionary lugger *Herald*, and coral on a fang of rock scraping along the hull makes an ugly sound. And to reach the Strait that bore the name of the Spanish navigator Torres, who sailed through it in July 1606, Cook had to navigate the most treacherous unknown sea in the world, between the Queensland coast and a thousand miles of Great Barrier Reef.

About fifty yards from the monument was a big hole. In the side of this shaft was a drive, a tunnel into the hillside. It did not go in far, but farther than we did. The old mine began to squeak and smell, until it was full of the squeaking and the stench of nested bats.

A surveyor-explorer named Embley had landed on Possession Island more than a hundred years after Cook did, in 1895. Embley had ". . . observed a quartz reef, containing visible *gold*, standing out boldly from the coral. He traced this reef to the highest point on the island [it is by no means the highest point], the point on which Captain Cook had set up his flagstaff. . . . Mr Embley and others worked the reef for some years. The first shaft was sunk where Captain Cook's flagstaff had been planted." Nobody knows exactly where it was planted.

Anyway, Embley's was a rich mine and Logan Jack, from whose *Northmost Australia*[1] I have been quoting, gives official figures for the mine's yield, in four years to 1901, of no less than 2,480 ounces of gold. Which would have been worth a pretty penny then and today would bring over $75,000.

"Had Captain Cook caught sight of the gold which lay beneath his feet when he landed on Possession Island [Logan Jack goes on], could the boldest flight of fancy have ventured to predict the future history of Australia? If, instead of convicts in the southern part of the continent, the first settlers had been gold miners pushing their relentless way from the extreme north and making stepping-stones of one fresh goldfield after another, along what lines would the occupation of the continent have developed?"

Thursday Island, instead of Sydney, as the capital of the new colony? Britain's convicts, who could no longer be sent to Virginia because of the American War of Independence, having to be sent

[1] Notes will be found at the back of the book.

somewhere else, perhaps to a place in Africa that was under consideration before Cook sailed into Botany Bay? (You don't send convicts to
an Eldorado.) Gold, the begetter of greed and violence, bringing
new conquistadores down on an empty Australia before Britain had
time to settle in and garrison it? Outnumbering Americans, perhaps,
Anglophobes to a man at that time, pouring across the Pacific to grab
nuggets with one hand and tear down the Union Jack with the other?
Bombarding warships of the old enemy, France, moving in? Chinese
teeming down from Asia in overwhelming numbers? Perhaps it was
just as well that Cook was no geologist.

To speculate was interesting, but more interesting, I thought, was
the process of discovery and what it amounted to. This, more than
history, had decided me to go to Possession Island, which to Cook
was only a landing-place for a formality of flag-raising, and to Embley
meant a fortune in gold.

Possession Island showed how little, and how much, first-footing
or first-sighting could mean. So did another place a hundred miles
south from it, down the western side of Cape York Peninsula,
Duyfken Point.

Duyfken (Little Dove) was the name of the first recorded European ship ever to come to the Great South Land, in 1606 (six months
before Torres the Spaniard came). From the discovery of this New
Holland by Willem Jansz, commander of the yacht-sized *Duyfken*,
the Dutch gained nothing. Whereas the British gained an immensely
valuable dominion from Cook's coming, a century and a half later, to
the much better-favoured eastern coast.

What Jansz had found was country without a whiff of spice or
other trade to it, poor-looking, malevolent with naked blackmen who
grew no crops and built no houses and, when a boat from the *Duyfken*
went ashore, slithered out of the trees and killed a Dutchman. Coming
to the continent's western edge ten years later, Dirk Hartog was faced
with a desolate shore; and Hollanders after him came upon little but
shoals in the west and swamps in the north. Tasman found the sought-
for route south of New Holland and through to the Solomon Islands,
and though he discovered on the way Tasmania and New Zealand, he
brought back nothing about the continent to leaven the Dutch disappointment with it.

It was left to England's Cook to find the eastern coast and, taking a
boat up the river that enters Botany Bay, report good soil and "as fine
a meadow as ever was seen". Joseph Banks, the *Endeavour's* botanist,
was less enthusiastic at first, but commended the discovery as being, at
least, a land fit for convicts to live in.

Port Jackson, which Cook had named but not entered, Phillip, the
first governor, found to be "the finest harbour in the world", and in

1788 the settlement of Sydney was founded just west of where the multi-million-dollar Opera House rises.

From Sydney, settlement spread slowly and painfully across the backwall mountains, up and down the two thousand miles of coast that comprised Cook's *New South Wales*, and to other edges of what another admirable navigator, Matthew Flinders, called on his charts of its coasts *Australia*.

The continent that was to become one country stretches from snowy mountains through desert to jungle, with the greatest of coral formations lining one coast, the flattest of treeless plains bordering another, the largest of monolithic rocks rising red at its centre. Peopled anew, it came to husband hopfields hedged with English hawthorns in its southern appendage, sugarcane on a lush coast of its tropical north, wheat spread across its westward plains, and more sheep than any land has ever pastured were added to the animals of a country where the native fauna ranged from penguins—through the oddest of leaping marsupials and egg-laying mammals—to crocodiles. Australians made six colonial States into an independent common-wealth, and pioneered ballot-box voting for the better government of a country of one people speaking one language; and, although Aus-tralians may speak it not quite as Englishmen or Americans do, they speak it uniformly, without any regional difference between the speech of a lighthouse-keeper on Cape Leeuwin and a cattleman two thousand miles and more away on Cape York.

To the Cape York vicinity we must, briefly, return.

MATTHEW FLINDERS, who set out from Sydney in 1802 in the *Investi-gator*, rounded Cape York and sailed down its western side and gave Duyfken Point its name. In the bay the Dutch discoverers had come to, Flinders recorded sighting "some remarkable red cliffs" (PLATE 4).

Those red cliffs are the coastal edge of the world's biggest deposit of bauxite, the ore of a metal not known to the world of Flinders. This metal the English chemist Humphrey Davy in 1809 christened "aluminum" (and for some reason the English changed this to "alu-minium"). But it wasn't isolated as a metal until 1825 or marketed before 1850. Flinders, then, can hardly be said to have discovered in 1802 the great aluminum/aluminium bonanza. Or even the red cliffs, which the *Duyfken's* Dutchmen must have seen in 1606.

Into the red-cliffed bay runs a river discovered by, and given the name of, Embley, our exploring surveyor who discovered Possession Island's gold. At its mouth stands now a mining town with the aborig-inal name of Weipa (pron. Weepa). Weipa was formerly a mission station. The man who went out with the Presbyterian missionary and found the site for Weipa mission was J. T. Embley. That was in 1895.

By then the world well knew the metal that was contained in bauxite.

So we might say, as Logan Jack did of Cook: Had Embley known the wealth, greater than gold, that lay beneath his feet when he stood there at Weipa, the twentieth-century history of Australia might have been different.

Bauxite was recorded in the Weipa region in 1902 by a Queensland Government geologist, but the area wasn't prospected until 1947. Assays then and two years later could have been regarded as promising commercial-grade bauxite. However, some more specimens requested from the missionaries proved low-grade, and Queensland's Government geologists shook their heads over Weipa.

In 1950, soon after the war in which Australia was doubtless saved from invasion by American bombers blasting a Japanese fleet in the Battle of the Coral Sea, the official journal of the Victoria Returned Servicemen's League, *Mufti*, said Australia should give the top of Cape York Peninsula to the United States. It could be a "second Alaska" and "provide Australia with an American defence base". Of this proposal to raise the Stars and Stripes over a hunk of the peninsula that could have included Weipa nothing more was heard. Which was just as well for Australia, in view of what happened in 1955.

Harry Evans, a Consolidated Zinc geologist on loan to the Frome-Broken Hill Company, was prospecting the Weipa area for oil. He was also mindful of a memo from his chief, Maurice Mawby, that field geologists in north Australia should "keep an eye open" for bauxite deposits. When Evans (who knew nothing of the earlier finds) found bauxite outcrops near the Embley River he looked for more along the coast, which showed him so many miles of bauxite cliffs that, he wrote: "I kept thinking that, if all this is bauxite, there must be something wrong with it."[2]

It was high-grade bauxite, and subsequent prospecting proved reserves of 3,000 million tons of it. Bauxite has been bringing only about $3.50 a ton. But at that price there was $10,000 million (or, by U.S. count, over ten billion American dollars) worth at Weipa.

The continuum becomes one of history, with the historian writing: "In 1970 Australia was the world's largest exporter of bauxite, and Weipa the world's biggest bauxite mine."

THE NEW AUSTRALIA

Decade of the Drill

AUSTRALIA has been virtually rediscovered in the past ten years, the sixties. The new exploration of the continent—vertical instead of horizontal, geophysical rather than geographical—has uncovered vast hoards of mineral wealth, along with reservoirs of oil. It is no overstatement to say that the country that stepped affluently into the seventies is a New Australia.

Rediscovery of what Australia amounts to has happened before. Two hundred years ago Cook found that the New Holland the Dutch had considered valueless had an east coast worth settlement. It happened again after 1813 when a way was found across the Great Divide of mountains that walled the miserable convict settlement at Sydney, and the Squatting Rush followed to the western sheep pastures. And again in the middle of last century, when Australia became the "shining Eldorado"[1] of those who surged to the first Gold Rush.

Let us not belittle history by equating the deep-boring drill with the wave-cutting prow of Cook's barque, the seismic gear plumbing the earth by sound waves with the great navigator's sextant cocked at the sun; and we do not have to see new *Endeavours* in the shape of floating oil rigs. Yet the finds that have come from probing the down-under dimension of the country (which Americans have long thought of as Down Under) have been tremendous, and today's iron is going to be worth demonstrably more than the gold of all Australia's yesterdays. The new potential promises greater changes in the economic and social shape of Australia than have been wrought before. And it is being said, by authoritative as well as optimistic voices, "The surface has only been scratched."

Be that as it may, look at what has been discovered in the sixties:
► Mountains of high-grade ore in Western Australia. To gain an idea of the value of the new iron mountains, consider this: If all the gold found in all the Australian goldmines from the first gold rush in 1851 up to 1900 could be resold at today's price, it would bring 3,000 million Australian dollars.[2] Two of the new Westralian iron miners,

Hamersley and Mt Newman (which only began operations at the beginning of 1969), already hold contracts to *export* iron ore worth more than $A3,700 million within the next fifteen, not fifty, years.

And this is from a country that, until 1960, banned the export of iron ore because it reckoned as only enough for Australia's own needs its reserves of 370 million tons. An estimated 500 million tons of 64 per cent ore is in Hamersley's Mt Tom Price Mine alone. And Hamersley's managing director[3] has estimated that the reserves of lower-grade (about 30 per cent) ore in the Pilbara region would add up to the staggering figure of *100,000,000* million tons! This is 500 times the known reserves in North America.

In 1971 Australia became the third-largest producer of iron ore in the world, next to the Soviet Union and the United States. (In the mid-sixties it had been in thirteenth place.)

▶ Oil. The Australia that used to import all its petroleum found, in 1961, the first of two commercial oilfields (Moonie) in southern Queensland. Within the sixties four bigger fields were brought into production, three of them offshore from Victoria in Bass Strait and one at Barrow Island off the coast of Western Australia. This oil in 1971 supplied more than half of Australia's petrol requirements.

▶ Natural gas has been found in far greater quantity than the country can use or market at present. Estimated Australian reserves of eight trillion cubic feet in 1969 (considerably more now) had an estimated value of $250 million. Natural gas has replaced coal gas in domestic use in Brisbane and Melbourne and Adelaide—and will in Perth and Sydney.

▶ Bauxite. The pre-sixties importer of the pebbly red ore of aluminium has become the world's biggest exporter of it. Weipa's apart, there are other deposits on Cape York Peninsula, and on the Gove peninsula of Arnhem Land—where what will be the third-largest town in the Northern Territory has now arisen—and in Western Australia development is proceeding of big bauxite deposits on Admiralty Gulf and in the Darling Range.

▶ Nickel. In 1966 Australia was producing not a single ton of the high-priced mineral that hardens steel and makes it stainless.[4] By 1968 it had discovered enough nickel at Kambalda in Western Australia to have contracts for Western Mining Corporation to supply Japan with nickel concentrates worth $64 million. By 1971 this company's estimated nickel ore reserves (which are of higher grade than Canadian) have increased five times to over 17 million tons.

Few stockmarketeers in Australia and Britain will forget the sensational rise in 1969 of the shares of another nickel-finding company, Poseidon N.L.—from cents to $190 on the eve of the company's report, which was to the effect that it had proven ore reserves of four million tons. Further exploration is likely to produce richer nickel lodes than are presently known.

▶ Uranium. Announced as the "world's richest" in 1970, the uranium reserves at Nabarlek in Arnhem Land (N.T.) were down-graded in 1971 to about 9,000 short tons of uranium oxide, worth nearly $108 million—still an exceptionally rich mine prospect, with its potential not fully explored.

▶ Copper. Sixties exploration showed significant new deposits. The great new find was on Bougainville, one of the Solomon Islands that are part of the Australian-administered Territory of New Guinea. Conzinc Riotinto of Australia (C.R.A.) estimated its copper ore reserves on Bougainville at *more than nine hundred million tons.*

▶ Coal. Unglamorous black stuff but very important industrially, it has been second in value to lead as a top Australian mineral export. Huge new deposits are being mined in Queensland, which will outstrip New South Wales as the main coal producer.

▶ Manganese, essential in steel production. The United States is a have-not nation, so is that other great steel producer, Japan. Major Australian deposits of high-grade manganese are, since 1967, being mined at Groote Eylandt in the Gulf of Carpentaria.

▶ The sand minerals. Man can fly into space and to the moon only because rockets and spacecraft can be made of a light-strong metal called titanium. The making of titanium requires rutile, a mineral found abundantly in Australian beach sands. Australia is now the chief producer of rutile, which is also the best of substances for making paint white. Also, supersonic aircraft manufacture requires rutile-titanium. As well, there is Australian abundance of zircon, which has uses as varied as in cladding nuclear reactors and tanning leather and making body deodorants; ilmenite that yields paint pigments; monazite that is a major source of the phosphor in colour television tubes.

The New Australia's mineral-wealth catalogue also includes:

Scheelite that makes tungsten. Tin that has become so high-priced. Antimony that hardens the lead in car batteries and printer's type. Molybdenum of the high melting point, sought by the steel industry. Vanadium, another high-priced steel-improver. Big phosphate deposits await development. Diamonds are being explored for, and have been found. Salt production is increasing so rapidly in Western Australia that exports of salt could soon become worth more than the decreasing exports of gold.

What, then, does the New Australia's bonanzaland amount to? Nobody knows yet.

But what *is* known has been summed up thus: "*Australia possesses the richest deposits of ore resources in the non-Communist world.*"[5]

Who Shares the Wealth

QUESTIONS will already be occurring to the realistic reader, and the first may well be this one:

Q.—How much does Australia get out of this, really? Aren't the big mining developments largely owned by overseas interests, and isn't it to these that most of the profits will go?

A.—Different authorities have given differing answers to this question. Some put the percentage of overseas interests in Australia higher than did Sir Ian McLennan, who is chairman of Australia's largest company, the Broken Hill Proprietary Co. Ltd, when he said in late 1969: "Australian industry has developed to its present extent, and this particularly applies to recent mineral developments, only with the help of substantial financial assistance from overseas. . . . Currently this figure runs at about twenty-seven per cent. It is certainly not overwhelming."

Irrespective of who owns the mining enterprises, their profits are taxed by the Commonwealth Government at a rate that is now 47½ per cent, plus royalties. As the then Prime Minister, Mr Gorton, said in 1970, "We get half the profits from any discovery".

The highest possible Australian equity in the country's natural resources is, of course, from the Australian point of view, desirable. Here the history of B.H.P. itself is heartening. When it decided to set up an Australian steel industry the company was seventy-four per cent overseas owned. Now only about sixteen per cent of its shares are held abroad.

What seems to me the best-reasoned statement on this matter came from T. M. Fitzgerald when he was the highly-regarded financial editor of the *Sydney Morning Herald*. He wrote: "Broadly speaking, overseas capital that is invested in potential export industries cannot fail to be of net benefit to the Australian balance of payments. The more successful the project, the more will the ultimate export proceeds exceed in amount the dividends remitted overseas." He added that there were important exceptions. "The case can be quite different if most of the capital funds are raised locally in borrowed form and the equity is held abroad", and, "The most serious risk in confining the ownership of Australia's great mineral reserves to overseas hands is in the potential conflict of interests on the degree of industrial processing to be carried out locally. It may suit foreign owners to continue indefinitely drawing raw materials from the great Australian quarry." It was up to Australian governments to provide specifically against such dangers, while also recognizing that this was the time for

Australia to, as Tom Fitzgerald put it, "take in all the overseas fuel it can to carry the national workload".

In Weipa's bauxite the Australian shareholding is now ten per cent. It is thirty per cent in the Gove bauxite development: seventy per cent of the money is from Swiss Aluminium. It is high, sixty per cent, in Mt Newman's iron. In the even larger Hamersley Iron project it is less, 11·5 per cent. As against the drain-off of dividends to Hamersley's overseas investors, it was estimated that the company would soon be paying $100 million a year company income tax into Canberra's coffers. And, of course, such companies spend scores of millions on Australian products and labour.

The biggest nickel developer, Western Mining Corporation, is an Australian company with predominantly Australian shareholders. In the oil discoveries Australian equity is about fifty-fifty. As to oil exploration, overseas firms had financed just over half of it.

In March 1970 the president of one of America's largest commercial banks, Dr Gabriel Hauge of the Manufacturers Hanover Trust Company, forecast a heavy increase in American investment in Australian mining ventures.

Australian import of capital had risen to $1,100 million by the year 1968 and in 1971 was expected to top $1,500 million.

Q.—How lasting are these mineral deposits likely to be? Will the iron work out, as the gold did at such places as Hill End and Coolgardie, and the prospering Tom Prices and Newmans of today become comparable ghost towns in twenty years' time?

A.—As to the iron deposits, Western Australia's former Minister for Industrial Development, Mr Charles Court, told me in Perth: "Provided that we do not make the mistake of selling only our highest-grade iron ore—and the plan is to mix the 64 per cent ore with second-grade from satellite deposits—then towns like Tom Price and Newman could go on for ever."

The same could apply to Kambalda nickel; but one can hardly be dogmatic and say that it will. As to bauxite, the vast Weipa deposits are expected to last at least a hundred years. Arnhem Land's known bauxite reserves are less than Weipa's; but one can hardly think that $35 million is being spent at Gove to build the town of Nhulunbuy if there is not substance to the statement of Nabalco's chairman, Mr David Griffin, that it will "in all probability, be there for ever".

Q.—Will the bonanzas of mineral wealth make Australia a better country for Australians to live in, and a better country for migrants to come to?

A.—The short answer is "This *should* happen."

There is the possibility of easy affluence breeding heedless hedon-ism, and of the crassest kind of materialism taking over in a country where bricklayers and builders of garish bungalows are, now, likely to earn more than schoolteachers and booksellers. It is good that the typical urban Australian family man has a house he is paying off, not renting, and that he owns a car (the ratio of car ownership is next-highest to the U.S.A. and Canada) and his wife has a washing-machine and there is likely to be a telephone as well as television. It is not good that he lives in a country where the provisions for social services, medical and dental care and, above all, education fall markedly below those of a much less affluent country about two-thirds the size of Tasmania, which is Denmark.

There is now every material reason why life in Australia for the majority of Australians—for whom life is already very good in com-parison with most other countries—will be better. Hopefully, in-creased spending on education and cultural amenities will broaden the definition of what "better" means: so that gaucherie does not grow in proportion to prosperity, Sydney does not end up looking like a harbourside Las Vegas, the litter of beer and soft-drink cans does not deepen along country roadsides, and authorities do not remain blind to the ugliness that has been created on the urban and rural scene.

As TO MIGRANTS, an unwarranted assumption overseas could be that Australia will need millions upon millions more people to bring its bonanzas out of the ground. Machines do most of that now, not men. It is not to be expected that immigration will increase in proportion to the increase in the country's wealth of natural resources.

There is a small, but growing, school of thought in Australia that discounts heavily the value of immigration and attacks pungently, if not always plausibly, the Australian immigration policy. This group's best spokesman[6] argues thus: Immigration has not served to "fill Aus-tralia's empty spaces": in fact, the rural population has declined. It does not provide any meaningful bulwark of manpower for Austra-lian defence: "Numbers no longer decide wars." Bringing out migrants—who must be housed and their children schooled and social-medical services for the family provided—had cost Australia, over the past five years, something like $1,000 million.

What this anti-immigrationist omits from his concern (and he admits that he does) is the ethical consideration, the moral obligation to extend to others the opportunity to share a better life than their own countries can provide. He also ignores the fact that, in Australia's condition of near-full employment, there *is* a labour shortage. (The Australian unemployment figure in early-1970 was only about one per cent.)

Immigration will not only continue. There was a planned intake of 140,000 new settlers for 1971. The great majority of migrants have been from the United Kingdom and Ireland. Most of the others have come from Greece, Italy, Yugoslavia, Holland, Germany. Those I talked to in the new mining towns were mainly British, and they were glad they had migrated.

American migrants, of whom Australia gets relatively few, appear to be in different case. Many of them go back to the States. This seems to be mainly because the new life means initially (unless they come with capital) a downward adjustment in living standard. The average British migrant doesn't expect immediately to have a car, which he didn't have in England; whereas the American is used to having one, and when he finds that his Australian wage does not allow the hire-purchase payments, because cars cost much more in Australia, then he feels an intolerable deprivation.

Moreover, America to nearly all Americans is the best of all countries; so those who leave it are frequently the chronically disgruntled types. Some are Negro-haters escaping to a white society that they find on arrival has a low boiling-point and does not share their indignations, and has a casual acceptance of laws and trade union edicts that irk the uptight American. In my opinion, Australia could use many more Americans of the type it too seldom gets, the ones for whom opportunity would outweigh irritation.

The population of Australia, which now stands at $12\frac{1}{2}$ million, is expected to be 15 million by 1980. The leading Australian demographer[7] did not expect it to exceed 20 million by the end of the century. Some others think it will be more.

That stimulating British scientist, Professor Fred Hoyle, in 1969 proffered the opinion that Australia already had enough people. He added, "There is grave danger in Australia striving to become a great and powerful nation like the United States . . . it is too horrible to contemplate."

The professor was being, perhaps, more provocative than profound. But the argument that Australia needs population quality, rather than quantity, is a hard one to confute.

It is as well to dispel any illusions that Australia feels today, as it once did, that it must "populate or perish", or that Australia is fearful now, as it once was, of millions of Asian eyes cast covetously on its "empty North", or that an all-welcoming Statue of Liberty has been shifted, in spirit if not in substance, from New York's harbour to Sydney's.

A Change in Shape

THE NEW mineral discoveries are so changing the traditional shape of the Australian economy that it is no longer true to say that Australia "rides on the sheep's back".

Wool, for so long the main export on which the country has depended for forty per cent of its income, was still worth over $800 million in an average year. But minerals exports topped $1,000 million for the year ended June 1970.

"It is by no means impossible that mineral exports could reach a figure of $2,000 million a year by the mid-seventies," said the then Federal Treasurer (now Prime Minister), Mr William McMahon, in 1969. If that increase is achieved—and the 1971 estimate is over $2,600 million—minerals would be worth to Australia as much as all the wool, wheat, meat, dairyfarm and other agricultural produce combined. Iron could be worth more than wool by 1980. So could bauxite.

There would never again be the same dependence on the rural sector. Which was just as well, because overseas demand for wool and wheat in the years ahead is, to say the least, uncertain.

The industry based on Australia's 180 million sheep—14½ sheep to every Australian, more sheep than any other country has, though the U.S.S.R. is now challenging Australia's lead—has always had its problems and its perils. It has survived such disasters as the drought of 1944-5, when nearly a quarter of the New South Wales flocks died, and a third of Queensland's. It had maintained a high place in the Australian economy despite the onset of synthetic fabrics.

The financial year ended June 1971 showed the wool industry in real trouble. Australia's wool cheque, which used to be around $800 million, was about $230 million down on the previous year's $652 million. Production had stayed high, but prices went so low it looked as though, despite all schemes to prop the industry, one woolgrower in five would have to get off the land. Some $200 million in Government aid was said to be needed to resettle these and keep many others in the industry. Flatly, Australia had too many sheepmen and too many sheep, especially in the marginal-rainfall areas.

There is no doubt whatever that man-made fibres will continue to cut into wool's market, not so much because the synthetics are better but because they are cheaper. Costs of production are the crux of the wool industry's problem. These are likely to keep rising, and the price of wool is not. A sword of Damocles appeared to "hang by a synthetic thread" over an industry becoming less and less profitable. But the threat to wool no longer amounted to a danger that could let the lifeblood out of the Australian economy.

Wheat had been grown to such glut proportions, in Australia as in North America, that much of the harvests remained stored and un-marketable. Had China's seasons been better and Communist wheat farming more efficient, and had Australia followed the American line of not selling to the unspeakable Reds, the Australian wheatfarmer's situation could have been, by 1970, desperate: as it was, it was bad. In short, the minerals boost to the Australian economy could not have come more opportunely.

It would be to over-simplify this economy to represent it only in terms of what could be gained from under the ground or grown on top. Unrealized overseas was the growth of Australian manufacturing. Most Englishmen and Americans (and not a few Australians) are sur-prised to learn that Australia has exported telecommunications equip-ment to more than forty countries, and to more than sixty it has exported well over 100,000 of the Holden cars it makes in such num-bers that they dominate the Australian road scene. The 100,000th export Holden was shipped to Thailand in 1967. In the same year ninety-seven Australian-made Ford Falcons were sold to one taxi company in, of all places, Osaka. But it was mainly through big buying of raw materials that Japan replaced Britain as Australia's best customer.

Australia, with one-sixth of its exports manufactured goods, had joined the top dozen of the world's trading nations. Almost as many industrial plants were going up as mines were going down.

"Australia's future could be of dazzling proportions," said visiting Sir Val Duncan, British chairman of the giant Rio Tinto Zinc Cor-poration that was a heavy investor in the country through its sub-sidiary, C.R.A.

There were, naturally enough, some sceptics and finger-waggers, and economists who saw inflation shoals ahead. Only fantasists ex-pected a straight-smooth sail to South Utopia. But prosperity was not just a solid shape on Australia's horizon: a lot of it was here and now.

Nobody was cynical enough to say of Australia what had been said of Brazil: "It is the country of the future—and always will be."

"THE WAVE of the future rides in the Pacific," an American industrial-ist declared after a 1969 visit to Australia.

Impending, though, was a change in the conception of Australia as a Pacific country. Geographically it has never been just that, anyway: as much of its coast is washed by the Indian Ocean.

Into the Indian Ocean, not into the Pacific, a port in the north-west of the continent was in 1970 shipping a greater export tonnage than the port of Melbourne or even the port of Sydney. Port Hed-land, the biggest iron-ore outlet was, only a few years ago, a scruffy

little sun-seared township sitting disconsolately on the shoulder of
Western Australia and making news only when a cyclone hit it. Today it is probably the fastest-growing town in Australia, and epito-
mizes the recent progress of the fastest-growing State.

Western Australia, the largest part of the Australian Commonwealth, with an area that makes Texas look small and where the
British Isles could be tucked away in one corner—and which entered
the seventies with a population still not quite one million—is the State
that will come last in this book. Which is probably as well, to avert
anticlimax.

Western Australia is the "comingest" State. It is where the big iron
and nickel discoveries, and of oil as well, have been made. Where new
towns have sprung up that have yet to get their names onto most maps
of Australia. Where the living standard is rising faster than in any
other State. Where the capital, Perth, has been growing at three
times the rate of Sydney. And only the day before yesterday, or so it
seems, it was the Cinderella State, the Commonwealth's mendicant
that was hardly more productive than South Australia or tiny Tasmania.

"In fifty years, or less, Western Australia will be the most important economic unit of the Australian Commonwealth." So Mr Charles
Court, then Minister for Industrial Development, said to me in Perth
in October 1969. He could be right.

It is in Western Australia more than anywhere else that one is conscious of the necessity to "re-think" Australia. From their schooldays,
eastern Australians have been conditioned to think of the western
side of the continent as afflicted with a paralysing barrenness. So much
of it has been stamped, on the maps, with DESERT and ARID. Wrongly
so, in parts, I was to find. (Mr Court, who had been instrumental in
having these labels removed from his State's cartography said, "Anybody in my Department who puts 'Arid' on a map gets the sack!")

Now, with the new mineral discoveries, we have to reorientate our
thinking about even farthest-inland areas of Western Australia that
get so little rain one would hardly hesitate to mark them "Arid", if
not "Desert". Not only is a huge part of the State still untested as to its
possible resources of artesian or other underground water—and is also
a region of sedimentary basins that may contain oil—but these tracts
that have been thought of as worthless are quite likely to be loded
with more iron and, conceivably, enough nickel to plate the streets of
Perth.

IT IS ALSO PART of the change that some Australian truths have turned
into myths.

The typical Australian in the outback has long been envisaged (and even continues to be pictured on book jackets) as a leathery, bush-bred, middle-aged, cattle-station stockman in a wide-brimmed hat. He is now a construction worker or a mining-machine operator, still in his twenties, who grew up in an Australian city (or he may have grown up in Scotland) and he wears a peaked but brimless "hardhat", a plastic safety helmet. He has come to exist, only in the past decade, in much greater numbers than cattle station workers—who are, in any case, mostly Aborigines or of Aboriginal blood in the north, where so many of the cattle stations are.

Nor is it any longer true to say that bar talk in the Australian pub is likely to be confined to discussion of the merits of racehorses, foot-ballers, cricketers. The Stock Exchange, which used to be the preserve of the manager class, has become the concern of clerks and carpenters. (True, a lot of small investors suffered burnt fingers in the 1970-71 fiscal year.)

Still another change is one that writes "Rubbish!" to a statement about travel in Australia that was only too true no longer ago than the fifties: "Outside the cities and the big towns it is just about impossible for the tourist to find decent accommodation."

Motels have mushroomed all over Australia, and these more than anything else have transformed the tourist-accommodation picture.

Tourism being an aspect of the New Australia that is a major concern of this book, it needs an introductory section to itself.

The Tourist Exploration

AUSTRALIA remains, by world standards, a scarcely-explored tourist country. True, it is much more travelled than it was.

Australians, those of them who could afford the experience, have been great travellers to Europe and, in the last ten or fifteen years, to Japan; and it is understandable that they should want to visit the founts of Western civilization and to see Asian exotica. But they have not shown themselves very adventurous in exploring their own country as tourists.

That attitude is passing, but not passing quickly enough in a country that *needs*, as never before, its people and especially its urbanites to get out and see the New Australia and become involved with it and aware of its challenges. Unless they see for themselves the Australia they think of as lying Beyond the Black Stump they are unlikely to believe that there are places out there where they could live as well—or even better in respect of income and housing—as they live in the cities or large towns, where eighty-three per cent of all Australians live. New towns that can get all the truck drivers and drillers they need, either from the intake of migrants or by the lure of high wages, also require such people as schoolteachers, doctors, dentists, lawyers, chemists, geologists, librarians, accountants, journalists, and maybe computer programmers. These seldom come off migrant ships. They will have to come from somewhere, or Australia's development will be spragged by its new industries and communities not being properly staffed at all levels.

The reason why more Australians will see Australia, and more tourists will come to it from overseas, is a new one: the country is, suddenly, exciting. It has, or is getting, a new image that koalas and kangaroos could never provide.

This image can, of itself, attract the adventurous. But it will not attract their friends if they go home and tell of discomforts and inefficiencies that went hand-in-ungloved-hand with what they found rewarding.

I may sound enthusiastic about Western Australia today, but I was much less so when I was there on two earlier occasions. As recently as 1967, I stopped off in Perth, with my wife who hadn't seen the West, on the way back from India, and we were booked in to what was then the leading hotel, the Adelphi. It couldn't have been drearier. It was like a badly furnished mausoleum where you were denied even peace: we arrived off an Air-India plane at two-thirty in the morning and at seven-thirty a maid banged on the door with cups of stewed tea we hadn't ordered.

The Adelphi has been pulled down. Next to where it was has risen the Parmelia. This is, in its décor, the best hotel in Australia: and for food and service I found it in 1969 almost the equal of Intercontinental's Southern Cross in Melbourne.

Brisbane in August 1971 got its first international-standard hotel, the Crest. Two years earlier its accommodation standard had jumped with the building of one of the Parkroyal Motor Inns, which I heard were very good from friends at Cooks whose business it is to know such things, and I stayed at several. Such establishments are higher in their buildings, their accommodation standards and, of course, in their prices, than the ordinary motels. Some of those are much more ordinary than others, much less hotel-like than a Parkroyal or a Travelodge. [Parkroyal was taken over by Travelodge in 1970.]

It has been claimed by Australian motel interests that the standard of motels in the country is higher than in the United States. This could be true, for one reason: the Australian motels are newer. They incorporate improvements that hadn't been thought of when most of the American motels were built.

However, Australian motels, on the whole, are not designed and

c

furnished with much aesthetic sense. The exceptions are as rare as are Australian motels with any Australian character—which should not be too hard to contrive in a country that had a good colonial architecture.

So many of the motels I stayed at looked as if they had come off the drawing board of the same young architect and were colour-schemed and furnished by his vivacious young wife, who thought that the guests would never find their rooms unless the door of No. 16 was painted pastel yellow, No. 17's pastel pink, and No. 18's pastel blue.

Not nearly enough Australian motels have been granted liquor licences. Few have the little bar most travellers would welcome; some cannot even serve wine or beer in their dining-rooms, which are often the best places to eat in country towns. They soon get licences if they happen to be brewery-owned. The hand of the big breweries lies heavy on the land.

For what it provides, the average motel is not expensive. Tipping is minimal, being conditioned by package-deal coach tourists who figure they have paid in advance all they need to pay: so the bringer of the breakfast tray is pleasantly surprised by twenty cents. These places are porterless, and it is best to travel light. At least, in most motels in "country" Australia there are no stairs to climb; but the two-storey type is increasing.

I stayed at dozens of motels in the course of recent travel, and found them clean and comfortable. Their principal offence is that they tend to blanket roadsides with garish billboards, and they thrust out from their feature-happy façades neon signs so big and blatant that these look as though they were designed at Luna Park, and with the intention of stopping an eighty-mile-an-hour motorist who had defective vision and, also, wore sunglasses at night.

AUSTRALIA, the one country that is also a continent, is as big as fifty-nine Englands. It is about the size of the United States without Alaska and Hawaii. It is half as big again as Europe without the European Russia part.

In a country so big air services are the traveller's boon. Australian airways' route mileage is nearly four times that of the 25,000 miles of railways. Their safety record is one of the highest and their fares among the lowest (about seven cents an air mile) in the world. The two major airlines, known as Ansett and TAA, employ the kind of jetcraft that can fly the 2,000-plus miles between Sydney and Perth, with stops, in under six hours.

Since February 1970 it has been possible to take the modern Indian-Pacific transcontinental express train from Sydney right through to Perth in about sixty hours. Different widths of line in different States

—laid down before Federation when the colonial States were virtually different countries—used to necessitate train-changing at borders. Standard gauge tracks between the capital cities are new. All Australian passenger railways are government-operated. Rail-passenger service has not been of a standard comparable with what airlines provide. It is improving.

Tourist coaches have come up fast as a major carrier of travellers Australia wide. Self-driving stretches with car, caravan or camping-van can be long and arduous, on roads that will not be all sealed right round Australia before the mid-seventies. Mechanical breakdown miles from anywhere may prove highly expensive, if towing to a repair point is involved. Getting stranded on some off-the-highway Never-Never track can be hazardous in parching heat. Northern Territory tourist literature warns motorists never to leave their cars to seek help: they may lose their bearings and perish from thirst—and would not be the first to have done so.

Early in the planning of this book I thought I should take a car (and had practically decided what make and even what colour it should be) and drive myself over much of the route I proposed to cover. This plan I abandoned for these main reasons: (i) I should be travelling in too individualistic a manner, too different from the way most Australian tourists travel when they go more than five hundred miles from home. So, for them, the book would not record a relevant experience, and for overseas tourists it would not be of much value at all. (ii) If I drove I should be cutting myself off from people who knew the country well and could tell me about it, as coach drivers could, and from other tourists, whose reactions to places would be of interest. (iii) Being driven, I should be able to observe better and jot down more notes of the at-the-moment kind that are more valuable than the written-up-at-the-end-of-the-day record. (iv) Driving that precluded air-hopping would take too much time. (As it was, travelling mainly by air and tourist coach, the travel took eight months.)

So, instead of figuring which was the best car to drive I switched to finding out which was the best tourist coach service to travel by. People of reliable judgment in the travel business said, "Pioneer". This is the most extensive of the coach networks, and is owned by Ansett Transport Industries, which has the most extensive air network. With Ansett-Pioneer (and some other carriers) I came to the kind of arrangement that, probably, has saved me from becoming the Southern Hemisphere's best-travelled bankrupt.

At this point I want to repeat something I have said in print before. I review countries and their services very much as a drama critic reviews theatre: the fact that he is given a free seat places him under no obligation to praise the play or the performers. It is up to the "show" to be good. Anyone who expects of a travel writer that he should, in return for complimentary or discounted transport or accommodation, refrain from criticism is, in effect, expecting of that writer that he should write a dishonest report.

I travelled in Australia in 1969-70 about 35,000 miles. Of that distance, 17,500 miles were by air; 14,000 road miles by tour coaches, mainly, and private vehicles; 3,050 miles by rail; and there were some relatively short boat trips. The coverage, though it is wide, is still very selective. Areas and places were selected after a good deal of inquiry and advice as to which were likely to be the most rewarding. The two top-rated areas of tourist Australia, the Great Barrier Reef islands and the Red Centre, are prospected pretty thoroughly. Capital cities are examined but, since there seems little point in leaving Metropolis to stay in Urbanville, not many provincial cities and towns are included descriptively. The book does not pretend to be, as Osmar White's *Guide to Australia* was,[8] a comprehensive compendium of places. It looks at industries only where these are significant to the New Australia, or uniquely Australian, as black opal mining is. To have been right round Australia years before was an advantage when it came to selecting places distinctively Australian.

WHAT IS NEW about travel in Australia?

Ayers Rock isn't new, it is ancient, but there is a whole new plan for tourism in the Red Centre. History is, obviously, not new; and of Australian history there is little, relatively. Appreciation by Australians of what history there is—*that* is new; and the overseas tourist may well find the exhibiting of this history, where the exhibition is good, more interesting than he expects. What is at Swan Hill in Victoria is both new and good—the best outdoor historical museum in Australia. The goldmining ghost town of Hill End in New South Wales is a hundred years from being new—but its being taken over by the State, and proclaimed the first Historic Town, is certainly new.

Some places I went to are not on the tourist track yet: Weipa in Queensland, B.H.P.'s manganese mine at Groote Eylandt in the Gulf of Carpentaria, Gove and Oenpelli in Arnhem Land of the Northern Territory, Barrow Island and Mount Goldsworthy in Western Australia were among these.

Such places can be expected to become accessible to tourists, just as the industrially spectacular open-cut iron mines at Mt Tom Price and Newman are already.

I did not go to those off-track places in any spirit of one-upmanship. They were essential material for a book to be called *The New Australia*. Recognizing this, the people in control gave me access and accommodation. But I am glad to have these places in at the edges of a tourist-Australia picture that is expanding to the extent that any book about the country today is likely to be out of date tomorrow—unless it is a today-and-tomorrow book.

"WHAT OVERSEAS VISITORS, especially the Americans, like most about Australia are the people. They say we're so friendly." After hearing this many times from travel-trade buffs, I still remain surprised.

Not that Australians are unfriendly. But I have found Americans friendlier in America, and have not known Australians to be as hospitable to strangers in Australia as Greeks were to me in Greece. That, though, is not really the point of the matter. It was *Greece* I went to Greece for. Switzerland was, to me, far more fascinating than the Swiss, and Iceland than the amiable Icelanders. Much as I like the warm-hearted Italians, the Venetians never impressed me as Venice did, any more than the smiling Nepalese measured up to the sight of the Himalayas standing white in the sky to the north of Katmandu.

Am I to believe, then, if I don't believe that Australians are super-people, that Australia has so little to offer the foreign traveller that the best thing it has is the Australian? No, I think that when Americans—or Englishmen—say Australians are so friendly, they are being polite, with that politeness they habitually *express*, as when Americans say after a conversation with someone they have just met, even if the conversation has not been particularly interesting, "Been nice talking to you." Australians, who are less polite, have no equivalent.

I also think that American and English tourists, owing to the distances involved in Australian travel and to the short time they customarily schedule for their stay in Australia, seldom see the best things the country has to offer.

I cannot believe that Australians, as a tourist attraction, are any match for the Red Centre, or see why Australian blokes should be regarded (except perhaps by a nymphomaniac) as more "beaut" than Australian beaches. Nor can I see my countrymen as being as exciting as the superb architectural sculpture that has risen on a point of Sydney Cove and deserves a far grander name than the "Opera House".

Perhaps there are two kinds of travellers—people-lovers and place-lovers—and I belong in the second category. A scene-happy misanthrope, as distinct from the type that wouldn't mind missing the Matterhorn so long as he "got to know" the Swiss? I don't *think* so. . . . True, I have never regarded *The proper study of mankind is man* as the truth of truths. But neither have I felt like going farther than Sartre and saying, *Hell is other people. Heaven is other places.*

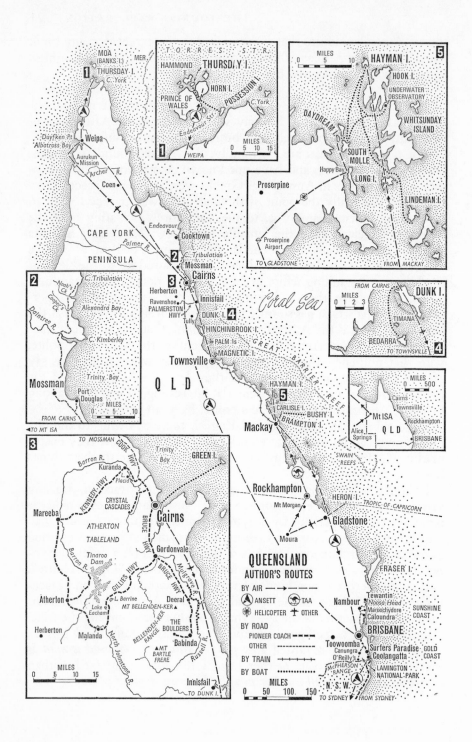

MOA (BANKS I.)
THURSDAY I.
C. York

1

Duyfken Pt.
Albatross Bay
Weipa
Aurukun Mission
Archer R.
Coen

CAPE YORK
PENINSULA

Palmer R.
Endeavour R.

Cooktown
C. Tribulation
Mossman
Cairns

Herberton
Ravenshoe
PALMERSTON HWY
Tully
Innisfail
DUNK I.
HINCHINBROOK I.
PALM Is.
MAGNETIC I.

Townsville

QLD

Coral Sea

GREAT BARRIER REEF

HAYMAN I.
CARLISLE I. BUSHY I.
BRAMPTON I.

Mackay

SWAIN REEFS

Rockhampton
Mt Morgan
HERON I. TROPIC OF CAPRICORN
Moura
Gladstone

FRASER I.

TORRES STR.
MER.
THURSDAY I.
HAMMOND I.
HORN I.
PRINCE OF WALES
POSSESSION I.
C. York
Endeavour Str.
WEIPA
1
MILES
0 5 10 15

HAYMAN I.
HOOK I.
UNDERWATER OBSERVATORY
DAYDREAM I.
WHITSUNDAY ISLAND
SOUTH MOLLE
Happy Bay
LONG I.
LINDEMAN I.
Proserpine
Proserpine Airport
TO GLADSTONE
FROM MACKAY
5
MILES
0 5 10

2
C. Tribulation
Noah's Ck.
Cooper's Ck.
Daintree R.
Alexandra Bay
C. Kimberley
Trinity Bay
Mossman
Port Douglas
FROM CAIRNS
MILES
0 5 10
◄TO MT ISA

FROM CAIRNS
MILES
0 1 2 3
DUNK I.
TIMANA
BEDARRA
4
TO TOWNSVILLE

MILES
0 500
Cairns
Townsville
Mt ISA
Rockhampton
Alice Springs
QLD
BRISBANE

3
TO MOSSMAN
COOK HWY
Trinity Bay
GREEN I.
Barron R.
Kuranda
L. Placid
KENNEDY HWY
CRYSTAL CASCADES
Mareeba
ATHERTON TABLELAND
Barron R.
Tinaroo Dam
GILLIES HWY
BRUCE HWY
Cairns
Gordonvale
Lake Eacham
L. Barrine
MT BELLENDEN-KER
Deeral
Atherton
MULGRAVE R.
BRUCE HWY
THE BOULDERS
Herberton
Malanda
North Johnstone R.
BELLENDEN-KER RANGE
MT BARTLE FRERE
Babinda
Russell R.
Innisfail
TO DUNK I.
MILES
0 5 10 15

QUEENSLAND
AUTHOR'S ROUTES

BY AIR ——→
ⓐ ANSETT ⓣ TAA
HELICOPTER OTHER

BY ROAD
PIONEER COACH
OTHER

BY TRAIN +++++

BY BOAT ••••••

Nambour
Tewantin
Noosa Head
Maroochydore
Caloundra
SUNSHINE COAST

BRISBANE
Toowoomba
Canungra
O'Reilly's
McPHERSON RANGE
Surfers Paradise
Coolangatta
GOLD COAST
LAMINGTON NATIONAL PARK

N.S.W.
TO SYDNEY FROM SYDNEY

MILES
0 50 100 150

QUEENSLAND

What Happens at Weipa

WEIPA is a good example of what happens in the New Australia when a big mining company goes about putting a new industry in the economy and a new town on the map.

The west coast of Cape York Peninsula, where Evans's prospecting in 1955 revealed the huge bauxite deposits, was the backblocks of one of the least-settled regions of the continent. The land, thinly forested with eucalypts, is flat and stoneless: the only boulders are agglomerations of the pebbly red bauxite. The Aborigines who live there have no word for stone or mountain.

Planning had to be from scratch, and total in concept. The two thousand-plus square miles of country that Comalco[1]—the company managing the enterprise—leased from the State of Queensland in 1957 had not even been fully mapped. The sea approaches to Weipa, through Albatross Bay, were so inadequately charted the main markings were still those of Matthew Flinders. Surveys and soundings had to be made, tides measured, currents traced, wind and weather patterns recorded.

The job of locating and designing the port installations went to Dutch consultants, Royal Netherlands Harbour Works Ltd. A scale model of Albatross Bay, an extensive outdoor construction with running water simulating tides and currents, was made at the University of Delft. Hollanders determined how much dredging would need to be done to bring in 40,000-ton ships to take away the bonanza bauxite from the first place their forbears in the *Duyfken* put on the map of New Holland that was considered worthless.

Problems that Weipa's population would face, physically and psychologically, were researched, by the Transvaal Physiological Research Laboratory in South Africa as well as the Australian School of Tropical Medicine. A firm of architects and town planners began a study of what kind of houses would be best for a place with a temperature range of 70 to 95 degrees (F.) and 65 inches of rain that fell mostly in monsoonal December-March. Colonies of Weipa ants were flown down to C.S.I.R.O.[2] laboratories in Canberra, and their appetites for certain building materials observed.

Water supply had to be located, from rivers and underground. Soil samples—as well as ten thousand bauxite samples sent for assay—went south for analyses that showed what trees, shrubs, vegetables, grasses would grow well at Weipa if introduced.

The State provided the town's school, hospital, police station, at a cost of a million dollars. The company spent $4,600,000 on housing and such recreational facilities as the community hall with the club-canteen, swimming-pool, tennis courts, sports ovals, bowling-green. All the town buildings are of brick. From bauxite clay, the bricks were made on the spot. The design of the houses is functional but attractive, the dun-pink colour of the bricks offset with white veranda posts. Roofed and louvred with aluminium and wide-eaved against the sun, the houses are all-electric, sewered, fly-wired. Planned and sited to give cross ventilation, the rooms also have ceiling fans. The houses have lawns and gardens: motor mowers whirr and hose-sprinklers play as in metropolitan suburbs. The women go to shop at a well-stocked supermarket called the "mini-market". (One of them said, "It's just that you always see the same faces there, never anyone different. But I do like it here at Weipa . . . yes, I like it.") Bread came fresh from the bakery. Mail and newspapers arrived daily by air. Movies were shown in the community hall. Men worked six days a week and earned high wages, and bought their beer at city prices.

Five hundred people were at Weipa when I was there in mid-1969. Give it five years (Mike Joll, the personnel superintendent said) and there would be five thousand. That would mean such things as a high school. (It is now built and being used.) But the present town could become just a satellite of a larger one.

By 1974 Comalco expected to be doing more than mining and ship-ping bauxite. An alumina refinery would be built at Weipa. Instead of shipping out ten million tons of the gravelly red ore, it would be turned into about five millions tons of powdery white alumina—a big saving in cost of shipping to the smelters that turn each two tons of alumina into one ton of aluminium metal.

The cost of the alumina refinery looked like being well over three hundred million dollars. It made you blink—money of that mag-nitude being spent where fifteen years before there wasn't anything, or prospect of anything, but a mission with four earnest Presbyterians trying to Christianize and civilize a few hundred Aborigines at a place on the map that was just an unregarded wrinkle of the Australian con-tinent's apparently useless Big Finger.

I FLEW up Cape York Peninsula four hundred miles from Cairns to Weipa. Population and the lush green cultivation of sugarcane dwindle. Jungle with treetops as dense as cauliflower thins to gum-forest interspersed with sand plains the rainy season turns to quagmire known as "wet desert". There are some cattle stations.

The telegraph line to Cape York cuts a thin swathe north from Coen, which was a tin-mining township when I landed there twenty years before; but mining had just about finished. Gold-mining there used to be, from the days of the Palmer River rush a century ago that gave rise to the supply port of Cooktown. In the Big Finger's ninety thousand square miles there were only three thousand whites until Weipa sprang up.

Ansett flew to Weipa six days a week from Cairns, but I was in the company's plane that supplements the airline service, takes personnel in and out, and flies Comalco errands in the north. There was no proper road through to Weipa yet, only a track that required vehicles to have four-wheel-drive, and unbridged rivers made it impassable in the Wet.

The Piaggio's pilot, Les Nind, took a westerly course so that I could see where the "red cliffs" of Flinders began. The Archer River below, we came to the coast at Aurukun Mission, which had a good reputation and survived in a region where Government was taking missions over. Aboriginal children waved up at us. Just north of here the red cliffs began (PLATE 4). Vividly, they edged a turquoise sea that at one place showed the wavering image of a huge shark.

Weipa proclaimed itself in planes of red earth the mined areas had cut geometrically into the dark bushland. Red lines of roads linked these and the town pattern of houses set in rectangles of green. You didn't have to look for the bauxite. It was everywhere, apparently, under the tree cover, under your feet. The plane landed on it.

I was fitted into an accommodation niche in the Weipa pattern. My "donga" (room) in one of the six-room singles blocks looked out at a satin-smooth sea. But the blue between the paperbark-trees was edged with blackish mud and the water was unsafe for swimming. This was June, midwinter in the Sydney I had left, but Weipa has no winter. The days were pleasantly hot with sun, the nights balmy. (November-March would be a different story.)

The manager, Peter McLeod, I found in the late afternoon drinking beer with his workers in the club-canteen. He was a no-nonsense, literate, likeable man of forty-seven who, aside from his job, could do anything from flying the company's Piaggio to arguing philosophically, if that is what we did at his house between drinks until midnight.

Only the families seemed to have any sense of belonging. The singles were itinerants, there to make money for some purpose that was centred elsewhere. Eating (cheaply and well) in a central dining-hall, showering in the ablutions section of each block, doing their own laundry in the block's washing-machine, the single men lived communally and quite differently to the family men in the houses. Of their sex lives I know only that, at Weipa, the singles were discouraged from flying up to Thursday Island, which had a bad name for V.D., but travel was facilitated to farther-off Cairns. There were very few single girls at these towns.

The uniformity in style of building made less for monotony than for harmony, I decided. A company town could look more attractive than other outback towns. Nobody built sub-standard houses. Nobody, because they weren't allowed to, painted the roof grass-green, or "picked out" the front door and the window trims in baby-blue, or indulged a featurist passion for a very fancy front fence. There were no fences. And no billboards or blatant shopfront signs.

MINING BAUXITE is simple, if you have the gear. Big Caterpillar bulldozers tear down the trees. Then the 'dozers get behind bigger-longer Cats called scraper loaders, and together they rip off the couple of feet of topsoil overburden. That exposes the bauxite, which may be six or more feet deep. The Hough machines called payloaders get into this with their scoops that shovel eight cubic yards at a bite. They dump the pebbly red stuff into Haulpak trucks that take fifty tons at a load and charge off down the roadways trailing clouds of red dust from wheels with tyres that stand higher than my six-feet and cost nearly a thousand dollars each.

At the elevated dump station each truck's ribbed pan that looks too weighty to tip, but turns out to be moulded of aluminium, cascades more bauxite down a hillside of ore. What are called apron feeders get this onto a conveyor belt that runs to a crushing station where lumps are reduced to small pebbles that are then wet-screened, and what washes away as slurry is pumped to mined-out areas where it settles down as filling. Trees were already growing ten feet high on some of this rehabilitated land.

The bauxite thus beneficiated (treated ready for refining) at the rate of a thousand tons an hour, then goes onto another conveyor belt that runs up onto the long boom of the stacker. From this it pours onto the peak of the red stockpile mountain that, when the sun is going down, looks like Hell's idea of Fujiyama.

All this mining and mechanical clatter-and-churn and dust-raising goes on miles from the township.

While I was at Weipa the ore carrier *Lake Eyre* came in. Within minutes of its tying up at the wharf, the great boom-arm of the shiploader had slewed into position, the conveyor was conveying, and bauxite was pouring into the ship at the rate of three thousand tons an hour. The ship would sail the same day for Comalco's alumina/

aluminium making plant at Bell Bay in Tasmania. Even more of Weipa's bauxite went to the Queensland Alumina plant at Gladstone. Shipments were also going to Japan.

"This year we'll ship nearly five million tons," Corny (Cornelius) Durham, the marine superintendent who had taken me down to see the loading, said.

Weipa's port, where in the mid-fifties there wouldn't have been anything except a few native dugout canoes, was what C.R.A.'s chairman, Sir Maurice Mawby, had said it would become—the biggest bauxite port in the world.

I had met Sir Maurice Mawby in Melbourne. Extraordinary business capacity seldom goes with such charm of manner as he had; but then he was not at all the usual tycoon. His office wasn't hung with photographs of the huge C.R.A. undertakings he controlled, such as the Zinc Corporation's lead-zinc-silver mine that was the largest at Broken Hill, or Hamersley in Western Australia that looked like becoming the world's biggest iron mine, or what might turn out to be the greatest of all copper mines, on Bougainville: C.R.A. was in everything, from smelting to power-supply, to aluminium and uranium and phosphates.

The pictures behind his desk were sensitive drawings of Aboriginal children by Elizabeth Durack. To one side a very long and large glass case displayed, in front, a superb rock collection of mineral-rich specimens. Back of these were rows of books, old and rare ones, many of them to do with Australian exploration.

Looking across the desk at this immaculate man with the smooth grey hair who had had so much to do with master-minding enterprises spending $1,600 million, and who would soon retire at sixty-five as C.R.A.'s chief executive, I decided to resolve a doubt and said, "I should know this, of course, but—you *are* Australian?"

"I was a barefooted boy at Broken Hill, and used to be able to track a lizard over a rock. And that might be more than some of the Aborigines you'll see up at Weipa can do nowadays."

FOUR HUNDRED ABORIGINES lived at what had been the Weipa Mission until the Queensland Government took it over in 1966 from the Presbyterians, who had neither the money nor the staff to run it properly. Now it is the Weipa Aboriginal Reserve settlement.

Out of ninety adult men sixty worked for Comalco or the company's contractors. They got white-man wages and most were earning around $70 a week. One had bought a Valiant Safari Wagon and several had Holdens.

Comalco had provided, at a cost of some $300,000, sixty-two houses, nearly all with three bedrooms. The houses were of aluminium. Perhaps a dozen had a look of home-pride, with neat curtains and some garden and lawn cultivation. The postmistress was an Aboriginal woman, Elsie Cooktown.

The settlement ran just over a thousand cattle. The land would "grow anything, given water". Papaws and bananas flourished in some of the house gardens. But the manager shook his head when I asked if the settlement had an agricultural future. "Farming is not in them."

The school standard, he said, was good. "I'd say their intellectual equipment is O.K. but they don't get the same educational aids as our kids get."

I also talked about the Aboriginal people with Bill McGuffie, who had been twelve years at Weipa: he was there on the early surveying. A "bushman true" who was born at Cooktown, the son of a Batavia River goldminer, he knew the natives from long contact. As stockmen they were good, but "horse killers".

"They'll ride a horse to death, and then just take the saddle off and walk away. No feeling for creatures. The blackfeller will ignore a dog starving beside him. You've got to get them in school very early to teach them to be any different."

Yesterday Island

I HAD BEEN to Thursday Island twice before. The last time was twenty years ago, just after the war. The Army had given the place a rough time: drunks' bullet holes in the Federal Hotel's ceiling, and the ultimate loutishness of a piano being shoved off the balcony to smash it open to get wire to go trolling for kingfish.

Yet, with less peeling paint and fewer rusty iron roofs, T.I. was still much as I remembered it, or appeared to be as the boat came in from flat Horn Island where the plane lands. From the airstrip a bus lumbers down to the launch, and the trip in takes longer than the flight up from Weipa. Nobody hurries at T.I.

The place had changed little because not much had happened to change it. The new industry, cultured pearls, used the same lugger-diver means of getting oysters to grow pearls in as were used when Thursday Island was the main pearlshell port of the world. Pearls were never the mainstay; pearlshell was, in the days of pearl buttons. Plastic buttons had taken the market of the pearly kind, including those that used to have reddish streaks on the back and were not cut from pearlshell but trochus, a conical shell striped on the outside. As for the trade in *bêche-de-mer*, the long sea slug that made a gelatinous soup the rich Chinese swore by as a restorative of virility—well, you might say, "In China they don't have lich men or elections any more." Industrially, Thursday Island had become an outpost underwater factory of Mikimoto's Japan. I thought I should learn something about cultured pearls while I was there. And did, later on.

The luggers were fewer. I missed the fleet of lean two-masters, prows sheathed with a band of copper against the reef's bite, that used to ride offshore: the most picturesque craft that ever put keel to water round the coasts of Australia. And found myself looking, from the launch, for the wongai-tree. Locally famous, the wongai-tree grew misshapenly beside the road opposite the Federal Hotel, on the edge of the beach that ran down into low-tide mud. It turned out to be thicker in the trunk and leaning more than ever.

The coconut palms that streamed their fronds like tattered green banners in the sou'-east tradewind that blew for six months of the year—they could bend their slim trunks to the wind and spring upright again when it stopped, but not the old wongai that was laden now with its plummy fruit that looks like loquats dyed in burgundy. It was said by the chocolate-skinned islanders, "You eat fruit of dat wongai-tree, you gotta come back to T.I." I didn't recall eating any, but here I was. This time I did eat a wongai-plum, and should be surprised if I see Thursday Island again.

Without the Federal Hotel it would be unimaginable. The first time I stayed there, in 1931, the then proprietor, Jack McNulty, still had the register signed by survivors of the wreck of the *Quetta*. That had happened in 1890. A Royal Mail steamer sailing a calm sea on a moonlit night, passengers serene on the decks or dancing to the ship's orchestra—when, suddenly off Albany Island, the *Quetta* was ripped open by a pinnacle of uncharted rock and sank in three minutes. The moon-silvered sea closed over the lives of a hundred and thirty people, of nearly three hundred who were aboard. Some of the survivors had subscribed to the building of the steepled white wooden church, T.I.'s most significant edifice, the Quetta Memorial Cathedral. It is perhaps the smallest cathedral in the world. It would be a tourist attraction, if tourists came to sleepy-scruffy Thursday Island.

I was given a lift to the Federal by Father McSweeney who was at the wharf with the Catholic Mission truck to pick up young Father Flynn who had been my seat companion on the flight from Weipa, where one or other of the priests went regularly to celebrate Mass. The old bar had been decorated with a rorty mural that didn't worry Fr McSweeney as we downed whiskies before dinner.

In the hotel dining-room, where the two priests had their dinner when they weren't across at their Mission on Hammond Island, there seemed to be almost as many plastic flowers as there were frangipannis and hibiscuses on the island. A flowering vine of plastic garlanded the shiny turtle carapace hanging on the wall, but spared the oleograph of Jesus that was the mark of a good R.C. establishment, run by old Mrs Villalba, her son Joe, and son-in-law Eddie Sue San and their respective wives. To wait on the tables there was a soft-footed girl from Murray Island, which to me was Mer and memories.

MURRAY (I much prefer its native name, Mer or Mäer) is an island I should like to have gone back to. It lies about a hundred and fifty sea miles north-east of T.I. It is at the head of the Great Barrier Reef: one might call it the crown. The coral growth at Mer (says the authoritative C.M. Yonge[1]) grows with a luxuriance "seldom equalled, and probably nowhere surpassed, in any other coral region in the world".

I have never seen, at any of the other Barrier Reef islands I have now been to, coral so variegated, so lovely in form and so vivid in colour.

Nor have I seen, or have reason to believe there exists, any other Australian island as beautiful as Mer. If I may again quote Yonge: "The beauty and luxuriant vegetation of Mer cannot be portrayed in words. Only Samoa [of the Pacific Islands, Dr Yonge later visited] can be compared to it, and the climate of Murray Island is infinitely superior to the oppressive steamy heat of Samoa."

What makes Mer's vegetation so lush is that it is a volcanically formed island. The resort islands farther down the Barrier Reef are, most of them, continental islands, marooned hunks of the mainland; or they are flat coral islands built up by the accretion of sand on coral reef and vegetated by bird-dropped seeds and the odd coconut drifting ashore and taking root. Neither kind can have the fertility of Mer's red-brown soil that comes from lava disintegrating, or such impressive contours as its old crater and its black bluffs of lava rock give to Mer.

The most picturesque and truly tropical and best-coralled island of the Great Barrier Reef that is said to be Australia's top tourist attraction, Mer had never had a tourist on it.

It was certainly the least accessible of islands, and its terrain unsuited to an airstrip; but there were flying-boats, helicopters, hydroplanes, Hovercraft. It must be, I thought, that the Queensland Government would not allow any tourism because the island, which had a population of about five hundred Torres Strait Islanders when I was there thirty-odd years ago as a young newspaperman, was a Native Reserve. A permit was necessary to go there.

Would tourist industry necessarily "ruin" Mer and be to the islanders' detriment? There was practically no industry as it was, plastics having put down the pearlshell and trochus the islanders used to fish with their cutters. The able-bodied young men had had to leave to find work on the mainland: gangs of them had worked on building the new railway lines of the big iron mining companies over in Western Australia. So the young women were bereft of husbands, or seldom saw them. Mer's population that had grown to 1,000 had fallen to 600, and the island was, by all reports, in no happy state. Why not, then, some tourism, intelligently undertaken and controlled? Building and staffing guest lodges (palm-thatched not tin-roofed ones, and aesthetically built to suit the environment), running tourist boats and servicing the flying-boats or whatever—and entertainment dancing the islanders were so good at—would create jobs on the island. The men would not have to go away to earn, the women would be happier, and there would be more of those delightful brown children I remembered.

Queensland's Director of Aboriginal and Island Affairs, Mr Pat Killoran, came up to Thursday Island two days after I did: in fact, it had been arranged in Brisbane that we meet there. Pat, as he became over the first beer at the Grand, was a towering figure with a big voice that expressed dynamically positive attitudes. I got an unequivocal answer to my question about tourism for the island I had thought his paternalistic Department must regard as sacrosanct.

"Yes, we'd allow tourists at Murray. I wish someone would come up with a proposition to invest a million bloody dollars there!"

POLYCHROME has always been the word for Thursday Island. A mixture of races is manifest to any stroller down its sleepy streets. Cingalese, Chinese, Malays, Filipinos as well as Europeans and T.S. Islanders, had for a long time lived there and given their mutations to a multiracial population.

I bought my newspapers (along with the remaining paperback copies of the only novel I ever wrote,[2] which began in the Thursday Island of 1890) at the shop of "Nissi" Mendes, whose father came from Ceylon and had Portuguese in his ancestry. Nissi Mendes left the shop to his wife and ran me over the island in his car to such places as he thought I should see, or that I wanted to see again. Up onto Millman Hill that gives the best view; out to the new-to-me "suburb" called Tamwoy with about three hundred Torres Straits Islanders (who had left their own islands in increasing numbers to settle on T.I.); to the cemetery where I wanted to see if the termites, who build pointed mud mounds higher than gravestones, had spared any of the tall wooden markers with Japanese calligraphy wriggling down them. Yes, there were still a lot of those divers' gravers. Japanese divers like Kinzayomen Kamei, who was the "king" diver of his day and was always called King. Tomo, who inherited the title, found King dead in thirty-two fathoms, out in the Darnley Deeps that took so many of the lives that were part of the price of pearlshell.

CULTURED PEARLS. My notebook says: "Went down to Cape York Pearling Co. and talked to manager Arnie (Arnold) Duffield. They plant a nucleus like half a marble—made from a 'stone' that grows in a Mississippi River mussel—inside the gonadal sac of the oyster, together with a fragment of mantle, the outer part of the oyster's flesh that excretes the nacre we call mother-of-pearl. Operation performed by Japanese experts (who do not teach the technique to others). Not 50 per cent of operations succeed: more than half the oysters die. If they survive, chances are about 20 to 1 against growing a good round pearl. Hundred transplants wouldn't produce, on average, more than two pearls. Live oysters the lugger divers bring in are hung in baskets in the sea until required. Operated on, they're hung again, then put down on the bottom, usually, on platforms that can be raised. In Japan oysters for culturing are grown from spawn; in Australia, not cultivated. Australian oyster is larger, can produce larger pearls. Japan buys them for centrepiece pearls in necklaces. Problem is to match colour to Japanese pearls. Cultured pearls often said to weigh less than natural pearls: actually, cultured are slightly heavier. Experts cannot say whether a pearl is cultured or natural by looking at it. Same nacreous creation. X-ray can tell by revealing the different structure of the nucleus."

Fifteen luggers were employed getting oysters and pearlshell (twenty years before there were nearly sixty working shell). The few hundred tons of pearlshell now produced goes mainly to Germany, to the jewellery trade. In the packing sheds you still hear the *clack-clack-clack* as the sorted shell is tossed into heaps.

THE NIGHT before I left I had some drinks and then dinner with Peter Pinney and his wife, Sunny. Peter's adventurous autobiography runs through *Dust on My Shoes* and such other books as *Who Wanders Alone*, *Anywhere But Here* and *Restless Men*. He was crayfishing at Moa (Banks) Island, where many of the islanders were descended from Pacific "blackbirds" brought to Queensland to provide Kanaka labour on the canefields; and when that stopped they were settled in Torres Strait. (On this island wolfram deposits estimated to be worth $30 million have been found and mining these will probably revolutionize the Torres Strait economy.)

In the early morning there was no sign of life on the Pinneys' boat as the launch for Horn Island chugged out past it with the passengers for the Ansett plane that would take me to Cairns.

4/QUEENSLAND *These red cliffs on Cape York Peninsula are where the Dutch made the first discovery of Australia in 1606, and were noted by Flinders in 1803. The red is bauxite and, at Weipa, has given rise to what became in 1970 the biggest bauxite mine in the world, operated by Comalco.* BELOW: *Bauxite stockpiling—vivid in the sunset's glare—at Gladstone where it becomes alumina (and, at Bell Bay in Tasmania, aluminium).*

Sugarcane farms spread lushly across the coastal plain near Cairns, backed by mountains clad in the jungle Australians call "big scrub".

5/QUEENSLAND

Burning the cane, to get rid of trash and make harvesting easier, is done in the evening and gives drama to the night scene. Near Mackay.

The Tropical North

THE CORAL SEA is a lighter-than-Mediterranean blue, a beautifully paled azure that is the exclusive dye of tropical seas. From the plane, the cloud shadows on it look almost purple. The long coast is a riband of sand. Behind this the lush green savannah of sugarcane spreads its field-pattern across the red earth that goes back to mountains clad in jungle. The range, for the most part, stands back and allows enclaves of coastal plain; at Cairns it puts out a dark paw that barely leaves room for the airport.

The northmost city of Queensland is central to the most richly tropical region of Australia. This is where, an English author once said, "the cream of the Continent rises to the top of the milk".[1]

Cairns does not look or feel like a city, which its 29,000 population is supposed to make it. Palms wave, poincianas deck their feathery green with vermilion glory (in November), frangipannis flourish like the flaunting hibiscuses, bougainvillea riots and crotons glow—but these do not make Cairns the brilliant tropical garden city it could be. It lets its commerce thrust too much against the visitor's eye.

Cairns, nevertheless, is the tourist's natural base. The accommodation we had (Claire, my wife, joined me in Cairns) justified its Sydney recommendation of the Trade Winds Motel.

It was mid-June, the Australian winter month when the temperature at Cairns hovers pleasantly between 63 and 79.

BEHIND CAIRNS the mountains rise two and a half thousand feet to the most fertile plateau in Australia, the Atherton Tableland.

In a continent that is one of the oldest land masses on earth, and so much of the country has been worn down to plain and denuded by the weathering of a thousand million years, this is a region of relatively recent volcanic activity. The lava has crumbled into rich soil. The craters have filled with rainwater and turned into lakes.

There are two ways for the non-driving tourist to get up to it. The best way is the rail way. The little diesel train takes about an hour and once it leaves the flat its fourteen-mile climb becomes that of a truly scenic railway. If there has been heavy rain you may have to close the windows against spray from a waterfall right beside the track. The line took four years and nineteen lives to build through rain-forest on mountainsides so steep that there had to be fifteen tunnels on the way to Kuranda.

We had done this Kuranda rail trip before (Cairns was part of our honeymoon, rather many years ago) so we went up by motor-coach on Pioneer's one-day Atherton Tableland tour. Near the top of the

D

winding road is a memorable panorama of the rich sugar-plain, far below, spreading to the sea. Most of the coach passengers joined the coach from the train, at Kuranda.

Kuranda's railway station, perched above the Barron River, is said to be the most picturesque in Australia. The roofs that are central to the platform are cocked-up instead of sloped-down and their undersides are hung with baskets of ferns and orchids. A traveller's-palm grows on the station and much of the rest of the platform is smothered in coleus and poinsettia—which is not, of course, an indigene, but Queensland surely has as many poinsettias as their native Central America: they are in almost every garden from Brisbane north. The handsomest exotic of the north is the African tulip-tree that hangs lanterns of lit-vermilion blooms in its dark-green foliage.

The coach runs into drier country (forty inches of rain a year as against the seventy-five Cairns gets). The bushland is blobbed with ochre-brown clay anthills. Mareeba appears, the tobacco-growing town, and has little to reward the eye. Hundreds of Holdens are angle-parked in the main street and some cassata-coloured houses attest the Italian-Yugoslav element in the population. Atherton is better, but not better enough. This is a region that yields magnificent timber. Are there no architects who know how to use it?

The landscape near Atherton is superb: fields of maize and the dairy pastures, with patches of residual jungle interspersing a panorama humped with seven knolls that are the cores of seven ancient volcanoes. The coach driver says that the red topsoil is over a hundred feet deep, and one can well believe him, such is the fertility of the Atherton Tableland. The air is cooler up here than it is in Cairns, and summer temperatures are more comfortable, with less humidity.

To establish agriculture and dairying must have involved a herculean task of clearing the "big scrub". The Australian who says *bush* for forest uses *big scrub* for jungle. A downright nationalist in speech, he has scorned exoticisms and tended to give things his own earthy labels. A "flock" of sheep is Pommy talk: the Aussie's word is *mob*. He won't have "herd" either, and uses *mob* for cattle as well. "Ranch" is too Yank, so (he'll make a bleached-out word do, rather than borrow a bright one) he speaks of a *station* or a *property*. Inveterately the under-stater, he used to refer to the mountain range behind Cairns as *The Bump*. If his cattle rush off they don't, ever, "stampede": it is simply a *rush*. There is not a single "gulch" in all the Australian's terrain, but many a *gully*; and no "monsoon" in his meteorology, only *The Wet*. His eucalypts are *gum*-trees. Beverley Nichols once wrote, with a curled English lip, that Australians were the kind of people who called mimosa *wattle*.

John Atherton, the Atherton Tableland's pioneer, was an English migrant from Wigan in Lancashire. He trekked from near Armidale in New South Wales more than a thousand miles to Central Queensland back of Rockhampton, with sheep. Then he pushed on farther north, with cattle. He was also the first man to find tin in North Queensland. When he found his prospector's dish rich with tin, the story goes, he shouted to his mate, "Tin! Hurroo!"—and that was the genesis of the name of the huge dam the coach comes to for luncheon, Tinaroo.

From the Tinaroo Lake Motel you look out over a blue expanse of water three-quarters the size of Sydney Harbour. It irrigates a lot of tobacco land.

ONE OF THE HIGHLIGHTS of this tour is the Curtain Fig. It is hard to credit that a bird dropping a seed that takes root in the fork of a giant tree could cause so much trouble for the tree, and create such a tourist attraction.

The seedling fig lowers tenuous roots to the ground. Gathering strength from the earth, the roots thicken and multiply, until it is a behemoth among parasites that has a stranglehold on the host tree. The tree isn't strangled yet, but its trunk has been curtained by a thick palisade of roots sixty feet high and extending far to one side of it. As the strangler-fig crushes the life out of the tree it feeds on the rotting wood and bark.

The doomed tree rears in an area of Big Scrub that is the haunt of the cassowary, a flightless bird that stands five feet high and is also found in New Guinea and a few Indonesian islands. It has black emu-like feathers ending at a neck of electric-blue skin, with red wattles, and on top of its head is a bony protuberance like a casque, used to butt its way through the jungle. Its big feet have long claws, and it is on record that a youth was killed by the kick of a cassowary. This very shy bird does not appear for Pioneer tourists. Neither does the Golden Bower-bird, which is unique to Queensland and "builds between two trees a wall of twigs which he decorates with flowers. These he is forever re-arranging with his bill to suit his fancy. . . ."[2]

"Tree-kangaroo" sounds odd—kangaroos up in the branches instead of bounding along the ground? All kangaroos and wallabies evolved from animals that came down from the trees. *Dendrolagus*, the tree-kangaroo, for some reason went back to living arboreally. This was not easy because, while living on the ground, his long tail had lost its prehensile character. There are two species in North Queensland jungles, living on foliage and wild fruit. They are dull in colour whereas some of the kinds in New Guinea have handsome bright-brown fur. The forelegs are longer and stronger than those of ordinary kangaroos, and the back legs shorter.

This is also good (if that's the word) python country. Pythons here can grow to twenty feet. Some travellers might prefer to see the kind of worms rooted up by wild pigs. They are red, green, blue, phosphorescent and up to four feet long. We didn't see any of those either.

"Malanda Jungle," says the coach driver. A fine stand of roadside Big Scrub is part of the property of a family who came from England and whose name is—English. Peter English comes out to the coach and introduces his two Aboriginal helpers. Diminutive Davey Douglas, reputedly aged eighty, is spry enough to do corroboree dances for the visitors. The other one, Paddy, shins up a tree with a rope of lawyer cane round his middle. Both throw boomerangs, which they also sell to tourists. They have shed trousers and put on loincloths and painted themselves with white markings for our coming.

Incidentally, the returning boomerang was hardly a weapon, but an implement of sport, a plaything. "Its main use as a weapon is when it is thrown to simulate a hawk on the wing, generally over a flock of ducks or parrots which are being netted by hunters."[3]

WE CAME to the small lakes, the craters that have filled with water, beautifully sky-blue on this sunny day. They are called Eacham and Barrine and lie four miles apart. Both are girt with thick jungle in which are such trees as rosewood, tulip-oak, varieties of other oaks and beeches and walnuts and pines, silkwood, pigwood, cheesewood, penda and cherry-penda, umbrella-trees, lillipillies and the red-blooming flare-tree. And ghittoe, which the wily bushman gathers in rain-time because ghittoe, which he calls "kerosene wood", will burn wet. It is an excellent wood for fishing-rods and archery bows and during World War II it made propellers for Air Force crashboats, and wore like metal. Beside Lake Barrine stand enormous "twin" kauri-trees, twenty feet in girth and both over 135 feet in height.

Stories that the two lovely lakes are interconnected would appear to be nonsense; but no one has yet explained satisfactorily why, come deluge or dry, their water levels remain almost constant.

The coach does a round trip and descends to the coastal plain by the Gillies Highway, which was one of the most difficult of Australian roads to construct and has two hundred and forty bends in twelve miles. We stopped, in the late afternoon, to look down on another panorama of the sugarfields (PLATE 5).

"A fine view now," the driver said, "but in a few weeks time you won't be able to see the Mulgrave Valley for smoke. They'll start burning the cane about four o'clock." (PLATE 5.)

In Sugarland, fire is put through the cane to burn out the trash and reduce the leafage, to make it easier to cut: it also ousts the snakes and rats. The fires that make the night dramatic are lit in the late afternoon because the wind tends to drop then, and the cane must be cut as soon as possible after the burning or it deteriorates. So in the morning the cutting begins—but only about ten per cent of the harvesting is these days done manually, with gangs of hard-muscled canecutters (like the two in Ray Lawler's play *The Summer of the Seventeenth Doll*) slashing down the burnt canes with long hooked knives and getting blackened all over in the process. Mechanical cane-harvesters have largely replaced them.

Planting has also been mechanized. Machines chop the cane into short lengths, dip each in a mercurial solution to ward off nematodes and insects, plant the cane, give it a dose of fertilizer and tamp down the earth on top. It grows as high as sixteen feet and, in June, some varieties were in flower, or perhaps it would be better to say in "plume". The arrowy plumes are a silver-beige with a hint of lavender, and very lovely such fields are, especially when they are seen against the sun in the early morning or when the sun is going down, their delicate tops glistening.

THE TOURIST in North Queensland should travel, if he can, another spectacular road—two of them, in fact, but the Cook Highway I'll come to. The Palmerston Highway climbs the Palmerston Range, through some magnificent Big Scrub, back of Innisfail. Both road and range bear the name of an insufficiently known Australian—one who, in my view, has a better claim to fame than murderous Ned Kelly of the iron hat—Christie Palmerston.

A Victorian farmer's son who went as a young man to the Palmer River goldfields, Christie Palmerston stayed in the North, living in the jungle and with the Aborigines. He became a superb bushman, and has been called the "Prince of Pathfinders" and "Queenland's Robin Hood". Neither title sits well on him, but it is hard to think of one that would.

Christie Palmerston had done unlawful things, but no policeman wanted to arrest (even if he could find) the bushman who saved a sick prospector's life, tracked down and rescued men who became lost in the jungle, explored to their headwaters half a dozen rivers, found the Upper Russell goldfield, guided two hundred Chinese through the jungle to it, discovered the Daintree Pass and blazed the track from the Herberton tinfield down to where Port Douglas was established. And when the government wanted a trail cut down the range to Innisfail, Christie Palmerston cut it. The charges against him remained in police-station pigeonholes and he came to the respectability of a government job—which he might have ended his life in, if he hadn't been the Christie Palmerston who went to Malaya and died of fever there, in 1893, in the jungle.

DEERAL, at the mouth of the Russell River, thirty miles south of Cairns, is the second-wettest place in Australia, with an average of 172 inches to Tully's 179.

Not too surprisingly, then, when we went on a Pioneer coach-launch trip to the Mulgrave-Russell Rivers it was raining. Not heavily enough, though, to obscure the beauty of the cruise—riverbanks massed with such rain-forest as only such rainfall and tropical heat can raise: a multi-green upsurge of trees overgrowing each other and tangled with vines, an arboreal host stopped by the river and hanging out over it. Reflections there were, but subdued by the day's heavy overcast. On a sun-bright day it would all be double-imaged in the water's mirror. Round-leaved cotton trees, related to hibiscus, in their flowering season deck the jungle with yellow blooms. Spanish-moss beards lichened limbs of high trees that tufts of the spindly Alexandra-palm wave over in triumph of their struggle up to the light. The mangroves send long aerial roots spiking out of the mud. Rain pits and rings the river and dances on it.

Here and there the jungle breaks and you see cane farms coming through to the river's edge. Arthur Shepherd, who runs the big launch, has protested against this scrub-cutting that, if it goes on, will ruin the rivers scenically. But, he says, his objections have been passed from the Department of Tourism to Lands, to Forestry and back to Lands, and on to the legal eagles who point to a loophole in the law that is supposed to preserve a two-chain belt along the banks, but doesn't.

It is much the same with crocodiles, he says. Tourists like to see wildlife and a few years ago you could count on seeing at least one croc. on every trip. "A big fellow used to sit on a sand spit and take no notice when I came right alongside him." The professional shooters have been allowed to take just about every croc. in the two rivers.

After lunch on the launch we get back on the coach and go to a place called The Boulders. Here you walk half a mile along an easy, natural track through fascinating rain-forest to where a creek cascades over some sculptural boulders.

Another tour includes a walk to what are called, enticingly, the Crystal Cascades. Cairns has such notably good, soft water that tourist ships used to carry it back to Sydney to hairdressers who wanted it for rinses.

The Boulders walk is better, but along the Crystal Cascades track I was glad to have pointed out by the coach-driver who came with us a bright green leaf with a serrated edge, which is *not to be touched*. It is of the stinging-bush. Horses that eat it go mad and have to be shot. The underside of this innocuous-looking leaf is covered with minute hooks, and the pain these inflict is intense.

"You must see the Daintree country," said Paul Kamsler of the Trade Winds Motel. "No, you can't take one of the tours—they only go as far as Port Douglas and Mossman. Anyway, you need a four-wheel-drive vehicle. We'll lend you one."

I said that I'd like to go with someone who knew the country.

"I'll get on to Harold Peake, our doctor. He's got a Land Rover."

Dr Harold Peake and his wife Deirdre picked me up early, and I liked them immediately. We sped up the Cook Highway that hugs the shore past some pleasant beaches. With the sugar-town Mossman seventy-five miles behind us, we came to the Daintree River. It is a fine jungle-bordered stream, on which a boat was stalking a reportedly enormous crocodile. The punt came and we crossed and proceeded to a point where four-wheel-drive was engaged and even Dr Peake got slightly lost. At an isolated house an old man who kept whanging his stick at barking dogs put us onto the track that crossed Cooper's Creek and then, after a climb to a superb panorama, Noah's Creek. We went along a half-made road bordered by luxuriant jungle. The only habitation for miles was a beach-fronting hut admirably built of thin tree-trunk lengths complete with lichened bark. It was empty, and the builder had not thought it necessary to put on a door. Beyond that we shortly ran out of negotiable road. Deterred by a stretch of muddy water that appeared endless and of uncertain depth, we returned to the beach near the admirable hut.

Big-leaved trees cast their shadows on a beach that was humanly untracked but was, nevertheless, patterned. The patterning was elaborate and all done in bead-sized balls of sand, by small crabs. A jungled mountain rose behind this beach and from its trees bright blue butterflies fluttered down and courted our picnic cold-box, which was bright blue. Our beach looked out to a photogenic islet. At the distant north end was Cape Tribulation, so named by Cook, because "here began our troubles" when the *Endeavour* was holed on a reef.

This was much too idyllic a spot to think then, but I've thought it since: What a man was this Cook who, having sailed half-way round the world into unknown seas could record that here his troubles "began", in a sailing ship of 366 tons, a converted coal-boat half the size of one of the Sydney ferries that ply to Manly. Holed badly, the *Endeavour* was saved by being "fothered", and only one seaman aboard, John Monkhouse, knew the technique of fothering: oakum and chopped wool were bagged into a sail, lightly sewn so that when the sail was drawn over the hole the suction of the water broke the threads and pulled the oakum-wool into the hole and plugged it. By this esoteric piece of seacraft was the *Endeavour* saved for beaching and repair at what is now Cooktown—and Cook preserved, and Australia settled when it was.

ON THE WAY BACK from the beach that is in Alexandra Bay, after recrossing the Daintree and passing through some fine sugarland that comes right to the edge of Mossman, we turned off the Cook Highway four miles to Port Douglas.

Port Douglas began in 1877, before Cairns did; but Cairns got the railway, and the miners' supply port declined down to a fishing place that now lived largely off tourism, and shipped shell jewellery all over the world. It looked sleepy but had, on the bay side, a couple of good restaurants up on the hill that gave a glorious view across the sea to mountains in the Daintree region. The American Consul in Brisbane, who was staying at our motel in Cairns, particularly recommended the food at a restaurant called Island Point.

As you drive in there is a notice: TO PORT DOUGLAS BEACH, *the Best Beach in the World*. It is certainly one of the longest, and the sand is hard enough for cars to run on it. For me, the world's best beach would need to have surf. No North Queensland beach has, because the Great Barrier Reef bars the rollers coming in.

The Barrier Reef Islands

CORAL. What is it? A dictionary defines it as a hard calcareous substance, and an encyclopaedia as an order of marine animals. Both are right—even if it is confusing to think of corals as creatures that build houses of coral.

There are other coral creatures that do not build stony little dwellings. These are "soft" corals, and there are many soft corals as well as hard corals round the Great Barrier Reef Islands. They are of the class called *Alcyonaria*, a nice word and we could use it for the soft corals but for the fact that, although all soft corals are Alcyonaria, all Alcyonarian corals are not soft. Some soft corals are very beautiful; others are scungy things that look like slimy brown rubber. There are some rather ugly hard corals, too, but many are enchanting in form and colour.

People used to speak, and some still do, of the marvels wrought by the coral "insect". The creature is an animal, a polyp. The polyp is, in form and behaviour, a sea anemone (which one guide used to pronounce as Annie Moan). A polyp may be only as big as a pinhead, and a microscope necessary to see that its mouth is ringed with flower-like tentacles. As all sea anemones are, the tiny animal is a carnivore.

The tentacles are equipped with batteries of "nettle-cells"—minute harpoons that shoot microscopic shrimp-like creatures and paralyse them with the poison on the barb.

The "true" coral polyp builds by taking in calcium carbonate from the seawater, secreting this as a limestone substance and excreting it through its skin. This hardens into what we might call a cup, tube, sarcophagus or house: it is usually called the creature's skeleton, but it is a "skeleton" mainly on the polyp's outside. It is more of a "house".

Most coral creatures are very small and live in colonies of thousands with their houses (technically *corallites*) cemented together, and they build on top of the houses of polyps that have died. They multiply, profusely, by laying eggs and exuding fertilizing spermatozoa. Some bud and split themselves in two.

There are at least 350 varieties of coral in Great Barrier Reef waters. Some of the hard-coral kinds create formations like staghorns, brains, fans, miniature organ-pipes or hands with a hundred fingers. These corals are of many colours, and of colours different when the polyps are out to when they are in.

Corals are not exclusive to tropical seas. Cup corals grow on the south coast of England. Masses of branched corals have been dredged up from 300 fathoms (1,800 feet) in fjords in Norway. Corals even grow in Arctic and Antarctic seas. But only within the tropics (and at a few places outside them that have warm currents) are there coral *reefs*.

Reef-building corals live only in waters that are not colder than 65°F. and at depths the light can penetrate to, less than thirty fathoms.

THE GREAT BARRIER REEF that lies off the Queensland coast of Australia is not only the largest coral formation in the world. It qualifies for inclusion in any listing of the world's eight natural wonders. But that does not answer the question: What is it?

Most coral reefs are either isolated growths or reefs that fringe the shores of, mainly, islands. Barrier reefs are at a distance from the land. New Caledonia, Fiji, the Society Islands, the eastern end of New Guinea and some islands to the north of it, all have barrier reefs, and there is another round some islands between Madagascar and Africa. But their extent is nothing like that of the Great Barrier.

The Great Barrier Reef's extent depends on what the term signifies. If it means that squiggly line appearing on most maps, stretching from off-Bundaberg to up near the Gulf of Papua, then practically all the people who say they spent their holidays on the Great Barrier Reef are liars: they were never on it.

The Great Barrier Reef isn't one reef, but very many. We might think of this coralline shelf of the continent as a veranda on the north-east of the Australian house. An underwater veranda, with a lot of seats on it, the islands. If the coral reefs are thought of as veranda-boards, then a lot of the boards are missing. The veranda's edge is broken too: the Great Barrier Reef is not continuous, and in about a dozen places the channel breaks are big enough for shipping to get through. But, broken-edged or not, it is still a rampart against which the Pacific rolls in from depths of as much as 6,000 feet to make a flurry of white along barrier reefs that are often said to enclose a "lagoon", where the depths are seldom more than 200 feet. It is less a lagoon than a labyrinth.

It is often said that the Great Barrier "covers an area of 80,000 square miles"—which is quite an area: England's-plus-Scotland's, close to Victoria's and a bit more than the U.S. State of Nebraska's. The outer reefs *enclose* about that area.

However, it is still a marvellous veranda, and one may wonder how Australia, uniquely, came to have it. What seems to have happened is this—and the theory put forward by Evolution's great man, Charles Darwin, in 1842, has more than held its own against other theories: the east coast of Australia slowly subsided, at a rate that the reef-building coral was able to keep pace with. That there was subsidence is beyond doubt. All the high islands in the Great Barrier Reef region are marooned mountain tops.

Of the six hundred islands, and islets, about two hundred are coral-reef creations, coral cays. Two sizeable and well-vegetated cays are among the seventeen islands that have been developed for tourists. One cay, the farthest north, is Green Island; the other, the farthest south, is Heron Island. I propose to do a north-south rundown on the islands I went to, so Green will come first.

But before proceeding to what we may fairly call the Barrier Reef Islands let me make a couple of points:

(i) At first sight the coral reefs, as they appear at low tide beyond the beaches of those islands, are disappointing. The fact that you can see the coral protruding means that most of it is dead.

(ii) Close exploration of these reefs will usually reveal many wonders and beauties in the deeper pools and over the edge of the reef.

(iii) Unless he or she has diving gear, the tourist will not see coral gardens and tropical fish as these appear in magazine colourplates and movies taken by underwater photographers. However, the non-diver can still see some good coral by going in glass-bottomed boats, when the sea is smooth and the weather sunny.

(iv) Most tourists—there is nothing derogatory about the word: it simply means people who tour and, by and large, they are superior people to the people who don't tour—most people, then, are not avidly interested in nature: if they were, cities like New York and London and Tokyo would not exist. The majority of Barrier Reef Islands visitors are primarily winter-escapers to warmer climes, vacationers whose idea of relaxation is lazing at the swimming-pool, suntan seekers, social gatherers, "fun" people. Old or young, this majority take the view that damned if they're going out on that mucky-looking reef expanse and risk coral cuts that are hard to heal on the chance of seeing aquarium-type fish in coralled pools and finding a bailer shell and a cowrie.

Although I do not feel at one with these people, I am glad they have that attitude. More than 300,000 tourists a year are going to these islands, and their reefs are being crunched over by rather too many feet as it is. If the majority-people left the swimming-pools and the bars and were as concerned with reefing as they are with lazing, afternoon napping and having amours, then the reefs would have too many people on them and be a mess.

In token of gratitude, I propose to review the Barrier Reef Islands with these people in mind. My personal preferences and prejudices will inevitably show through, but I hope to give an idea of how well the island resorts cater for the people they cater for. Readers, of whatever stripe, who wonder which island to go to should be able to identify themselves as Dunk Isle people or Daydream people, Hayman people or Heron people, South Molle swingers or Brampton-for-me types.

Two QUESTIONS may well be worrisome to any intending Barrier Reef-goer who reads the newspapers: (i) are all these reefs being devastated by the starfish called the Crown of Thorns? and (ii) what about cyclones such as the one that hit the Whitsunday Group islands (Hayman, Daydream, South Molle) in January 1970?

As to (i) the 1970 answer is "No—but. . . ." The Crown of Thorns starfish (*Acanthaster plancii*) which grows to over twenty inches across, feeds on the live coral (PLATE 7). Covering coral with its up-to-twenty arms, the starfish extrudes its stomach and ejects juices that dissolve the living coral. Its depredations, on reefs off Cooktown, were first reported in 1959. In some years before 1968 it destroyed about seventy-five per cent of the live coral at Green Island near Cairns. This devastation was checked by divers and boatmen gathering up and destroying at least 25,000 of the starfish. When I was at Green Island in mid-1969 one of the boatmen who had been engaged on this task said he had not seen a Crown of Thorns for about eighteen months, and he pointed out live coral that had regenerated.

Other reef infestations reported in 1969 were, in the north, off Magnetic Island and, in the south, below Heron Island. Neither at Heron Island nor anywhere else did I see one specimen of the Crown of Thorns. But that proves nothing. The Green Island infestation is evidence enough that the starfish can be of plague proportions and do enormous damage to the coral.

Although a professor of the University of Sydney who had done a geological survey of the Great Barrier Reef said that he did not believe it was in danger of destruction "by man or any other creature", a University of Queensland zoologist, Dr Robert Endean, warned repeatedly that the Crown of Thorns was a serious menace and not enough was being done to combat it. Government spending on the problem in 1969 was $30,000—not much alongside the $400,000 the United States was spending to stem Crown of Thorns infestation in its trust territories in Micronesia.

As to (ii), cyclones are not normally a hazard in the Barrier Reef islands. When they do occur it is in the months January-April. "During the first four months of the year these cyclones appear to have their origin in the neighbourhood of the South Pacific Islands. . . . However, only a small percentage reach Australia, the majority recurving their path to the west of New Caledonia."[1]

Damage to tourist installations on the Whitsunday islands wrought by Cyclone Ada on 17th-18th January 1970 was exaggerated in early news reports. Considerable havoc was wrought, but the buildings on Daydream Island were not "flattened", nor were those on Hayman Island "two-thirds destroyed". Trees and other vegetation suffered badly. These resorts were operative again by June–August.

GREEN ISLAND

SIXTEEN MILES off Cairns lies a coral cay, thirty-two acres in extent, that Cook called Green Island because it was "low, green and woody". Its being little more than an hour away by launch makes Green very popular with day-trippers. You can stay there, as we did—though only overnight—at the Coral Cay Hotel, which has about thirty reasonably priced cabins, some with private facilities, in a picturesquely palmy setting. The dining-room wasn't good.

At the wharf I talked with Blake Hayles whose family has long run the launch services to Green and also to Magnetic Island, and they own the hotel on Green. He said he had spent $1,100 getting rid of the Crown of Thorns starfish, paying ten cents apiece for them.

It was a bad day, raining. The island on the horizon grew, as we approached, out of a grey sea. It was still the green *cabochon* I remembered, and the sand beach on the north side still as white, but as bereft of bathers as the sky was of the sun that, when it shone, made the water specially blue and translucent. The long finger of jetty was longer than ever.

With other raincoated tourists we huddled in under the canopy of one of the glass-bottomed boats—launches with two long rectangular boxes you sit round and peer down through the glass. The boatman knew exactly where the best coral was, but when we were over it the coral was anything but spectacular: there was no sun to light the depths. There was not much colour apart from some branching heliotrope and blue staghorn coral which, the boatman said, had grown in the year and a half since the Crown of Thorns was conquered. He said the coral was "regenerating nicely".

The rain lashed into the boat on a strong sou'-easter. Claire, who had not been to Green or any coral island before, said, as we returned to the jetty, "Is that all? I thought—well, I expected that the coral would be more than it is . . . more like Kenneth Slessor's verse."

> *Flowers turned to stone! Not all the botany*
> *Of Joseph Banks, hung pensive in a porthole,*
> *Could find the Latin for this loveliness,*
> *Could put the Barrier Reef in a glass box*
> *Tagged by the horrid Gorgon squint*
> *Of horticulture. Stone turned to flowers . . .*[2]

Half an hour later my wife was exclaiming over the coral she was seeing, and I was taking photographs of the fish swimming in and out of it. That butterfly cod—its spines were poisonous, yes, but wasn't it gorgeous! As though disdaining to use the lacework tail for swimming, it fanned its striped body through the water with pectoral fins that trailed from its side like red-and-white plumes. Could there be anything else so baroque in all the tropical seas? And, if I wanted a picture of the wrasse, here he was, coming out from behind that waving pink-and-green soft coral! How different was his design from the butterfly-cod's, German-contemporary as against Renaissance. And his body's colour like crème-de-menthe, in the bottle.

> *. . . put the Barrier Reef in a glass box*

Yes, we had gone to the island's aquarium, called Marineland.

What would you see, though, if you went down, rubber-suited and flippered like a frog, off the end of the jetty? At the end of the jetty is the Underwater Observatory. You enter through a shop stacked with all the shell-made things you have never wanted to own and dyed pieces of dead coral in plastic boxes, and go down stairs into the big cylindrical tank with portholes. Outside the portholes the coloured fish—no butterfly-cods but many another kind—are swimming at eye level through the stacked-up coral. The fish move past because move they must in their endless quest of food—some of which is provided daily by the Underwater Observatory's proprietors, two intrepid hunting-and-diving-type Australians, Vince Vlasoff and Lloyd Grigg.

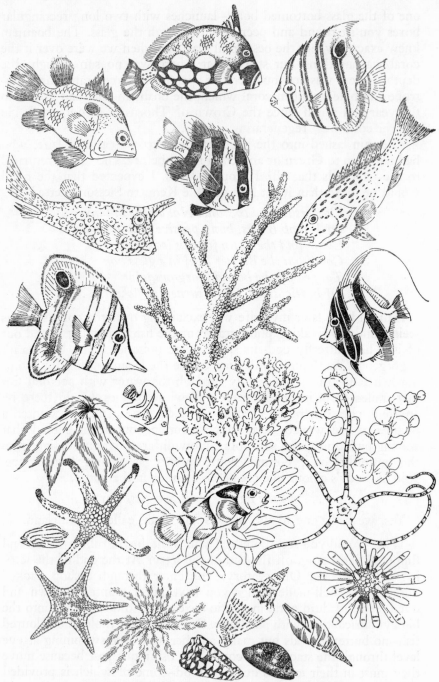

SOME BARRIER REEF MARINE-LIFE FORMS

—Drawing by Claire Simpson

They built the huge tank at Cairns and towed it out and anchored it with railway-line steel driven eight feet into the coral.

There is a cinema on Green Island. The programme never changes, nor should it. This theatre screens only, and exclusively, several films made by Noel Monkman. He was so good that much of the under-water photography that won an Academy Award in 1952 for the Hollywood film *The Sea Around Us* was Noel Monkman's. Nobody else got such shots, not only of the beauties, but of the grim realities, such as schools of trevally rounding up, like a wolf-pack, shoals of sardines. Noel Monkman had died, aged seventy-three, the month before we came to Green Island.

Noel and Kitty Monkman were akin, though different in type, to "Beachcomber" and Bertha Banfield of Dunk Island or, as Cook called it, Dunk Isle.

DUNK ISLE AND BEDARRA

FROM CAIRNS we flew in thirty-five minutes to where, in E. J. Ban-field's words, "Two and a half miles off the north-eastern coast . . . is an island bearing the old English name of Dunk."

Banfield, largely because of his appreciation of the great navigator, joined with officialdom in retaining the Cook-given name of Dunk rather than the native name of Coonanglebah. So says Alec H. Chis-holm in his introduction to a new edition of *The Confessions of a Beachcomber*.[3]

Edmund James Banfield, who was born in Liverpool, came in infancy to Australia where his father founded a newspaper in Mary-borough, Victoria, on which the son worked. He subsequently over-worked, to a state of nervous exhaustion, as a journalist on the Towns-ville *Daily Bulletin*. After looking at a number of islands, he selected Dunk to withdraw to, with his wife (they were childless) in 1897, when he was forty-five. As he puts it, ". . . a weak mortal sought an unprofaned sanctuary—an island removed from the haunts of men—and there dwelt in tranquillity, happiness and security" for twenty-five years. His *Beachcomber* book (1908) was acclaimed overseas as well as in Australia, and he followed it with *My Tropic Isle*, *Tropic Days* and the posthumously published *Last Leaves from Dunk Island*.

Banfield died on the island, aged seventy-one, in 1923, and his wife Bertha was alone for three days before a passing ship saw her distress signal. They are buried together on Dunk, and their rustic grave has the simple dignity of lichened stone that blends with the lichened rain-forest. The epitaph of the Beachcomber who went aside from the world to live is from Thoreau: *If a man does not keep pace with his companions, perhaps it is because he hears a different drummer. Let him step to the music which he hears.*

Alec Chisholm, the author and ornithologist who had spent some time on Dunk with Banfield, returned in 1967 to unveil a portrait of him and was "disturbed by the thought that 'development' may have grievously affected the once-tranquil island". He found that the Avis Air Charter Company, the lessees of 360 acres, had developed the tourist portion in a way that merged with the 6,000 other acres of National Park.

The saddle-backed island that rises, jungle-clad, to nearly nine hundred feet may be only six square miles but it looks larger. Beyond the west-end curve of Brammo Bay there is nothing at all of habitation, nothing but rain-forest growing down to virgin shoreline. ters at the back.

At the bay's edge we could see, as we came in, a long russet-brown wooden bungalow, or so it appeared. This contained two luxury suites that had been given the lordly Dunk names, "Earl of Halifax" and "Earl of Sandwich". The manager, Francis McIlree, who met us at the airstrip, said that he had intended us to have one of them. But the two couples who occupied both had become enamoured of the island and had said, "Oh, no, we're not getting out. We're staying another week!" So we were accommodated in plainer quarters.

By the 1971 season Dunk had eighteen luxury suites (its accommodation capacity increased to 120 people) and had put in a golf course and added archery and clay pigeon shooting ranges.

The occupants of the first two luxury suites had come from Melbourne in their own chartered plane, complete with pilot. They were about to take off for a trip to Cooktown, and squeezed me in. The weather that forced us back to Cairns was but a foretaste of what was to come.

IT SAYS A GREAT DEAL for Dunk Isle that we enjoyed our stay there of five days during which *eleven inches* of rain fell.

Most of this rain came down in one great deluge on our first night. The lounge-bar was open-sided to the bay and a torrent no guttering could cope with streamed down as a solid curtain of water. Somebody laughed and asked, "What are you going to write about this place?" and I could think of no answer but, "Probably list it under Great Australian Waterfalls."

This was at the end of June, normally a "dry" month—dry for Dunk, that is. The island averages 120 inches a year, which is well over four times the Melbourne mean of 26 inches. Yet, Banfield averred, Dunk had fewer days of rain than Melbourne does, or Sydney or any Australian capital except Adelaide. When it rained at Dunk it *rained*. As to temperatures, the calendar page turned over to July while we were on Dunk, and July is the coolest month with an

Largest and most popular of Barrier Reef resorts is Hayman Island. Guests could sail gay catamarans on the bay called the Blue Lagoon.

Daydream Island is a small one with a large swimming-pool set with an island bar. Buildings shown were restored after cyclone damage in early 1970.

7/QUEENSLAND *Coral viewing with snorkel and goggles at Heron Island, most southerly of the Barrier Reef resorts.* BELOW LEFT: *The "Crown of Thorns" starfish (specimen is about 20 inches across) feeds on live coral and kills it. Extent of the starfish's depredations on the Reef has been exaggerated; but its ravages (unless checked, as at Green Island) could be most serious.* BELOW RIGHT: *Beautiful fish of the Reef.*

average of 57 degrees. January is the hottest, with an average of 87.

The tourist who wants to walk through tropical rain-forest that quite merits the name of jungle—and on Dunk you can walk twelve miles of well-graded paths—can hardly expect to do so in an Alice Springs climate. The profligacy of its vegetation is a distinction of the island, and so is its bird-life. Not as many species are to be seen in winter as in summer, but the big tree in front of the dining-room was usually a-twitter with wood-swallows and white-ears and pigeons. When I was walking to Coconut Bay a scrub-turkey, the black mega-pode, flapped up onto a branch with a raucous cry. There were many butterflies. I didn't see any animals. Banfield wrote that there were only echidnas, rats and bats on Dunk; but some young men who went up to Kootaloo, the mountain-top in the west of the island, said they saw three wild pigs, one a large black-and-white boar.

Apart from the discouraging daytime rain—not heavy but rather persistent—over the first couple of days, the feeling I got about Dunk Isle was that it was a place to relax and unwind rather than one for energetic excursions. A walk along the beach towards the western point of Brammo Bay had such rewards as watching nothing move except a crab and the water lacing up on the sand and, in a breeze, the tracery of shadows the casuarinas cast. When you stood on the point's sandspit you were as a figure on the edge of an empty stage in an empty theatre, with the scenery of islands withdrawn on a silky blue sea—except Purtaboi, an islet that lives out in the bay and looks as though it has escaped from a Japanese print and taken on a disguise of tropical greenery. A balm seeps up from the mulchy earth and down through the coconut's fronds, softening *Dunk* so that it ceases to rhyme with *plunk* (PLATE 3).

Low tide in the bay bared a messy reef. By glass-bottomed boat you can get good coral; and by foot you can get to good oysters.

As to food, Dunk's dining-room was particularly good when we were there. *Papaya* was always present for breakfast, and not only fresh-fish dishes were well-cooked. The wine list was gratifying, and meals pleasantly served by decorative young women who had gone to Good Schools and thought it fun to do waitressing on a working holiday, provided the resort was *their* kind of place. Dress was infor-mal, coatless. If it was cool enough to wear a cravat at dinner-time you wore one, but never a tie. In fair weather, dinner would be served out under the palms and trees, with flares. There were never more than about fifty guests at Dunk. It had its *cachet* and was, on 1971 price-check, the most expensive of the Barrier Reef resorts.

There was no organized night entertainment: you made your own amusement or read a book. By day there was safe swimming in the

E

sea, or in the pool. The fishing was, reputedly, good—as it is every-where on the Barrier Reef: I am not a fisherman. As amateur beach-combers we were rewarded on the first day by a fine nautilus shell and on the second found eight spectacular sea-stars washed up on the beach, the smallest of them six inches across and the largest nine. Collected for a colour photograph, they were subsequently returned to the sea.

Most Barrier Reef resort islands offer excursions to other islands, and on the third day we went across to Bedarra, three miles to the south of Dunk.

BEDARRA ISLAND is a gem. Had I been Banfield I think I might even have preferred it to Dunk to settle on. But that is partly because of a personal liking for small islands, easily-encompassed ones: Bedarra is less than a square mile in area. Also hindsight comes into it, because I am thinking of Bedarra as it is now, Bedarra of the beautiful path that winds away, through a bower-like profusion of tropical growth, from the pleasant little building where guests had their meals. Bedarra catered, then, for only ten people.

The resort's owner-proprietor, Ken Druitt, was a cheerful, casual, down-to-earth Australian type who saw no point in being ambitious. Apart from a cabin, there were two well-separated bungalows that were only a few steps from a sand beach that was, at any tide, per-fect for swimming.

Ken Druitt gave me a nutshell history of Bedarra: The first pur-chaser and settler, in 1912, was a Captain Allison, a great swimmer: he used to swim a mile and a half to the in-between island, Timana, walk round Timana and then swim another half-mile to Dunk. Ivan Menzies, the long-time Gilbert and Sullivan star, bought the island with the idea of setting up there a Barnardo Boys' Home. It was sold to a London chemist named Harris, who sent out trunks of trinkets to trade with the natives Bedarra didn't have. He never set foot on his island, though he got to Dunk. A French banker and an Englishman named Greatorex came into possession and a bungalow was built where Druitt's place is and Italian workmen made, with great artistry, the paths. On a bay on the other side of the island, at Hernandia Beach, an admirable semi-colonial house was built and there John Buist of Bingil Bay, who had become part-owner of Bedarra, was host to the late Australian Prime Minister who was so fond of spearfishing, Harold Holt, and his wife, now Dame Zara Bate. The house and the segment of island that went with it was bought by a Victorian grazier, Colin Scott. A painter, Noel Wood, who had his own house in a bay opposite, had been living in the Scott house as caretaker.

Wanting to see more of Bedarra than we were able to on the day trip across from Dunk, I returned to it, by Ken Druitt's speedboat, the following day and walked across to the house at Hernandia Beach. The artist was absent but his brother was there and he kindly showed us the house and the garden with its orchids and, at the edge of it, the largest megapode's mound I have ever seen. It must have been twenty feet across, and had been used, to local knowledge, for thirty years.

The jungle-fowl is (like the scrub-turkey and the mallee-fowl) a strange bird. To save itself the job of sitting on eggs to hatch them it expends great energy in scratching up a hill of earth and decaying vegetation that, fermenting, generates warmth and incubates the eggs the bird buries in the mound. Although the jungle-fowl is smaller than the domestic fowl it manages to lay an egg nearly three times the size of a hen's.

FROM DUNK ISLE you can fly, in half an hour, to Townsville. For about a quarter of the eighty-mile flight you are looking down on the forested slopes of what appears to be a mountainous jut of mainland— indeed, Cook named it *Mount* Hinchinbrook(e). But it is mainland marooned, a large island that has between its western shores and the coast the picturesque Hinchinbrook Channel. There is no settlement or tourist development on Hinchinbrook Island: it is a national reserve.

Ahead, the sea is scattered with the islands of the Palm Group. The big one, Great Palm, is a government-run Aboriginal community.

MAGNETIC ISLAND

TOWNSVILLE, with over 70,000 population, is too urban-industrial to have very much to enchant the visitor—except at night when, from the towering summit of Castle Hill, the city spreads out its jewellery of lights.

Queensland's second-largest city is a place with an admirable winter climate. Its daytime temperature averages 76 degrees in the coolest month, July; and its rainfall of only 43 inches a year (nearly all in January-March) makes it much drier than Cairns. From Townsville a lot of packaged tours run inland, up and down the coast, and out to the islands.

Locally there are the tropical Queen's Gardens to see; a town common thronged with water-birds and dancing brolgas (the Australian crane, a fine grey bird that stands nearly five feet high); and, here and there, some pleasant buildings such as Buchanan's Hotel with its white iron lace (sadly marred by a big signboard plastered across its façade and some beer advertisements), and the more massive Victoriana of the Customs House and the Queen's Hotel.

We installed ourselves in Townsville's newest and best accommodation, at Lowth's Hotel, which was capital-city standard and had an excellent dining-room. The copper refinery I did not propose to visit, much less the meat-cannery; but I did want to see the new university. [The University College of Townsville became the James Cook University in April 1970 when Queen Elizabeth went there during her Australian tour and granted Royal Assent to its becoming autonomous.] So I called up an old colleague, Colin Roderick, its Professor of English.

"Come out!" he said. "Magnificent campus we've got here—you must see it."

The setting was 650 acres of bushland at the foot of Mount Stuart, and here Townsville's university was in process of creating what could be the most interesting campus in Australia. The Humanities Building, the Basic Sciences complex, the Library and the Students' Union were particularly impressive. It was expected that there would be about two thousand students by 1975, and two-thirds of them would come from outside the Townsville region.

While it was still only a college of the University of Queensland, Townsville had shown such initiative of its own as to set up the Foundation of Australian Literary Studies, sponsored not by the Government or by the Universities Commission, but by the community of Townsville, led by the resolute Professor Roderick.

"Townsville is booming, and will go on booming," he said, waving an arm at the city from the veranda of his hilltop house.

It did, indeed, appear that the "Sleeping Giant" was waking up. You could see the giant—his prone figure formed by the contours of the hinterland mountains. The "Sleeping Giant of Townsville" showed up well when you looked across five miles of blue water from the heights on Magnetic Island.

"MAGNETICAL ISLAND" Cook called it, because the *Endeavour's* compass was swinging about, and he thought it was being affected by magnetic ore contained in the rocks of the island. But this could hardly have been the case, because no navigator since has had the same compass trouble.

The trouble with Magnetic Island—although only from the viewpoint of the vacationist who seeks to escape madding crowds and familiar environment utterly—is that it attracts too many people. It has attracted about eight hundred who live there, making it almost an island suburb of Townsville. Hotels, motels and many guest-houses accommodate another populace of vacationers in the winter season, and there is a daily influx of trippers from Townsville, only thirty minutes away by launch.

RAINFALL OF BARRIER REEF ISLANDS

These figures (except the approximations in bold type) are from the Queensland regional office of the Commonwealth Bureau of Meteorology. They are based on "data available and, where there are insufficient records our best estimate of the long-period annual averages". Annual average totals are, mostly, high in comparison with Sydney's 47 inches and Melbourne's 26; but, the Meteorological Bureau says these can be "deceptive from the tourists' point of view, for most of the rain falls in the first three months of the year" and there is not a great difference in the number of wet days at Cairns (146), Melbourne (143) and Sydney (150).

The top line monthly figures are approximations, to the nearest ¼ inch. The lower line figures show actual average points (100 points = 1 inch).

	January	February	March	April	May	June	July	August	September	October	November	December	ANNUAL
Green I.	**19** 1872	**16½** 1643	**19** 1905	**9½** 947	**5** 496	**4** 417	**2½** 255	**2** 208	**1½** 134	**¾** 72	**3** 288	**6½** 645	**88** 8855
Dunk I.	**21** 2079	**23** 2325	**23½** 2334	**13½** 1332	**8** 789	**5½** 560	**4** 420	**3** 307	**3** 305	**3** 320	**5½** 548	**7** 717	**120** 12036
	(Clump Point figures, also representative of Bedarra I.)												
Magnetic I.	**11½** 1158	**13½** 1351	**9½** 940	**3** 296	**1½** 159	**1** 124	**¾** 79	**½** 39	**½** 40	**¾** 77	**2** 196	**3½** 340	**48*** 4804
	(* Cape Cleveland figures, representative of Eastern part of Magnetic I. The Western part's rainfall is estimated at about **40** inches.)												
Hayman I.	**9** 933	**13** 1299	**9** 881	**8** 790	**6** 614	**4** 417	**1½** 143	**¾** 77	**1½** 143	**½** 40	**2** 201	**2** 185	**57*** 5723
	(* By method of ratio with surrounding stations, long-term average annual rainfall is estimated at **65** inches.)												
Lindeman I.	**14½** 1446	**13½** 1355	**11½** 1165	**7** 716	**5½** 528	**4** 378	**1** 112	**1½** 155	**½** 51	**½** 60	**2** 216	**5½** 539	**67** 6721
S. Molle I.	**14½** 1438	**17** 1709	**16½** 1635	**2½** 269	**4** 391	**1½** 151	**½** 67	**½** 65	**0** 0	**1** 116	**2** 220	**4½** 459	**65*** 6520
Daydream I.	**16** 1609	**6½** 654	**12** 1195	**4½** 441	**3½** 339	**2** 201	**¼** 23	**⅛** 13	**½** 63	**1½** 153	**2** 218	**½** 63	**50*** 4972
	(* By method of ratios with surrounding stations, long-term average annual rainfall is estimated at **66** inches.)												
Long I. (Happy Bay)	**15** 1509	**19** 1933	**13** 1333	**9** 897	**5** 511	**3½** 366	**1** 112	**1½** 169	**¾** 74	**1** 108	**2** 195	**6** 591	**78** 7798
Brampton I.	**13** 1311	**12½** 1260	**12** 1188	**6** 592	**3½** 370	**2½** 268	**1½** 160	**1** 102	**1½** 156	**1¾** 179	**3** 289	**6½** 648	**65** 6523
	(Mackay figures are given as representative of Brampton I.)												
Heron I.	**5¾** 573	**4¾** 479	**4½** 433	**3½** 334	**4** 399	**4** 380	**2** 187	**2½** 232	**¾** 71	**1½** 142	**3** 284	**3½** 342	**39*** 3876
	(* By method of ratios with surrounding stations, long-time average annual rainfall is estimated at **40** inches.												

However, there are nineteen square miles of this island with many bays and beaches, and solitude is to be had by those who like it. A lot of people don't, and for them Magnetic has much to offer: golf-course, bowling-green (made of rubber), rentable boats and cars and Mini-Mokes, fishing excursions, and the "Fabulous Magnetic Island Marine Gardens"; in fact everything from a TAB betting shop and a telephone exchange that can get you London direct to churches, taxis and three buses called Nippy Nell, Galloping Gertie and Flighty Flo. It's that kind of place.

Magnetic advertises itself as the "Sunshine Island"—and well it might if what I was told there, and what appears in one of its tourist leaflets, was true. "Average rainfall, 22 inches" (which would make it the driest-sunniest place on the eastern coast of Australia). Another leaflet said 43 inches, which is near the actual figure.

Rainfall figures for the Barrier Reef Islands, which are tabulated on the following page, are based on what was compiled for me by the Queensland branch of the Commonwealth Bureau of Meteorology, to whom I appealed for information that tourists needed to have. The information was nowhere in print.

TARIFFS at Barrier Reef resorts are surprisingly moderate. Magnetic Island's are specially reasonable. A resort called "Alma Den", on Alma Bay, where you walked out onto the best swimming beach on the island, was only $7.50 a day, meals inclusive. It was run by a particularly pleasant couple, Mr and Mrs Charles Thomas, catered for about forty people, and welcomed families with children.

Charles Thomas, who was president of the Magnetic Island Tourist Association, ran us all over the island, and it was more attractive than I had expected. The heights—the central mount rises to 1,628 feet, and there are others—gave panoramas of bays with huge granite boulders piling up to forests of pines and other trees more tropical. Horseshoe Bay was rather flat, though it had plenty of beach and was good for shells. Three bays you could walk, but not (then) drive, to—Arthur, Florence and Radical—looked charming. Although the island had twenty-five miles of bitumen roads that were extending all the time, the greater part of it was still undeveloped National Park wilderness, with orchids on the trees and koalas (not indigenous) in some of them, and a lot of bird-life. A big melaleuca was alive with brilliant parrots. Rock wallabies were there, too.

Coral was at its best, Charles Thomas said, at Arthur Bay. We went into the Marine Gardens and saw even more brilliant specimens than were at Green Island's aquarium of the "decoy" fishes that live with sea-anemones. Why should this scarlet-banded fish be snuggling in among the poison-shooting tentacles of an anemone that looked like a big white dahlia with waving petals? The bright fish was immune, and protected from predators by their dread of the anemone's batteries of paralysing darts.

No sea growth was stranger and more decorative than one that looked like a bag of opaque white plastic pinched in at the top and with a flower growing out of it, and had its sides painted in patterns of scarlet and Reckitt's blue. It was a "Deepwater Sea-cucumber".

The harlequin-fish looks harlequinesque. But the the angel fish is surely misnamed—unless angels can be thought of as striped yellow, blue and orange.

WE RETURNED to Townsville and that evening took the 9 p.m. "Sunlander" train to Mackay, in order to reach without delay the fly-point to Hayman Island. We had a first-class sleeper, which was first-class as to comfort, but there was so much jolty stopping and shunting sleep was difficult. Scheduled arrival at Mackay was 5.47 a.m. Could we have morning tea at 5 a.m.? No, only at 4.30, the conductor said. (Since then the Sunlander timetable has been changed and this train now departs Townsville at 6 a.m. and 3.25 p.m. and arrives in Mackay at 2.19 p.m. and 11.40 p.m.)

Mackay's Caravilla Reef Motel, of the Travelodge chain, could not have been more welcoming to guests arriving at an ungodly hour.

HAYMAN ISLAND

THE HELICOPTER that flies to Hayman Island from Mackay is a Sikorsky that takes twenty passengers. The trip, about forty-five minutes, directly over the Whitsunday Passage with a couple of dozen islands to the east, is a beautifully scenic flight on a blue day. You can pick out with a map the other resort islands of the group—Brampton, Lindeman, Long (Happy Bay), South Molle, Daydream. Beyond the biggest, Whitsunday, with nothing of development on it, and sizeable Hook Island, the 'copter whirls down to Hayman.

Physically, it is an island two miles long, in shape like an elongated upside-down Tasmania, with a horseshoe mount that rises, lightly timbered, to eight hundred feet. All the development was at the bay-curved southern end. The Royal Hayman Hotel spread a wide complex of single-storeyed accommodation and playgrounds tropically set with palms and bright shrubberies. It fronted the sandbeach of what was called, inevitably, the Blue Lagoon. The whole of this end of the island is encompassed by a coral reef.

Hayman, the biggest and best-publicized of Barrier Reef resorts, could take 370 guests. Owned and air-serviced by the Ansett organization, it had been created in a mould that was not so much Australian as—and this undoubtedly appealed to most Australians—Hawaiian-exotic, but it was losing this image and gaining its own character. No longer was it advertised with a colour brochure with beautiful girls swathed in sarongs and leis. Fascinated as we were by those colour pictures of Beautiful People doing Exciting Things, I wondered whether this would attract tourists to the island or make them think they were too unglamorous to go there unless they were 36-24-34 females and possessed wardrobes such as the glamour-girls and glamour-boys (all models) were wearing. I was, it appeared, quite wrong in harbouring this doubt. The manager assured me that not only did ordinary people come to Hayman in droves, but they had bought thousands of copies of the brochure-book at a dollar a copy.

Hayman could keep tariffs down, because the resort was a big-turnover enterprise. The visitor could be expected to spend extra dollars on everything from drinks to cruises, big-game fishing excursions, clothing (at the Island Shop), souvenirs, snacks, water-skiing and more drinks while watching the entertainments provided, or between dances, or when they were letting their heads go or meeting their neighbours on Corroboree Night.

THE 'COPTER came in crabwise to the heliport by the long jetty. Sun-tanned young men with their first names on the pockets of their Hawaiian-style shirts had the luggage off very smartly and on to the mini-train we boarded. The HAYMAN ROCK-IT had red-and-white-striped carriages, matching the striped-sails catamaran on the bay the hotel fronted (PLATE 6). Fellow passengers off the chopper were a mother and daughter, a chummy Merry Widow, two dapper gents, a rapt honeymoon couple, a brace of Jewish businessmen with their wives—and four young men with long hair and mod. clothing and a hundredweight of gear, which meant they had to be either a band or a film crew. They were a film crew, there to make Hayman the setting of another of those cigarette TV-cinema commercials that must be very confusing to those who wish to be "in" smokers, because the "in" people are not only constantly travelling to "in" places—they are constantly changing their brand of "in" cigarettes.

The Rock-it train rocked gently along its narrow line past hibiscus and frangipanni, and what appeared to be several stuffed birds. Curlews have a habit of standing utterly moveless on one leg and looking at the world mournfully with long girlish eyes, as though stunned by some secret sorrow. We became quite attached to Hayman's curlews. Their cry is a weird sort of wailing.

We were accommodated in one of what are called the Frangipanni Lodges, white-painted double units reached by a picturesque path.

There were beach-fronting Hibiscus Lodges at slightly-higher tariff, and we took it as a compliment that there were three hibiscus blooms and fruit tastefully arranged on the dressing-table of our Frangipanni. Golden Orchid Lodges cost least, and one can hardly expect a greeting of three golden orchids. We arrived in mid-afternoon and looked at the useful little booklet, *Hayman for the Layman*, that gives light-heartedly and with the utmost tact, information on all matters, including what is the expected wear at dinner. In 1967 men were expected to wear in the dining room at evening ties, but not coats. In 1971 ties were no longer expected at dinner.

At other meals, anything except swimming costume. On special nights, such as Oriental Night, would everybody please dress up in the Oriental costumes, provided without charge.

WHAT DID WE DO at Hayman for five days? Here is a sort of diary:

Day 1. Bay being so shallow at high tide, a sand flat at low, swam in pool. Liked pool being saltwater not fresh. Film crew adopted us, bright-minded bunch. Had dinner with them, and, later, drinks in ballroom-lounge. Claire retired, I went with sparky crowd to palm-thatch hut with bar at end of beach, called Hernando's Hideaway, which had dim-lit ambience. Small combo played specially well. Good idea this: people who want to party-on and dance into small hours can, without noise disturbing others.

Day 2. All-day cruise to Lindeman Island. [See next section on South Molle/Lindeman.]

Day 3. Claire went reefing while I talked to manager André Maestraecci, who clearly knows what he's at. Ask why is Hayman so popular? *A.* "Barrier Reef resorts give people a lot for the money. We give *more.*" To what extent do people come to see coral? *A.* "Australians don't come specifically to see coral. But overseas tourists *will.*" What coral will they see? *A.* "Coral viewing *par excellence* is still the problem. The best coral is over the edge of the reef, on the side of it. For the non-divers, someone has to come up with an underwater craft people can sit in and see it at eye-level. Meanwhile, our new glass-bottomed boat will do a good job. The coral's good off Bali Hai, the little island where we have barbecues when the weather's right."

Joined Claire on reef, where tide still out. Only patches of coloured corals, mainly blue-tipped staghorn and heliotrope-edged massive rounds of brown. Hundreds of bêche-de-mer, torpid, wrinkled, like foot-long naked caterpillars. Pick one up (quite harmless) and it eviscerates sticky white threads. If molested it is likely to void its whole intestines. Able to move only sluggishly on tiny sucker-feet (like starfish), saves its life by presenting predator with its insides. Grows a new set—"within nine days" in one case recorded by Roughley.[4]

In afternoon walked to Blue Pearl Bay (1¼ m.) on west side. On the way, a fine lookout across Whitsunday Passage. Very little rain-forest, more savannah country, with Norfolk pines near shore and decorating very picturesquely a rocky islet this end of BP Bay, which had no other visitors. Not a good beach, shingle of broken coral bits, many curiously holed; found one like miniature Henry Moore sculpture. Water very blue but stony bottom uninviting and not warm enough this late afternoon to swim. Near islet, quail-like birds whirred up from grass, and piebald fish-eagle hovered. On way back found a vine covered with hundreds of black-and-white butterflies, settled or fluttering prettily.

Day 4. All-day excursion to Hook Island (underwater observatory, coral viewing) and South Molle. [See next section.]

Day 5. Rained all morning. Cleared. After lunch swam and sunned at pool. Talked to some people who had walked round island (4½ m.) and said very enjoyable walk. Fishing party came in with good catch, which chef will serve them for dinner. Said they saw a school of forty manta rays—biggest the boatman had ever seen.

Had dinner in Gold Room. Here you pay, but charges very moderate as taken into account you're missing paid-for meal in general dining-room. The filet mignon was excellent.

Showy entertainment complete with forty-foot Chinese dragon and games. Feed your partner rice and first with empty bowl wins a prize.

Day 6. Pack to leave. Talk at lunch with Mr Maxwell Macauley, ardent amateur conchologist from Nhill, Vic., who thinks Whitsunday Islands best for shells and comes regularly to Hayman. How does he find them? "Track them like a blackfeller." He knows what they live on, so looks for particular sea vegetation, then looks on nearby sand for shellfish tracks, then digs. Most of his best finds have come from under sand.

Half-day excursion launch to South Molle will make a special call at nearby Daydream Island and drop us off there.

[Revisiting Hayman in mid-1971 I found the resort much as it was before the damaging cyclone of January 1970. Vegetation that took such a battering had regenerated amazingly: indeed the place seemed to have more palms, bougainvillea and crotons. André Maestraecci was beaming as before and running the Hayman operation in a way that was clearly to the satisfaction of at least nine out of ten vacationers. This time the weather was perfect and I returned to mid-wintry Sydney with a suntan gained in four days.]

LINDEMAN AND SOUTH MOLLE

NOT HAVING STAYED on these two islands, I can give only impressions of them gained from going ashore on launch excursions from Hayman.

Lindeman has been run as a tourist resort by the Nicolson family since 1930, when the pioneer settler, Angus Nicolson—who ran cattle, sheep and goats on the island—set up the first palm-thatch cabins with washbasins and carbide lamps for eight guests. It has been maintained in such good repute that when Princess Alexandra of Kent made an Australian tour in 1959 she spent four days there. Five years earlier, Queen Elizabeth and the Duke of Edinburgh had left the Royal yacht to picnic on a beach just across the channel, on Seaforth Island. This looked to be a much better beach than the one where the resort was, and Lindeman guests went across to it when the weather was not as windy as it was the day we landed.

Coconut palms lined Lindeman's beach and there were particularly attractive tropical shrubberies and trees in the vicinity of the swimming-pool. Away from that, Lindeman looked pastoral rather than tropical, although, beyond its grassy slopes, forest covered its 695-foot Mount Oldfield, which must give a superb panorama of the island-studded sea. So many islands were in its vicinity that Lindeman provided a lot of cruises, and those to the nearer islands were inclusive in a tariff that ranged (1971) from $11.50 to $22.50. Some of the accommodation needed refurbishing according to a stockbroker-type and his wife who left Lindeman on the launch that took us there and came to Hayman, where they later told me they were happier. Lindeman takes only about forty people. There is a daily (except Sunday) air service between Mackay, half an hour away, and the airstrip on the island.

On the Hayman cruise to South Molle we went first to Hook Island where an underwater observatory had been set up. Possibly because it was fairly new, it did not have the variety of fish and coral to be seen at the Green Island observatory. Glass-bottomed boats did coral viewing. There was plenty of coral growth to be seen but a number of people expressed disappointment at not seeing coral in its picture-book colours.

SOUTH MOLLE would appear to be the swingers' island, even though the man I talked to in the office protested that it had been misrepresented as a place that catered only for the uninhibited young. "We get a lot of older people, too," he said, "and expect to get more, or we wouldn't be putting in a bowling-green." For us, the generation gap gaped so wide there was the feeling of walking into a milk bar that served hard liquor. Doubtless the décor we thought gaudy appealed to others as gay.

The island, attractive in itself, is about the same size and shape as Hayman. The beach in front of the coconut palms that waved over the gay cabins was rough with coral shingle; but there was a notably large swimming-pool. Beyond the pool was a six-hole golf course and tennis courts. South Molle was taking up to 240 guests, at rates on about a par with Hayman's, though ranging a little higher for air-conditioned suites. Three or four cruises a week were included in the tariff.

What South Molle had that greatly appealed to us was the best collection of Barrier Reef shells we saw anywhere, together with shells from other parts of the world. This remarkable array of 13,000 specimens had been gathered together, the girl attendant said, by a Swiss of seventy-odd, George Sax. I thought she said "Sex"; but that was probably because I had been given a copy of the *South Molle Grapevine*, a roneoed sheet of gossipy tidbits full of adolescent innuendoes and jokes like one fly saying to another, "Hey! You forgot to do your man up!"

DAYDREAM ISLAND

THERE ARE THREE Molle islands (named after an early lieutenant-governor of the New South Wales colony) and on the other side of uninhabited North Molle is an attractive slip of pine-forested island only a mile or so long and a couple of stone-throws wide. This is West Molle which, since about 1950, has borne the much more glamorous name of Daydream Island. Here we spent four days.

At Daydream as at Hayman (where the Ansett operation moved to from Daydream, for reasons that had more to do with the problem of freshwater supply than with the limiting size of the island) the resort theme was South Sea Island glamour. Daydream did not try to match Hayman's diversified entertainment of Oriental Nights and Left-Bank Paris Nights: it concentrated on providing a kind of Instant Hawaii on Australia's coralled doorstep. It was short on swaying palms but long on swaying hips of comely food servitors; and it was at least a day before I got used to navels winking at me while I took a serving of salad, from midriffs bare between sun-tops and sarongs at dinner and grass skirts at luncheon.

When the wind was not too blowy, luncheon was served beside what was claimed to be (and life is too short to check this one) the largest swimming-pool in the Southern Hemisphere. The pool was Daydream's free-form centrepiece, with the resort building surrounding it, and in the middle of it was a concrete island where you could haul up from swimming and have a drink at the palm-thatched "Island Bar" (PLATE 6).

Indoor drinking was also atmospheric, the lounge bar being flanked with a king-sized mural of Hawaiian glamours, and there was another one in which Captain Cook featured. There was no lack of big-leaved tropical plants or of guitar music with a tropical beat at night. By day there was piped music that, at times, we should like to have turned off. The accommodation, not gaudy, was very good—spacious rooms with "private facilities" and picture-windowed to the sea view at the back. Considering what was inclusive—all meals (which were good), entertainment, free cruises and so on—tariff was very reasonable.

Daydream Island as we saw it was created by a millionaire with childhood memories of bread-and-dripping in the slums of Nottingham. Bernard Elsey came to Australia with his parents at the age of five. He was, in 1969, a very fit-looking man in his sixties who did not drink, smoke or gamble, and had two ex-wives. He made enough money to retire early, from his business of being sole Queensland distributor of three successful breakfast cereals. Having retired to a large motor-yacht, he became bored with the inactivity and ran his boat for tourist cruises from the Gold Coast, the Australian Miami near Brisbane. When tourists asked him where they could find a hotel with bath-attached rooms and a swimming-pool—and there weren't any—Bernard Elsey built some. He became one of the Gold Coast's big developers, and that made him his million.

He spent half a million dollars on the Daydream Island he opened in 1968, having solved the water-supply problem by installing a desalination plant. To the island he took his Gold Coast success formula of brighter-than-bright and gayer-than-gay exotic décor and do-what-thou-wilt sophistication in modern comfort at moderate prices. Not surprisingly, the place built up good business in its first year, and became most popular with honeymoon couples.

THE BEACH fronting the resort on the western side (the east-side beach was useless for swimming) was of coral shingle, not sand; but rubber li-los were liberally provided. Most guests swam in the pool.

There was another beach, called Sunlovers' Beach, that could be reached only by water. "If your suntan stops where you wish it didn't," the Daydream brochure said, there was this secluded beach where you could "sunbathe *au naturel*". It was implied that Sunlovers' Beach was not for mixed nude bathing or even mixed topless bathing; but on sale at the island shop were male briefs that consisted only of a pouch and two strings, and the most minimal of mini-bikinis.

The bay was better for water-skiing than coral viewing. Diving and snorkelling gear could be hired. Most Daydreamers saw their coral at a place on the nearby mainland, reached by the island's big launch, called Mandalay Coral Gardens. Here an interesting couple, Shirley and Basil Keong, cultivated their own coral garden in a pool they had built, which was washed over at high tide. Divers both, the Keongs had brought in coral from the reef and transplanted it to the pool, where they had twenty-four varieties growing, interspersed with starfish, bêche-de-mer and clams.

For Hawaiian Night, the Saturday feast-entertainment, guests were encouraged to wear the available sarongs and, in the case of men, lap-laps. Leis were everywhere, and the staff were either grass-skirted or flower-shirted. The big moment was when the roast pig was borne in flaming. The food served was good. On another evening the girls who waited on the tables turned mannequins and modelled casual clothes from the island shop. Every night was a cabaret night until, at least, eleven-thirty; and there was talk of building on the tip of the island a place such as Hayman had in Hernando's Hideaway, where dancing could continue out of earshot, and there would be a bar, of course.

By day the more energetic Daydreamers could climb up a short track to the viewing place called, after Mr Elsey, Bernie's Lookout.

Daydream has its heliport, from which the Ansett helicopter lifted us to Proserpine. From here Claire had to return to Sydney.

BRAMPTON ISLAND

As AN ISLAND, Brampton had an attractiveness that was quite special. As a resort, it catered for those unspecial people, Mr and Mrs Every-body. In order to discover how attractive the island was, you had to walk around it; and the Everybodys would rather talk than walk.

I had heard about Brampton being "such a friendly place", and thought this referred to an atmosphere created by Brampton's friendly management; and, in part, it did. But the friendliness was also built up, as assiduously as polyps build coral, by the kind of people Brampton attracted: people-loving people who liked to be seated six or eight to a table in the dining-room; Bingo-loving people who looked forward to the nightly Bingo game in their quiet moments, which were few because they believed that friendship was a flower that would parch and wither unless it was watered incessantly with talk.

The palmy grove the resort centred around was very attractive, and you walked through it to a particularly good beach. There were other beaches, but this north-facing one was not only the sunniest and most sheltered but had the broadest sands and the calmest bay. The idea of leaving the excellent "home beach" for a change of scene—or to have a beach to yourself or selves—this made sense to very few Brampton-goers (thank goodness). PLATE 8 shows the other side.

In short, Brampton could be the right island to go to for what most people who went there would consider the wrong reasons.

MACKAY is where you fly to Brampton from, in twenty minutes. The island has an airstrip quite adequate for the Twin Otter operated by TAA.

Brampton's operators were also the operators of Roylen cruises. "Cruise 'n' Stay" holidays were very popular. A vacation of, say, two weeks could begin or end with a five-day cruise on one of the Roylen twin-screw cruisers that were 112-feet long and took twenty-five people in two- or three-berth cabins at about $90 each. The cruise visited, usually, ten islands. The rest of the fortnight could be spent on Brampton.

On arrival at Brampton, I was made welcome by one of the island's two hostesses, who put a paper lei round my neck; but that was as far as the Hawaiian bit went. A small train trundled guests and luggage to the complex of resort buildings, where I had one of the older-type two-unit bungalows, with a front veranda facing onto the palmy-flowery grove that was so attractive. At the back it had "private facilities" behind louvres. Modern suites were available.

It was a beautiful day—the first really good day in weeks, the hostess said. Barrier Reef weather is not necessarily the succession of balmy, sun-filled days many visitors expect it to be. If this beautiful weather held there would be, next day, a cruise to the Outer Barrier. (It held and there was.) I made for the beach, swam, baked and watched the water-skiers cutting parabolas in the gilded sun-path across the water.

Dinner that night was a barbecue at the beach, and as I came down to it the sunset was in the last flush of its glory. Casuarinas brushed the foreground with their long dark hair. Islands retreated across the shining stage of sea, from black silhouettes to grey. Soon the flare-pots were licking the night with tongues of flame.

Such a setting, I felt, deserved a better barbecue: better steak, for a start, and cheese after to go with the red wine—which only I appeared to have. No wine was available, so I had gone up to the bar and got a bottle and several glasses; but the people I sat next to declined politely, except the island's sketch artist, who did portraits for a dollar.

Later, at the bar, I talked to some of the young Bramptoneers. The island got its percentage of swingers—the boys on beer and the girls on brandy-dry or Bacardi-and-Coke—in a bar somewhat reminiscent of South Molle's but with small billiard-tables instead of pin-machines. Some went off to dance, others to barrack a horse in the Race Game. Bingo they regarded as for oldies.

The main purpose of going to the Outer Barrier was to walk about on flats of pristine coral. For such a cruise the sea must be calm (otherwise people won't go, from fear of becoming seasick). The sun needs to be shining (or they won't go either). The cruise launch must leave at a time (which cannot be before breakfast) that will bring it to the Outer Barrier at low-low tides (low tides can vary by several feet). Odds on this confluence of conditions occurring are rather long.

On this cruise the weather condition was perfect, but not the tide at the reef that spread from a coral cay called Bushy Island. This was fifty-two miles from Brampton.

On top of the big launch I found a sunny, shielded spot behind the life-jacket crates and settled down to watch Brampton get lost astern behind its bigger neighbour, Carlisle Island; and then did a spot of gull-watching. Gulls with their immaculate breasts accented by bright red legs and beaks; their prim look that makes pigeons appear to belong to the avian *demi-monde* (until the scraps go overboard and the gulls swoop on the wake, shrieking like fishwives). Gulls that come to be watched by perching on the radio aerial and teetering there, six or seven in a row. Gulls hovering, gulls at their most watchable as they hang in the air on the beautiful bow of silver-white wings with the sun through them.

After lunch I went into the wheelhouse to look at the chart. The man at the wheel said, "That's Bushy, right ahead." An hour later the island was being served up from the sea as a helping of thick green vegetation on a plate of white sand. By this time I had found two kindred spirits, nice women, both schoolteachers. We were in the first boat off and had checked the time of the last boat back. There was coral to be seen as we came into the shallows, but it was brown coral. Far out, a thin line of white water marked the edge of the Great Barrier Reef.

The coral cay had no uncovered reef to walk on, owing to the tide's not being low enough, so we walked round the island: it wouldn't be half a mile. The trackless beach had ever-mysterious flotsam: that grey slab of wood with the rusted bolt through it was part of what and came from where? The water was like liquid glass and the sand was strewn with shells, not in great variety but especially numerous were small heliotrope cowries. We gathered shells.

Deciding to swim, we did so with sandshoes on because of the near coral, which was dead and nothing to look at. There was just enough depth to swim, but no use for the goggles and snorkel I had brought.

Pulling shorts over wet bathers, we went into the vegetation that was jungle-thick in patches with big glossy-leaved trees crowding the pandanus and coco-palms. There was a corrugated-iron hut with an ancient fuel stove in it and a rusted refrigerator.

Brampton Island is attractively formed, with quiet blue bays you can walk to on the other side from where the resort is developed.

Heron, a true coral island, is flat and its sandy soil grows these pisonia-trees. Thousands of noddy terns come to nest in them in October.

9/QUEENSLAND *Coal-mining has developed at Moura by the use of this monster $13 million "walking dragline" to remove overburden. The bucket takes 200 tons.*

Felling a large hoop-pine in forest south of Mackay.

When we got back to the cruise launch, a glass-bottomed boat had been lowered overside and was taking parties out for coral viewing. We were seeing a lot of blue staghorn coral but not very much else when a well-dressed European, who was obviously disappointed at not looking down into something like a colourspread from the *National Geographic* magazine, said to the boatman, "We can go back now", and the boatman took us back to the launch. I stayed in for a second trip that showed very good coral formations on the edges of deep holes, big spreads of tabular coral with mauve and yellow and some pink, luxuriant soft coral waving, and vivid-lipped clams, but few fish because the propeller scared them away.

On the way back to Brampton, darkness brought out a quarter-moon among the brilliance of stars that blaze in the south-world sky where the Southern Cross hangs, four big stars and a small one.

NEXT DAY, with lunches picnic-packed, the two schoolteachers and I walked round Brampton. I doubt if it is more than five miles, but we managed to take all day over it, what with reefing at Turtle Bay (not good), sunbaking on the beach at Dinghy Bay (three people were fishing, and thereafter we saw no others); not getting oysters at Oyster Bay (we had forgotten to bring an oyster-knife); swimming and lunching and swimming again; climbing over the ridge to Western Bay where we found a scrub-turkey's mound and eavesdropped on the male bird serenading his hen in a voice with rattles in it; then going up a well-graded track through eucalypts, and over the top to where we heard rude-sounding noises that turned out to be coming from wild goats, very shaggy and long of horn and given to standing on their hindlegs to eat trees. On the way down we slowly finished the drink I'd brought while watching a superb sunset's backdrop of colour to the pewter cut-outs of islands to the north.

Next morning, Fitz McLean, who runs Brampton, was flying across to Mackay in his own plane and took me with him.

HERON ISLAND

FARTHEST SOUTH of the islands I stayed on, Heron Island was only two miles up from the Tropic of Capricorn; but it looked more tropical than a lot of the continental-type islands to the north. It is a coral cay, one of nine in the Capricorn Group, and the only one developed for tourists.

Heron was not luxuriously developed in the Daydream style, and it hadn't the Dunk Isle *cachet*; so it was not for sophisticates. Although it had Bingo at night, I didn't see it as for Mr and Mrs Everybody, either. It was certainly not for swingers. Heron was for nature-lovers, coral-reef fossickers, snorkellers, skindivers (but not spear-gunners:

F

spear-fishing was prohibited), underwater photographers, bird-watchers (and, in the season, turtle-watchers), anglers, water-skiers, barefooters and casual dressers and unfussy eaters (though the food was f.a.q.-plus with fresh fish every day), and plain-lazy people who, when they weren't swimming or prone on the sand, liked an island small enough to walk round in half an hour.

The reason why Heron Island—which lies forty-five miles off Gladstone, which is six hundred crow-flight miles south from Cairns —has winter temperatures that seldom go much below seventy degrees becomes apparent in Yonge's statement about the coral that surrounds it: "That reefs can flourish here at all—and the coral, though it may grow more slowly, is just as luxuriant as that of the more northern reefs—is the result of a warm current that flows down inside the Barrier."⁵

When Dr Yonge was on Heron in 1929 it had only a turtle-soup factory. The scientist predicted then that the day would soon come when "the sand cays of the Capricorns will each possess its hotel or guest house", reached by "fast motor boats" from the mainland. Until 1969 Heron could be reached only by the launch from Gladstone that took five hours. Now you could board Airfast's helicopter and be there in forty minutes (for $18 as against $9 for the launch).

As to accommodation, Heron was changing. The old-style was the small fibro cabin, such as I had, with no running water, or even a jug to hold drinking water brought from the tank tap. One row of motel-type units, with "private facilities" and television, had been built. (In 1971 there were two types of motel units on Heron.)

There ought always, for the people who like this, to be a Heron Island without concrete paths but just sand underfoot as you meander to the dining-room through the pisonia-trees, none of which, I hope, will be cut down to put in a swimming-pool: even at low tide one could swim in the sea. Nor would I want Heron to have some smart type of assistant-manager instead of Robert Poulson's offsider, Vivian Bylund, who was so knowledgeable to go reefing with.

As YOU FLY to Heron from Gladstone you see spreads of reefs in isolation and reefs extending round two islets on the route, and when you are near Heron you fly over the big oval formation of Wistari Reef. Its pattern is fascinating and, in colour, beautiful—not from any colour that can be seen of the coral itself, which all looks brown or beige, but the shallow water over the reef is pale turquoise and jade. The indigo of the deeper water round the reef is edged with a line of waves breaking white.

A small harbour like a long pool has been blasted through the coral so launches can come in to Heron, and this is an excellent place to swim at any tide, although there are more sheltered places when the sou'-east is blowing and the tide is high. The water here was so blue on sun-bright days that it used to reflect a wash of blue on the under-wings of the white herons planing low over it in search of fish.

The herons that give the island its name are always to be seen there whereas some of the other birds that frequent it are migratory. Mutton-birds (shearwaters) and white-capped noddy terns come to Heron in great numbers to nest. The mutton-birds possibly come from as far away as the Aleutian Islands that stretch off Alaska. They usually arrive on the same date, 11th October, and always between the eighth and the eleventh; and how this incredible precision comes about through processes of instinct is still mysterious. The adult birds leave Heron in April, and the young follow them. Noddy terns flock to the island over approximately the same period as the mutton-birds, but not all the terns are migratory; some are always there.

The hostess, Roberta Noonan, took parties through the island that is thick with, mainly, pisonia-trees, though there are many pandanus palms as well. Pisonias occur in many parts of the tropical world and the species in Australia thrive in coral-limestone sands. The tree has a sticky seed and has propagated itself on these cays by its seeds sticking to the wings of migratory birds. Sometimes so many seeds stick to the wings of the noddy terns that the birds cannot fly out to catch pilchards, and they starve and die. "And yet," as Roberta said, "it is the tree they choose to nest in." The big-leaved pisonia spreads out a butt like the misshapen hoof of a gigantic horse; it grows in contorted shapes, and it gives fine shade; but the wood is soft and soggy and will not burn. PLATE 8 shows pisonia-trees.

On this walk my foot sank through the sand into a burrow just under the ground—one of the innumerable nests of the mutton-birds. They are not the same type as the mutton-bird of Bass Strait, and would not be taken for food even if they could be: the island is a National Park. In the bird season the island becomes rather smelly, I was told, and the nights noisy with the mutton-birds mating.

FOR REEFING it is advisable to wear rubber boots or canvas ones of the gym. type with ankle pads, and also socks, in case your foot goes through the coral crust when you walk over it or your legs are scratched by the edges of clumps. Coral cuts turn septic and are very slow to heal: it is as well to pack an antiseptic such as Metaphen, which comes handily in a very small bottle. Cloth gardening gloves are recommended, and you need a stout stick. The best place to go to on the reef flat is called the Blue Pool, where you need goggles and snorkel or, at least, a glass-bottomed box. (These things, even reefing sticks, could be hired at the Heron Island shop.)

I had been reefing on my own, but it was much more rewarding to
go out with Vivian Bylund. Even the bêche-de-mer which lie about
plentifully in the sand patches between the corals became more interesting. Not only could they throw out their insides and grow a new
set but, Vivian said, bêche-de-mer made good beaches. The creature
ingests sand to extract its food from, and if it takes in rough coralline
sand at one end what comes out the other is finer sand. What turtles
ate was this soft green weed, turtle grass. This yellowy-brown sea
anemone was quite different from those bright-coloured ones like
dahlias: it contained a chemical that produced insanity in humans,
Vivian Bylund said; and *that* fish—he hadn't seen one of those for a
while!—was the venomous sea-scorpion, a kind of lesser stonefish.
Although the reef's beauties far outnumber its "nasties", it is as well
to know something of those.

I have yet to see, outside of aquariums, the dreaded stonefish. Not
only was the "warty ghoul" (as Banfield called it) particularly hard
to discern, so like an indented stone is it—a most unfishlike fish that is
not only hideous in form but such a poor swimmer it usually lies
torpid and collects a disguise of sea-growth on its body—but stonefish
were, fortunately, rare. "In twenty years of walking this reef, I've
seen four," Vivian said. The venom—injected from spines that rise
erect on its back if the stonefish is disturbed—is not, as is sometimes
stated, invariably fatal. Worse is the sea-wasp. This jellyfish has killed
forty people in Queensland waters, but it is not a hazard on the Barrier Reef, according to Gillett.[6] Cone shells, live ones, should be left
alone. Several of the species (notoriously, the Geographer Cone) are
inhabited by a shellfish that protrudes a toothed tongue with glands
of poison that had been fatal to two people, a man in 1935 and a boy
in 1970.

When Viv Bylund turned over flattish hunks of coral rock to show
what lived under them there were sometimes patches of crimson and
other colours, as on an artist's palette. Our best find was a handsome
nudibranch (sea-slug) that was navy-blue, yellow and black. All
stones turned over were carefully replaced. It is better to walk the
channels than crunch over the platforms of coral, not only because
you may go through it, but because a lot of the reef "cementing" here
is a covering of pretty pink growth that should not be despoiled by
reefers.

As Bob Poulson confirmed, "Most coral, after all, is brown"—and
he admitted that many Barrier Reef visitors expect far more coral
colour than they see. At Heron, though, there was more colour than
I saw elsewhere.

The Blue Pool was near the edge of the reef (PLATE 7), not very deep and perhaps twenty feet long. There was some coloured growth on its sides and long-spined black sea-urchins. But the fish that had been trapped there when the tide receded were its main attraction.

When I got in and floated with goggles and snorkel I was seeing a pellucid small world with such beautiful inhabitants as electric-blue Demoiselles with golden tails, wrasse in their rich green, the black-and-yellow striped Moorish Idol, a parrot-fish that had a coat of as many colours as the bright angel-fish had stripes. There were some other varieties, one of them banded black and white: notes and memory are here poor substitutes for the underwater camera I did not possess. The water, so still below, was surging on top with the strong wind that, on this sunless day, made it damnably cold out of the water; but it was well worth that discomfort.

The Wistari and Heron Reefs are so rewarding for divers that every November a four-week Australian Skindivers' Festival is held at the island.

ON HERON there is a marine research station, set up by the Great Barrier Reef Committee. It is a small—too small—operation, the staff consisting, when I was there, of an American marine biologist, Stephen Domm and his wife Alison.

The Domms had done a guide-booklet for visitors to Heron. In it they tell of the female turtles coming up the island's beaches in December-March to lay a hundred or so eggs that hatch out in about eight weeks. As the tiny hatchlings make for the sea they are picked off by gulls in the daytime and at night by the scavenging ghost-crabs that "appear to relish their orgy of destruction, for they kill more of the turtles than they can consume" (according to McNeill).[7] So the chance of a baby turtle reaching the age of seven years—when the Green Turtle has a carapace about three-foot-six long and may weigh over two hundred pounds—is about one in a thousand. Apparently the hatchlings make for the sea because they are drawn to the light on the water. They also make for the lights of the resort, and have to be gathered from cabin doorsteps and taken in buckets of water along the beach well away from the lights and released in the sea, where other predators await them.

Steve Domm told me that he had not seen a single Crown of Thorns starfish among the Capricorn coral. He had seen only two triton shells, which Dr Endean regarded as the predator that could control the devastating starfish: Domm didn't agree.

Two other Americans were at Heron Island while I was there— a Texas oil man, Ray H. Marr of Dallas, with his nephew, Chris. They were both ardent divers and underwater photographers and were most enthusiastic about what they had seen.

When I asked young Chris what he thought of Australia generally, he said, "I think it's wonderful the way you get to know people just by their first names."

Gladstone and the Moura "Monster"

AT GLADSTONE, before I went to Heron Island, I had a look at what happened to Weipa bauxite—how the red pebbles were turned into white powder that made aluminium. And that was only part of a look at what had happened to Gladstone.

Queensland Alumina Ltd had in 1967 begun operating a $160-million refinery at a place an English writer had found to be, only two years earlier, "a torpid, easy-going little country town".[1]

New Gladstone had 13,000 people and a million pieces of steel reared up in mammoth cylinders called flash tanks and digestors and precipitators at Queensland Alumina. It had by its harbourside not only red mountains of Weipa bauxite but black mountains of stock-piled hinterland coal, and silver-grey mountains of beach-mineral ilmenite. It had a new hotel too modern to be called a pub, a drive-in cinema, and an annual Festival with floats and a Queen. It had Japanese sailors (ashore from the ore ships) whose behaviour was exemplary, and other seamen from other ships who weren't to be blamed entirely if Gladstone had a teenage delinquency problem (which I was told it had, but police and clergy subsequently denied this). So many ships were coming into Gladstone Harbour that now it was handling more cargo—mainly coal, bauxite, alumina, petroleum, grain sorghum, wheat, caustic soda, beach minerals, meat—than all the other east-coast ports of Queensland together.

A town does not just take off like a rocket: there has to be a pro-pellant. In Gladstone's case the name of the propellant was W. R. Golding, M.B.E., F.R.G.S., the Mayor and, for the past thirteen years, president of the Harbour Board. This tall and elderly man's father was at Gladstone when the town was born in 1854.

"Mr Gladstone" hoped that fertilizer and sulphuric acid plants would join the alumina refinery and the huge coal-loading installa-tions on the verge of his Harbour Board's new harbour. He also thought about making an attractive environment. He got a tree-planting scheme going, and most of the trees he planted himself.

AFTER being run round the new Gladstone by its mayor, I had lunch at a three-storeyed motel on the town outskirts with Queensland Alumina's Noel Wootton, whose title was not *Public* Relations Officer but *Community* Relations Officer. Q.A.L. worked hard at "relating to" the Gladstone community. C.R.A.'s Sir Maurice Mawby was Queensland Alumina's chairman. The partners in this Gladstone enterprise were Kaiser of U.S.A. (44 per cent), Alcan of Canada (20) and Pechiney of France, Europe's biggest aluminium maker (20), Comalco (16). For a Golding to get a $200-million plant (as it soon would be with extensions) for Gladstone, there first had to be a Mawby to get those big overseas companies interested in processing bauxite in Australia.

Bauxite is processed into alumina by grinding it fine and then dissolving the alumina content with caustic soda. Alumina stays in solution, red mud is drained off. Filtering produces a precipitate that is dried into a crystalline white powder—a million tons of it a year, worth about $50 million. In May 1970 plans to *double* this output were announced. The expansion would make Gladstone's the largest alumina plant in the world. Of the 650 staff (which would be expanded to 950) very few were to be seen within the plant. So much was automated that operatives barely outnumbered maintenance men. The plant ran twenty-four hours a day, seven days a week, and industrial relations were good: they had to be.

"If the plant stopped," Noel Wootton said, "the cost of getting it running again could be a million dollars."

WHEN THE HELICOPTER from Heron Island brought me back to Gladstone there was a small plane waiting for me, a Cessna I had chartered. I do not normally charter planes, but Moura, ninety miles inland, was a hard place to get to in any other way; and Paul Grubb, the Ford dealer and air-charterer at Gladstone, had quoted me, for a two-hour trip that would deliver me to Rockhampton after Moura, a price so very reasonable ($40) that I was not surprised to learn that he was also the District Commissioner of Boy Scouts.

Drought had parched the cattle-country hinterland we flew over. Beyond the brigalow plain appeared a low range of light-coloured hills. As we came closer to these hills I could see that nothing grew on them, they were formed of loose earth. The "range" that stretched for miles was man-made. The hills were piled-up overburden that had covered, to a depth of about fifty feet, a great seam of coal. The dark floor of the open cut was rather like a black river running through a pale ravine, except that it had toy-sized trucks and bulldozer-loaders on it.

The coal was being mined by Thiess Peabody Mitsui. The company that held contracts to deliver $400-million worth of coal to Japan by 1977 was 22 per cent Australian-owned through the holding of Thiess Bros (the brothers in the 1920s were small farmers who couldn't afford to buy a chaff-cutter); 58 per cent American (Pea-body Coal); and 20 per cent Japanese (Mitsui). The government-built railway line from Moura to Gladstone had cost $27 million.

However, I hadn't chartered a plane to see a coalmine, even one that was a major reason why New South Wales would soon be running second to Queensland as a coal producer. What I wanted to see was the thing that had built this range of dirt so that the miners could get at the coal. And there it was, looking anything but toy-sized from the air, this monster machine called a Walking Dragline. (PLATE 9.)

There was no bigger earth mover in the world than this American-made Marion Type-8900 Electric Walking Dragline. It looked like a huge crane except that the boom (which was 275 feet long) stuck out of what was, when you were close to it, like a five-storey building. The building was a power-house, stacked with motors that added up 33,000 horsepower. The main thing the motors had to do was swing the boom and haul the bucket that hung off the boom on cables as thick as my leg. The bucket itself weighed a hundred tons. It scooped up two hundred tons of earth at one bite, tearing it out of the side of the open cut it was making, and making another dust cloud when it tipped the earth on the summit of its latest hill. The cost of this mechanical behemoth was not a million dollars, it was *thirteen million* dollars. It weighed six and a half thousand tons. And it walked.

The monster walked because that was the only way it could change its position. No wheels or tracks could have borne its weight. Its "feet"—one either side of the great round turntable it sat on and moved round on—were eighty-foot-long slabs of rectilinear steel. They lifted about seven feet off the ground, then they moved forward about seven feet. If it needed to be moved to another place to dig another open cut it could walk there at the rate of eight hundred feet an hour.

The Cessna's pilot, John Phillips, had whizzed me round and round while I shot photographs, then landed on a cattle-station's airstrip and an arranged car had come out with the mine's personnel manager, W. H. Chapman, and taken us to where I could see the dragline close-up. It was so big that you had to stand back about two hundred yards to get it in a photograph. I asked how many people ran it, and the mine man said, "Three. An operator, an oiler and another man." Three-man shifts worked it twenty-four hours a day, seven days a week.

As I looked at the dragline the bucket stopped its dragging-digging, swung over and lowered down to come to rest not far from us. The room I work in at home would have fitted inside it, easily.

"Smoko?" I queried.

"No. You're going to be lucky. I'm around here all the time, and I haven't seen it walk in a week. It's going to walk now."

And walk it did, the feet going slowly up and then down again and the whole building-sized thing heaving forward one seven-foot step. Then it went back to work on its range-building.

ON THE FLIGHT to Rockhampton I looked down on a crater-like hole in the ground, an open cut so big it made the town on its rim look small. This was the once-great gold mine that is still a gold mine but is now principally a copper mine—Mount Morgan. It is a wonder a film scenarist hasn't got on to the Mount Morgan story: it is such a lode of drama.

The story could start in 1880 with the wife of a feckless stockman, Sandy Gordon, begging the Morgan brothers who owned the cattle station to give Sandy, whom they had sacked for his drinking, another chance. If they did he'd show them where there was gold. They did, and the rich Mount Morgan mine was born. The Morgans got a lot of gold. Then the mine seemed to be petering out. The day he sold half the shares in the mine for £88,000, "Fred Morgan was so delighted with his shrewdness that he shouted champagne to all comers in Rockhampton," says the brilliant historian of Australian mining, Geoffrey Blainey.[2]

The buyer of the Morgan shares was a red-haired, English-born, Westminster-schooled Rockhampton solicitor, William Knox D'Arcy. He was soon to be the richest man in Australia, his shares worth over £6,000,000, his dividends from Mount Morgan's gold such that he could buy a house in Grosvenor Square in London, a country seat, a box at Royal Ascot and entertain a hundred guests in his private enclosure at Epsom. Melba and Caruso sang at his parties. The miners winning the gold got seven shillings a day, which was reckoned good pay in the nineties.

The other major shareholders were the brothers Hall. Walter Hall became so rich that his wife was able to bequeath a million pounds to found, in Melbourne, the Walter and Eliza Hall Trust. This, subsequently, was able to spend more than a million on the relief of poverty, the advancement of education and religion, and the setting up of the Walter and Eliza Hall Institute of Medical Research at the Royal Melbourne Hospital.

William Knox D'Arcy, living it up in London, became interested in searching for oil. He thought of drilling in Australia, but decided there could be no oil there, so he concentrated on the Middle East, in Persia. Now the Mount Morgan mine wasn't doing nearly so well and, having paid out all its profits in dividends, it was having trouble meeting the expenses of changing over to a copper mine. Indeed, if its financial position had been known, D'Arcy's shares would have plummeted. In 1904 a very worried D'Arcy pleaded with the management

in Australia to cut costs, save money. Mount Morgan's resourceful
mine manager devised a system of timbering tunnels and mining
chambers that was much cheaper.

D'Arcy, whose Persian explorations had struck oil that had very
soon ceased to flow, had spent £225,000, and in 1905 was at the end
of his financial tether. He was about to approach the French Roth-
schilds for a loan when the British Admiralty (concerned that Britain
had no oil worth mentioning) stepped in. A British company would
finance further drilling on the D'Arcy leases in Persia. And Burmah
Oil did, for three years, without result. Having spent what it thought
was enough, Burmah was about to pull out when, in Geoffrey
Blainey's words:

"At four in the morning of 26th May 1908 the drill tapped oil,
which spurted above the derrick and bathed the drillers and crew.
They had found the largest oilfield then known and on that field
began the gigantic firm known successively as Anglo-Persian, Anglo-
Iranian and British Petroleum. . . . It was the wealth of Mount Morgan
and the fact that it was held in few hands that gave Britain a prize
that even in 1956 was providing nearly half of its income from overseas investments."[3]

It was a great year for Britain, 1908, and a great one for D'Arcy,
who got nearly a million pounds' worth of oil shares; but not a good
year at Mount Morgan. The cheaper form of timbering had seemed
safe enough, even the miners thought it was: until in September one
tunnel roof caved in and crushed seven men to death, and in November thousands of tons of rock smashed down through the timbers of
another roof and five more miners died.

In Rockhampton, where I had to wait for a TAA plane, I had some
drinks with a couple of local identities who had been at Daydream
Island when I was there—Bevan Verney, who had told me not to miss
seeing Moura's Walking Dragline, and John Nott, who was developing Keppel Island as a tourist resort. The hotel we were at was the
Criterion, balconied with iron lace. Its publican used to be Fred
Morgan, and it was here that he shouted champagne for all when he
sold the Morgan shareholding in the Mount Morgan mine to the man
who, more than anyone, got Britain her Middle Eastern oil, sheiks
their Rolls-Royces, a million Persians their jobs, and today's United
Arab Republic the avid support of the Soviet Union.

"She's Booming at the Isa"

IN ALL THE INTERIOR of Queensland north of Brisbane—an area as big as Britain-France-Italy combined—there is only one city. And that is only a city by Queensland definition, which says over 18,000 population can constitute one.

"Yair, the Isa's been a city since sixty-eight," says the Australian miner in the pub. He speaks of Mount Isa as the Isa, just as Charters Towers is spoken of as the Towers and the Brisbane suburb of Wollongabba as the Gabba.

"Twenty thousand people here now. And she'll grow a lot more yet, she's booming." The Australian miner turns to the Finnish miner he is drinking with. "Soon be like bloody Brisbane, won't it, Vic?" Veikko, the Finnish miner, grins and nods.

"S'pose they told you—" he says it off-handedly in a deprecating, wouldn't-want-to-skite tone (but he's making darn sure that somebody tells you)—"it's the biggest bloody city in the world."

"Thass true," Vic the Finn says, looking at you.

The area administered by the Mount Isa City Council is bigger, by several thousand square miles, than the Netherlands. It used to be part of the Shire of Cloncurry. This was felt to be too much like the tail wagging the dog. Apart from the fact that Cloncurry had only a few thousand people, the Isa had the Mine. It employs 5,000 people.

Mount Isa Mines was not only Australia's biggest producer of copper. It looked like becoming, perhaps by 1975, the biggest miner of silver-lead-zinc in the world. Those four ores were coming from one great mine. Another huge lode of silver-lead-zinc was to be developed. This Hilton mine would mean a satellite town for another five thousand people out here in the dry brown porcupine-grass country where the Leichhardt River seldom flows.

The nearest city to Mount Isa is Townsville. The milk comes from Townsville, 600 miles by rail in refrigerated vans, after it has come 280 miles by road from farms on the Atherton Tableland. In terms of distance this is like London getting its milk from Vienna: it is the longest milk run in the world.

Vegetables come by rail and by air not only from Townsville but from Brisbane and Adelaide, a thousand miles away. South Australia's capital is a little closer than Queensland's is to Mount Isa.

"It's not as though we couldn't grow our own vegetables," the locals tell you. "The rainfall may be only fifteen inches a year, but there's tons of water, what with Lake Moondarra—look at the flower gardens, look at the lemon-trees. Some blokes do have a backyard plot of vegetables. But you couldn't make a go of it commercially. You couldn't pay the wages."

In October 1970 a new wage agreement gave Mount Isa's underground miners the highest earnings of any workers in Australia—$9,300 a year (almost $180 a week). A tradesman on shift work got $7,158 and an unskilled worker went up to $6,220 (say $120 a week). These figures included prosperity loading and bonus that, together, were worth $26 a week when I was there, and have since increased.

I said to an M.I.M. man, and knew that I was leading with my chin, "So everybody gets twenty-six dollars a week 'isolation money'."

"You've got to be joking! What isolation? What are we isolated from? The races? On every Saturday. High school for the kids? We've got one—two, there's a tech. college as well. Good shops for the women, clubs for the men—Rotary, Apex, Lions, Jaycees—golf, bowls, tennis, all the sports, even archery, stock-car racing, the lot. Movies, plays the Mount Isa Theatrical Society puts on—"

"No television." (Mount Isa has TV now, since the end of 1970.)

"Well, not *yet* there isn't. And when we get it I suppose people won't read twenty thousand books a month from the town library."

"*City* library."

The M.I.M. man laughed. "That helped, you know. The prestige bit. People saying, 'Oh, we're a *city* now. . . .' Next letter to Mum down south: 'You've always said you don't see how we can live up here so far from the *city*. Well, Mum, we've got news for you—'."

"Yes, they must have liked that. What about being so far from the sea?"

"If you mean swimming, sailing, power-boating, water-skiing, fishing, we've got Lake Moondarra [PLATE 10]. And every family has a car. They shoot up to the Gulf for week-ends. They think nothing of eating up the six hundred miles to Townsville when they go on vacation. They'll go down to the Gold Coast if they feel like it."

"The Gold Coast. That's twelve hundred miles each way."

"They do it. You people from the south, you let a bit of distance jolly well scare you! We're used to it up here."

"Well, I like that, John—from you!"

"Just another Pommy bastard who's turned into an Australian one." John was from London.

The sense of isolation is there, nevertheless. And what Mount Isa does about it is interesting. On a look-out hill beside the town is a big signpost bristling with pointers that point in every direction and to everywhere. The pointers tell how many hundreds of miles off are TOWNSVILLE, BRISBANE, ALICE SPRINGS, ADELAIDE, DARWIN, SYDNEY, MELBOURNE—and that it is almost four thousand to TOKYO, 9,398 to LONDON, 10,001 to NEW YORK, the distances to EDINBURGH and NOUMEA and MERAUKE in New Guinea and to a dozen other places, including 4,787 to the SOUTH POLE and 7,650 to the NORTH POLE and 12,117 to RIO DE JANEIRO. A citizen can look up at this signpost and think of Mount Isa, all distances measured from it, as the centre of the world.

There is a second reason why Mount Isa Mines pays high. It can afford to. Its profit increased, for the year 1968-9, by *one hundred and sixty-five per cent* to $27 million. And the mine went on to *double* that to $55 million profit for 1969-70.

There was a time when the Broken Hill Proprietary could have bought control of what has been called "a second Broken Hill" for £500,000. In 1926 the mine was being hawked in London. It was saved from closure by J. L. Urquhart whose companies owned mines, smelters, steelworks, riverboats, sawmills and factories in Russia until, in 1917, the Revolution took them. Urquhart put what money he had left into Mount Isa, which swallowed the lot. Urquhart went to New York and saw Senator Simon Guggenheim, president of the giant American Smelting and Refining Company, who agreed in 1930 to put in £500,000. Mount Isa swallowed that, too, and six months later the Americans had to put up another £600,000. After they tried to sell their "white elephant", as it was considered, and could find no buyer, the American company put in still another £500,000. Such were its debts and loans that Mount Isa Mines didn't pay a dividend until 1947, and then only because the price of lead went up. World War II had made the mine's copper highly economic, but the end of the war saw it still deep in debt. The man who made Mount Isa the great mine it is today was the present Australian president, Sir George Fisher; but it was American money that sustained it, when no other money was forthcoming. It was still 52.6 per cent American-owned.

It was actually predicted in 1943—and by a most reputable Australian geologist—that within ten years Mount Isa would be a ghost town. Sir George Fisher told residents in November 1970 that the mine would still be going strong in their grandchildren's day.

"MOUNT" is rather a big word for any of the hills in ranges that don't look as high as the Isa's "trademark", the slender striped smokestack of the mine that fills in the farther side of the picture you see from the look-out with the signposts (PLATE 10).

The look-out was named for John Campbell Miles. He was "one of those jacks of all trades who wandered the outback . . . wiry, quiet and temperate . . . liked to watch the billy boil and the sun rise . . . decided to go to the Northern Territory and maybe prospect for gold . . . reached the dead copper town of Mount Elliott and saw a billiard table standing in the sun where once a hotel had stood . . . chipped a lump of rock that was black and honeycombed and unusually heavy

[lead] . . . wondered if he had found another Broken Hill. . . ." Professor Blainey writes Australian mining history very well.[1]

That was in 1923. Miles's samples assayed an average sixty per cent of lead. A rush to the field started. Miles got a good cheque and faded from the scene. His bushman partner, Bill Simpson, worth £30,000, took a taxi the 1,200 miles to Brisbane, where he went on a bender and didn't see the car that killed him while he was crossing the street.

When John Campbell Miles died his ashes were buried under a vividly coloured hunk of ore at the base of a memorial clock-tower in one of the main streets of Queensland's newest city. At night lights shine on it through cylinders of copper artwork.

There is a good deal of copper art in Mount Isa, and just about all the rest of it—the "Seven Seas" mural in one of the hotel bars, a more imaginative mural called "Night in the Bush" in the dining-room of the Barkly Hotel that uses bush wood with copper, the picture of the mine in etched copper that hangs in the Base Hospital, an abstract called "Universe", and the copper-rod murals at the Mount Isa Airport—all these were the work of a Czech who had left Prague in 1948, when Communism came to his country. The former teacher of graphic arts in Prague, Vladimir Pinsker, whom everybody knows and calls Val, was now Staff Artist at M.I.M.

Only half the adult Isans were born in Australia. Fifteen per cent came from Britain. The next largest immigrant group, just ahead of the Germans, were the Finns, about 1,100 of them.

"They make damned good citizens," said Bill Weigh, the mayor. So did the Germans, who had just built themselves a posh new Concordia Club. There were also Dutch, Greeks, Spaniards, Estonians, Latvians, Poles, Yugoslavs, Hungarians, Swiss, French, Italians.

Giuseppe (Joe) Vaiente was born just outside of Verona. He had cut sugarcane on the North Queensland coast, saved enough money to buy a share in his uncle's cane-farm, gone home to Italy and got married, stopped off at Mount Isa on the way back and saw opportunity there. He started with a small guest-house, and since March 1969 a good place to stay in Mount Isa was the Verona Motel. The Premier of Queensland had opened it. Its restaurant served the best barramundi (flown in from the Gulf) I have ever eaten and the accommodation was first-rate.

THE MINE itself attracts tourists to Mount Isa, especially in the winter months when the days remain warm and the skies are a rainless blue. Visitors are given a guided tour of the mine. I was shown the smelting and some other operations (few visitors are taken underground) but did not go on the tour. People who did told me the M.I.M. guide was particularly good.

Explanation of the mining and smelting of the copper-zinc-silver-lead, without seeing the processes, is like hearing only the soundtrack of a film; it cannot convey much. And, in a modern mine like this one, so much is automated. Hauling the skips—filled with up to twenty-four tons of copper ore, hauled at the rate of 220 skips a shift—becomes an electrical operation, with the skips denoted by lights on a control panel. Every Tuesday the hauling cables are X-rayed: this shows if any of the interior strands of the wire ropes are fraying. The blast furnaces and convertors are always dramatic when the molten metal pours into one of the "kettles", glowing red and sending out a wave of heat and a wreath of pale smoke in the dim iron hall.

Mount Isa is Queensland's biggest industrial enterprise and one of Australia's largest: the twelfth-largest mine in the world, although, as silver mines go, it is the second largest; and the largest in the world mining silver-lead and copper, which do not usually occur side by side as they do here. Of these metals the most valuable production was of copper, with lead second and silver third. The mine was producing about 90,000 tons of copper a year. Of all minerals it had, still in the ground, something like $7,000 million worth at prices ruling at the end of 1970.

As well as the new Hilton mine that is expected to double production five years or so hence, Mount Isa Mines could be working, in the near future, what may be the biggest lead-zinc deposit in the world. This lode is at McArthur River across the border in the Northern Territory.

When I flew out of Mount Isa it was to go to the Northern Territory (or return to it, rather, for I had flown in from Alice Springs) and the Connellan Airways plane landed at McArthur River. While it was refuelling I talked to a surveyor from the Department of Mineral Resources. He said that diamond drilling had established that the zinc-lead lode was very extensive. Yet the outcropping on the surface was so small that the exploration team had nearly missed it, and drilled it only as an afterthought.

It is not enough to find a vast lode of ore. It must be of a grade that is economic before it is worth mining. Having mined it, you must be able to treat it, extract the metal. The McArthur River lead-zinc was said to be very complex, difficult to treat. M.I.M. was working on that. It was the kind of difficulty they had encountered, and overcome, before.

If McArthur River was a "goer" there would be a big new town on the map where at present there was nothing to the north except sleepy little Borroloola with an Aboriginal mission, a welfare officer and a

Latvian crocodile shooter who lived in a galvanized tank, not even a pub any more; and to the south there was Brunette Downs cattle station, which was twice the size of Delaware. M.I.M. already knew where it would build the port that would have to be built on the Gulf of Carpentaria, to ship out the ore, and approximately what it all would cost, $200 million.

THREE of the four hotels in Mount Isa had the distinction of being in the ten biggest beer-sellers in Australia. When I "did the pubs" with Val Pinsker, he introduced me to Herb McHugh, the publican of the Mt Isa Hotel, whose beer purchases for the year ran to the staggering figure of $520,929.

"Second in the State," he said proudly.

There were some Aborigines or part-Aborigines in the bar and I asked if they were notable beer drinkers. Herb McHugh shook his head. "Wine is what they want—and they won't buy anything that hasn't got a bright red label on the flagon. They reckon the redder the label the better the wine."

From cashing their pay cheques, which they had to endorse, the publican had found that there were still a number who could not write. These "signed" with a thumbprint. Those who could write were likely to sign such names as Sam Tuesday or Tuesday Johnson, and there was one named Tuesday Friday. I didn't think this or the thumbprints or the red-label wine funny. Australia's failure to educate its Aboriginal Australians is a national disgrace.

THE FLYING DOCTOR SERVICE of Australia, which has gained renown world wide, began spreading its "mantle of safety" over the outback when, on 2nd August 1927, the first flying doctor trip was made from Cloncurry. It was to Mount Isa to treat an injured miner.

Nowadays Mount Isa is a base for the Royal Flying Doctor Service, covering a large area of Queensland and the Northern Territory. The same radio system as the base doctor used to prescribe treatment for patients at isolated cattle stations and mining camps carried the lessons of the School of the Air to children in remote areas. There are now about a score of these bases, and more than a thousand outposts with two-way radios.

Waking Brisbane, Sleepy Koalas

QUEENSLAND'S BRISBANE, from the point of view of overseas visitors— not that it was getting many—was the most "typically Australian" of the State capitals.

Mt Isa's world centres on the mine with the striped chimney: it has proved one of the richest copper-silver-lead producers in any country.

Lake Moondarra, a big blue eye in what used to be an arid-faced landscape, gives Mt Isa's citizens plenty of water, and water-skiing as well.

11/QUEENSLAND *Rainbow lorikeets, as tame as they are vivid, flock in thousands to morning and evening feeding at Currumbin Bird Sanctuary on the Gold Coast.*

American servicemen who in World War II spent leave in Brisbane, or were attached to General Douglas MacArthur's headquarters there, found Sydney brighter and its girls less inhibited, but Brisbane was just "so Australian"—as Australian as those sleepy, slowpoke, kinda-cute koala bears up the river at Lone Pine.

Urban Australians from Sydney and Melbourne looked on Brisbane with less tolerant eyes. It was, they were inclined to say, not so much a city as Australia's biggest country town—essentially provincial in its friendliness and philistinism, its casualness and cultural lag. It was also —worst sin in their book—wowserish. Wasn't its largest hotel, the Canberra, run by the Temperance League, and if a beer bottle or whisky flask was found in your dreary room you were warned, or even asked to leave? Brisbane might be able to boast the best City Hall in Australia, and it had some other nice Palladian public buildings, but, its critics used to ask, where was its Conservatorium of Music?

It might have a rather beaut winter climate, but it had no beaches, being twelve miles up the Brisbane River, which put it a hundred miles beyond the pale to Sydneysiders—half of whom lived no nearer to Sydney beaches than half Brisbane's suburbanites were from the sandy shores of Moreton Bay, where they went swimming when Sydney was shivering. Brisbane, being halfway tropical, *must* get more rain than Sydney, Sydneysiders firmly believed. (In fact it gets an average three inches less rain than Sydney's 47 inches.)

BRISBANE 1969 was, naturally, changed from the Brisbane I had last taken a close look at twenty years before when I was there to do a radio documentary programme about it for the A.B.C. Then, 400,000 people had lived in Brisbane, a third of all Queenslanders. Now 700,000 did, out of 1,800,000 Queenslanders, a higher percentage. Booming Townsville-Gladstone-Mount Isa had not managed to decentralize the prosperity of the Brisbane that was still the tap to the Queensland bonanza barrel.

Not only were there such changes as trams gone, trains dieselized, Conservatorium of Music provided; and a new theatre for live plays going into, of all places, the State Government Insurance Office building (hence its name, the S.G.I.O. Theatre). Doubling its population meant that Brisbane was doubling its size. Wherever I looked from my tenth-floor room, cranes were angling on the city skyline, adding high (well, sixteen-storey) new buildings to the ones that had already reared in a city where the tower of the City Hall used to reign unchallenged.

The Brisbane accommodation picture had changed greatly, for the better. The Parkroyal Motor Inn where I was staying had suites of international standard, with service to match and an excellent dining-

G

room. It was when I went down to dine that some gas went out of the New Brisbane balloon.

When I ordered a half bottle of wine with my dinner, the waiter explained that there would be a slight delay. A young man had to hop on a motor scooter and race off to a hotel to buy it. The Parkroyal, a top tourist asset to the city, had been open a month, but its restaurant's liquor licence had not yet been granted.

Of the forty-five restaurants listed, in 1969 only thirteen were liquor-licensed.

So when, in Sydney in the third week of February 1970, I opened my morning newspaper I could hardly believe what I read:

SWEEPING QLD
LIQUOR PLANS

BRISBANE, Wednesday.—A meeting of the joint Queensland Government parties today approved sweeping liquor reforms.

The Liberal and Country Party parliamentarians agreed to: *Sunday hotel trading throughout Queensland; admission of women to all public and other bars; establishment of non-residential taverns; licences for live theatres.*

Queensland, the slow one, had suddenly jumped out in front with more liberal liquor legislation than any State in Australia had. The proposals became legislation in April 1970 and were hailed, rightly enough, as "a great boost to tourism". Liquor licences would be granted to all restaurants of good standard, and night clubs could serve liquor until 3 a.m.

The Crest International, Brisbane's first luxury-standard hotel—with 24-hour room service and convention facilities for 700—opened for business in the city's heart, King George's Square, in August 1971.

Lennon's Hotel, for long the main one, is to be pulled down and the Federal Hotels propsal was to erect, on another site, a new Lennons of international standard.

BRISBANE began, as a convict settlement in 1824, soon after the explorer John Oxley had found a "not ineligible site" up the river from Moreton Bay, which Cook had named after the Earl of Morton; but Cook's biographer, Hawkesworth, slipped in an "e". The fervid Scot who was then Chief Justice of New South Wales named the new place Edinglassie (a combination, y'ken, of Edinburgh and Glasgow), but official noses wrinkled at this and the name soon became that of Governor Brisbane. It was part of New South Wales until 1859. The new State—which was to be called Cooksland, but Queen Victoria preferred Queensland—started (according to its first Governor, Sir

George Bowen) with sevenpence-halfpenny in the Treasury; and a thief broke in and stole that. A century later Queensland was producing $150-million worth of sugar a year and a third of all Australia's beef.

The visible sign of Brisbane's convict origins is the round stone Tower Mill that stands up on Wickham Terrace. It has long been referred to as the Observatory, though it was never used as one. The sails the windmill was fitted with originally, to grind corn, would not turn; so it became a treadmill worked by hapless convicts in leg-irons. In 1935 two experimenters with television established themselves in the top of the old tower, and from it were transmitted the first telecast pictures in Australia.

The modern Tower Mill Motel that now dominates Wickham Terrace took its circular shape from the old mill. I stayed there, and liked it, in June 1971. It rises ten storeys to a very good restaurant-with-view.

There is a revolving restaurant within the 24th floor of the S.G.I.O. Building.

The tourist walking about in Brisbane will locate himself more easily if he remembers: The ladies run one way, the gentlemen the other. Streets named Ann, Adelaide, Elizabeth, Charlotte, Mary, Margaret run parallel and Edward, Albert, George, William run crosswise. Between where Albert meets Ann and Adelaide stands the City Hall. Its tower is no longer the viewing place it used to be, tall new buildings having blocked off parts of the Brisbane panorama. The roof garden was a Kindercraft Centre where mothers could leave babies and children under the age of six while they shopped; and so could tourists with infants avail themselves of this service, which the Brisbane City Council subsidized. Since the women on the staff worked voluntarily, charges were a nominal twenty-five cents for the first hour and ten cents an hour thereafter, plus "nappy service, 15 cents a day". The Kindy, as it was called, could take 126 children. (Sydney City Council's child-minding centre takes only half as many.)

Brisbane was friendlier than Sydney to the stranger, a less urban and more suburban place. The very atmosphere seemed to be brought into the city each morning by the people who came to work from suburbs with names as natively Australian as Kangaroo Point and Coorparoo, Toowong and Indooroopilly (and others as non-Australian as Merthyr and Highgate Hill), and when they went home in the evening this atmosphere went with them, leaving a sort of vacuum. The city itself created no ambience such as night-time Sydney with its effulgent King's Cross, where people live within the city to a far greater extent than they do in Brisbane.

The taverns the new liquor legislation allows would do something to fill the vacuum tourists abhor. Brisbane would become less censorious of theatre like *Hair* and, sipping a glass of champagne or a Fourex beer at interval, people would chuckle over the old days when magazines allowed in other States were banned in Brisbane. Yet it would be a pity, I thought, if New Brisbane modelled itself on Sydney.

Brisbane had a wonderful chance to create eating-drinking-entertainment places with Queensland-Australian, warm-climate character.

The Brisbane City Council was in the position of controlling the whole 384 square miles of metropolitan area, whereas in other State capitals authority was divided between the councils of many municipalities. Under a master plan conceived by its Lord Mayor, Alderman Clem Jones, Brisbane in 1971 was "having a heart transplant [with such new buildings as the Crest International Hotel at its centre] that "may make it the best-planned, best working urban centre in Australia, Canberra included," according to one writer.[1]

Brisbane's suburbia was at least distinctive. Whereas the Sydney pattern was of red-tile roofs of boxy brick bungalows, up here it was of corrugated-iron roofs, commonly painted green, on weatherboard houses that were high on stilt-like supports. This arrangement not only raised the house for cooling breezes to blow through it and under it, and frustrated termites. The space beneath provided garage, laundry, dad's workshop, and a wet-weather drying area and play area for the children. Often it was screened in front with lattice, against which grew the ubiquitous poinsettia, offering up its scarlet on skinny arms, the sensuous white florets of the frangipanni, and the flamboyantly lovely hibiscus—though these were all too often the "double" variety, a monstrous mutation.

"Brisbane I find a very pleasant place to live," said Austin Lloyd of the Tourist Bureau as he drove me up through the natural parkland to the summit of Mount Coot-tha. And looking down from this 900-foot mount, across the river serpentining its way towards the city-centre on a tongue of land, with the nearest bend making a glorious green campus-front for the University of Queensland at St Lucia, and far more trees remaining in the suburbs than Sydney has preserved, Brisbane looked, indeed, a pleasant place to live—for the average man, who didn't care whether *Hair* was allowed to be performed there or not.

QUEENSLAND is, without any doubt, the Australian state with the greatest potential for tourist development. (The other area of great potential is the Centre, out of Alice Springs, but this is only a region not a state.)

But what does *Brisbane* have to attract the tourist—the Australian tourist from the south, mainly, and the tourist from overseas?

The main thing Brisbane has is a far better winter climate than any other Australian capital city. Its thermometer runs an average maximum of 78°F. in July—which doesn't mean that you shouldn't take your topcoat, because the average-minimum is 50. But Brisbane is warm when Sydney is wrapped up and Melbourne is shivering. This climatic benison is mainly of interest to Australian travellers: tourists from the northern hemisphere come mostly in their winter which is the Australian summer. Even American tourists who came in winter were still routed through Canberra to Melbourne, because Brisbane lacked the kind of accommodation Melbourne had in Interconti-nental's Southern Cross Hotel. That situation should change by 1972, and if American visitors in our winter are happier, as well as warmer, in Brisbane than in Melbourne, they will tell their friends, and Brisbane will be really "in the money".

But, what do they *do* in Brisbane, and what does the Australian tourist from Sydney-Melbourne-Adelaide-Hobart do?

Within a hundred road miles of the city are: The Gold Coast, that stretches from Southport, forty-seven miles south-east; the Sunshine Coast that goes north as far as Noosa; the Darling Downs with Toowoomba, eighty miles west; and, due south about sixty miles, the remarkable mountain-top Lamington National Park.

Within twenty miles are the beaches of Moreton Bay. Out from these shores are resort islands. The American survey team that reported on Australian tourist development in 1965 recommended "that the development of Stradbroke and Moreton Islands near Brisbane should be planned on a long-range basis while the land is still fully available". Miners of the beach minerals (rutile, zircon, ilmenite) have long been at work on Stradbroke. Perhaps there is room for them and tourism, too, as Stradbroke is a large island, thirty-eight miles long. Moreton Island has what are claimed to be the highest sand dunes in the world. The American survey team clearly had it in mind that these islands could be developed as resort lands that would not repeat the gaucheries of the Gold Coast.

The best excursion Brisbane offered was up the river to the Lone Pine Koala Sanctuary. The *H.K.F. Report*[2] rated this as "one of Australia's fine visitor attractions". Lone Pine is the best place in Australia for American visitors to see those "cute Australian native bears", the koalas. The Queensland koala is the most appealing of all: it is smaller, only half the weight of the Victorian koalas on Phillip Island, lighter in colour, softer in fur, more "cuddly" (PLATE 13).

CAM REID (he was christened Claude Alexander Miller), who began the Lone Pine Sanctuary, was a boy aged seven in 1898 when, coming from Sunday School in the Brisbane suburb of Enoggera, he saw some bigger boys aiming a .22 rifle at a koala in a tree. He rushed in to stop them shooting it, and got his face punched.

The utterly harmless, inoffensive and most vulnerable of unique Australian animals was slaughtered almost to extinction. In 1908 sixty thousand koala pelts passed through the Sydney market. In 1924 *two million* koala skins were exported from eastern Australia. In 1927 the Queensland Government licensed ten thousand trappers who destroyed so many koalas that 600,000 pelts were exported under the names of "beaver" and the remarkable phoneyism of "Adelaide Chinchilla".

Cam Reid, who was then thirty-six and had had a bad time as a soldier in World War I, was running a small dairy farm on the Brisbane River and doing tourist trips on the side. He couldn't stand the open-season-on-koalas horror of 1927. In that year, on his farm, he started the Lone Pine Sanctuary.

He started with four bears. Ironically enough, he could not get the slaughter-permitting government's permission to keep more than four in captivity.

All Reid knew about koalas was that he liked them. People he asked for advice predicted that the bears would die—as they would have if Cam Reid and his wife had not tended them with such care and followed them through the bush, watching which eucalyptus leaves they ate. Of the 370 varieties of Australian eucalypts koalas eat only eighteen kinds. Of these only seven are their sustenance. The others are either medicine or, as Cam Reid put it, "like sweets are to human beings". His four bears thrived and began to breed. A "maternity ward" was built for them. It all cost money. Reid opened his place to the public, but didn't charge admission. He put out a collection box. At the end of one Sunday afternoon the box yielded two shillings and sevenpence.

Before World War II Australians were uninterested in koalas. According to Cam Reid (who was still running the place when I first went there), American servicemen were the ones who put his Lone Pine Sanctuary on the tourist map.

"The American boys used to come to Lone Pine in droves, with Australian girls—who told their families where they had been, and people started to think, 'If it's good enough for the Yanks. . . .' Then the rush was on."

Cam Reid brought tourists up-river in his own boat. He trained an Alsatian dog, "Strongheart", to carry a koala on its back. He added other animals, birds and snakes to his fauna park. He bred his koalas to the number of fifty. An American doctor offered £450 for one, because his son loved it so. Reid explained that, without its diet of certain leaves, the bear would die of starvation.

The koala is not, of course, a bear. It has no animal relations, though it may have had the same ancestors as the ground-burrowing wombat and the long-tailed possum. A marsupial, it is only three-quarters of an inch long at birth. It lives on two teats in the maternal pouch for six months. It continues in the pouch for two months more, then it comes out and is hugged to its mother's body and carried on her back. Essentially a tree-dweller, the koala is clumsy on the ground. It moves about mainly at night. By day it is usually found sitting slumped in a tree fork, asleep.

The Reids (Cam, who had grown old, had two sons running Lone Pine) sold the sanctuary in 1964 to the Robertsons. It is now being run, and run very well indeed, by two intelligent young men, Pat and Paul Robertson. They had migrated from England in the fifties with their father, who had become a successful builder in Brisbane.

The koala's aboriginal name means "doesn't drink". Cam Reid held that koalas got all the liquid they needed from gum leaves, and that their kidneys could not cope with water. The Robertsons saw koalas drinking during the hot weather, and now they put bowls of water out for them.

The Robertsons' truck travels seventy miles to get the right leaves, of which the average adult koala chews up about two and a half pounds daily. There were 120 koalas at Lone Pine when I was last there, twenty-five of them still in the pouch: as well as kangaroos, emus, wallabies, wombats, Tasmanian Devils, quokkas (Western Australian short-tailed wallabies no bigger than hares), dingoes, and many kinds of birds and some snakes. The Robertsons release some of the koalas they breed, in natural parks where their food-trees grow. Koalas are now totally protected.

It is often written of the koala that it has an "appendix" six feet long. This intestinal tube is not comparable with the useless human appendix; it is a functional digestive tract, Pat Robertson said. There is a stage when the young koala eats a little of its mother's faeces, to take in bacterial organisms its metabolism requires.

Paul Robertson (who showed me how to hold a koala properly: cup your hand under its bottom so that it feels secure) said that his favourites among the animals in the sanctuary were not koalas and kangaroos, but possums and wombats. The possums at our place (now rare, for the bush that adjoined has been urbanized) have always been as cheeky as the magpies; but, on much slighter acquaintance, I can well understand his affection for the waddly wombat, which needs more protection than it is getting.

Because wombats burrowed under rabbit-proof fences, the Victorian Government had been paying out $9,000 a year for wombat scalps—and irrespective of whether they were trapped near fences or in forests where they did no damage at all. One gets the impression that politicians dependent on the "country vote" will agree to anything that gives a farmer's son some pocket money.

That in 1924 two million koalas were killed for their pelts may suggest that they were greatly abundant on the eastern seaboard, although they were already extinct in Western Australia; but this was not the case. They are slow breeders as well as slow movers and, because of their daytime somnolence, so vulnerable that they probably would not have survived the Aboriginal hunters but for the fact that koala flesh is so eucalyptus-flavoured it is inedible.

Anatomy of the Gold Coast

A CAUTIONARY TALE: Back in the Dreamtime of Australian Tourism, in the Year Nineteen Seventeen, an Estate Agent had some Land to sell at a place the Aborigines knew as Umbigumbi. It was a good place to Go Fishing, from the Beach and in the Nerang River at the back of the Beach. Along the River there was Mud and Mangroves and also Mosquitoes.

The main beach at Umbigumbi was called Main Beach and, being South of Southport, some people said it was South Southport. The Estate Agent did not Think Much of these Names.

What we want, to Get Them In, he said, is a name that means Surfers Paradise. He Thought and Thought, but the only Name he could Think Of that meant Surfers Paradise was Surfers Paradise.

That will Do, he said. Other People said, You have to Put In an Apostrophe and make it Surfer's Paradise or Surfers' Paradise, but the Estate Agent said, No I don't. And Surfers Paradise the name has Remained.

When the Road Went Through a Showman named Mister Cavill bought a piece of Another Estate called Southport Estate and put up a Hotel. He called it the Surfers Paradise Hotel, Southport, but in the Year Nineteen Thirty he Dropped the Southport. The place had become Surfers Paradise, and it was Popular, but it did not Boom until the Year Nineteen Fifty-two.

In the Year Nineteen Fifty a Writer came to Surfers Paradise and he looked at Mister Cavill's Hotel of Texture Brick, which had many Tropical Shrubs and was A-Twitter with Birds in cages, and he Walked About and came to the Muddy Banks of the River at the Back. The Writer said, I don't Think Much of This. And when he heard the Prices the Estate Agents were asking, for even the Land that Faced the Mud, he said, Ridiculous, and, No wonder that a Brisbane Journalist wrote that only the Rich could afford to Live Here and sarcastically christened the place the Gold Coast.

The People who Lived there Liked this name and puffed out their Chests and said, We live on the Gold Coast. And More and More people came and Bought Land at the Fancy Prices. The Writer of course did not Buy Any. He thought the place was Rather Vulgar as well as Greatly Over Priced. That was two years before the Boom began and the price of Land at Surfers Paradise went Sky High.

So the Writer did not become a Rich Man and he has to Write Books, and always Put In the Apostrophes.

THAT I THOUGHT Surfers Paradise "rather vulgar" in 1950 in no way alters the fact that the Gold Coast has become in 1970

—Destination 1, in travel-trade parlance, for Australian tourists and some overseas visitors, mostly from New Zealand, bringing to the area $35 million a year.

—A city, the City of the Gold Coast, stretching twenty beach-fronted miles from Southport (47 miles from Brisbane), to Coolangatta on the border of New South Wales, with a population of 60,000 permanent residents (expected to increase to 100,000 by 1975).

—A resortland with accommodation for 80,000 tourists at one time, in some 2,600 accommodation units of motels, blocks of flats, "serviced apartments", guest-houses and eighteen hotels.

—Australia's most highly developed tourist area as to entertainments and attractions—two of them (Marineland and Skiland) of international standard, and two (Currumbin Bird Sanctuary and Fleay's Fauna Park) of special Australian interest.

—The best-value tourist area in Australia, because of its particularly reasonable tariffs.

—A holiday region with a winter climate that is about six degrees warmer than Sydney's and ten degrees warmer than Melbourne's: average maximum of 72 in April-September, with average minimum of 53. The rainfall (54 inches), is, however, higher than Sydney's and twice Melbourne's; but, as ever when we go north, it is rain less evenly distributed, and more likely to be *rain* and less likely to be drizzle. The wettest months are January-February-March, the driest June-July-August.

IT IS NOT its winter climate that draws most people to the Gold Coast.

High Season is mid-December to the end of January, coinciding with the end-of-year school holidays. February-March-April (with

Easter) and the May school holidays are next-busiest. Then late-August to mid-September (school holidays again). In mid-September to mid-December there are lots of "Vacancy" signs. But the off season, in any protracted sense, is winter, late-May to mid-August. Off-season tariffs may be only two-thirds of high-season's. But even high-season rates are relatively low.

The accountant of a Sydney suburban bank tells me: "In January I manage to get my holidays, when the kids have theirs from school—we've got four kids—and we drive up to the Gold Coast. We don't stay at Surfers Paradise. Burleigh Heads is a better bet for the family man. It's nearly six hundred miles each way, and, with running around, we might do fourteen hundred. Adding in the cost of gas and oil, it still costs me less for three weeks up there than it would to go to some much-nearer resort in my own State. And we think we get a better holiday. There's more variety, more places to go, more things the children enjoy, and we can go to a different beach every day if we want to. We're all for the Gold Coast."

There are, in fact, twenty-one beaches. As to tariffs, in off-season June you could see signs hanging out saying "$2.75". The official accommodation guide listed some motels with rooms with showers, telephones, swimming pools, even squash courts and lawn bowls, for as little as $7 a day each (double occupancy $10) in the high season. Of the variety of attractions there is no question either.

Nor is there any question that for every hundred people who are attracted to this Australian Miami, this elongated Blackpool, there are perhaps ten people who are repelled by it.

As I came into the area from Brisbane, on a Skennar's coach, there was a butcher's shop. It had five signs proclaiming itself, in everything from paint to neon, as a butchery—on the glass, on the cantilever awning, above the awning, on the side wall; and right down the front, vertically, it was a MEAT EMPORIUM. This was apparently all right in the eyes of the City Council of the Gold Coast.

If you come into the Gold Coast from the other end, as I did on a Pioneer coach from Sydney, you find the gaucherie wrought by advertising signwriters and builders is pitched in a different key. All is jazzily gay with candy colours as you are whacked over the retina with the fact that you have arrived in what the brochure calls Australia's Holiday Playground. Although this is also described as "modern Australia's corroboree ground", the Gold Coast is about as Australian as a Coca-Cola bottle or a Mexican's mule. The hooks that catch its tourist trade are heavily baited with exotica. The coach drove past holiday flats or motels with such names as: RAPALLO, BALI HAI, COSTA RICA, SANTA MARIA, CABANA, MOANA, SUN VALLEY, MANDALAY, SHALIMAR, FLORIDA CAR-O-TEL, RANCH MOTEL, MARDI GRAS.

Midway along this twenty-mile strip is Palm Beach, with streets named Tahiti, Sarawak, Hawaii, Timor, Bali and Manila. Broadbeach, on the other hand, is sturdily British with avenues named Elizabeth, Charles, Phillip, Margaret, Alexandra, Chelsea and Britannia.

Architecturally (if that's the word) the design of many Gold Coast motels and flats is something one imagines being done by young draughtsmen in flowered shirts and sunglasses in offices with injunctions dangling over their drawing boards in the form of mobiles that say: *Taste is Waste!—Make it Bright, Never White!—If It's Plain, Do It Again!* and *Are You Sure You've Annoyed Robin Boyd?* (Boyd is the author of the book *The Australian Ugliness*.[1]) Eye-stopping effect is achieved by putting in lots of panels in the walls that divide one unit's balcony from the next, and having the panels painted different colours.

SURFERS PARADISE—or Surfers, as it is commonly called—is where the Gold Coast peaks, physically as well as in its character. Two-storey apartments rear to eight-, ten-, sixteen-storey blocks. The sophistication that goes with $136 million worth of Gold Coast investment sets in. The shops are slicker and the boutiques are boutiquier.

The brassy blonde that is Surfers piles up a high hair-do of signs, advertising everything from sun-cream to restaurants. What has begun to happen here has happened, long since and large scale, from Kings Cross in Sydney to Times Square and Piccadilly Circus and Tokyo's Ginza and Paris's Place Pigalle. Vulgarity, when its voltage becomes sufficient, generates vitality. Commercialism, with its clutter of sign-boards and coloured neons at night, creates visual animation that excites the uncritical eye. A sort of sub-culture is created, in which music is something that comes from a carousel, the advertiser and shopkeeper provide the art gallery, and the lurid paperback takes the place of literature—and not only for the holiday-making hedonist.

This city of 60,000 permanent residents didn't even have a public library. (In a civilized country such as Denmark, the council would be required by law to provide one.)

The last time I was on the Gold Coast I thought I should stay at a place typical of Surfers Paradise and I went to one of Bernard Elsey's four Beachcomber places, the Tiki Village Boatel-Motel. The "boatel" part is because this place is, in the words of its brochure, not only "in the heart of Surfers Paradise" and "only minutes from the rolling surf" but is also right on "Australia's finest skiing waterway", and launches moor at its steps. This waterway, which is bridged across to the lush development of Chevron Island, is the Nerang River—where twenty years earlier I had sniffed at the mud and mangroves. Just along from the Elsey operation was a sixteen-storey block of apartments. The south-side windows of these would look down on what used to be swampy scrubland on the other side of the river. Bruce Small had waved over this a wand of money made from selling Malvern Star bicycles and turned it into a development called the Isle of Capri, and himself into a millionaire.

"Isle of Capri", of course, oozes glamour. Bernard Elsey was a touch more original. *Tiki* was the name of a Polynesian god or Adamlike ancestor hero of the Maoris of New Zealand, who is given squat and large-headed form in small greenstone carvings. The Tiki in front of Mr Elsey's Tiki Village, in ochre-coloured cement, assumes the proportions of Easter Island stone idols and there are a number of lesser open-mouthed and saucer-eyed tikis in the grounds and décor, which is Polynesian in character. Coco-palms wave and crotons glow round the curvaceous Blue Lagoon of a swimming-pool (PLATE 12). At the side of the pool lunch was served, and you could sunbask on cushioned benches set out on banks of terraced lawns with backwalls that kept off the wind. My double room was spacious, not gaudy, and provided with all facilities including refrigerator, radio and television. The double-occupancy rate (1971) in the "holiday" season (Christmas Eve to 21st January and at Easter and May and August school holidays) is $10 including dinner and breakfast, or you could have full-board for $11 a day. When rates are as reasonable as that—and good service went with them—nobody should wonder why Surfers Paradise, and the Gold Coast in general, attracts so many tourists.

Earlier I had stayed at the Chevron Hotel where a high-standard room was $13 a day single ($11 double), which was also very reasonable for what you got, and what could be had in the hotel's purlieus. (These rates, in 1971, were a dollar or so higher in peak season.) Sophisticated drinking was well provided for in its Birdcage Bar, and its Golden Peacock Restaurant (which was not, as it sounds, gaudy) had the reputation of being the best place to eat in Surfers Paradise.

The hotel also had a Pink Elephant Bar, which was little more than a swill area for young swingers and, on its other frontage, the South Seas Lounge. These were strictly for the budget trade. The Pink Elephant served lunch for $2 and the South Seas, which provided dance music and entertainment, had dinner for $3 including cover charge.

It was calculated in 1970 that a visitor's day-to-day expenses covering hotel accommodation, meals (including dinner with wine) and sightseeing/entertainment would cost $9.90 a day on the Gold Coast as against $13.60 in Sydney.[2] (In 1971 it might be 15 per cent more.)

Convention trade had become a big thing at Surfers, with the Chevron having a convention hall that could take a thousand people; and it could do barbecues for five hundred. It occurred to me that some of so many away-from-home males were pretty sure to seek sexual adventure while in this "playground" atmosphere; and that if there were any place in Australia where the call-girl system was likely to operate this was it. "No," I was assured. "Quite unnecessary. We have so many enthusiastic amateurs."

THE BEACHES are, of course, the Gold Coast's main natural attraction. They are not, however, all that the region has to offer. The nature lover need drive no more than thirty miles to be in the rain forest of the Lamington National Park in the mountain hinterland (but that we'll come to in the next chapter).

Surfers Paradise beach was fairly well sprinkled with browning bodies when I was there in June and there appeared to be nearly as many when I returned in the third week of July, a winter month when nobody swims in Sydney except a few Spartan types. I went to the beach on a bright sunny day and found the water on the chilly side of "bracing", but quite bearable, though the surf itself wasn't raising any waves big enough to ride. The breeze had a nip to it but recliners could be hired in the lee of canvas screens and, thus sheltered, one could sunbake quite comfortably.

In these winter months the Surfers symbol, the "Meter Maids"—girls in gold lamé bikinis with stitched-on coins, who are employed by the local Progress Association to pop five-cent pieces into time-expired parking meters at which visitors' cars are standing—they were not in evidence. The nights that followed sunny days could be distinctly cool. Winter, though, is drier than summer to the extent that the rain average for July-August-September is only a third of the twenty inches for January-February-March. I asked the amiable manager of the Tiki Village which time he considered best and he said, "September to November. You get fine warm days, the nights are pleasantly cool, and it's quieter."

OF GOLD COAST ATTRACTIONS in the entertainment sense there is a gamut that runs from the top spectacles of Marineland and the water-ski show through animal and bird parks to a waxworks and such Antipodean colonies of Disneyland as Santaland and an Australiana place that is part boomerang-factory; there is, near Mermaid Beach, a chair-lift up to an excellent view of the coast and a far-from-excellent restaurant; down at Kirra there is Gilltrap's Auto Museum, which is very good; over at Tweed Heads, Jack Evans has his Porpoise Pool; and every weekend the International Motor Circuit goes *vroom-vroom*.

Marineland is an outstanding show because David H. Brown, who directs and comperes it, is more than a showman; he is an intelligent man who has been studying marine mammals for twenty years and knows so much about them that a number of papers he has written about dolphins, whales and seals have appeared in scientific journals. An Englishman, he was in charge of the marine section at London Zoo before going in 1952 to California where he was curator of mammals at Marineland of the Pacific.

After I had seen the Marineland show in the morning I returned in the afternoon to talk to David Brown. To me, the highlights of the show were the dolphins' spectacular leaps from the water, in unison—there would be three or four high in the air together (PLATE 12). Demonstrable as their intelligence and their skills was their trainer's rapport with them—which was such that they seemed to enjoy throwing a ball from the water, retrieving rubber rings from the pool even when they were blindfold with suction cups over their eyes, and doing their remarkable "tail walk" along the surface of the pool. A pilot whale, "worked" by John Reynolds, was also astonishing. It was about ten feet long and weighed over a ton, yet it would not only thwack its tail at the command signal, but leap vertically clear out of the pool.

"WHAT I WANT," David Brown said, "is a killer whale, a true killer whale *Orcinus orca* as distinct from what is called the false killer whale *Pseudorca crassidens*. They can sometimes be taken in a net in Puget Sound when they come in after the salmon. Contacts I have in Seattle are trying to get me one."

Their spectacular size apart, whales in general and "killer" whales in particular did not sound to me nearly as interesting as dolphins. David Brown explained that the dolphin is really a small whale—and the killer whale (so called because it is such a voracious feeder) is a large dolphin.

"The killer whale," he said, "is the most intelligent creature in the sea, even more intelligent than the dolphin." There were six in captivity in the United States and he had studied them at Marineland of the Pacific.

"They are most remarkable animals, and their affinity to humans is quite equal to what we find with dolphins. They'll let you ride on their back. They'll lick your face. They are most precocious and learn very quickly. I expect to be able to train a killer whale in four months to leap from the water—and when you see three tons of whale hanging straight up in the air—that's really a sight!"

Such a whale would work with dolphins, always providing that it was well fed and that the dolphins were assigned a minor role. Its ego was highly developed, its sensibilities such that, if left alone and denied human attention in its captivity, it could become psychotic and even get ulcers.

David Brown got his three-ton killer whale from America, and it was put in the Marineland pool towards the end of March 1970, at a cost reported as $20,000. Ramu, as it was named, would not eat. Every attention was given it, but in April the whale died. An autopsy showed that it had a haemorrhaging gastric ulcer.

Porpoises are also of the mammalian order that includes whales and dolphins. Between porpoises and dolphins there is no sharp scientific distinction, but porpoises are smaller and haven't the dolphin's beak. In America the bottle-nosed dolphin is called a porpoise and in Australia dolphins are usually referred to as porpoises. Hence the name of Jack Evans's "Porpoise Pool" at Tweed Heads. This was an entirely different, and much less spectacular, type of show, with Evans clowning and aiming his entertainment at a largely juvenile audience.

Skiland of Australia, the water-skiing performance, had skiers, both men and women, of great skill. One of the more extraordinary feats, performed by two of the men, was water-skiing without skis. They were towed along at high speed behind the launches with no support but the soles of their feet.

Currumbin Bird Sanctuary is where a couple of thousands of the paint-box parrots called Rainbow Lorikeets flock, morning and evening, to be fed. Tourists are handed plates containing a mixture of honey, water and bread, and when the birds descend they are likely to perch on anything from the fence behind which people are seated to the plate rim or the visitor's hand or even head, so used have they become to the human presence. It is a remarkable and vivid sight (PLATE 11). It all began, in 1947, with Alec Griffiths finding a few lorikeets in his garden trees and setting out food for them.

THE MAN who runs Fleay's Fauna Sanctuary, a mile or so off the main road near Burleigh Heads, is not only a dedicated naturalist, a former schoolteacher who became a Bachelor of Science and was director of the well-known sanctuary at Healesville (Victoria). David Fleay—a tall man now in his sixties who handles a tiger snake as calmly as a joey kangaroo—was the first man to breed in captivity that most extraordinary of Australia's creatures, the platypus.

The platypus is so anciently primitive in the scale of animal evolution that it is not so much one "living fossil" as several. Its name is from *platus*, the Greek for "flat", and flat it is (rather like an elongated hotwater bottle) in its furred body—perhaps twenty inches long in an adult—something like a beaver's, but having a beak like a duck's, except that the beak is not so much bony as leathery. It can swim like a turtle under water for about twenty seconds; then it needs to

breathe. In common with birds, it has only one vent for generation
and excretion, which makes it a monotreme, but it is truly a mammal,
meaning that it has *mammae* (milk producing glands).

What fazed zoologists overseas—and it took them until 1884 to
accept the fact—was that the platypus did something that seemed incredible in a mammal: it laid eggs. It usually lays two, and the eggs
are not shelled like a bird's but softly leathery like a reptile's. And it
suckles its young, without having any teats: the milk oozes through
the pores of its skin. The duck-bill is a voracious eater of worms, tad-
poles, small crustacea and, in captivity, eggs. It nests in a riverbank
burrow it digs. Its forefeet are the only ones it uses in swimming, and
these are less like feet than webbed hands. The hindfeet of the male
have a spike with a gland of poison, making the platypus the only
venomous mammal. The only other surviving monotreme in the world
is also Australian, the porcupine-like, ant-eating echidna, which also
lays eggs.

There were, of course, many other animals, along with birds and
snakes, at David Fleay's Fauna Sanctuary, all of them native to Australia and New Guinea.

"New" Coast and Old Wilderness

NORTH OF BRISBANE about sixty miles the town of Caloundra looks
across to Bribie Island and inland to the strange peaks of the Glasshouse Mountains. There are eight miles of good surfing beach hereabouts. A number of other excellent beaches stretch for the next thirty
miles to the promontory of Noosa Head.

This "Sunshine Coast", as it is called, is developing apace as a tourist
area. Our next-door neighbours in Sydney—who regard Surfers Paradise as "ghastly"—are by no means the only people who much prefer
the Sunshine Coast to the Gold Coast. They have been going each
winter up to Alexandra Headland or to their beloved Buderim (which
is a short drive inland) and their only complaint is that the region is
becoming "too popular". However, in comparison with the Gold
Coast, this new coast is practically virginal.

I have not stayed on this coast, but have toured along it, and it
looks recommendable for a quieter type of holiday than the Gold Coast
offers, and one that was even less expensive. The quickest way to get
there from Brisbane is to fly to Maroochy airport which is close to
three resorts that practically adjoin midway along this coast,
Maroochydore, Alexandra Headland and Mooloolaba. The place I
had proposed to stay at (before my enemy, Time, said, "No!") was

Dolphins at Marineland, near Surfers Paradise, perform amazingly for their trainer, marine mammalogist David Brown.

At Surfers Paradise this bank of the Nerang River was mud and mangroves before the developers moved in. This is Tiki Village "motel-boatel".

13/QUEENSLAND

Koalas were so ruthlessly slaughtered for their skins that "Cam" Reid set up the Lone Pine Sanctuary on the Brisbane River. Queensland's are the soft-furred, smaller, "cuddly" kind. LEFT: *A 1970 American tourist with one at Lone Pine.*

the Boolarong Park Inn overlooking the ocean at Alexandra Headland, because I had heard such good reports of it from three sources.

The tour I took covered 250 miles in a day in a minibus and is not recommended. It became interesting, though, when the Glasshouse Mountains came into view. Cook, in one of his more imaginative moments when he wasn't naming things after Their Lordships of the Admiralty, gave these isolated peaks their name. They are massive upthrusts of trachyte, a volcanic rock that has in its structure feldspar crystals, and they may have appeared to reflect the sun.

There are eleven of these striking mountains and the peak that rises straight up from the plain nearest the tour route is called Tibrogargan, who was a giant in a violent and somewhat tedious Aboriginal legend about their formation. At its foot was a pineapple plantation with a notice outside: *Pineapples 50 cents a dozen.* A dozen!

The approach to Nambour is through sugarcane country, and the landscape suddenly turns to green loveliness in the Nambour Valley. The town of Nambour is growing into a city; but cane "trams" still trundle across its main street on rails of fifteen-inch gauge. Cane-cutting here is still done manually.

A less spectacular crop began to clothe hillsides: this was ginger. Buderim (pron. Budderim) is the only place in Australia that has a ginger factory. Tourists are welcome to inspect the process on work days: this was a Sunday. Buderim's surroundings are lushly attractive, and I can well understand why Mr Next-Door—who would rather the bowling green than the surfing beach—likes to go there.

We cut through to the coast, to Coolum. The land boom was on, but prices hadn't gone sky-high yet. An Alexandra Headland estate has since been advertised in Sydney papers as the paradise to retire to, at $2,000 a plot. At the place where we had an awful lunch, Peregian, beachfront allotments were selling at $2,000 and looked to be well worth it. The white-sand beach there, with hardly a house to it, stretched for miles. Whether beachfronts should be sold, or reserved to the public domain, is a question the Queensland Government should consider.

There was good sea scenery, and some nicely uncrowded caravan parks, on the eight-mile run to Noosa, which would appear to have a considerable tourist future. At present it attracts mainly fishermen, who seem always to be the first to find a good place, and the ones who begin its ruination by putting up ugly shacks. Noosa (if there is such a place: there is Noosaville and Noosa Heads as well as Noosa Head) has so far preserved itself from the uglification that has set in at farther-on Tewantin. It has, as the view from a lookout called Tingirana shows, a lot to offer, with its surf beach, its river, its nearby lakes, its scenic coast, its National Park, its caves and, across the water

H

from Tewantin, at a place called Teewah, cliffs of coloured sands. Actually, the tour I took was called the Coloured Sands Tour. But we never saw them. The tide was wrong, so we couldn't get across.

"I've been a farmer all my life," said Friedrich Dreier, obviously of German descent, who made pictures out of the coloured sands, pictures held in place with glass. The tour called at his place. He didn't, thanks be, do "scenes" in coloured sands. He did abstract designs, and had classified sands of thirty-five different colours.

On the way back we came through the Maroochy area. The onsurge of tourism is such that in July 1971 East-West Airlines began an air service twice weekly from Sydney direct to Maroochydore. Here an eleven-storey block of apartments and shops had risen, and the State Minister for Tourism said in opening this Maroochy Sands Complex, "I have not the slightest doubt that by 1980 tourism will be Queensland's most valuable industry."

BACK IN 1937, when I was a young newspaperman, a Stinson airliner flying between Brisbane and Sydney crashed in the McPherson Range near the Queensland border. My news editor said, "Charter a plane and get up there", which I did. In this small plane we were flying over the ruggedest rain-forest country I had ever seen, looking vainly for a sign of the wreck, which had not been found. We hit a downdraught (as, it transpired, the Stinson had done) and dropped two hundred feet. The photographer with me cracked his head on the cabin roof and said he was damned if he was going to die for the Sydney *Sun*. So we gave it away and landed at Beaudesert, where I asked a cattleman, who was sitting on his hunkers rolling a cigarette, "What do you call that wild country we've been over?" and he said, "We call it the Lost World."

That afternoon my paper's headline screamed AIR CRASH IN "LOST WORLD". The name thus given currency has gone onto the detail maps for part of the region then known as Lamington Plateau and now called Lamington National Park.

The man who found the wreckage of the airliner (the pilots, whom I knew, were both dead, as were three of the five passengers) and who guided the rescue team in to bring out the two survivors, was a superb bushman who lived up in these mountains. Bernard O'Reilly became something of a national hero at the time, and subsequently wrote a popular book, *Green Mountains*[1] about the region and how five young O'Reillys, his brothers, came there as pioneers in 1912-13 and hacked paddocks out of the forest that was, in part, jungle. Then, in 1915, the whole surrounding area was declared a reserve, a National Park. So the O'Reillys could not extend their holding. So they turned the homestead into a guesthouse—Green Mountains is the name of it, though it is usually known simply as O'Reilly's, and the O'Reilly family still runs it.

The O'Reilly country is bushwalker country primarily. But it is also a fine mountain-top place just to sit and relax and look across vast valleys, unspecked by habitation, to contours of the range that were sharp in the crystalline air and bright blue on the beautifully sunny and still July afternoon I was there. Ninety miles of walking tracks have been made by the Forestry Department, and there is limited access to some places by four-wheel-drive vehicle such as a younger O'Reilly took me in to one of the many waterfalls.

Antarctic beeches one may expect to find in western Tasmania; but they are here, too—lichened giants perhaps three thousand years old, survivors from another climatic age. A delight of a road winds in to O'Reilly's through a tunnel of sub-tropical rain forest. Orchids grow in profusion, more than forty species. Fern-fringed pools lie in gullies clad with great trees hung with ropes of liana vines and gripped by strangler figs, and the coolness creates the feeling that you are in air-conditioned jungle.

Birds, hard to see in habitat of such thick vegetation, include the Albert lyrebird, and the Rufous Scrub-bird, which is rather like a lyrebird in miniature, and the dazzlingly lovely Regent bowerbird.

Some of the birds, not least the scrub turkeys, come about the house, where they are fed, and so do possums and wallabies. The appealing Pretty-face wallaby, as well as the pademelon and the whiptail kinds, is here. All birds and animals are, of course, as much in sanctuary on O'Reilly lands as they are in the surrounding 49,000 acres of Lamington National Park.

The coach from Brisbane took about three hours to make the seventy-mile run to O'Reilly's. It stopped for morning tea at Canungra, a one-pub township which had the wartime training school for commandos and to prepare Australian troops for jungle-fighting conditions in New Guinea. From Canungra the climb begins in earnest. Although the road winds dramatically along ravine-sides in places, the bush is familiarly eucalypt and nothing quite prepares you for the jungle-track entry to where O'Reilly's sits neatly on its plot of green three thousand feet up. It seems higher, because the view is so wide of a mountain world you are atop of. On this brilliant day I felt I had emerged, miles above the frenetic Gold Coast, into a realm of utter peacefulness where, if I reached up, I might almost touch the sky.

There is another reputedly good place in the area, Binna Burra Lodge. Hike-minded visitors often walk the fourteen-mile track between the two and, having stayed at one place, go back to Brisbane via the other.

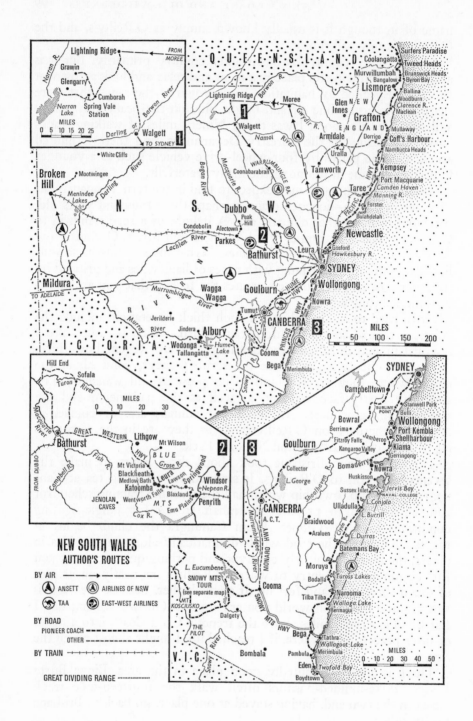

Inset 1 (top left):

FROM MOREE

Lightning Ridge →

Narran R.

Grawin

Glengarry

Cumborah

Spring Vale Station

Narran Lake

Barwon River

MILES
0 5 10 15 20 25

Darling or Barwon River

Walgett

TO SYDNEY

Main map:

Q U E E N S L A N D

Coolangatta

Surfers Paradise

Tweed Heads

Murwillumbah

Bangalow

Brunswick Heads

Byron Bay

Lightning Ridge

Barwon R.

Moree

Glen Innes

N E W

Lismore

Ballina

Woodburn

Clarence R.

Maclean

Walgett

Gwydir R.

Grafton

E N G L A N D

Mullaway

Coff's Harbour

Namoi River

Armidale

Dorrigo

Nambucca Heads

White Cliffs

Uralla

Tamworth

Kempsey

Bogan River

Coonabarabran

WARRUMBUNGLE RA.

Taree

Port Macquarie

Camden Haven

Manning R.

Broken Hill

Mootwingee

Macquarie R.

N.   S.   W.

Dubbo

Forster

Bulahdelah

Menindee Lakes

Darling River

Peak Hill

Condobolin

Alectown

Newcastle

Lachlan River

Parkes

Leura

Gosford

Hawkesbury R.

Bathurst

SYDNEY

Mildura

R   I   V   E   R   I   N   A

Wagga Wagga

Goulburn

Wollongong

TO ADELAIDE

Murrumbidgee River

HUME HWY

Nowra

Murray River

Jerilderie

Tumut

CANBERRA

Jindera

Albury

PRINCES HWY

MILES
0   50   100   150   200

V   I   C   T   O   R   I   A

Wodonga

Tallangatta

Hume Lake

Cooma

Snowy R.

Bega

Merimbula

Inset 2 (Blue Mountains):

Hill End

Sofala

Turon River

Macquarie R.

MILES
0   10   20   30

FROM DUBBO

GREAT   WESTERN

Lithgow

Mt Wilson

BLUE

Bathurst

Fish R.

HWY

Grose R.

Campbell R.

Mt Victoria

Blackheath

Medlow Bath

Leura

Lawson

Springwood

Katoomba

Wentworth Falls

Blaxland

Windsor

Nepean R.

JENOLAN CAVES

M T S

Emu Plains

Penrith

Cox R.

Inset 3 (South Coast):

SYDNEY

Campbelltown

Stanwell Park

Bulli

SUBLIME POINT

Wollongong

Bowral

Port Kembla

Berrima

Shellharbour

Fitzroy Falls

Jamberoo

Kiama

Goulburn

Kangaroo Valley

Gerringong

Collector

Bomaderry

L. George

Nowra

Huskisson

Shoalhaven R.

Sussex Inlet

Jervis Bay

NAVAL COLLEGE

CANBERRA

Ulladulla

L. Conjola

A.C.T.

Braidwood

Clyde R.

L. Burrill

Araluen

L. Durras

Murrumbidgee River

MONARO HWY

Batemans Bay

Moruya

Cooma

Bodalla

Tuross Lakes

SNOWY MTS HWY

Tilba Tilba

Narooma

Wallaga Lake

Bermagui

Bega

Tathra

Wallagoot Lake

Pambula

Merimbula

Bombala

Eden

Twofold Bay

Boydtown

MILES
0   10   20   30   40   50

Inset (Snowy Mountains, bottom centre):

L. Eucumbene

SNOWY MTS TOUR
(see separate map)

MT KOSCIUSKO

Dalgety

THE PILOT

Snowy River

V. I. C.

Legend:

NEW SOUTH WALES
AUTHOR'S ROUTES

BY AIR ——→

Ⓐ ANSETT   Ⓐ AIRLINES OF NSW

Ⓣ TAA   Ⓔ EAST-WEST AIRLINES

BY ROAD

PIONEER COACH – – – – – –

OTHER - - - - - - - -

BY TRAIN +–+–+–+–+–

GREAT DIVIDING RANGE ·················

NEW
SOUTH
WALES

Down the Coast to Sydney

THE NAME "New South Wales" is one that Australians are as used to as Americans are to "New York". Yet, if we think about it, the name seems almost ludicrous.

Cook, apparently, didn't call the new land anything when he formally took possession of its whole eastern coast at Possession Island, and Banks was still referring to it in his journal as "New Holland". In Cook's journal, written up on the voyage home, he twice referred to it—this land with the coast that had everything from seals to crocodiles on it—as "New Wales". Why he chose that name we don't know: perhaps some southern cliffs or an estuary reminded him of a conformation seen from a collier coasting in to Carmarthen. Cook scratched out one journal entry of "New Wales" and substituted "New *South* Wales".

This was adopted as the name of the convict colony Phillip was sent out in 1788 to found and govern—and it was regarded as taking in a good half of the Dutch-discovered continent, along with Tasman's "Van Diemen's Land" (Tasmania). Relating this vast area to South Wales, a mere fragment of the British Isles—or to a whole new Wales in the south, for that matter—was rather like calling a kangaroo a new mouse.

Even when other colonies were cut out of this enormous hide of land, and New South Wales was reduced to its present size, the naïve name was as inappropriate as it is now irremovable. And Cook—of whom anything would be forgiven by today's New South Welshmen if he had done no more than discover Sydney's surfing beaches— wasn't even a Welshman.

Of New South Welshmen (if one may tie this attenuated tag to the State's whole population) there are now about four and a half million, over one-third of all Australians. The most populous of the States is also the most productive, both as to primary produce and manufactures. It used also to produce more than forty per cent of Australia's mineral wealth: but that economic distinction has now gone, literally, west. It has the largest capital city, Sydney, and the two largest Australian provincial cities, Newcastle and Greater Wollongong, the big steelmakers. In these three urban areas live two-thirds of the State's people, about a quarter of Australia's.

It is one State but two distinct regions. The fertile littoral is, from the north, greened with banana plantations, sugar and dairying and is clean-sky country until we come to smokestacks at Newcastle. After Sydney it goes on to more dairyfarms and then smokestacks again and dairypastures again and fishing ports: over-simplified, but that is broadly the picture.

Behind the well-named Great Dividing Range lies another country. The land beyond the fringe is drier, flatter and, most of it, browner. It grows sheep, wheat and cattle in that order, has flourishing provincial cities and some factories; its south-western irrigated region spills a cornucopia of fruits; and in the far west it has the most famous of silver-lead-zinc mines. However, it is not much use overseas visitors asking the average coast-dweller what New South Wales is like out at Broken Hill, or even just over the mountain barrier at Bathurst, because it's ten-to-one that he has never been to either place, never seen a sheep shorn, never seen a kangaroo that wasn't in a zoo or a fauna park. The State's sea-edged side is its attractive front garden, and few want to leave it to play in the big backyard.

No country that tourists come from to Australia in any numbers has States or other divisions as large as Australia's. Although New South Wales is only fourth in size among the States, and occupies little more than one-tenth of the continent, six Englands would fit into it, and it could swallow Texas or two Japans.

HAVING FLOWN between Sydney and Brisbane a dozen times—and it is, indeed, a fine coast scenically from the air with its wave-frilled beaches and its lush green riversides of pasture and cropland—I thought I should see the North Coast right through by road.

I got on a Pioneer coach in Sydney, but propose to describe the route in reverse. The Pacific Highway route, that is: there are two. You can also go by the New England Highway. That inland way shows such places of special interest as the university city of Armidale, and Queensland's Toowoomba. At least we shall get to Armidale, later.

So we have gone from Brisbane and said, "Good-bye, Gold Coast" and crossed over the border of New South Wales and the shining Tweed River that is named after the one bordering England and Scotland. The coach soon comes to Murwillumbah, "place of many possums".

Australia is indebted to its Aboriginal Adam—whom some white Australians still think of as no more than a feckless primitive—for so many place names that come off the map with a uniquely voiced and often a singing quality. Listen to some other Aboriginal names of places in New South Wales: Araluen, Bundanoon, Cambewarra and Coonabarabran and Cootamundra, Dorrigo, Eurunderee, Gerringong, Jamberoo, Kiama and Kurrajong, Leura, Mandurama and Merry-winebone (pron. Merriwinnabone), Pokataroo, Quandialla, Tarra-wonga and Tumbarumba, Ulladulla and Uranquinty, Wilcannia, Yarramundi. The tribal languages of this region were especially euphonious. Not invariably so, of course: Bumblegumbi, meaning "broken limb", is hardly mellifluous. But is there a lovelier name in any language than Araluen? Its soft stream of syllables means "place of running water". The poet Henry Kendall bestowed the name on his daughter.

As backdrop to Murwillumbah, the main town of the lush Tweed Valley, there is the picturesque jut of Mount Warning to nearly 3,800 feet. This is rich sugarland and bananaland, as well as dairying and timber, country.

Brunswick Heads, bearing one of those nostalgically imported names, we soon come to. I have a cousin living there who swears that its native name must have meant "plenty of fish". A keen rod-and-line man, he is never likely to return to living in Sydney. Big tourist development in this attractive sea-and-river area, only forty-four miles south of Surfers Paradise, began in 1970, with American capital. Wendell-West, of Seattle, Washington, who have created whole resorts in the United States and Hawaii, began the creation of Ocean Shores, and planned to provide such amenities as a $500,000 beach club and a $300,000 marina for yachts, and sell "recreational real estate" at $4,000 to $10,000 a lot.

A seventy-five-miles-long stretch of top North Coast calls itself "Summerland" and is proving alluring to southern tourists who don't want to go as far as Queensland but seek sub-tropical warmth.

Round Bangalow the landscape is like some part of the English shires that has suddenly sprouted bananas—and, if you come when the fruit is ripening, bright blue plastic bags. These enclose the big "hands" of the fruit to filter the sunlight's ultra-violet rays. The bananas are picked green and ripened in gas ovens. This is also pine-apple country.

We leave the coast for Lismore, a city (pop. 20,000) with its prosperity built largely on butter, cheese, milk and cream, and there are no more contented cows than those that graze hock-deep in the rich pastures sprung from the silt left by the Richmond River's flooding over its virid banks that contain it, on this fine day, as such a blue and peaceful stream. The water once rose five feet up the wall of the place where we lunch: you can still see the mark.

South from Ballina near a town called Woodburn there is a monument, and an Italian flag waves. New Italy was the name of a settlement that was the Australian aftermath of the grandiose scheme of a go-getting French nobleman, the Marquis de Rays, who in 1880 convinced a mass of Italians that they would make their fortunes by migrating to New Ireland, a nethermost appendage of New Guinea. Many died of fever, and New South Wales succoured the remnant, who were given land in this area, to the subsequent benefit of the Australian sugar industry.

Here we pass out of "Summerland" and, coming to Maclean, find a sort of Little Scotland. The first settler was a Cameron, and there is many a Mac growing sugar or potatoes or maize on the verdant flats of the Clarence River and bananas on the hillsides, or harvesting the sea for fish. The Clarence River, another fine one, flows by Maclean and winds up to Grafton (pop. 16,000), one of the most liveable-looking provincial cities in Australia. Grafton's "Jacaranda Festival" in November, when these trees shed their feathery green and deck themselves in heliotrope-blue, was probably the first of Australian civic festivals of this kind.

WE GO BACK to the coast and, on this three-day tour to Sydney, stay overnight at the Suncoast Motel among tall gum-trees at a place called Mullaway. Next morning, after about twenty miles, we come to a town that really has the tourist in its sights—Coffs Harbour. The name sounds a touch bronchial, but could be more so—Korff's Harbour, after its first settler, a Captain Korff. "Coffs", as it is known, is the largest timber-shipping port in Australia, and also the greatest banana-grower; so it might be thought that it doesn't really need the tourist dollar. But it is after it and getting it, in a big way.

Coffs Harbour is far enough north of Sydney (363 road miles), and of Newcastle, to offer vacationing urbanites a complete change of landscape—banana-clad hillsides backing its miles of surf beaches and merging with high stands of sub-tropical forest as in Bruxner Park reserve, and a scenic hinterland of range country towards Dorrigo and beyond. It also provides the southerner with a longer season of bathing at tolerable temperatures. Apart from fishing, a prime attraction, it has better-than-usual sporting facilities for golf, bowls, tennis, excellent caravan parks for those who like caravan parks, and over a thousand beds of tourist accommodation, at moderate rates. Every hotel in town had been remodelled—at the behest of the most active tourist association on the whole North Coast, with the livest wire of a tourist officer I have ever met, Peter Wulff, who whizzed me round when I returned to Coffs Harbour via Armidale. Coffs incarnate, he streamed statistics about the place that had doubled its population to 10,000 in ten years, built this new bridge, that new Olympic Swimming Pool, planted trees here, improved there, and now rated its tourist industry a bigger earner than timber or bananas.

There was the Biggest Banana in the World—a concrete, yellow-painted gaucherie to walk through. Bruxner Park, though hardly the "dense jungle" of the tourist brochure, had splendid trees, and an interesting fauna park called Kumbaingeri had been developed. There was also Jarrett's Shell Museum, which must surely be the only shell museum set up in a banana plantation—the biggest one in the district. I ended up well dined-and-wined at the elaborately appointed Star Motel.

Short-term, Coffs Harbour will make a lot of tourist money. Long-term, I am inclined to fear for it. Originally it was a badly designed town, or two towns, and it needed to call in a top-grade planner; and to think again about its policy of *laissez-faire* progress that was letting anybody build anything that looked "smart".

The unmentionable four-letter word in North Coast tourist literature is r-a-i-n. Coffs Harbour averages 65 inches of rain a year; some rain falls on 123 days (one in three); the wettest months are February and March, the driest September and October.

Down the coast from Coffs is Nambucca Heads, which is particularly picturesque, has a superb panorama lookout, is a smaller and less "developed" place, and averages 55 inches of rain. This is about where bananaland ends.

SIXTY-SIX MILES farther south we stopped for lunch at Kempsey. At the Allandale Guest-house a rather special bedroom had a beautiful four-poster cedar bed and a century-old, huge chest of drawers in most cherished condition. Alas, the fine red cedar of the region is nearly all gone.

Billboards proliferated against the bushland, crudely and gaudily advertising coast resorts and, mainly, motels, along the road down to Port Macquarie, where we spent the night at one of the twenty-odd motels, the Macquarie. The place gets a lot of vacationers and night-stop tourists.

Next morning rain poured as we set out for a coach tour of the town that is one of the oldest in New South Wales, having been founded at the mouth of the Hastings River as a convict settlement in 1821. Australia's most renowned convict, the architect Francis Greenway (who in England had forged a contract when bankrupted in the building business) is locally regarded as having designed the Anglican church, St Thomas's.

Although the Port Macquarie district gets winter frosts that wrote *finis* to its namesake governor's attempt to grow sugarcane there, its red volcanic soil gives it rich green vegetation, and its scenic hinterland is splendidly timbered. Moreover there is a pocket of superb primeval rain-forest, preserved as a 77-acre sanctuary under the name of Sea Acres.

The highway goes inland from here, to Taree on the Manning River, calling itself "the town to retire to". From there it goes still farther inland—from a coast that deserves a splendid sea-hugging scenic highway. So one does not see the region of Camden Haven, which a friend of mine has picked out as the place to retire to; or fishermen's Forster, which sits between lake and sea. Instead, we go on through the timber town of Bulahdelah, and nothing much happens scenically that side of Newcastle.

Newcastle is terribly important, I know. It has the steel foundries, the huge power plants (with coal right underneath them), the greatest concentration of heavy industry in the land. But it has nothing for the traveller unless he wants to see blast furnaces in B.H.P.'s steelworks (which the traveller who hasn't seen other blast furnaces, as this traveller has, probably should see) and is welcome to see them on a guided tour.

Beyond Newcastle is Lake Macquarie, of which our good driver remarked that, Wangi Wangi powerhouse and all, he considered it the most beautiful lake in Australia.

This side of the crossing of the Hawkesbury River—a glorious waterway of which more will be heard in the chapter on Sydney—the traveller should look out for what our driver-commentator, Ronald Finlayson, described as "Australia's largest wildflower". The Gymea lily commonly grows fifteen feet high and bears a globular head of red flowers. The blooms can be six inches across. The Gymea lily occurs only from the mid South Coast of New South Wales to southern Queensland. It is totally protected.

Between the Hawkesbury and Sydney there is, scenically, nothing notable on the highway, but the bushland and some of the suburbs passed through are more eyeworthy than they are if you come into Sydney from any other direction.

"When you come to Sydney"

Dear Helen and Joe,

When you come to Sydney I shall probably be in Bali or back in Japan, much as I should like to be here and have you spend as much time with me as I spent with you in New Jersey and New York. I'll also probably be travelling when Robin D. of London makes his first and long-overdue appearance in my home city. And I'll bet I'm in Hong Kong or somewhere when that young couple in Perth who were so nice to me there have piled enough pennies for the transcontinental jump to the holiday they've promised themselves in Australia's biggest-oldest-brightest city.

This letter, then, can maybe serve all three parties, and others. Though to write of what Sydney has to offer two long-travelled American "senior citizens", a middle-aged English publisher, and a young Australian couple—all looking at the place with different eyes and wanting different things of it, and at three different income levels—it's not going to be easy: but here goes . . . .

First, you have to arrive. If you come by air I am happy to say that you (but not you from Perth) will not be stepping from the plane into that old Topsy of an international terminal we've been red-faced about for years at Kingsford Smith Airport, Mascot. We have a new ultra-mod. terminal that can stand comparison with those of major cities overseas.

The drive into the city, though charmless, is now expresswayed in part, and you will be only minimally assaulted by the odours of an industrial area that is an ugly introduction to Sydney.

If you come by sea, and you enter through Sydney Heads on a blue, sun-sparkled morning—or are doubly lucky and come in on a bright summer Saturday afternoon with enough nor'-easter to heel the sailing boats that are everywhere weaving white and coloured warp to the weft of the ferry-boats' shuttling—then this is jackpot Sydney, indeed: you've hit the finest way of all to come to my place. (Admittedly, I share it with two and a half million other people.)

The Harbour, this waterway that is longer and lovelier than you can see from the ship and which you must promise to explore further, this is Sydney's glory. A superb foyer to a less-than-superb city is water-floored from the Heads up to the Bridge (PLATE 16).

Renowned the Sydney Harbour Bridge may be as the biggest arch bridge in the world (though not the longest: its 1,650-feet span is twenty-five inches shorter than that of the Bayonne Bridge in New York) but it is no great aesthetic sight, our webby great "coathanger" with at each end a spiritless (and functionless) pylon. The swing of grace, such as distinguishes San Francisco's Golden Gate bridge, ours lacks. It will be poised at what may look, from the ship, like the end of Port Jackson; and, indeed, it is not unlike a huge arched portcullis that could slide down between its gate-pillars of pylons and cut you off from the rest of the waterway, which goes on and on, narrowing as it pokes finger-bays into the land, wriggling round islands, industries, oil-tanks and peninsulas, and finally disappearing up two rivers, the rather fashionable Lane Cove and the less-fashionable Parramatta.

You'll come down the Harbour past, on the southern side: Watson's Bay, where the house still reigns supreme above the home unit block, and you'll see more white than usually obtains beneath our ubiquitous red-tile roofs; then the big bow-window of Rose Bay; exclusive Point Piper and Darling Point, with towering apartment blocks; very "with-it", as to shopping, Double Bay; and smaller yacht-crammed Rushcutters Bay and Elizabeth Bay. A few beaches and parks apart, we have preserved for public use little of this foreshore: it is built on to the waterfront with expensive houses and ever-increasing apartment towers.

On the northern shore you'll have glimpsed a wedge of subharbour that is the ferry-entrance, surfless side of Manly. The bifurcation of the waterway into Middle Harbour is lost to view behind the jut of Middle Head which, like the gaunt sandstone sentinel of North Head, is an entrenchment of the defence Services, but they're moving out, it'll all be parkland! A finger of bushland, Bradley's Head, points out at you, and beyond Ashton Park's foreshore density of eucalypts there is treeland oddly interrupted by hints of habitation: it is inhabited by animals—Taronga Zoo Park. Beyond the zoo are some nice bays and points. The contouring of the harbour shores is so good that it is no wonder that we, in our antipodean adolescence, have been unable to match its nature with our planning and building. Still, you may grant that there is a very liveable look to Mosman Bay and Cremorne Point. And, I venture, Kirribilli Point that holds the Governor-General's residence when he is in Sydney, Admiralty House, you'll be charmed by (though not by subsequent bricks-to-the-waterfront Kirribilli). You will be aware that, on the other side, there are the Botanic Gardens lawn-carpeting down through the trees to Farm Cove. Beyond the crenellations of Government House, the city-proper thrusts up towers of office blocks. All the higher martellos of metropolis have risen only in the sixties. But by now—before you reach Circular Quay where your ship will berth at the maritime terminal on the Quay's far side—you will be looking at *It*.

It is the new architectural astonishment of the southern world. So unconventional that it's been close to unbuildable, "building" seems no more adequate to it as a word than "Sydney Opera House" is as a name. It is virtually all roofs and no walls, except fronts of topaz-coloured glass, and within it will be not one theatre but three (one for cinema) and a concert hall—and that opera will sometimes be performed in it is not at all as important as the still-to-be-finished structure itself, about which books are already written, one of them titled *The Other Taj Mahal*.[1] The Italian genius of engineering, Nervi, may castigate all such structures as this great one by the Danish architectural genius Joern Utzon as "anti-functional", but the point is that it isn't intended to be primarily functional. You, Helen and Joe, have got your Metropolitan Opera House in Lincoln Centre and what have you got: another beaut box. We've got a wonder—Australia's first man-made wonder, an architectural sculpture fit to be bracketed with our monolithic natural wonder, Ayers Rock. Its shape is like that of no other building on earth, and is usually compared to something on the sea. We call them "sails" or "shells"; but "cowls" might be a better word for these long-pointed convex neo-Gothic arches given third dimension, bowing at one end to the city and at the other to the harbour that is proud to reflect them. You know what we've got, worshipful of the performing arts here on Benelong Point in Sydney? The first secular cathedral.

Come back, come back in 1973 when the Opera House is to open. What it will open with we don't yet know. It ought to be something new and stupendous, commissioned now for the occasion; but our State Government is mainly concerned with proving that its local architects can finish this fantastic structure as well as it could have been finished under Joern Utzon if Utzon had not left or been, in his own words, "forced to resign" after disagreements with his client, the Government, about ways, means, costs, co-operation, acoustics, seating and date of completion.

The Opera House that was no more than some design sketches —so incomplete that Utzon almost did not send them in for the world-wide 1957 contest he won—was originally estimated to cost less than $8 million and was to be finished to open in January 1963. That it will cost not less than $85 million before it opens in March 1973, if it does, is not due to mad extravagance. It is simply because the Opera House is the kind of unprecedented building it is: Ove Arup, the chief consulting engineer, called it a "masterpiece" and a structural "miracle". The miraculous necessarily costs far more than the mundane. The money in this case has been extracted painlessly from a rather affluent public that likes to gamble, by means of Opera House Lotteries.

Its cost *is* staggering, but the Opera House will be of vast worth, not only to Sydney culturally but as a tourist attraction, and valuable beyond measure to the "image" abroad of Australia as a country where such a building can happen.

The exterior is virtually complete, to Utzon's design; or, rather, his re-design of the shells to uniform curvature. His original design was, I think, aesthetically superior, but the constructional complications imposed by the varying curvatures were too many to add to a project that was beset from the start by a legion of structural problems.

The interior, and the glass walling under the shells or cowls, is being completed with the Sydney architect Peter Hall in charge of design. I have no doubt that the final result will be good, very good. Whether it will be as good as Utzon would have made it, had *he* finished it—that is a question many of us may ask; but how can there be an answer?

Whatever the main curtain goes up on, the curtain itself should be magnificent. To the sun-motif design of the Australian artist John Coburn it has been handwoven from Australian wools on the Aubusson tapestry looms in France, at a cost of $78,000.

So YOU'RE HERE, however arrived, and to get to your hotel will have made acquaintance with the Sydney taxi-driver. He is not really a "type", since he may be anything from a benign Australian oldster to an intense young Italian to a long-haired University student earning his fees with nightwork. However, you will, with luck, encounter at least one driver who characterizes his calling with the sardonic humour that is so Australian.

As an example of this, a car in front of the taxi stops suddenly, does a U-turn and pulls in at the other kerb. Our taximan leans out of his window: "And where did you ever get a bloody driver's licence—out of a Weetbix packet?"

John O'Grady, who under the name of Nino Culotta wrote a very funny bestseller about an Italian migrant and his Aussie workmates called *They're a Weird Mob*,[2] told me that, on returning from a trip to Europe, he got off the ship and said to a taximan that he wanted to go to the suburb where he lived, about fifteen miles out of the city, Oatley.

"Oatley!" The driver looked at him. "Gawd, I wouldn't go that far on me holidays!"

You had best stay, I think, pretty centrally in the city. Robin's firm can afford to put him at a posh hotel, and I don't think he'll do better than the most modern, biggest (428 rooms) Wentworth.

For you who won't be here on expense account, I'll try to suggest somewhere adequate but less costly.

There are high-bracket hotels and other kinds, and motels and serviced apartments, in the King's Cross area, about a mile east of the main city. More of them, in fact, are there than in the city proper. It's livelier up there, at King's Cross, more sophisticated, night-bright, cosmopolitan, colourful. The Cross, as we call it, deals in everything from luxury to low life. Pricey apartments with city-harbour views at Kingsgate, the Chevron or the round-towering Gazebo motel; $12-a-head dining at the plushy Chelsea restaurant; commendable eating for less than half that at many places; stay-open delicatessens that stock everything from *blutwurst* to *mortadella*; way-out fashions; *avante-garde* theatre; striptease and all-male girl shows; available ladies and other sextroverts; gents of no fixed occupation; longhairs, leatherjackets, skinhead hoodlums and grassy-eyed weirdos. Unless you are roving-eyed swingers, which you aren't, I'd say that King's Cross is very all right for a visit, but you don't have to stay there. You young'uns from Perth might fascinatedly disagree and make it your headquarters for Week One—and I wouldn't blame you. But I don't see you, J & H, in Sydney for the Australian version of Greenwich Village with a dash of Times Square, any more than I see Robin D. wanting other than passing acquaintance with the local Soho-Piccadilly Circus. I see you as more interested in the lovely dandelion of night-lit water that is the El Alamein Fountain at the top of Macleay Street than in striptease shows. Which reminds me of a very Australian story:

Call him Bert: "She was a great night at the R.S.L. [Returned Servicemen's League Club] the other night—big turn, slap-up dinner. After, one of the fellas says, 'How 'bout we go somewhere, eh? Ever been to the Pink Pussy Cat?' Heard of it, o' course, and you know me, be in anything. So down we go, 'bout half a dozen of us, to this striptease joint at the Cross. Holy mackerel, I never seen anything like it in all me life, didn't know it went on! Sheilas stripped to the buff you might say—things like thimbles on their tits and a patch o' glitter down there, but they might as well have been starkers. Some real good-looking sorts, too, and talk about sexy—wow! . . . But you'd never get me going to none o' those places no more, or not unless I take to the spirits. All you can get to drink is bottled beer."

Priorities are really laid on the line. Sex is all right, but what Australia's beer-loving Berts are really devoted to comes straight from the keg.

Back to accommodation. If you don't stay in the King's Cross area, in the city heartland your choice is more limited. Not that there aren't hotels aplenty there, but they are mostly interested in bar-trade not bed-trade, and *Australia Accommodation Guide 1969-70*[3] lists only ten places (hotels, motels and serviced apartments). Fewer than that are in the area I think could suit you best, which is downtown Sydney. I choose it for these reasons: (i) it is close to the Harbour and the ferries (you should go on the Showboat Cruise and to Manly and Taronga Park) and to Wynyard railway station and the buses for the northern beaches; (ii) it is handy to the main shops, theatres, cabarets and a goodly selection of restaurants; (iii) it is fairly close to Martin Plaza, where traffic has been ousted and the city has got itself, at last, a gay heart.

Main-street Sydney 1971 is not, let's face it, an enchanting city to explore. What it could be like in 1980—and it has a real chance to be exciting—is not relevant here and now. Nowhere are the two main streets strands of any distinction. Pitt Street, the chief shopping one, is narrow and, thanks to the number of blatant hang-down signs, looks like an Anglicized Hong Kong. The one long street in Sydney with any dignity is Macquarie Street, which we'll come to.

My point is that you are best located where you can get *out* to where the good places are. Remember, this is an essentially Harbour-divided and sprawled-out city, blessed with a quite exceptional beach coast. Being somewhat unsellable on the proposition of high-density living, in spacious Australia, I like it that way, the harbour being the harbour it is, the sprawl spreading into the bushland we have and, of course, the beaches being the beaches they are.

So I am inclined to recommend: For Helen and Joe, the Wynyard Travelodge in York Street, if $22 isn't too pricey for a double in this 1969-new box of twenty-odd storeys with city-harbour views, roof-top swimpool (but you'll eat better out). Or (and this might do also for the Perth couple if they aren't bedazzled into King's Cross accom. at around $15), a serviced apartment at not-new but favourably-regarded Marton Hall in Margaret Street. Fully equipped (including cooking facilities) and serviced daily, these 140 flats cost, for the ones with some view, $70 a week (that's $10 a day for two people). (Rates are for 1971.) Underneath is a good (though not cheap) restaurant, La Potinière, which will send up meals: liquor from Pfahlert's Hotel next door. Opposite is a small park. Marton Hall is the only place in my picked area to get recommendation in the *Enjoy Australia on a Budget* booklet.[4] I know of it mainly because my publishers favour it to put visiting authors at. I haven't stayed there, or anywhere in Sydney: where you live you don't.

In this area other restaurants I can commend are the Summit (of which more anon), the French Tavern (v.g. food and atmosphere), the Angus Steak Cave, nearer the Quay the Chalet and one called

14/NEW SOUTH WALES *Opal of the distinctive Australian "black" variety has been found only at Lightning Ridge, and at Grawin, where this big shaft-dump is. A rich opal find was made in 1971 at Glengarry, three miles away.*

LEFT:
Veteran opal-gouger Maurice Claire at Grawin showed me a gemstone he found at Lightning Ridge. He valued it at $3,000.

RIGHT:
Two fine black opals showing red "fire", with others including "whites" (which lose colour in photographs).

Snow sports have boomed in popularity in recent years at roof-of-Australia resorts near Mt Kosciusko and over the border in Victoria.

Wallagoot Lake, a dreamy part of the Far South Coast where there has not been much tourist development yet, but there is great potential for it.

Six Bulletin Place. In Angel Place, a first-rate stool-sitting meal is to be had at the Oystermen's oyster bar. This, to me, is the best place to eat the best of all Australian foods, our Sydney rock oysters. (I should also mention a laminex-tabletop fish café at Circular Quay called the Sorrento. In my experience, its oysters have been excellent and its prawns particularly fresh and good.)

If, having tasted our Sydney (Rock) oysters *naturel*, you still don't like oysters—for you pity wrings my heart. They are unquestionably the world's best: I must look down the nose at America's Blue Points and England's Whitstables, and dismiss out of hand any oysters Japanese. Not that ours are fully appreciated by Australians. They are served, in top hotels, on silver platters of ice, which effectively freezes out some of their delicate flavour. They are served with a dishlet of sauce, usually concocted with tomato catsup, into which you are expected to dip them: never do. A drop of squeezed lemon, a grain or two of pepper is allowable.

Other distinctive Australian foods you are entitled to expect to eat in Sydney: alas, they are hard to come by. It is easier to find Greek *moussaka* or Indonesian *nasi-gureng*. I know of only one restaurant, the Summit, where you can be sure of finding on the menu our finest big fish, *barramundi* (flown down from the tropical north), and kangaroo-tail soup which, much as I deplore the slaughter of kangaroos, I have to admit is delicious, even if conscience precludes me from ordering it. Queensland mud crab, large and delectable, seems to have disappeared with the demolition of the old Wentworth Hotel. Tasmanian scallops are scarce in Sydney, and even in Tasmania. Sydney lags behind Melbourne in the provision of eating-places with Australian character, though, even there, it may be more in the décor than the menu. But you can more easily get in Sydney than in other States that excellent fish called John Dory.

A lobster is not a crayfish, it's bigger, but "lobster" and "crayfish" are the same thing on Australian menus. Ask if it is *local*: if it is, it is better, meaning very good. "Shrimps" we don't say, only "prawns", and the big ones are "king" prawns. Fresh-cooked, and not iced, they are succulent.

Best way to acquaint yourself with the overall pattern of the city is by going to the top of Australia Square. The square name attaches to a building as round as a gun-barrel, currently the tallest (560 feet) in the land. There is an observatory section, where the view costs a dollar; but I suggest you splurge and dine at the top, at the Summit restaurant. It is pricey: you are paying for being 47 floors up and for the machinery that revolves the restaurant, slowly: one revolution takes an hour and three-quarters. Book well ahead. Assuming

I

summertime, say that you'll be there half an hour before sunset; insist on a windowside table and try to arrange that it be one that, when you get there, has the Harbour Bridge in view. That way you'll see the best of the harbour and the city in daylight.

Waste no time at all on uptown Sydney. Beyond the wedding-cake Victoriana of the Town Hall is a dreary area. Uptown Sydney could be good in 1980: there's an impressive plan for its redevelopment, including park areas it sadly lacks today. And, when you go up William Street to King's Cross, try to see past the present ugliness of a street we talk of turning into, by 1980, a splendid boulevard, "Sydney's Champs-Elysées".

HISTORIC SYDNEY. A relative term, of course, historic; but don't forget that our colonial beginning, for thirty years after 1788, was in the Georgian era, a good one architecturally. Have a look at what we call the Rocks area, near where the Bridge begins.

Maybe the best thing to do is this: Take a half-day, morning coach tour that begins with a run through the Rocks: it doesn't stop anywhere, except perhaps for photographs. If the area interests you, return to it on foot. Take with you, for guidance-with-map, an excellent leaflet called *Historic Sydney* prepared, in conjunction with the National Trust, by the N.S.W. Tourist Bureau: you can pick it up at the Bureau's office, which is in the plaza part of Martin Place. If you go back to the Rocks, go into the lovely old Garrison Church and allow some time for the Argyle Arts Centre, where artist-craftsmen are at work and where you are most likely to find some worthy souvenir of Australia.

A large part of the Rocks area is slated for redevelopment that, on the plan, looks imaginative and will preserve the best of the Old Sydney there, in contrast to new towers of offices and apartments, a huge tourist hotel and a large and lively pedestrian mall. At a cost of some $500 million, the Rocks will be, the planners say without a blush, "recreated over the next fifteen years into an urban complex on a magnificent scale, challenging all previously known concepts of city environment". This development, along with the Opera House on opposite Benelong Point, should do a lot for Sydney's front door.

The best of the rest of historic Sydney begins in Macquarie Street near where Hunter Street ends.

Perhaps you should have strolled through the Botanic Gardens first, entering them near the crenellated Conservatorium of Music (once the stables of nearby Government House), and emerged opposite the Library. Anyway, continue along Macquarie Street towards King Street. At your left is State Parliament House, finished in 1817 as part of the Rum Hospital, so called because the contractors were to be paid with a monopoly of the lucrative rum trade. On the other side of the sandstone pile that is Sydney Hospital, another part of the original Rum Hospital is known as the old Mint building. Both parts are two-storeyed with wide verandas, columned and bal-conied in colonial style. The Mint is much the better of the two.

At the King Street end of Macquarie Street, look left to Hyde Park Barracks (1817), now a law court: unhappy additions have left little more than the gable-with-clock to admire of its design by Francis Greenway, the convict architect who was free-pardoned for this work by a well-pleased Governor Macquarie. Look right now, down King Street, to Greenway's finest monument, St James's Church (1819) with its greened copper spire. Inside the adjacent Law Courts—from which bewigged barristers robed in black silk emerge—is a beautifully preserved cedar staircase not many people know about: you can go in. But the loveliest staircase in Sydney you will find by going downhill-and-left into Onslow Avenue when you go through King's Cross. It curves up in the elegant oval entrance hall of Elizabeth Bay House, an 1832 Regency mansion by another distinguished early architect, John Verge. And have a look at what has been done to recreate period-Sydney elegance at the nearby Town House hotel.

The coach tour I recommended will take you for morning tea to Vaucluse House, the home of the statesman-explorer William Charles Wentworth, whose mother was a convict girl and who vigorously fought for responsible government and the Constitution won for New South Wales in 1853; and he was one of the trio of explorers who first crossed the Blue Mountains. Vaucluse House, though, was built in 1804 by an extraordinary Irish adventurer trans-ported for abducting an heiress, Sir Henry Brown Hayes. Finding too many snakes about for his liking, Hayes imported tons of turf from the Ould Sod made snake-free by the blessed St Patrick, and hopefully surrounded his house with this as a barrier of protection.

Vaucluse is, according to one survey, top of the "elite" list of suburbs, ranking above Point Piper, Darling Point, Bellevue Hill and Killara, which is nine miles in on the north side of the harbour. Killara has more trees and better gardens (trees are taller and soil better away from the salty harbourside). Vaucluse and the others have the views, and there is more white stucco and paint in these less arboreal eastern suburbs: Killara sticks to brick. Vaucluse your coach will pass through, either going to or returning from Bondi Beach.

Bondi, the suburb, looks brash where it isn't dowdy and has as few charms as trees. Bondi, the beach, happily divorced by a grassy stretch from the shop commerce of Campbell Parade, is superb. Or so I thought as I looked at it under the sun of an end-of-summer May day, its crescent sweep of sand both wide and long, a beach strand deservedly famous and fit to receive the blue-green Pacific that hilled itself rhythmically offshore and curled and broke into racing fronts of white that bore in the hardy board-riders at each end of the beach and a few body-surfers in the middle—a good, medium surf, not wildly living up to its Aboriginal name (actually "Boondi") that meant the noise of breaking waves.

I felt that I was *seeing* Bondi for the first time. In midsummer you can't see it, the beach, for people. The sand turns into acres of flesh, and the wedding of sea and shore is lost in a dark confetti of bathers. I had the absurd feeling that its summer-Sunday horde—all those mums and dads and kids and bikini birds, and big bronzed studs and undersized stableboys from Randwick and skinny hippies and blue-jowled louts and paunchy businessmen—they were somehow unworthy of such a beach. But it is the thought that is unworthy, isn't it? So I feel like saying: Bless 'em all, Bondi the Beach, receive them to your sands, be the place of weekend godhead to clerk and factory-bencher, and the classless Elysium of the waitress from the clattery café. Receive them to your waves, and preserve them from your rips and undertows beyond the DANGER signs. Especially bless your lifesavers, the young men who voluntarily serve and thresh out in the belt at the end of the reel-line to rescue a hundred swept-out surfers on a bad Sunday. And, while you're at it, bless the surfboard riders, right down to their ankles and shins made knobby from board bumps, for the way they go on to master such waves as have wiped them out and out and out again—until they stand up whizzing and twisting and knowing such speed sensation that, without benefit of machines, used to be known only to ski-champions of the snow. You'll love to watch them.

Watch also, if you can, a surf carnival on one of the beaches—and near Sydney there are thirty-five miles of surf-pounded sands. There's the strutting march-past of each competing team, the races, the bringing in and resuscitation of dummy half-drowneds, and the surf-boat races—which, in a big surf, provide spectacular capsizes. But the boys with the coloured skull caps tied to their heads always bob up unbrained by overturned boats and flying oars.

Sharks, but sharks, you say? They are undoubtedly out there. I've heard the sharkbell ring, though not many times, and seen the surf emptied till the scare was over. Consider, though, the millions of entries into these so-called "shark-infested" Sydney waters in a year—and the last shark tragedy at a surf beach was in 1936.

You could leave the coach tour at Bondi, get a taxi, say "Watson's

Bay" and add "Doyle's"; and have yourself as good a fish lunch as you can get in Sydney, at an outside table, at this restaurant fronting a small beach, beside the Watson's Bay Hotel, where you must buy your bottle of riesling or hock, because Doyle's isn't licensed.

Take a bus back towards the city. At Rose Bay is a highly expensive restaurant, Caprice, built over the water so the night-view from a windowside table is rather magical, but I don't like its décor much. A "floating" restaurant, the Captain Cook, is moored nearby. In 1970 it won a "restaurant of the year" award. (The award for the best cellar went to the Coachman Restaurant. Several gourmets swear by the Five Doors, where I've eaten well.)

Stop off at Double Bay. It has been called "probably the most vital and unique shopping centre in Australia". Forgive the "most unique".

Past Double Bay and before Rushcutters Bay, if you go left up Glenmore Road, away from the water, you'll come to Paddington; preferably by taxi to Underwood Street and start walking from there. As in the Belgravia area of London, terrace houses in what used to be a working-class suburb just above slum level have undergone transformation in the past decade. Parts of Paddington could now be called "fashionable", if the word were not a dirty one to the new residents, many of whom are connected with the arts.

These Victorian houses, perhaps ninety years old, two-storeyed on twenty-foot frontages, are balconied with cast-iron lace and restoration or renovation has done many of them proud.

Paddington is also very good art gallery country. Be sure to see the Bonython Gallery. Good restaurant territory, too, is hereabouts.

In the city area I should have directed you east of Macquarie Street and across the Domain to the Art Gallery of New South Wales. It has the best collection of Australian paintings anywhere. Don't miss the work of such artists as Tom Roberts, Drysdale, Dobell, Nolan.

THE BEST LINE of railway to live on is the North Shore one, over the Bridge and up four-five hundred feet of undulant land to the most favoured sector, between Killara and Wahroonga.

See this quiet, green, rather civilized suburbia, I suggest, on the way to what lies beyond it—Kuring-gai (or Ku-ring-gai) Chase and the northern beaches that I prefer to surf at because, apart from their being handier, they are not as crowded as Bondi-Bronte-Coogee-Maroubra, and the background bush is not all razed and built over.

I've looked over the *Coach Tours around Sydney* booklet the Tourist Bureau puts out, and the one that seems recommendable is No. 8, Hawkesbury River/Kuring-gai Chase/Koala Park (9.30 start, returning 5 p.m., $5). This will take you through Killara and at

Pymble you'll see our best-treed suburbia along Pentecost Avenue; then there's a ten-mile run, with lots of bushland left along it, to the northern beaches. From Newport you go on to Palm Beach, glimpsing on the way Pittwater that entranced its christener, Governor Phillip.

Palm Beach (twenty-six miles from the city) is where some of our richer citizenry can afford to maintain expensive houses they use only at weekends. It is a good beach and the background is specially pleasant, there being no shops here (except one hideous food stall), and the sand extends to where the peninsula you are on ends in a hammerhead called Barrenjoey, topped with a lighthouse that shines out over Broken Bay, which leads into the Hawkesbury River, where you are going. By launch, from the Pittwater side of Palm Beach, you cruise (lunch aboard) past Lion Island and scarps of ochre-ish sandstone, and dense hillsides of gums rise darkly from what, on a blue day, is a peacefully beautiful waterway.

At Bobbin Head, where the ferry launch brings you, at the head of Cowan Water, you rejoin your coach, and return to Sydney via Koala Park at Pennant Hills, and here you'll see koalas and kangaroos under better conditions than you will at Taronga Park.

If you feel that you would rather explore on your own Kuring-gai Chase, a 36,000-acre national park, you can, with a rented drive-yourself car. (We drive, Joe, on the *left* of the road: the wheel is on the right-hand side.) In that case go to the Visitor Information Centre, about a mile beyond Bobbin Head (and close to another koala sanctuary). This helpful setup of the National Parks and Wildlife Service can tell you anything from what-tree-is-that to where you can leave your car and go down a track to picnic beside a sequestered bay with, maybe, oysters on the rocks (small but succulent: take an oyster knife) and where there's a fireplace if you need one to grill chops, or where you can find Aboriginal rock carvings.

Have a good day—round-tripping with the coach tour or on your own. Sydney is for enjoying. And not just as a city but as a place with untrammelled edges, where the Bush puts up its crooked arms and invokes a spirit of timelessness that makes the G.P.O. in Martin Plaza seem very far away as you fiddle with a twig of cuppy gum-nuts, "read" the trunk of what we call a scribbly gum, and smell the sun's warmth on the eucalypt-leaves you look down through to blue water. But don't expect it to be very quiet. You are likely to be laughed at by kookaburras, carolled at by musical magpies and, on a hot summer's day, have your eardrums drilled by the song of cicadas.

Blue Mountains and Beyond

OF THE BLUE MOUNTAINS that begin about forty miles back of Sydney the traveller is entitled to expect two things: that they are blue and that they are mountains.

Of their blueness, at a distance, there is no question. Of their being mountains there is no question, either, in the mind of the hiker craning up at vertical cliffs from the Jamieson Valley to the south of the two main resort towns, Katoomba and Leura.

But this is not the way most sightseers see the Blue Mountains. They see them from on top. They look down and they look across. And what they see, thus, usually leaves viewers greatly impressed—as well as surprised that so much of the scenery is *below*.

Blue Canyons could be a better description than Blue Mountains. The region is a riven plateau rising to about 3,500 feet at the highest part at Mount Victoria, eighty miles from Sydney. This great mesa-like upthrust of sandstone and shales has been cut through by water-courses and divided into a series of plateaux. River gorges have widened into valleys through eroded rock falling away from the cliff faces. The fallen rock piles deeper and deeper at the foot of the cliff and forms a slope that geologists call a talus—rather like a hillside going up to the base of a medieval castle with walls rising sheer to the battlements. Close up, there is nothing blue about these mountain walls. In some places the cliffs are, due to ironstone stain-ing, rust-red and tangerine and purple-brown.

The blue haze arises (PLATE 18) because the valleys are floored with forests of eucalypts, and when oil from these trees is vapour-ized into the atmosphere it has the effect of intensifying or "scatter-ing" blue-light rays, particularly in valleys as enclosed as these are. (Similarly, dust particles intensify red light, so the sun low on the horizon looks redder.) The mountains-valleys are at their bluest—and the coloured cliffs at their brightest—just before sunset.

KATOOMBA is the town we immediately connect with the Blue Mountains. It is the tourist centre, and tourism virtually its only industry: and not such a prosperous one as it used to be before New South Wales vacationers became so sea-happy that the coast is now where three out of four spend their holidays.

People who like the Blue Mountains so much that they wouldn't live anywhere else travel daily the sixty-eight miles from Katoomba to Sydney offices by train. It takes about two hours by the fast train known as The Fish (because, the story goes, many years ago the driver's name was Herring, the fireman's Salmon and the two conductors were Pike and Trout). Actually, there was a hefty driver named Heron whose nickname was "The Big Fish".

Katoomba is, these days, more or less merged with mile-away Leura, which is where I prefer to stay. Anyone who plays golf, as I used to, could hardly find a lovelier course, scenically, than Leura's. Handy to the links there used to be only guest-houses. Recently I was glad to find, near by, the Leura Motel which—in spite of its having that "over-dressed" look that red texture-brick confers on any building—proved to be an excellent establishment of its kind.

At Leura you get a superb panorama from Sublime Point, and the Bridal Veil Falls are very good, if there is sufficient water going over. There are many waterfalls—long ones, too—down these precipices. Leura has some streets of pleasant houses people have retired to behind trees that colour beautifully in autumn. In one of these streets, Denison, you will find "Everglades", a gardened place of distinctive loveliness that the National Trust has acquired.

Between Katoomba and Medlow Bath (where the enormous, touristically ancient Hydro Majestic Hotel is worth visiting because its position overlooking the Megalong Valley is so scenic), by the roadside is the Explorers' Tree. It was marked by the party that in 1813 succeeded in crossing the mountain barrier, led by Blaxland, Wentworth and Lawson (hence mountain towns named Wentworth Falls, Blaxland and Lawson, passed through on the way up to Katoomba).

Even today there is no more than a ribbon of development across this plateau of the Great Dividing Range, and there are no towns on either side of those strung along the railway line. There can't be, as you see when you come to Blackheath and go down to the edge of an enormous chasm. Here is Govett's Leap—and some Australian visitors think a bushranger named Govett made a desperate leap here on his horse. In fact, Govett was a surveyor and the waterfall you see going over a precipice is the "Leap".

The Blue Mountains climate is pleasantly cooler than Sydney's in summer, and much colder in winter, when snow sometimes falls. It can be at its best in spring and autumn. Rain is fairly evenly distributed, though more falls in the summer months, and often as a misty drizzle. Katoomba gets an average fifty-five inches a year, and some rain falls on one day in three. Lovers of the Mountains find Sydney air soggy most of the year, and extol the "bracing" and "exhilarating" quality of their higher (and unpolluted) atmosphere.

SIGHTSEEING. There is, of course, the quick and effortless way of seeing Blue Mountains sights without even staying there. Coach tours leave Sydney each morning and return you for dinner. By lunch-time you are at Katoomba, at the most renowned of all viewing places, Echo Point; and you can have a three-course lunch for under a dollar-fifty in a gaudily touristy restaurant which does, however, revolve and provide through its glass walls a scenic panorama and a close view of the most-photographed of all mountain formations, a trio of eroded pillars known as the Three Sisters.

After lunch you can swing across the valley-head where the Katoomba Falls plummet, in the "Skyway" cable car, and ride what is said to be the world's steepest scenic railway—and it feels like it— 750 feet down into the Jamieson Valley: this takes only seven minutes.

Much is missed if the Blue Mountains are experienced only from the top and at motorized eye-level. It is great walking country (when I was much younger a party of us had a fine time hiking from Katoomba to Jenolan Caves). Even the not-so-young, if they have remained reasonably fit and agile, should consider doing at least the Federal Pass walk, which is about four miles and takes a couple of hours. The easiest way is to go down from near Leura Falls by well-graded steps and, having walked along through the tree-ferny track at the foot of the cliffs to near Katoomba Falls, ascend by using the scenic railway.

The Blue Mountains resorts are not expensive. Even at the Carrington Hotel in Katoomba—lately renovated but retaining its baroque statuary and still redolent of its naughty-nineties grandeur when your wicked Uncle Henry spent an illicit weekend here with a girl in a feather boa—even at the Carrington you could in 1970 get bed and breakfast for $6; more for suites, of course.

THE JENOLAN CAVES are as spectacular as the stories of their discovery are dubious.

It is said that a bushranger named McKeown robbed travellers over the mountains road in the late thirties of last century. One of his victims, named Whalan, determines to track the outlaw to the hide-out McKeown must have in rugged unexplored country beyond the valleys to the south of Katoomba. Whalan comes upon a great arch (now known as the Grand Arch entrance to the Devil's Coach-house). Through this he enters into a small hidden valley where, lo, there is a hut, obviously the bushranger's. Whalan returns with police troopers, McKeown is captured, the great open cave he found is made known, and the discovery of a marvellous labyrinth of "dark" caves follows.

The only trouble with this good story is that there appears to be no historical record whatever of a bushranger named McKeown.

However, it is the scenic worthiness of the caves that matters.

Jenolan's caverns may not rank with those of Carlsbad in New Mexico; but they are recognized as the best in New South Wales and, indeed, so far as caves are known and developed, the best in Australia. I have not seen abroad better stalactite and stalagmite formations.

Jenolan (153 miles from Sydney) is usually reached by turning off the Great Western Highway beyond Mount Victoria. The road twists down to the impressive slant of the Grand Arch entrance to the Devil's Coachhouse, and you pass through this to the Caves House.

What, it may be asked, is New Australia about Jenolan Caves? The standard of accommodation is. The Caves House, commodious and fully licensed—and operated in exemplary style by the State tourist authority—was regarded in 1970 as the best-value country hotel in New South Wales, with first-class accommodation and good meals inclusive for $10 a day.

Also, there is a new look to some of the caves. From being tramped through for years by hundreds of thousands of visitors, formations had become discoloured and grubby-looking by dust settling on wet limestone. Several caves have been expertly "steam cleaned", and shine again with a pristine quality.

A VISION FOR BATHURST

The citizens of Bathurst, the provincial city that lies 130 miles west of Sydney on the other side of the mountains, picked up their newspapers one day in October 1969, and nearly dropped them. They were astonished, as well as delighted, at what had been said about their inland city in the State Parliament—and said by a Sydney politician, the Member for Manly, Mr E. D. Darby, M.L.A.

What he had said was that Parliament should move to Bathurst, and Bathurst, not Sydney, should be the capital of New South Wales.

Mr Darby's argument was that the present State Parliament House was an "archaic shambles", a new one would have to be built soon, and it should be built outside Sydney, which was already congesting itself into a town-planners' nightmare.

Bathurst, having held Mr Darby's proposal up to the light and seen in it everything from undreamt-of prestige to boosted property values, hugged the scheme to its civic bosom and promptly formed a Bathurst-for-Capital Committee. If the nation could be governed from much-farther-inland Canberra, why should it be thought bizarre that the State could be run from Bathurst?

Irrespective of how much sense decentralization might make, I could not see our State politicians voting themselves out of Sydney and over the range to Bathurst, and so giving reality to Mr Darby's vision of the Queen opening a splendrous new House of Parliament there on the 200th anniversary of the State's and Australia's founding in 1988.

However, I could see why Mr Darby had picked Bathurst.

THE AMERICANS who compiled the *H.K.F. Report* on Australian tourism's potential wrote: "The rolling sheep country beyond the Blue Mountains is very appealing. Bathurst is a charming town [city, actually, population 18,000]. The main street's beautiful galleried buildings, with their decorative wrought iron . . . are irreplaceable. The new civic centre with its art gallery and auditorium is typical of Australian thinking, and would interest visitors."

"Charming" Bathurst? No one word can describe the place. Bathurst has an interestingly split personality. Essentially sedate, in a way that becomes Australia's oldest inland city that was founded in 1815, before Melbourne, it nevertheless reverberates quite frequently to the roar of racing cars tearing round its international-standard circuit on Mount Panorama. Traditionally pastoral-agricultural, it also cans food, makes the cans, has engineering works and manufactures footwear and furniture. So culturally conscious that it erected as its war memorial a "Singing Tower" when the only other carillon in Australia was Sydney University's, Bathurst still tolerates the ugly signboard and shopfront. A considerable educational centre—it has not only high schools but a teachers' college, and the Mitchell College of Advanced Education—it had yet to produce a well-written account of itself. A city set in countryside that could hardly be more Australian, you enter it through an avenue of willows that grew from cuttings brought from Napoleon's exile isle of St Helena, and find English elm and ash dropping autumn leaves round a Machattie Park greenhouse renowned for its tropical begonias. It has on its outskirts fine old homesteads of the squat-tocracy—and at No. 10 Busby Street, hard by the railway yards, the most unassuming dwelling of an Australian Prime Minister, the late J. B. (Ben) Chifley; the semi-detached cottage he lived in from when he was a loco-driver going off with his tin tucker-box to when he was being limousine-d home from The Lodge at Canberra.

Near Bathurst (though nearer to Orange) is Ophir, where gold discovered in 1851 by Edward Hargraves—an English-Australian who had been a "forty-niner" in the gold rush to California—started the gold rushes that were to change the course of Australia's history and double its population in five years. When gold was discovered there were no railways in Australia. A group of Americans who had gold-rushed to Victoria decided that Australian coach services could be much improved by introducing American hickory-wood coaches with leather springs, such as Wells Fargo used. Freeman Cobb from Massachusetts headed the syndicate that brought out the Yankee coaches and in 1853 Cobb & Co. began. Cobb and his partners soon sold out (Cobb returned to the States to become a Senator) but as Cobb & Co. the firm went on. By 1870 its coachlines, criss-crossing eastern Australia from Melbourne to Cape York Peninsula, were travelling 28,000 miles a week and harnessing 6,000 horses a day. Another American, James Rutherford from New York State, came to head Cobb & Co. and he moved its headquarters, in 1862, from Bendigo to Bathurst.

World War II's big Army camp at Bathurst turned into a migrant reception centre; and many migrants, liking the district, made their homes there. German builders were responsible for the top motel, where I overnighted in November 1969, the Bathurst Motorlodge. The appointments had quality, not the usual flashiness: nowhere was the improvement in country accommodation better exemplified than in this first-class place.

I arrived after midnight by the late train from Dubbo. A supper tray was waiting in my room, and the information that "Miss Eyre has arrived and will see you in the morning." Gwen Eyre, my cousin, had come up from Sydney to drive me to a place I knew, and she had reason to know better than nearly anyone—Hill End.

"NEW" HISTORIC HILL END

HILL END, fifty-two miles north of Bathurst by the most-used road, is where the Old Australia's first big mining boom really got up and glittered. Alluvial gold was rich in pockets. But the big wealth was underground in reefs.

Reef mining began at Hill End. The first stamper battery in Australia,[1] hauled over the mountains by bullock- and horse-teams, was erected there in 1857. Soon there were others, and the ore they were crushing was coming mainly from Hawkins Hill—and some say (though it is hardly verifiable) that Hawkins Hill was the richest five acres of earth in the world.

The richest strike of all was to come from the mine where two Germans, Beyers and Holtermann, had already struck gold so good that the shares had rocketed. In October 1872 a blasting disclosed a "jeweller's shop" wall of gold, and from this a tooth-shaped slab four-feet-nine high and weighing over a quarter of a ton was hauled up out of the shaft. It was filled with some 3,000 ounces of gold that today would be worth about $100,000. It was not, as it is often termed, the biggest "nugget" (a nugget is a lump of alluvial gold). It was simply the largest known gold mass ever brought to the surface anywhere in the world.

So Hill End is historic, no question of that. No wonder, either, that it has now been declared by the State to be a Historic Site—the only town or village in New South Wales to be thus marked for preservation.

The Hill End that a century ago had eight thousand people, twenty-eight pubs and two newspapers—is it today, with hardly more than a hundred people and one hotel, more than just another "ghost-town"? I think so; and it is a place I became involved with at an early and impressionable age.

When I was six years old my mother sold the private hospital she had in Sydney and we went to Hill End and lived there until I was twelve. From Bathurst we went out by a coach that had *Royal Mail* emblazoned on the side, and I sat up front with the driver, my feet resting on a nine-gallon keg of beer for the Royal Hotel, which was to be our home for the first years because my mother's sister had married its proprietor, Oswald Forbes Eyre. His brother, Hal Eyre, had become the foremost political cartoonist of the day in Sydney (*Eyre Jr*, Harry Eyre, cartoonist for the *Sydney Morning Herald*, is his son); and my uncle Oswald had become the unlikeliest of mining-town publicans. A gentle, sensitive, big man with perfect manners, he never swore and his English-pink cheeks blushed at bar-room bawdry. Gwen, my cousin, carried on the hotel after her father, and then my aunt, died. The Royal, built in 1872, passed out of Eyre hands some years ago and is nowadays owned by the State authority, and it has been gazetted as a Historic Inn.

Two-storeyed, with iron-lace balcony and veranda posts: I was to find it still much as I had known it. In the dining-room were the same pictures—Queen Alexander, and Grandfather Eyre in Masonic regalia. The staircase still the same lovely cedar, and the cedar bar.

Holtermann is in the bar: Bernard Otto Holtermann, partner with Louis Beyers in the mine of the Great Nugget that was more than a nugget. Holtermann, the man of many parts, stands lithographed beside the gold-tooth rock that is almost as tall as he is, on a poster advertising *Holtermann's Life-Preserving Drops*, which were supposed to cure everything from asthma to dysentery and gout. Always the showman, Holtermann, when the golden slab was hauled aloft, wanted to buy it to exhibit it: he offered £10,000, but the company wanted £12,000, and so it went into the crushers. With his fortune made, Holtermann became interested in photography, and a historically marvellous collection of wet-plate photographs he commissioned and exhibited abroad was unearthed in Sydney in 1951 and is now in the Mitchell Library.

But Beyers, what of Beyers, whose name is not mentioned in

some encyclopaedias that write of the famous Australian "Holter-mann's Nugget"? Beyers was a miner when Holtermann was only a hotel waiter. Beyers took the other young German into mining, and Beyers was working the Hawkins Hill mine without Holtermann when the first rich strike was made. And the modest Beyers was the man who endowed Hill End with its greatest charm.

His way of saying thank-you to the town that had given him riches was to plant a mile-long avenue of trees through it. He had lindens brought from his native Germany and there are oaks, elms, planes, chestnuts, walnuts, pines and hawthorns both white and pink. In places the trees meet across the road and make a leafy canopy, and Beyers Avenue is, of course, an autumn glory.

BEYERS AVENUE still looked beautiful to me as we drove into Hill End from the Bathurst Road that meets the avenue half-way down.

On the way from Bathurst we had picnic-lunched by the Turon River under a fine big brow of cliffs called Wallaby Rocks, just through Sofala, which is gold-famous, too, and picturesque with the willowed Turon River winding through. This was "The Turon", the alluvial Eldorado that used to have almost as many Chinese diggers as white—even more than there were at Tambaroora, three miles from Hill End on the Mudgee road. Tambaroora faded sooner: now there is nothing there, except the cemetery.

To return to a place where one spent a healthy and happy-enough childhood is to risk being disenchanted. I wasn't.

There are people who say the real Hill End is already dead, and what you see now is a Hill End embalmed for tourists. They are right, I suppose, in a way. I knew the real Hill End, or part of it. The last of the bowyanged miners working the last of the mines, some with "dusted" lungs. Kids I went to school with who wore singlets made of calico flour-bags and, when the white frost of winter forbade bare feet, hobnailed boots with no socks. Houses where the bedding was hessian sacks. Huge, marvellous bonfires on Empire Day, and sapling gums tied to shop veranda posts as Christmas decoration.

Forty years ago Hill End was a nothing. When I came to Sydney to go to high school and, asked where I came from, replied, "Hill End", people always said, "Where's that?" Thirty years went by, and I began to hear about Hill End. The artists, well-known ones, had discovered it.

Donald Friend was the first. In the early fifties he bought a miner's cottage (which he still owns though he lives in Bali now) and he lived there, off and on, for years (and wrote a delight of a book about the place[2]). Donald introduced Hill End to his painter friends:

"Tas" (Russell) Drysdale and Margaret Olley stayed with him. Paul Haefliger who was the *Sydney Morning Herald's* art critic and his wife Jean Bellette, both painters, bought a cottage they used to go up to before they went away to Spain. Then in 1962 one of our top abstract painters, John Olsen, returned from overseas and was looking for a place that was "truly Australian". He went to Hill End in company with Guy Warren and a couple of other artists, and found it "beaut". Hill End was the inspiration of Olsen's renowned series of paintings called "The You-Beaut Country".

The difference between the long-haired and the short-haired tourists was that the artist types were content to look and cerebrate and do their own thing creatively about it. The others felt that they must be doers in the sense of engaging in some activity relevant to the place, some shared pastime akin to sport. Their thing at Hill End is fossicking for gold, by panning for it. They buy (at the store) a small pick and a prospector's dish. This is a shallow thin-iron pan, rather like an oversized frying-pan without the handle and having a rolled edge and, usually, a groove called a riffle below the rim. With the pan three-quarters full of washdirt they dig from a bank (up to about fifteen pounds of dirt) they squat at the edge of a creek or waterhole. They wash the clay away by puddling and swirling and tipping the dish and get rid of the gravel, after careful peering at the bits of washed quartz, in case they are throwing out a nugget. Finally they are left with just a streak of heavy black sand in which may glint a few heavier specks of gold. With more luck, they'll get a piece the locals will say is a "coupla 'weights" (a pennyweight is one-twentieth of a troy ounce, worth about $1.50).

A camping area with the usual facilities had been set up (by the Hill End Citizens' Association) for tents and caravans. More and more tourists could be expected—Hill End was one of the rare places where character wasn't smothered under commerce—and demand for more accommodation. Probably the solution will be, in part, motel-type accommodation added at the back of the Royal Hotel. The State authority should, and probably will, see to it that any such building is in keeping with the place.

Hill End, or most of it, is now in the care of the N.S.W. National Parks and Wildlife Service. This is about the only organization I know of in Australia that can be trusted to put up a well-designed signpost. It also outfits its rangers with uniforms that are attractive and command respect.

Any historic place needs to be interpreted to the visitor. There would be much better visual interpretation of Hill End's history when the old hospital's restoration was completed and it was turned into a Hillendiana museum.

On the way out to Hill End my cousin had said, "We've got to see the old roasting pits."

What "roasting pits"? I had never heard of them. Neither, it turned out, had she, until when she was told of the discovery in about 1963 of the remarkable construction that had been overgrown with blackberries on Alpha sheep station, about eight miles from Hill End. Harry Hodge describes them in his Hill End *Guide* booklet[3] as "easily the most historic and important evidences of the past in the district".

The roasting pits were built in 1857 by Cornish miners, to crack exceptionally hard stone small enough for the crushers to cope with it. So well built were they that they stand today much as they did a century ago, and they are unique in Australia.

IT WAS TIME TO LEAVE, most reluctantly. At the hotel the ebullient Dita Cobb was writing for her newspaper column: "Hill End, darlings, is for raving about" and, "The Royal is a beaut old pub." The proprietress, Mrs Davis, gave us lunch (which they don't usually serve) in the huge kitchen. Then Gwen headed her VW towards Bathurst by a different road, known—and with some reason, still—as the Bridle Track.

This road winds steeply down to the Turon. The river is unbridged and you may not get over the concrete crossway if there has been much rain in the mountains. You go along the river, past towering Sailor's Bluff to its junction with the Macquarie. Then the road follows that. You look down through casuarinas onto sunstruck water with white-glinting rapids, and across to plunging hillsides. There is, for the first twenty miles of the forty, hardly a sign of habitation—but lovely riverside spots for peaceful camping. There is nowhere to get petrol if you run out, or food or drink; we passed only one other car, and the road was rough in places. There are a few station gates to open before, near Bathurst, you get back on the bitumen. But, scenically, this little-used road is one to remember.

OUT AMONG THE JUMBUCKS

THE AMERICANS, twenty-two women and eight men, all of them retired people, are sitting on logs in the shade of bluegums beside the Macquarie River near Dubbo. On their laps are cardboard lunch-plates, and a thin smoke drifts from the fire that has barbecued the steaks and chops they are tucking into.

Each of the tourists is wearing, tied round the neck, a white bib: it is made of plasticized paper and on it is printed JOLLY SWAGMAN TOUR and the words of three Australian folk songs, *Click Go the Shears*, *Wallaby Stew* and *Farewell to Old England* (about convicts sailing for *Botany Bay*). But not the words of our folk anthem, *Waltzing Matilda*, beginning:

> Once a jolly swagman camped by a billabong
> Under the shade of a coolabah-tree,
> And he sang as he watched and waited till his billy boiled,
> "Who'll come a-waltzing Matilda with me!"
>
> Down came a jumbuck to drink at the billabong . . .[1]

Perhaps the tour organizers baulked at explaining to Americans—or to Japanese, with whom this tour is also popular—what a *swagman* was (a wayfarer or hobo with his belongings in a slung blanket-roll, a swag), a *billabong* (a lagoon-like effluent of a river), a *coolabah* (a rough-barked eucalypt), a *billy* (a tin can with a wire handle, for boiling water), what was meant by *Waltzing Matilda* (taking the road with a swag, known as Matilda), and that a *jumbuck* is a sheep.

Before lunch there were drinks. "Whisky, sir. Scotch or Bourbon?" . . . "I'll take an Australian beer." And the hostess had gone round with a big pressure-pak can asking everyone if they'd like a spray: "Our flies can be very friendly." Now the tourists are drinking their billy tea.

"Is this what you call a *billy*?" I am asked by a jolly American whose swag is a three-hundred-dollar Canon camera, as he helps himself to another cup of black tea. I, the only Australian in the tour party, say that a billy is smaller and round: this black oval thing is called a dixie. He laughs, "Dixie? Good old Dixieland! Now what kind of an Australian word is *that*!" Fair enough. Actually *dixie* is Indian (Hindu, not Red, Indian).

"I noticed that the driver, when he made the tea, he hit the sides of the dixie with a stick." He tapped it, I say, to settle the tea-leaves to the bottom. "That so? . . . Y'know, this is all right, eating out here in the bush. Something a little different for us." He lights a cigar and unties the bib and looks at it. "Why don't I fold this in my pocket and take it right back to the States? Souvenir of being in the Australian outback." Maybe I blinked. "This *is* what you call the *outback* isn't it?" At Dubbo, not really. If you went on west for another thousand miles you'd be just half-way across the country.

Dubbo is 260 road miles from Sydney and an hour's flight by the Fokker Friendship of Airlines of New South Wales, which runs this one-day "Jolly Swagman Tour" for overseas tourists, only, whenever the numbers are offering. (I, wanting American reaction to Australia, have been allowed to join it.) We had left Sydney at 7 a.m., got in the waiting coach at Dubbo airport, and been taken to breakfast at the Amaroo Hotel in the main street of Dubbo, which

K

calls itself the "Hub of the West", meaning the Western Plains. It is 17,000 people surrounded by wheat, wool, fat-lambing and cattle-raising, pigs and poultry, vegetable-growing and orchards. The principal in-town industry is the abattoirs. Looking down Dubbo's main street (the handsome Civic Centre is not in view) I can see nothing exceptional or unexpected.

"Esther," an American woman behind me says to her companion, "did you notice as we drove in—all the druggists are *chemists*. And there are just so many *banks*, why they're as common as grocery stores!"

This morning the coach ran out of Dubbo with the driver giving a commentary and some of the Americans asking each other, "What did he say?" because their ears are not attuned to Australian voices. Not that they were missing anything but the usual parochial particulars about how many bowling clubs and motels there are, and the size of the R.A.A.F. storage base. What they want to know about is the country: even such basic things as why a eucalypt is called a "gum-tree". (Strictly, it isn't one. Acacias and liquidambars are trees that have true gum, and what oozes from eucalypts and becomes like hard treacle is a quite different substance. But "gum-tree" is the name Governor Phillip used and we are stuck with it.) The driver has seen so much Paterson's Curse that he doesn't mention what that spread of purple flowering across a paddock is; and so many galahs that he doesn't say the name of the pink-breasted grey parrots the Americans are exclaiming about.

However, everybody is happy when, twenty miles out, we get to Avondale station. This 1,620 acre property the Americans would call a ranch grazes 2,500 Corriedale sheep, along with Hereford cattle, and grows oats as a fodder crop. Jack Payne who runs Avondale is close to seventy but doesn't look it. He is a real countryman, strong and leathery, with an unaffectedly cheerful grin and sun-wrinkles round the eyes that look out at everything with dispassionate practicality from under his wide old hat. The tourists feel at ease with him as he casually takes them round a yard of cows and heifers with one big bull in it and says such things as that, owing to the good feed, this year the calves are very big. He has to bring cows in, the first-calving heifers especially, to assist any difficult births. "What do you do? You rig a pulley-block on a tree, and you rope what you can of the calf. Rough, but it's the only way."

His market for cattle? "I'd say most of 'em end up as meat in your American hamburgers. Yes, even that big bull over there—the one with the curly forehead. Forty cows he's got, forty wives. He'll be hamburgers. But he's had a good life."

They'd like to see the dogs work sheep? He calls out what could almost be the same name twice: Smiler is the bitch, Shiner the dog. They are Border Collies. Just outside the gate is a mob of sheep.

"The dogs'll bring 'em in through this gate," Jack Payne says as Smiler and Shiner race out, eager for the work they know so well. The sheep want to go any way except towards the gate where all the tourists are standing, but the dogs are behind them and round them, manoeuvring, racing from one side to the other, sharing the work so that they are never both at the same place. When the mob is moving gatewards the dogs are on the ground, almost crawling as they edge them forward, ears up, tongues lolling, never a bark.

A ewe breaks away and Smiler is after it, alongside it, she jumps at it—and the air splits with Jack Payne's whistle. Smiler stops as though shot. One whistle means *Stop!* He shouts "Smiler!" and she is off again, and brings the runaway back—properly, with Payne growling, "Smiler, I'll tan your hide." The dog must not touch the sheep. Soon they are all baa-ing in through the gate where the people are, Smiler working like mad to make amends, Shiner doing a steady job.

I ask Jack Payne why has he given them names as alike as Smiler and Shiner. "They know which one I call." How does he train them so that they don't do the wrong thing. "With a stick."

The Americans loved the sheep dogs working. The women would have liked to pat Smiler, but Smiler wouldn't come. A sheepman's dog is one man's dog. And they were so much taken with Jack Payne that the hostess asked him and his wife to come in and have dinner with the party at the hotel that evening, which they did. It was a good gesture and the tourists liked that too.

BEFORE WE LEFT the barbecue-lunch place on the Macquarie River there was the Aboriginal. He was well-dressed—yellow pullover and a felt hat—and he first of all played music on what is surely the world's simplest instrument, a gumleaf held between the lips. I've yet to see a white man do this, though I suppose it can be learnt, like throwing a boomerang.

The Aboriginal man threw boomerangs (which were for sale) and the American tourists were invited to try their hands at throwing. He showed them how to hold the boomerang, by one end with the point of the curve towards you and held vertically: you throw it outwards, straight, not slanted and upward as you might expect.

Then we coached again, out to a fat-lamb property called Cockleshell Corner. Bill Jackson was a youngish sheepman and he and his wife, in slacks, bid the party welcome in an uneffusive Australian way. He said he knew they had come to see sheep-shearing, and so they would. But he had some lambs to attend to—"marking and so on"—and would they like, first, to see that? "Why, yes," they said.

"Lambs" is an emotive word to women, except sheepmen's wives. I don't think any of the Americans knew that "marking" is castrating.

Sheep were in the pens, and the visitors exclaimed as the dogs ran across their backs to get to the other side to help with the cutting out; but, being unnecessary here, the dogs were whistled out of the pens. Mrs Jackson worked a gate at the end of a race so that when a lamb came it was diverted into the lamb pen.

Bill Jackson picked up a gangling little lamb that was all legs and tail-waggle and as appealing as a young lamb can be. He carried it to an empty pen where he had set up the marking cradle. Into this the lamb was clamped on its back and held there helpless, bleating.

"We use a rubber ring," the sheepman said, stretching the ring on an applicator like a pair of pliers. "The ring is less cruel." He did not mention the old way of marking, still in use on some stations, which is to slit the scrotum and take the testes between the teeth and yank them out. He put the stretched ring over the lamb's woolly little knob and it flipped off tight round the base (I think the men all winced: I know I did) stopping the blood circulation. The testicles would atrophy and eventually drop off.

Another rubber ring was slipped over the lamb's tail. A knife appeared in Bill Jackson's hand and with a quick slash he docked off the tail just below the ring. There was a horrified "Oh!" from some of the women and a piteous bleat from the lamb.

This lamb was blind in one eye, from foxtail grass that has a needle point and will pierce the eye of a sheep when it is feeding. If you've got foxtail grass in your pastures, you've got it: Bill Jackson knew of no way it could be eradicated.

The sheepfarmer then scratched the lamb's chest and immunized it against scabby mouth. He injected it with 500 c.cs of whatever it is that prevents pulpy kidney. He took the branding pincers and snipped a piece, the station's distinctive mark, out of the lamb's left ear, which bled a little on to its face. The air felt damp with sympathy as the lamb was released from the clamps and lifted down. It staggered off and lay down miserably in the grass.

"He feels pretty sad now, but in about twenty minutes he'll be up and running around," Bill Jackson said. "Now, have you got all the photographs you want? Like me to do another one?"

There was a quavering chorus of, "No."

IN THE SHEARING SHED two heavily-woolled ewes are waiting to lose their fleeces to Fred Powell, an Aboriginal shearer. He catches his sheep under the forelegs and sits it up and back, so that when he is bending over shearing its belly the forelegs are tucked under his left armpit and the ewe's head is clamped behind them against his thigh.

The whirring clippers go so closely over the belly you can see the teats standing up, yet so skilfully that there is never a nick. His left hand pressed firmly on the sheep's shorn abdomen, he takes the clippers through with a curving rhythm and the wool rolls back from the sides in an unbroken mass. Now he has the sheep down sideways and wedged against his feet as he does the "long blow" down the flank. The ewe feels his mastery and does not try to struggle. The wool piles on the floorboards (PLATE 16).

In no more than about two minutes a white-naked sheep, looking half the size it was and almost skeletal, is being knee-shoved away towards the chute and Fred is ready for the next one, which is shorn in the same way, without a pause, without a cut, every movement cool and co-ordinated. The Americans are very impressed, as well they might be. A "gun" shearer is something to watch.

The tally board in the shed, still there from the shearing that finished two months ago (a few sheep are held back for visitor demonstrations) shows that one shearer, Barry, did 127 in a day. He has a way to go to match the great Jackie Howe's record in 1892 at Blackall in Queensland—321 sheep in 7 hours 40 minutes. And that was with hand blades, not machine clippers. Machine shearing was an Australian invention.

The Americans all wave to Bill and his wife as the coach goes off. On the run back to Dubbo the shadows of the box-trees are lengthening across the pastures and galahs are flying up from the road verge in pink-grey clouds of wings, but no kangaroos.

We go to the Fauna Reserve in Dubbo's Victoria Park (PLATE 16). The joeys looking out of kangaroo-does' pouches or leggily getting into them are a delight to the tourists, who are given food for them, and a tin of corn for the cheeky big emus to peck into; and they are shown snakes and such lizards as stumpy-tails and blue-tongues. Then a stop is made at the Pioneer Museum, which is in a most elegant old (1877) building. The museum is interesting but, to Americans who are used to a higher standard of display even in their provincial towns, it amounts to nothing much. Too many exhibits, too little interpretation. There is no catalogue.

The visitors are taken to the R.S.L. Club, and invited to have a drink "on" Dubbo. Some cannot resist playing the poker machines that stand, batteries of them, round the walls and are the financial stay of so many clubs in New South Wales. The Americans get the message that Dubbo is "friendly", likes having them visit the place—even to the extent of sending along a couple of its shire councillors to the dinner later at the hotel, to say a word of welcome. After dinner they fly back to Sydney.

What C.S.I.R.O. Spells

AT PARKES the wheatlands of the western plains were, in the late afternoon of a brilliant May day, beautiful. In paddocks ornamental with kurrajong-trees the young crop was as green as the earth, in the sunset flush, was crimson. But this was not really what I had come to Parkes to see.

Fifteen miles out, the car had turned off the main road and, appearing higher than the horizon of low hills, was this great soup-plate in the sky. That is what the aerial of the radio telescope resembles at a distance; locally it is called the "Big Dish". When it resolves itself, at close quarters, into an openwork mesh of steel mounted on a round concrete tower, it looks enormous. The "dish" is, in fact, an acre in area: its diameter, 210 feet, is only five yards short of the width of a football field. (PLATE 16.)

Britain's radio telescope at Jodrell Bank near Manchester is bigger, but not better. The newer Australian instrument has improvements that give greater accuracy. It is the largest in the Southern Hemisphere, and is housed at what is called the Australian National Radio Astronomy Observatory. The great dish is also a symbol.

The huge radio telescope at Parkes is the most visible, if not the most valuable, manifestation of what science is doing in the New Australia, through the nation's principal research organization, the C.S.I.R.O.

This body began in 1926 as the Council for Scientific and Industrial Research. At that time the exploration of outer space through radiophysics was not even thought of as part of its function: so perhaps we should leave the Parkes telescope and come to it later, in sequence. In the beginning the C.S.I.R. faced problems that were very down-to-earth. As it says: "*The cattle industry was ravaged by pleuropneumonia and the sheep industry by black disease, pulpy kidney and liver fluke. Fence posts rotted and rabbits multiplied. Huge tracts of land mysteriously failed to support pasture growth. Insect pests ruined crops of grain, fruit and vegetables. Manufacturing was at a low level; and the average Australian citizen wore a shirt made in Manchester, shoes from Northampton and drove a car made in Birmingham or Detroit.*" That statement needs to be read over again, almost memorized, in order to appreciate what the organization of trouble-shooters that started out in rented premises with forty-one scientists—and now has about two thousand of them and its own establishments all over Australia—has accomplished at the *primary* level.

Cattle that were getting pleuropneumonia are now getting about two million doses a year of a vaccine that prevents it. Sheep losses through "black disease" have been cut by an estimated ninety per cent. Pulpy kidney has been prevented by injection, and a lot has been done about liver fluke, and footrot.

A disease called "staggers" was traced to the toxic content of a valuable pasture, *Phalaris tuberosa*, and it was found that "staggers" could be prevented by dosing with cobalt. Now millions of sheep carry in their paunches "cobalt bullets". Similarly, C.S.I.R.O. investigation of "coast disease" that was wasting and killing sheep in South Australia showed that this was caused by deficiencies of copper and cobalt.

Fences no longer rot if their posts are of the treated timbers recommended by the C.S.I.R.O. that saved the Postmaster General's Department $4,000,000 a year by showing how telegraph poles could be made longer-lasting.

"*Rabbits multiplied.*" It was a bad day for Australia, and eventually for rabbits, when they were introduced from England. It was estimated that, before 1951, rabbits were eating as much feed as 70 million sheep. The only solution appeared to be some plague that would decimate the rabbit population. In South America it was discovered that a virus disease, myxomatosis, was lethal to European rabbits. C.S.I.R.O. work with the virus in Australia reduced the number of rabbits to about one-tenth of what it was—and in 1952 the value of increased primary production from sheep alone was $70 million.

Why pastures failed on far-from-arid land, the C.S.I.R.O. discovered, was because the soil lacked such nutrients as phosphorus, copper, cobalt, molybdenum. In South Australia this research resulted in more than a million acres of land, regarded as useless, being made productive by adding to the soil trace elements of copper and zinc.

Insect pests could be reduced by spraying with such compounds as DDT, but the residual toxicity killed birds and useful insects as well; also, the pests became resistant to it. Not only is the C.S.I.R.O. developing new insecticides that look like being as effective as DDT, without its drawbacks: the organization has gone to the scientific forefront in combating pests by non-chemical and biological methods, such as introducing predators. A wasp from South America now eats the grubs of the moth that can ruin Australian potatoes. The green vegetable bug is no longer a problem because of an introduced parasite. Dense stands of lantana bush are being attacked by introduced insects. The "bad" Sirex wasp that eats softwood timbers is being eaten by introduced natural enemies.

If graziers in North Queensland find the buffalo flies there less pestiferous to their cattle, it may well be because the C.S.I.R.O.

liberated in this region, in 1968, dung beetles. The night-working beetles carve up cattle dung into pellets they carry away and bury, to be food for their larvae. So they deprive the flies of cowpats as breeding grounds—and in doing so clear pasture for the better growth of grass; and the buried pellets of manure enrich the soil. It is possible that similar beetles might eventually control the pesky bush-fly also.

IT WAS JUST AS WELL that in 1936 the Commonwealth Government decided to extend the scope of the C.S.I.R. to take in problems of secondary industry. Three years later Australia was at war and was being called upon to manufacture things it had never produced before. So clearly valuable was the Council's work then that after the war, in 1949, it was reconstituted as the Commonwealth Scientific and Industrial Research Organization, with a much broader base and bigger budget. What the C.S.I.R.O. has done since would take a whole book to tell. Even then, the problem would be to explain some of the work in layman language.

A self-twist spinning machine, a quite new concept in textile spin-ping, was perfected by the C.S.I.R.O. in 1970, and is now being manufactured under licence in Melbourne. It spins ten times faster, and occupies only one-fifth of the space of conventional machines.

The C.S.I.R.O. could be more concerned with interpreting its work to the community and with making it easier for writers about Australia to list even highlight achievements of those scientific divi-sions whose work is relatively easy to understand.

Wool the Division of Textile Industry has made moth-proof and shrink-proof, "non-iron" and "permanent-press" by what is called the Si-Ro-Set process. Other countries are using these Australian-developed processes, and paying patent royalties for doing so.

Fuel cells have been developed that generate electricity by using simply methyl-alcohol and water. Prototypes were, in 1970, under test by the Postmaster General's Department and had run unattended for six months in remote areas.

"A.A.S." instruments. A new Australian industry, the making of sophisticated scientific instruments, has grown out of an original invention by Dr Alan Walsh of the Division of Chemical Physics, in an area of science called atomic absorption spectroscopy. In the field of mineral assaying, one recently developed instrument in the hands of one operator, is reported to be capable of analysing, in one day, two thousand rock samples. The instrument can determine simultaneously (at a cost of about a dollar a sample) their content of nickel, copper, silver, zinc and lead. Such Australian-developed

The "Big Dish" radio telescope at Parkes and its smaller partner in the C.S.I.R.O's radio astronomy detect and measure emissions of energy from the sun and stars.

BELOW: *Sheep shearing is demonstrated to American tourist visitors at Dubbo.*
LOWER RIGHT: *One of the tourists holds a joey kangaroo at the local fauna park.*

Sydney, showing the downtown section, the Harbour Bridge, Kirribilli Point in foreground, and (centre left) the coming wonder, the Opera House.

The Blue Mountains are less mountains than canyons of a riven plateau. Blue
haze is from eucalypts exuding oil droplets in a walled area.

Near Albury, waters of man-made Hume Lake combined with fertile land and
autumn colouring to produce this scene at Tallangatta.

instruments are being made under licence in U.S.A., Japan and a number of European countries, bringing royalties of over $500,000.

One representative of an overseas manufacturer of the Australian-designed equipment, on hearing of Dr Walsh's recent radical improvements to the model he had been manufacturing, blurted out, "Damn you, Walsh—you've made all our apparatus obsolete again!"

In 1971 a C.S.I.R.O. team with a spectrometer-equipped van was developing "neutron prospecting". Instead of chemical analysis of diamond drill cores, a probe armed with a neutron source that excited gamma radiation in the drill hole could test it much more quickly and less expensively.

Powdered butter. In 1962 the Division of Dairy Research discovered how to make this form of butter that retains just as much butter-fat as ordinary butter, but remains stable in hot conditions and is so much easier to mix with other ingredients for bulk cooking, as in cake-making. This is only one of a number of food "firsts" the C.S.I.R.O. has achieved—mechanized cheese-making is another. It also showed that the ripening of bananas could be delayed by sealing bunches in polythene bags.

Tropical pastures are being greatly improved by C.S.I.R.O. work with Townsville *stylo* (the new name for what was called Townsville "lucerne"—a drought-resistant plant, which is not a lucerne, from Central-South America, first naturalized in the Townsville region in 1903). Cattle have fattened up to twenty times better on Townsville stylo than on native pasture. A tenfold increase in beef production over large areas of North Queensland is anticipated and, in some areas of the higher-rainfall country of the Northern Territory "Top End", the increase (a C.S.I.R.O. spokesman said in 1970) could be *fifty times.*

Rain-making. The first artificially-induced rain ever to hit the ground fell in New South Wales after a cloud seeding experiment in 1947. In other experiments since then, many falls have been precipitated by silver iodide smoke released from aircraft. Rain-making techniques are not applicable to coastal areas or the cloudless outback. However, in areas up to 200 miles from the coast, experiments have measured increases of up to 20 per cent of the natural rainfall. Australia has led the way in such rain-making.

Water purification. In 1966 C.S.I.R.O. scientists came up with a quite new process for removing the minerals from brackish water, by trapping impurities in beds of plastic beads called "ion-exchange resins". The beads could be cleansed and regenerated easily.

Fishing. Tuna fleets in 1967 were supplied by the Fisheries and Oceanography Division with maps showing sea surface temperatures and other conditions favouring the occurrence of tuna. The increased catch was worth an extra $100,000.

Dried fruits. Through microscopic study of grapevine buds, the Horticulture Division was able to predict sultana yields ten months in advance. Harvesting costs were reduced by spray-treatment of the fruit so that it could be shaken from the vines instead of having to be picked.

Radio astronomy. The C.S.I.R.O's Division of Radiophysics was given that name during World War II to disguise the real nature of its secret work, which was radar. In 1946 its scientists discovered that (a) the sun had an atmosphere enormously hotter than had been supposed and (b) powerful radio waves are emitted from the vicinity of sun-spots. Australia has become a leader in the new science of radio astronomy, which it did much to pioneer. Recognition of this came from the United States in the form of donations amounting to $600,000, by the Carnegie Corporation and the Rockefeller Foundation, towards the $1,600,000 cost of the Parkes radio telescope.

The Ford Foundation subsequently contributed $US630,000 (more than half the cost) towards a unique solar observatory set up at Culgoora in northern New South Wales in 1967. Ninety-six radio aerial "dishes" each forty-five feet across are equally spaced round a circle nearly two miles in diameter. They form a radio-heliograph, and are automatically steered to follow the sun. The radio waves they pick up are fed through an electronic complex and become pictures on a television screen of activity on the sun's surface. Such pictures occur at the rate of one a second: previously a picture of the "radio" sun had taken forty-five minutes. The whole of the equipment was designed by the brilliant Dr J. P. Wild and his colleagues.

Australian radiophysicists are thus able to study, in much greater detail than was possible before, the violent solar flares that release energy millions of times greater than that of H-bombs, and the correlated radio "outbursts" that are often followed by blackouts in short-wave communications. Also they are concerned with sun explosions emitting streams of protons that could be lethal to space travellers.

Chief of the Radiophysics Division was an outstanding scientist, Dr E. G. Bowen, who stressed the need for a big radio telescope such as the C.S.I.R.O. got at Parkes in 1961 after it was discovered (in 1951) that there was radio emission from hydrogen atoms. Optical telescopes could give only a very limited picture of what was going on in a universe in which hydrogen atoms were "the basic building bricks". Radio telescopes could "see" through the clouds of stellar dust that obstruct the optical astronomer's view. They could detect in outer space "radio stars"—which were first detected by Australian radiophysicists. The Parkes Catalogue of Radio Sources is the most complete in the world. Over four hundred of these sources have been identified with visible objects. Most of the other radio emissions probably came from galaxies too faint to be recorded on photographic plates.

The precise determination of one radio source, made at Parkes, led to the discovery in 1962 of the first of the objects called *quasars*. These had appeared to be stars but are (according to one theory) enormously more luminous, emitting up to a hundred times the energy of the brightest galaxies. According to another theory, quasars are debris of a "local" explosion in space and their luminosity is because they are relatively near—"a mouse two feet away, not an elephant a mile away". Either way, quasars are a vital element in the controversy over whether the universe is expanding, in accordance with the Big Bang theory, or constant, as those aver who hold to the Steady State theory.

The Parkes radio telescope is also trained on the pulsating radio sources (*pulsars*) first reported by Cambridge radio astronomers in 1968. Pulsars are the source of most cosmic radiation, according to Professor C. B. A. McCusker, Professor of High-Energy Nuclear Physics at the University of Sydney, the scientist who in 1969 reported the discovery of sub-atomic particles called *quarks*. Professor H. Messel, head of the Sydney University School of Physics, said at the time that the discovery of the quark would rank in importance with the discovery of the atom and nuclear fission. Sydney experiments were going on in 1970 to confirm the existence of quarks. All scientific progress in Australia does not, of course, stem from the C.S.I.R.O.

THE VISITOR to the Parkes radio telescope will have its operation described to him simply by sitting down in one of the "talking chairs" in the tourist-lounge near the gate. He will also see that the Big Dish has a smaller brother, a radio telescope of 60-foot diameter, and that this is movable and can be positioned anywhere along a thousand feet of railway track. It is called an *interferometer* and is used in connection with the big aerial to which it can be "slaved" to point in the same direction.

When I first saw the Big Dish it was tilted. Next morning it was horizontal. At certain times (observation programme permitting), usually on Sundays, visitors can inspect the control tower.

"We are proud of our Big Dish," said Mr W. F. W. Painter of the Parkes Development Association.

There are, of course, other things to see in and near Parkes, and

Bill Painter gave up a day and a half of his time to show me some of them. The view from Memorial Hill is, when the countryside is as verdantly green as I saw it, a superb panorama of wheatlands and pasture beyond the town of 10,000 people—a town which has, incidentally, two first-rate motels, the attractive Coach House and the Caravilla Motel (where I stayed, and found the management most pleasant and the food very good: it should be liquor licensed).

Beside the railway line near Parkes is a building a quarter of a mile long, a bulk wheat terminal that stores four and a half million bushels. It takes three weeks to fill it with wheat and, alas, six months to empty it, which is too expensive and no more terminals are being built of this kind known as the "Wheat Elephant". When an inch of rain falls on its enormous galvanized iron roof, which goes right to ground level either side, the run-off is sufficient to fill a 119,000-gallon storage dam.

We drove out through the old gold-mining towns of Alectown (near the radio telescope) and Peak Hill where there was a huge open-cut mine, derelict, and where an Aboriginal named Harold Keed had, with the assistance of the Department of Decentralization, set up a boomerang factory.

We picnic-lunched among gums and galahs by the Bogan River and went on to where, on Murray Leach's property, Coonardoo, are some Aboriginal rock paintings. They were not particularly good ones, but in New South Wales any Aboriginal painting is a rarity and something to be preserved. These were not easy to find. But vandals had found them and daubed red paint over them.

We saw no kangaroos. They had all been shot out.

Parkes began as a gold-miners' canvas town called Bushman's: in 1872 its name was changed to honour the Australian statesman, Sir Henry Parkes, whose library is in the local historical museum. This museum had the best carved Aboriginal burial tree I have seen. For the rest, it was pretty much a mess and needed to discard at least half the gallimaufry of exhibits, and call in an expert to display and interpret the best.

From Parkes I flew to Sydney in an hour and twenty minutes by the East-West Airlines.

Broken Hill Is On Its Own

THE MAN FROM MELBOURNE on the tourist bus was a civil engineer whose appearance suggested that he had prospered since he left Broken Hill thirty years ago. He had not been back since.

He looked down Argent Street, the main street of the "Silver City", with some distaste. He said: "By God, you know, it hasn't changed much. These Broken Hill people, they just haven't kept up with the outside world."

It would doubtless be argued from Broken Hill that it sees no good reason to change, and that the outside world has not kept up with it. Does the representative worker in Melbourne earn $100 a week, as the average Broken Hill miner does? (And it is by no means uncommon for him to earn $150 a week.) In what other city can 30,000 people afford 13,000 cars? Where else in Australia does a medical scheme ensure the family free medical attention and hospital treatment including operations—and a tooth filling for a dollar at the Dental Clinic? "Broken Hill," they might say, "is on its own", meaning out in front.

Broken Hill is on its own in a more literal sense. It is part of New South Wales geographically; though with Sydney seven hundred miles away, and Adelaide only half that distance, it has always been more a part of South Australia commercially. Politically it isn't part of anywhere. What the Government of New South Wales might decide about wage agreements or hotel hours means nothing to Broken Hill: it decides its own. Traditionally the most Australian city in Australia, Broken Hill is less than integrated with the rest of Australia.

I could see what the returned native from Melbourne meant. "City" had come to mean a heterogeneous population: Broken Hill had remained exceptionally homogeneous. Cities have tall buildings (even Dubbo, a town with only half Broken Hill's population, has a seven-storey block), cantilever awnings, and lots of brick-and-tile: Broken Hill stays below the level of its mine-heads, retains veranda posts, and many of its houses are still of corrugated iron. Politically, it is a radical city: in many ways it is rigidly conservative. Socialist cities, after the first flush of change, are like that. Not that Broken Hill has socialism, but it has the nearest thing on the Australian scene to a "dictatorship of the proletariat". It is a trade-union society.

It is a strongpost of semi-socialism living in peaceful and prosperous co-existence with the capitalism of four big mines working such rich lodes of silver-lead-zinc that they can afford to give the workers what the workers want in payment and conditions. Not that this happy state has come about as a natural consequence of the mines' wealth. It represents a fought-for and hard-won victory. The man from Melbourne could remember five hundred hungry miners marching down Argent Street, and being told by his parents, when he was a boy and said he was going to another boy's house, "Don't *eat* anything", because there wasn't enough food.

The workers won, after a lot of strikes. The on-top miners' unions stayed vigilantly determined that the hungry days would never come again. They by-passed the arbitration system and negotiated their own contracts with mines that had no chance of getting non-union labour. The mines agreed to share their wealth by adding to wages a bonus related to the price of lead (the "lead bonus" in 1970 was over five dollars a shift, and has been much higher). The mining unions consolidated their strength by getting all other local unions to affiliate with them in a body called the Barrier Industrial Council.

"The B.I.C. runs Broken Hill." This is often said, and it is broadly true. And Broken Hill, through the B.I.C., looks after its own. You don't—if your job is within the province of the Workers' Industrial Union—go to Broken Hill to get a job. You won't get one because you aren't a local: you either have to be born there or to have lived there for eight consecutive years and be a member of the W.I.U. (which controls about twenty per cent of all jobs). That you may be capable of doing the job better than any local applicant can be beside the point.

"Yes, it's a walled city," Joe Keenan, the president of the B.I.C., said to me, and added that in a workers' society that is the way it had to be.

Joe Keenan was shortish, solid, black-haired, about fifty, vigorous and intense, and he looked you straight in the eye. When he was telephoned and told that I wanted to talk to him and I heard, "You'll be there at five o'clock?" it was typically Broken Hill that "there" didn't mean at his office but at the pub where he regularly drank. Finding him would be no sweat: you simply told the barman or anybody you were looking for Joe Keenan, and he'd be pointed out. He was, and you shook hands and he said, "Have a drink, Colin", and you said, "Thanks, Joe", and the barman set up another beer. No "mister" business.

Any argument about whether Broken Hill was a closed society and why was anticipated. Having said it was a "walled city", Joe Keenan went on to say: "We're all the same here. We dress the same, we talk the same, we think the same, we meet always in the same places, the mine or the pub. We're bonded together. There's got to be this bond. Working in a mine, a situation can come up any time where your life can depend on the fellow you're working with thinking of you, and his life can depend on your thinking of him. There *has* to be this thinking of the other fellow."

Individualism was, therefore, dangerous. The union couldn't accept an outsider and figure on instilling into him this thinking-of-the-other-bloke. It was something bred in the Broken Hill bone.

And yet—and this had Joe Keenan worried—there were Broken-

Hill-breds who didn't have it. The young ones, the youths coming into the workforce.

"Their thinking's odd," Joe said. "They haven't got this thinking about others. They can dress as they like—that doesn't worry me—and they can think what else they like. But they've got to have the bond in their minds, they've got to think of others!"

COLIN JACK who runs West Darling Tours didn't agree with the Melbourne engineer who said Broken Hill hadn't changed much in thirty years. In the seventeen years he had been there, he thought it had changed dramatically. "When I came Sulphide Street was all rocks and dirt, and look at it now." Sulphide Street, Chloride Street, Oxide Street—the names were redolent of what Broken Hill lived by.

An odd local feature of miners' housing was the number of fluted columns or column-ettes supporting verandas. Apparently, an Italian was the first to introduce this particular form of home "beautifying" that makes Robin Boyd so annoyed, and the columns were so much admired that he made a mould and cast them. But supposing that he had set up a sideline business of casting and selling not only columns but cement swans for the front lawn and fancy pots, while still retaining his job as a miner (or any other job), he could have been in trouble with the Barrier Industrial Council. Still, the B.I.C. president, Joe Keenan, is a professional musician as well as a miner.

The wife even of a working miner was not allowed to take so much as a part-time job. This ". . . condemns active-minded women to long days of boredom and frustration," said Elspeth Huxley in her book.[1] However, Broken Hill has few jobs to offer married women, anyway, I was told.

Allan Coulls, the City Librarian, thought that Elspeth Huxley had "met some very disgruntled women". He added, "I don't agree that Broken Hill is tied down by unionism. What the B.I.C. does is all to the good of the city."

FOR THE TOURIST there were the Monday-to-Friday afternoon tours of the "Mines, City and Flying Doctor Base" and a different half-day tour each morning, except Thursday when there was a full-day tour to Mootwingee, all operated by West Darling Tours. In Broken Hill even tourism took the weekend off.

The city tour was adequately conducted by a woman guide-driver, who introduced herself as Laurie. She told of the discovery of the mineral riches on what the explorer Sturt had called "a broken hill" of the low Barrier Range in some of the most desolate country he had ever set eyes on. Charlie Rasp, a German boundary rider on Mount Gipps sheep station, found in 1883 what he thought was tin and formed a syndicate of seven men whose leases became those of the Broken Hill Proprietary Company, now the largest company in Australia. A one-fourteenth share in the mine was traded for ten old bullocks worth about forty dollars—and was to become worth in 1887 a million and a half dollars. The first B.H.P. crushing of 48 tons of ore yielded 35,600 ounces of silver—740 ounces to the ton!

In the New Australia's mineral boom we have been astonished at Poseidon nickel shares going to $280: in February 1887 B.H.P. shares changed hands on the Melbourne Stock Exchange at £409.

B.H.P. today is not at all engaged at Broken Hill, and hasn't been since 1939. All B.H.P. owns there now is a huge heap of slag. The principal mine operator is Conzinc Riotinto of Australia. C.R.A. has the biggest mine, the Zinc Corporation's, and also New Broken Hill.

On the bus tour you stop by the Zinc Corporation mine and see miners coming off shift from a cage that lifts eighty-four at a time from the bowels of the earth. Beside the cage is a big board headed SCORE. It lists time lost through accidents in the mine and the record of accident-free working days.

I had been at Broken Hill before but, like the man from Melbourne, not for thirty years. I was there then only two nights and during the one day I was taken to play golf, and just about all I remembered of it was that, on the golf course, you drove off by mounting your ball on the bottom section of a wax-match box: the ground was too hard to drive a golf tee into. The "greens" were of sand and still are. But there is now greenness in Broken Hill that was unknown then, because now there is the water supply from the Menindee Lakes Scheme—which provides Broken Hill with its weekend playground, seventy miles away, for sailing, motor-boating and water-skiing. The water has also made parks.

The city is now surrounded by a regeneration area. Tree planting has reduced the dust. Within the city the new school buildings are impressive. When we passed the jail Laurie said, "We don't have any serious crime. The jail is only for drunks." The B.I.C., with its all-seeing eye, doesn't approve of crime—and, to a quite remarkable degree, Broken Hill is crime-free.

The Flying Doctor Base is visited on this tour. Every week-day afternoon at four o'clock tourists could be present when the doctor at the microphone treated his far-flung patients by radio. Not that you heard the details, but it was explained that a woman had just called in from a station and said, "A young man has been kicked on the shin by a horse. I've bathed and bandaged the wound", and the doctor had told her what else to do. Another woman reported the condition of her sick daughter who was on penicillin, and the doctor changed this to 250 milligrams of another antibiotic.

The doctors at this base treated about three thousand cases a year by radio, and they flew 60,000 miles in the three aircraft the base had. Their "practice" covered half a million square miles, which is five times Britain's area or Colorado's. They could be at the bedside of the farthest-out patient in two hours, or send the plane to bring the patient in to hospital.

Then there is the School of the Air. Since 1956 it has been broadcasting lessons to children living in isolation within the same half-million square miles, some of them on lonely stations across the borders of Queensland and South Australia. The teacher talks to each child and each can reply to questions. The teacher has no visual aids to work with, and cannot gesture or point: everything has to be conveyed by voice. Yet the School of the Air puts on small plays and the children dress up and take part. A Friday morning tour took visitors to watch it in operation.

I WENT DOWN the Zinc Corporation mine. Ordinarily tourists can't do this. First you change, completely, into company-provided underwear, socks, boots, boiler suit and a hard hat with a lamp on it that attaches to a battery on your belt.

The cage rocked and swayed as it dropped a thousand feet to Level 18. Jack Bayne, the boss of that level, took me up and down ladders and through timbering along drives that were wet underfoot. I said it was no place for anyone who had had a few drinks, and he agreed: "Do the right thing and you won't get a scratch in fifty years. But there's no margin for error. If a man comes on shift with a hangover I send him home."

We came to where a pair of brawny miners had fired a face and brought down a lot of rock they were clearing out. They did this with a mechanical scoop that ran on a wire rope pegged into the rock-face. The scoop appeared to fling itself at the rock like a demented thing, in contrast to the solid calm of the man working it. Between the two men, who had mined together for years, you could feel the "bond" Joe Keenan talked about.

These men worked on contract. Bosses like Jack Bayne got salaries, but all the underground ore-winning was contract work, paid by how much ore was produced: $18 for a five-hour shift was common, plus lead bonus, plus cost-of-living allowance. Starting work on the face at 8.30 a.m. they were out of the mine by 3 p.m. Underground miners were the high earners, the status workers.

Broken Hill was building a Cultural Centre. In the Charles Rasp Memorial Library it had a good one—and it was the first *free* library in New South Wales. There was also a library (it was locked) in the Musicians' Club, which had two thousand members, who didn't

L

have to be musical. A cacophonous battery of poker machines had given rise to its modern building.

MOOTWINGEE, eighty miles north-east of Broken Hill, is one of the few places in this region where permanent water can be found, and so it was a camping ground of the Aborigines. The rock engravings they have left there are certainly the best in western New South Wales, and there are rock paintings as well. An area of twelve hundred acres has been proclaimed a Historic Site. Since I was there the National Parks and Wildlife Service has set up a Visitor Information Centre to interpret the place to tourists.

Laurie was again the driver-guide of the West Darling Tours minibus. The bitumen ended where signposts said TIBOOBURRA 199, PACKSADDLE 99 and we turned off the Tibooburra road. The gravel ran through a flat landscape of ochre-brown earth clumped with dusty-green saltbush and sparsely treed with piebald eucalypts and spindly mulga. Several emus appeared near the road and raced away. The largest of flightless birds except the ostrich, they can run at thirty miles an hour.

On either side the road-edge glinted with beer bottles and cans. Tourists, I supposed, had tossed their share of these from cars, but locals would have been responsible for a lot, and one was left with a feeling of prevalent loutishness. I wondered if it would not be possible for the B.I.C. to declare the vice of litterbuggering the land-scape to be an anti-union activity.

We stopped at Yanco Glen Hotel, which seemed to be all there was to Yanco Glen, and was signboarded: LAST WATERHOLE THIS SIDE OF THE BLACK STUMP.

Although the land looked too arid to feed stock—about the only green things were the vines of the useless paddy-melons that were nearly as plentiful as bottles by the roadside—there were several sheep stations along the route. The last of these was Mootwingee Station, and when we were through its second gate we saw the first live kangaroos, a family of three. There had been some dead ones, killed by cars, along the road.

"Not many roos left in these parts now. Shot out," Laurie said, and, country woman though she was, added, "I cry when they're shot." The buck and the doe and the joey had stopped and were sitting up looking at us. When they do that I always feel that there is something wrong with any man who can pump bullets into them.

AT MOOTWINGEE the land heaves up into rugged formations of dark-reddish rock. The run-off from the slopes of these forms waterholes in rock pockets. Not large in this dry time, they would always have been enough to sustain the Aborigines and bring in the game to drink: and make some grass at the verge, apparently, because *Mootwingee* means "green grass".

Some of this rockland, which is quite extensive and thrusts picturesquely against the blue sky, is conglomerate and other slopes are of shattered stone in flat slabs. Many of the trees are native pines.

The overhangs of ledge caves gave the tribe shelter and their back-walls provided places for the Aboriginal artist to paint the things of his "Dreamtime". One such is called the Snake Cave, and here in red ochre the Rainbow Snake has been depicted and it measures twenty-eight feet long. As I have written in another book:[2] "The Rainbow Serpent moves through the myths of tribes over all Australia. To the black man the big snake is nearer to godhead than any other creature of his earth."

There are also stencilled hands, such as are to be found on the coast near Sydney. They were done in two ways: by dipping the hand in red ochre or pipeclay white paint and pressing it on the rock; or by taking a paint mixture into the mouth and spraying it round the placed hand to leave its outline.

The rock engravings are much more numerous, and better, than the paintings. They are done on flat slabs of quartzite, by pecking with a very hard rock such as ironstone. The largest figure is of a kangaroo that measures forty-two inches. Some human figures, apparently of hunters, are roughly depicted and there are petroglyphs of emus, lizards, a speared wallaby, an owl and curlews. We still know little of why these engravings were done and when they were done—last century or thousands of years ago.

On the way back to Broken Hill more kangaroos were seen—they come out to feed in the late afternoon—and some wild goats. When the last embers of sunset had died on the horizon of the wide brown plain and darkness fell, the headlights of the bus picked up two white objects in the middle of the road ahead. They were sheep, newly dead, one with its belly ripped open. Some speeding motorist was responsible.

Laurie had a feeling for nature and she enlivened the long ride home with such stories as how, after the district got sixteen inches of rain in 1957, the beautiful Sturt Pea had bloomed across the land gloriously, and at one place along the Menindee Road the flowers were so thick you couldn't help treading on them, and she had counted a score or more colours, including lavender and black and spotted ones as well as the usual scarlet. All this "desert" will bloom, given water. Ordinarily, it gets only nine inches of rain a year.

Because she felt she had a party that day of people who were specially interested, Laurie had shown more of the area than she usually did, taking us to off-track formations such as Mushroom Rock. Being so generous with her time had made the tour's return later than it had ever been. We did not reach Broken Hill until nearly eight o'clock.

At the place where I was staying (the Grand Private Hotel, clean, modestly comfortable, without private facilities, and only $6.95 a day with all meals) dinner was off. This was not the fault of the proprietress. Dinner-time was six to six-forty-five because the Town Employees' Union required that after seven o'clock staff be paid double time. Dinner was also off where others in the party were staying.

So we went to a café. It was unlicensed, and I was deputed to go to a hotel to get some wine. There was a choice of only two brands of claret, neither of them good ones, and no burgundy at all. I settled for one of the clarets, and the hotel would not accept a Travellers' Cheque (Commonwealth Bank) in payment. Back at the café, when I asked for cheese instead of dessert an astonished waitress exclaimed, "Cheese! We don't serve cheese."

Broken Hill had two newspapers, the *Barrier Miner*, which had to fight its way for circulation, and the B.I.C.-backed *Barrier Daily Truth*, the Labour paper, which didn't have to worry, because its circulation was guaranteed by the requirement that every unionist *must* take it; and if there were two or more unionists in the household, two or more copies were delivered.

From the touristic point of view, Broken Hill's most interesting scenery is sociological, and, if it became part of the ordinary Australia or the New Australia, it would be less interesting.

New England's Armidale

No TWO AUSTRALIAN CITIES are less alike than Broken Hill and Armidale. One is out at the end of the western plain, hot, arid, industrial and mining-proletarian. The other is three thousand feet up on the northern tableland, chilly, lush, academic and pastoral-patrician. One is, in this short-historied land, Old Australia. The other is, by name and nature, New England.

As the name of the region that has Armidale as its centre, New England is surprisingly appropriate. In autumn the Armidale landscape glows with the colours of what Australians think of as "English" trees, to the extent that the visitor might almost be persuaded that the native eucalypts were outnumbered by elms, oaks, poplars, claret ash, willows and silver birches. Usually in winter there is at least one snowfall (it is the most northerly region in Australia to get snow) and red-breasted robins pop up on the postcard scene.

Sheep and cattle station properties have such names as Gostwyck, Chevy Chase and Dangarsleigh. Driving past Dangarsleigh, the Armidale man who was running me round said, "A few hedges and you would think you were in England"—and another property of the pioneer Dangars, called Palmerston, was in fact hedged with hawthorn. Gostwyck had a family church with its brickwork covered in Virginia creeper, and a splendid avenue of elms leading up to the homestead.

About all that was needed, I thought, to complete the New Englishness was one of those tripwire names (like Oxford's Magdalen pronounced Maudlen) for the stranger to fall over. It was there. The Dumaresq River was always spoken of as though it were spelled Dumerrick.

Armidale's population of 16,500 included over two thousand students and staff at the University of New England—the only one of the State's five universities to be situated in a rural area and, although it became autonomous only in 1954, next-oldest to the University of Sydney. New England's university buildings are too Australian-contemporary in their architecture, and there are too many gum-trees on its extensive campus that is three miles out in a pleasantly countrified setting, for Armidale to be thought of as an Australian Oxford. But English university traditionalisms are there. There is talk of "Town and Gown", and the functionary who showed me round the campus retains the title of Yeoman Bedell. Within the campus park deer mingle with kangaroos.

The six established faculties are Arts, Science, Rural Science, Agricultural Economics, Economics and Education. I asked the Vice-Chancellor, with whom I had lunch, Professor Zelman Cowen (who has since gone to the University of Queensland) what had happened to his proposal of a Faculty of Natural Resources. There appeared, at this time, to be a need for this. Natural Resources was a going concern, Professor Cowen said; but the Universities Commission had not favoured it as a Faculty, only as a School.

I wondered if the academic staff yearned to be at the universities in Sydney instead of "out on the country", and asked Professor John Hardy of the English Department how he liked Armidale. "After living in Brisbane, Oxford and Toronto, I'm completely sold on the place," he said. "There's a nice feel to Armidale. You buy a new car because you want one, not for keeping up with the Joneses. It's not big enough to be bourgeois."

Not only its university made Armidale an educational centre. It had six secondary schools, including the prestigious T.A.S. (The Armidale School), and the first country Teachers' College was established there. This is interesting to the non-academic visitor mainly because of its art collection, the bequest of Howard Hinton. When I was a young art critic for a Sydney newspaper in the thirties I used to see Howard Hinton round the galleries and regarded this quietly spoken man, who was in the shipping business, as a wealthy patron of the arts who sometimes went to Europe and bought paintings there to add to his big collection that was probably housed in a mansion. In fact, he lived, a bachelor, in two small rooms of a boarding-house. The collection of more than a thousand paintings he gave to Armidale Teachers' College in 1929 includes works of all the major Australian artists of his period (along with a Rembrandt etching and a Rodin drawing) and is today valued at over $2,000,000. Howard Hinton died in 1948, and when his estate was wound up it amounted to seventy-four shillings. He had spent all his money on art and given the pictures to galleries. In the case of the Teachers' College, he thought that if young teachers were brought into daily contact with good paintings this would serve to raise the level of art appreciation.

I HAD FLOWN to Armidale from Sydney on the East-West Airlines service that takes an hour and a quarter. It was the first time I had been to this provincial city that had been a city since 1885 and had two cathedrals and a burgeoning tourist traffic that was sustaining eight motels and eleven hotels, of which Tattersall's, where I stayed, was regarded as the best. I liked Armidale at once. Dangar Street, dipping down to the willows of Dumaresq Creek, is surely one of the pleasantest streets in rural Australia.

It would appear that the place was named, about 1839, by a District Commissioner for Crown Lands, George MacDonald, after Armadale, the Scottish home of the Clan MacDonald on the Isle of Skye; but he misspelt it as Armidale.

As was said earlier, the preservation of local history is, in Australia, new. Armidale has an excellent Folk Museum in a delightful iron-laced building and in it you can see such early apparatus of the wool industry as shepherds' crooks and a "watch box", rather like an outsize dog-kennel, where the shepherd slept within the sheepfold on bitter nights.

Such museums are usually under the auspices of the local historical society, but Armidale's was directly a concern of the City Council —which, the Mayor (Dr John Failes) told me, was possibly the only council whose aldermen included a Professor of Classics, who was also an Anglican clergyman, and was addressed as Reverend Professor Alderman Bishop.

There is also in the museum a £400 REWARD police poster for the capture of the notorious bushranger who was known as Captain Thunderbolt. Had he been just plain Fred Ward, horse-thief, who escaped from Cockatoo Island jail in Sydney in 1863 and "held the northern roads" until Constable Walker shot him in 1870, probably he would have faded from memory. But "Thunderbolt" is a power-ful name. At Uralla, where the bushranger's grave is a tourist attraction, the Commercial Hotel had changed to the Thunderbolt Inn. I had lunch there and this is indeed a hotel of distinction, not because of its name but because, on its balconies and between the tops of its veranda posts, it is so decorative with the iron lace that the Phoenix Foundry at Uralla was long famous for casting. Some of Sydney's best iron-lace came from Uralla.

I did not go to Thunderbolt's grave. Anyone who set out to prove that the Australian ethos reeked of cultural adolescence could rest his case on the homage paid to bushrangers. As Russel Ward (who is Professor of History at the University of New England) has said in his excellent pocket-book history, *Australia*,[1] the bushranger Ned Kelly is firmly entrenched in Australian language, literature and art, but some great Australians are forgotten men.

Incidentally, when I was talking to Professor Ward at the univer-sity, he made an observation I thought both interesting and true. The American image of America, he said, was still the log-cabin-to-White-House one, though it was a long time since Lincoln, and American presidents this century had usually been men of means with anything but log-cabin backgrounds. The average Australian, this historian thought, had a much better chance of becoming a captain of industry or Prime Minister than the average American had of becoming a tycoon or President.

Worth seeing at Uralla is Harry Wooldridge's "Rock-Hunters' Rendezvous", which a Melbourne geologist who has travelled the country widely rated as the most comprehensive, though not the biggest, rock collection in Australia.

The region was, and still is, rich in minerals. Hillgrove, a mile off the Grafton road, once had three thousand people and two mines that yielded gold worth $1,600,000. It had gone down to a forlorn few houses, less than a ghost town—but by mid-1970 scores of new houses had arisen at Hillgrove. However, New England Antimony N.L. had to close its mine early in 1971.

THE LANDSCAPE out of Armidale can suddenly and quite dramatic-ally change. You are driving past rolling hills of English-green pasture so good that it comes as no surprise to learn that the property over there, Bayley Park, a couple of years ago got the world-record price of 410 cents a pound for five bales of its wool. Or you are admiring the rich black soil and Santa Gertrudis cattle on St Helena. Then, having turned only the shortest distance off the road, you are staring down into an enormous canyon.

The tableland is edged with gorge country. A great gorge cuts into the plateau about twelve miles from Armidale and from the top of this a creek hurls its water a thousand feet down the cliffside. Dangar's Falls, as these are called, were more impressive than Wollomombi Falls and Chandler Falls in Wollomombi Gorge, twenty-six miles out—but, as a gorge, Wollomombi is the more spectacular. It is so vast, and so deep that the waterfall nearest the lookout point takes a plunge of fifteen hundred feet.

Wallamumbi station (spelt thus) is the oldest and largest beef cattle stud in Australia. Its owner, P. A. Wright, was the father of the distinguished Australian poet Judith Wright, born there in 1915.

Thirty miles on, towards the coast, is a wide tumbling of waters down several cascades, the picturesque Ebor Falls. Before this, if you turn off to the New England National Park and go on nine miles, past the trout hatchery on the Serpentine River, you come to Point Lookout. From 5,250 feet the land falls precipitously into a great valley.

It was swimming in mist the day I was there; but on a clear day, the people who were driving me the 120 miles to Coffs Harbour said, you could see to the coast's Pacific blue. Without that, the view across the New England National Park wilderness was impressive enough.

You go on through Dorrigo, green, high-rainfall range country of timber and potatoes. Stopping in the township, we picked up a young geologist who had been working on local antimony leases. He appeared to think the lode was full of promise.

New South Wales, which two years before was producing almost half Australia's mineral wealth, had slipped back to producing little more than a third of it on 1969 figures, because Western Australian production had advanced so much. But, such was the rise in the level of prospecting activity in 1970, it would not have been surprising to see a mining resurgence in New South Wales. However, in 1971 this had not come about on any major scale.

The Ridge's Rare Opal

THE MOST BEAUTIFUL and most valuable form of opal has been found only in Australia—and here it has been found only in a relatively small area of northern New South Wales, in the vicinity of Lightning Ridge.

It is called black opal to distinguish it from other opal of lighter hue called white opal. "Black" is a misnomer and so, for that matter, is "white". A quality stone of the rare black opal blazes with colour. It can have "flashes of liquid flame that in an instant give way to sapphire blue or slip into molten green as the angle of light alters". Having described it thus, a leading Australian opal dealer, the late Percy Marks, went on to say, "Black opal beggars all description." An American connoisseur of gemstones, writing years ago in the *Saturday Evening Post*, said, "It is more beautiful than diamonds or rubies. Australian black opal is, without doubt, the finest gem in the world." (PLATE 14.)

Mexican "fire opal" is next in brilliance to Australian black opal, though its fire is orange rather than the red that glows and flashes in the best Lightning Ridge gems. However, no bright colour exists in opal at all as pigmentation, any more than it does in a prism.

The colour comes from light refraction caused mainly by minute cracks and cavities in a silicate deposited between rock layers by volcanic action. This matrix is relatively translucent in the case of light opal, and darkened with impurities in the case of the black, which makes the refractive colour more brilliant. Sometimes a grey section of a gemstone is cut away and replaced by a backing of black "potch" (matrix) or onyx, making for better colour. Many gem opals in rings and brooches are of this non-solid kind called doublets.

Opal fields are usually indicated by stones found on the surface, "floaters". That had happened at White Cliffs in western New South Wales a couple of years before a bushman named Charlie Nettleton in 1891 was shown some "pretty stones" picked up by the wife of the boundary rider on Angledool Station near the Queensland border. He found more of these floaters near Lightning Ridge, so called because a mob of yarded sheep there was struck by lightning.

Nettleton prospected, sank a shaft and sent 100 ounces of opal in the rough to a buyer in Sydney—who offered ten shillings (a dollar) for the lot. The buyer said this opal was "too dark" to be valuable. Nettleton told him to send it back. Subsequently, in 1903, he worked his way overland to White Cliffs where one of the pioneer diggers on that field, E. F. Murphy, had set up as an opal buyer. Murphy was a fine judge of opal, and a fine man: I knew him in his eighties and he says in his book,[1] of which he gave me a copy shortly before he died some twenty years ago, that he was offered by Nettleton "a parcel of opal of an entirely new variety—very dark, although it did have some good colour". He "thought the stuff had possibilities" and bought it on behalf of the leading dealer, T. C. Wollaston of Adelaide, who "said to go on buying the opal, and that he would introduce it".

Wollaston was to find that European buyers were very chary of accepting Australia's fiery dark opal, because of the traditional image of precious opal as light-hued. In Paris they would not buy it at all, but Wollaston got some dealers to display it and left it to be sold on commission. Its spectacular beauty gradually overcame prejudice, and such men as Lord Northcliffe, the English newspaper magnate, became avid collectors of black opal, which could come from nowhere else but Lightning Ridge, where every stone in Northcliffe's collection was originally bought by Murphy.

The second Lightning Ridge strike was made by Mick Cantfell and his brother in 1904. Mick was a straight old bushman of seventy-five with a blackened pipe in his grin when I talked to him in 1948, and he said, "We struck it all right. It was like putting yer pick into a jeweller's shop. A woman's stocking full we had, gem stuff, beautiful stone. Took it to Sydney, and got a hundred and fifty quid for the lot. Migawd, if I had it today I could buy the Sydney Town Hall and the clock with it!"

TODAY (1970) top quality black opal's value is far above that of light opal. An outstanding stone could be expected to sell, on the field at Lightning Ridge, for $400 a carat (say, $60,000 an ounce). When it had further cutting and polishing and was mounted and displayed in a shop-window or showcase it could be priced at not less than $1,000 a carat.

Australian light opal comes nowadays mainly from the South Australia fields, Coober Pedy and Andamooka: White Cliffs is almost abandoned. Light opal in its finest form may sell for $1,000 an ounce on the field, and it is usually sold in the rough, not cut and polished.

A crystalline opal of 220 ounces, the largest found in Australia, was unearthed at Andamooka in late 1969 by four miners with a bulldozer, and sold in Adelaide for the record price of $168,000. The stone, in two pieces, was christened the "Desert Flame" and it became part of the Australian exhibit at Expo '70 in Japan. The Commonwealth Government was reported to have insured the "Desert Flame" for $1,400,000.

Andamooka I saw as a young newspaperman in 1935, soon after opal had been found there on a sheep station so stony-barren that it couldn't feed a sheep to a square mile and the station homestead was forty miles from the front gate. The small plane I was in—chartered by a strange Canadian buyer (Prosper J. Ralston, "The Man With the Harp") to visit all the opalfields—was the second aircraft to land at Andamooka, and only a few gougers were working where today there is a town. We were the first to land (the late Pat Hall was a superb pilot) at Coober Pedy, where about fifty people were living underground like rabbits in a warren; but their dug-out homes in the side of a low hill were cooler than above-ground shacks would have been in that sun-scorched desert. One tunnel-like entrance was sign-boarded POST OFFICE and COMMONWEALTH BANK OF AUSTRALIA. The only above-ground structures were the oldest inhabitant's bush hut and a ten-by-ten one of corrugated iron, for the policeman who visited the place every month.

Now Coober Pedy in 1970 has nearly two thousand people and a tourist motel—and in mid-1970 it was having a crime wave, with an unsolved murder of an opal buyer, mine-robbings galore and other ugly violence.

LIGHTNING RIDGE is plain country of reddish earth glinting with quartz fragments. The trees are mainly coolabah and the bastard sandalwood called budda, with the wild-orange known as emu-bush. From the air, the ground out from the town looks like the creation of a colony of worms, holes with dirt heaped high round them, pale earth, pinkish.

Visitors from Sydney could fly, on four days a week, by Airlines of N.S.W. to Walgett and thence go 48 miles by road. On Mondays you could fly right through to "The Ridge", as I did, using the 7.10 a.m. Airlines of N.S.W. service to Moree, where it connected with Davey Air Services' smaller plane that landed me in Lightning Ridge shortly after ten o'clock.

When I had last seen the place, in 1948, its population had dwindled to three hundred, and the gougers were mainly aged pensioners, working the old ground of existing holes because sinking new shafts was beyond them. The main layer of what is called "opal dirt" may be anything from ten to fifty feet down, and after sinking three or four feet it is usual to strike six feet or so of concrete-hard rock, "shincracker"; and then maybe twenty feet of softish sandstone. After he had bottomed on clay "opal dirt" the miner drove in under the roof of rock, gouging carefully with a two-pound pick by the light of a candle stuck in the ring of an iron spike called a "spider". He hoped to hear his pick clink on a nodule or seam of stone, which usually turned out to be valueless "potch" (matrix). If he got a "nobby" he'd clip the ends of it with a pair of pincers, and if he saw colour he'd put it in his tin. (And they still mine that way in some shafts.) All the dug rock and dirt was laboriously hauled by hand to the surface in buckets, by a windlass. With no new ground being worked, finds were few and some old-timers were reduced to "noodling" the dumps for a nobby that might have been missed. (Some tourists do this.)

Now there were two thousand people, about five hundred of them mining. The Ridge was still a one-pub town, with the pub improved and rechristened the "Diggers' Rest". But a new motel, called the Black Opal Lodge, had risen opposite; another motel was building and a third contemplated. There was a modern bowling club and new amenities in the caravan park, and an excellently simulated opal mine had been set up as a tourist attraction.

Tourists had discovered Lightning Ridge and, when the road from Walgett was sealed, what was already a big trickle was expected to swell to a torrent of visitors. After all, for a certain type of vacationer, it was one of the most characterful, cosmopolitan, exciting and at the same time relaxing places in Australia to spend a holiday. Or was it, still?

In the Diggers' Rest bar there were still "characters", not old ones such as I remembered, but young men in clay-stained jeans, and beards, some shirtless. In the middle of one group—The Ridge was still cosmopolitan—was check-shirted Alex, the "Boy from Berlin", who had struck it rich at the Nine-Mile. But the young German had excitedly made for the pub and talked of his luck and spent three days celebrating. When he went back to his mine the ground all round it was pegged, and the newcomers got more opal than he did.

Nobody knew Alex's second name, and that was typical. Who, in The Ridge of yesterday, had ever known the other names of Whistling Sam, Liverpool Jack, Andy the Frenchman, The Count, Bagboots, Big Ben or the Jimmys—Whispering Jimmy, Silent Jimmy, Peanut Jimmy, Carney Jimmy (who lived on a species of lizard known as the carney) or Jimmy the Murderer (who killed his pet monkey in a fit of rage and never forgave himself). Now there were locals nicknamed Horizontal George and Vertical Bill, and less than half of the miners were Australian-born, I was told. Six of them were Americans, and later I was to talk to Frank the Yank. "The Ridge" hadn't changed very much in character.

Opal mining had changed. Jackhammers were making much shorter work of the "shincracker" band. Windlasses were gone from most working shafts: the dirt-mounded field thrummed with generators' power that flung the bucket up and over an arc arrangement to empty it onto the dump or into a perforated drum called a rumbler, that revolved and sieved away a lot of the dirt. What was left went into

THE RIDGE'S RARE OPAL   157

a truck that was driven off to a dam where the opal dirt was
"puddled". The dam, filled from bores, was surrounded by old cars.
Their engines were harnessed to pump water and to power puddlers.
Something like a washing-machine with perforated sides, the puddler
revolved and washed the dirt to a mass of rough pebbly stones. None
of these were likely to show more than a fleck of opal colour: the
gem, if it is a gem, is like a nut hidden in a dirty shell. The man at the
puddler has to be an eagle-eyed expert to pick nobbies from the
pebble mass. I watched one of the most experienced miners on the
field, "Speck" Rush, puddle a truckload of opal dirt. This took fifteen
minutes, and at the end of that time he had picked out six "nobbies"
that possibly contained precious opal. "Speck" Rush—who looked
sixty and also looked in the pink of health—would clip them later.
Tourists often came to noodle the puddlers' dumps in the hope of
finding a nobby that had been missed. A Lightning Ridge schoolboy
found one that sold for $3,000.

I had been, years ago, down a shaft and watched a gouger picking
the clay by candlelight in a drive less than four feet high. This time
I went down the mine "Speck" Rush had, in partnership with a vigorous young Dutchman, Alan Vroom, and I walked about a spacious
underground chamber with electric light and watched contract
miners working for Rush-Vroom filling the mechanized buckets.
They were moving out four hundred buckets of earth, a day.

You don't ask an opal miner how much he is making. I should
think, from some opals "Speck" Rush showed me which he hadn't
had to sell, that they were doing well. A mine near by was said to
have struck opal to the extent of $48,000 worth.

Dudley Jolly, who had taken me to see his friend the amiable
"Speck" Rush, was one of a new category of Lightning Ridgers—
the escapees from the commercial ratrace. Dudley had had in Sydney
a frenetic job in newspaper advertising management. He came to
Lightning Ridge for a week-end, caught opal fever, yearned for the
clean-aired, easy-tempo life and—"Well, I gave the city away. Best
thing I ever did, and my wife agrees." He mined for a while, but the
businessman in him saw opportunity in the town, and he opened a
clothing store, which had done well.

A doctor had sold his good practice in a Sydney suburb and turned
opal miner—"I'm taking the advice I used to give my patients." A
former bank clerk from Melbourne had made enough to be able to
afford to take trips abroad to the last two Olympic Games. (But old
Foley Kite, aged eighty-seven, out at the Nine-Mile, had been digging,
when he wasn't shearing, for sixty-eight years and had never found a
really good stone.)

Near Dudley Jolly's shop was the house of one of the seven resident opal buyers, Edward Bourchier. The green lawn in front was such as I'd never seen before at Lightning Ridge, grown with bore water that came out of the ground hot and provided hot water at the hotel and the town bathing pool. Ted Bourchier confirmed that up to $400 a carat had been paid on the field for top-quality black opal, but the highest he had paid was $250 a carat, and $100 was fairly usual—and some of that could end up at $1,500 a carat in a New York jeweller's, he said. Ninety per cent of Australian opal was exported—"a pity to see nearly all the beautiful stones leave the country"—mainly to the United States and to Japan, where "green-fire" stones were in high favour. Usually black opals that flash with predominantly red fire, or those with a harlequin mix of colours, were the most highly valued. Most of the stones Ted Bourchier bought he re-cut for export. They had to be of *cabochon* (domed) shape: a flat-faced stone, whatever its quality, was regarded as looking too much like a doublet.

A company's proposal to mine with bulldozers had been stopped by local protest and State Government opposition. "The town would have died." Leases could be pegged up to a hundred feet square, and some areas were reserved where anyone could try their luck for the dollar it cost to get a Miner's Right at the police station. Tourists like to do that and, now that there was motel accommodation, Ted Bourchier thought that Lightning Ridge would really boom as a tourist resort. "For travellers this is something different, and a tip-top place to come to in winter." (In summer it is very hot, and pestiferous with flies.) I asked if he thought Lightning Ridge would go on producing opal at the rate that had been increasing each recent year.

"In my opinion this field has still only been scratched, and it could go for ever—even though millions of dollars' worth of gemstones have come out of just the claims round the Leaning Tree."

The Leaning Tree is three or four miles out. At a shaft near by a strong-bodied young Slav, Steve Terzic, was shovelling dirt that came up in automatic buckets from three other Croatians down below. He wasn't saying how much opal they had won but said, "Over the year you do better than working for wages."

"Frank the Yank" Brown looked a happy man, if I ever saw one, as he leant against the doorway of the neat cottage he had built out among the opal dumps. A carpenter from Washington State, he had migrated to Australia and, after working around, found his niche at Lightning Ridge. Jean, his Australian wife, was one of two nurses who had tired of nursing and tried opal gouging. Wearing only shorts and sandals in the summer's heat, he seemed to exude contentment from his tanned torso as he gazed fondly at the infant daughter Jean was holding.

"Yeah, I'm happy here," he said.

He was opal mining in partnership with an Australian, he said, and, "If I want to work, I work. If he wants to work, he works. If we want to work together, we work together—or we work alone. He says to me, this Aussie, 'You think Australians are lazy, don't you?' and I tell him, 'No. I think you work in a relaxed sort of way. I've gotta believe that, because I want to be like you. This life is for me.' "

OPAL MINING wasn't as laboriously primitive as it used to be; but I couldn't help wondering whether it couldn't become more mechanized.

However, since I was there a Sydney man with a lot of experience on the Lightning Ridge field, George Dewhurst, has gone to work with a big Calweld drill that sinks a shaft three feet in diameter in a fraction of the time it takes with a jackhammer and gelignite. The hard, long labour of getting down to the opal dirt is the limiting factor that has kept so many miners on old ground. So a big drill that can bite down to sixty feet, as the Calweld 150-B type can, would appear to be the answer, if operating costs weren't too high. The driller could be contractor as well as miner, sinking shafts for others. And such a truck-mounted drill could greatly extend prospecting. Beyond The Ridge there are hundreds of square miles of potentially opal-bearing country that has never had a pick in it.

If another black opal field exists—and it seems to be against all reason that the most precious form of the gemstone is confined to the Lightning Ridge area—George Dewhurst looks the likeliest of men to find it. In fact, he thought he may have already found it. And not near Lightning Ridge, but about two hundred miles to the west.

WEST OF LIGHTNING RIDGE

"THE GRAWIN" it is usually called, this opal field that is hardly far enough from Lightning Ridge—about 23 miles south-west—to qualify as a separate black-opal region. On maps that show it at all it is simply Grawin, thirteen miles beyond the little township of Cumborah on the Walgett-Goodooga road. Grawin is less than a village, has neither pub nor post office, only one small store, no electricity or water taps or other amenities for camping and caravanning tourists. When I was there in December 1969 there were about sixty people scattered over the field, living mainly in humpies.

At Lightning Ridge they will tell you that, although some beautiful light opal has come from here, Grawin black opal is rarely a true black, more often a smoky grey, and that it is subject to cracking. But they have to concede one of the most famous "named stones" ever found came from the Grawin. This was the "Light of the World".

Billy Klein and Kurt Stevens found it, eighteen feet down, in 1928. It cut to a flat round about the diameter of a tennis ball; a "show opal of fine quality with a lovely pattern of red and green in the black surface", Murphy called it. The miners were offered £1,200 on the field for it but wanted £3,000. After it had been exhibited in Europe and very widely publicized, which collectors don't like, Stevens sold his half share to Klein for £200 and Klein sold the "Light of the World" to Percy Marks for £600.

Other famous finds included the "Flame Queen" from Lightning Ridge (1915), shaped like a poached egg, with a brilliant bronze-red dome as the "yolk". It was sold to a Brisbane jeweller for £92, changed hands at £500—and, over twenty years ago, the collector who came by it valued his "Flame Queen" at £5,000.

About the luckiest opal diggers ever were two shearers named Simpson and Reece who came to Lightning Ridge one Saturday morning in 1945 and by midday Sunday they had twelve stones including beauties that were named "Bird of Paradise" and the "Rising Sun". The buyer Jack Francis offered up to £1,775 for the lot—but the deal wasn't closed until he added "12 packets of tobacco and cigarette papers and 12 boxes of matches"[1]: it was wartime, and these items were rationed.

At the Grawin I met Maurice Claire (PLATE 14) who had recently come there from Lightning Ridge where he had found a blue-green stone of 105 carats, an oval gem nearly two inches wide. He went to his tin humpy and got his opal and held it for me to photograph. Maurie Claire, a resolute-looking character, said he was determined to hang onto his opal until he got the price he reckoned it was worth, $3,000.

RAY NEWTON was no opal gouger but a sheepman. His Spring Vale station, 17,000 acres with a good deal of cypress pine growing on it, was fifteen miles from the Grawin. This modest-mannered country-man and his pleasant wife, Pamela, had decided to cater for tourists.

Their station was only a thirty-mile run from Lightning Ridge and tourists could drive over there, though they might well prefer to fossick for opal at the less-visited Grawin. They could see how a sheep property worked, and Ray would drive them out to Narran Lake, a wild-life sanctuary with birds galore, kangaroos, emus and wild pigs (photography only: no shooting). The Newtons called their operation "Pineopal Lodge" and, having heard good report of it, I went across from Lightning Ridge to spend a night there. Ray Newton picked me up and drove me over.

For tourists the Grawin centres on Ron Garnier's place, which is a place like no other. Ron, a plumpish ex-drover, ex-Lightning Ridge gouger who doesn't look right without a glass in one hand, and usually looks right, has a rambling sort of corrugated-iron residence that has grown from the original tin hut of Stevens and Klein who found the "Light of the World". The walls of Ron's open-sided main room were covered with photographs of opal mining identities, racehorses, Aborigines, plus newspaper clippings, mottoes and admonitory witticisms he has lettered, and there was a scatteration of opal specimens, curious old bottles and other oddities. Outside, Ron indulged a passion for exterior decoration. He had made from empty bottles, never in short supply, a memorial to his old mate Bunny Woods, whose tipple was methylated spirits. (Ron doesn't mind muscat topped with beer, but no "metho".) Bunny's memorial was also home to a family of cement pixies and, since real flowers don't easily grow, Ron had planted some plastic ones.

It was dark when we got to Pineopal Lodge. As to accommodation, it was one wing of the Newtons' white weatherboard homestead plus several units of the kind of fully-furnished instant housing that is becoming increasingly used in the Australian outback: city-built with all mod. cons from air-conditioning to bathroom with hotwater and the flushing bowl, to 'fridge and fluorescent lighting, innerspring mattress, linen even, and spanking kitchen with oven stove and shiny with laminex; even the television set. Like caravans grown up to apartment size (one was two-bedroomed), the metal-framed "units" are simply hauled in by road and set down. The family-sized one rented for $55 a week. You brought in your food and drinks and did your own cooking, barbecueing the evening steak outdoors.

Sitting out under the trees round the homestead in the evening was very peaceful. One of the six guests, who in Sydney was the manager of a sporting club cacophonous with poker machines, leant back with a can of beer in his hand and said gratefully, "God, isn't it quiet."

The highlight excursion was by conducted tour only, needing Ray Newton's four-wheel-drive Toyota and his local knowledge. We left with Ray at 4.15 a.m. The object was to be out at Narran Lake at dawn.

I admit to never having heard of Narran Lake. Yet it is claimed to be the largest natural lake (dams have created larger man-made ones) in New South Wales, normally nineteen miles long by about six wide and quite shallow.

This dry-country bush supports only thin-trunked trees—even the cypress pines are seldom large. Mostly there are supplejacks, grey-leaved myalls, wilgas, buddas and whitewoods. Ray Newton knew every tree I asked the name of. The stars faded in a sky that would remain cloudless, and the day would, later, grow hot.

M

Wild-life breakfasts in the early light. Grazing kangaroos sat up and looked at us, then took off away from the vehicle's noise in long rhythmic bounds. A few rabbits popped into burrows. Ungainly emus—they always give me the impression of being as small-brained as they are big in body—fled on the large-footed legs that made them seem clodhoppers after the ballet kangaroos.

There were brolgas, dancing. With a lift of his long grey wings, the male springs off the ground like a dancer in a slow-motion film, and gives the female such a performance that an egg never had better excuse for getting fertilized. And we saw a great many galahs. The commonness in inland Australia of these rosy-breasted cockatoos with wings of the softest grey, tends to blind us to their beauty. They rise from their feeding grounds and wheel away in a pink-and-grey swirl.

"Galahs are clever," Ray Newton said. "Below where they nest in a tree they'll eat the bark off to make it too smooth for lizards to climb up and get their eggs."

The sun rose, striping the flat land with the long shadows of what trees there were. And, just before we got to Narran Lake, the first wild pigs appeared. We must have seen at least twenty pigs.

When we got to the marshes that merge with the lake the bird life was abundant. Plovers were strident at the edges and out on the sun-gilded water were ducks and swans, ibis and cranes and lotus-birds with their thin scarlet legs. On the lake itself there were more bird congregations and, in the distance, a fleet of sailing pelicans.

THE NARRAN LAKE VISIT, through private property, was disallowed in mid-1970. (It may be resumed: it should be.) But something else has happened only eleven miles from Narran Lake, fifteen miles from Pineopal Lodge and five miles south of Grawin.

A new, and rich, black opal field was discovered in September 1970 at a place called Glengarry. In mid-1971 four hundred gougers, mostly from Lightning Ridge, were on this new field where more than a million dollars worth of "black" (mostly green) opal is said to have come out of the ground. One stone, named the "Orient Queen" was reportedly valued at $150,000.

That afternoon Ray Newton drove me the thirty miles in to Walgett, and I took the Airlines of New South Wales plane that flies in a couple of hours to Sydney, by way of Coonabarabran. About twenty miles west of Coonabarabran (300 road miles north-west of Sydney) rise the Warrumbungle Mountains. I had seen them before only at a distance, when flying between Sydney and Brisbane.

The Warrumbungles are, I think now, the most spectacular mountains in New South Wales and, next to the Glasshouse Mountains in Queensland, the most spectacular in eastern Australia. Although they form part of the Great Divide they have, like the Glasshouse, their special character from volcanically created contours. Some peak up to three thousand feet, and one to almost four thousand. Pinnacles, rather than peaks, have been created by volcano mountains weathering away to leave only the great plinths of hard-lava rock that were the cores of craters. Belougery Spire and The Needle are outstanding examples of this, but perhaps the most remarkable formation of all is the jaggedly-sheer narrow upthrust called The Breadknife.

It was a good clear day, perfect flying weather, and I asked the captain of the Friendship if he would veer a little from course and come over the middle of the Warrumbungles. He not only did that but came down to five thousand feet; and I was allowed the best of all views from the cockpit cabin. The Breadknife was just down there abeam of us, and huge Crater Bluff and, set amid this craggy splendour, the white telescope-dome of an astronomers' eyrie, the Siding Springs observatory.

Warrumbungle National Park, which encompasses these mountains, now has roads, hiker trails, shelters and some accommodation. More and more people are realizing what a scenically grand vacation area this is in the central-west of the State.

The Snowy Scheme and Kosciusko

THE PIONEER COACH that headed south from Sydney that bright autumn morning was capacity-full with forty-five passengers. Most were women, as is usual enough on these tours; but the proportion of elderly women was uncommonly high. This was because a party of fourteen members of a suburban Age-Pensioners' Association was aboard. When we stopped for lunch, at Bowral, one of these caused consternation.

She was sitting at the same table as I was at the Von Nida Motel, this grey-haired woman with the lined white face who moved slowly and lacked the chipper chatter of her companions. They spoke to her as people often speak to others who are not well and called her by some Christian name I forget: Mary will do. I shall call her Mrs Term: she had an incurable illness, which we have come to euphemize as a "terminal" one.

Halfway through the meal poor Mrs Term's head dropped, and she was so shockingly ill that I feared she might die on the spot. Two of the other pensioners came to her aid, one crying, "Her tablets! Where are her tablets?" These were found, and before we were due to rejoin the coach Mrs Term said she was feeling better.

I happened to be sitting next to one of the two women who had helped her, and was told that Mrs Term had been given only six months to live.

"She *would* come, you know. I said to her, 'Don't you think, Mary, the trip [it was the Four-day Canberra and South Coast Circle Tour] could be a bit too much for you?' But she said to me, 'Nell, I'm going. It hasn't been too easy to save up the forty dollars, but I've got it,' she said. 'I want to see Canberra before I die.'

"She said that what she'd *really* like was to have taken the six-day tour. The one that goes on from Canberra and round the big Snowy Mountains Scheme."

Why, I asked, was Mrs Term so keen to see the vast Snowy complex of tunnels through mountains, dams, power-stations with turbines and dynamos. Certainly it was a great project, but one that I thought would be mainly of interest to men.

"Oh, I don't know why exactly. Read about it, probably—Mary's always been a reader—and sort of caught her imagination as you might say."

Why would 70,000 tourists, nearly all of them Australians, go to see the Snowy Mountains Scheme in that 1969 year? There had to be something more than the prospect of seeing dams and generators to set them off in the first place. What that "something more" was may well have been indicated by an Australian economic geographer when, in 1963, he concluded a critical appraisal of the economics of the whole Snowy Mountains hydro-electric and irrigation scheme with a statement that didn't have to be entirely correct to be significant:

"The primary worth of the Snowy is psychological. By this undertaking the Australian people have shown that they are capable of taking the long view. And they can justify this action by the argument that this is an act of national consolidation. Perhaps not an economic act, but neither was Anzac. Nor was Canberra, although it is rapidly becoming so. Through a national affirmation of faith we have gone a long way towards creating a Snowy Mystique. . . ."[1]

This critic knew that his argument—that the needed electricity could be generated more economically from coal-burning stations than from hydro ones—would not prevail. He knew, even before his figures were convincingly refuted by the Snowy Mountains Authority, he was pea-shooting at a monument our national consciousness wanted reared as an act of faith and prideful achievement; and that he was powerless against the Snowy Mystique which, with completion since then of so much of the project, has turned into a Snowy Revelation. Whatever we call the scheme's attraction, it had entered the mind of Mrs Term and scores of thousands of others.

ON THE WAY to Bowral the coach captain on this tour had given quite a good commentary. In introducing himself at the start of the trip he had, as drivers always do, asked the passengers to call him by his first name. So he was "Reg".

Before Bowral was reached we had passed through Campbelltown, which had developed fast from farmland and then a sort of far-flung Sydney suburb to "New South Wales's newest city" with 26,000 population.

Near Menangle a machine called a Roto-Lactor milked fifty cows every ten minutes (300 an hour) on the dairy property of Sir Denzil Macarthur-Onslow, whose ancestor, John Macarthur of Camden Park, in the early 1800s was the father, more-or-less, of the Australian wool industry (although he did not, as many Australians think, introduce the first Merino sheep). As Reg said, the country is too wet for sheep, and they would probably have all died of scab and footrot if the crossing of the Blue Mountains in 1813 had not opened the way to more suitable pastures.

After leaving Bowral—the well-favoured rural resort that was picturesque with its English trees in autumn colours, and is cold enough to grow the tulips that bloom in October for its Tulip Festival—the coach takes the Highlands Highway that misses blissfully historic Berrima but runs through Bundanoon, which is also lovely. You are then about a hundred miles from Sydney.

A couple of hours on from Bowral the provincial city of Goulburn is the afternoon-tea stop. Goulburn has a white-stone Gothic cathedral church (St Saviour's) designed by Edmund Blacket, the remarkable self-taught architect who has been called "the Christopher Wren of Australia": Blacket was responsible for fifty-eight churches and the splendid main building of the University of Sydney (1860). There is not much else of distinction in the sheep-country city of Goulburn, but it valiantly seeks to attract tourists by holding an annual Lilac Time festival—which has to be held in early October when the Six-Hour Day holiday makes a long weekend. But the local lilac is seldom, if ever, then in bloom. So Goulburn has to import lilac from Adelaide, and use plastic lilac for some of its festal decorations.

Collector, farther along the road, used to have a characterful pub: its décor was based on the curious Australian adoration of bushrangers and it was called, if memory serves, the Collector Arms. Now it screamed "BUSHRANGER HOTEL" and had annexes for food and drink of the vulgarest kind of catchpenny modernity. We didn't stop there but went on towards Canberra.

The countryside is sheepland, of which Reg said: "The finest wool-producing country in the world, though it may not look it. A bit of sourness in the country is good for wool, and sheep do better if they have to forage around for their feed. The Merino here grows wool right down the length of the leg."

Then you come to Lake George which, as Reg said, is peculiar. It is a lake, and then it isn't, and then it is a lake again. The tops of a fence built across it when it was dry land protruded from shallow water that was for years permanent and deep enough to encourage the building of launch jetties. Lake George is subsided land on a geological fault-line that occasionally causes earth tremors in the region.

So here we were, nearing the national capital—and my inclination is to go on and write of Canberra, in sequence. But to include Canberra A.C.T. (Australian Capital Territory) in a section headed *New South Wales* would be rather like including Washington D.C. in a chapter about New York State.

"THE SNOWY SCHEME", as we call it, has been named by the American Society of Civil Engineers as one of the "Seven Wonders of the Engineering World".

It has often been compared with the mighty American water scheme created by the Tennessee Valley Authority (T.V.A.). The Australian project has been directed, since work began on it in 1949, by the Snowy Mountains Authority (S.M.A.). After twenty years of work the tourist can see much of it finished and operating and the shape of what is to be completed by 1974.

To understand what the Snowy Scheme is we need to understand what Australia is—in terms of water. Australia is the driest of the continents, mainly because it has few masses of mountains to precipitate rain and give rise to rivers. (The outflow of *all* the Australian rivers in an average year is less than two-thirds of the Mississippi's.) However, the coastal belt of eastern Australia has plenty of rivers and is not usually short of rain or in need of irrigation, because of the long corderilla called the Great Dividing Range. In the south-eastern part of this well-favoured littoral half the population of Australia lives, and most of the heavy industry and factories are concentrated, mainly in two group-sectors—one that takes in Newcastle-Sydney-Wollongong in New South Wales, the other in Victoria round Melbourne-Geelong.

Between the two lies the highest part of Australia, called the Australian Alps, and part of these are the Snowy Mountains. Snow is here useful stuff for irrigation—of the country inland, west of the mountains—because the water is stored frozen during the best-rainfall months and melts later, when there is more need for it, to swell three westward-running rivers the mountains give rise to.

The trouble was that much of the snow melted into the Snowy River (and some tributaries such as the Eucumbene)—and the Snowy ran off the wrong side of the range, flowed south through part of Victoria that needed no irrigation, and wasted its water into the Tasman Sea. Was it possible to divert the Snowy's water into three rivers that flowed west into the water-needy country? The Murray, which is Australia's biggest river, has to water nearly all the borderland between New South Wales and Victoria, and then go on to do a further irrigation job in South Australia, which hasn't another decent river to its name. The Murrumbidgee has much irrigation to do before it joins the Murray. The Tumut River feeds into the Murrumbidgee.

It *was* possible to have a Snowy Irrigation Scheme; but not economically feasible. There were not, and never would be out there to the west, enough farmers, of fruit or whatever, to pay for anything like the cost of such irrigation. And, though subsidy for development is often essential, there was no future in spending a dollar on water to grow a dozen oranges that would sell off the farm for fifty cents. However, if the water for irrigation could also be used to produce something else—something essential that the millions of people living on the coast would buy—then the Snowy Irrigation Scheme could be feasible. That other product was water-generated electricity, to provide power and light to industry, transport, dwellings. So the irrigation project was reckoned as likely to be economic as an ancillary function of what is primarily a vast Snowy Mountains Hydro-Electric Scheme. Of the $800 million total cost, not more than about $120 million will have been spent on making it an irrigation scheme as well.

What the Snowy Scheme will do when it is completed:

—Seven power stations will have a total capacity to generate 3,740,000 kilowatts of electric power. (One kilowatt, 1,000 watts, is about 1.3 horsepower.) That is more power than the whole of New South Wales has been using in winter, and would sell for an estimated $50 million a year.

—Thirteen major dams (the largest, Lake Eucumbene, will fill to eight times the area of Sydney Harbour) will have the capacity to store nearly 7,000,000 acre-feet of water. (One acre-foot is as much water as will cover one acre to a depth of one foot, about 272,000 gallons.)

—The extra water that will augment the Murray and Murrumbidgee Rivers (about two million acre-feet a year) is reckoned sufficient to irrigate 1,000 square mile of dry country, which might grow produce worth $60 million a year.

THE MOST DRAMATIC part of the work of making the Snowy River's waters flow the other way today's visitor does not see. The principle was, "First trap the water, then divert it, then use it." You see how it has been trapped, behind huge dam-walls. You see how it is being used, to generate electricity. But you cannot see what diverted it from dam-lakes to power-stations—great tunnels that were driven through the mountains.

The under-mountain tunnels were the costliest part of the project, and the most dangerous work. They are all finished now, the eleven main tunnels and the lesser ones—nearly a hundred miles of tunnels altogether. They cost about two million dollars a mile in money;

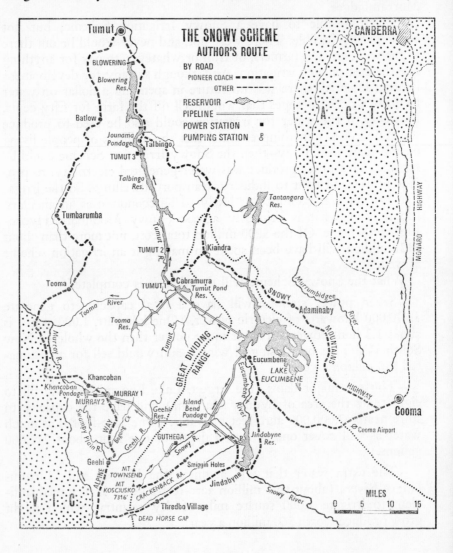

19/NEW SOUTH WALES *The Snowy Mountains Scheme has created many lakes—this one is formed by Blowering Dam near Tumut—to produce hydro-electricity and provide irrigation. Costing $800 million, the scheme will be complete in 1974.* BELOW: *Murray I power station and (at right) Tumut I, which is underground.*

20/CANBERRA A.C.T. *The national capital, showing the Civic Centre with parking areas and, in the background, part of Lake Burley Griffin.*

21/OPPOSITE PAGE ▶
The Captain Cook Memorial Jet began shooting up 450 feet from Lake Burley Griffin in 1970.

Red Kangaroo. Shooters have taken a heavy toll.

LEFT: *Pet, 50-pound wombat near Canberra.*

Bright, in the valley of the Ovens River, is particularly attractive when autumn mints its gold in the town's avenues of elms and poplars.

Lake Buffalo, another of the water storages that transform the countryside, mirrors hills and the branches of drowned trees.

and every mile and three-quarters cost a life. Fifty-four men died in the course of boring and blasting the Snowy tunnels, nearly all from misfiring explosives and falls of rock. Yet that grim figure is less than half the fatality rate per mile on the Mont Blanc railway tunnel through the European Alps.

The tunnels are either round or horseshoe-shaped and are up to twenty-four feet in diameter. The longest, the one that feeds the Snowy's waters into Eucumbene dam, is over fifteen miles, and the Eucumbene-Tumut tunnel is only a mile or so shorter. Time and again the Snowy Scheme tunnellers beat the world record of 362 feet for a six-day week of round-the-clock shifts: they advanced at up to 541 feet a week. Even so, the Eucumbene-Tumut tunnel took three years.

Men from many countries have worked on the construction; and some of the contractors have been American or French. Balts, Italians, Slavs, Dutch, Germans have been part of the workforce of more than 6,000. The flags of twenty-seven nations fly beside the park in Cooma, the country town that boomed into a new life when it became Snowy Scheme headquarters.

I had left Canberra at 7 a.m. on a Murray's coach that traversed seventy-two miles of sheep country and got me to Cooma in time to join the 9 a.m.-departing Pioneer three-day Snowy Mountains tour of about five hundred miles.

It was the third week of April, before the snow season began.

DIARY: Out past Cooma airport where, soon as good snowfalls begin, there'll be 25 planeloads of skiers a day flying in (coach-captain, Frank, says). Into Monaro (Ab. word meaning "treeless") grazing country, knobbed with big boulders. Climb 2,000 feet up Eaglehawk Hill. Landscape now littered with grey carcasses of felled trees.

Approaching Lake Eucumbene. Construction township here, where now only two-three houses, had 3,000 people. Houses moved to last big dam of scheme, Talbingo. Seeing part of Eucumbene storage lake—four times area of Sydney Harbour now, and only half full. Dam-wall ahead is 381 feet high, half-mile thick at base. Frank says some companies wouldn't tender for dam job because of four-year time limit. A U.S. company, working 24 hours a day six days a week, completed it in 23 months!

Off coach, onto launch for lake cruise. Across there, down under, is drowned town of Adaminaby. Ahead what was a hilltop has become Hallstrom Island, and on it are *white* kangaroos, the albino ones Sir Edward Hallstrom bred: see five of them feeding. Lunch on launch. Left-over bread to mallard and teal ducks that cluster round. On left-hand shore, fishing lodge of N.S.W. Governor, Sir

Roden Cutler. Lake is stocked with trout. Snowy Scheme's supplementary benefits: biggest lake in State, and a whole new tourist area.

American construction co. (Frank says) tunnelled into mountain, filled tunnel with 65 tons of gelignite. Whole mountainside fell out and provided nearly a million tons of rockfill for dam-wall. Region must have trembled; also conservationists. Can't have Snowy omelette without breaking ecological eggs. Think Big: have trouble doing that. Still, new fauna. Ducks in the wilderness.

Eucumbene River fills, with aid of snow, this great reservoir and next one we come to, Jindabyne. Again, old township of Jindabyne, which was on the Snowy, is drowned. New Jindabyne, town-planned for S.M.A. by Prof. Denis Winston, is attractive with characterful shopping mall colonnaded with stone pillars, and one sign says TRADING POST. Jindabyne Dam was another American job. Water that fills the valley where once the Snowy coursed shines placidly blue against brown hillsides it laps. Jindabyne pumping station pumps water into one tunnel system that feeds the Murray.

Enough engineering for a while; now we are headed for Mt Kosciusko [named after a Polish patriot by 1840 Polish explorer, Strzelecki]. Enter Kosciusko National Park, largest in Australia, 2,500 square miles [nearly the size of Devon in England and bigger than the U.S. State of Delaware].

Into the ski-resort area, now centred beyond the slopes where stood the burned-down Hotel Kosciusko I learnt to ski at. Landscape, soon to be snow-whitened, is blasted-heath, round-rocked country, with snow-gums. Lunch (good) at Royal Coachman ski lodge at Smiggin Holes. First fresh snow atop Mt Perisher. Snow-sports boom had produced in Perisher Valley three hotels, a dozen commercial ski lodges, 53 private lodges.

Charlotte Pass, 6,039 ft. Some trees and signposts just beginning to take on a glass-edge of ice. Now beyond the treeline. Fascinating landscape of lichened rocks and heath: not seen it uncovered before.

Coach grinding up through a thick mist. No snow, but roadside heath whitening, beautifully, as with a great frost, and pools glazed with ice. Rawson's Pass, 6,960 ft. Visibility about twenty feet. Only 300 feet, a hundred yards, to the summit of Kosciusko (7,314 ft), highest point of Australia. But Frank, excellent driver, is beaten by the mist that blinds his road. "In this," he says, "I can't safely go farther", and stops.

Some of us get out. Cold, it's freezing—literally: a shivering English motorist who's been tailing the coach in an unheated car has a thermometer in it showing 30 degrees, two below. Look what's happening to the heath and earth. Wet with the mist, being iced by the freezing wind, getting perceptibly rimier, glassier, icy-whiter, leaf and stem losing green and suppleness, mosses frosting over, lichens' colour erasing. Then, as a flurry of snow comes, stones changing their hardness to a fur of soft whiteness.

Suddenly realize what I'm seeing: The birth of Winter, death of Summer, the earth in white-bright mourning for itself as it goes into its snow-grave for six-months' burial. Then resurrection, wild-flowered, in the Spring.

RETURNING through Perisher Valley, stopped for a drink at the Man from Snowy River Hotel. Décor here could have done better by the "Banjo" Paterson ballad's hero who outrode all others in a round-up of wild horses. Pity that some of the developers of this popular skiing valley couldn't have used better architects and been less inclined to gaudy gimmickry.

Thredbo we come to next morning after overnight at Ski Rider Lodge, Wilson's Valley (which wasn't very hot: the heating system failed in the night). Thredbo Village very attractive in this steeper-sided valley, particularly when looked down upon from chair-lift some of us took to top of the Crackenback Range. Brilliant blue day. Alpine Hotel looks of admirable standard, with a golf course going in. Eight ski lodges. Chair-lifts and ski-lifts.

Coach climbs to Deadhorse Gap (wild horses, brumbies, were found frozen to death in a blizzard about sixty years ago), 5,190 ft, the watershed. Steep descent down rugged side of Snowy Range, with more timber, fine straight alpine ash. Look across to the Pilot (peak of over 6,000 ft) where Murray River rises, beginning as a wild mountain torrent its 1,600-mile course to the sea.

Winding descent ends in Victorian borderland; a lush green valley. Small river running through—it's the young Murray.

North now to Geehi (pron. Jee-hi). From one lookout, areas of forest appear reddish-brown, as though singed by bushfire. A stick-insect has appeared in countless numbers and, ringbarking branches, defoliated the eucalypts.

Murray 1, largest of completed Snowy power-stations (PLATE 19). Enter the humming Hall of the Generators, ten of them, or what shows of them, their tops in line, identical, immaculate, cyclamen-red steel. Make obeisance, from the visitors' gallery, to a million kilowatts. Think a mechanistic-minded visitor from outer space might well mistake Murray 1 for an Earthlings' cathedral. Only two acolytes attend the ten omphalos-like steel-and-concrete, red-and-white altars, so automated is everything in this steely, shining, surgically-sterile place of the servant-god that springs to our aid when we snap on a light switch, electric frypan, TV set. His body lives down there under the concrete, his blood is roaring water that comes down the mountainside in a perspective-pattern of huge pipes, to whirl the turbines that whirl the generators into creating electrical energy.

Lunch at Khancoban—another attractive S.M.A. dam-town with greensward, rose-garden, swimpool, where in 1960 were only grazing paddocks. Westward, we cross a broadened Murray River into Victoria, briefly. Country plush-green, lovely. Fat cattle contentedly eating themselves on to the dinner plate. A hillside specked with white. Quartz? Not also up on dead-tree boughs, surely. White cockatoos. On through one-pub Tooma and renowned-for-its-rodeo Tumbarumba. Some rabbits, but not a single kangaroo. Very Australian blackboys (grass-trees) and briers with exotic red berries. Past a station property called WILLIGOBUNG (Frank says couple of owners failed on it: new one named it wondering if he'd go bankrupt, too: looks prosperous). Regiments of reafforestation pines, then apple orchards signal approach of Batlow, famous for its cider. Tour sometimes visits Mountain Maid cannery-cidery but it's too early in apple season. Sinking sun blazing through the run of roadside trees on the way to Tumut, overnight stop.

Departing Tumut next morning, another perfect day, admired its remembered poplars: Tumut has beautiful trees, oaks included. But why is Tumut River now so narrow? Its flow's shut off by Blowering Dam, which soon to see. Countryside looks very good. So do SANCTUARY notices in country where every farmer's boy grew up to own a .22 rifle and no bird was safe on its bough.

Blowering Dam appears (and be damned to "dam"; it's a lake). Like it that the Snowy Scheme has put these wide blue eyes in the face of this far-from-the-sea landscape, where the only waters previously were river-wide. Now the Tumutites can come out and go power-boating, sailing, water-skiing. Blowering Dam has created the second-largest lake in the whole Snowy Scheme (PLATE 19).

Biggest dam-wall of all will be 530 feet high [imagine it 90 feet higher than the top of the arch of Sydney Harbour Bridge is from the water]. See it under construction at Talbingo, where third-largest reservoir lake will be. Australian contractors, Thiess Bros., are tearing sides out of mountains to get 19 million cubic feet of earth and rockfill.

New Talbingo town, set up for S.M.A., using housing hauled from places where constructions completed (houses were made to come apart in the middle), has another of Prof. Denis Winston's attractive shopping centres.

Between Talbingo reservoir, which will be a long widening of Tumut River, and adjoining Jounama Dam (being built by French company), will be biggest-of-all Tumut 3 power-station. Able to generate 1,500,000 kilowatts, half as much again as Murray 1.

Leave the Tumut and cross a high plain, uninhabited since gold-mining days. (Surprising that all the Snowy Scheme tunnelling and excavating hasn't turned up any gold deposits.) Miles and miles of dead trees—killed by a bushfire in 1963. Frank: "Two fishermen on the Tumut River were careless with their campfire, and burned out 250 square miles of country." At noon reach Kiandra, where ski-lodge recently burnt. An 1890s gold-rush town shrunken to a hamlet with one pub that served awful lunch of tough curried steak.

On to Cabramurra, highest town in Australia (4,880 ft) where completion of two smaller reservoirs and Tumut 1 and Tumut 2 power-stations has reduced 3,000 people to a couple of hundred. Many bright-painted houses stand empty; some have been hauled off to Talbingo. Coach descends mountainside so steep that making of road down—flanked by spectacular gorge—was itself a major achievement. At the bottom, Tumut 1 power-station—underground, inside the mountain. Inspect this (PLATE 19).

After stop at Cabramurra, a hilltop has a big switching station. Insulators glitter like beads on a giant's abacus. And, like framework giants, the steel transmission towers march across the mountains carrying the power cables high on their widespread metal arms.

Back through Kiandra and down the Snowy Mountains Highway. Occasionally a gnarled old candlebark-tree with patches of vivid red bark to its trunk. Through new Adaminaby that replaced town drowned in Eucumbene. Two churches, dismantled stone by stone, were re-erected at unremarkable site the townspeople opted for. Frank says it could have, should have, been re-sited beside Lake Eucumbene.

At 5.30 we're back in Cooma. Been a good tour, over a route mainly made possible by Snowy Scheme's provision of hundreds of miles of good roads in what was untracked wilderness. Might do it again in few years, when Scheme's all finished down to Talbingo's long lake. Perhaps in January when, I'm told, the Kosciusko country is prettified with snow daisies, alpine bluebells, yellow billy-buttons, other wildflowers including one called, engagingly, purple eye-bright.

To the Far South Coast

HAD I GONE ON from Canberra on the coach-tour with Mrs Term and her pensioner friends, it would have brought me to the Mid South Coast at Bateman's Bay. This is an attractive area; and there are a few charming havens for visitors and vacationers on what might be called the Near South Coast that begins within twenty miles of

Sydney and ends, as the railway does, at Nowra's river. But the loveliest part of this region is from about Moruya to Merimbula: the Far South Coast.

By train you could flash down to the railhead in a good express, and there are bus services on from Nowra. You could fly Sydney-Merimbula direct in about an hour: and for the motorist it was just on 300 miles from Sydney.

It was possible to see the South Coast, on a passing-through basis, in daylight, in the course of two-day coach tours between Sydney and Melbourne; or on one of the round tours between these two capitals that take seven or more days and, in the case of Pioneer tours (only), traverse the Princes Highway as part of their route. All of these coach tours made an overnight stop at Merimbula.

That so many people in Australia (about half a million people a year) are now using coach tours does not mean that there are still not a lot of people—people who like to travel and can afford to, if it's not too expensive—who have never been on a coach tour. Of these, I feel, only a dwindling minority of rugged or snooty individualists are still standing four-square behind a prejudice inscribed *You'd never get ME on a conducted tour.* The majority would probably be interested to know: How good are these tours? How expensive, or inexpensive, are they? Who operates the best of them? What kind of people are you coached up with?

The "How good?" answer will vary with the tour and with the operator. Indeed, the enjoyability of the same tour by the same operator can vary markedly with the personality and knowledge of your coach-captain (as the driver-commentator is called), with the people in the coach party, the type of coach used, and the weather and road conditions.

In Australia, Pioneer are easily the biggest of the coach-tour operators, and definitely not the cheapest. Their fares could be the highest, though not by much in this highly competitive business. It appears that, in buying coach tours, you pay more/get more, pay less/get less. I cannot speak from personal experience of Pioneer's competitors' tours; nor do I think that Pioneer tours I have been on could not have been better. However, if they were not the best offering I do not think a travel service of the calibre and stature of Cooks would say they were, and give them so much business.

As to cost, this was evidently a prime reason for coach-tours' popularity. The "dearest" were still very reasonably priced. The four-day Canberra–South Coast round tour from Sydney (the one I got off) was only priced at $44.50 (less five per cent discount to pensioners, nurses, Servicemen) for a trip of about five hundred miles, with morning-afternoon-evening sightseeing in Canberra, all meals, two nights' accommodation with "private facilities" (shower, toilet) at the Wellington Hotel in Canberra (which has a good rating) and a night at the Bateman's Bay Motel (highly rated).

Round tours of seven or more days (by Pioneer) from Sydney with stop-overs in Canberra and Melbourne were costing in mid-1970 an all-inclusive $13 + a day to around $16 on the "Red Carpet" tours that were the best accommodated (Parkroyal at Canberra instead of the Forrest Motor Lodge) and the ones most likely to have some overseas visitors on them. If you wanted a room to yourself instead of shared accommodation it cost about $3 a night extra.

The international traveller would find the main differences between European coach tours (such as I took in Italy, Greece, Austria, Germany, Spain, Denmark, Norway) and Australian were: (i) in Australia the coach-driver also gave the commentary and "looked after" the passengers, whereas in Europe drivers only drive and the rest is the separate function of a commentator-guide, who may be male or female; (ii) most of the passengers on regular (not specially arranged) Australian tours are Australians, whereas in Italy or Greece you seldom travel with Italians or Greeks but with other foreigners; (iii) accommodation is most often in motels not hotels, is newer, better as to modernities, though with less "character"; (iv) the Australian tours are cheaper.

To get men who were, as a first essential, skilled and safe coach-drivers and also had the knowledge and diction to give a good commentary, and the personality and temperament to keep a coachload of forty people happy, was clearly difficult: the talents needed were so disparate. As the numbers of overseas visitors grow (and they are growing rapidly), I think it will be found both desirable and economic to introduce highly-qualified non-driver commentators on some higher-priced coach tours that not only American and European visitors will prefer and be able to afford. A lot of sufficiently affluent Australians could patronize these as well, particularly the better-educated.

As to what kind of people travel on coach tours, all kinds do. An average party of thirty to forty on a Pioneer tour might include six retired business-trade-professional men and their wives; several widows travelling together or with women companions; a widower or two and a couple of unattached young men; a honeymoon couple without much money; several pairs of vacationing nurses or typists or, if it is school-vacation time, female schoolteachers; two middle-aged couples who habitually holiday together; one dedicated photography hobbyist (male); one funny-or-unfunny type (either sex) who cracks jokes and laughs a lot; one gentlewoman who knows the names of roadside flowers; no children (except during school holidays) because the child fare can be 85 per cent of the adult fare; no infants-in-arms.

Coaches of the Scenicruiser or Super-Clipper type ride comfortably, have adjustable seats, are air-conditioned, and noise is minimized by their being rear-engined. A desirable, non-tiring day's run is 200/250 miles, five to six coach hours spread between stops for morning and afternoon teas, lunch, sightseeing, photography. On long tours, such as the Darwin-Perth "Nor'Wester", stretches have to be longer; but a "comfort stop" is made about every two hours.

Seating is "rotated", meaning that twice a day you move back one seat, and those at the rear come to the front. It is usual to give a coach-captain who has made the trip enjoyable a gratuity; and this might well be reckoned at the rate of half-a-dollar a day.

As THIS SOUTH-BOUND COACH was leaving Sydney via the Princes Highway suburb of Kogarah, our coach-captain (David) drew attention to—not that it's easily missed, with its fountains and flags flying—a large and lavishly featurist building that represents a New South Wales, even an Australian, social phenomenon. This was the $2,250,000 St George Leagues Club which, David said, was referred to as the Taj Mahal of its kind.

A footballers' club only in name, it had marble floors and eight bars. In an entertainment hall members were regaled by cabaret stars the Leagues Club imported direct from overseas or by boxing bouts or a symphony orchestra. It had a gymnasium carpeted wall-to-wall, sauna baths, squash courts, indoor bowls—you name it. All these amenities were nominally free to the 20,000 members who paid only five dollars a year. The cost of this extraordinary pleasure dome was not met by the profits on the quarter-million gallons of beer quaffed there annually. Most of the club's revenue, which ran to a couple of million dollars a year, came from its batteries of poker machines, the baroque "one-armed bandits" that so encourage gambling hopes that insertion of a few more ten- or twenty-cent pieces will "crack the jackpot".

We cross the George's River by the bridge from the point called Tom Ugly's: Tom Huxley appears to have been the early settler's name the Aborigines pronounced as Ugly. Sydney can be said to be left behind when a road fork is reached just beyond Sutherland. We stay on Princes Highway. The other road skirts the sea more picturesquely from Stanwell Park to Thirroul.

Sublime Point is a major reason why we have been travelling the native-named Illawarra district in terms of *Warra* (a high place) rather than *Illa* (near the sea). To take the coast-clinging road would mean climbing up Bulli Pass, 1,200 feet in a couple of miles, to the lookout of the mountain scarp that commands one of the finest panoramas in Australia. The view of a coast scalloped with bays and beaches stretches far, far to the south—how far depending on how clear the day is. Below lies coal-mining Bulli; and, farther on, the narrow coastal plain has lost its rural green under the spread of the great smoke-greyed industrial complex of Wollongong–Port Kembla, and the housing expanse of Greater Wollongong's nearly 200,000 people. The view from Sublime Point is not as sublime as it was when industry had obtruded less upon the natural scene. The tallest smokestack in the Southern Hemisphere (of the Electrolytic Refining & Smelting Company at Port Kembla) looks not very big from this distance and height, and is still a smokestack.

B.H.P. will, by 1973, expand its Port Kembla steelworks with the huge four-year expenditure of $300 million. As the area grows industrially bigger must it also grow uglier?

There is a good deal else in the Wollongong–Port Kembla urban area that is quite unnecessarily ugly. Some of it stems from attempts to "brighten up" an industrial environment. At Unanderra, admirably enough, there were flower boxes on the railway station—but the flower-boxes had been gaudily painted different colours. Smaller industries cluttered the roadside with some of Australia's worst sign-writing, adding to the uglification of the outskirts of what was the third city of New South Wales.

Yet there are many charms along this route, and more if you can get off it and explore. To the motorist I commend the odd enclave of sub-tropical rain-forest at Minnamurra Falls: you turn off Princes Highway at Kiama and go up what is one of the loveliest places on the South Coast in a green season, the Jamberoo Valley. At Kiama itself there is the spouting natural wonder of the Blowhole, spectacular in times of a savage sea.

South of Kiama, scores of coral trees, leafless in winter, project jets of scarlet bloom. Cabbage palms hoist their heads on trunks like poles. Green hillsides swoop beneath the hooves of gorging dairy-cattle. Some beaches are beautiful, and Gerringong's is so long and firm that in 1933 Kingsford Smith took the *Southern Cross* off it to fly to New Zealand.

Nowra (pop. 10,000) sits at the wide mouth of the Shoalhaven, a river that goes back into wilderness where it courses rugged gorges and attracts the intrepid canoeist. In this tourist-alluring hinterland, too, is Kangaroo Valley and the scenic Fitzroy Falls.

Jervis Bay, about twenty miles south, is a splendid natural harbour like a mouth open between two jaws of rugged peninsulas. The lower of these is part of the Australian Commonwealth Territory: Jervis Bay was defined as the Federal Capital's access to the sea, the

N

port of Canberra. But Canberra never went in for trade and all that eventuated at Jervis Bay was a training college of the Royal Australian Navy (and even that was removed, for economy's sake, to Victoria in 1930: in 1958 it moved back). Tourist resorts, much favoured by fishermen, have grown up at Huskisson in the middle of the bayshore, and at Sussex Inlet (where we once had a fine family holiday) that runs, behind the A.C.T. part, into lake-like St George's Basin. Pioneer's four-day circle tour took in Jervis Bay, but this one didn't.

What could revolutionize Jervis Bay, make it a bustling port and spread a population of at least 15,000 round it, was the proposal announced in August 1969 by the Armco Steel Corporation. One of the U.S. steel giants, Armco planned to establish a $300-million steelworks at Jervis Bay. This formidable competition for Australia's great and only steelmaker, B.H.P., was expected to eventuate if a feasibility study showed that Armco could secure sufficient coking coal in the region and sufficient iron ore supply from the West.

Another big development would come if the Commonwealth Government confirmed its intentions to establish Australia's first nuclear power station at Jervis Bay. This could cost an estimated $130 million.

The lunch stop was at Ulladulla, 143 miles down Princes Highway from Sydney, at the Marlin Hotel, which is typical brewery-texture-brick architecture of the forties. The Italian professional fishermen have their fleet blessed at the start of the season by the local priest.

Just before Ulladulla, the coach skirts one of the loveliest of a number of inlets that sandbars turn into lakes, Lake Conjola; and, when you go on, there is Lake Burrill and, farther down, Lake Durras, just before you get to Bateman's Bay on the Clyde River's charming estuary, which is lake-like in itself. Bateman's Bay's oysters and lobsters are particularly good. Out in the bay, the Tollgate Islands, or islets, sometimes have penguins on them.

Seventeen miles on is another river-mouth town, Moruya, its oyster-growing backed by dairylands and timber.

We are over 200 miles from Sydney as we go on towards Narooma. Like Bermagui, farther south, Narooma came into prominence as a big-game fishing resort when, in the 1930s, the American author Zane Grey interrupted his writing about two-gun riders of the purple sage to come to Australia, and he caught many marlin off these two places. Narooma, on the highway, is the more picturesque and popular tourist town; but the Tuross Lakes on the way down from Moruya are drawing more and more campers and caravanners to the edges of their still and shining waters. Down the road from the lakes is Bodalla, where early Australian dairy-farming was greatly improved on the 38,000-acre estate of Thomas Sutcliffe Mort, pioneer industrialist. Bodalla markets a good cheese.

Motorists who turn, past Narooma, at a signpost saying MYSTERY BAY will be glad they did so, for Mystery Bay is as alluring as its name. It has curious rocks, some with burnt-orange lichens, and a beach with parti-coloured pebbles, black and white ones. Its mystery had to do with the strange disappearance there in 1880 of a government geologist, Lamont Young, who was English, his German assistant and three fishermen they had gone out with. The fishing boat was found among the rocks, stove in with stones, from the inboard side. There were signs that the men had not drowned but landed. Although Young's parents appealed to Queen Victoria, who asked the Governor of New South Wales to expedite the search for the missing men, and a large reward was offered, not a trace of the five was ever found. One theory was that they were kidnapped and carried away on a mysterious schooner that had been moored there, the *Magic*.

Bega, the "capital" (pop. 4,000) of the Far South Coast was little more than lights when we reached it, for this tour was in the last week of May and the days had contracted to early darkness.

Merimbula, that night, was only the Black Dolphin Motel. But this was a motel designed with such character that it was nominated by *Architecture and Arts* magazine in 1961 as one of the year's ten best Australian buildings. The architect was Robin Boyd.

The South Coast, as the *HKF Report* on Australian tourism puts it, is "renowned for the quality of food produced. This could be exploited as a tourist attraction." The Merimbula oysters I began dinner with (slightly stronger in flavour than Sydney's, but none the less delectable, and perhaps a little larger), followed by an excellent local-Lobster Newburg, substantiated the American opinion.

IN THE MORNING, just across the road fronting the Black Dolphin, the lake was still as glass. From the high gums on the opposite shore came the chinking of bellbirds.

The bus coming from Merimbula airport, taking passengers from Sydney the twenty-two miles into Bega, picked me up. The editor of the *Bega News*, Alan McGregor, was to run me round.

Surprisingly, there was no regional tourist centre with a tourist officer. Alan McGregor said, "This is primarily a dairying district —though there's timber as well and Bega cans fish and makes such things as furniture as well as very good cheese—and the country people are unwilling to pay rates to build roads and such for tourist development. They say they get from it only marginal benefits."

What I saw of the area indicated that there was room for the kind of development that protected the widespread natural beauties of seashores and lakesides at the same time as it gave access to these and provided more accommodation of Black Dolphin standard.

Tathra (pron. Taathra), eleven miles from Bega, was its port before road transport ran the steamers out of business. The attraction is Tathra's surf beach, a safe one and good enough for a State surf carnival to have been held there. It swept away in a mile-long arc that had not a sign of habitation behind it. At the settled end about 700 people lived. It had camping-caravanning areas, and one motel.

Wallagoot Lake (not to be confused with Wallaga Lake near Tilba Tilba) you turn off the Tathra road to get to. Boats and water-skiers it had at weekends, but on this weekday it was utterly peaceful, with nothing to disturb its double-imaged shores and cloud reflections except, in the distance, some black swans and herons, and nearer shags (cormorants) watching for fish. From where we were I could see only one house (PLATE 15).

Merimbula I now saw much more of. It is lakeside and seaside beautifully joined. The lake's far edge is duned with white sand behind a beach where the rollers come in.

Beyond the town (where 800 residents were submerged during midsummer holidays under a tourist population of thousands) was a point from which you look across the wide sapphire-blue inlet to Pambula. In the foreground, beyond red rocks, was the picturesque and historic Old Wharf, thronged by holiday families fishing.

Pambula is a couple of miles from the ocean; but Pambula Beach, now the road to it had been sealed, was developing fast under the name of Jiguma (which, if pronounced *Jigooma*, could sound better than the local usage, *Jiggima*).

Eden, the coast's last town before Victoria, is less than a paradise. The townscape reflects something of the rigours of the fishing-fleeters' lives. Yet there is a good looking golf course/country club. A small cemetery a century old saddens the salty air at the edge of a nice-enough beach on the ocean side. We went up the steep hill that leads to the look-out across Twofold Bay.

Gazing across this splendid natural harbour, one could understand the grandiose scheme of Benjamin Boyd to make it the great port of a new Australian State, with Boyd Town as the capital. Bank-founder, big-time pastoralist, Kanaka-importer and owner of ships that in-cluded his whaling fleet that worked out of Twofold Bay, Ben Boyd had built a lighthouse that still stood on the far point as a derelict square tower.

Six years before, Claire and I had overnighted at Boyd Town at its Seahorse Inn (Boyd built about 1846 what was described as "a splendid hotel in the Elizabethan style" fronting a beach, along with a Gothic church that was in ruins, and some brick houses that had vanished). The Seahorse Inn was full of Victoriana and creaking stairs up to curious bedrooms, and it was run at that time with a roystering informality we much enjoyed.

I flew back to Sydney with Airlines of New South Wales from Merimbula.

The Riverina's Albury

THE RIVERINA is considered nowadays to be the region bounded by the Lachlan River and part of the Murrumbidgee down to the Murray, and by the Murray as far east as Albury, and then by a line north from Albury up to Condobolin, taking in Wagga Wagga (which Australian usage shortens to just the one Wagga).

It is a diverse region of mainly wool and wheat except at its green heartland, the M.I.A. (Murrumbidgee Irrigation Area). If the Riverina had a "capital" it would surely be Wagga, the largest inland city of New South Wales.

The Riverina is a very important part of Australia as to productivity, but it is hardly the scenic Australia tourists go to—except in its Murray Valley corner round the Victorian-border city of Albury.

THE OVAL WINDOW of the T.A.A. Friendship—it had left Sydney at 8.50 a.m. and called at Canberra—framed a picture of lush green landscape and a great hook of blue water as the plane lowered for an eleven o'clock landing at Albury (pop. 27,000).

Lake Hume, when the waters rose in the valleys behind the dam-wall in 1936, was the biggest reservoir and man-made lake in Australia. It retained that distinction for twenty years; then Victoria got a bigger reservoir at Eildon, which has been overtopped by the Snowy Scheme's Lake Eucumbene, which will be only half the size of the Gordon River water storage under construction in Tasmania. All the same, Lake Hume with two and a half million acre-feet of water in it, which the two States share, is large enough to have 250 miles of foreshores, and has much increased the scenic attractiveness of this Murray-side area. Albury had an active tourist bureau, whose executive director Fred Willson White (since resigned) was at the airport to meet me.

Albury had changed greatly since I had last seen it. In the main street the new Civic Centre had not only a very good block of Government offices set in gardened lawns, but a big regional library and the elegantly modern Civic Theatre that doubled as a convention hall. Its botanic gardens had improved to the extent that they had won prize after prize. The suburban housing in North Albury had a metropolitan rather than a provincial look. It was a sun-bright Sunday with closed shops—in which an affluent community is said to spend more per capita than in any other Australian city except Sydney and Newcastle—and the air of early May was still warm, with an edge of crispness. Autumn had found elms to turn golden and claret ashes were in their glory.

A party of Japanese travel agents had recently been there, Fred Willson White said, and they had seemed impressed with the city and what they had seen beyond it. He had taken them out to a sheep station to see shearing and sheepdogs working. They had also liked the food served at the official luncheon, with sherry, claret and riesling all made in the district.

"I think you'll like the country round the Hume Dam," my host said; and didn't mind my saying that a "dam" is something tourists may not feel inclined to give a damn about, and their interest could weary at "weir", but everybody loves lakes, so let it be Hume Lake.

The lake is eight miles out of Albury, or the beginning of it is, and on the way I saw countryside so lush I hadn't seen its greenness surpassed in the English shires or the U.S. State of Vermont. The sheep, which are whiter than you see out on the western plains, were up to their woolly bellies in pasture and the cattle sleek in clover. For much of this the big dam-lake was responsible.

Hume Lake was more than blue beyond the green. It was more than a waterway wider than the Murray River had ever provided for boating and water-skiing; more than a place for the angler to catch redfin (English perch) and trout; more than a looking-glass for golden poplars at its edges to reflect their colour in, as they did at Tallangatta (PLATE 18). It had, in parts, a character that came of its being a man-made lake with trees that were not all submerged when the dam was built and the waters rose in the valleys. Some, near the edges, lived on with water halfway up their trunks. Those that had succumbed to their roots being underwater, or had been ringbarked dead before the water came, were in places thickly enough together to make a strange water-forest of upflung bare branches double-imaged in reflection.

There were birds, but not as many as I should have liked to have seen. Fred Willson White said: "It's proclaimed as a sanctuary, but you know what shooters are. . . . We have rangers, and anyone seen with a gun is promptly prosecuted."

It was about thirty miles to Tallangatta—re-sited on higher ground, for the old town had drowned—and we could have driven at least forty miles along the lakeside in the other direction. We stopped for the tea Mrs Willson White had brought, and watched the sun go down. The big gums on the bank blackened into silhouettes against the tangerine glow, and a thousand dead trees had their dark branches raised above the sunset-coloured water.

NEXT MORNING, having slept comfortably at the New Albury Hotel, I was driven ten miles west to Jindera. We drew up at what looked exactly like an old-fashioned general store. The signboard proclaimed it WAGNER'S STORE.

P. C. Wagner was a baker from Rothenburg in Germany who migrated to Melbourne in 1864. Although Albury takes its name from an English village in Surrey, it had many German migrants as its pioneer settlers.

When modern Albury had decided to set up a historical museum it hadn't done what most places do—which is to collect anything and everything that looks antique or curious or "valuable", even though it has no more relationship with the district than Japanese lacquer-ware—and bung the whole collection, under a tacky frieze of old photographs, round the walls of a local hall. (Nothing can *not* be displayed or the donor would be offended.) The Jindera community had wisely selected a theme, in this case German settlement, and set its museum in and around the restored Wagner's Store.

The store was stocked, on the shelves behind its two long counters, not only with bolts of old materials and bottles of what you can't buy now, but with many other articles that customers walked in and bought a hundred years ago—and because their setting was real and right, they were much more interesting than the same things would be in a conventional museum. Family rooms had been authentically furnished, wall-papered, picture-hung: the parlour with its German-pewter candlesticks; the music-room with its old Edison phonograph; the girl's-room with floral china on the dressing-table; the nursery with a carved wooden German cradle; the laundry with its early wooden washing-machine and goffering irons for frilly bonnets. Outside, a slab hut had been rebuilt from original timbers of several huts pioneers had lived in, and was furnished with the ruggedly simple things that served them.

Since I was at Albury, a trout farm, the first in New South Wales for the commercial sale of trout, has become a Lake Hume tourist attraction. And the city is getting a fine Civic Centre.

From Albury I went into Victoria; but the narrative needs to go now to the Australian Capital Territory, to Canberra.

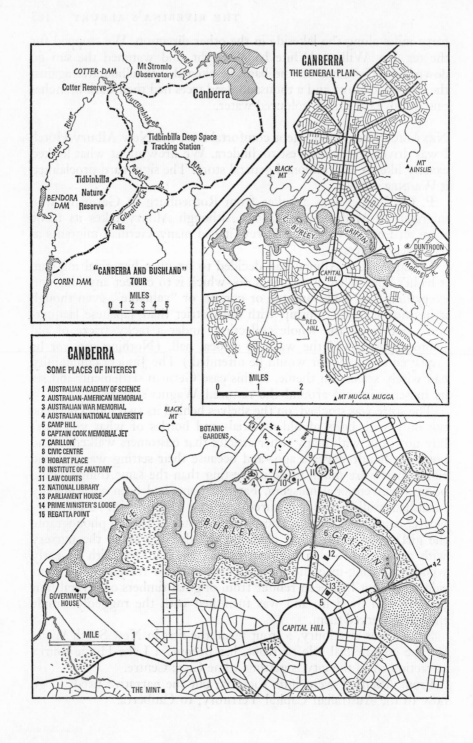

CANBERRA
THE GENERAL PLAN

MT
AINSLIE

BLACK
MT

L. BURLEY

GRIFFIN

DUNTROON

CAPITAL
HILL

Molonglo R.

RED
HILL

MUGGA WAY

MILES
0   1   2

MT MUGGA MUGGA

Molonglo R.
COTTER·DAM
Mt Stromlo
Observatory
Cotter Reserve
Canberra
River
Cotter
Murrumbidgee
Tidbinbilla Deep Space
Tracking Station
River
Poddys
Tidbinbilla
Nature
Reserve
BENDORA
DAM
Gibraltar Ck.
Falls
"CANBERRA AND BUSHLAND"
TOUR
CORIN DAM
MILES
0 1 2 3 4 5

CANBERRA

SOME PLACES OF INTEREST

1   AUSTRALIAN ACADEMY OF SCIENCE
2   AUSTRALIAN-AMERICAN MEMORIAL
3   AUSTRALIAN WAR MEMORIAL
4   AUSTRALIAN NATIONAL UNIVERSITY
5   CAMP HILL
6   CAPTAIN COOK MEMORIAL JET
7   CARILLON
8   CIVIC CENTRE
9   HOBART PLACE
10 INSTITUTE OF ANATOMY
11 LAW COURTS
12 NATIONAL LIBRARY
13 PARLIAMENT HOUSE
14 PRIME MINISTER'S LODGE
15 REGATTA POINT

BLACK
MT

BOTANIC
GARDENS

LAKE
BURLEY
GRIFFIN

GOVERNMENT
HOUSE

CAPITAL HILL

MILE
0   1

THE MINT

CANBERRA A.C.T.

Optimist at the National Capital

CANBERRA is, from any of the four eminences that flank it, a most viewable city. A resident said, as we stood among the tourists on Mt Ainslie, "Even if they can't *say* it they come to *see* it." He had winced at a woman's calling it Can*berra* instead of *Can*-ber-a.

Its pronunciation as much a trap, for overseas visitors especially, as Brisbane being Brisb'n and Melbourne Melb'n, Canberra is nevertheless a good and properly Australian name for the national capital. Some awful names were suggested—Wheatwoolgold, Democratia and Marsupalia among them—and the chosen "Canberra" was kept secret until the christening ceremony in 1913 by the Governor-General's wife, Lady Denman, who had been told the official pronunciation, and it came from the English lips of Lord Cowdray's daughter as a clipped *Can*-b'ra, with the final "a" soft.

To the Aborigines, who were driven off this good sheep country, the name was what the white man spelt variously as Canberry, Canburry, Kamberry, Kamberra, Kembery, Caamberra and, possibly correctly, Nganbirra. Its meaning is usually given as the appropriate one of "a meeting place". However, John Gale, a Queanbeyan journalist who first suggested this site for the capital, spent years trying to find out the true meaning and became utterly convinced that it was "a woman's breasts", from the two mounts we call Mt Ainslie and Black Mountain. Which could be appropriate if Canberra becomes the nurturing place that I am going to suggest, optimistically, it could become.

This optimism about Canberra's tomorrow—such as I am quite unable to feel about Sydney's or Melbourne's—comes of looking at Canberra's yesterday and Canberra's today. Early, it was "knocked" unmercifully. In 1908 the most Australian voice of the time, the *Bulletin*, roared against the proposal to plant the national capital in a place where there was nothing but "a handful of hovels in a howling wilderness". (One of the hovels was 40-roomed Yarralumla, now the Governor-General's residence, another was Duntroon, the sheep-station homestead of the rich Robert Campbell, and St John's Church has been there since 1845.) After the city's 1913 christening and commencement, the same voice said, "It is practically certain that within the next twenty years the entire outfit will have to be shifted"; and, after the Royal opening of the Commonwealth Parliament, "It is a city of shams and makeshifts. . . . Wool has been pulled over the eyes of a continent."

Born of State jealousies and parochial wrangling (the Senate voted for a Tumut site, the House of Representatives substituted Bombala, and in 1904 the Federal Parliament actually passed an act establishing the site near Dalgety on the Snowy River, but New South Wales would not grant the land: it was too far from Sydney, from which, by law, the capital had to be not less than 100 miles), Canberra was about as wanted as a bastard child. Australian apathy was such that not many people turned up at Parliament House for its opening on 9th May 1927 by the Duke of York and, afterwards, workmen had to bury 20,000 meat pies that had been ordered for the crowds that didn't come.

Even the parliamentary motion to establish a national capital was not moved by an Australian, but by the colourful King O'Malley, described by an opponent of Labour as a "goat-bearded, tail-coated Yankee", founder of the phony Waterlily Rock-bound Church of the Redskin Temple of the Chickasaw Nation (to get his land made tax-free as church property, when he was a real estate dealer in Kansas) and also founder, in Australia, of the Commonwealth Bank.

Canberra was designed by an American, the Chicago architect Walter Burley Griffin (in conjunction with his wife, who had also worked with Frank Lloyd Wright, with whom Griffin was in partnership). King O'Malley, as Minister for Home Affairs, had called for designs in an international competition with a first prize of £1,750. The succeeding Minister (W. O. Archibald) described the design of the gentle-mannered, idealistic Griffin (I knew him) as the work of a "Yankee bounder" given to "grand theorizing, moonshine and dreaming". A departmental board rejected Griffin's design as impractical and drew up its own—which was so appallingly bad that three hundred Sydney-led architects petitioned the Government to "Save Canberra".

Back in office, King O'Malley endorsed the Griffin plan. Griffin, who was enchanted with Canberra—"a beautiful site for a city"—was Director of Design and Construction. But departmental bureaucrats frustrated him at every turn, and Prime Minister "Billy" Hughes got rid of Griffin in 1920.

The city's design, though watered down and whittled at, is still essentially Burley Griffin's. His plan still comes in for criticism: but "If ever there was a city planned to be above Featurism, to be grandly and wholly united, it was Canberra," writes Robin Boyd.[1]

Most of suburban Canberra's good-standard housing has been unimaginative; but suburban streets took cues and curves from Griffin's design and are not soullessly straight to a grid plan, and they are well-planted with trees and shrubs.

"The plan of Canberra is of a garden city in which the garden is more emphasized than the city," W. K. Hancock wrote in 1929.[2] This was true because Griffin's concept had been changed to, officially, "a garden town, with simple, pleasing but unpretentious buildings". It was a case of plant now, build later. Peach and prunus blossomed but little did in the way of city masonry. In the Depression years of the thirties Canberra could still not be considered viable. When World War II came it had only 11,000 people. Stultified by wartime shortages, Canberra was still, after the war, "six suburbs in search of a city" and Commonwealth public servants were still strongly resisting transfer from Melbourne and Sydney to the "bush capital". Garden-town Canberra did not become Canberra City in terms of 20,000 population until 1950. Five years later, it was getting in a mess. The English planner Sir William Holford was called in and he recommended the controlling authority set up in 1958, the National Capital Development Commission.

Only in the twelve years to 1970 has a city of real consequence grown up in the Canberra garden. The laggard has leapt, the blueprint burgeoned, and the population exploded—tripled, in fact, from 40,000 to 130,000. In those recent years the capital has gained its most notable buildings—and Lake Burley Griffin.

The lake has transformed Canberra, giving it a broad blue sash to its middle instead of just the string of the Molonglo River. Mr (Sir Robert since) Menzies, one of the staunchest believers in Canberra's destiny, said in a recording I made with him in 1948, the year before he began his seventeen years as Prime Minister: "The plan will assume coherence, and the city will acquire its full character, only when the lake scheme is carried out." (PLATE 20 shows a part of the Lake.)

The unbelievers were the ordinary Australians. The look of the Canberra of the past few years has helped to change dramatically the attitude of those who derided the place—or whose fathers or grandfathers did—as everything from "a good sheep station spoilt" to a "waste of money" and, of course, a "white elephant".

Nearly a million of them, in a year, as well as a lot of overseas visitors, are going to see it, and spending about twelve million dollars to do so.

FROM THE LOOKOUT eminences you see, I think, the most impressive Australian city except Harbour-glorious Sydney as seen from a plane that is about over North Head; but when the plane lands in Sydney disillusion sets in, aesthetically, and when you land in Canberra it doesn't.

From Black Mountain is the view of Canberra I like best (it is where I took the photograph that makes the book's end-papers, but the National Library is more distant than it appears in the tree-fork because I used a telephoto lens). From Mt Ainslie you look down along that over-stated avenue from the War Memorial towards, on the other side of the lake, Parliament House (temporary since 1927). You need to imagine, over there, a far finer Parliament House built, behind the present one, on Camp Hill. There will be a national monument on Capital Hill. Beside the lake, opposite the National Library, will be the National Art Gallery and the High Court of Australia.

Within the lake, which is crossed by smoothly-designed bridges, you see several islets on one of which is a carillon tower, a present from Britain. You also see the high plume of water that can jet 450 feet, like the one that shoots up in Lake Geneva (PLATE 21). The banks of the lake are too shaven, in parts. Stiffness, not dignity, is created by fleshing with formality the ribs of a good formal plan. Canberra needs to unstiffen its sinews and dance a little along the paths of its design.

Before we leave the lookouts, I had better concede that there are Australians who are unlikely ever to like Canberra, because they see it only in terms of politics. Some there must be who glower down on Lake Burley Griffin and see, rising from its waters, a creature not unlike the Loch Ness Monster except that it has the face of the Prime Minister, is fat with swallowed tax dollars that rightfully belong to the States, and has as many loops to its ugly back as there are letters in CENTRALISM. Perhaps it is as well to have such one-eyed angry Canberra-watchers, for there is always the possibility that the monster exists.

THE LIST that follows of Canberra's "tourist attractions" does not put them in order of their popularity with visitors. (If it did the Australian War Memorial would be No. 1.)

PARLIAMENT HOUSE. If you live in a country, I think you should see its national parliament, in process of government if possible. If parliament is not in session you will at least get a better look at the two Chambers, on a guided tour, after passing through King's Hall, hung with portraits of Royalties and Prime Ministers and paintings of historic parliamentary occasions. The House of Representatives takes its green décor from the House of Commons in England, the Senate Chamber its red from the House of Lords—although it is modelled on the American Senate. The Speaker's Chair in the "Reps" is a copy of the one that was in the Commons, which presented it along with the Mace and replicas of its dispatch boxes. When the Chair in the House of Commons was destroyed by bombing in World War II it was replaced by the Australian Government presenting a copy of its Chair. Displayed in a glass case filled with argon gas to preserve it is the only Magna Carta document outside Britain.

THE NATIONAL LIBRARY. To the scholar and student it is a treasure-house of more than a million books and a million other accessions in print, manuscript, map, painting, photographic, film or sound-recording form (including Cook's journal, the first pamphlet printed in Australia, the log of the *Southern Cross*, and a history of Jesus in Chinese). To the visitor the new (1968) library is primarily a stately building admirably sited beside the lake. White marble clads the peristyle columns of what Walter Bunning of Bunning and Madden, the architects, saw as being "a contemporary derivation in the spirit of classical design . . . a calm quiet building of heroic scale".[3] The foyer is splendidly decorated with tapestries, Australian in motivation, by Mathieu Matégot of France and stained glass windows designed by the Australian artist Leonard French.

THE CAPITAL'S DEVELOPMENT COMMISSION DISPLAY at Regatta Point showing Canberra's proposed development over the next twenty years should perhaps come first: it is a good place to begin your tour. Behind the Regatta Point pavilion you can see how the big COMMONWEALTH PARK project has progressed from stage one with its Rock Valley: in 1970 it was developing the third-stage Marsh Garden with streams and pools, and later there will be an avenue of fountains and scented gardens; but this 80-acre development will take until at least 1975 and perhaps to 1978 to complete.

CANBERRA BOTANIC GARDENS, completed in late 1970, are entirely of *native* plants and trees.

THE INSTITUTE OF ANATOMY. The part of the Institute that is open to the public is really a museum—and not only an anatomical one with the racehorse Phar Lap's fourteen-pound heart in a bottle and the more interesting and well-illustrated anatomy of the platypus. The ethnological side has remarkable collections of Aboriginal artefacts and art, and also good exhibits from Papua–New Guinea.

THE AUSTRALIAN WAR MEMORIAL. Still the top attraction with visitors, 550,000 went through it in 1969, making seven million since it opened in 1941. It is less a memorial to all the Australians killed in the wars they fought for our freedom than it is a museum that depicts war as much less real and savage and tragic than war is. To catalogue a painting, *The Gunners*, as, "This shows the battered crew of an 18-pounder field-gun taking punishment and giving as good as it gets" makes carnage appear to be no more than a somewhat sporty by-product of courage. To euphemistically classify bayonets and Mills bombs as "Technical Exhibits" is to ignore the reality of their being things for gouging human guts and blowing bodies apart. War isn't a battle-scene diorama with a couple of face-down, acceptable dead. Nor is war Will Longstaff's so-popular painting, *The Menin Gate at Midnight*.

THE MINT. The most modern in the world, the Royal Australian Mint has an impressive long building excellently arranged for visitors to see how our coins are made. But don't expect this kind of money-making to be exciting.

THE AUSTRALIAN ACADEMY OF SCIENCE. Not usually open to the public, but what matters is the exterior, the most striking building Canberra has to show. It is wholly a dome, of copper-clad concrete, 150 feet in diameter and arched all round where it rests in a ring of water. It is very "right" for space-age science; and I wish Canberrans would stop being so denigratingly Aussie and forget their funny-name "Eskimo Embassy" for this Sir Roy Grounds structure.

THE AUSTRALIAN-AMERICAN MEMORIAL, commemorating the part the United States played in saving Australia in World War II, is an eagle-topped aluminium pillar.

"ETHOS", one of two sculptures in the admirable CIVIC SQUARE—THEATRE CENTRE, sculptures the spirit of the Canberra community as Tom Bass sees it.

THE AUSTRALIAN NATIONAL UNIVERSITY is a high-level one, its Institute of Advanced Studies consisting of six research schools. Among the advanced students awarded research scholarships and working for Ph.D. degrees are many from abroad. The School of General Studies, a teaching university with five faculties, has about 4,000 students. Architecturally, the A.N.U. has been described as "thirty-seven buildings in search of a university". Visitors (who are asked to provide their own transport) can go into the grounds, but enter the buildings only if they are with the weekday (3 p.m.) conducted tour.

For the rest: GOVERNMENT HOUSE, Yarralumla, can be seen but is, naturally, no more open to inspection than is the Prime Minister's Lodge. CHURCHES one hardly goes to Canberra to see, though coach tours set great store by the one moved stone by stone from Sydney where it used to be a railway mortuary with trains running through what is now its aisle. (Cosmopolitan Canberra—about a quarter of the population is overseas-born—has a mosque, attended by Diplomatic Corps and Asian-student Moslems.) At night one can dine well at the CAROUSEL RESTAURANT atop Red Hill with a fine view of the city-lights pattern and peaceful pools of neonless dark. Canberra's eating-places (the Chantilly restaurant is a good one) are much better than they used to be. Friday's late-shopping night is about the best time for the stroller to savour the city.

CITY SIGHTS TOURS, such as Pioneer and Mini Tours run, take you past the EMBASSIES. Architectural purists led by Robin Boyd (with whom I usually agree) find it a farce of Featurism that many of the embassies and legations should have built in national style—the American Embassy in the Williamsburg manner, the Japanese one Kyoto-modern, the French "a sort of ranch-style Petit Trianon" (Boyd), the South Africans going all Dutch-Colonial, the West Germans being grimly Bauhaus, and the tiger-motif Malaysians wildly Asian. It seems to me pretty innocuous—a kind of Outdoor Museum of Exotic Architecture, very popular with tourists as the exhibits pop up among the Australian "lovely homes" of suburban Forrest-Yarralumla-Red Hill. After all, the Diplomatic Corps of forty-eight countries' representatives is very much part of Canberra, and there is no more reason why they should wear Australian dress architecturally than that the Indian women should not go shopping in saris.

THREE SATELLITE TOWNS to Canberra will be created, one in the south-western suburbs by the building of WODEN TOWN CENTRE. It will cater for 90,000 people when its shopping mall is opened in 1972. The thirty major buildings planned (one will be twenty-two storeys) will take until 1980 to complete. A similar project, still on the drawing-board, would develop at Belconnen, six miles north-west of the main city.

The most interesting outer-Canberra project is what is being called unofficially, SWINGER HILL (not a mod. name, Swinger was a surveyor) in the suburb of Phillip, near Woden Centre. If Ian McKay, the Sydney architect, succeeds—and his plan has great promise—in housing 2,500 people happily in 700 good-looking dwellings on 63 acres (that is 40 dwellers to the acre, with few of them in flats), he should be knighted, at least, for solving the greatest problem of the average married man in metropolitan Australia: how to live in a good environment within an hour of the city when he can't afford the quarter-acre-block house and there is nothing else offering except "home-units" he doesn't want to put his family in. Row houses, stepped houses and courtyard houses, the majority single-storeyed, will make up most of the Swinger Hill "medium-density housing development". Most houses will have courtyard space equivalent to 27 by 30 feet (many people don't want a lot of garden). Fifteen varieties of dwellings are contained in a strongly irregular plan with open space meandering in to a large-ish "Common" beside the community centre. Windows will be placed to maximize privacy. And, of course, the wiring will all be underground. Houses of twelve squares, with double carport or garage, are expected to cost under $15,000, land included. The first houses will be built for the National Capital Development Commission, with the idea that private enterprise will carry the scheme on.

In the Woden region's most prestigious suburb the land that was selling (leasing, rather, for 99 years: you can't buy land outright in Canberra) for up to $8,000 a block was once all owned by the grandfather of Keith Green. "Little did grandfather know when he sold it"—grandfather after whom Mt Green, farther out, is named—said the grandson. He was a small tour-operator, Green's Tours. He drove the bus himself and did the commentary; and my recommendation of his "CANBERRA AND BUSHLAND" TOUR is partly conditional on his still doing so, because, although the itinerary was good in itself, Keith Green was an exceptionally knowledgeable commentator on the Canberra area, where he was born and bred. In fact, he had been commissioned to write the local history of the region round Rock Valley (near Tidbinbilla), which was once his family's property.

His all-day tour of about a hundred miles went to Mount Ainslie lookout [now accessible to big coaches also]; out past the Royal Military College, Duntroon ("It costs the country $40,000 to put a cadet through to graduation as a first-class lieutenant," he said). Then there was the launch-cruise part, starting on the willow-lined Molonglo, with many cormorants, and winding out on to Lake Burley Griffin. Keith Green knew not only the names of such autumn-coloured trees as the pin-oaks and claret ashes that beautified the drive along Mugga Way but, when we were in the countryside, which eucalypts were red-gums and which were candlebarks and yellow-box. He said there were fifty varieties of gums in the A.C.T., which is 900 square miles and still half of it virgin bush.

"This creek began as a sheep track. Erosion slowly did the rest," he said, bolstering a conviction of mine that, in the long run, sheep-raising ravages the country much more than mining does.

After a picnic lunch of sandwiches at the top of picturesque Gibraltar Falls, the tour went on to the Corin Dam (much bigger than the nearer Cotter one) up a high road where ski-runs were being opened up only forty minutes' drive from the city.

We went then to TIDBINBILLA NATURE RESERVE, which is 25 miles from Canberra. This conserves 11,500 acres of upper-valley country and its fauna. Lyrebirds, kangaroos, wallabies, echidnas (spiny-ant-eaters), possums, gliders and wombats are indigenous. Emus had been introduced in the fenced area and were so tame that they stalked visitors for food handouts. There were lots of approachable kangaroos, and koalas had been re-introduced.

This was near TIDBINBILLA DEEP-SPACE TRACKING STATION, one of three in the A.C.T. that track satellites in orbit and space vehicles. This one has a 200-ton aluminium dish antenna and is operated, for the Government, by a company whose name would hardly have been believable twenty years ago, Space Tracking Pty Ltd. "It's tracking now, so we can't go in," Keith Green said. His tour returned to Canberra via pine-forests and the Cotter River Reserve, where the poplars' autumn gold was beautiful to look back upon in the sunset light of a perfect April day.

Overseas tourists could see sheep-station life (shearing, sheep-dogs working) in the vicinity of Canberra. The average tourist (caravanners apart) spends only one night and two days there. It seems to me worth longer than that.

It had about thirty hotels and motels. A 16-storey hotel, Noah's Lakeside, being built on London Circuit, would have (by 1973) convention facilities. Canberra was becoming a centre for conventions.

At first, as visitors, we may not be precisely aware of what makes the Canberra scene, urban or suburban, different. What we are not seeing, as much as what we are, contributes to its being agreeable to the eye. We are not seeing power wires overhead, or telephone poles, only light standards. We are not seeing roadside hoardings, or shop-fronts and building-sides plastered with advertising signs. Or fences to the houses, or TV aerials on their roofs. In short, there is less clutter, a blessed absence of components of the Australian Ugliness.

CANBERRA could be the city from which the rest of the New Australia learns to improve the quality of its life. It could be the exemplar of the good environment. It could be the influence that makes a materially well-off society also a well-civilized one.

Even to say that this *could* be Canberra's role takes a lot of optimism. However, I feel that it could, for two reasons:

(i) The growing change in the Australian attitude towards the once-scorned national capital; the acceptance of, and even admiration for, Canberra by those who have looked at it lately; the recognition that it has become a place of learning as well as legislation, of good-living as well as of government it used to be wholly identified with.

(ii) The change in Canberra-the-community; its becoming the

o

kind of "quality" community that *could* take the role of society-improver.

Canberra is no longer the Australian equivalent of the Washington D.C. that used to be called "Uncle Sam's company town". Today hardly more than half of the Canberra workforce is Public Service engaged in the business of government. And of that half a goodly proportion is now highly-educated and includes many university graduates. As well as being part of government, they are part of what I can only call the cultural Canberra.

"Cultural" is used in its broadest sense, much broader than "to do with the Arts", broader even than any meaning that embraces the "Two Cultures" and, so, takes in the scientists at the C.S.I.R.O. as well as the professors and lecturers in the Humanities at the A.N.U. I don't mean just academically cultural, either. What I do mean comes from the simplest definition of "cultured", which is "improved". So Canberra's cultural community would include not only the teachers at its College of Advanced Education but the students training there to be teachers or technologists or public administrators. It would certainly include the Public Servants who had to do with framing regulations that said, in effect, *No roadside billboards* and *No noisy powerboats on Lake Burley Griffin, only ferries and sailboats* and *Yes, we can have medium-density housing at Swinger Hill.* It would take in the horticulturists responsible for the best of the tree-planting.

Canberra has, of any Australian city, the highest proportion of people who might thus be called "cultured" or "improved". Their quality comes, in part at least, of good education and good environment. Both of these desirables are provided in better measure in Canberra than in any other Australian community.

It could be called the Lucky Capital of what has been called the Lucky Country.[4] The Canberra community not only has Australia's best-standard housing and schooling, but the highest average income. It is also the city with the least pollution and noise. (It has practically no industry, except building.) It has, for a community of its size, easily the highest number of groups or clubs interested in broadly cultural activities; and a particularly low rate of crime and juvenile delinquency. It has a better daily newspaper than is produced in cities of twice its 140,000 population; Newcastle and Wollongong to name two. In short, Canberra is the most civilized place in Australia. And the best definition of "civilized" is simply "enlightened."

Could such light as Canberra has be reflected? Is it reflectable to much bigger Australian cities with problems of industry and slums Canberra doesn't have, and with the abrasive interaction of a less homogeneous citizenry of lower average income and education?

I think that Canberra *could*, although it is not a large community, be effectively active in improving many an aspect of the national condition. Moreover, this privileged community has a *noblesse oblige* responsibility to extend the kind of "improved" society it enjoys. A highly articulate community, it could be much more vocal than it is about social uglinesses existing beyond the A.C.T.

I like to think that from the precincts of the "Ethos" statue in Civic Square will come a spirit motivated by an active and unafraid social conscience that will win great respect for Canberra as the city with the community that did much to distil and distribute a better ethos for the New Australia.

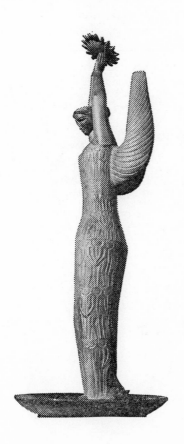

"Ethos"

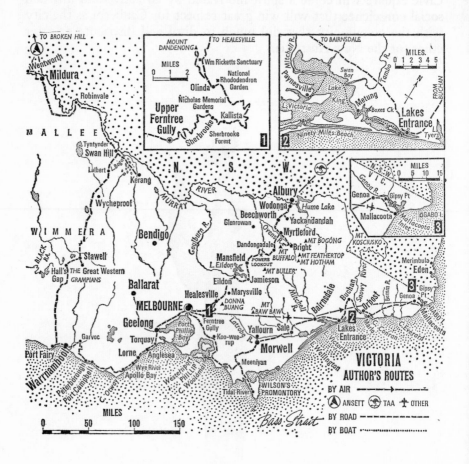

VICTORIA
AUTHOR'S ROUTES

BY AIR

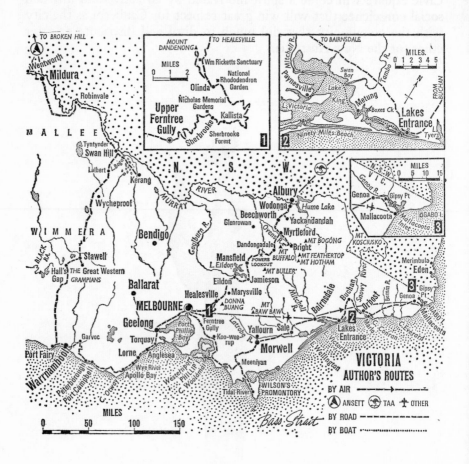 ANSETT   TAA ✈ OTHER

BY ROAD

BY BOAT

VICTORIA

Beechworth doesn't need Ned Kelly

YACKANDANDAH is a place I felt I had to go to, after leaving Albury in New South Wales and proceeding into Victoria to explore it by car for several weeks. Even though it was not on the direct road to Beechworth, which was to be the night stop, who wouldn't want to go to a place named Yackandandah?

Exploring Victoria by car makes good sense. The smallest State of mainland Australia has some twelve thousand miles of first-class roads, lacing more variety of scenery than other-Staters realize Victoria has. I was not driving the car. Lindsay Howe was. Lindsay Howe was a quiet-mannered young man who was an excellent driver and also very tall—a slim six-feet-five-and-a-half. He was the photographer of the Victorian Tourist Ministry.

We left Albury after lunch in a Ford Cortina from Avis Rent-a-Car and, twenty miles down, turned off to Yackandandah. The main street was having a sleep under its oaks and elms. The bar of a one-storey hotel, with *Est. 1859* on its sign, had one customer. He looked Italian and I learnt that he was Vittorio Reghetti, from Verona. When invited to finish his beer and join me in one (Lindsay drank squash) the woman behind the bar said, "If you buy Victor a drink, he's always likely to eat the glass."

I said I'd pay for the glass. Vittorio said, "You want me to eat it, I will." I said I didn't *want* him to eat it. He said he felt like eating a glass and added, "Unless I have a few beers I can't eat it." I asked how long he had been eating glass and he said since he was four years old, and he could also chew up razor blades. He opened his mouth and showed gold-capped teeth: chewing glass had broken them. I asked why he didn't suffer from lacerated throat and insides. Vittorio said, "Is all right", which didn't explain much.

Anyway, when he had finished his beer he bit a hunk out of the side of the glass, and another and another, and crunched the lot up. Glass-chewing makes a horrible noise. He swallowed the fragments, washing them down with another beer. I do not understand why Vittorio Reghetti is not dead but have no doubt that he is alive and well and tobacco-farming at Myrtleford, forty miles down the road

from Yackandandah. His tobacco, he said, would make him about
$6,000 that year. "Best year since I come to Australia", which was
in 1952.

VICTORIA has, as they say, a lot going for it, although it is the
smallest mainland State, only three per cent of the continent's area.
England and Scotland would fit comfortably into Victoria, as would
Kansas; but thirty-four Victorias would fit in the map of Australia,
nearly four of them into New South Wales. Yet Victoria has been
producing one-third of Australia's wealth. From the "small giant"
tucked down in the continent's south-east corner comes a fifth of
Australia's wool and wheat, nearly a third of its red meat and more
than a third of its fruit, half its butter and root vegetables. From its
factories come a third of all Australian manufactures, including more
than half the textiles and nearly half the clothing. And Victoria has, in
Bass Strait, easily the biggest fields of the new bonanza—oil.

Of every hundred Australians twenty-eight live in Victoria: twice
as many as live in a Queensland, which is seven and a half times
larger. Next to New South Wales (4½ million), Victoria (3½ million)
is the second most populous State. Why? Victoria's topography
creating a better spread of rivers and rainfall and good soil does not
entirely account for this population position. Those factors were
there, but people weren't in any great numbers until after something
happened—in California.

To go to the Californian gold rush that started in 1848 thousands
of men left Melbourne in what was still the Port Phillip District of
New South Wales. Victoria did not become a separate colony until
1851, the year that Edward Hargraves, who had returned from
California, found the gold that started the rush to New South Wales.
More men left the new colony. Melbourne was becoming denuded.
Desperately, its mayor set up a committee that offered a reward for
gold discovery in Victoria. This was quickly taken, discoveries multiplied, and the population rush-off became a rush-in, of optimists
bound for such goldfields as Ballarat and Bendigo—including 20,000
who came in from California. Where there had been 76,000 people
when the fifties began there were, ten years later, over half a million.

In the "fabulous fifties" Victorian goldfields produced one-third of
all the gold produced in the world. This enriched the colony by
more than £100 million. When the gold began to give out, as it soon
did, Victoria had the money to start industries to employ its thousands of workless gold-miners. Many of the luckier ones bought land
and stayed to grow wheat or wool. Business surged ahead. Melbourne
became a bigger city than Sydney in 1860, and stayed bigger until
after the turn of the century.

BEECHWORTH, which we soon came to, was one of the gold towns that founded Victoria's prosperity. And what a town it was—and, for that matter, is. The fine old stone and iron-laced buildings in its quiet main street are only some of twenty-seven worthy structures classified by the National Trust, and, mostly, well preserved.

Of Australian historic gold-mining towns (Victoria's Ballarat and Bendigo are cities), Beechworth retains a fabric of its colourful past that makes what Hill End (N.S.W.) has seem only a fragment.

"Colourful" is the unavoidable word for Beechworth's past. The best man to tell about it was Roy C. Harvey, the dedicated curator of the Burke Museum, after Robert O'Hara Burke, who was captain of police here in 1856, four years after Beechworth began. The Burke of Burke and Wills, the ill-fated explorers, was never considered by his Beechworth troopers to be a good bushman.

"The Golden Horseshoes story is true in every particular," Roy Harvey said, shaking his head over a guide book's suggestion that there may have been only gold paint on the shoes of the horse Daniel Cameron rode through Beechworth on the day in 1855 when he was elected to the Victorian Parliament. He rode at the head of a procession of gold-diggers called "Monkeys", who affected black woollen trousers, Crimean shirts with bright neckerchiefs, Wellington boots and silk sashes. "Why, we even know where the gold for the shoes came from —'Big' Johnson's claim, the Woolshed, richest on the field. He was the 'Monkeys'' leader and 'shouted' three hundred bottles of champagne when their candidate won. The rival crowd were called 'Punchers' and wore moleskins. All carried revolvers in their belts, and some diggers in the procession had banners embellished with devices of solid gold."

He went on: "And that's wrong, saying that in fourteen years Beechworth produced only three million ounces of gold!" I blinked at the *only*. "That was just the official return. With what was sold privately, we've accounted for 4,121,918 ounces in the first ten years. That's over three tons of gold."

Beechworth remained so rich that in 1873 there is record of a procession beside which the marches of the "Monkeys" and "Punchers" pale. The processional order is given as: Company of the Field of the Cloth of Gold (mounted); Heralds (mounted); carriages carrying those dressed as Kings, Ambassadors, Peers of the Realm, etc.; German Brass Band, Pages, Standard-Bearers; German Knights (mounted) who were German immigrants in costumes and armour specially sent out by the Crown Prince of Prussia. Then Yeomen of the Guard, more Emperors, Dukes, etc.; Hibernians with a £70 banner; Oddfellows, Rechabites, Kentucky Minstrels, Jacks-in-Green, and at the end—the Chinese, surpassing all others in splendour and cost, 250 Celestials, every one in brilliantly coloured silks (two of the costumes specially imported from China cost £800).

At night the Chinese staged what reads like a fireworks display unparalleled in Australia "with several huge and marvellously illuminated fish that floated across the sky with tails and fins flapping".

Some of the Chinese regalia is preserved in the museum, together with portions of the carved joss house—which Roy Harvey found built into a farmer's sheep pen, and restored and re-painted. He had added a thousand exhibits in the past year to the remarkable (but getting overcrowded) museum that displayed everything from an excellent collection of aboriginal weapons to theatre posters of opera and the American dwarf "General Tom Thumb" appearing in the local theatre in 1858, to a bronze fountain that at banquets played not water but eau-de-cologne ("*The Fountain plays Every Day at the* LONDON TAVERN, *the Coolest House in Beechworth*")—to a replica of Ned Kelly's suit of armour, "correct to the last bolt and bullet dent".

Made of ploughshare steel and weighing ninety-five pounds, Kelly's armour consisted of an eye-slitted helmet like a nailcan over the head, a torso encasement and, suspended from the front of that, a curved plate that covered the groin but didn't reach to the knees. It was cumbrous, and the wearer could barely use a revolver, much less a rifle—and he could still be shot in the legs, as Ned Kelly was at Glenrowan, where he was captured and his career ended in 1880.

[Australians know who, if not what, Ned Kelly was. For the overseas reader: Edward Kelly (born 1855, hanged 1880) was the son of an Irish convict transported to Tasmania who, when emancipated, took up a small farm selection north of Melbourne. His mother was of another Irish family, Quinns, some of whose male members had criminal records. "Red" Kelly died when Ned was eleven, and he had to leave school and help alleviate the poverty of a family with seven other children. Ellen Kelly moved her brood to near Glenrowan. When he was sixteen Ned already had a criminal record for violence and (probably unjustly) for horse stealing, though he became an arrant horse-thief later, with his step-father: his mother remarried, to a Californian. He is always referred to as a "bushranger" (a bail-up man operating from a hideout in the bush) but does not typify the Australian outlaw of that kind. The Kelly Gang he led included (with their ages when outlawed and Ned was 23) his brother Dan Kelly, 17; Steve Hart, 18; Joe Byrne, 21. Ned Kelly shot and killed three police, and Byrne murdered a police informer. They robbed two banks and, after capturing the police there, took over the N.S.W. town of Jerilderie. Only Ned survived a police siege at Glenrowan Hotel in 1880. Mainly, it was his grotesque armour that made him loom larger-than-life in Australian legend. He is a mythic figure in high-level Australian painting (Sidney Nolan) and literature (Douglas Stewart's verse-play), and has been made dramatically courageous in popular books and films. "Mind you die like a Kelly," his mother said when he went to the trial that could only end in his execution, when he was twenty-six. "Game as Ned Kelly" has gone into the Australian language as a term signifying bravery.]

In token of the thousands of Chinese who were on the goldfield, Beechworth's cemetery has not only about 1,500 of their graves but remarkable structures called the "Chinese Burning Towers". The name is misleading: Chinese were never cremationists. The twin hexagonal peak-topped towers, with oval openings low down, were used for roasting pigs for the funerary meal and paper prayers were burnt on the altar they flank.

On the red-berried hedge beside the Chinese graves, the grey cockatoos, called gang-gangs, found only in south-eastern Australia, feasted and shrieked. The males have scarlet crests.

We went then to the Powder Magazine, a walled granite building that gets an "A" National Trust classification and has been very well restored. Before it was built, two miles out of town, in 1859, the miners kept their blasting powder in their huts.

An elaborate Victorian-Italianate façade still stands of the Ovens Goldfields Hospital, the first (1856) hospital between Melbourne and Goulburn in New South Wales, and for years the only one. It, too, is of granite, as are the main-street buildings; the local granite is light-coloured, almost "warm". The Supreme Court, Gold Registrar's and Gold Warden's offices and Sub-Treasury form one of the best groups of old buildings in Victoria.

The iron-laced, veranda-posted Commercial Hotel proved a good place to stay. Its old coaching stables were being turned into a carriage museum.

Beechworth clearly has a big tourist future, and an already considerable tourist present: the Burke Museum had had 30,000 visitors that year and 2,000 lapidaries had convened there at Easter and gone gem-rock-gold hunting. Autumn, when I was there and the introduced poplars and claret ashes were coloured, was probably Beechworth's best time; though, being nearly 2,000 feet up, it is not hot in summer. It won a money prize as Victoria's "Ideal Town" in 1928 (and again in 1932) and used the money to begin to form Lake Sambell, which has transformed a mining-ravaged area.

In short, Beechworth has attractions enough without promoting itself as "The Heart of the Kelly Country"—which it wasn't. The Kellys never lived in the Ovens River country but on the other side of the King River about ten miles from Glenrowan, which is forty miles from Beechworth.

Beechworth's only connection with Ned Kelly is that one of his gang, Joe Byrne, came from there; the police informer Aaron Sherritt whom Byrne murdered lived there; and Ned Kelly was twice in Beechworth jail. He was in Benalla's jail when only fourteen, charged with beating a Chinese named Ah Fook and taking ten-shillings from him: case dismissed, on the evidence of young Kelly's associates. He was again in Benalla jail at fifteen, charged with being an accomplice of an egocentric but not bloody-minded bushranger named Harry Power, whose horse-holding apprentice Ned undoubtedly was; but this case was also dismissed for lack of evidence. On a third charge, when he was still fifteen, he was not so lucky. Ned got three months for "indecency": he had carried to a hawker's wife, Mrs McCormack, a packet of calf's testicles (the McCormacks had no children) with a note the court found to be obscene (Kelly didn't write it). On a charge of assaulting the hawker he was fined £10 the Kellys couldn't raise, in default three months jail, and bound over to keep the peace. At sixteen he was sentenced to three years in Pentridge jail, Melbourne, for receiving a stolen horse. The sentence was savage, and it would appear that Kelly did not know the horse was stolen.

He emerged from jail to find his own horses stolen and his mother remarried to George King from California, who later deserted her. Ned worked honestly as a timber-cutter for three years before joining King as a horse-stealer. This fact does not square with the usual story that Kelly was so embittered and socially antagonized by his unjust jailing that he couldn't go straight. Nor, even if it be conceded that one or two police false-witnessed against him, does his subsequent bloody-mindedness towards all policemen and his hatred of all land-holders better off than "the poor", and his predatory attitude to their property, become excusable—much less admirable. Nor is it true to say, as is said in Beechworth and Glenrowan, "Everybody around here was on Ned's side." Some small-holders were awed by the gang and frightened not to assist it, particularly after the killing of the informer Aaron Sherritt. But no less than twenty-six land-holders had banded together and offered reward for the capture of the horse-stealers; and, after the killing of the police near Mansfield, not only troopers, but townsmen with them, came out to risk gun-battle in hunting the Kelly Gang down.

A PIECE of national furniture the New Australia should get rid of is the pedestal that has for so long elevated the image of Ned Kelly as a folk hero.

He was not just an underprivileged, high-spirited young man driven to desperadoism by social and legal injustice and police persecution. He was not at all a chivalrous bushranger in the Dick Turpin romanticized-highwayman tradition. The Kelly Gang had hide-outs in the bush but they were never highwaymen, never stuck up a single stagecoach. Ned, whose police record as a youth shows him to have been less than a Robin Hoodlum, was mainly a horse-thief: he admitted stealing two hundred horses and changing their brands (a cruel business that was sometimes done by first burning off the old brand with the bottom of a red-hot frying pan). Leading a gang of flash young larrikins, he graduated to bank robberies and holding up a sheep station and, with much exhibitionism, the New South Wales town of Jerilderie, where one of the two banks was. But the crimes he was hanged for, when he was twenty-six, brand Kelly as not just a bandit but a gangster; and Byrne's cold-blooded killing of Sherritt without a word had no fair-go Australianism to it: it was Mafia-type murder.

Charged with the murder of three policemen—one (Lonigan) he recognized as a personal enemy only after shooting him dead; Sergeant Kennedy, who left five young children; and Trooper Scanlon he had never seen before—Kelly said that he shot in self-defence, as three of the four police tried to shoot him after they had been called upon to surrender and disarm. (Although he carried a rifle and a revolver, in his writing[1] Kelly actually complained about the police having guns: they were "only supposed to carry one revolver and 6 cartridges in the revolver". Moreover, the shotgun he took from the police after he shot Lonigan, his enemy, he wrote that he "loaded with bullets instead of shot".

Hindsightedly, it was foolish of the police, when gun-covered by the gang, to fight. It was also extremely brave of them: gamer than anything Ned Kelly is recorded as doing. Certainly gamer than his walk out in his armour at Glenrowan, after he had made his Confession to a priest who went into the besieged hotel. He did not then, as is popularly believed, do gun-blazing battle: he hid and reconnoitred for four hours before he fired a few shots, with difficulty because he had been wounded in the arm and hand while in the hotel. Brought down and captured, he was asked by the police to send in a message to Dan Kelly and Steve Hart (Joe Byrne was already dead) telling them to surrender. He is said to have replied: "They will not mind what I say. The heart's gone out of them. They won't come out fighting like men . . . they're only boys. . . ."[2] (The two, apparently, shot themselves, or each other.)

The Glenrowan stationmaster was game when he refused to stop the special train the gang knew the fourth killing (Sherritt's) would bring, full of police. Kelly compelled workmen to tear up part of the track, to derail the train, on which there were also newspaper reporters. He is quoted as saying, in a book by an admirer,[3] "I did not give a bugger who was in it; but I knew on Sunday morning there would be no usual passengers. If I were right again, I would go to the police barracks and shoot every one of the bloody traps and not give one a chance."

We know Ned Kelly was violent, but when and where was he ever valiant? Was he not, basically and obsessedly, vicious?

The most damning evidence of his vicious character was never given in court. It was written by the man himself. He wrote a screed of 8,300 words and, when the gang held up Jerilderie, he sought to get it published in the local paper, but the editor could not be found. This has become known as the *Jerilderie Letter*. It attempts to justify his career, but is quite unconvincing because it is such a raving, self-pitying, bragging, fanatically-Irish, naïve and violent document. It is not only packed with hate for "a parcel of big, ugly, fat-necked, wombat-headed, big-bellied, magpie-legged, splay-footed sons of Irish Bailiffs or english landlords which is better known as officers of Justice or Victorian Police". It contains shocking intimations of savagery, and even sadism. A few extracts will suffice. (I have introduced punctuation to clarify meaning, but the words are verbatim.)[4]

Police informers could expect to be *pegged on an anthill with their bellies opened. Their fat taken out, and rendered and poured down their throats boiling, will be cool to what pleasure I will give them and any person aiding or harbouring or assisting the police in any way.*

Of police "persecution" of his mother, whose house was clearly a rendezvous for horse-thieves and allegedly a sly-groggery: *They knew well I was not there, or I would have scattered their blood and brains like rain. I would manure the Eleven Mile with their bloated carcasses. . . .* He finishes the sentence with: *. . . and yet, remember, there is not one drop of murderous blood in my veins.*

Of his fight with Trooper Hall who sought to arrest him for assaulting the hawker McCormack: *I straddled him and rooted both spurs into his thighs.*

Again, of public assistance to the police: *If I hear any more of it, I will not exactly show them what cold blooded murder is, but wholesale and retail slaughter, something different to shooting three troopers in self defence and robbing a bank.*

And the paranoic final passages: *I give fair warning, to all those who have reason to fear me, to sell out and give £10 out of every hundred to the widow and orphan fund, and do not attempt to reside in Victoria. . . . Neglect this and abide by the consequences. . . . I am a widow's son outlawed, and my orders must be obeyed.* (Kelly's underlining.)

On these, his own statements, I think the case for the prosecution of the Ned Kelly Myth could rest.

Of Bright, Skiing, and Kangaroos

A FLASHING, TROUTY STREAM, the Ovens River comes in to meet the highway that brings us to Myrtleford. The rich valley grows more tobacco and hops than any other in Victoria and boasts the biggest grove of walnuts. We can see the tobacco leaves drying, wrinkled and bright-brown, through the ends of the high grey corrugated-iron driers. One of these could belong to Vittorio the glass-chewer met at Yackandandah.

At the end of the valley and to the south, Mount Buffalo towers a granite head that winter will soon be whitening with snow. We enter the shire of Bright, and then the road slips through the ranges—past apple-orchard slopes, more hopfields and tobacco and dark pine forests—and into the town.

It is a town you wish its namesake, the great English reformer and pacifist John Bright, could have seen. Now, with the autumn sunlight minting its gold in the poplars and planes and chestnuts, so peacefully; not in his own time. The man who said "Force is no remedy" would have been horrified at what happened in the Buckland Valley in 1857, when the white miners drove the Chinese brutally from the gold-diggings and burned their huts and shops.

On this day of May it was so still in Bright that yellowed leaves could be heard settling on the pile that had accumulated on the roof and bonnet of a Holden parked under an English elm.

Autumn was Bright's beautiful season and, in the early morning, there were such delights for the colour photographer as the view of the mountain-cupped town from a lookout (PLATE 22) and children going along a high path against the light that made a golden canopy of an avenue of elms, the road soft with their fallen leaves.

"We're getting a hundred thousand visitors a year," said Mrs A. Delaney, who was very active touristically.

MOUNT BUFFALO is no more than thirty miles from Bright, right to The Horn (5,645 feet). It is not only one of the Victorian winter skiing resorts—which add up to a bigger area of snow than Switzerland has (PLATE 15). Buffalo is a national park that draws tourists in other seasons—and the terrain is quite different to that of Kosciusko in New South Wales.

Great boulders of brown granite pile one upon the other in mounds, and there is much more forest. In the striking view The Horn commands, the tree-clad mountains spread darkly towards the barer heights of Feathertop (6,306 ft) and Hotham. (Victoria's highest mountain is Mount Bogong, 6,508.) In the smooth boulders and monoliths of granite, you feel the ancientness of the Australian land.

Eight miles back from The Horn, past still Lake Catani where there is skating in winter and Tatra Inn that looked to have good ski slopes, is the Mount Buffalo Chalet. Just down the path from it I saw a lyrebird, and heard another in the gully below.

Snow sports in Australia are older than Europeans or Americans may easily credit. "By 1862 skiing was well established at Kiandra [N.S.W.] with races for all, including the Chinese," says the *Australian Encyclopaedia*; whereas the *Britannica* has skiing beginning as a competitive sport in Norway only about that time and in California not until 1870. There was even some tourist skiing near Mount Hotham in 1863. But it did not become widely popular until after World War II. I was at Hotham in the thirties: you climbed up the range on horseback from pretty Harrietville and skied in as best you could across the Hotham Heights to the one chalet. Now you go by one of two roads to three chalets and twenty ski-lodges; and, instead of herringboning up a hill for twenty muscle-aching minutes to run down in two, you take a chair-lift or a T-bar. However, the most popular Victorian snow resorts are not up at six thousand feet on the "roof of Australia"—it is still rather an area for the expert (not that I was ever one)—but at Mount Buller where the slopes are easier, and Falls Creek with runs that are more wind-protected and very well equipped with ski-lifts. Nearer Melbourne there is skiing at Mount Baw Baw, Lake Mountain and, after a heavy snowfall, at Mount Donna Buang, a mere sixty miles from the capital.

LEAVING BRIGHT, we went back through Myrtleford, where I bought almonds and chestnuts to munch, and Lindsay Howe fresh-picked persimmons and carrots to take home, in a shop that also sold Italian newspapers. We drove south via man-made Lake Buffalo. The surrounding hills and the branches of drowned trees were double-imaged in the water as in a mirror (PLATE 22).

Then down through green Dandongadale (how does a place get a name like that?) and (repeat the question) Gentle Annie's Gap, and out to Power's Lookout. The bushranger Harry Power, the young Ned Kelly's mentor, could have seen so much country and what was moving on its string of road from this vantage point with an eagle-beak rock pointing at a fine panorama. In the white trunk of a foreground gum-tree someone had cut large initials.

The afternoon's highlight was the view from a lookout near Jamieson of Lake Eildon (pron. Eeldon). *Part* of the lake, rather, for the drowned valleys that make Victoria's biggest man-made waterway run off in all directions and their blue gets lost to the eye behind dark-forested mountains. It is three and a half times as big as Sydney Harbour, and its 320 miles of shoreline outline a shape so fantastically irregular on a large-scale map that, trying to describe it, I came up with "like a splattered Don Quixote being thrown into the air from the back of a thin splattered dragon". Its configuration made it ideal for boating: there were so many secluded arms you could *putt-putt* into and explore. It also meant that the lake poked its way into a large tract of country and was accessible to the inlanders at a number of points, not just from the holiday resort town of Eildon, where the main boat-harbour was and you could hire launches and even drive-yourself houseboats. The lake is stocked with brown and rainbow trout, of which the hatchery at Snobs Creek breeds two million fingerlings a year; and there is no closed season.

Victoria is the only mainland State where you are never far from water. This is not only because it is relatively small and its main boundaries are a thousand miles of sea coast in the south and the continent's major river, the Murray, in the north. It also has, compared to the other States, many more lakes, natural ones as well as man-made.

Victoria also has very fine forests. The eucalypt called mountain ash (*E. regnans*, meaning "reigning") is truly a monarch among trees. Indeed, it is the tallest hardwood tree in the world, taller than the famous karri of Western Australia, though the karri is greater in girth. Mountain ash grow up straight as poles and, being high-branchers with not much canopy, fairly close together. Authenticated measurements of Victorian trees showed one of 375 feet, another of 326 (as high as the C.R.A. building in Collins Street, Melbourne). They, alas, are long since destroyed and the highest known is one of just over three hundred feet in a "sample acre" of mountain ash preserved near Marysville.

However, I was to see many mountain ashes reigning on the foot-hills when I toured up from Melbourne to the Dandenong Ranges and Healesville. The Dandenongs one can regard as in the environs of Melbourne, its back garden-wall. Healesville, though, forty miles off and more northerly, is hardly to do with Melbourne. We ran through it that night and I returned to it later; but I think it should come in now.

HEALESVILLE has become so synonymous with the fauna park, a few miles out of this smallish (pop. 3,500) resort town in the lower mountains, that the reserve is often referred to as the Healesville sanctuary instead of the Sir Colin Mackenzie Sanctuary.

The town was named for a Victorian premier of last century, the sanctuary for a great Australian anatomist. He was one of the "menders of the maimed" after an infantile paralysis epidemic before he became interested in the anatomy of Australian fauna.

When I went to the 78-acre sanctuary that attracts about 350,000 people a year I had not read the comments of the American surveyors of our tourism in the Harris-Kerr-Forster report, where they say, "We were disturbed by the aesthetics of the sanctuary." I began to be disturbed at the front gates. These were hung with such a plethora of ill-lettered signs that it is a wonder this ugly entrance, complete with strands of barbed wire, didn't get its picture in such books as *Australian Outrage*[1] or *Look Here!*[2]

Inside, the tourist literature about birds and animals being kept "in their natural surroundings" became a bad joke as one passed wire enclosure after wire enclosure (some donated by commercial firms, who got their names writ large). A wombat was trying to clamber up the sides of a grim concrete pen. The lyrebirds' place was much better, with rustic wood instead of harsh grey wire.

Surely the prosperous State of Victoria can afford to exhibit Australia's unique fauna—in a sanctuary that gets hundreds of thousands of visitors a year, at fifty-cents admission for adults—on a non-commercial, plug-free basis. But it is the "Olympic Tires Platypus Exhibit" you see, and the "Olympic Tires Koala Exhibit". The wading and swimming birds come to you by the financial courtesy of General Motors-Holden and you picnic in the "Swallow and Ariel Picnic Area". No wonder the American tourism-survey team wrote that it felt "more effort could be given to making the whole excursion to Healesville a better experience".

In zoo-like cages, pens and ponds, all kinds of other Australian birds and animals are here, from kookaburras to goannas, tiger cats to Tasmanian devils, which we can consider in Tasmania, from cockatoos to kangaroos, which let us consider now.

KANGAROOS are the same kind of animals as wallabies, which are smaller, and wallaroos, which are mountain- or rock-kangaroos and mid-sized: the roan-coloured wallaroo is called a euro. The tree-kangaroo (mentioned in a North Queensland chapter) is different, almost like a little bear. The family includes hare-wallabies and rat-kangaroos, one species of which is the potoroo: these are rare, but there are more in Victoria than anywhere else. They are all *macropods*, meaning "long-footed".

The smallest of the rat-kangaroos is only about a foot long plus a six-inch tail, and the director of Taronga Park zoo in Sydney has said he would give "part of his soul" to have a Musky Rat-Kangaroo which lives in the Atherton Tableland of Queensland—if it still lives and has not been added to the six species of kangaroos that Australians have, so far, made extinct. And at least another six are in danger of becoming so.

Largest of the kangaroos is the Great Grey or Forester. An exceptional "boomer" (old male) could stand seven feet high and weigh two hundred pounds. Yet when born this animal would have been little more than an inch long. It would have made its way (perhaps with assistance from the mother's lips) up into the pouch, and there attached itself limpet-like to one of the four teats kangaroos have, although multiple births of more than twins are very rare.

The most widespread of the larger kangaroos is (or was before the slaughter) the Red Kangaroo of the inland plains (PLATE 20). Only the male is reddish: his doe is a smoky-blue and called the Blue Flyer. One of these graceful animals, when pursued by a horseman across a dusty plain where the tracks were checked afterwards, made ten leaps of 37 feet, then cleared an eight-foot fence with a leap of 42 feet. But kangaroos will not ordinarily jump a fence more than five feet high. Some are able to travel, when pressed, at thirty miles an hour. Their tails are balancers and, at speed, never touch the ground. The original American-written script of the Fox film *Kangaroo* (on which I worked as Australian script adviser) had "thumping thousands" of kangaroos eight feet high attacking a cattle station and killing several of its defenders. Kangaroos are not belligerent, though a hunted one, cornered, will stand on its tail and rip with the long fourth claw on its hind feet (the rest of its toenails don't amount to much). Or, taking refuge in a creek, it will grasp an attacking dog and hold it underwater to drown. But kangaroos are not hunted by horsemen and dogs any more.

The jeep-type vehicle that goes out to get night-feeding kangaroos has spotlights (illegal in Queensland, but used there) and telescopic-sighted rifles on padded gun-rests. The light-blinded kangaroo has no chance—not even of instant death. For the skin market, a shot in the hip marks the hide less than a chest shot. When the shooting is over it is finished off. Does are good value: they may have a joey in the pouch. Two skins are better than one, even if the second is only small. And there is that much more meat if the shooters are towing, as they usually are, a mobile freezer. The business not only disgusts me. It disgusted an American woman game hunter who wrote about it in *Sports Illustrated* a few years ago. Virginia Kraft's report was reprinted in *Life* under the heading *Kangaroo, Goodby*, and quite a few million Americans and others must have read (even the Spaniards read it under *Adios, Canguru*) the writer's verdict that Australia, "a nation so dedicated to the sporting life, is also so singularly amoral about its wildlife".

The big slaughter began about 1959, in New South Wales. In that

P

year the president of the N.S.W. Graziers' Association (Mr T. M. Scott) said there were two million kangaroos in the State's western division and each was eating as much as two sheep; therefore kangaroos were costing the State the wool from an extra four million sheep, worth £6.3 million. Having shorn his four million hypothetical sheep, Mr Scott then killed them for mutton worth £8 million; and he somehow came up with the figure of £150 million as what kangaroos had cost *Australia* in the fourteen years since World War II. This statistical exercise (which left out of account so many factors, from rainfall to rabbits to prices) was taken quite seriously. Since then C.S.I.R.O. scientists have established that (*a*) a kangaroo eats only about as much as one sheep, not two, and (*b*) much of its food is herbage that sheep don't like, and only to some extent and some of the time are kangaroos in direct competition with sheep for food.

This is not to say there weren't sheep-raising areas where the number of kangaroos had increased to such pest proportions that they menaced the sheep-raiser's livelihood by semi-starving his sheep, particularly in times of drought, and drinking the sheep's water in shrinking dams, when the creeks they normally drank at were dry; and that kangaroos did not have to be shot to save the sheep and to aid the economy. But that is not the reason why they have been slaughtered in millions, in good years and bad.

It was found in 1958 that there was a good market abroad for kangaroo meat, as well as for kangaroo skins. West Germany took nearly half a million pounds of it in 1960 and the market has since extended to Britain, Hong Kong, Malaysia and other countries. Kangaroo meat by 1965 was a million-dollars-a-year business, ahead of skins, for export alone. Domestically, there was such demand that it was estimated at the end of 1969 that pet cats and dogs in Sydney alone were eating a hundred tons, equivalent to nearly 10,000 kangaroos, a week, mainly in the form of canned pet-foods.

Some of the meat sold abroad is for human consumption, and it is dubious that this should be allowed. Shooters had to work more cleanly after the Germans rejected much of the meat sent them, but a prominent Australian zoologist[3] wrote in 1965: "There is still grave risk of *Salmonella* infection [a form of botulism, "sausage poisoning"] to any person who admits kangaroo meat into the kitchen."

The Commonwealth Government refused even to set a limit to the kangaroo meat traffic. At the same time it maintained the fiction that Australia regards the animal in its national coat-of-arms as "protected", by allowing so few live kangaroos to be exported to zoos abroad that Sydney's zoo had in 1969 orders that it would take six to eight years to fill. But the same zoos could buy any quantity of dead kangaroo to feed their lions.

As of mid-1970, Victoria and New South Wales "protect", by law if not by deed, all kangaroos; but permission is given to landholders to destroy them if they are shown to be pests. South Australia and Tasmania have extended open seasons for shooting all but two kangaroo species. Western Australia declares red and grey kangaroos to be vermin in certain areas of the State. Queensland allows unlimited shooting of nearly all the larger macropods by anyone possessing a shooting permit. In any State, simply asking for a shooting permit usually gets one if the applicant is a landholder.

Drought having helped shooters decimate the New South Wales kangaroo population in the years 1959-66 (C.S.I.R.O. Division of Wildlife Research figures showed kangaroo density dropping in three years from 8.6 to 2.7 to the square mile in Murrumbidgee areas), the professional shooters moved into Queensland and gave the Great Greys what they had been giving the Reds and Blue-Flyers.

SOME C.S.I.R.O. SCIENTISTS of the Wildlife Research Division appear to believe that kangaroos can best be preserved by "farming" them, i.e., letting them graze with sheep and cattle as stock, and then killing (sorry, harvesting) them for their high-protein meat and their valuable hides.[4] The same proposal has come from other quarters.

Looked at with one half-closed eye, the scheme has economic merit. Fencing might be something of a problem, but not necessarily so: you could stock with joeys, who could be hamstrung, or given neat little weights on their legs. Maybe tail-docking would help. And, of course, to raise a really good breed of heavy meat-yielder, only the best buck joeys could be left uncastrated. Wild (or "brumby") kangaroos would need to be shot out to prevent them leaping in and getting at the doe stock.

I cannot quite see why I regard this whole idea as so revolting when it has obvious advantages. We would always have lots of kangaroos to show tourists who instead of being taken to a zoo or fauna park could be shown over a kangaroo farm—although not, perhaps, at "harvesting" time.

Moreover—and this would really solve what could be a problem— if the tourists who buy hundreds of thousands of those cute toy koala bears found out that these were made (as they are) from the fur of dead kangaroos, it wouldn't matter. They would not feel badly about buying them, and would go on buying them, because they would know that the kangaroos had to die anyway.

All the pussycats could have their kangaroo pet-meat. And anyone could wear a kangaroo-skin coat with no more conscience than is now felt about wearing cow-skin shoes. Because the only way that Australia could preserve its unique, emblem animal that used to bound across its plains was to treat it like sheep and cattle and raise it to kill it.

Melbourne in its Own Write

A GOOD MELBOURNE WRITER can write of Melbourne so that the city is endowed with a charismatic quality, a kind of *mana*. Nobody else can do this: you have to live there. Unless it is known that the writer lives in Melbourne the *mana* cannot generate. Nor can it if the writer writes only about Melbourne. It has to be a tale of two cities, Melbourne and Sydney.

Fascinating as this is as a literary process in articles and book chapters by Melbourne writers, it might be even more effective if done as a TV documentary.

The Melburnian commentator begins by showing you Sydney, and telling you how beautiful its Harbour is, how superb its beaches, how zesty its spirit. Then he shows you aspects of Melbourne, and damns them. He derides unmercifully its inferior weather, its sober-sidedness on the one hand, its football mania on the other. He warns you that Melbourne's trams are terrible and hopes you never have to take, either, a train from Flinders Street Station because, "Just look at that building—isn't it hideous!"

The viewers, surprised and titivated by the *Praise Sydney* part, find their mystification at the *Damn Melbourne* sequences turning towards downright pity for the poor devil who says he lives there. But they *can't* pity him: there is nothing at all "poor devil" about his stance or speech; he looks about as pitiable as a man who owns a couple of Rembrandts, and as contented as a cat with a saucer of warmed cream. And, just before the break for the commercial, Man of Melbourne says quietly, with an enigmatic smile, "This is where I *prefer* to live. . . ."

The effect is potent, stunning. The audience can draw only one conclusion. Melbourne must have merit indeed, a worth that weighs so much in the mind of this clearly intelligent man that the city's lack of Sydney's natural beauty and zest is more than counter-balanced; Melbourne must have attractions so major that the things he went on about, the lousy weather and all that, are minor consider-ations of no real countervailing consequence.

The audience can hardly wait for the commercial to be over and Man of Melbourne to come back on screen and tell them about Mel-bourne's great merits and attractions. The commercial is, of course, not about Melbourne. Melbourne has been established as needing none. At this point, if any city needs a commercial it is Sydney. Sydney has begun to take on the image of a snazzy two-tone sports car with a bikini-girl getting in, standing beside a dove-grey Rolls-Royce Phantom, of which the salesman has said that one of the demisters isn't working perfectly and has pointed out a few tiny scratches on a hub-cap.

This sounds like cleverly calculated literary trickery creating an illusion that upgrades Melbourne and downgrades Sydney. I don't think it is. When Robin Boyd, the good Melbourne architect who is also a good writer, writes under the heading *Why I Love Melbourne*,[1] it comes through bell-clear that he *does* love Melbourne. And there are other Melbourne writers whose writings show an affection for the place that is undeniable, and who, I quite believe, would rather live there than in Sydney. Sydneysiders will be inclined to say that these Melbournophiles rationalize, and maybe they do in some ways, but since when was rationalization not part of love? It may also be that Sydney is easier to love than Melbourne is (or its setting and some of its surroundings are: as Man of Sydney I am unable to love the city between Circular Quay and Central Railway), but love for a woman of character can be deeper than for a pretty girl.

ROBIN BOYD begins by saying that he often feels that Melbourne should be given back to the blacks, from whom a half million or so acres were "bought" in 1835 by John Batman who traded to the Aborigines for it blankets, knives, looking-glasses, tomahawks, beads. (The Government refused to ratify the "purchase".)

There is, Boyd writes, subtle beauty to Melbourne's bayside and valleys but "nothing to compare" with Sydney's site or, for that matter, Perth's or Hobart's. Suburban Melbourne has "some of the most depressing tracts of man-made Australia". Its "manic-depressive" weather is its "standing joke". Yet the furnace winds from the north in summer, and the wild cold ones that rip down Swanston Street, are part of weather that "provides all the contrasts and stimulation one might ask for, and more than any other single quality give the entirely artificial creation that is Melbourne the character it has today." Then, after that interesting bit of ambivalence, comes love:

"Melbourne's pride is Collins Street and it is—at the top end at any rate—the most civilized of urban streets in this country. I am tempted to go further than that and say, in the Commonwealth of Nations. . . ." And Melbourne has Alexandra Avenue ". . . sweeping past the magnificent Botanic Gardens by the river, the leaves of its trees touching overhead. Or nearly. It is as gracious an avenue as you will find anywhere—this time I'll say it—in the world.

"Melbourne city was ringed with beautiful parklands last century. The view of it over the tops of those parks from the inner ring of suburbs is similar and somewhat superior to that from the upper floors of the apartments lining Central Park, New York." Yet only one tall building has gone up to take advantage of this view, and that was built by a Sydney company, Boyd adds.

Melbourne, he says, will be "the last capital city to change the rules on censorship, capital punishment and ceremonies performed in uniform"—and that attitude he obviously deplores. *But*—"I think that every creative movement of any importance in Australia during the twentieth century has had its origins in Melbourne." He does not say what these movements were but invites the reader to think the claim over, in terms of "painting, creative science, medicine, theatre, architecture, even film". And, he says, "The place which produces the most original ideas is the moral capital of Australia." (And did that remarkable statement cause a single Sydneian to jump down the Boyd throat? Sydney was not even listening.)

Robin Boyd goes on: "The rivalry between Sydney and Melbourne is not the joke the overseas visitor thinks it is. It is real and it is an important stimulus."

Stimulus need not arise from rivalry: it can come of a desire to emulate. If this eminent Man of Melbourne says Sydney is a stimulus to his city, I accept that it is; although I had thought of Melbourne as being pretty much self-winding.

As to the rivalry—it simply isn't there. It is a hoary made-in-Melbourne myth. "Rivalry" means competition, for some prize or honour—in this case it would be for being the better city. Sydney doesn't enter, it doesn't compete. And since you can't have a one-rival rivalry any more than a one-person wedding or a one-knight joust, the rivalry Melbourne may think exists doesn't. I wish it did.

If Sydney saw Melbourne as its civic rival surely it would have shown some sign of trying to match Melbourne's art gallery—even the old one, before the magnificent new Arts Centre arose. When did Sydney ever try to do anything to the city so that some part of it rivalled the dignifiedly pleasant "Paris end" of Collins Street, until in late-1970 it decided to create a permanent Martin Plaza? Show me an Italian restaurant in Sydney that has ever felt the challenge to be as good as Melbourne's Florentino. And where are the south-looking Sydney hoteliers who are concerned that their service should be better than, or for that matter as good as, one gets in Melbourne at the Southern Cross?

Sydney has, let us face it, this superiority complex. It doesn't, though, wear this with hauteur. It is not six-foot Sydney looking *down* on five-foot Melbourne. It looks straight over Melbourne's head and, most of the time, doesn't know it's there. Melbourne does not look *up* to Sydney—but at least it looks at it.

Robin Boyd ends with, "In spite of the warts on Melbourne's face I love it. But I love it more because Sydney is just over there." I wish that Sydney thought of Sydney in terms of Melbourne (with its beautiful Arts Centre and parklands) being just over there, instead of merely being rude about the place, with jokes as corny as, "Melbourne's well laid-out"—"Well, it's time it was, it's been dead long enough." In point of fact, Melbourne is badly laid out—on a dull and rigid grid plan. It was laid out by a surveyor from Sydney. (This was no part of the chicanery Melburnians see Sydneians as so apt to perpetrate. Surveyor Hoddle did this in 1837, when Melbourne was part of New South Wales, only two years after Batman set up his village.)

A MELBOURNE POET, Chris Wallace-Crabbe,[2] has written that when a Melburnian looks at his city, "There is little about the place of which he can really boast, except for its ubiquitous prosperity and its eminence as the world capital of Australian Rules football."

[This national code of football is also strongly supported in South Australia, Western Australia and Tasmania. It evolved after, in about 1856, a Victorian pastoralist's son, T. W. Wills, returned from Rugby school in England and said Rugby football was "unsuitable for grown men engaged in making a living".[3] Australian Rules is, nonetheless, a hard game—it allows bumping, but not tackling or tripping—and a fast one. There are no scrums, line-outs or passing; the ball must be bounced within every ten yards. It is spectacular with "flying" for marks. Rugby followers deride it as "aerial ping-pong", and Rules fans call Rugby "open-air wrestling".]

Melbourne (Wallace-Crabbe goes on) "has little of the simple Colonial Georgian architecture which lends grace to older cities like Sydney". Sociologically, "As an interesting contrast to its general moderation and decorum, Melbourne has a well deserved reputation for political extremism, or at least vigorous dissent", and, "The Public Schools of Melbourne and Geelong have long had a reputation of being more educationally advanced and less exclusive than their counterparts in New South Wales." However, Wallace-Crabbe finds, the arts in Melbourne are of little consequence to the citizenry, whose abiding interest is sport. "Sport is the golden calf." He hit Melbourne so hard in the *Current Affairs Bulletin* that there were protests that he hit it too hard. *But* he said that, if Melburnians' attitude to the city could be summed up in a phrase, it would be the Johnsonian one (which, of course, puts it on a par with London), *"Sir, when a man is tired of Melbourne, he is tired of life."*

Osmar White, in his text for the book *Melbourne*,[4] was precluded from using the tale-of-two-cities technique. This big book was for not only the English-speaking overseas market as well as Australians, but for translation into French, German, Italian—and to show Melbourne in terms of Sydney would have been meaningless to people who didn't know Sydney. It is the definitive book on Melbourne and will probably bring more migrants to the Australian capital that already has the biggest migrant population.

Gordon De'Lisle, who provided the photographs for *Melbourne*, was under no such restriction when he became writer as well as excellent photographer in his *Introducing Australia*.[5] He manages to make Sydney sound more exciting than I have ever found it. (Is it really "breathtakingly bustling . . . Australia's centre of forbidden delights . . . gay . . . a swinger!"—and is Melbourne really so slow-moving, proper and unswinging that Sydney looks like that to Man of Melbourne?)

Believing firmly that Sydney sees Melbourne as its rival, De'Lisle finds Sydney "petty jealous of those virtues that are special to Melbourne: stability, charm, peace, conservatism, introversion, introspection." This doesn't work. The Sydney he has depicted wouldn't know that those qualities were ones to be jealous of. However, his city of special virtues irks this Melburnian in so far as Melbourne is "pruriently prudish" about such things as bare nipples, even in magazine depiction, and a plaster figleaf was mooted for a replica of Michelangelo's "David" when this was exhibited in Myer's department store.

When I was last in Melbourne an "all girl baretop revue" was advertised (as Melbourne's only one of its kind) at The Ritz at St Kilda, an unlovable bayside suburb. Moreover, it would appear that Melbourne is a bit of a hussy at its great spring racing carnival when the horses run for the Melbourne Cup at Flemington and the ladies contest what is called "Fashions in the Field", about which Gordon De'Lisle is most censorious: this "started as an elegant conception but currently functions as a graceless outlet for fashion extremes, whose bared breasts and thighs distract from excellent racing".

I have never been to a Melbourne Cup. It must be, with the Melbourne gentry in their grey toppers and the sassy young ladies of fashion, quite an occasion on the course: it certainly is off it. No other Australian event stops work in offices, and practically halts traffic in the streets, as this one does for about ten minutes on the afternoon of the first Tuesday in November, throughout the rest of Australia (in Melbourne, Cup Day is a public holiday). It is the only time of the year I place a bet and buy tickets in sweeps. Anyone engaged in authorship is inclined to look upon horse-racing as a very minor form of gambling; but for perhaps an hour on this one day of the year I, too, am inflamed with a national fever and at one with the great tense, merry mob of real-Australians. For this I have to thank Melbourne, its Cup. No other Australian occasion binds us so.

The myth that Melburnians are an inhibited people is regularly shattered (only to be as regularly repaired) on winter Saturday afternoons when Melbourne Cricket Ground is turned into their Colosseum by the gladiators of Australian Rules football. Osmar White (who holds that they have inhibitions that are here purged: "Rules" provides catharsis) writes: "No class seems to stand aloof. Secure in the anonymity of the crowd, the barrister howls as loudly as the butcher's boy for the blood of the umpire" and "you will see the Melbourne mob in a state of unrepentant emotional nakedness."[6]

This spectacle I haven't seen, either. What *have* I seen in Melbourne, then, and what words of my own have I about what I have seen and liked?

THE FIRST THING a tourist, and particularly an overseas tourist, is interested in is the hotel or other place where he or she will stay. On four visits to Melbourne during 1969-70 I stayed once at the Commodore Motel out at Queen's Road, which is quite a good one and not cheap, and three times at a hotel (where I had stayed before) that can be sixteen to sixty per cent dearer, and is the best hotel I have stayed at in Australia. So I'll begin with—

The Southern Cross Hotel. Although it is backed by Pan-American Airways and the management techniques are American, the atmosphere isn't; nor is it English, though the elegant main dining-room is called the Mayfair Room and the Club Grill is oaky-red-leathery and a hall porter named Arthur has much the same manner as Fred at Brown's in London; and, of course, it isn't Australian because it has a Coolibah Coffee Shop. It is international, one of the fifty-odd Inter-Continental hotels that include such good ones as the Okura in Tokyo, the Mandarin in Hong Kong and are right across the world from Jerusalem to San Salvador. I've found Southern Cross service to be particularly good. I don't know as much about the food as I should because whenever I eat in the Club Grill I am inclined to order the same two dishes I like so much, *Heart of Palm Vinaigrette* and the *Roast Prime Rib of Blue Ribbon Beef*, which is the best beef in Australia, or at least it tastes the best to me. Something to do with hanging it and slow-roasting it, to bring out and keep in the flavour.

So you are in Melbourne, perhaps in accommodation more economical than the Southern Cross, and you want to see what Melbourne has.

Walk along the top of Collins Street, and see why Melburnians love it as they do. There is, indeed, a touch of the Boulevard Madeleine in Paris, with the plane-trees and the umbrella'd tables under them, and nice little boutiques and galleries, and you look up to the Doric-columned portals of an impressive Parliament House.

Stage One of the Victorian Arts Centre, the National Gallery is in St Kilda Road on the other side of Prince's Bridge across Melbourne's small, muddy-but-loved river, the Yarra. The building may, at first glance, look fortress-like and penitentiary-plain. But it is graced with an arch entrance over which the State's coat-of-arms is well sculptured and the moat-approached arch reveals glass that is less glass than a permanently-running curtain of water. The Australian architect, (Sir) Roy Grounds, contrived, with water, this fine contrast of fluidity and solidity of the Victorian bluestone, a blue-black basalt that looks good and lasts for ever. The rest of the great concrete structure is veneered with this. It has to be remembered that, whereas the Sydney Opera House has looked like the Opera House since the "sails" were formed, the Victorian Arts Centre will not look like the Victorian Arts Centre until a more-graceful-than-the-Eiffel tower rises up at one end of it, 415 feet to a gold-tipped spire. Beneath the tower will be a theatre complex and restaurants.

As an art gallery building, Melbourne's must be one of the best in the world. There may be new ones in Europe or America that are as superbly functional and as strongly aesthetic, but none that I have seen is so spaciously uncluttered, so unobtrusively well-lighted, and so provided with areas of carpet and viewers' seating that one can stay for hours and still emerge untired.

The interior plan is broken with courtyards. The Sculpture Court has a Rodin and a Henry Moore figure, and the Asian Court has beautiful Japanese simplicity of stones, water and bamboos. The Great Hall (see PLATE 1) has a magnificent (and largest-in-the-world) ceiling of coloured glass by Leonard French. There is quite a good restaurant on the top (third) storey. Sydney's Opera House will be the country's most exciting building; but it is mainly the work of a Dane. Not that that really matters, but Victoria's Arts Centre (expected to be completed in 1973) will be Australia's finest expression of Australian-created architecture and Australian concern with a broad spectrum of the arts.

The art collection is the most comprehensive in Australia and the most valuable, because of the Old Masters it contains (these include three Rembrandts, a number of Venetians, Titian among them, and an El Greco). It is stronger on British painters (three Gainsboroughs) than on French Impressionists. The Australian painting collection is good but no match for what is in Sydney at the Art Gallery of New

South Wales, where such painters as Dobell and Drysdale, and even Victoria's own Tom Roberts, are much better represented.

The Parks and Gardens. Melbourne's are so extensive they could take up all the tourist's time, and are not distinctive enough to warrant that, even if its Botanic Gardens are the best-landscaped and the best-planted in Australia. King's Domain has the excellent and unconventional Sidney Myer Music Bowl where the performers are tented in metal and 100,000 people, on seats or the lawns, can listen to open-air concerts. The Treasury Gardens become, across a street, the Fitzroy Gardens, with Captain Cook's cottage brought from Yorkshire.

Suppose we stop walking, and go to dine. I like very much the Florentino restaurant in Bourke Street, its food, its atmosphere, its service; and, for what you get, it is not expensive. The Walnut Tree in William Street I also found good, and it is interesting-looking, this "little" place of Louis Fleyfel's. At his big place, Le Château in Queen's Road, the décor is a bit much for "Australia's Most Elegant Restaurant", as it advertises. André Simon was so enthralled by a crayfish entrée at this very expensive place that he changed the name of the dish to *Langouste Excelsis.* Local gourmets seem to like Maxim's in South Yarra. There are many good places.

"You must have lunch at Jimmy Watson's," a Melbourne friend said. "It's a Melbourne experience." So we went out to the near, unfashionable suburb of Carlton, to a building something like a two-storey warehouse, which had had a Robin Boyd facelift, and at the back it had a nice little courtyard where, having bought your steak on the premises, you could cook it yourself if you wanted to; but few people did that. The place was without frills and thronged with all kinds of people collecting food and carrying it to tables—Parini-suited business-execs, students in jeans from the nearby university, a Cabinet Minister could have been there and a grave-digger from Melbourne Cemetery which is in Lygon Street, as Jimmy Watson's is; and there were well-dressed women, a hippie-girl or two and the odd social butterfly. We had two oxtail casseroles for $2.50 and a bottle of very-drinkable claret for seventy cents, bought at the wine counter where you enter.

Jimmy Watson had a wine shop. He served no food. His son, Allan James Watson, decided to, and he runs the place—and so personally that he said, as he pulled wine corks himself at the entrance counter, "It is not going to get bigger. I won't have a place where I don't know all the people who come here and can talk to them." Jimmy Watson's was open from ten till six. Lunch finished about 3 p.m., but you could get rolls and cheese with your wine throughout the afternoon. It is indeed a Melbourne institution.

IT IS AN AUSTRALIAN TRADITION, in writing about Melbourne, to say how "English" it looks. It can hardly be said to be English unless England can be said to be Victorian, meaning Queen Victorian—and, of course, England has had, thank goodness, quite a few other monarchs and other architectural styles. Sydney had a lot of Victorian buildings, and houses, too; but more of them have been demolished than in Melbourne, which is now getting rid of them at a great rate, the good with the bad. It has preserved, though, the amazing Gothic-accented Victoriana of the E.S. & A. Bank (1883) with its banking chamber that must be seen to be believed.

Out along St Kilda Road the gingerbread mansions are crumbling in the fingers of the developers. Within the city, B.H.P.'s Big Box will draw itself up to its full height of forty storeys in late 1972. C.R.A. has reared its tower at the top of Collins Street. And with Imperial Chemical Industries, General Motors–Holden's and Ford also having their headquarters in Melbourne, it would be hard for Sydney to dispute this city's claim to be the financial capital of Australia.

Sydney appears to remain unworried by anything Melbourne achieves. Told of the Victorian Arts Centre, a Sydneian is likely to jerk a thumb in the direction of the Opera House and let it go at that. Told that in a roll-call of Australia's leading painters he would probably hear more Melbourne names (Fred Williams, Leonard French, Arthur Boyd, Albert Tucker for starters) than Sydney ones, the Man of Sydney might well say no more than that these artists must be mad to live in a cold place where the clouds leak all the time. (Melbourne gets little more than half Sydney's rainfall, 25 inches as against 47, but it gets it more often and less copiously. Melbourne's average hours of summer sunshine are more—7.9 to Sydney's 7.1, but in winter it gets only 3.7 hours to Sydney's 6.1, and its average winter maximum temperature is 57° Fah. as against Sydney's 62, its minimum four degrees colder than Sydney's 47. In summer there isn't more than one degree between them in average maximums but changeable Melbourne's minimum goes eight degrees lower to 56.)

So Melbourne's weather is not much help to anyone trying to get Sydney to throw off its cloak of harbour-blue smugness, and pick up Melbourne's gauntlet.

But does Sydney know that Melbourne is better for fashion shopping? . . . "What, Myer's?" . . . No. Though Melbourne's Myer's, remember, now owns Sydney's Farmer's. How about Georges? . . . "Never heard of it" . . . (Georges probably *is* the best fashion store in Australia). Take a look at the makers' labels on the clothing of some of Sydney's best-dressed women and you'll find that more of

the good garments are styled and made in Melbourne than in Sydney
... "Oh, you mean Norma Tullo?" ... Not only Tullo.

Maybe if I tell the story of the anti-football movement. . . .

Keith Dunstan, Melbourne's most widely-read newspaper columnist, got sick of not being able to hold a conversation that didn't
degenerate into talk about football, and he (this was in April 1967)
asked his editor if it would be O.K. to write something anti-football.
The editor, a staunch Geelong supporter, blanched and knuckled his
brow but finally agreed. Dunstan wrote a mild par about being fed
up with the footy obsession. Letters came in, and more letters, supporting his attitude.

The Anti-Football League was formed. Badges were made, bearing the A.F.L. emblem, a red unbounceable thing like a pregnant
brick. Abusive letters also poured in to the paper, some saying that
the red badge was not of courage but of Communism, others calling
upon A.F.L. members to get out of Victoria. But so many Saturday-
afternoon-footy widows, frustrated music-lovers and others joined
(one man wrote, "I will join. All my family will join. Even my dog
will join") that—aided somewhat by the money from badge sales
going to charity—membership climbed to 17,012.

Melbourne's anti-footy movement was killed off, very cunningly,
by treating it as a joke. Football fans began buying the A.F.L. badge.
Keith Dunstan knew the game was up when the captain of the
Richmond team that had just won the Grand Final turned back his
lapel to show a badge and said to the columnist, "Aren't you proud
of me?"[7]

For Sydney to ignore Melbourne's new (1970) fifty-million-dollar
international jet airport at Tullamarine is one thing: Sydney has no
real reason to worry on that score. But I cannot believe that my
city will remain heedless of the menacing implications in the anti-
football story. Melbourne is clearly a schizophrenic city, and schizo-
phrenics are well known to be dangerously clever. Especially if they
have a sense of humour.

It is high time that, in Sydney's interests, rivalry with Melbourne
began.

THE DANDENONGS AND LYREBIRDS

AT THE BACK OF MELBOURNE, and much nearer to it than the Blue
Mountains are to Sydney, rise the ranges that Victorian tourism likes
to call the Blue Dandenongs.

The ranges begin only twenty miles out, and within thirty you are
at the 2,077-foot summit of Mt Dandenong. So it is quite possible to
work in Melbourne and live in the Dandenongs, or at least, with an
hour's electric-train ride, live at Ferntree Gully, which nearly 40,000

people have turned into an outer suburb, but where there is, never-theless, a fine national park. Here the splendid mountain-ash and grey-gums pillar a forest they share with peppermint-gums and mess-mates and, of course, tree-ferns.

These heights are rich with volcanic soil and some parts get nearly twice Melbourne's rain. So what is a highly attractive nature area is also a specially attractive one to the horticultural buffs, who have made the Dandenongs a place that is also distinguished for its beauti-ful private gardens.

Sherbrooke Forest, which has more columns of mountain-ash than Ferntree Gully, is where the tourist who is prepared to take to the walking trails has his best chance of seeing, or hearing, lyrebirds. Ordinarily these are very shy, but here they have become somewhat accustomed to humans and are less so. However, if you only hear one, and it is a highly-vocal male *Menura superba*, it can be more rewarding than seeing a hen that is about fowl-sized with brownish feathers but has no ornamental tail. Any bird call you hear, whatever its sound, may be a lyrebird's. *Menura* is a superb mimic. It was after watching one perform an amazing repertoire here in Sherbrooke Forest that the ornithologist R. T. Littlejohns wrote: "Every sound is easily produced and unstrained . . . the screech of the black cocka-too passes smoothly to the rich note of the currawong; equally accur-ate and attractive are the faint trebles of the thornbills and wrens. There seems no sound too difficult or too elusive to be reproduced in that remarkable throat . . . Now a flock of parrots flies over, and our bird interrupts his normal singing to mingle, with evident relish, imitated parrot notes amongst those of the flock. Again, when his nearest neighbour commences the usual feeding call, he leaves what he is doing to break in and finish the stanza with him. . . . Suddenly the placid singer lifts his head and sends forth . . . a kookaburra *chorus* as complete and prolonged as any quartet of natural kooka-burras ever uttered. How the notes of more than one kookaburra are reproduced simultaneously, or apparently so, is inexplicable."[1]

This bird did not display its tail at all; but subsequently, in Sher-brooke Forest, Littlejohns got an extraordinarily good picture of a lyrebird displaying. Although the bird was head-on to the camera, nothing of its head or its body could be seen; they were entirely screened by the fern-like feathers of the tail coming right forward over the bird's back and touching the ground in front. Curving out from each side at the rear were the thick major feathers, like the sides of a lyre—these can be thirty inches long and are a silvery colour marked with golden-brown—that give the bird its name. Actually (says Alec H. Chisholm) the tail is rarely held in a way that re-sembles a lyre, and then only briefly.[2]

Early, the male birds were slaughtered for their feathers—"men hawked the tails in baskets about Sydney suburbs in the 1880s".[3] The bird is now well protected and in no danger of becoming extinct. Gould thought the lyrebird, rather than the kangaroo, should be Australia's emblem.

Near the village of Sherbrooke ("Pop. 100. Accommodation: one kosher guest-house, three-guest houses—"[4]) there was a sign by the roadside, DRIVE CAREFULLY, LYREBIRDS CROSS. This had worried a motorist's small daughter: she thought the car might be attacked by bad-tempered lyrebirds, and asked what had made them so cross.

Near Olinda is the National Rhododendron Garden, at its best in November. The trees were very fine as we wound up to the summit of Mt Dandenong, where there is a lookout with a panorama of Melbourne and the Ministry of Tourism was in process of building a revolving restaurant.

I went twice to the Dandenongs, the first time on a Mackenzie's Tours coach and again with Lindsay Howe driving.

ON THE SECOND RUN we turned off near Mt Dandenong to the William Ricketts Sanctuary. This is maintained by the Victorian Government, through the Forests Commission, with the help of private citizens, and, in the words of the leaflet, "it offers the unique spectacle of a sculptor's art in a natural forest setting. Mr William Ricketts, a young musician with a passionate love of nature and intense desire to discover his true vocation in life, came to the Dandenong Ranges, where he purchased $4\frac{1}{2}$ acres of steep forest land, and set about the task of interpreting in clay the aboriginal theme."

Ricketts has exceptional facility as a sculptor of Aborigines, mainly in terms of their faces and torsos merging into tree trunks or rocks. It is unfortunate that sentimentality sometimes sprouts out of their shoulders in the form of wings.

However, this is religious art. William Ricketts is an intensely religious man who somehow manages to believe fervently in God as creator of all things separate and at the same time believe pantheistically, "I am an integral part of my environment . . . separateness is the enemy of true religion." He proclaims "a righteous anger" against despoilation of the Australian bush and slaughter of its fauna.

The nice woman at the entrance ("I am here because I love William and all he stands for") had read some of my books, and she suggested that I should go up and knock on the studio door and introduce myself. So I did and mentioned that the first book I wrote was about the Aborigines.

"I read no books!" William Ricketts said, his pale blue eyes piercing in a pale sharp face. He added, unnecessarily I thought, "I have

never seen the sculpture of Michelangelo!" Then he was away—
about science and technology turning the world into an antheap,
and about the "burners and killers" of the bush. He was terribly
angry, and declared, "I am going to fight them all—alone!"

He showed us his latest sculpture. It had piles of slaughtered
animals at the foot of two cross-like objects, between which a man,
obviously himself idealized, stood holding a lot of animals protectively. As a work of art, it was vulnerable to criticism, though the
detailing of the animals bespoke great skill of eye and hand. As a
sculptural tract in the cause of conservation, I was all for it.

The Good Waters of Gippsland

MALLACOOTA INLET I had a hunch would be good. It beckoned from
the map, from just across the Victorian border. "Mallacoota" was the
only town name along perhaps two hundred miles of coastline below
Eden in New South Wales. The inlet, shaped rather like a widened
Sydney Harbour, sprawled into eleven thousand acres of national
park.

The inlet was referred to as "a large and picturesque stretch of
landlocked water in the extreme east of Victoria";[1] Mallacoota itself
as, "a tiny [pop. 215] seaside holiday settlement much favoured by
keen anglers and nature-lovers. One motor hotel, one guest-house,
holiday flats available."[2] *Mallacoota* the name (Ab. "place of many
waters") was an attractive one. And Mallacoota the place was in that
area of Victoria east of the Snowy River called by a native word for
"east", *Croajingalong*.

It was off-track, which was good; but not so good as to getting
there, unless I drove down from Sydney. I could drop off the Pioneer
Express coach at an ungodly hour of the morning at a little place on
Princes Highway called Genoa, and probably get car or bus transport for the other fifteen miles when the local Genoese woke up.
Then I found there was a Commuter Airlines service from Melbourne, where I'd be, to Mallacoota. (Unhappily, this service went
out of business: I hope it is revived.)

Leaving Melbourne at nine forty-five, the Piaggio landed at Bairnsdale and it was just after noon as we descended to Mallacoota.

By now I knew more about the Mallacoota region from a brochure
that detailed the abundant fauna in its national park. What the brochure didn't say anything about (and how could it?) was the people.

A FINANCIAL ANALYST with the Ford Motor Company the man who

Old Murray River paddlewheeler "Gem" has become exhibit, restaurant and art gallery at Swan Hill's best-in-Australia outdoor Folk Museum.

23/VICTORIA

Mallacoota Inlet is a fine waterway near the New South Wales border, not too thronged with vacationers as yet, and with some lovely still reaches.

Near Port Campbell the sea has sculptured pillars from the coastline and left them standing out from the coast. There are others to the west.

Lakes Entrance at the Gippsland lakes that stretch behind the long land-finger of Ninety Mile Beach and are very good waters for a boating holiday.

met me at the plane no longer was. He had opted out of metropolitan industrialism. Ron Radak and his wife Margaret, who used to teach German to Italians in Venice and now taught school at Mallacoota, were the proprietors of the Bekta Holiday Flats where I stayed, very comfortably.

Another Ford man, John Murray, an English aeronautical motor engineer, had come to the Radaks' as a guest. He now had holiday flats of his own.

A former consulting engineer in lighting, Peter McGrath kept Mallacoota's general store—it sold everything from can-openers to gasoline, pharmaceuticals to fishing-gear. He had come on a fishing trip, caught three mullaway, barbecued them and was having a beer afterwards at the Gipsy Point Hotel we'll come to. He had said to his wife, Jo: "Why don't we get out of the ratrace?" and she had said, "What'll we buy?" He asked the publican, who told him the store at Mallacoota was for sale. Peter McGrath said, "Let's buy the bastard", and they did, and had never regretted it. Also, Peter said, Mallacoota was about twelve degrees warmer than Melbourne in winter.

The publican, Douglas Davis, was a dentist who had come to Mallacoota on holiday and, hearing that the hotel up at Gipsy Point was for sale, bought it. Now two of his regular visitors were Sir Henry Bolte and Sir Arthur Rylah, both ardent anglers. So far they had stayed in the business of being Victoria's Premier and Chief Secretary. But a High Court judge had built a house there and one felt that just about anyone in Melbourne could decide to "give it away" for Mallacoota, population now 250. Tourist population at the height of the summer season, 7,000. As well as the holiday flats (the ones I saw, Bekta and Blue Waters were good standard and not expensive) there was a big camping-caravanning reserve on the fore-shores outside the national park.

Most came to fish, for bream, flathead, snapper, whiting, tailor, sole, flounder, luderick, garfish, gurnard, and the big mullaway that can be thirty, even fifty-five pounds. (The local professional fishing was largely the adventurous business of diving for abalone.) But there were also miles of fine beach on the ocean side. You could play golf, on a course that in the late afternoon was likely to be shared, as I saw it, by a mob of kangaroos. And wallabies were feeding just outside when I got up in the morning at Radaks'. In April (when I propose never to go there, though I think the place will see me back) there was duck-shooting, which Mallacoota can surely get along without. What else the place had, and what I liked most, they showed me when they took me out on the National Park Ranger's boat. And *there* was another happy man—the ranger, Ken Morrison,

Q

who said, "I wouldn't swap jobs with anyone."

You can hire boats, of course, but not the *Mako* that had two 100 h.p. motors that ripped it through the water at forty knots.

THE WAKE of the Ranger's boat was beautiful, not just a flurry of churned-up lake, but three hills of white water and two green troughs between, with the central hill fanning out over the other two farther back, sculpturally, the pattern reforming as fast as it dissolved into big ripples that arrowed out across the inlet behind and accentuated the placidity of the waters ahead. I was glad the wake was like that, because I felt guilty about "doing" Mallacoota on this quick-look basis. I should have liked to putter over, in a boat with just a few horse-power, to the Goodwin Sands island which is such a bird haven. I should like to have a look at where the Spotted Dog gold mine was and the old cemetery of the early settlers. I should like to go up that creek to the right just where Ken Morrison cut his two hundred horses down to a water-walk and we glided past the emerald point of the dairy-farmer who brought his milk in every morning to Mallacoota and sold it from his boat. The water here was such a mirror (PLATE 23).

Then we are roaring away again, up through the Narrows between what they call the Bottom Lake and the Top Lake. We land briefly. The bush isn't very special, but what it contains is.

"We have two hundred species of birds round here, a few more than that in fact—including the lyrebird," the Ranger says. And he names birds I have never seen or, if I have, not being bird-expert, didn't know them—the pied oyster-catcher, red-billed and red-legged, the rufous whistler, the musk lorikeet and a dozen others that don't include king parrots, rainbow lorikeets, pelicans, spoonbills, spine-bills, satin bower-birds, whistling eagles, yellow-winged honeyeaters, egrets, black cockatoos, bronze-wing and wonga pigeons, teals, terns and swamp harriers and the rare ground parrot that is here so rare that Ron Radak says he has seen the aerodrome alive with them.

"We have a lot of the gliders," Ken Morrison goes on, getting to the animals and beginning with these beautiful small possum-kinds with membranes between their limbs and body that enable them to volplane from tree to tree. The largest here, the dusky glider (it is black and white), is eighteen inches long with a tail even longer, and it may glide a hundred yards from a high treetop. They have the sugar-glider that loves sweet saps, as does the fluffy glider that shrieks as it glides. The tiny feathertail is smaller than the one Eric Jolliffe, the joke artist, used to carry in his pocket, and it can be bedded down in a matchbox.

You have less chance of seeing one in daylight (I did once, but only because it "flew" from a tree that was being felled) than you have of spotting a marsupial mouse. These pouched "mice" aren't really mice: in fact, some species live on mice. But they are among the more interesting fauna here. The tubby wombat is plentiful and the larger possums and there is also the porcupine-like echidna. And some snakes. I looked hard at Goanna Bay but it was hardly to be expected that I'd see a tree-trunk decorated with a six- or seven-foot-long goanna of the kind called a lace monitor. Platypuses are not uncommon, in the Bekta River to the south of the inlet.

We sped from the Top Lake into the wide winding Genoa River and came to Gipsy Point where the hotel is run by Doug Davis, the no-longer dentist. He talked of four-pound bream and a giant thirteen-pound flathead and the fifty-two-pound mullaway that had been hooked by a visitor in February. But I'm afraid I was looking over my drink at—kangaroos. They had come out to feed at, unusually, half past three in the afternoon.

When we got back to Mallacoota, and I had been shown a lovely old house and some of the better tourist flats, the sun was turning the inlet tangerine. The powerful abalone boats were tearing in to a tricky crossing of the entrance bar. Then, after I had watched the tree-silhouetting on the headland and kangaroos hopping on the golf course, these people had me to dinner. And, in the course of that one of them said, "At Gipsy Point, what did you think of that wonderful old kangaroo?" I shook my head. "Don't tell me you didn't see him—the 'roo that comes in every day, hops right into the bar. He has his potato chips, then he has his two apples, and he has his glass of beer. Then he stretches out in front of the fire."

I said: "And then he gets up, orders a double whisky and says to Doug Davis, 'See what the 'roos in the back room will have'."

"No, no, I'm not kidding." He turned to others at the table, who confirmed the story. "He comes in every day—this time of the year, between four o'clock and four-thirty."

That was when I recalled one of my hosts saying at Gipsy Point, "It's four o'clock. We'd better be getting back. There's some things we'd like you to see in Mallacoota."

I LEFT, reluctantly, with Councillor Evans and his wife, Councillor Evans. Max Evans was a dairyfarmer from Bairnsdale and his wife Patricia was the first woman councillor in Bairnsdale's hundred years of local government. She was also the secretary of V.E.D.A. (Victorian Eastern Development Association). They had come to Mallacoota to drive me to Lakes Entrance. On the way we had lunch at Cape Conran.

There was no road to Cape Conran on some maps. The road there was had just been sealed, but not right to the beach. Twenty years before, there was nothing at this pleasant beach but the grave of some drowned sailors who had been washed up from a wreck, and an Orbost grazier built the first of the few holiday cottages there were at Cape Conran. This grazier, Jack Lynn, was now the president of Orbost Shire Council. He was garfishing when we arrived, but soon came up to join two other councillors and the shire secretary and some wives and children in what he called his "gathering room". Soon there was a great grilling of steaks and chops and sausages and quaffing of whisky and beer, even a speech or two.

We stopped near Marlo and looked at the Snowy entering the sea.

On the sea horizon was a strange shape that wasn't like a ship. I asked Max Evans what it was and he said, "The Glomar rig". Out on that oil rig, one might say, the grandsons of the stockhorse-mounted, whip-cracking, hard-riding Man from Snowy River were pushing levers that would power-drive lengths of drillpipe into the seabed in the quest for another of the Bass Strait wells such as had produced Australia's greatest flow of oil.

There is beautiful country round Orbost. The town's Council Chambers deserve a better, less signboard-stricken main street. The road to Buchan could not have been greener at its sides.

There are limestone caves at Buchan (which sounds Scottish, but is from the Aboriginal *bukken*). We got there after the caves inspection time. The caves are "undoubtedly the best in Victoria"—Osmar White. Buchan's autumn-coloured trees were lovely, and it is in good rock-hunting country, and marble country. The ranger said there were 900 tons of Buchan marble in London buildings.

GIPPSLAND, the best-endowed province of Victoria, was not discovered, as he claimed, by the Polish explorer Count Strzelecki (who named it after the colonies' Governor Gipps), but a few months earlier in 1840, by a Scotsman named Angus McMillan who called it "Caledonia Australis". The mountains may have reminded him of his homeland, but the lakes he came down to are nothing like lochs.

The lakes of Gippsland are a very extensive system of waterways. How extensive I was to realize when Keith Mason, the mayor of Bairnsdale (the big town just north of the lakes) flew me over them in his private Cessna. The lakes are connected, except Lake Tyers, and part of the system is a long canal-like stretch of water behind the extraordinary sandspit that fronts the ocean as Ninety Mile Beach. Landing on this from the Bass Strait surf, you could run up a sand dune and down the other side into water like a quiet river. An even more remarkable feature is what are called the "silt jetties", built up as streaks of land within the lakes by the silt carried down by the

Mitchell and other rivers. The long sandspit edge to the coast (similar to the one that forms the Coorong in South Australia) finally breaks near its western end where, just inside the break, is the resort town of Lakes Entrance. (PLATE 24, looking beyond the town.)

Lakes Entrance is, according to its tourist booklet, "Victoria's holiday paradise". Admittedly it is becoming paradisial in the Surfers Paradise sense of the word, what with the big sign of the Sparkle Motel going sparkle-sparkle and a Cozee Caravan Park and Bulmer's bully El Torito Motel-Flats and enough feature-happy architecture to make Robin Boyd run right off the end of the pier. Doubtless, a southern "Surfers" is what most Lakes Entrance business people want it to become: I think it's a short-term view. However, Lakes Entrance will make a lot of money before *kitsch* (a useful new word for bad taste) catches up with it. The other two lakeside tourist centres, farther in, Paynesville and Metung, looked better; and might even boom without being blighted.

Not all Lakes Entrance's two thousand residents are busy servicing a tourist population that was up near 40,000 during the Christmas holidays. Some man the trawlers of Australia's biggest fishing fleet.

The really big fish that were enriching the region were straight out there where you gazed from the lookout above the town—Halibut, Marlin, Kingfish, Barracouta, were the names of offshore oil-fields that were flowing 150,000 barrels a day in 1970; and Halibut and Barracouta were expected, between them, to double that production in 1971 and supply sixty per cent of Australia's oil needs. However, at that rate the Bass Strait reserves would not last more than fifteen years; so the drilling rigs afloat out there needed to bring in some more big oil fish. Tuna field proved commercial in 1971.

IT IS POSSIBLE to have a memorably good time on the Gippsland Lakes. That is what I had for two days. Nothing happened of my own arranging; everything came as a series of pleasant surprises. A diary would read something like this:

Motor cruiser *Circe* waiting at L.E. when arrived with Evanses, 6 p.m., rather tired. Whisky in other hand, met aboard: Murray Graham (Bairnsdale barrister, president V.E.D.A.), Keith Mason (timber-miller, mayor of Bairnsdale), Jim Coate (owner-skipper of *Circe*), his son-in-law Charles Heath (estate agent). Informal, relaxed, cheerful company. Felt brighter as white *Circe* glided seven miles through mild-aired dark to Metung Hotel. Very good dinner with Vic. wines; then hotel prop. George Stephenson produced *Liebfraumilch* from surprising cellar. Much ribald singing, Bairnsdale's mayor in particularly good voice.

Expect to sleep aboard, but no. About midnight, *Circe* heads into quiet creek where we have use of W. P. Heath's enviable built-over-the-water bungalow, Hove To, with all mod. cons.

In morning see how idyllic this spot (Boxes Creek) is, also that Jim has caught some of the bream swimming beneath the veranda boards, which Chas. Heath proceeds to fry in already-made beer batter. Usually prefer fish grilled but breakfast tastes so good get recipe for beer batter: Mix two parts plain flour to one of self-raising flour to creamy consistency with (flat) beer. Add pinch of salt and a preparation, Yolkene, to give bright-golden colour. Best if batter is left for hour after mixing.

They've worked out that *Circe* can't show me, in the time I have, what I should see. So a speedboat whooshes up, Charles takes it over, off we go at 40 knots. Down to the town, past tourist anglers drifting for flathead, past an island with kangaroos.

Rip back up the lake, past where Tambo River's mouth puts out long lips of siltland, to Swan Bay. Black swans rise before our coming, heavy in take-off, water trailing from their feet.

"School of dolphins!" Murray Graham sights them. Charles throttles back, crawls in towards where the black dorsal fins are curving-out, curving-under, one behind another. Formation's gone, motor's scared them. No. Here's one coming up right beside the boat. Another sleek black, billed body curvetting alongside, air-bubbling the blue-glass water. "They like a game," Charles says. Boat plays it with them.

More black swans take off as we whizz up Lake King [the smallest lake, 35 square miles; Lake Wellington is 55] to four-mile-long silt jetties at the Mitchell River's mouth, a double-spit of built-up fertility almost cutting the lake in two. Then back to last night's Metung, to look at Joe Bull's shipyard. Builds four- and six-berth motor cruisers he hires out, thoroughly fitted, hot showers, everything, provisions in 'fridge if you want. Charts, of course, and advice. "Best fishing months are May to November."

Forty-knot it up to where *Circe* will be now—Paynesville, in strait made by lake's largest island, Raymond, that used to have lots of koalas until, nine years ago, big bushfire. Paynesville's attractive, developing fast. Airstrip that Keith Mason says is only one in Australia where private planes can land and taxi almost to door of first-class hotel-motel, where we have excellent lunch.

Then—farewell and thank you, Jim Coate, Charles, *Circe*. Driven by Murray G. to Bairnsdale airport, and Keith-the-mayor's Cessna takes me up and over where I've been and where I haven't.

Stayed night at Murray Graham's. Bairnsdale in green dairying-sheep-cattle-timber country that looked good from air, Mitchell River winding through, lots of platypuses in it, Murray says. Treed lawns right down middle of widest main street. Pop. 8,500. More than just "civic-minded", very history-conscious about whole region. Publishes magazine produced by district's schoolteachers. Article about Bairnsdale school being perhaps first to teach observational nature study. Another about Morwell high-schoolers learning Esperanto. Mental vigour going on, not confined to bright hosts.

Power Valley, Bass Strait Oil

EIGHTY THOUSAND TOURISTS a year—more than twice as many as flock to the Gippsland Lakes in the Christmas holidays—go to Yallourn to look at lignite.

Lignite is brown coal, low-grade coal, crumbly damp deposit that is two-thirds water. Dried, it pulverizes to a powder so inflammable that NO SMOKING outside the car is a rigid rule for visitors to the huge open cuts where water sprays constantly as the coal is mined by machines that dredge out two thousand tons an hour, twenty-five million tons a year. With little overburden, mining is easy, at a production cost of only one dollar a ton.

The biggest single deposit of brown coal in the world is what Victoria has, stretching down the Latrobe Valley that lies ninety miles east of Melbourne. And what those 80,000 visitors see is the biggest centre of power and fuel production in the Southern Hemisphere.

It is impressive, this 500-million-dollar undertaking of the State Electricity Commission. What mainly drops the tourist's jaw is the size of the open cut at Yallourn. To go round it is an eight-mile drive. And that enormous mouth in the earth is gaping wider and wider, towards the town of Yallourn (pop. 4,500).

"The town will have to go," the S.E.C. man who was showing me round said. "The coal under it is worth more than the town is. We own it, all the houses; the S.E.C. even owns the hotel. The people have been told. A new town will be built to rehouse them and—Yallourn was started in 1921—they can expect that the new low-rental houses will be better. But some people don't relish the prospect of leaving their gardens and having to make new ones."

About 7,700 people are employed by the S.E.C. in the valley. The other town, Morwell, is much bigger and newer, post-World War II. The other big open cut is here, four miles round. Deeper than Yallourn's, it has reserves of lignite figured at 850 million tons. So it won't soon be depleted by the terraces going wider and deeper down there in the vast hole where the bucket-wheels of the dredgers are chewing out the dark-brown coal and sending it along the conveyors to rail trucks that go off to the plant that presses it into hard little mini-bricks of fuel. The briquette plant is very big, but larger still is the nearby towering electrical power plant that has an appetite for 50,000 tons of raw lignite a day.

Hazelwood power station is the newest and biggest of three that generate from brown coal four-fifths of Victoria's electricity. It has cost $300 million. Its chimneys, eight in a row, are higher than thirty-storey buildings. The water of its cooling pond is an expanse used for yachting.

You get noughts, like spots, before the eyes when the S.E.C. man talks of the Latrobe Valley power output. By 1978 the requirements may be as much as 23,300 million kilowatt hours, so booming-expanding is Victoria's secondary industry. A new power station is rising.

It will be called Yallourn "W", and the "W" could stand for "whopping". The S.E.C. has a picture of how it will look when completed, which should be in late 1973. Yallourn "W" will have only one tall stack, more than a hundred feet higher than Hazelwood's chimneys. But it will have two curved cooling towers, so wide that a thirty-storey building of average width would fit easily inside each of them; and so high that such buildings would barely poke out at the cooling towers' tops.

WESTERNPORT (it used to be two words) is about 70 road miles from Morwell. It is a big harbour that in the late fifties was "of little significance"[1], with farming country round it and the largest town Koo-wee-rup (pop. 839). By 1964 another encyclopaedia[2] had raised it to the status of "a tourist resort". Since then it had got oil and fertilizer plants. But those are only the beginnings of the Westernport industrial happening.

B.H.P. and G.K.N. (Guest, Keen and Nettlefold of U.K.) have signed up with a gratified Victorian premier (Victoria has never had a steelmaker) to make steel at Westernport. Beginning with a $92-million cold strip mill, which the Lysaght subsidiary was expected to have in production in 1972, the steel enterprise would, by 1985, Sir Henry Bolte said, add up to a thousand-million-dollar investment.

B.H.P. announced in mid-1970 a profit of close to $60 million. "That," the Financial Editor of the *Sydney Morning Herald* wrote, "contains only the first trickle of the coming torrent from oil, gas and iron ore."[3] $22 million of B.H.P's 1971 profit was from oil and gas.

The oil production platforms out in Bass Strait I had arranged to fly over. But when I got to Sale airport, on the way to Yallourn-Morwell, it was raining and the clouds were so low down that the pilot shook his head and said, "Today you'd see nothing. It's so bad the seagulls are walking."

Bass Strait weather can mean mile-a-minute gales whipping up thirty-foot waves. Nevertheless, forty-odd wells had been drilled by the floating rigs, all except six of them by the Esso-Hematite Petroleum (B.H.P.) partnership that struck gas in its first well in 1965. Now the score on commercial fields was: Halibut and Kingfish (oil), Barracouta and Marlin (oil and gas), Snapper (gas). The two rigs, incidentally, can drill directionally as well as straight down. Wells drilled at an angle may bottom as much as a mile apart.

Five production platforms had been built near Welshpool. These steel islands (PLATE 25 shows Barracouta) are anchored by driving 42-inch piles down their hollow steel legs and 200 feet into the sea-bed, which may be a couple of hundred feet below the waves. The above-surface structure has the capacity to collect oil or gas from perhaps twenty wells and tank-treat the oil to get rid of sand and water in it. Then it is sent ashore (forty-fifty miles in the case of Halibut-Kingfish) to treatment plants near Sale; the same with the gas. Thence, crude oil is piped 117 miles to a tank farm near Melbourne. Liquid gas (propane, butane) goes to a treatment plant on Westernport. The natural gas that Melbourne cooks with goes by a direct 108-mile pipeline to the gas companies there.

It is expected that the Bass Strait oil and gas development will save Australia $300 million a year in foreign exchange.

More than half the oil being refined in Australia in 1971 was coming from Bass Strait and other Australian oilfields.

The "Prom", and the Penguins

WILSON'S PROMONTORY is, to many Victorian nature-lovers and bush-walkers, simply, "the Prom". They love this Land's End of Australia, this peninsula of wilderness that is not so much the southernmost tip of the continent as an appendage, a would-be island you can drive to across a broad isthmus—and, having got there, feel more than 150 miles from Melbourne. It is all a national park.

The Prom is not for the average tourist. There is no hotel or motel; but there are about twenty "lodges" that rent cheaply. Those who want to go there for a day, to see if they might like it for a week, will have a longer day if they do as we did and overnight at the nearest hotel-motel (which was well run) at Meeniyan.

"There was a proposal to build a big international-style hotel on the Prom. Half were for it and half wanted it kept a natural wilderness," said Paul Brennan of the tourist development authority, who had picked me up at Sale, as we drove down the 46 miles from Meeniyan next morning.

When we got on to the Prom the road ran out of bitumen, and the Prom was very shortly to run out of road. Mountains (well, some are over 2,000 feet and you're at sea-level) loomed. Paul stopped to show me Whisky Bay, an attractive beach outcropped with smooth granite boulders, and Squeaky Bay where the sand is very squeaky underfoot.

Tidal River is the name of the place where the Ranger's office, the store, the lodges, the camping-grounds are. The bush we had come through was ordinary-Australian, thick with tea-tree, banksia, casuarina. But, apparently, the Prom had better, or worse, bush than that. The Ranger was in a state of concern over a party of hikers on a three-day walk who were twenty-four hours overdue in emerging from what he called, "very rugged country, no tracks—I'd think twice about going in there myself".

The National Parks Officer said that if the Prom got more than five thousand people as stayers or visitors at peak-holiday time the place was in trouble as to water and garbage disposal. So, nature-lovers' love of Wilson's Promontory was about to bring to Tidal River a $30,000 incinerator.

Dispose-of-it-yourself disposal methods couldn't be trusted. It was part of Boy Scout rules, in Victoria at any rate, that if a Scout in the bush felt the "call of nature", he should afterward burn his toilet paper, and not leave it as litter. No longer. One Scout fired the forest floor as well and burned out six hundred acres.

An ecological problem was that the more nature-loving tourists that came the more were likely to encounter a snake in the bush and kill it—and thus reduce the number of snakes that kept down the rats. The rabbits had to be poisoned because they were eating out the food of the wallabies and the deer. Wombats and the possums were fairly abundant. The great menace was the bushfire. Yet the promontory seemed to have recovered remarkably from the many fires that had ravaged it. The flora was interestingly varied along what is called the Whale Rock Nature Walk, which was only about a mile and easy.

From Tidal River the road takes a loop and stops on the slope of Mt Oberon (1,845 ft). You walk up the rest of the road, about three miles, and the last few hundred yards are goat-track, with good growth of the pink heath that is Victoria's floral emblem. The view from the summit has granite-bouldered uplands inland, and a grand vista of sea with marooned humps of islands.

I was glad I went to Wilson's Prom.

PHILLIP ISLAND I am glad I went to, too, although I did not see anything of it in daylight—nor did I much want to after reading an
article by Dr Stephen Murray-Smith, whose judgments are generally
respectable, headed "THE MINI PARADISE GOES TO HELL".[1] He said that
shacks were uglifying the island to the water's edge and, although
Cape Woolamai remained beautiful, trees had been slaughtered right
and left, and it had become a kind of Koala-land Coney Island. There
are many koalas on Phillip Island—bigger, furrier koalas than the
Queensland ones that appealed to me at Lone Pine Sanctuary near
Brisbane.

Penguins, rather than koalas, were what I had come to Phillip
Island to see. Penguins (there are none in the northern hemisphere)
are usually associated with the Antarctic, tuxedo-birds ambling down
ice floes to fish-dinner. It is not generally known overseas that southern Australia is the habitat of the fairy penguin. *Eudyptula minor* is
only about a foot high, has a teal-blue back, the rest whitish from
the feet to just underneath the eyes. These engaging little creatures
have become a major Victorian tourist attraction, even a highlight
for overseas visitors. In 1970 more than 120,000 people a year were
coming to watch what was called Phillip Island's "penguin parade".

Seven-o'clock arrival on a mid-May evening was a little late, but,
happily, so were the penguins coming in from the sea. A spotlight
was directed at the water's edge from the beachside wooden hut
where the manager of the Penguin Reserve tells the gathered visitors
about the penguins over the public address system. This did not
worry the birds, they were used to it; but an unfamiliar sound such
as a baby crying frightened them, Mr West said and, while we
waited, told me more about fairy penguins.

They are quite at home on the sea, where they catch fish—pilchards, whitebait, small garfish they'll round up "like sheepdogs do
sheep". Flightless, of course, like all penguins, they'll swim thirty
miles out, and stay out on the sea for up to five weeks at a time. In
August they come ashore to mate—same mate if they'd had one
before, same burrow in the grassy sand dunes. In September they
nest, and a pair will take turnabout on the eggs that hatch within five
weeks. Then both parents go out and, returning stuffed to the throat
with fish, regurgitate this to their young. So they are seen coming
in from the sea in their greatest numbers between November and
March. The numbers lessen as the young are weaned from being fed
daily to three times a week, twice, once. Hunger forces them to fend
for themselves when they are about four months old. Some are
banded then, and Phillip Island young ones have turned up hundreds
of swimming miles away at Victor Harbour in South Australia. But
what do we see now in May?

Suddenly appearing out of the small surf, their white fronts picked up by the spotlight, a group of fairy penguins is gathering on the sand. The first ashore tend to wait for the others. They waddle up the beach, within a few feet of the front-row visitors, making for their burrows as unerringly as they made for this particular spot of land from the sea where some may have been for days or weeks. The earnest, wing-out waddle, on those wide-apart white feet, is enchanting.

The fairy penguins have adjusted to being tourist attractions. At first they wouldn't come ashore if there was a light. So flashing torches were used to keep them in the water until the sightseeing crowd built up. Then, when they came out of the water in the dark the spotlight hit them. This was traumatic, the reserve manager said.

"An organized system of spotlighting they can accustom themselves to has made all the difference. The colony has increased greatly, to over five thousand."

Scenic Coast to Port Fairytales

A TEXAN named Gerd Ledermann who toured Australia with his family wrote that when he asked Australians he had met abroad about their country they invariably said, "Pretty good place to live." But "never a word about the beauties of the place. . . . Yet here we were discovering a wonderland."[1]

What Ledermann (who now lives in Australia) wrote about finding, to his surprise, that the country was not only liveable but in many parts beautiful was printed in conjunction with a colourphoto that did not depict Ayers Rock or an island of the Great Barrier Reef, but a coastal scene near Port Campbell that is reached by the Great Ocean Road. It runs along the Victorian south-west coast from Torquay to Peterborough, and the team of American experts who surveyed our tourist attractions rated it as one of the finest scenic roads in Australia.

The same survey did not even mention Geelong, Victoria's second largest city; nor had it, in New South Wales, mentioned Wollongong, which has a bigger population than Geelong's 120,000 and is also highly industrial. Geelong, with its imposing classical-columned City Hall, has particularly good parks and gardens, but it has so many industries that it cannot expect to be Meccasville for the tourist as well. So, after just a quick look at Geelong, we went on and down to the Great Ocean Road. Lindsay Howe, the six-foot-five-and-a-half photographer I had come down from Albury with earlier, was driving the Avis-rented Valiant.

Torquay, where interstate surf-club championships have been held, Anglesea, Bell's Beach (venue of the 1968 board-riding champion-ships) and Lorne are reckoned the best surfing beaches along this coast. Some smaller ones, even more recently developed than Bell's Beach, are also highly favoured by the board boys.

Anglesea spreads its houses back from the beach onto bushy hills. Lorne is, in the same way, even more attractive. It is not only a popu-lar vacation place but many well-endowed people have retired to live there and they have preserved fine eucalypts round their houses. Forest comes down to Lorne's back door from the Otway Ranges that shelter it from the cold south-westerlies and give it a mild winter climate.

We stopped a few miles past Lorne where the road bends round Mount Defiance and makes a lookout point. A plaque said that the Great Ocean Road was built to commemorate those Australians who served in the 1914-18 war. But it was hard to take one's eyes from the eastward view, where the habitations were lost from sight in the inlets between a succession of points of land the mountains put out, like crocodile-heads drinking the sparkling sea. There was another view a little farther on that had our cameras out again, down the scalloped coast towards Cape Otway.

The small resort of Wye River looked good in prospect. Then we came to where a brochure said "Unspoiled beauty of the bushland and ocean scene complements the charm of this pretty holiday village". Empty drink cans lay littered everywhere.

I wonder how an Australian would get on if he tried to emulate a travelling salesman in Sweden named Per Ögren, who got sick of seeing the sides of the roads he travelled littered with cans and bottles. By the beginning of 1970 the admirable Ögren had, in eighteen months, induced no less than 364 Swedish shopkeepers to buy back empty cans and bottles at one ore (a fifth of a cent) apiece. Several other shops were paying five ore (a cent). One of the shops paying one ore had bought over 100,000 cans ($200 worth) and carted them to garbage tips, in the interests of a less-littered Sweden.

THE COAST NEAR PORT CAMPBELL we came to after lunching on delectable local crayfish at the fishing town and family-type resort of Apollo Bay and then going inland, the road serpentining through forest and fern, rising to plushy green buttocks of dairyland, and then going back down to the sea again.

About eight miles this side of Port Campbell (which is only a small resort) you turn off the main road towards the sea. And come

to a coast as scenically remarkable as I think I have ever seen anywhere. (In Lebanon, near Beirut, there are similar land forms standing in the sea, and the Swedish island of Gotland has its *raukers*, but
what is here near Port Campbell makes much more dramatic scenery.)

We could not have come at a better time. The sun that blazed in
from near the horizon was gilding to almost-orange the biscuit rock
of the sea pillars. The sea had sculptured these out of the land and
set them apart from it. Those to the east, and a near headland like
the curiously eroded one we stood on, were fired with colour against
a cobalt sea (PLATE 24). In the other direction, against the light, the
pillars stood up shadow-dark on a sea where the blue and the foam
white had been sun-transmuted into silver.

The tall islands, some eighty feet high and not more than twenty
through, some peaked, some chunkier "stacks", are called, rather
absurdly, the Twelve Apostles. There may be twelve of them now.
There will in time be fewer, for the sea cuts them down faster than
it cuts out new ones from a coast of "Tertiary rocks . . . rather soft,
consisting of loosely consolidated beds of clay, sand and limestone".[2]
A headland is undercut in the middle, forming it into a bridge—one
of these remains (and is called, of course, London Bridge). Such a
bridge is eventually worn away and collapses, to leave a pylon standing in the sea that goes on mindlessly sculpturing the forms that in
the evening light looked so strangely beautiful standing out among
the long breakers that were running in to foam and lace on the sand
at the foot of sheer cliffs. The shadows crept up the sides of pillars
and headland, slowly extinguishing their sunfire colour that was so
vivid against a background of mauve clouds piled in the eastern sky.

This extraordinary coast was, for all its beauty, a cruel one to
ships. No fewer than seventeen vessels are known to have been
wrecked on the stretch between Cape Otway and Port Fairy—which,
in a direct line, is only about eighty miles. A rock island near the
London Bridge formation sank, in 1878, the *Loch Ard*, a spanking
iron-hulled clipper on her maiden voyage to Melbourne; and of
seventy people aboard only two survived. Some others are buried in
a tiny cemetery near a spectacular gulch the sea has cut in the cliff,
called Loch Ard Gorge. My notebook says it "Leaves Tasmania's
Devil's Kitchen for dead".

DARKNESS descended and drew down mist with it. Lindsay Howe
nosed the car cross-country through a shrouded landscape towards a
little inland place I had elected to visit named Garvoc.

At Garvoc I would, with luck, find a friend who is a much better
writer than I am, Hal Porter. Although I knew he was at work on a
novel, I didn't think he'd mind a visit; and he didn't at all, when we

finally found him, alone on his brother-in-law's farm at Garvoc. (In *The Literature of Australia*³ Porter ranks as "one of the most arresting stylists to appear in Australia since the Second World War".)

Hal, who was in his fifties, has two usual forms of address: Lindsay Howe was "young man", I was old enough to be "dear boy". He has a deceptive air of being charmingly disorganized, and writes in sobriety in a meticulously neat and efficient caravan set in the commodious homestead's garden. When he does hit town he is the loved menace of his friends, and is wildly the playboy who can drink whisky daylong and nightlong. He agreed to come with us to Port Fairy in the morning, and when we got to Warrnambool, Victoria's fourth-largest city, he described it as "preposterously prosperous". Which I've no doubt it is (or *was*, the way rural economics are going).

Australia's leading trousers-maker, Fletcher Jones, has a factory at Warrnambool, called Pleasant Hill. The grounds of this are extraordinarily gardened and open to visitors who like Wishing Wells and notices. The notices everywhere say everything from *You are nearer to God in a garden . . .* to *F.J. left Bendigo for the Western District in a two-horse hawker's wagon early in 1919 . . .* to *Postcards on Sale at "F.J." Shop 4 Blocks Down Town.*

From "F.J.'s" to Port Fairy is eighteen miles. "Rich country," Hal Porter says. "It's a great lava plain. Look at the black, black soil and the potatoes growing. We're in the Irish belt. We mustn't pass the Killarney pub. . . ." Lindsay Howe says we should stop first at Tower Hill, and we do.

Tower Hill is a hilled piece of landscape with a lake in what was the crater of perhaps the most recently active of Australian volcanoes in the Victorian part of this ancient land. The rich soil grew a profusion of trees and nourished abundant wildlife—until the pioneers, in cutting down most of the first, destroyed most of the second. Conservationist conscience set in, surprisingly enough, back in 1866. Then it was declared a reserve and, in a well-intentioned move to make amends, native trees were replanted and exotic animals introduced. Goats ate the gum-seedling trees, pheasants were promptly taken by hawks. Now, more intelligent restoration of the ecology is going on and—what with the ducks already back and Robin Boyd's architecture of the round Natural History Centre—Tower Hill looks like becoming a very interesting stop seven miles west of Warrnambool on the Princes Highway.

By the roadside, as we go, there are stone cottages straight out of Ireland, blank faced, no Australian-veranda nonsense. Of course we stop at the Killarney Hotel. And what names would there be chalked on the board by the pool table in the bar but Lenehan, Moloney,

Dwyer, Ryan. And what on the wall but a map of Ireland. With a map of Scotland stuck up beside it, by the proprietor, McKenzie.

"I know it's hard for you, Mac," Porter sympathizes with McKenzie. "All these potato diggers—every night the leprechauns are in. Even the kids born and bred here have the brogue."

McKenzie nods and says the last farm sold brought $550 an acre. Twenty-five tons of spuds to the acre it would grow—and the *onions!* His burr long lost, he is getting a touch of the brogue himself.

"Belfast" was for many years the name of Port Fairy we are now headed for. The renaming seems to have been done by a Sydney solicitor named Atkinson, who became virtually the owner of the town. Belfast it is no longer, but, "The Troubles, the legends, the blarney, the donnybrooks, the charm—they are all still around here," Hal says as we pull in to Port Fairy.

CHARACTER there is aplenty in stone, charm there is not quite so much of, and blarney there certainly is at Port Fairy. It is given to telling tourists Port Fairytales about its history.

A leaflet I got says, under the heading "VICTORIA'S FIRST SETTLE-MENT", that a Captain James Wishart took shelter there in his cutter *Fairy*, and gave its name to the haven, in 1810. According to the *Australian Encyclopaedia* the *Fairy* didn't arrive until 1827; and Henniker Heaton[4] gives 1828. Wishart didn't stay, nor did he form a settlement before, at Portland. The sealer William Dutton built a house and lived in it in 1829 and erected more buildings in 1832 (he left in 1833). Port Fairy's Whaler's Cottage, built for two of Wishart's men, and still standing, dates from about 1836. By which time the Hentys—whalers who also had sheep—had established the first permanent settlement at Portland in 1834, the year before Batman came to Port Phillip, where the first settlement in what is now Victoria was unquestionably made in *1803* by David Collins, with convicts and free settlers, who built houses where Sorrento is now: but Collins transferred his people to Tasmania. Port Fairy's "first settlement" claim is nonsense.

Another fairytale has to do with the wreck of an apparently very old ship of about 100 tons, built of mahogany. This was found in about 1836 near Port Fairy. It has become, in the tourist leaflet, "the wreck of the Spanish galleon, *Santa Ysabel*, the famed 'Mahogany Ship' which strayed from the Philippines route in 1595".

There is not, as far as I know, the slightest evidence to support the claim that this wreck (which has been buried under sand since about 1880) is the *Santa Isabel*, a ship of the Spanish explorer Mendaña's 1595 expedition to the Santa Cruz group of the Solomon Islands. The *Santa Isabel* disappeared when the volcano island of

25/VICTORIA *Oil was Australia's great lack, and a substantial part of its new prosperity rests on the six "production platforms" of Esso-B.H.P. in Bass Strait: this one is Barracouta. The first Bass Strait well drilled by floating rig in 1965 produced a big gas flow. From Barracouta both oil and gas are piped 20 miles to the mainland. The yellow square is where helicopters land.*

An "English" beauty invests the Tasmanian rural landscape in the island's north and midlands. This scene is at Table Cape near Wynyard.

Near St Helens, on the east coast, Binnalong Bay is a small fishing port and resort where the rocks are vividly coloured with lichens.

Tinakula was in eruption and was "probably destroyed by volcanic shocks".[5]

Nor can I substantiate the local statement that Port Fairy "was at one time the busiest [port] in Australasia outside Sydney". Maybe, as the same leaflet says, it was "expected to become Victoria's largest port", and maybe, for that reason "The Anglican church was planned as a cathedral": St John's Church, 1854.

Now here Port Fairy really has something to boast about, and barely mentions. Not the church itself—which is all right, but its architect was no Greenway—but the small relief sculptures on it, by a Scottish stonemason named Walter McGill. Hal Porter knew of these and had long admired them, and took me to see them. There is a head, beside the front door of the church, a face topped by a small crown. Although it is ravaged and noseless, it stamps Walter McGill as an artist so good that he is, I think, the great unknown of Australian stone sculpture. Another sensitive door-side head remains and some others, rather high up on the building, that look good from below. McGill also did the font in the church. But the church door was locked.

Memo Port Fairy Historical Society: Forget "first settlement" and *Santa Isabel* (or *Ysabel*). Protect the work of Walter McGill. Please put a small, tasteful shield-roof over the heads by the church doors for a start, so they don't erode further; and move that ugly pipe-conduit that runs right beside one. Find out all you can about who Walter McGill was and what else he did where. His work is the best thing you've got.

That last statement is rather a big one, though I'll stick by it. Port Fairy also has: (i) The Caledonian Hotel, 1844, believed to be Victoria's oldest continuously licensed hotel and in very good shape indeed, nicely restored—except that it doesn't have to be called *Ye* Old Caledonian Inn (and will the brewery please take that big FOSTER'S LAGER sign off the front). Worth going upstairs to the dormered rooms where Lindsay Howe couldn't stand upright, and to see the old shingled roof under the iron one. (ii) A Court House rated "A" by the National Trust, in a generous mood. (iii) Captain John Mills's 1850 cottage. (iv) The Whalers' Church, whale tusks inside the door. (v) The old A.N.Z. Bank that is a particularly good building.

Port Fairy lives off fishing—mainly crayfish, flake (which is shark) and barracouta—and tourism. Land prices had soared, and a fishermen's cottage had just been bought at a nice figure by wealthy Americans. It was getting to be an "in" place, somewhat to the disgust of H. Porter who said it used to be "enchanting" as I took a picture of him beside an old milestone that said "4 MILES TO BELFAST".

R

We had lunch in the bar of the Caledonian and left Hal there, and lit out for the Grampians.

The Grampians at Hall's Gap

IF YOU STOOD on the summit rock of Mt Everest you would be, as well as cold and famous, nearly eight times higher than if you were atop the highest peak of the "noble range of mountains" the explorer Thomas Mitchell discovered and named, from the ones in Scotland, the Grampians.

But Everest is teen-age rock, as age goes geologically, compared with Grampians sandstone. This was formed about 250 million years earlier—not that the Grampians mountains have been weathering down for that much longer. Their sandstones were laid down in a lake. They were heaved up rather later than those of the rest of the Great Dividing Range—of which the Grampians in western Victoria are the tail-end. They rose as three tip-tilted ranges running north-south and sloping sharply to the east, more gently to the west.

Some of the scarps give the impression of being stacked up in great blocks of eroded stone of just the ruggedness to make the Grampians the best of schooling grounds for rock-climbers. And some of these hard sandstones have been even more popular with quarrymen. Victoria's Parliament House and the Melbourne Town Hall and General Post Office are all built of Grampians freestone.

The Grampians region has abundant wildlife. Nowhere else did I see so many kangaroos; and it is rich in other animals, including rare species, and birds. Also, Laseron calls it "a botanist's paradise".[1]

What I liked immediately when we drove in to Hall's Gap, the tourist centre, was that it looked blessedly unlike a tourist centre. The few shops, the not-many houses, the excellent camping-ground and the accommodation places were unobtrusively strung out and subordinate to the red-gums, stringybarks and messmates that reared high all round and right to the road's edge—such a change from places where everything has been axed away to the point where the tallest roadside thing is a telegraph pole or a signboard. The forest is part of the town: which is so right for an area where the attraction is the wilderness.

If you wanted water with your wilderness there was plenty of that, in a number of reservoir lakes, for the parched Wimmera and Mallee regions to the north are watered from the Grampians. Lakes such as Bellfield have been stocked with fish, and we heard of a fourteen-pound trout being caught in one of them.

As a tourist area the Grampians had once been very popular; then, like the Blue Mountains of New South Wales, it had become less so. Now that twelve councils had formed an association to promote it, the area was coming back strongly, and not only with walkers, rock-climbers and amateur naturalists and gem hunters. Much of this resurgence could be due to the work of Ian McCann, who was with the council at Stawell, the nearest big town—a man so interested in the natural history of the area that he had 5,000 colour photographs, and he really knew what it had to offer. May was a cold-ish time, and there were few of the wildflowers that are the glory of the Grampians in spring. I asked Ian McCann, who came over from Stawell, what were the best months.

"Round Hall's Gap, from early September to early November—last year the flowers were late and better in November. In October you can't miss."

WE STAYED at the well-run Grand Canyon Motel that, when it went up at the end of 1967, was the first new building at Hall's Gap in years. The Grand Canyon (must our christeners be such copyists?) was a gorge about three miles away. It is a mistake to "build up" a gorge with a name like that in an area where the highest mountain is under four thousand feet. Still, an American girl who had left last week had been "thrilled" with the Grampians.

The place to stay before Fred Conboy put up his modern motel was the one hotel, with the exotic name of Le Château and a reputation for a well-stocked bar. It was doing bar business in a corrugated iron shed: it had been burnt down. The amiable proprietor said that as many as fifty kangaroos could usually be seen feeding in the paddock next door in the early morning.

"So the other morning this chap with a movie camera drives up. His wife stays in the car, and when he says 'Now!' she leans on the horn. Of course, the kangaroos take off. That's what he wanted—action for his movie. Don't blame me if the kangaroos aren't there tomorrow morning."

There are some introduced deer, and Ian McCann was caustic about the "deer stalkers". They had come in and shot two deer that were tame. "You could have shot a cow just as easily." Then they parked their Mercedes and Jaguars and had a "venison barbecue".

Next morning in the paddock beside the hotel I "shot" at least twenty kangaroos, and we weren't there long. Nine are sitting up looking at the telephoto lens in one picture, and there were a number of others feeding farther down. I got some more down the road, one in mid-flight over a fence, and others bouncing along in that wonderful motion that is like that of no other species of animal on earth. Yet the sensibility castrates can stop it with a bullet and call that sport.

We went out to Dairy Creek where there are many koalas, but we didn't see any. We heard lots of birdsong. More than 150 species of birds have been recorded in the Grampians, from wedgetail and whistling eagles and peregrine falcons to three kinds of kingfishers that aren't kookaburras (even the rare red-backed one I've never seen). The bird man who has yet to add to his sightings the brilliant spotted pardalote or the emu wren, the yellow-tailed black cockatoo, the boobook owl or the migrant rainbow bird (in spring and summer) is assured that they are all in the Grampians.

The mammal-man will want to see (and who else wouldn't except a friend of mine who says he has no interest in any animal uncooked!) the "soft-furred smoky mouse" which is no ordinary cheese nibbler. According to Ian McCann, it is seldom found outside the Grampians, though it has a relative living in Western Australia. There is also the potaroo, the rat-kangaroo half the size of a rabbit, lots of echidnas, platypuses in the creeks, but no wombats. Among the reptiles, the harmless white-lipped snake is common, as are lizards, from "bicycle lizards" (they get up on their hind legs and scurry off like a frantic bike-rider), stumpy-tails and blue-tongues, to the geckos, skinks and the legless lizards. The numbers of lace monitor goannas had been reduced by "vandals", for whom there should be a much dirtier word.

Going down a gorge of purple-brown sandstone we came upon rock-climbers learning how to scale overhanging scarps with the aid of a rope. Even though it was beginners' stuff, it looked quite dramatic. They were a nice group who had brought with them into the gorge their pets, a cat that had curled asleep on a rock and a grey parrot that disapproved of the whole exercise very loudly.

Aboriginal paintings are to be found in the Grampians, though at some distance from Hall's Gap. What is called Bunjil's Cave, in the Black Range about 20 miles away, had been classed by the Curator of Anthropology at the Museum in Melbourne as the "most important site so far reported from Victoria", as to Aboriginal painting. The figure of a fat man, with two dogs, has been reliably established as that of Bunjil, a tribal deity who "warmed the sun, and the sun warmed the earth, which opened and the blackfellows came out".

Wines at Great Western

WINE is very much part of the New Australia. A beer-drinking people who used to be inclined to dismiss wine as "plonk", Australians now drink more wine than the English do—and the biggest increase has been in the consumption of table wines.

England used to get some pretty bad Australian table wines, and stick to French ones. Nowadays there is no good reason why this should be so. According to the author of *The Wines of Australia*, ninety-nine per cent of the average French vintage is consumed in the year it is made into wine and, Harry Cox goes on to say, "its general quality is not as high as the average quality of Australian wine".[1]

Unquestionably, the Australian quality has improved a great deal in the past twenty years. Average Australian reds may have an "earthy" quality, but the best are very good, and some of the whites are superb. English acknowledgement of their merit was the House of Commons members' dining-room agreeing, in early 1970, to stock six Australian wines the House Wine Committee had tasted and found good: Houghton's white burgundy, Orlando Barossa riesling, St Thomas burgundy, Chalambar burgundy, Yalumba Chiquita sherry and Galway Pipe port. (All good wines, and widely available ones in Australia, but not necessarily our best-availables.)

Today's Australian investment in wine-making runs to well over $100 million. The widespread viticulture in the southernmost quarter of the continent, increasing in acreage all the time, had the earliest of beginnings. Vines came on the First Fleet. John Macarthur was no less a pioneer of wine-growing than he was of wool-growing: with the aid of vine-dressers he had brought from France, he was producing 27,000 gallons of wine a year in 1827. Four years earlier Gregory Blaxland, the Blue Mountains explorer, had produced a Parramatta wine that won a gold medal in London, Australia's first award: it has had many such since.

Victoria's first permanent settler, Edward Henty, planted vines at Portland in 1834. In the 1850s the chief wine-growing centre in Australia was Rutherglen, south of the Murray River—and South Australia might not be the leading wine State it is today if the Victorian vines had not been, at the end of the century, devastated by *phylloxera* (an American louse that eats the vines' roots). Victoria still produces some very good-value wines. It once produced a dry red from Lilydale, near Melbourne, that so bamboozled Paris Exhibition judges that they gave it the prize for the best *Bordeaux*.

GREAT WESTERN sounds a big name for the little township where a big Seppelts winery is, eight miles down the road from Stawell. The place was originally given the name of what proved to be the most famous failure among early steamships, *Great Eastern*; but as it was in the west of the State, this was changed to Great Western. An intrepid young Frenchwoman, Anne Marie Blampied migrated with her teenage brother in 1852 and went to the Beechworth goldfield, where she at least found a husband, another French migrant named Jean Trouette. They went west for gold, to Stawell, and Trouette, who knew wine-making from France, planted the first vines at Great Western. He made good wine, but died early and his St Peter's winery did not long survive the death of his son, asphyxiated in one of the vats. The vineyards and cellars called Great Western were begun by the English brothers Best, and expanded by Hans Irvine who, with the aid of a Frenchman who had worked for the House of Pommery, in 1892 made Australian champagne (if we take the designation as valid for any such type of sparkling wine made outside the Champagne province of France: it isn't in France, where "champagne" I saw in the making in the Loire district had to be called Monmousseau).

The House of Seppelt bought out Irvine in 1918 and so further extended the wineries enterprise begun by Joseph Ernst Seppelt who migrated from Germany with his family and workmen in 1849 to South Australia to grow tobacco: he found that vines grew better.

It was a Saturday afternoon when we went to Great Western, so no work was going on in the winery. But the manager, Mr L. R. Francis, was there to show us round. He had been making wine for forty-five years and gave the impression that he had been doing it with probity as well as knowledge. Seppelts, big as it is, is not as big in wine-making as Penfolds, Lindemans and McWilliams. But it has a reputation for consistency in its Moyston claret and Chalambar burgundy, both bottled and cellared at Great Western.

Great Western champagne has won the most local awards. Harry Cox seems to think that McWilliams will take its palm away, though Australian champagne, he says, "is only a shadow of the French".[2] Australians are inclined to order "champagne" as though it were a one-type wine; but the usual sweet champagne and the dry *Brut* are as different as sauterne and riesling.

OTHER WINERIES we shall be looking in at in South Australia, but the process of wine-making doesn't vary much and can be described briefly as it is at Great Western.

The grapes are picked (end of February to April) and crushed, the stalks separated out. The juice-skins-seeds, called "must", is pumped into vats to ferment, with yeast that turns the grape sugar into alcohol, or evaporates it as carbon-dioxide gas. So dry wines are fermented longer, until almost all the sugar is gone. Fortified sweet (dessert) wines, e.g. port and frontignac, are made by adding brandy spirit that arrests fermentation and leaves sugar. Sweet sherry, much the same. Dry sherry gets its special character, in casks, from "flor", a yeast culture developed from grape bloom. The fermented wine is "racked", allowed to settle. Then it is clarified and brightened with "fining", often a volcanic clay called bentonite, which has no taste or smell and attracts particles in suspension. Finally it is filtered.

For white wines, the principal varieties of grapes used here are Riesling for riesling and hock, Pinot Blanc for chablis, Semillon for sauterne. The Seppelts reds are mainly made from Cabernet Sauvignon grapes for claret, Shiraz (also called Red Hermitage) and Pinot Noir for burgundy. All grape juice being colourless, it is the dark grapes' skins that give the red. When this is sufficient the wine is run off to complete its fermentation. The skins and seeds, called the "marc", are part of what brandy is pot-distilled from. "Black" grapes, their juice separated smartly from the skins, can be used to make white wines, including champagne.

Champagne-making is complicated. The wine has to go through a second fermentation in the bottle. While this is going on each bottle, head down in what are called "riddling tables", has to be turned by hand, every day for four or five weeks.

"A good riddler can turn 25,000 bottles a day," Mr Francis said. Then the stopper is unclipped, the sediment shot off. The bottles go to a machine that injects a sugary liqueur—unless it is *Brut*, the dry kind made of top quality juice. This doesn't go on the market for four or five years: the other champagne is only two years old.

The cellars at Great Western make it a particularly interesting winery to go through and it gets many visitors. The "drives" into an ancient river bed that was found to underlie the upper rock were begun by Best a century ago and extended at least a mile by Hans Irvine. In some sections the old brickwork at the sides is of a beautiful colour (classified "A" by the National Trust). Mould hangs in soft black stalactites from the ceiling. The bottles are deeply furred with deposits. The wine in the cellars included 360,000 bottles of champagne, and three times as many others.

The oak for the great oval-fronted casks that mature the Moyston claret, and some other wines, has had to be imported from the U.S.A. and France: no Australian timber is suitable.

What They Did at Swan Hill

STANDING on Big Hill that overlooks Stawell, you may be looking at the kind of town that could endure in parts of the New Australia where recent mineral finds may work out, as Stawell's gold mines did.

Not only did the Frenchman who came for gold plant the vines that led to Great Western's winery. The clay that stopped yielding much gold gave rise to the Stawell Brick Company; and the gravels and sands to Ridge's Ready-Mixed Concrete. Grand-daughters of miners the stations stocked up with sheep to feed are working at the North Western Woollen Mills.

Stawell was prosperous enough to give itself in 1969 a centenary present of a new Town Hall clock, with bronze figures of two gold-cradling miners that are animated every hour to a folk tune played with Westminster chimes. Back in the gold days it gave a good prize to the best sprinter at the Easter sports meeting. The Stawell Gift has been for nearly a century Australia's most renowned professional footrace. So all the gold towns didn't end up as ghost towns: look at Stawell. Look at Ballarat and Bendigo.

This book will not look at either Ballarat or Bendigo. In order that it shall not end up as thick as the old family Bible or as a book that says too little about too many places, lines have to be drawn—and one line goes through highly industrialized urban provincial centres of large population. (Ballarat has 60,000 people and over 300 factories; Bendigo, 40,000, has a lot of industry as well as being a huge sheep-market.) However, if a place does something new and notable to re-present its history to the traveller, then that warrants inclusion. Ballarat Historical Park, a very big project, was still in the project stage, however: no part of it was even nearing completion. But a good deal of it should be open in 1971.

Ballarat's new presentation of its history to the tourist involved building replicas of historic buildings to virtually re-create a mining town. The period of the Eureka Stockade, which was Australia's only "revolution" (1854), will be portrayed with Bentley's Eureka Hotel the miners burnt, and the Victoria Theatre where the flamboyant Lola Montez performed her spider dance, and the office of the *Ballarat Times* whose editor the dancer horse-whipped for writing of her as a strumpet. So the tourist who is travelling Victoria in 1972 has good reason to go to Ballarat.

We were headed for Swan Hill where the best of Australian folk museums was. To get there from Stawell you drive north through the eastern edge of the Wimmera country that grows most of Victoria's wheat. The towns signal their presence far ahead, on the long straight line of the road, by wheat silos thrusting up out of the flat landscape as great concrete-grey cylinders. It is wide-sky country, owned by the sun. When the Grampians have disappeared behind and you are north of Wycheproof, there is never a mountain to impede the vigilant sun's getting up in the morning or hide its last glaring from the western horizon, where the Mallee country lies; and seldom does a raincloud cover its blazing eye.

The sun had gone down on a thirst we assuaged at the dusk-wrapped little silo town of Lalbert. There was nothing New Australia about the Saturday-afternooners filling the bar with talk of nothing but football; the half-gape at strangers entering, and the side-bets about how tall Lindsay Howe was; the old "Where y'from?" instant friendliness; the drunk reciting bush verses in your ear; the print in the tatty lounge of the Man with the Donkey still bringing in the wounded at Gallipoli.

Mentally, Swan Hill, though less than thirty miles away on the Murray River, was in another country.

BLACK SWANS were noisy on the river below the hill where the explorer Mitchell camped in 1836, and named the place from the swans that kept him awake. Nowadays, Swan Hill is very much awake, in that term's best sense. Not in the sense of what happened when the town of Tocumwal, on the New South Wales bank of the Murray farther east, woke up to the value of tourism. To hook tourists, Tocumwal suspended over the main road a very large and coloured fibreglass Murray codfish.

Swan Hill gets more tourists in a week-end (about $5,000 worth) than Tocumwal—which is on a major highway as well as on the same river—gets in a month. The plastic cod may be a stopper, but what is there to stop for? Swan Hill would never have thought of putting up a plastic swan. The tourists come because of what Swan Hill has done as a result of thinking about Swan Hill, primarily, not about tourism. It is hard to credit that this could be: but take the word of Sir Roy Grounds, the architect of the Victorian Arts Centre and Canberra's Academy of Science, who became so interested in what the Swan Hill community was trying to do that he is also, without fee, the architect of its folk museum: "These people were not concerned with tourism, or with money to be made out of tourism. They wished to record their history, and to creatively improve their environment."

The first surprise sprung by this community of fruitgrowers, wheatfarmers, fat lamb raisers, wine- and butter-makers and some factory workers, was back in 1947 when its population was 4,305. The Swan Hill National Theatre began staging an annual Shakespeare Festival! They were presenting *Twelfth Night* as theatre-in-the-round by 1967.

That was the year Swan Hill won the Develop Victoria League's triennial contest as the "Premier Town" of the State. It ran away with the "Cultural Activities" section of the contest, scoring 97 per cent, by having no less than fifteen cultural groups, including the Swan Hall Film Society and the Swan Hall *City* Orchestra. That's right. Two years earlier, still with only 7,000 people, this exceptional town had got itself proclaimed a city.

At the same time as it was being Stratford-upon-Murray, the mini-city of Swan Hill was doing highly practical things that were to win it the "Rural Development" section of the premier town contest. It had the best storage for farm products, a fruit processing plant uniquely capitalized, and forty-five businessmen and growers had backed a feasibility study that showed that Swan Hill justified a food processing plant. More prosperity would come of this to the town that had been prospering for years—and in 1961 had been irked by the feeling that perhaps it should be a bit ashamed of itself. It had forgotten the people who put Swan Hill on the map in the first place. As a former mayor said, "We were almost shocked by the fact that we had no memorial of any kind to our grandparents who opened up this part of the country."

What to do about the pioneers? Incorporate a memorial in the form of restored farm machinery in the design of the new library, as the local historical society suggested? With maybe a small historical art gallery as well?

The good thing Swan Hill did then was to do nothing—until it had got the best of advice on what it should do. Councillor Ross Mellor (then a schoolteacher) and the then Town Clerk, Robert Pugsley, talked to Eric Westbrook, director of the National Art Gallery of Victoria, telling him the historical background and what remained from pioneer days.

Eric Westbrook suggested the folk museum, and an old Murray River paddlewheel steamer as the nucleus of it. There were further talks with such people as Professor of Architecture Brian Lewis and then with Roy Grounds about what form the museum should take. Grounds said it should be an outdoor re-creation of the pioneer's way of life, a whole village with actual buildings brought in from wherever they could be found and re-erected faithfully, together with the machines and implements the early settlers worked with.

The scheme got under way with a borrowed "fiver" paying the deposit on the old three-decker paddle-steamer *Gem*, the one-time pride of the Murray. It took nine months to get the *Gem* up the now-less-navigable river to Swan Hill and a lot more than the $4,000 it was bought for to restore it. But the whole scheme was obviously such a good one that Victoria's Premier came up with a grant of $100,000. The State's contribution, at mid-1970, had grown to $250,000. But more than twice that much money had then been spent on the Swan Hill Folk Museum—$600,000 in fact. Much of the $350,000 came from the local Council and community; most of it from the Swan Hill Folk Museum itself.

Figure at close to a dollar a head the revenue from 120,000 visitors in 1969, and the 200,000 that Ross Mellor (no longer a schoolteacher, now manager of the enterprise) told me in August 1970 it would get in that year. Project such figures into the future and the great expenditure makes great sense. And, though the folk museum began as an act of civic conscience, it has become such a tourist attraction that even the Government must be getting a lot of its money back in increased taxation from increased earnings of moteliers, car service stations, butchers, bakers and others who share in the big tourism revenue.

Let us look at what Swan Hill (pop. now 8,200) has in its vaunted Folk Museum.

You ENTER a park where the old paddle-wheel *Gem* (PLATE 23) floats in a landlocked basin beside an arm of the Murray called the Little Murray at Horseshoe Bend. It is a beautiful old boat that can hold a candle or two to any riverboat that plied the Mississippi. Built in 1876, the *Gem* did so well as "Queen of the River" that in 1890 the vessel was cut in half, the halves dragged apart by bullock teams, and a centre section added to make it larger. It flies two flags, one of them the "Murray River Flag"—Union Jack in one corner, a five-starred Southern Cross quarter in the other, over blue and white stripes representing the flow of the Murray. (Such a flag was flown on the first paddle-steamer to come up the Murray to Swan Hill in 1853.)

Aboard is, apart from the Folk Museum's offices, an art gallery. And the Riverboat Restaurant where I had what was undoubtedly one of the best meals I ate in Victoria.

Go ashore and you step into the nineteenth century to an extent that doesn't happen when you step into the kind of Australian out-door historical museum that has a Cobb & Co. coach in a shed. The coach is here, but so is the Cobb & Co Agency, authentic to the things on the counter. There is a blacksmith's next door to shoe the horses—not a simulated smithy's but a real one brought in from Lalbert, with the tools used by THOS. THOMPSON, BLACKSMITH &

FARRIER (all the signwriting is period-perfect). In the wheelwright's shop next door to that an old man is wood-turning platters and dishes: tourists buy them. KIMM'S BARBER SHOP is no longer in Swan Hill's main street: it is here. "REWARD" notices are on the wall. They are still being printed next door at the "ECHO" PRINTERY near by, as souvenirs. The printery, with all its old type, was brought in from a place down near Castlemaine. No mean feats these of acquisition, transportation, re-erection; but what the museum makers found even more gratifying was getting Towaninnie station homestead on site—complete with its original mud-brick kitchen.

The old house was built, fifty miles south, in 1848, and built in a manner said to be unique to this part of Australia, "drop-log" construction. (Posts with slots cut in them were set up at six-foot intervals. Tapered logs were dropped down the slots and the slots held these firmly in place.) The roof, as Australian as a swaggie's slouch hat, spreads down to make a veranda all round. Hessian-lined inside, and papered over that, Towaninnie homestead has been given authentic period furnishings.

The "Iron House" came from England, prefabricated there and shipped out for assembly to relieve the housing shortage of the goldrush period. It is from South Melbourne, where it once housed the Commandant of Marines. But nothing could be more indigenous than the stable built of mallee roots (the mallee is a spindly dwarf eucalypt with a big rootstock) grubbed from the ground by the early wheat sowers.

To clear the land the pioneers used to break down the scrub for burning by hauling across it with bullocks a "mallee roller" (such as you see at the folk museum's entrance) made from a section of a big tree's trunk. A later clearing method was by chains drawn over the land between two traction engines, which had many other uses. Swan Hill has what is believed to be the largest traction engine ever brought to Australia. It has a whole collection of early agricultural machinery and implements, vintage tractors, harvesters. Three of these were Australian inventions—the stump-jump plough, the stripper that took the heads off the wheat and threshed out the grain, and the first harvester that winnowed and bagged the grain as well —invented by H. V. McKay, a Victorian farmer's son, when he was only eighteen.

Other vintage vehicles range from a red-gum jinker with wheels of solid wood to an Indian hawker's van such as used to be a common sight in the country districts and a Furphy's farm water cart curiously inscribed with the Pitman's shorthand symbols for *Water is the gift of God—Spirits the concoction of the Devil.*

There is much more to the Swan Hill Folk Museum than I have

described, and eight buildings have been added since I was there—including a post-office that is being made fully operative with nineteenth-century equipment.

The folk museum is to have its own old-style theatre: Sir Roy Grounds and Tom Brown were working on this. Adjoining land was to become much more than a fauna park. It would be developed as an "Environment Park" with the C.S.I.R.O. and other interested bodies researching and restoring its ecology.

Most ambitious project of all, the folk museum was to become a *son-et-lumière* spectacle at night—and the only one in the world where the audience moved. The spectators, who normally see such sound-and-light presentations from a seating area, would be taken round the area in soundless electrical vehicles.

SIR ROY GROUNDS was still, as he had been for some seven years, coming to Swan Hill about once a month for consultations and working on the project as its honorary architect—and I was given a rather earthy example of what it has meant to have his guidance and thinking. The Folk Museum Committee had said to him, "With attendance increasing the way it is, we'll have to build new and bigger lavatories. And they'll need to be where people can find them easily."

As I heard the story, the architect nodded, sighed, cogitated and said, "Well, if they need to be prominently sited, we'd better put them here", and he pointed to a position just inside the entrance. "But, we have to make the building disappear. First we make it round—no corners to jut against the eye. Round and brick. Then we clad the outside with mallee roots. Good, local, pioneer material—and the same colour as the earth. All they really need to see is MEN and WOMEN."

There is a message here for all the local councils that vote money for "erection of toilet blocks" at local spots frequented by tourists and in doing so disfigure these places with blatant box structures (labelled LADIES and GENTS), never thinking beyond brick or concrete to natural materials that blend with the surroundings.

Indeed, there are a lot of lessons to be learnt by other Australian communities from Swan Hill, and particularly by those towns that are trying to attract tourists (and what town isn't?).

As Sir Roy Grounds has said, "If a community thinks in terms of its environment first, tourism will come as a bonus. Such a community will get more tourists than the one that thinks first about tourism, and destroys its environment in the process of trying to attract tourists."

Another Miracle at Mildura

THERE IS MORE to Swan Hill, of course, than its Folk Museum. Ten miles out is Tyntynder Homestead, built in 1846 and a kind of folk museum in itself. Its walls are still in part the original logs of Murray pine; family portraits of the Holloways who bought it in 1876 from the Beveridges—Andrew Beveridge was speared by the Aborigines —hang in rooms of fine old furniture that includes the piano that Burke (or Wills) played on when those ill-fated explorers passed through in 1860. The bushranger Morgan was a horse-breaker on the station and another outlaw, Gardiner, stole its famous black stallion. Tyntynder (meaning "song of birds") is a storybook place.

Ten miles down the highway in the other direction is Lake Boga, a Murray Valley playground that provides even yachting, and which Swan Hill's shire council was making even more attractive by planting a thousand or so trees. Pelicans as well as swans were here.

On the way to this lake I asked the shire president, Peter Heighway, what else he was, and he said he had a "fruit salad farm". He grew peaches, apples, apricots, plums and grapes. His crops were almost disease-free because of the low humidity; and because locally grown seed was virus-free there was a big export of lettuce seed, especially, to the United States. How fruits and vegetables came to be grown in an area of less than twelve inches rainfall is a story I propose to leave until we get near Mildura.

There are other natural lakes hereabouts, including Lake Kangaroo, where the pioneer settler's name was Gorton. The property owned by John Grey Gorton did not see him very often those days: he was, then, rather busy being Australia's prime minister.

These lakes were "a great place for duck shooters—you get as many as 4,000 guns out at the opening of the season". (Victoria had 40,000 registered duck shooters.)

Kerang, farther down the highway, is a greater place for ducks and shooting them, and for birds generally. Here I talked to two local men who feared that the ducks would be shot out because their breeding grounds were going. "Birds are all we've got at Kerang," they said. "If we keep destroying their habitats, we'll end up with beaut roads for motor cars, and nowhere to go."

Where they wanted to go to, it turned out, was to places where there would always be plenty of ducks, to shoot. So they were fighting the Irrigation Commissioner who wanted to drain one swamp and a farmer who was trying to turn another swamp into grazing land. Both swamps were also breeding grounds of other birds such as ibis. Fred Wilkinson and Des Thomas, these duck-shooting conservationists, would have been horrified at the thought of anyone shooting ibis. (Farmers' friends, 5,000 ibis could eat a ton of grasshoppers in a day.) Or almost any other birds of the 240 species they said the district had, except, of course, the fourteen varieties of ducks—although they wouldn't shoot the rarer varieties of these, either. Other shooters who flocked to Kerang in the duck season would hardly be as discriminating.

Blasting at a flight of ducks with a shotgun and caring only about how many you bring down and not caring a damn about how many fringe birds fly off with a pellet or two in them to die afterwards, slowly—I am unable to see this, or any other form of bird or animal killing, as sport. If "cropping" (that nice euphemism for killing) becomes necessary then let it be done by professionals, who should be highly paid for doing a rather dirty job.

Over-breeding can, in the case of water birds, be controlled by egg gathering: Des Thomas showed us a colour slide of accessible eggs spread over fifty acres of reeds. Seven hundred ibis nesting in McPhail's swamp had left their eggs because irrigation had stopped the water flowing. And there was hardly likely to be a duck plague, to judge from Fred Wilkinson's chart showing wildlife areas that had been lost in the past four years through farming activities.

AT ROBINVALE, seventy-five miles down the Murray from Swan Hill, is a McWilliam's winery that is one of the most modern in the Southern Hemisphere. Anything less like the winery at Great Western would be hard to imagine. There is not an oak cask, much less a cellar cobweb, in the place.

The building, with a curved roof of corrugated iron, looks about as romantic as a quonset hut. Inside there is nothing to be seen but concrete and machinery. There is not even a vat you can poke your nose into: the vats are wall high, of concrete lined with wax. You don't even see any grapes—they are loaded into the crushers from an outside dock—or any wine until a slab is lifted in the concrete floor, and there it is fermenting underneath. McWilliam's at Robin-vale make a sweet sherry, a lot of brandy, and their white wine called Lexia.

"We used about 7,000 tons of grapes this year, averaging 120 gallons of juice to the ton. We only use the 'free run' of the juice—that's the initial pressing, the best. Skins and seeds are got rid of automatically," Mr Max McWilliam said.

Storage cellars? It wasn't necessary to store the wine made by this modern process. The Lexia they were making would be on sale by

Christmas. Would I like to try it—the Lexia that was coming through the pipes now?

I knew their Lexia. To me it had a sweetish edge. "Not really," Mr McWilliam said. "It's bone dry, but the Gordo grape it's made from carries that *suggestion* of sweetness."

I tried it, the new '69 Lexia. It still had, to me, that edge of undryness—which so many people like, anyway, as in a moselle. It was better than any Lexia I had tasted before. In fact, for a wine of its type, it was superb. Delicate, but with volume of flavour; good bouquet as well.

And yet it was made in this great shed full of concrete and metal and flexible plumbing like firehoses snaking across the floor to what looked like sewer vents, where the only "atmosphere" was the air that didn't even have a decent grape-musty smell.

"It doesn't seem right," I said to Lindsay Howe as we got back in the car.

OLIVEHOLME, the biggest olive grove in Australia, was just along the road. It produces, off five hundred acres, more than half the olives we grow and most of the olive oil we make, though not nearly as much as is imported.

After the ultra-modern winery, it was almost a shock to find that the method of harvesting olives hadn't changed. Migrant Italians, men, on ladders, were beating the olives off the trees with long sticks. (Soon after I was there Oliveholme introduced mechanical treeshakers that harvest 60 trees an hour at half the manual cost.) The trees, planted in 1950, were bigger than much older ones I had seen in Italy, Greece, Spain. The olives looked very good.

It was also orange-picking time. The bright globes of fruit were thick in the dark, glossy-foliaged trees. The pickers' bags were soon filled and piled into the trailer boxes behind the tractors. And beans: beyond a field of melons the bean pickers were busy. Grape-picking was over. But on either side of the road stretched some of nine thousand acres of vines the Robinvale district grows to make not only wine but currants and raisins.

"Robinvale has been the most successful soldiers'-settlement area in Australia. They've been making six thousand dollars a year off a thirty-acre block," Max Hunt of Robinvale said. He wasn't a grower, but had the electrical store. He was interested in "growing" tourism and showed us the area he was planting with trees and lawn at the riverside to make a private caravan park. Beside his house was the heaviest-bearing grapefruit tree I had ever seen. And the rainfall was—?

"Eleven inches."

So that, in terms of the rainfall map, all this cornucopian country-side is in almost-arid Australia.

Max Hunt took us down to Lock 15—"One of the best locks on the Murray."

This, of course, was what made it all possible. Irrigation.

"MILDURA" meant "red earth" Aboriginally. The Mallee country the Murray River bounds here was once described as a "Sahara of hissing, hot winds and red driving sand"—an overstatement. But the explorer Mitchell called it "one of the most barren regions of the world".

The city of 14,000 people is approached along a wide avenue handsomely planted down the centre with red-gums, prunus, pop-lars, acacias, palms, and gardens bedded with the brilliant red Sturt Pea. The sides are planted, less handsomely, with motels; but it is an impressive strand. Fittingly, it is Deakin Avenue.

Alfred Deakin, who was to become Australia's second prime minister, went to California in 1884 to study irrigation. His report on *Irrigation in Western America* was so impressive that the United States Government reprinted it. While there, Deakin met the Cana-dian-born Chaffey (pron. *Chay*fee) brothers, George and William, who had been responsible for the big Californian irrigation schemes. He so interested them in the possibilities of irrigating Australian lands that George Chaffey came to Australia. When he saw the Murray River he sent for William, who sold out their Californian interests and joined his brother at Mildura. Here they were to have a twenty-year lease of 250,000 acres of land, providing that they spent £300,000 in improvements.

It sounded a good deal, but the land, populated mainly by rabbits, was then worth so little that the Mildura Run pastoralist company had rented land at a penny a year for fourteen acres and still failed, along with the bank that backed it. Also, New South Wales regarded the Murray as its water and was loath to let the Chaffeys have it. In short, the deal, coupled with the Victorian depression of the nineties, ruined the Chaffeys. But it made Mildura.

George Chaffey knew that the land was all right, if it was watered. A brilliant engineer, he designed a pump so revolutionary in prin-ciple that the big British engineering firm of Tangey's agreed to make it, but would take no responsibility for its working, and would not put their name on it: it was cast with CHAFFEY on it. The famous pump, which worked perfectly and is enormous, can be seen on the river bank opposite the Mildura Arts Centre.

Chaffey Brothers Ltd having wound up in 1895, George, aged

S

fifty, returned to the States, where he transformed the Colorado Desert and ended up as a rich banker.

William Chaffey stayed on. He so inspired a rather disgruntled community by his hard work that the irrigation scheme flourished, he paid off his creditors, became mayor of the town, and started the Australian Dried Fruits Association that was the core to Mildura's prosperity. Before he died there, in 1926, he had done more than any man to make Mildura the green heart of one of the richest regions of Australia. The city put up a statue to William Chaffey. His brother deserved one, too.

The Chaffeys were prohibitionists, and their agreement with the Victorian Government made it virtually impossible to start a hotel. Australians got round this by starting liquor-licensed clubs. The Mildura Working Man's Club was certified in the *Guinness Book of Records* as having the longest bar in the world (285 feet). Then, in England, Butlin's holiday camp at Bognor Regis got 430 feet of bar—which Mildura says is not a "single bar" like the one it has now increased to 295 feet 10 inches or almost a hundred yards long.

There were still only four hotels (I stayed at the Grand) and just about every able-elbowed Milduran was a member of one or more clubs. The working Man's Club had 9000 members, male and female.

Mildura was getting 300,000 visitors a year. Surprised by the figure, I asked what tourists did, and was told that (apart from the fact that Mildura had the biggest winter-time bowls carnival in Australia) the main attraction was a two-hour trip along the Murray River on a paddlewheel steamer. So we paddled up the Murray on the *Melbourne*. The captain was a nice man, but it is expecting much of a good captain to be also a first-rate commentator. The Murray's banks, though here and there charming, are ugly in parts with tin sheds and pumps. The river is, scenically, better near Renmark in South Australia. Mildura could do much to make the Murray scene, and the steamer trip, better than it is at Mildura.

You could still be left wondering what Mildura had that was in any way outstanding—if you did not go to the Mildura Arts Centre.

AN ARTS CENTRE, not just an art gallery, Mildura truly has. A theatre is part of it. It was the theatre part that split the community in two, with so many Mildurans saying, "We don't need it" or "We can't afford it" that the mayor who was in favour of it came close to being defeated at the council elections. Now Mildura is very glad it has this part of the Arts Centre that a tourist leaflet lists first under the city's "principal attractions".

Thomas G. McCullough is young, ardently intelligent, bearded and from Belfast. He came to Australia and taught art and was one of only two people who took a diploma course in museum making. Mildura was lucky enough to get him as director of its Arts Centre complex that opened in 1966.

William Chaffey's charmingly nineteenth-century house, or mansion, *Rio Vista*, is the ideally uncluttered museum of local history. Conjoined, in contemporary architecture, are the art gallery and the theatre, which had presented the national ballet, a Pinero play, Filipino dancers, the Bath Festival Chamber Ensemble and the Yarra-Yarra New Orleans Jazz Band and a lot of lectures. In the gallery the art Mildura had—much of it Brangwyn and Orpen paintings given by a local collector—was so well displayed that the collection looked better than it actually was. The gallery ran many special exhibitions—it even got a show of Sidney Nolan—and it sent works of art out on tour.

Knowing that no gallery is really strong on Australian and New Zealand modern sculpture, Tom McCullough decided to make sculpture Mildura's distinction. Aided by donations from firms, he managed to make the triennial Mildura Prize for Sculpture the biggest offered to sculptors in Australasia.

Art critics and art dealers from the capital cities had to travel to Mildura to see what was accepted as the country's most important sculpture exhibition. Sculptures entered for the prize were displayed within the gallery and on its front lawns. Eyes popped at such a winner as Kitching's avant garde *Phoenix II*, parts of which were a washing machine agitator, a Ford Thunderbird's tail-light and children's playballs, and runner-up *Slotzyman and Slotzywoman*, which a local farmer described as "like two Holden engines making love". B.P. (the petroleum company) bought both for the gallery. Mildura City Council bought others.

In the Sunraysia district—the name is a brand name that seems to me to make the Mildura-centred region sound like a box of dried fruits—this cultural vitality coming out of the Arts Centre must have a yeasty effect. And perhaps there is—with so much agricultural machinery about, old and new—a readier acceptance of "mechanistic" sculpture than there would be in some other places.

Nowhere in the world has a machine been so publicly respected as at Wentworth, just down the Murray on the New South Wales side, Sunraysia's oldest town. Wentworth has the only memorial ever erected to a tractor—the model of a Ferguson F.E. 20, raised high on a stone base. The "Fergy" tractor helped build the levee that saved the town from the river's 1956 flood.

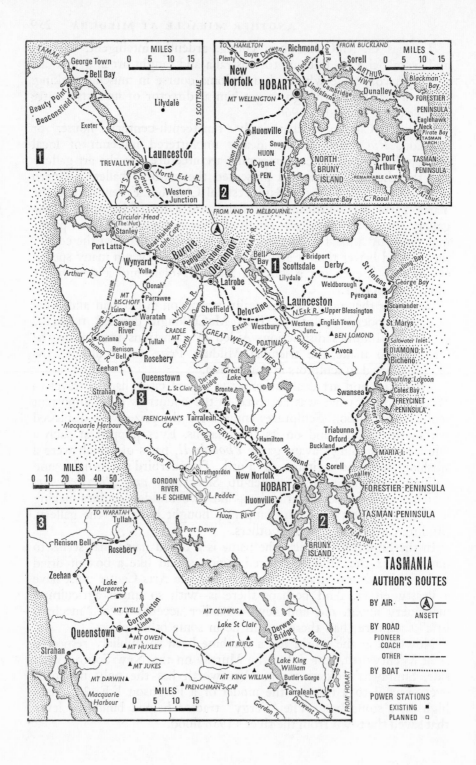

Inset 1:

TAMAR
George Town
Bell Bay
Beauty Point
Beaconsfield
Exeter
Lilydale
TO SCOTTSDALE
TREVALLYN
Launceston
North Esk R.
S. Esk R.
Cataract Gorge
Western Junction

MILES
0 5 10 15

Inset 2:

TO HAMILTON
Plenty
Boyer
Derwent R.
Richmond
Coal R.
FROM BUCKLAND
Sorell
New Norfolk
HOBART
Riston
Cambridge
Lindisfarne
ARTHUR HWY
Dunalley
Blackman Bay
FORESTIER PENINSULA
Eaglehawk Neck
Pirate Bay
TASMAN ARCH.
MT WELLINGTON
Huonville
Snug
HUON PEN.
Cygnet
NORTH BRUNY ISLAND
Port Arthur
TASMAN PENINSULA
REMARKABLE CAVE
Huon River
D'Entrecasteaux Channel
Adventure Bay
C. Raoul

MILES
0 5 10 15

Main map:

FROM AND TO MELBOURNE
Circular Head (The Nut)
Stanley
Port Latta
Boat Harbour
Table Cape
Burnie
Penguin
Ulverstone
Devonport
TAMAR R.
Bell Bay
Bridport
Scottsdale
Derby
St Helens
Binalong Bay
George Bay
Wynyard
Yolla
Latrobe
Lilydale
Weldborough
Pyengana
Arthur R.
Oonah
PIPELINE
MT BISCHOFF
Parrawee
Luina
Waratah
Sheffield
Deloraine
N.Esk R.
Upper Blessington
English Town
Scamander
Savage River
CRADLE MT
Wilmot R.
Exton
Westbury
Western Junc.
St Marys
Corinna
Pieman R.
Renison Bell
Tullah
Forth R.
Mersey R.
GREAT WESTERN TIERS
POATINA
South Esk R.
Avoca
BEN LOMOND
Saltwater Inlet
DIAMOND I.
Bicheno
Zeehan
Rosebery
Queenstown
Derwent Bridge
L. St Clair
Great Lake
Bronte
Swansea
Moulting Lagoon
Coles Bay
FREYCINET PENINSULA
Strahan
FRENCHMAN'S CAP
Tarraleah
Ouse
Hamilton
Triabunna
Orford
Buckland
Oyster Bay
MARIA I.
Macquarie Harbour
Gordon R.
DERWENT RIVER
Richmond
Sorell
Dunalley
FORESTIER PENINSULA
GORDON RIVER H-E SCHEME
Strathgordon
L. Pedder
New Norfolk
HOBART
Huonville
TASMAN PENINSULA
Port Arthur
Port Davey
Huon River
BRUNY ISLAND
FROM HOBART

MILES
0 10 20 30 40 50

Inset 3:

TO WARATAH
Tullah
Renison Bell
Rosebery
Zeehan
Lake Margaret
MT LYELL
Gormanston
Linda
MT OLYMPUS
Lake St Clair
Derwent Bridge
Bronte
Queenstown
MT OWEN
MT RUFUS
Strahan
MT HUXLEY
MT JUKES
Lake King William
Butler's Gorge
FROM HOBART
MT DARWIN
MT KING WILLIAM
FRENCHMAN'S CAP
Tarraleah
Macquarie Harbour
Gordon R.
Derwent R.

MILES
0 5 10 15

TASMANIA
AUTHOR'S ROUTES

BY AIR
ANSETT

BY ROAD
PIONEER COACH
OTHER

BY BOAT

POWER STATIONS
EXISTING
PLANNED

TASMANIA

The Prideful One Per Cent

"AUSTRALIA is a large island off the coast of Tasmania" is the kind of howler one can easily imagine a Tasmanian schoolboy writing.

The implications are not, after all, very different from those of a Tasmanian author who characterized his fellow islanders as a "proud people" who "like to be known as 'Tasmanians' rather than losing their State identity, under the group name 'Australians'."[1]

Tasmanians, numbering almost 400,000, are three per cent of Australians living on an island that is a little smaller than Scotland, a little larger than West Virginia, and not quite one per cent of Australia. Clearly, they must be proud of something other than their numbers—as many people live in three Sydney outer suburbs—or their State's size.

Historically, Tasmania is proud of being the second-oldest-to-New-South-Wales settlement (1803), and the first State to be granted its own separate colonial government (1825). It remained, officially, Van Diemen's Land (its discoverer, Tasman, in 1642 having given it the name of the Governor-General of the Dutch East Indies) until 1855 when it became "Tasmania", honouring the Dutchman who never knew he had found an island, and left no mark. Tasmania is proud of its historic sites.

It is not proud of having started life as a penal settlement, but neither is it ashamed of its convict past, which was common to the other States except South Australia and Victoria—which, the islanders will tell you, was "colonized by Tasmanians", Batman, Fawkner and Henty having gone across from Van Diemen's Land.

It might be tactless to ask why these intrepid settlers of Bass Strait's other side left Tasmania; or why, if, as a Tasmanian rhapsodist insists, "Nature gave the island only the best from her bag",[2] more people don't live there. Tasmania can answer smartly that the State has a density of population second-highest to Victoria's; but relative density in one of the world's most sparsely settled lands doesn't mean much. Tasmania has lived long with the problem of attracting new population and not losing Tasmanians to the wider opportunities of the mainland, from the time of the Victorian gold rush in the 1850s.

Discovery of tin, gold, silver, copper and zinc in Tasmania stemmed the outflow in the seventies and eighties. Depression and drift began again about the time of Federation—which rather put the little State in the position of a dinghy competing in a yacht race. The Commonwealth had to come to its rescue and give it a financial tow. It was getting a good economic wind behind it when World War II broke out. Post-war, Tasmania was no longer exporting people but importing industries. These were attracted because the island had developed its great natural resource—water—into electricity.

Of this transformation Tasmanians are, with reason, proud. The one-per-cent island has, from its roofs of mountains, thirteen per cent of Australia's rainfall run-off. That potential has been utilized by damming rivers and lake outlets and piping the water down mountainsides to so many big power plants that, by the end of 1972, Tasmania will be generating about one-third as much hydro-electricity as the great Snowy Mountains Scheme will when it is completed in 1974. No mean feat for a State with less than one-fifth of Melbourne's population.

And when Stage 1 of the Gordon River Power Development is completed in 1975 at a cost of another $100 million there will be a further huge addition to the power Tasmania is able to sell so cheaply that it pays Comalco to ship its bauxite 2,400 miles from Cape York to Tasmania and do its aluminium-making near Launceston.

"Three Units for the Price of One," Tasmania's Hydro-Electric Commission advertised to lure mainland manufacturers to come across and add their factories to those that were already making in Tasmania such things as confectionery, carpets, paper, woollen yarns, canned foods and hand tools. "The old image of Tasmania as a rural backwater has been shattered in the past decade," boomed the H.E.C.

THE TOURIST looking at a map of Tasmania—which is shaped like an eroded shield—sees many English or Scottish names on it: Hampshire, Queenstown, Hamilton, Campbell Town, Ross, Sheffield, Hastings, even Runnymede and Melton Mowbray. Aboriginal names are few, though some have been given to hydro-electric stations, such as Tarraleah and Waddamana and Tongatinah.

Tasmania has no reason to be proud of what it did to its Aborigines. These natives were of a type distinct from the mainlanders, and there were possibly no more than (estimates vary widely) 3,000 of them when the first white settlers came. By 1876 there were none. They had been killed off as though they were, today, kangaroos or wallabies or brush-tail possums or black swans or brown quail or wattle birds. (There were open seasons for all of these in Tasmania in 1970. Wombats could be killed at any time.)

The annual wallaby drive organized by the Avoca Football Club in May 1970 was considered a great success. It attracted a record 237 shooters who killed 1,237 wallabies—said to have been "ravaging" the pastures of a grazier who held something like 50,000 acres. For the footballers of Avoca, a small town in north-eastern Tasmania, the wallaby drive raised $500. It also raised wrath in the mainland Press. The Australian Wildlife Protection Council (whose president reported that one member of the Animals and Birds Protection Board of Tasmania was a skin-buyer) said that if any more Avoca wallaby drives were held his organization would, though reluctant to do so, urge people not to go to Tasmania for their holidays. (The 1971 drive killed more than 1,000 wallabies.)

It should be assumed, I suggest, by Tasmania's tourist authorities that one intending tourist in a hundred is a conservationist or "crank" (the terms are less synonymous than they used to be, and the species more numerous, on the mainland at any rate) who finds Tasmania's condoning this kind of wildlife slaughter off-putting. Tasmania's revenue from the estimated 104,000 tourists it got in the year ending March 1969 was about $10 million. So a one per cent loss would be $100,000—which is rather a lot of money to risk not getting from tourists so that the Avoca Football Club can get $500 from dead wallabies. Also most tourists like to *see* wildlife—and Tasmania is relatively short of it. Tasmanians have shot their Forester kangaroo nearly to extinction and had reduced the Flinders Island colonies of Cape Barren Geese, which are among Australia's rarest birds, to less than a thousand before they were protected.

On the latest figures mainland Australians were 88½ per cent of Tasmania's holiday visitors. American vacationists (four per cent of the total) stayed only one or two nights. Few New Zealanders, Australia's most numerous tourists from overseas, go to Tasmania.

The image that many mainlanders have of Tasmania is of a picture-postcard State, decidedly more "English" than any other part of Australia—and therefore a refreshingly different scene to that of their own States—cooler in summer, prettier in spring and autumn and altogether too cold in winter (except for skiers). The picture is fairly right, except that it leaves out of account that a great deal of Tasmania is mountainous.

Motoring tourists can bring their cars from Melbourne on the overnight-crossing ferries *Princess of Tasmania* and *Tasmanian*

Trader or from Sydney on the *Empress of Australia* (40 hours). Airlines offer fly/drive tours: you fly to Launceston, pick up an Avis car that costs only petrol for 700 rental-free miles, and then set off along a set route, with reserved accommodation as part of this package deal, which includes flying back to the mainland with the airline. In 700 miles driving you can see most of tourist Tasmania.

"Round" the island, in the tourist sense of the term, is about a thousand miles, with side-trips, and this can be done on a coach tour of ten to fourteen days, such as I did. The "round" trip offers the greatest variety of scenery.

Launceston to Eaglehawk Neck

COLONIAL TASMANIA's urban scene is best preserved at Hobart, just as the grim story of the convict era remains written in stone at Port Arthur to an extent that it nowhere is on the mainland.

In Launceston, Tasmania's second city—with over 60,000 people, it is half the size of Hobart—not very much is to be seen of the historical Australia that now exists so sparsely in the other States that Tasmania regards what it has left as a major tourist attraction. Yet Launceston, as a settlement, was only three years younger than Hobart, and older than Brisbane, Melbourne, Adelaide or Perth. It was founded in 1806 by Colonel Paterson, and Governor King called it Patersonia; but Paterson modestly thought it should be Launceston, after the governor's birthplace in Cornwall. The smaller city tends to regard Hobart as convict-bred. No convicts were sent to Launceston.

Launceston spreads its mostly wooden houses—commonly white-painted with dark-red iron roofs—on the hills at the head of the picturesque Tamar that is called a river but is more of an estuary, reaching forty-odd miles in from the sea to where, at Launceston, two rivers, the North Esk and South Esk, come into it. So there is a lot of blue in the Launceston scene, and a lot of flower-flecked green, for its main distinction is the extent of its parks and gardens.

Cataract Gorge is now more gorge than cataract, except after heavy rain. Tasmania's (indeed, Australia's) hydro-electric development began with the harnessing of the South Esk River where it knifes through mountains at the city's edge, taming its flow and making Launceston, in 1895, one of the first cities in the Southern Hemisphere to be electrically lit. It was the provision of cheap power-from-water that was to make Launceston the Bradford of Tasmania, the textile-making centre, the home of the big Coats-Patons (formerly Patons & Baldwins) wool-spinning mill. The other mills are not conspicuous and Launceston manages nicely to look much less industrial than it is. The walk along the side of Cataract Gorge remains remarkable for rugged beauty so close to the city's centre.

Launceston still has some good Colonial buildings to show, though these are fewer in the city (which didn't become one until 1888) than on its outskirts. Not so formally Georgian as nearer Franklin House (1838), and more picturesquely set and with a more "lived in" look, is Entally House, eight miles out. It dates from 1820, though subsequent alterations have given Entally the look of two houses (one called the Governor's Wing) joined together. It has been finely recreated as a rich settler's home of the 1820-1840 period. There is beautiful English furniture, truly "period", from before 1820. Some of it eighteenth-century, Regency, Chippendale, Hepplewhite.

Entally House was built by a son of Mary Reibey, who was one of Australia's, not Tasmania's, most notable convicts: the term is a harsh one for the thirteen-year-old Mary Haydock who tomboyishly took a Yorkshire squire's cob off to ride it, and was arrested (wearing boy's clothing) and sentenced to seven years transportation. Two years after she arrived in Sydney she married an enterprising ship's officer named Reibey, in 1794, and when he died at forty-two she became the colony's greatest businesswoman. She carried on the Reibey shipping fleet, managed farms and warehouses, erected buildings in Sydney's main streets. She grew so rich her grandson Thomas Reibey would accept no stipend when he was Archdeacon of Launceston. Leaving the Church, he became prominent in politics and was, for a time, premier of Tasmania, and, though ever a pillar of propriety, had one of the biggest racing stables in Australia.

What is said to be the oldest-established hotel in Australia, the Launceston Hotel, was begun in 1814 by Dicky White, who had been transported for being a highwayman. He also prospered as a pastoralist, auctioneer and racehorse-owner, played the violin and dressed like the figure on the Johnnie Walker whisky bottle. The upstairs lounge of this comely hotel in Brisbane Street is still probably the most comfortable place to drink in Launceston; and it has a reasonably priced restaurant called Dicky White's Bistro. These I discovered for myself the evening I arrived in Launceston, having flown in from Melbourne in under an hour, and gone to the Town House Motel, which was quite civilized and even had a bar.

The other places I saw as part of a coach tour (another Pioneer one), I joined in Launceston and continued with right round to Queenstown. It also went to a fauna park run by Monty Turner, who said his father had helped Walt Disney make a film and when it was finished Disney said, "Shoot the animals". The younger Turner asked could he have them, and that was the beginning of the place where he was exhibiting, among other fauna, the only two koalas in Tasmania (imported from the mainland: koalas were never indigenous), the rare golden possum, and Tasmanian devils. These unprepossessing, mostly-black animals are something like a badly-proportioned dog, with ferocious-looking teeth.

Another tour that can be taken during the day and a half spent in Launceston is along the Tamar by coach to Beauty Point (which doesn't do much to justify its name) and thence by launch on a not very interesting cruise past George Town, the original settlement at the estuary's entrance, and Bell Bay where Comalco runs Australia's first and largest aluminium-making plant, (which I was to see when I returned to Launceston).

The best part of this tour is the run through the apple-orchard country and past some lovely reaches of the Tamar between Launceston and Exeter.

Beaconsfield (which went under the brighter name of Brandy Creek until a Tasmanian governor thought that too undignified), near Beauty Point, was the richest of the island's goldmines and one of the richest in Australia—it produced more gold than Hill End in N.S.W. It was abandoned in 1914, not because the gold ran out but because water ran in. The crumbling walls of the old gold-smelting plant are grown over with ivy; but the gone-down town that was once the third largest in Tasmania has not lost hope that some big company will come along, get rid of the water by modern pumping techniques, and mine much more gold from the still-rich reef.

THE COACH rolled out of Launceston on a sparkling morning. This was the third day of April, the last month of Tasmania's tourist "season". Next week would see the last of the Pioneer tours until December.

The coach captain, Brian, was from Newcastle-on-Tyne, and a bit of his mother's Ireland, as well as Yorkshire, adhered to his accent. As his job required, he knew more about Tasmania than most Tasmanians. How much the new State Government houses we were passing cost, and how they were paid off: $14 a week for forty-two years. Why the houses were mostly wooden; three quarters of the island was still under timber. How much had been destroyed in the last big bushfires: 3,600 acres in an afternoon. Why there were only 500 miles of railways: too expensive to build more for a small population. He didn't know, though, why one sees relatively few birds: "They say there are over two hundred species.

I've been driving through the island for three years, and I don't know where they are."

We had been travelling through unremarkable country until, from a lookout the good Tasman Highway wound up to, there was a spread of Devon-green valley towards Scottsdale. We picked sun-warmed blackberries from bushes by the roadside, getting sweet-purple mouths and tiny seeds between the teeth. The road serpent-ined down to rolling fields of clover spotted gold with dandelions and clumped with pines. The soil reddened richly. Fields of potatoes gave way to flowers—acres of asters were blooming. Yates grew a lot of seed hereabouts. (At Lilydale to the west there was a big farm of lavender.) Round here, Brian said, the rhododendrons were a sight to see in December. Scottsdale was prosperous: you could tell from the standard of the farmers' barns—often better indicators than their houses are. And the district might flourish further from molybdenite mining, as Derby, farther along the road, once did from tin.

We neared Weldborough where the Chinese joss house in Laun-ceston Museum came from: Chinese flocked to Australia after tin as well as gold.

The road climbed on, winding. "Must have been surveyed by a snake," the wheel-twisting Brian said, and "I don't see much of this stretch. Too many bends to watch." A middle-aged passenger from Dubbo, N.S.W., declared: "People say, 'Take your car to Tasmania.' Not for me. I want to see the country—not just the flaming road through it."

The sides of the road have been getting denser and greener. At the top of Weldborough Pass we stop and go into rainforest, cool-climate jungle that in Tasmania comes as a surprise to many travel-lers. The light is dim and seems green as you pick your way through beech and myrtle, sassafras and towering swamp-gum, round rot-ting logs upholstered in moss like plush, and sprouting fungi.

Down to the pastoral valley of Pyengana, and we stop at a place where I buy leatherwood honey—which I have been trying to get in Sydney ever since, with occasional success, because it is the best honey I know, though some people don't like its strong, "smoky" flavour. Leatherwood, *Eucryphia lucida*—"its white scented flowers resemble single roses"[1]—grows only in Tasmania, I think; the same may also grow in Chile.

The road is less than enchanting from Pyengana to the coast at St Helens.

St Helens I fell in love with. Cupid was Johnnie Walker who used to work on a Sydney newspaper's sub-editors' table where subs were always saying that what they wanted to do was give away the race with edition deadlines and run a country pub. None that I knew ever did, except Walker who (avoiding the kind of inland small-town pub that would drive a city-bred sub. madder than edition deadlines) got himself what he has made perhaps the best place to stay on the Tasmanian east coast, the St Helens Hotel-Motel.

The town is the east coast's largest but still has no more than a thousand residents, though it gets a lot of tourists. It sits on placid George's Bay, an inlet sheltered by a long point. On the ocean side of this the Peron Sand Dunes (named for a French explorer) lined a sweep of lonely and lovely beach. At Binalong Bay the rocks round the little boat harbour were vivid with orange lichens (PLATE 26). As we drove back to the hotel the cray-boats sat moveless on a bay flushed pink with the sun's going.

The dinner I had could not possibly be served to package-deal coach tourists: it would cost too much. For the record, it was the best meal I ate in Tasmania, except that the local oysters are not comparable with those of New South Wales. The seafood chowder was specially good. The scallops—well, scallops are now hard to come by in Tasmania, which has over-fished its most distinctive seafood. Queen scallops are particularly rare. I got three—grilled. They were of a specially delicate flavour. Then I got a crayfish tail cooked in a sauce of burnt butter with parsley, chives and lemon. (Superb, and available, given forty minutes notice, at $3.50 then, probably more now.)

Next day was another blue one. We went on to Scamander, where the fishing is famed; but so it is all down this coast. From sheep-pastured seaside the highway goes inland to the coal town of St Mary's, then winds back to the coast at Saltwater River where, in convict days, there was an infamous coal-mine worked by the most refractory convicts, with cells built into the mine galleries. As we approach Bicheno, Brian points out to Diamond Island where, he says, there are fairy penguins. Because they eat so many fish, the professional fishermen "get among them and kill them", illegally. A warm current makes this part of the coast sixty-degrees mild in June-July.

Bicheno, now a popular resort as well as a crayfishing centre, was used as early as 1803 by whalers and sealers, who made the Aborigines club seals for them, and brutally misused their women. Yet there is a grave at Bicheno, tended now by the local schoolchildren, and the headstone reads: *Here lies Waubadebar, a Female Aborigine of Van Diemen's Land, Died June 1832, Aged 40 Years. This Stone is Erected by a Few of Her White Friends.* It appears that Wauba-

debar, a good swimmer, saved the life of the sealer she clubbed for
when his boat was wrecked; and for this she gained a degree of
white respect that would appear to have been unique. One can only
guess at how other Aborigines regarded this burial, for they always
cremated their dead.

THE TASMANIAN ABORIGINES, according to one theory, were a
Negrito people from the north who, before there was a Torres Strait
or a Bass Strait, preceded the mainland types into what became the
continent. Another theory is that they were descendants of a boat-
load of Melanesians who drifted 1,500 miles from New Caledonia.
Certainly they were different from the mainlanders: their hair
woolly, their lips not as full, and their language more rudimentary,
without any sibilants. Like the mainlanders, they were hunters with
spears and waddies, and used stone axes and bone awls. They never
had the dingo and, curiously, did not eat scale fish, though they
relished shellfish and sea mammals. They went naked, except for a
kangaroo skin over the shoulders, built huts and made distinctive
rock engravings.

Soon after the first military settlement was founded at Hobart in
1803 a party of natives, men, women and children, appeared near
the whites' camp, hunting kangaroos. A panicky officer ordered
them fired upon. About forty were either killed or wounded, and
the "Black War" had begun. The antagonized Aborigines retaliated
where they could, against sheep and settlers, when they were dispossessed of their hunting-grounds and subjected to white cruelties
Governor Sorell described in 1819 as "repugnant to humanity and
disgraceful to the British character".[2] In a Hobart newspaper of
1824 they were still "the most peaceful creatures in the world".[3]

Governor Arthur tried to round up, for their own protection, the
Aborigines who were left in 1830, and to segregate them on the
Forestier Peninsula. His "Great Drive", with 5,000 soldiers, police
and settlers stretched out in line, cost £30,000 and made the well-
intentioned Arthur a laughing-stock when it captured only one
man and a boy. It was not only that the bush-wily natives slipped
through the line: there were so few left to capture. A deeply
religious and courageous bricklayer of Hobart named Robinson
convinced Arthur, if nobody else, that he could bring in the remnant. Gaining the natives' confidence he did, over the next five years,
induce the several hundred left to come with him. They were taken
to a bleak island, off the north coast, and taught about God and
Heaven and Hell, and they were so miserable and sick they soon
died down to forty-four, who were removed to a squalid camp
near Hobart, where the blankets given them were "stolen by whites

or bought for gin".[4] The last Tasmanoid was not Truganini but an old woman living on Kangaroo Island in South Australia, where she had been taken as a girl by sealers.

Thus was Tasmania founded, on genocide as well as convictism.

AT SWANSEA we stopped for lunch at the renovated and modernized Swan Inn that was licensed in 1841. Historic Swansea is Meccasville for fishermen—bream, trout and deep-sea.

The hotel looks across wide blue Oyster Bay to Coles Bay in the long crooked finger of land called the Freycinet Peninsula. The name given by an early French navigator is one to remember: this peninsula is likely to develop in a few years into one of the most favoured resort areas in Tasmania. Granite peaks go up to 2,000 feet and on the ocean side of Coles Bay are alluring Sleepy Bay and Wineglass Bay; there are also the Friendly Beaches and Moulting Lagoon. Most of the mountainous peninsula is, happily, Freycinet National Park, already beloved of bushwalkers and naturalists. It is to be hoped that the developers don't make a mess of the rest of it.

Good green sheep country has piles of scallop shells in some of the paddocks. An echidna is seen by the roadside. Brian teaches his coach to sing *On Ilkley Moor*. We come to Triabunna, busy with fishing and once a whaling station and the garrison town for the penal colony on wasp-waisted Maria Island, where the Animals and Birds Protection Board of Tasmania is, admirably if somewhat belatedly, trying to preserve such fauna as the Forester Kangaroo and even "breed back" from small emus the dwarf Tasmanian emu that disappeared a century ago.

The road turns inland from Orford where a $1.5-million industry of extracting sodium alginate from seaweed has grown up since 1964. At the village of Buckland we go to a church with a remarkable stained-glass window. It is said to be fourteenth century and to have been an addition to Battle Abbey, founded by William the Conqueror near Hastings in 1094, and to have come into the possession of the Marquis of Salisbury who sent it out to the first rector of Buckland. Some authorities are dubious about its Battle Abbey origin; but it is still a magnificent window to come upon in a tiny place in Tasmania.

In the churchyard, a stone over the grave of an infant who died in 1852 has the epitaph:

Here lies the grief
Of a fond Mother
And blasted expectations
Of an indulgent Father

There is Break Me Neck hill and another called Bust Me Gall on the way to Sorell. A farmer has planted the roadside to his rich pastures with flowers. After a refreshment and "comfort" stop, we go east on the Arthur Highway and, just past Dunalley, come to what is really the most historic place in Tasmania, Blackman Bay. Here on 2nd December 1642 came Abel Tasman, with the war-yacht *Heemskerck* and the even smaller *Zeehaen* called a "flute". He made a landing, was surprised to see an animal track like a tiger's and—no natives were seen—steps cut five feet apart on tree-trunks, suggesting a race of giants. Tasman proposed to land again next day, but the weather was too rough. A ship's carpenter swam ashore with a flag, and the country was dubbed *van Diemenslandt* and Dutch territory. Cook, trespassing 135 years later, did not know it was an island, either. A Tasman monument stands on the bay shore.

THE MAP of this south-east corner of Tasmania shows a number of almost-islands. Narrow necks of land, such as the one we cross now (the only one cut with a canal) to the Forestier Peninsula, are also common to Maria Island and Bruny Island (each comes close to being two islands). The next narrow neck we come to—the one that joins Forestier Peninsula onto Tasman Peninsula—is the most written-about neck of land in Australia.

Eaglehawk Neck is only seventy-eight yards across. This made the peninsula, Governor Arthur decided in 1829, a "natural penitentiary". He sited his prison settlement on the southern inlet—both were named Port Arthur. Across Eaglehawk Neck dogs, with barrels for kennels, were chained. The cordon of hounds was the idea of Ensign Peyton Jones, in charge of the guard there. They were tethered so that at chain's-length they were nearly nose to nose. They were not there to tear escaping convicts to pieces, but to bark alarm to the guards of soldiery. So to escape meant swimming Eaglehawk Bay, or Pirate Bay on the opposite side. It was promulgated officially that the waters teemed with sharks, of which the man-eating types are rare in Tasmanian waters. There was also a network of semaphore stations to signal any attempts to escape.

Before reaching Port Arthur we hear about Australia's first railway. It ran for four and a half miles. The one small carriage was pushed by two relays of four convicts along the flat and up rises, and they rode it on the downhill stretches.

The Four Seasons Motel was the only one right at Port Arthur, which gets about 30,000 tourists a year. Even in April it was full, and short-notice bookings between December and March were impossible. There was another hotel, the Lufra, at Eaglehawk Neck.

Tasmania generally is short of tourist accommodation and in-season tours need to be planned well ahead.

Pre-Australia at Port Arthur

AN ENGLISH VISITOR, transported by rocket from London and set down at Port Arthur knowing nothing of its history, might well record his first impressions thus:

"This looks a pleasant bayside place, surprisingly English in atmosphere and with interesting old freestone buildings. The larger structures are more or less in ruins, including a rather enchanting church, set in a park as green as Ireland. A round crenellated tower over there is intact, and some white Colonial cottages look cherished and charming.

"To one side of the bay is a very long building, four-storeyed in part—it may have been commodious warehouses if the place was a port. In front of this is a sprawl of tents and caravans of holiday-makers—by no means the best part of the scene. On the rise at the back are remains of good stone buildings whose functions one can hardly guess at. Wholly preserved is what could be a small Town Hall or perhaps a Mechanics' Institute. Out in the bay I see a long point and, off it, an engaging small island.

"The area has been planted with English trees, and long enough ago for oaks, elms, ash and poplars to have grown into avenues round this park-like portion. The church, pointed with small spires, is a really choice little ruin, a latter-day Tintern Abbey in quality (PLATE 27). Must be interesting background to this settlement. I shall have to find out what it was."

That is how Port Arthur could look to a more innocent eye than most Australians bring to it, even if we still don't see it clearly. Some explanation for our English visitor:

"Port Arthur, sir, was a principal Australian penal establishment for convicts from your country and Ireland between 1833—when the buildings you see began to rise, though it was started three years earlier—and 1877, when it was abandoned. Van Diemen's Land became, as someone said, the 'jail of the Empire'. New South Wales agitatedly persuaded Britain to cease transportation to there in 1840. After that, now-Tasmania received 35,500 convicts making, in all, half the transportees to Australia. Only a minority ever saw the inside of Port Arthur. Government needed the skills of the educated. Settlers needed the labour of convicts assigned as servants. No women convicts were ever at Port Arthur.

Hobart's Tasman Bridge rides smoothly across the Derwent River, beyond which the capital is extending into the foothills of Mt Wellington.

Port Arthur, the one-time penal settlement, is an odd place to have produced Australia's loveliest ruin, the convict-built church there.

The strange "dead world in Technicolor" landscape near Queenstown. How it was produced by copper-smelting is explained. Now it is regenerating.

28/TASMANIA

Vivid copper-greened water and rock of an old open-cut of Mt Lyell copper mine, near Queenstown. The open cut still being worked was enormous.

"It was more than a jail. It was, at one time, the third-largest settlement in Van Diemen's Land, with many more buildings than you see now. Even in 1835 it had a coal-mine—which the convicts had a horror of working in, but it is untrue to say that they 'never saw daylight': they worked eight-hour shifts. It had shipbuilding yards; it made boots and shoes; it supplied timber and grew tons of vegetables produced by 1,100 convicts whose numbers were increased until in 1853, when transportation to Tasmania ended, it had 9,000.

"The long bayside building was the Penitentiary. The round crenellated tower, the Powder Magazine—near the ruins of the Guardhouse and Courthouse. The ruin beyond is of the General Hospital—and you can imagine convicts being taken to it after awful floggings. However, flogging ceased here long before it did as a regular form of punishment for misbehaving soldiers in the British Army. The substitute introduced at Port Arthur was solitary confinement in the Separate Treatment Prison's cells. Flaying the mind, as it were, instead of flaying the back. That building you thought of as a small Town Hall *is* the local Council Chambers, now, and also the dance-hall and cinema: it used to be the Lunatic Asylum.

"Much of what was called the Separate Treatment Prison still stands. The guide who takes tourists round will tell you that it was built in the style of the 'model prison' of England's Pentonville, which wasn't built until 1842, about the time this one was. I think its pattern was the earlier Millbank model, based on the reformer Jeremy Bentham's 'panopticon'. A central warder could watch five radial corridors with 44 cells. A prisoner needing attention pressed a lever that popped out his number and rang a bell over the warder's head. There were two 'dumb cells' where specially recalcitrant prisoners got no light and heard no sound.

"You are not, I'm sure, the morbid-type tourist who wants to see a flogging triangle and a gallows. Neither is here. There were no executions at Port Arthur; but many in Hobart.

"The point out in the bay is Point Puer (Latin for 'child', as you know) where there was a reformatory for transported boys. They were taught trades, and some became leading citizens of Hobart, or their descendants did. That 'engaging island' is the Isle of the Dead. *Isle des Morts* actually, but that seems a bit much for the burial place of some 2,000 convicts, so many of whom couldn't read or write, in nameless graves. About two hundred soldiers and other 'free' have headstones.

"A tourist launch goes out past the island and Point Puer. I shouldn't take much notice of a story about the 'Suicide Cliff' boys

T

threw themselves over, so awful was their lot. According to Coultman Smith (whose *Shadow over Tasmania*[1] paperback you can buy
at the kiosk-museum) one boy fell over the cliff and another was
pushed over for tale-telling.

"One of the charming old Colonial cottages was lived in by
William Smith O'Brien, who was exiled from Ireland for being a
leader of the 1848 uprising. With him came Thomas Francis
Meagher, who escaped from Tasmania to America, where he fought
against the British in the Civil War and ended up as governor of
Montana.

"The church is, as you say, enchanting—the loveliest ruin in
Australia. Originally there were thirteen spires—Christ and the
twelve Apostles. We aren't sure who designed it, probably the
architect James Blackburn, who was transported for forgery three
years before the church was begun in 1836. It is St Nobody's as to
name, and it was never consecrated—not because, as is commonly
said, one of its convict builders murdered another who was working
on the same wall, but because it was of no particular denomination.
There was room for over a thousand Anglicans and Irish Catholics
to be marshalled in on Sundays. And apparently they quite enjoyed
bellowing out hymns: it was the only time they could raise their
voices. They had chapel every morning—the 'solitaries' with hoods
over their heads, because not seeing a fellow-man was part of their
punishment. There was a Bible in every cell, though not much light
to read it by. But the Penitentiary had its library room and such
games as dominoes. I am not trying to minimize Port Arthur's
harshness; but there were, unfortunately, worse places."

MANY AUSTRALIANS are inclined to think of Port Arthur as the
oldest and most notorious of "Vandemonian" convict hells-on-earth.
In fact it was the second last to be established and, with all its
inhumanities, the best.

Although Charles O'Hara Booth as commandant (1833-44), who
did most to make and mould Port Arthur, was the stern disciplin-
arian the "System" required him to be, Governor Arthur described
him as "kind and humane" as well as "active and determined".[2]
(Arthur himself has been often described as one of Britain's greatest
colonial governors and, though a despot and a bit of a prig, he
was "essentially humane").[3] Booth was undoubtedly a man of
conscience.

That, at Point Puer, "boys of ten years were tied to the triangles
and lashed equally with hardened criminals"[4] appears to be untrue,
of Booth's time at any rate. The maximum penalty for misbehaviour
was "thirty strokes on the breech".[5] The strain of running Port

Arthur and Point Puer was too much for Booth, so he gave it up and took charge of an orphanage he ran with great efficiency until his heart gave out when he was fifty-one. Of Port Arthur after Booth it is difficult to find out very much. There is not, and there should be, an adequate and accurate guide-book to Port Arthur.

Macquarie Harbour on the West Coast was really hellish. Marcus Clarke's novel *For the Term of His Natural Life* reflects Macquarie Harbour's condition rather than Port Arthur's, which his fiction is often taken to portray as fact.

Colonel George Arthur, when he became lieutenant-governor in 1824, saw that sending the worst criminals to such a foul-weathered, hard-to-supply place as Macquarie Harbour was stupid. Also, there had to be a place—he saw the "natural penitentiary" of Tasman Peninsula as it—from which system-brutalized or brutal-anyway convicts would find it very difficult to escape and prey on the settlers, as bushrangers. Escapees, mainly from Macquarie Harbour and the infamous road gangs, were so numerous as bushrangers that 103 were sentenced to death in 1825-26. In the main they were vicious. The educated and audacious Matthew Brady was one exception (but Jeffries of his gang was a monster). Another was the "Tasmanian Robin Hood", Martin Cash, who was one of only four men ever to escape from Port Arthur.

IN THE MUSEUM at Port Arthur you see actual records of transportees (who were not necessarily in this prison). One sheet lists Irishmen, all given seven years for stealing a cow, a sheep, a lamb, a horse, a pig, the same for larceny, burglary, robbery (which were differentiated offences).

Joseph Parker, who probably had earlier convictions, was transported for life for stealing a silk handkerchief. Jane Horrocks, who got seven years for stealing a jacket, had previous convictions for theft and for being a prostitute. Sentence of death for stealing goods valued at twenty-five shillings from a rich man's house was commuted to transportation for life in another case. In 1843 James Lynch, aged nine, was sentenced to seven years transportation for stealing three boxes of toys. He was sent to Point Puer.

An extraordinary girl was the guide in this museum. Her manner was very lively. Her speech was un-Australian and sounded like Cockney. Showing a large and hideous man-trap, she said: "Needed a real good fertile possy this one, like in a garden. Break the bone in yer leg, for sure—I reckon it could 'ave you off at the ankle."

About body-irons, which were sometimes attached, as well as leg-irons, to convicts who time and again attempted escape, she was very bright: "No future in actin' rebellious and nickin' off, was there?"

The only men compelled to wear leg-irons were those who gave trouble, according to Coultman Smith. Leg-ironed men, obviously, were hampered workers who could not produce much. Their irons weighed, each, about three-and-a-half pounds. Yet, the author of *Shadow over Tasmania* says, you will see "heavy irons" exhibited in many parts of Tasmania today. "These were almost all manufactured at Port Arthur after the convict evacuation, by ex-convicts who made a small living by making 'convict relics' and selling them to the visitors." One old man sold at least a dozen of "the last cat-o'-nine-tails of the convict days", which he had made.

People insensitive enough to buy leg-irons or hang such an implement of suffering as a flogger's whip on their walls deserve to be gulled. And a tourist restaurant in Hobart, named the "Ball and Chain", does not, in my opinion, deserve to be patronized. No paraphernalia of convictism's cruelty should be used lightly as a commercial gimmick.

The Port Arthur dualism—relic of the bitter past and holiday place of the present—is strange. One wonders how people can set up tents or park their caravans under the Penitentiary walls for a week or a fortnight of fishing and fun. And, even, whether they should be allowed to.

Watching average-tourist reactions as one goes round with the guide can be depressing, as the tour itself is. Yet one feels a sort of duty to see the prison portions. Some sensitive people can't take it and leave the party. And Derwent Martyn who had been guiding there for twenty-five years told me, "Some women cry".

To Hobart: The new Monte Carlo?

THERE IS MORE to the Tasman Peninsula than Port Arthur. Not far from Eaglehawk Neck are three curious formations. Naturally rectilinear, like flagstones, are the bay-shore rocks called the Tessellated Pavements. A natural rock bridge, Tasman's Arch, has been cut through a cliff by the sea that has also hollowed out a great fissure called the Devil's Kitchen. At the Blowhole a notice warning STOP! DANGER — KEEP AWAY! is there because in 1956 a freak wave rushed in and drowned a young couple who were sightseeing on their honeymoon.

On the way to these sights is Doo-Town, a togetherness of houses that began with a wag from Hobart putting up a week-end shack he called IT'LL-DO. Anyone who winces at that is warned that the run through Doo-Town shows the whimsy to have proved so contagious that other fun-people have built houses there named DOO-NIX, RUM-DOO, LOVE-ME-DOO, DOO-LITTLE, DIDGERI-DOO, AF-2-DOO and—but that will surely do or doo. At least it's one place where you'd know exactly the kind of neighbours you'd have if you moved in.

Subsequently I went with Brian to where the sea had begun to make another Tasman's Arch by piercing the cliff with what is called the Remarkable Cave, because its opening is shaped like the map of Tasmania. It is down a great many steps and not a "must"; but the view from hereabouts towards Cape Raoul, with wave-cut cliffs of a rugged coast, was very fine. The distant point had vertical columns of rock called the Organ Pipes.

"Ah," Brian said. "You should have seen those columns before the Navy used them for target practice."

So it seems we have, or had, an H.M.A.S. *Vandal*.

On the way to Hobart the coach goes back through the rich pastoral countryside round Sorell, over the long causeway that crosses an arm of the sea called Pittwater and, from Cambridge, up to a historic town that looks the part, Richmond.

"The jail here in Richmond we don't go to," the coach-captain said, to, I think, everybody's relief. "It's the same type as the model prison you saw at Port Arthur." (If that is so—and Richmond's jail was built in 1825—why is it always said that the Separate Treatment Prison at Port Arthur was modelled on Pentonville's of 1842?)

A much better stop, if only to admire the fine iron lace that frills its verandas, is the Commercial Hotel, one of the best-looking colonial hostelries in Tasmania (although the renovators did not have to pick out the doors in such bold black and white).

Mellow Richmond has the oldest bridge in Australia still in use, convict-built across the Coal River 1823-25. Everybody takes, from the riverside below the photogenic old bridge, the picture of one of its four main arches framing the spire of Australia's oldest existing Roman Catholic church, St John's. However, Richmond's Anglican church, St Luke's (1824), is one year older. Its interior roof is interestingly like a boat's hull upside down. The broad arrow in the stone fitted with a mud-scraper at the entrance door tells you who did the building. Both of these churches, and some other early ones in Tasmania, have upstairs galleries, where the convicts in the congregation were segregated.

Hobart we came to across the bow-curve of the Tasman Bridge that replaced in 1964 the floating bridge of cellular concrete that used to pitch and roll when storms roughened the Derwent estuary that, on a blue day, is a beautiful waterway. With the Derwent and the massive backdrop of Mt Wellington, Hobart is the only capital that has a setting to challenge Sydney's. And you are much more conscious of Nature's hand, for it holds a city that is only one-twentieth Sydney's size, with 125,000 people. (PLATE 27.)

"Derwent" from the Lake Country; "Hobart" in tribute to the fourth earl of Buckinghamshire; "Wellington" for the Iron Duke—and soon we'll be in Salamanca Place because Wellington had a victory at Salamanca in Spain—and, having come through Risdon Vale and Lindisfarne, we are running through the gardens of Queen's Domain. At least there is Lenah Valley (*lenah* was Aboriginal for "kangaroo"). Admittedly the native name for the Derwent could have been a problem: it is given as *Teemtoomelemenennye*.

Hobart I had been to only once before and that was twenty years ago. Memory held little more than a place of sleepy charm where ships, and even fishing boats, appeared at the ends of main streets. They still do. And the yachts of the annual Sydney-Hobart race tie up in Constitution Dock just across the street from the Museum and Art Gallery, closer to the city's heart than if, in Sydney, they moored at Circular Quay.

The city had seemed to me then no city at all, but a place where Victorian red-brick merged with convict-cut Georgian stone in flat-fronted buildings near a dockside where you half expected to be button-holed by some ancient mariner who wanted to tell you about the whaling days—and would probably fall asleep in the process of doing so.

The sleepiness has gone. Salamanca Place, though, is still the line of old stone warehouses it was, an unrivalled vista of Colonial Australia. A pity it is lined with parked cars—but one of Hobart's boasts is that it was the first city in Australia to introduce parking meters. Another is that it was the first to liberalize the liquor law to 10 p.m. closing for hotels. But it doesn't want to be thought of as overly progressive. It needs you to know that it has the only Royal Tennis Club—the indoor, original tennis from Henry VII's time that later became lawn tennis—with, at last report, forty playing members. And the oldest theatre, the Theatre Royal that opened in 1837—and is Hobart's main theatre still! The cultural implication—that Hobartians a century and a third later can't fill a larger one—is appalling.

The new library is a glass-sided box: Hobart, like every other city, testifies that Germany, though it lost its big military wars, won the architectural one, directed from the Bauhaus by Walter Gropius

armed with a set-square. Charmless apartment blocks and a Travelodge have arisen in New Hobart. But Old Hobart charm is
retained at Battery Point, with its ring of colonial cottages round a
green at Arthur's Circus. In St David's Park early tombstones from
what was a churchyard are set up against the walls, the lettering
beautifully carved, fine serifs and all. And, in the old suburb of
New Town, Runnymede House is a colonial mansion-homestead
that is National Trust-worthy.

I HAD LOOKED FORWARD to seeing in Hobart a friend who has lived
there since he left Sydney in the early sixties to become Professor of
English at Hobart's university. James McAuley is usually ranked as
one of the three or four best Australian poets living.

(My first meeting with Jim McAuley, in June 1944, was note-
worthy. He, then 26, and another good poet, Harold Stewart, 27,
gave me a joint statement—it was published exclusively in the
Sydney newspaper supplement *Fact* I was editing—about how they
had perpetrated what is now regarded as the literary spoof of the
century. They had concocted, in one afternoon, between them—and
attributed to a non-existent Ern Malley (deceased)—a batch of
meaningless "modern" verse in the obscurantist style they both
deplored. They sent it, with a fictitious biography of Ern, to an
avant-garde magazine published in Melbourne, *Angry Penguins*—
whose editors were so impressed and excited that they brought out
a commemorative issue in tribute to the poetic genius of Ern Malley,
who was described in the Introduction by Max Harris, as "one of
the two giants of contemporary Australian poetry".[1])

McAuley had written of Hobart[2] that it was "a very nice place to
live in". It was a "human-size" city where one could walk or drive
home for lunch, and shopping was easier. But you soon learnt never
to ask for "four pounds of *potatoes*"—they were Brownells, or Pink-
Eyes or King Edwards or Bismarcks or some other kind, never just
potatoes. Shops were not open on Saturday morning but, "after
living in a mainland city where one wasted Saturday morning
simply because they *were* open, it is a great pleasure to get the
week-end purchases done by Friday evening and have a full week-
end of real leisure". With the beauty of Hobart's natural setting,
and the city's nearness to rural scenes, went fresh air that the few
industries, using electric power, did not much sully. Even the cold
winters were not a bother if you dressed for them.

He was appalled—although "much of historical interest and
aesthetic merit in Hobart's buildings" remained to reward the visitor
—by the "civic and commercial barbarism and indifference" and the

"loathsome tetter and scurf of later developments", and advised: "Tear down the present signs and hoardings, abolish all the atrocious advertisements and regulate the size and quality of new ones: insist that all buildings be properly maintained and painted, and that the painting be done in a colour range designed to establish a general tonality in place of discord." Excellent advice to any city or town.

The McAuley family had a roomy, oldish house with a lot of atmosphere, much of it of their making, at New Town. There I was invited to dinner, and found Jim and his wife still happy with Hobart the living-place. As to the people, "With all their virtues, the people of the south have something soft in the grain, a lack of initiative," he said.

Could he pinpoint any speech difference? Agreeing that it was extraordinary that Australians in Hobart spoke very much as they did in Darwin, he could think of only one distinctive Tasmanian idiom: older men who made their own cigarettes rolled them in what they called *tissues*, not "cigarette-papers".

We left the fireside and went up to St John's Park, where Jim showed me one of his favourite churches. It was built in 1838, and the façade of John Lee Archer's tower is of quite exceptional grace, and fine old lodges adjoin the church building. He was concerned that, in preserving what was old and good, we did not turn into "fuddy-duddy conservatives" facing away from our own age. He had written a poem that said this, very well.

THERE IS A NEW SMELL in the Hobart air. The city's distinctive aroma has been a blend of hops becoming beer at the Cascade Brewery and raspberries boiling into conserve at the Jones jam factory. Hobartians returning from the mainland or other places overseas are said to prefer this balmy fragrance of their homeplace to Chanel No. 5.

The new smell is of money, tourist money—and not just the accommodation dollars or the dollars spent in antique shops at Battery Point, or multiples of the 25 cents admission to the Van Diemen's Land Folk Museum in the old house, Narryna, in Hampden Road. The nose twitchings are in anticipation of the Big Dollar, the heady scent of millions, even of millionaires, just round the corner or, more accurately, just along the waterway at Wrest Point.

Wrest Point is the best, and biggest, hotel site in Australia. To match, in terms of Sydney, its six-acres of point going out into the Derwent would mean giving over to a hotel the end of Benelong Point, where the Opera House is, plus a bit of Government House gardens. At present the Wrest Point Hotel (where our coach party stayed) occupies the back portion of the little peninsula and the front is a guests-only domain of lawns and trees, with a private beach and a swimming-pool right on the point. Between this and the present hotel is to be built a huge new hotel-casino.

Roulette, baccarat (*chemin-de-fer*), blackjack (*vingt-et-un*); croupiers calling "No more bets" (*Rien ne va plus*) as they spin the wheel; jewelled women and mask-faced men winning or losing thousands of dollars in an evening—not in sophisticated Sydney but in "Tassy". The "Apple Isle" is to become the princeless Monaco of the Southern Hemisphere; and Hobart, of all places, its Monte Carlo.

Wrest Point's owners, Federal Hotels Ltd, a big concern, have said it will all come to pass, at a cost of $10 million. Latest plans for the building—the distinguished Sir Roy Grounds is the architect—show a round canister-like tower of a hotel rising seventeen storeys on a wide disc-like base that will be the casino. Originally, it provided for 369 bedrooms or suites, but the plan has changed almost as much as the opening date. This was to be pre-Christmas 1969 and has gone back to some time in 1973.

The first sod on the project was still to be turned, with ceremony, when in August 1970 the *Sun-Herald* of Sydney reported: "Some of Europe's wealthiest bankers, businessmen and gamblers are among hundreds of people seeking bookings for Hobart's $7 million hotel casino." Federal Hotels general manager, Mr J. Haddad, was quoted as saying, "The casino is making Tasmania world known. It has become Hobart's Opera House, not in cost but in conception."

Modesty, though, will have its place in the project. Applications from showgirls to act as scantily clad croupiers had been sternly rejected by Mr Haddad. Hundreds of applications from croupiers overseas had been received. The casino would have Australian croupiers. The Frenchman who is to manage the casino, M. Pierre Bax, was earlier reported as saying that there would be no James Bond business and "no females with a lot of exposed flesh".

The casino would have a bank of two million dollars and bets would be from 50 cents minimum to an upper limit. Mr Haddad added that there would be no poker machines. "We don't want the tone of the place lowered." (Monte Carlo's casino has poker machines, Prince Rainier having found them necessary; but I don't remember there being any at the casino at Nice. However, there was quite a bit of *décolletage* round the roulette tables, and prostitutes had infiltrated the small-stakes *boule* casino.)

I have nothing against gambling: it has, after all, provided the Sydney Opera House and the Stock Exchange form of it has funded the finding of so much of Australia's new mineral wealth. Inveterate gamblers, though, such as you see in the French Riviera casinos, I described in another book as "not the kind of people with whom I should want to be shipwrecked on a desert island".[3]

That swarms of them are virtually lusting to leave the tables at Nice or Las Vegas or Macao to fly to Hobart to plank the big roulette chips on zero *en carre*—this strains my credulity somewhat. But I feel sure the casino will be a roaring success with Pioneer coachmen betting *rouge/noir* or *passe/manque*.

Federal Hotels have doubtless anticipated a problem that might be phrased as: "No, no, Elmer, it's not Tanzania, that's in Africa, that's niggers. *Tasmania*, I said. It's down in Australia, like Noo Zealand is. And they got these Australian croupiers who don't know the tricks, they're honest like peasants, see. And Gus here's heard the pay-out is good, 'cause they're trying to build up the business. You know what, it's *summer* down there, right now! And they got fishing as well! Tuna? Sure, they got tuna—they use 'em for bait. How'd you like to catch a White Death shark, eh? Sure, the man says there's Tasmanians can mix a five-to-one martini. Look, how would I know if they got call-girls? We can always take our own dames. No, Elmer, you're not going to get punched down in the street by some boxing kangaroo. Look, here's a picture of the hotel. No, I didn't say 'Rest Point'—I know how you hate rest and scenery. It's got a W like in Wrestling. The place it's at is called *Hobart*. It's on this Australian island where they had apple-trees and sheep, but the sheep ate the apples, or something. Anyway, they're after our dollars, and we're after theirs."

APPLES were the core of Southern Tasmania's economy. One of the reasons that tourism was being pushed so hard as a revenue earner in 1970 was that the Australian slang phrase "She's apples" meaning "It's all right" was hardly applicable to the Tasmanian apple industry. It was, the chairman of the Australian Apple and Pear Board said, "in trouble".

South African and New Zealand apples had become increasingly competitive; the 1970 dock strike in Britain, leaving thousands of cases on the wharves, had cost the Tasmanian grower dear; better growing methods had led to over-production; Australian apples-pears exports were down twenty per cent in 1970—and the position would get much worse if/when Britain went into the Common Market.

Not that the apple industry was in any parlous state or that bull-dozers were headed for the orchards to root out apple-trees to grow something else—which was just as well for Tasmanian tourism. One of the most alluring sights the island State had to offer was the Huon Peninsula in mid-September to late-October, apple blossom time.

By April, when I was there, most varieties of apples have ripened, but the harvest goes on until early May and many trees were still balled and bowed with red fruit or the kinds that ripen green.

The driver-guide on the tour coach that went down the Huon Peninsula knew his apples—including a variety named Lady in the Snow ("One side's light green, the other's bright red, and the flesh is snow white").

Bligh of the *Bounty* planted apples and other fruits in 1788 at Adventure Bay on Bruny Island, and four years later planted more there because all except one apple-tree had been destroyed by bush-fires—which so ravaged the Huon Peninsula in 1967 that in a township with the cosy name of Snug almost all the houses burned, and there was widespread destruction of fruit-trees. Reconstruction had had to be hasty, and some of the farms had a makeshift, untidy look along the shore of the picturesque D'Entrecasteaux Channel. The tour skirts this and goes to Cygnet and on to Huonville at the head of the Huon River's lovely estuary.

Then we went to the summit of rocky Mt Wellington, where the autumn day turned wintry cold with a tearing wind. Low cloud was blanketing the renowned view of Hobart on the way up, but when we were at the top the clouds blew away and let the sun shine briefly on the city, and a rainbow reach down to it.

To the Strange West Coast

NEAR NEW NORFOLK, about twenty miles up the Derwent from Hobart, I once made a radio recording with a Mrs Helen Hillman, who was charmingly articulate and not long out from England. She said:

"The Australians on the bride ship told me, when I asked them about my new home in Tasmania, that I should find it just like England. It is like that, and yet it is different. It was April when I crossed from the mainland—April and yet it was autumn, a pale yellow glowing kind of autumn, a subdued changing over. . . . In the Derwent Valley, where we came to live, there were dozens of varieties of berries, sweeping avenues of poplars, and hedges of holly—at which my small English-born daughter snorted: 'Stupid! Holly and no Father Christmas!'"

"There were apple and pear orchards growing in rich Devonshire-like soil, and hop-picking was in full swing. It was so like a Kentish scene with the grey stone oasthouses built by convicts more than a century ago—I almost expected to see a gipsy caravan lurking among the shadows of the hop vines. But then there would be a reminder that this was Australia. A tall eucalypt, a gum-tree, would come into view, so unfamiliar to the English eye, giving the landscape that blue smoky-grey greenness that I have come to regard as the typically Australian colour.

"We have been here five months now and drifted from autumn to spring. Accustomed to the rigours of English winters, we have hardly been conscious that winter has come and gone. Already the wattle is in bloom. Mimosa we called it in England, and paid so much for small bunches from the London flower-sellers." Mrs Hillman ended by saying: "To the person who is seeking a country of beauty and opportunity, who likes the land and does not mind remoteness, Tasmania would seem to offer everything."

Her husband was an engineer at the Australian Newsprint Mills, at Boyer, just down-river from New Norfolk; and I had come to do a radio documentary on how this only Australian industry of its kind made paper out of pulped trees—huge Tasmanian swamp-gums —that overseas experts had said could not be made into paper: the wood was so short-fibred. With some imported pulp added to give strength and whiteness, the mills at Boyer make now about 100,000 tons of newsprint a year. It is a more interesting manufacturing process than some (tours can be arranged to see it), this turning what looks like porridge into paper. The mills are on the river because it takes 40,000 gallons of water to make one ton of paper.

This beautiful part of Tasmania, which produces four-fifths of all the hops the Australian breweries brew into all the beer Australians drink, centres on New Norfolk. It looks much more like New Kent, and its name was not born of nostalgia to do with Norfolk in England: its early settlers came across from Norfolk Island.

At New Norfolk was the Bush Inn. It was built by a man named Bush, began business right back in 1815, and is only months younger than the Launceston Hotel established by the ex-highwayman Dicky White in 1814. It is said to be the oldest continuously licensed (since 1825) hotel in Australia. It was probably stuck up by Tasmania's most notorious bushranger, Michael Howe, because he twice plundered the town before he was killed in 1818. That astonishing adventurer, Jorgen Jorgensen, "King of Iceland", convict and much else, must surely have drunk there: he was married at New Norfolk, at the church we'll come to. The Bush Inn is where an early

Methodist parson, Abraham Briggs, used to preach in the tap-room. It is where, in 1838, the Irish composer William Vincent Wallace wrote the lyrics of his opera *Maritana*; it is where Dame Nellie Melba stayed in 1924 and sang Wallace's *"Scenes that are brightest . . ."*; and a unique broadcast of *Maritana* was given from the inn in 1932 by the A.B.C. It is where in 1949 I saw, in the cellar, what was surely the most extraordinary collection of old liquors in Australia—Austrian maraschino of 1821, Napoleon brandy of 1848, eighty-year-old whiskies (one was Dewar's and Bullock's— before the makers became just Dewar's), Kummel with the Russian Imperial coat-of-arms on the bottle, square-bottle Geneva gin, absinthe brought in before it was illegal, cherry whisky, peach bitters, drinks I'd never heard of—the place was a museum of liquors. And this is where, on seeing the old Bush Inn again, I felt like tearing my hair and cursing the dunderheadedness of Tasmania's tourist authorities.

It wasn't any longer even called the Bush Inn. It had become the "Bush Hotel". Over the entrance to a depressing bar the new name glared from one of those ugly signs a leading wine-maker will put up for nothing because it also says, *Ask for Mardi Gras*. This history-book hotel with its lovely situation right on the river had been allowed to degenerate into charmless ordinariness, just another country pub. The latest proprietor said the fabulous cellar was gone before his time.

Why, if private enterprise was so inept and unimaginative, did the State not declare it a Historic Site and take it over? And call in a first-rate architect and decorator to restore it and make it the kind of characterful place to stay that is so sadly lacking in Tasmania—which was told plainly enough in 1965 by the American tourism experts that "one of its strongest visitor appeals is to be found in its historical evidences" and another in its "English atmosphere".[1]

Tasmania's oldest existing church is at New Norfolk, St Matthew's, built in 1823. It is mainly of interest because of its stained glass windows, all made in Munich, this century, and memorializing local identities such as the wife of Ebenezer Shoobridge who started hop production in the Derwent Valley.

In this church in 1831 the Danish-born Jorgen Jorgensen took a second wife. She turned out to be an alcoholic termagant who brought nearer the day when the man who had helped to found Hobart in 1803, and who had taken the first whale in the Derwent, was found drunk and dying in a ditch. Returning to Copenhagen in 1807 via Cape Horn, he had been lionized as the "first Dane to circumnavigate the globe" and given command of a Danish privateer assisting the

French. It was captured by the British, for whom he then worked as a secret service agent. Sent to Iceland, he deposed the Danish governor, proclaimed Iceland an independent British protectorate and himself king. He halved the taxes, introduced trial by jury, re-designed the national flag and was getting on well with the populace when a British sloop sailed in with a stiff-necked captain who deposed Jorgensen and returned him to London, where he embarked on a literary career. His writings included a treatise on how Britain could get rid of its National Debt, written when he was in a debtors' prison in London: he was an inveterate gambler, "my horrid vice" as he called it. He warned the British Government in 1812 of a French plan to attack Sydney; he was a spy in Spain and Portugal and an official observer at the Battle of Waterloo. Gambling got him in trouble again and, for pawning the bedding at his lodgings, he was sentenced to transportation. Back in Tasmania, he became, among other things, an explorer for the Van Diemen's Land Company, whose history he wrote, a police officer who hunted bushrangers, and an authority on the habits and language of the Tasmanian Aborigines. When he died in 1841, Iceland's one-time king was buried in a pauper's unmarked grave.

Jorgensen was Tasmania's most remarkable convict. More so than Thomas Griffiths Wainewright, a gifted artist and writer, who was transported for forgery. He had escaped charges of poisoning with strychnine, to get their money, his uncle, his mother-in-law and his wife's half-sister, whose life he had insured for £16,000 and whose death at his hands he excused by saying, "After all, she had such thick ankles."

HOPFIELDS line the coach's road, and pale gold spears of Lombardy poplars make windbreaks to the fields of poles and rigging for the vines to twine up and along. Brian says that it costs about $2,000 an acre nowadays to rig a hopfield. Hop-picking is finished for this year. The drying kilns for the hops, the oasthouses, look right in this little-England landscape; but they would be conical strangers in the country the coach is headed for.

Off the highway are two lovely spots, Salmon Ponds near Plenty and the Russell Falls at the entrance to the Mt Field National Park—probably the most photogenic waterfall in Australia. Hawthorn hedges stay with us along the road to sheep-raising, cattle-raising Hamilton. Then on to Ouse—and could any name be less Australian than this one that three English rivers bear? Here we leave the Lyell Highway and start climbing into Tasmania's "tiger country".

Not that we are likely to see the Tasmanian "tiger" or "wolf" or "hyena" as the unique-to-the-island thylacine was called, though no relation at all of tiger, wolf or hyena (it had some stripes to its rump). It is, or was, a marsupial. "Was" probably: the last reported sighting of a thylacine was in 1961. Yet in 1949 I held a microphone to a man named Fred Taylor, who began by saying, "I've 'unted every animal there is in Tasmania to be 'unted" and went on to say that he had killed twenty-three "tigers". Back in 1863 Gould predicted that the animal would be hunted to extinction, because it was a sheep-killer.

Butler's Gorge was where I talked to mighty-hunter Taylor, when the Clark Dam was being built to create big Lake King William. The water from it comes down from a power station there to one of Tasmania's major hydro-electric plants, Tarraleah (the Aboriginal name for Tasmania's nearly-shot-out Forester kangaroo). The pipes that make such a photogenic perspective down the mountainside, a six-in-a-row spectacular, start at five-foot diameter and finish at four: that increases the water pressure greatly. Outside the power station we inspect are some disused Pelton wheels. When the water rushes into the scoops it gives tremendous drive to generators that make Tasmania the all-electric island. Inside, the power stations are like the ones described in the Snowy Mountains Scheme chapter. Tarraleah is now (1971) only the third largest. Poatina, fed from the Great Lake, generates enough electricity annually to drive a one-horse-power motor for about 1,500 million hours.

We don't go to the Great Lake. We go, after lunch at Derwent Bridge, through landscape so alien to the hopfields and velvet green farmlands of the morning that we could be in another country. Beech-trees (myrtles) rear a hundred feet high, rain-forest rises out of fern, and cloud-mist moils round the summits of the rugged King William Range. We come to Lake St Clair.

I have been here before, to what the naturalist Charles Barrett declared was "incomparably the loveliest lake in the world". It isn't, when one thinks of lakes in Italy and Lake Akan in Japan's Hokkaido, and others; but it still could be, on a blue day, the loveliest lake in Australia. In this grey weather it offers little except the so-tame wallabies that come to the tourists' feeding fingers. You can't see at all—much less in reflection—Mount Olympus, or Mount Rufous where the dam engineer at Butler's Gorge said that he had had good skiing down its sides on Christmas Day, and up here on the roof of Tasmania was snow sport such as vanished in mainland Australia in September. The lake's shores are jungle-thick with myrtle-beech, pines, sassafras and leatherwood. We are getting out of eucalypt country, except for the mighty swamp-gum.

THE EARLIER TRIP across from here to Queenstown had been made unforgettable by the most fantastic landscape I had ever seen, and I described it as "like a dead world that's been hit by a rainbow. The mountains are naked—not a tree, not a shrub, not a leaf, not a blade of grass. And the colour is incredible—heliotrope, yellow, pink, lime-green, studded with wet black tree-roots like spiders. It is desolation in Technicolor, like some lunar scene by Disney."

This weird landscape, which was to reappear near Queenstown, was man-created in this way: The ore at Mt Lyell, which became Australia's greatest copper mine, was mainly composed of sulphur and iron (pyrites), and it was found in 1902 that the heat generated by the combustion of these could smelt the copper without using coke. The sulphur released as smoke from the furnaces poisoned what vegetation was left after the forests of trees that clothed these now-bare mountains had been cut out to provide wood for the mine and town. With the tethering vegetation gone, the topsoil washed away in the heavy rains the West Coast gets (100 inches and more a year). This exposed the coloured clays and rocks.

Since 1922 only copper concentrate has been smelted, and no longer is there the pall of sulphur. But it has taken twenty years of the rain that falls on an average 200 days of the year to leach the sulphur's poison out of the soil. In 1949 it was hardly noticeable that the vegetation was beginning to come back: the earth was still bare of scrub for fifteen miles around Queenstown. Now, led by a small, bushy tree called dorrel, it is creeping in over the denuded hills, like dark tufts of candlewick.

So the fantastic dead-world-hit-by-a-rainbow landscape does not appear until we are within a few miles of Queenstown, near the ghost of Linda, once the bustling town of the North Lyell Mine that merged in 1903 with Mt Lyell. Where the remnant of outpost Gormanston defies the surrounding multi-coloured desolation we see the first township since Bronte, fifty miles back along this roof-of-Tasmania road flanked by such peaks as Frenchman's Cap (4,756 ft). Now we are winding between the two mineral-loded mountains of the Professors Range, one named for Lyell the geologist, the other for Owen the zoologist: to the south stand Mt Huxley, Mt Jukes and Mt Darwin. There is an eerie grandeur to this raped and naked land, and paint-box colour in the roadside rock. (PLATE 28.)

We top the rise and there below is Queenstown.

QUEENSTOWN was born of the copper mines that were born of prospectors struggling up from the sea twenty miles away, through rain-sodden forests' mud, cold and mist, to search for gold. And gold they found in 1885 at the "Iron Blow". Not until eight years later

This pipeline across the Savage River goes on for 53 mostly-underground miles, carrying "iron soup" that becomes iron pellets at Port Latta.

Savage River's iron ore, mined in a wilderness, comes up to be stockpiled for turning into slurry that goes by pipeline to the north coast.

was this recognized as the outcropping of a huge pyritic orebody containing copper.

From this grew the biggest copper-producing mine in the British Empire, the largest in the southern hemisphere. With the North Lyell and West Lyell as well, the company that is still called the Mt Lyell Mining and Railway Company (though the railway no longer operates) has produced well over 600,000 tons of copper along with some 17 million ounces of silver and over 600,000 ounces of gold. Today, as a copper mine, it is second to Mount Isa.

The town lives by the mine. One in three of its 4,500 people—and that means the great majority of the men—works for the company. Despite such modern buildings as the 45-room Four Seasons Motel where we stayed, Queenstown still looks the part as an old mining town, with a lot of veranda posts propping up the past and more than a hint of the movie-set West. Wooden houses with red-painted roofs stand against great black slag-heaps that accent dramatically the colour in the bald-headed mountains.

Queenstown and the company live well together. Bosses and miners drink side by side in the men-only Gentlemen's Club. Blainey says in his book *The Peaks of Lyell*,[2] "The company has maintained full employment, cheap housing, a good standard of living, and an unrivalled health scheme; in the last forty years it is doubtful if the employees in any other large Australian mining field received such a high proportion of the wealth won from the mines. In the same period no Australian mining field has been as free from social and economic upheavals as Mt Lyell."

The open cut at West Lyell, the main producer, is an enormous hole two thousand feet across. The benches in its sides are stepped down six hundred feet to a "floor" where the electric shovels and Haulpak trucks look almost toy-size as they move about an area pooled with water that has been mineralized blood-red. The area clears. A siren screams, and the firing crew either race off in cars or run to the shelter of yellow "safety barrels". Rock-faces disintegrate in an explosion you feel with your feet a split second before the thunder reaches your ears where you stand up on top of the open cut. Then grey dust clouds billow up into the silence.

By 1974 the ore blasted and trucked from this great open cut will have topped a hundred million tons and, at 790 feet, the cut will have dug its own grave as an economic operation. It had been predicted that, by 1975, Mt Lyell would be finished. Now it was known that, at deeper levels, there was another 40 million tons of ore.

"We are going back to underground mining for the deep lodes,"

◀ 30/NORTHERN TERRITORY At Glen Helen, evening reflections in the Finke River.

the mine's general manager, G. F. Hudspeth, told me. "By 1974 we expect to raise the present annual production of 16,000 tons of metallic copper to 25,000 tons. Although underground mining is more expensive, it will win for us higher-grade ore than the 0.7 per cent we are getting now. We hope for 1.2 per cent." (Mt Isa's ore is around 3 per cent copper, but Lyell has for many years mined lower grades profitably.) The company would spend about $30 million by 1974 in expanding its output.

Because the Mt Lyell company's richest asset looked like being its 44 per cent holding in the Renison tin company, the huge Patino tin interests centred in Bolivia tried to buy it in 1963; but Patino were outbid by Boral Ltd, which soon afterwards sold its Mt Lyell shares to the British mining giant Consolidated Gold Fields Ltd's Australian subsidiary, which now owns sixty per cent of Mt Lyell.

THE ORE has to be ground to powder. Chunks of rock bigger than man-size shatter in a pit where the great vibrating manganese-steel cone of the jaw crusher works relentlessly. The pieces chute down to the ball mills, where cylinders bigger than locomotive boilers whirl with a vast noise as the steel balls inside them grind stone to dust. From this powder the copper is extracted by the flotation process.

Flotation was a revolutionary advance in recovering minerals from ores and its commercial application was, says Blainey, a "triumph of Broken Hill."[3] So it is "strange that most American histories, textbooks and encyclopaedias hail the process as a fruit of American ingenuity".[4] Simply stated, it means that, if the powdered ore is mixed with water and frothed by aeration, the required minerals can, with the aid of chemicals, be made to float and adhere to air bubbles. Recovering the froth recovers the mineral, and much more of it than earlier processes recovered. "In the last thousand years in metallurgy [says Professor Blainey] it stands with the cyanide process, and the Bessemer process, as one of the three greatest advances."[5]

What most tourists go to see, on an evening tour, is the smelting. A greenish sludge (the concentrate) goes into the huge blast furnace and comes out, when the furnace is tapped, as molten matte, about forty per cent copper. Great ladles of this are carried by cranes to the globular converters that "blow" it, by the Bessemer process, into what is called blister copper, 99-per-cent copper, that is cast into slabs. The pouring and running of the red-glaring stream of molten metal, always dramatic, is particularly vivid at night.

What the overnight visitor to Queenstown may not notice is the character bred in its people by a rigorous climate. The rain on three days out of five meant, when I stayed there awhile years before, that every second house's veranda was white-flagged with drying napkins (most mothers have electric driers now). But the climate was still a testing one, and Geoffrey Hudspeth still thought of his typical West Coast miner as different from the average Tasmanian. "He's tough-grained and rough-edged, but he has a lot of dignity. He's all-man, but he's mannerly to women."

THE GORDON RIVER is the reason I did not go on from Queenstown with this twelve-day Pioneer tour, but waited there for the next fourteen-day one that took in a cruise on this river that courses the uninhabited wilderness of central-west Tasmania. It empties into Macquarie Harbour, the place of the infamous old penal settlement.

There is, though, more to the Gordon River than that. It is Tasmania's Snowy River—plus. The Gordon River hydro-electric development will create, in the smallest State, the biggest water storage in Australia. Lake Gordon will be three times the size of the Snowy scheme's Lake Eucumbene. And what is being done, at a cost of $95 million, is only Stage 1. Further stages, still under investigation, could create a power-from-water development able to generate nearly as much electricity as the whole Snowy Mountains Scheme in New South Wales. Tasmania's bush-walking nature-lovers are sad, though, about the Gordon scheme. "Drowned" by the enormous new reservoir will be beautiful Lake Pedder.

The Gordon scheme's Stage 1 will not be completed until 1975. Although there is a road (a permit to use it was needed, and a toll had to be paid) in to the construction township, Strathgordon, it seemed rather early days to go there: one construction township can be very like another. The road may be scenic, but the weather is likely to be foul, because the rainfall in the area is around 150 inches a year.

The morning after the next coach party arrived we went down to where Strahan (pron. Straun) sits on Macquarie Harbour, lonely in its distinction of being the only developed port on the west coast of Tasmania. There is only one other big inlet, Port Davey in the south-west corner. The country behind it is still largely unexplored.

Strahan was once the roaring gateway to the minefields—where Mt Lyell's big developer, Bowes Kelly, rich from Broken Hill, gave a banquet in the sixty-roomed Palace Hotel, with French menus, waiters from Melbourne and a German orchestra. Now it has no more than 500 people. It still ships Mt Lyell's copper and pyrites that used to be brought down from Queenstown by an Abt rack railway, replaced now by the twenty-six-mile road. An unlikely grave at Strahan is that of Grattan Riggs, an old American actor Australian audiences loved, who is described as "founder of the Elks fraternity". He collapsed and died after a performance at the theatre at Zeehan.

We had come to Strahan for the scenic trip up the Gordon River on a splendid big launch, the *Evening Star*, newly built in Hobart at a cost of $200,000—such was the faith of its owner-skipper, Reg Morrison, in the tourist potential of what the Gordon had to show.

Macquarie Harbour, a big one, extends twenty miles from the narrow, tide-racing entrance, Hell's Gates, that could well have got its name from the convicts who were sent there from 1821 until 1883, when it was abandoned in favour of Port Arthur, which was a picnic-place for felons by comparison. Records showing that, in three years, 183 prisoners received 6,280 lashes were quoted by a horrified Quaker missionary[6] who went there in 1832, and who wrote: "Out of 85 deaths only 35 were from natural causes . . . 27 were drowned, 8 killed accidentally (chiefly by the falling of trees), 3 were shot by the military, and 12 murdered by their comrades. Escape from Macquarie Harbour was well known to be a very difficult and hazardous undertaking. . . . Out of 112 who eloped, 62 were supposed to have perished in the bush, and 9 were murdered by their comrades on the journey for a supply of food." In other words, they were eaten. Dunbabin[7] writes of Alexander Pearce, "once a seller of pies in Hobart Town", that he "assimilated half a dozen of his fellow prisoners who escaped with him from Macquarie Island".

Many convicts were employed on felling and floating to the prison islands logs of Huon pine they had to get ashore in waist-deep icy water, and the guards wielded whips on those who were laggardly. The worst characters were sent to Grummet Island or "Condemned Rock". There were cases of men killing in order to escape their living-death conditions by being sent to the gallows. One such murderer, named Trenman, when asked why he did not simply drown himself, replied, "Oh, if I kill myself I shall go to the bottomless pit of Hell. But, by killing another, I get sent to Hobart to hang, and the parson will attend me and I'm sure of going to Heaven."[8]

We saw on this cruise Grummet and Sarah (or Settlement) Island and a small, pretty island that was the convict burial place, but did not (as another launch party did) land at any of them. Not that I had the slightest wish to see relics of their horrible history.

The *Evening Star* went about eighteen miles up the Gordon River, on what Reg Morrison said was the "worst day for months— no reflections, and the reflections are what mainly make the trip beautiful". The sky was leaden, the clouds low, and there was a brief pelting of rain. The mists that would have risen on a sunny day still wreathed about the river and created their own grey mood of beauty.

The banks of the Gordon here are impenetrable rain-jungle—a furry-green matting of myrtle-beech, sassafras and what is called celery-top pine, with the brighter foliage of blackwood, and the leatherwoods that come into bloom in mid-summer.

And there were patches of "horizontal scrub". This bushman's barrier is a major reason why such tracts of western Tasmania are relatively unexplored. It is a skinny, prickly growth that may struggle towards the light for forty feet, then it collapses and its laterals root in the ground; and this horizontal growth grows up vertically again. So a dense interlaced mass is created that blocks all human progress—even a cassowary, if Tasmania had any, couldn't butt its bone-topped head through.

Reg Morrison, whose father used to get eighteen pence a foot for beautiful figured blackwood—which couldn't be floated down river (it sinks)—and who is himself a notable bushman, spoke of timbers with knowledge and respect. The Huon pine that grows only in Tasmania, and is an extremely strong and durable softwood, had drawn the first white men to Macquarie Harbour. A wooden plough of the convicts had been found in the scrub on Settlement Island, well preserved. Huon pine is impervious to the worm.

For the keel of his *Evening Star*, which he could feel pride in with good reason, this lean, grey-haired man had chosen the tree, near Huonville. A Tasmanian red-gum two hundred feet high and eight feet six through, it had stood for probably 150 years. "The ground shook when it fell. Eighty tons of wood dropped. Branches as thick as a man snapped off like matches."

The "king of Tasmanian rivers" as the Gordon is called, brings down a greater volume of water than any other, and on its 140-mile course cuts deep gorges through the mountains. But here, near its end, it is the tranquil mirror, on brighter days, of the primeval-looking forest that flanks it. Even on the sunniest day it is not blue. The red button-grass up in the hills dyes the rivulets that feed it, and the river has a strangely blackish hue.

Savage River's "Iron Soup"

OVERSHADOWED by the New Australia's iron-nickel-bauxite drama, "on the boards" in bigger States, is the mineralogical repeat-performance being enacted in the north-west of Tasmania—a mining stage that was considered almost as played out as the stage of the derelict Gaiety Theatre at Zeehan.

Zeehan was so silver-rich that, at the turn of the century, the town named after one of Tasman's ships was the fourth-largest in Tasmania. Its Gaiety Theatre was Tasmania's, if not Australia's, largest. J. C. Williamson sent over *The Sign of the Cross* to open it in 1899. Melba sang there, Nellie Stewart starred, and Houdini astonished packed audiences of a thousand.

The Gaiety still stands and—when Zeehan was reached from Queenstown by the Pioneer coach that seemed to round more bends than a road should have in twenty-three miles—I stood inside its raddled walls and looked at its baroque tatters. The long-since-seatless emptiness echoed with young voices and *bump* sounds. A trampoline was set up about where the Front Stalls would have begun and the kids of Zeehan, their go-karts parked in the Back Stalls, were bouncing, bouncing. And, indeed, some of the old bounce was coming back to the Zeehan that had declined to a museum-town and had looked like ending up as a ghost-town.

Two hundred new houses were going up in a place with empty, broken-windowed shacks. A truckload of carpenters dashed down the re-surfaced main street where the tourists were coming out of the decorative old museum building with *A.D. 1892, Zeehan School of Mines and Metallurgy* on its curling Victorian façade, and a very good collection of mineral specimens inside. Next to this, vintage railway locomotives stood, including some from the Emu Bay Railway that ran a one-carriage service up to Burnie. The Emu Bay Railway had just voted $5 million dollars for expansion.

The cause of Zeehan's revival was Renison Bell. This old tin mine had struggled for fifty years; then Mt Lyell put in a lot of money to prospect and work the deposits properly. "By 1963 it was clear that Renison Bell was at least another Mt Bischoff," Professor Blainey wrote[1]—and Mt Bischoff was the richest tin mine in the world! (Hence Patino of Bolivia's interest in taking over Mount Lyell for its nearly-half interest in Renison tin.)

In setting up to mine tin in a big way, Renison Ltd made, in the 1968 financial year, a spectacular loss of $910,902. In the next year it made a spectacular profit of $1,541,847. I hadn't fully realized what Geoffrey Hudspeth (who is a Renison director) had meant when he said to me at Queenstown, "The Tasmanian mineral boom is back."

Renison Bell, twelve miles up the road, regards Zeehan as a suburb to build workers' housing in. The Dillingham Corporation of America had done big plant-building but, as a town, Renison Bell looked scruffy and the Renison Hotel, where we had lunch, contributed to the Australian Ugliness in heliotrope and green.

The next town, Rosebery, which was also unlovely, was where the Electrolytic Zinc Company mined mainly zinc, but got silver-lead, copper and gold with it. Electrolytic Zinc was in the process of expanding its operations to the tune of $50 million.

Before the Murchison Highway was built in 1964 motorists had to put their cars on the train that runs to Rosebery, and "round Tasmania" coach tours were not possible. This Pioneer tour I had arranged to leave, to go to see the Savage River iron development.

The coach-captain, Bill Dyball, whose commentary had been on a par with his very good driving, obligingly ran the off-route five miles to Waratah. The other passengers, who were singing lustily, didn't mind at all this diversion to the semi-derelict town at the foot of worked-out Mount Bischoff where, in 1871, a prospector known as "Philosopher" Smith, a grave-mannered teetotaller with a long beard, found "the greatest lode of tin then known to man".[2]

Even Waratah was looking up. Ten miles farther down the road, at Luina, the Cleveland Tin Company had started mining a tin-copper lode. One of its workers I talked to in the bar of the Bischoff Hotel at Waratah urged me to buy Cleveland Tin shares: "They've just got on to real good stuff, mate. I know, see." Because he was drunk, I didn't buy any. The company trebled its previous year's profit in the next six months.

A new township had grown up at Luina. Fourteen miles farther down this lonely, forest-flanked road was the more dramatic development and the even newer township, of 1,500 people, at Savage River.

THE SAVAGE RIVER IRON deposit had been known since 1877. As an Australian, I naturally want to see my country's natural resources developed by, and to the profit of, Australians. But I cannot see how this iron could have been mined and marketed without the capital and the know-how foreign companies provided—$87\frac{1}{2}$ per cent of the capital, and know-how that makes this an iron operation unique in the world.

The iron is relatively low grade (38 per cent: in Western Australia there are enormous deposits running 64 per cent). The Savage River courses through gorges of a trackless wilderness so rugged and rainy that it was never even inhabited by Tasmania's "savages", the Aborigines. There is no port on the nearest coast, the west, the iron could be shipped from (Strahan is 125 road miles away), and Burnie on the north coast would have been a 90-mile road haul—with the kind of ore the Japanese, who buy most of our iron, wouldn't want, anyway. Many companies' experts had looked at the Savage River lode and shaken their heads.

Pickands Mather, one of the biggest iron miners in the United States and with much experience of low-grade ore, got interested in 1963. It spent two million dollars on a feasibility study, and talked to two of Japan's biggest steelmakers, Mitsubishi and Sumitomo (who formed the Dahlia Mining Co. that has a half share in the Savage River enterprise). Seven Australian concerns, including five big insurance companies, put in $4 million to own some of the other half (making 12½ per cent Australian equity) with other American companies, including Pickands Mather. This company, which manages the enterprise, showed that the iron could be got out to the north coast direct, by a means that has been used to transport other minerals and oil. But nowhere else has iron been "piped" as this iron is.

After $76 million had been spent on setting up, what began happening to Savage River iron in 1967, and I saw happening two years later and is likely to go on happening for twenty years, is this: The ore in these wild wet mountains is being mined, say ten million tons a year, and ground up as fine as facepowder. Magnetically, the iron in the powder is removed. The 69 per cent concentrate is then mixed with water. This "iron soup", slurry, is pumped into a pipeline nine inches in diameter that had been put across fifty-three miles of mainly-awful country. The pipeline goes to a north-coast place that is not yet on most maps of Tasmania, Port Latta. There I was to see it dried back to powder and turned into little balls of iron, pellets. Of this high-grade (67 per cent) pelletized iron, five Japanese steelmakers had contracted to buy 45 million tons in twenty years.

The pipeline from Savage River starts out as a thousand-foot-long "suspension bridge" slung across a gorge where the river itself is a white-flecked torrent four hundred feet below (PLATE 29). The pipe dives into a mountain—only for about six of its fifty-three miles is it above ground—and putting it through such country was an impressive job by Bechtel Pacific, the contractors, who also built the attractive company town. From 1,100 feet above sea-level the pipeline had to rise to 1,500 feet before it began sloping down to the coast—and any gradient of more than one-in-ten would mean flow trouble. All the preliminary experiments notwithstanding, the day the pipeline opened there were thirty or forty engineers standing round with bated breath, I was told.

It worked. Even so, there were teething troubles with the pumping by the four 600 h.p. motors that send the iron soup coursing through the pipeline at four miles an hour. And there were technical problems at the pelletizing plant. Both problems were bad for profits, but by August 1969 they had been overcome. The forecast two and a quarter million tons of iron pellets was loading into Japanese ships during 1970.

Savage River was off-track to tourists when I went there in 1969: now the visiting motorist can expect to be shown, at certain times, over the whole operation. Indeed, so concerned with problems of production was the American management that I had trouble initially in arranging to see Savage River. However, the chairman of Ampol Petroleum, one of the Australian partner companies, has been for years an excellent friend; and W. M. (Mac) Leonard did more than smooth the way. From the hotel at Waratah I was picked up by Ampol's area manager from Burnie, and Ken Johnstone not only took me to Savage River, but stayed with me there for two days—there is a good Savage River Motor Inn—and made sure that I saw everything at Savage River, and even the Pieman River beyond. (Incidentally, it was Ampol's former chief, Sir William Walkley, who suggested that I write a book called *Australia at Work*, which I suppose I am doing, though it is also *Australia for the Traveller*.) The mine staff could not have been more helpful and hospitable.

The mining operations were the now-usual mechanical ones that needed a work force of only 350 men. Electric shovels loaded Euclid trucks with those taller-than-I-am tyres—and their exhausts heated the undersides of the big trays, so that wet ore (rainfall is 90 inches) tipped out without mud remaining. "Autogenous" grinding mills used the fall of the ore to turn the machinery that ground it small enough to go into the ball mills. The plant worked twenty-four hours a day six days a week. The SAFETY RECORD board showed 35 days without lost time due to injury: previous best, 34 days.

When the Valiant with WML on its numberplate (Ken Johnstone was nobody's sycophant: he just liked Ampol's boss, W. M. Leonard) took me down the dirt road south-west of Savage River we came to a notice, PIEMAN RIVER RESERVE. NO GUNS OR DOGS ALLOWED. After a few miles of spectacular rain forest there was the fine broad stream of the Pieman River. It is, surely, the only river in the world named after a white cannibal—the convict Alexander Pearce, the former Hobart pie-vendor who was known as "The Pieman". After his third escape at Macquarie Harbour (he had eaten men before), Pearce "brained his companion with an axe, ate the tastiest morsels, and calmly signalled a passing schooner to take him to Hobart and the gallows".[3] Apart from the river there was nothing much at what is called Corinna except a Ranger's house bearing the name RUFF-E-NUFF.

On the way back what looked like a deformed kelpie dog, its head too big for its body, sprang out of the button-grass and raced along the road ahead of us, until it shot off into the marshy verge. It was a young Tasmanian devil. "Quite a few about here," said the gravel-trucking man we met farther up the road.

TASMANIA had shown me some fine pastoral countryside, as well as wilderness and the strange environs of Mt Lyell; but when the brochures rave of Englishness one is inclined to expect to see a match for Surrey's gentle hills of green.

This looked-for and loveliest Tasmania began, with Savage River well behind us, about Yolla, where we turned off the main highway. It wasn't landscape as tamed as the English shires, but the same velvet greenness swathed the low breasts of hills that were more often set with a dark pine-tree than nippled with coppices. Sometimes a field of newly ploughed earth too red for English latitudes dissected the farmland scene.

This pasture-and-crop country was to climax its beauty at Table Cape near Wynyard. There, with the blue sea as backdrop, the sun-bright landscape curved in the gentlest contours, and even the sheep in the foreground seemed part of a physical poetry (PLATE 26).

Before the quiet beauty of Table Cape there had been the roaring technology of Port Latta. The "iron soup" from Savage River's pipeline went into a $35-million plant and came out as a rattling stream of 67 per cent iron marbles. Dehydrated back to powder by the heat of a bank of furnaces, the iron built up into little balls in huge revolving cylinders. From a mountainous stockpile, conveyor belts took the pellets to the end of what must be the longest jetty that ever poked a skeletal finger out into Bass Strait. The iron is loaded for Japan into such ships as the *Tasman Maru* of 90,000 tons.

Of course, there is something else that could be done with these iron pellets instead of sending them to Japan. If a steel industry were set up in Tasmania. . . . In July 1968 the then premier of the State said: "Roy Hudson, licence holder of the [Savage River] area is actively seeking a steel producer to base a manufacturing plant on the remainder of the ore." (There is another big iron deposit north of where Pickands Mather are mining.)

In late 1970 it was reported that establishment of a Tasmanian steel industry, at Port Latta, was likely in the near future.[1]

FARTHER WEST along the coast a long cape projects like a half-leg and foot. The heel of the foot is a striking conformation that the explorers Bass and Flinders, who first set European eyes on it in 1798, named Circular Head. It is called locally The Nut—and being flattish-topped it is rather like a nut of the kind that goes on a bolt, not the kind you crack. At the base of The Nut sits, or straggles, the crayfishing town of Stanley. Here, at the Warrawee café, we had a delicious cray-tail lunch for only $1.25. Most of the tails go to the United States.

Then Ken Johnstone had to race me back to Burnie, to finish the journey on still another Pioneer coach. Booming Burnie, with its big new docks, has 15,000 people, making it Tasmania's third largest centre, just ahead of Devonport. Its biggest industrial plant is the Associated Pulp and Paper Mills (where the paper of this book was made).

It was then about four o'clock and I was not long in this coach— which had, for a change, a lot of young people—before we came to the overnight stop at Ulverstone, which thinks of itself as the tourist centre of the north coast, and is proud of its clock-topped war memorial that towers bulkily in the town centre.

Next morning, the coach was soon in Devonport. Industrialism hasn't, as yet, overlaid Devonport's attractiveness, for the country hereabouts is so lushly green that you have trouble picking out the golf-courses from the rest of it. What with textiles and carpets, Devonport was growing as fast or faster than Burnie.

The Mersey River comes to the sea at Devonport. The Forth we had crossed a few miles back. (Surely, with all these names, the emigrant from Britain must feel more at home in Tasmania than anywhere else.) Both rivers were being harnessed into what was to become, in 1971, Tasmania's greatest hydro-electric project yet. Seven great dams and seven power stations that had been building since 1963, at a cost that would be $104 million, have added 1,500 produced annually. This Mersey-Forth Development is, in fact, a bigger one than Stage 1 of the Gordon River Scheme. Down in the wilds, the Wilmot River of the Western Tiers has been diverted to flow eastward into the Forth through a mountain-piercing tunnel that, dug from both ends, met to within a small fraction of an inch, by the use of laser beams. The power stations are all fully auto-matic and remote-controlled from Sheffield, miles away, where the staff lives.

On this cloudless day we left the coast and ran down the Bass Highway in the direction of the centre of the island. The sheep were up to their bellies in pasture, and newly turned earth was the colour of the chocolate Cadbury's make in such quantity down at Claremont near Hobart. Hedges of hawthorn fenced the fields, and the Western Tiers rose as we neared picturesque Deloraine. A surveyor Scott, a descendant of Sir Walter, named it after the Deloraine in "The Lay of the Last Minstrel".

The sheep were fattest and woolliest near Exton, where there is a Dorset stud. But nowhere was the scene more English than at Westbury. It even has a village green, said to be the only one in the Southern Hemisphere, used in the traditional way for cricket matches and fêtes. And, looking much like a Georgian country house in the English shires, was column-porticoed Fitzpatrick's Inn. It served Devonshire teas (but, oddly for an inn, no liquor). There you could stay for five dollars a night and sleep among the antique furniture presided over by Miss Jenny and Miss Myra. The country-side continued in this mood towards Launceston—a Ben Lomond rose in the distance and to the north of this the map showed an Upper Blassington and to the west, somewhat unnecessarily, an English Town.

We turned off to Western Junction, which has the airport of Launceston. All the other coach tourists got off here and Ansetted away to Melbourne or wherever. I went on to Launceston. I had an appointment with Bell Bay.

BELL BAY is where you see what finally happens to that gravelly red bauxite mined up at Weipa on Cape York and turned into white-powderish alumina at Gladstone. Here, near George Town at the mouth of the Tamar, it becomes aluminium.

The $50-million plant of Comalco Aluminium (Bell Bay) Limited is enormous, and complex beyond any other I have been in. Even the P.R.O. who showed me round still thought parts of it "rather frightening". It was originally built in 1954 as a Commonwealth aluminium-maker and Comalco took over an operation less auto-mated than later ones are, so some of the 760 workers still had hard manual jobs at the electrolytic hearths and in the man-handling of aluminium ingots. No brief explanation can convey how this light-strong metal emerges as a result of a process that employs great cylindrical towers called precipitators; and the calcinator that looks like the chamber-barrel section of Gargantua's big brother's revolver; and a reservoir of liquid caustic; and an avenue of more towering cylinders called vacuum flash coolers. Suffice to say that 73,000 tons of aluminium would come out of it all that year to roof houses, make boats and beer cans, and wrap food in foil, among a thousand uses.

Comalco (Bell Bay) was the biggest single user of electricity in

Australia. It used more than the city and suburbs of Perth. It used thirty per cent of all the electricity generated in Tasmania. "Power failure", then, was a synonym for "economic disaster". And 1968 was a nightmarish year because, owing to unprecedentedly low rainfall in that year and a few before it, the water storage that made the hydro-electricity was so depleted there had to be severe power rationing in the all-electric isle.

So, what was the Hydro Electric Commission of the water-power State building at Bell Bay, right alongside its biggest customer? A $19-million powerhouse station that wasn't hydro at all, but thermal. (It will be fired by oil, and could change over to natural gas from the Bass Strait fields.) Bell Bay Thermal will add about half as much power as the Mersey-Forth project to the Tasmanian system.

This time in Launceston I stayed at the Commodore Motel, which was pleasantly situated and had a good dining-room (even if the scallops it served had to come from Port Phillip, the local ones being so scarce). For dinner I went to Dicky White's Bistro. The martini I got had bits of ice floating in it.

All those American tourists Tasmania wasn't getting wouldn't care for that, either. However, I decided, in the morning of a blissful autumn day with hawthorn berries reddening along the road to the airport and un-Australian trees dropping yellow leaves on green Wilton grass-carpet, they still might find a lot to like about Australia's little England and the other untamed Tasmania of mountains and wilderness.

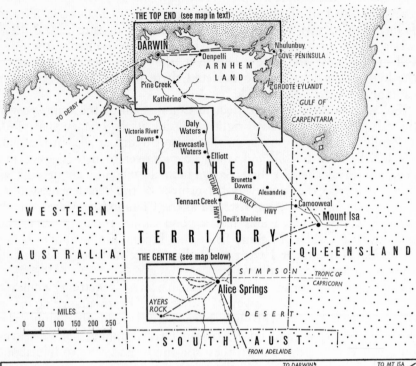

THE TOP END (see map in text)

DARWIN
Oenpelli
Nhulunbuy
GOVE PENINSULA
ARNHEM
LAND
Pine Creek
Katherine
Groote Eylandt
GULF OF
CARPENTARIA

TO DERBY

Victoria River
Downs
Daly
Waters
Newcastle
Waters
Elliott

NORTHERN

Brunette
Downs
Alexandria
Camooweal
Tennant Creek
Mount Isa
Devil's Marbles

WESTERN

TERRITORY

AUSTRALIA

THE CENTRE (see map below)
SIMPSON
TROPIC OF
CAPRICORN
QUEENSLAND
Alice Springs
AYERS
ROCK
DESERT

MILES
0 50 100 150 200 250

SOUTH AUST.
FROM ADELAIDE

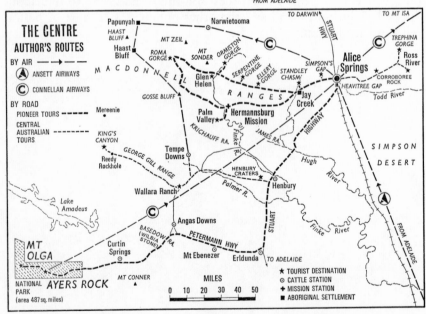

THE CENTRE
AUTHOR'S ROUTES

BY AIR →
Ⓐ ANSETT AIRWAYS
Ⓒ CONNELLAN AIRWAYS

BY ROAD
PIONEER TOURS ------
CENTRAL
AUSTRALIAN ------
TOURS

Papunyah
Narwietooma
TO DARWIN
TO MT ISA
HAAST
BLUFF
MT ZEIL
STUART
TREPHINA
GORGE
Haast
Bluff
ROMA
GORGE
MT
SONDER
ORMISTON
GORGE
Ⓒ
SERPENTINE
GORGE
Ⓒ
Ross
River
MACDONNELL
Glen
Helen
ELLERY
GORGE
STANDLEY
CHASM
SIMPSON'S
GAP
Alice
Springs
CORROBOREE
ROCK
RANGES
HEAVITREE GAP
Mereenie
GOSSE BLUFF
Jay
Creek
Todd River
Palm
Valley
Hermannsburg
Mission
KING'S
CANYON
KRICHAUFF RA.
JAMES RA.
HIGHWAY
SIMPSON
Reedy
Rockhole
GEORGE GILL RANGE
Tempe
Downs
Finke
Hugh
DESERT
Lake
Amadeus
Wallara Ranch
HENBURY
CRATERS
Henbury
River
Palmer R.
Ⓒ
Finke
River
MT
OLGA
Angas Downs
BASEDOW RA.
(WILBIA
STONE)
Curtin
Springs
PETERMANN HWY
Mt Ebenezer
Erldunda
TO ADELAIDE
STUART
FROM ADELAIDE
Ⓐ
NATIONAL
PARK
AYERS ROCK
(area 487 sq. miles)
MT CONNER

MILES
0 10 20 30 40 50

★ TOURIST DESTINATION
Ⓒ CATTLE STATION
✚ MISSION STATION
■ ABORIGINAL SETTLEMENT

THE NORTHERN TERRITORY

The Red and Future Centre

HAVING LOOKED at the States where five-sixths of Australians live in the east of the continent and in Tasmania, we come to that three-fifths of Australia where, down the middle and over in the west, there is only one-sixth of the population. If this book were two books it is with this wider, less-urbanized, more-outback Other Australia that Book Two would begin.

A map of Australia showing only the Australian States looks horribly incomplete without the Northern Territory:

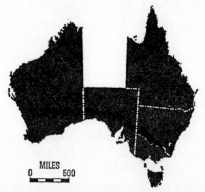

MILES
0   500

The reason why the Northern Territory lacks State status, has no more than an advisory legislative council and is governed from Canberra, is that this seventeen per cent of Australia cannot afford the apparatus of Statehood: it has only 70,000 people (twice as many live in the outer-Sydney shire of Sutherland). Nearly half the Territory's 70,000 are in the capital city of Darwin, the fastest-growing capital in Australia. The principal other place where the Territory has a clot of population is Alice Springs, with over 9,000.

More than a third of the people in the Northern Territory are black (Aborigines) or coloured. Darwin has a polychromatic population unusual in the "White Australia" resented by Asians—who have been astonished that Darwin's mayor, and president of the N.T. Legislative Council, was Mr Harry Chan, a locally born Chinese.

There was a time when there were many more Chinese than whites in the Territory, in the 1880s. The fourth settlement (three earlier ones had been abandoned) in what was then called the Northern Territory of South Australia attracted so few whites and labour was so short that the government brought Chinese in as coolie labourers. They found gold, which attracted more, and Chinese labour, mainly, built the Territory's only railway.

It was so hard to people the region that free passages to it were dangled in Devon and Cornwall (few takers); Mennonites, a Russian religious sect, were offered land (they went to Canada); an Australian emissary was sent to India to try to attract Hindu settlers (he didn't); and, finally, the Reverend Wilton Hack was deputed in Tokyo to "make known to the Japanese the advantages of the Northern Territory . . . . Should they desire to emigrate, the Government would pay their passages, but each must bring a year's provisions".[1] No Japanese came. Later some did, as pearl divers. And in February 1942 they came in bombers that devastated Darwin, killed 243 people and wounded more than 300 others.

Ironically enough, it was the Japanese as enemies who were responsible for the Northern Territory's being "colonized" to the extent it is today. The 7,000 whites who were in it when war broke out grew, within two years, to over 100,000—and though the great majority of these went away when the war ended some stayed in the Territory, or returned to it. They were mainly soldiers, airmen and navy garrison, construction workers and road builders—who built the bitumen Stuart Highway up from Alice Springs and the Barkly Highway from Tennant Creek to Camooweal in Queensland. Only since these roads have been built has the ordinary motorist or coach tourist been able to go to Darwin. And, of course, the Territory's produce could be trucked out, and it was no longer dependent on shipping to get such things as building materials and beer from the south. Although there had been air services, the highways did much to end the Territory's isolation and lessen what Blainey has called the "tyranny of distance".[2]

Airlines, we say, "annihilate distance". But although we can fly Adelaide-Darwin in about four hours it is still 1,700 miles of not only distance but *difference*. Adelaide is more southerly than Capetown, and Darwin is high in the tropics, nearer to the Equator than

Tahiti is. Darwin, in what we call the "Top End" of the Territory, is truly northern Australia.

Alice Springs isn't. It isn't even in the tropics, but just below where Capricorn cuts through. The Territory round Alice Springs is not northern, any more than it is southern or eastern or western. It is, geographically, dead centre. But not the "Dead Heart". It is not a "dead" environment—and touristically it is very much alive, because there are the best of reasons for tourists to go there.

The Centre is only half the distance from Adelaide the Top End is. Yet the Centre is actually *more different*, in appearance, from the Australia where most Australians live. They live with the green of trees—which the Centre has, but not nearly so much. They live with the blue of sea, harbour lake, river—the Centre's blue is all in its sky. The main, dramatic difference is that it is the *Red* Centre.

Although its redness establishes it as a place that is no place like home, redness is not in itself a sufficient attraction. I once saw from the air the Simpson Desert, at sunset, so red it looked like the back-yard of Hell. Unforgettable, but more awful than alluring.

What makes the Centre a "must" for the traveller is that the red-ness comes in such wondrous forms of rock. Ayers Rock is the most spectacular single natural wonder inland Australia has to show, the greatest monolithic rock in the world. "The Olgas", as they are called, are even more extraordinary as rock forms.

An American survey team of travel experts who went through the area in April 1969 considered Ayers Rock and the Olgas among the outstanding natural features in Australia and the world.[3]

Indeed, these experts gave the Centre such priority as a tourist attraction that their main report recommended that Alice Springs, instead of Darwin, be made the entry point to Australia by some international airlines flying from Honolulu, Japan, Hong Kong, Singapore and Djakarta in Indonesia.

The proposal to bring international airlines to Alice Springs as their first Australian touchdown is unlikely to be adopted in the near future. Direct Sydney–Alice Springs flights are likely to be scheduled by the winter of 1972.

In 1969 the Centre had about 30,000 visitors, of whom approxi-mately 6,000 were from overseas. Projecting from these figures, the American survey team estimated that if accommodation and trans-port facilities were extended and improved (in ways they recom-mended) the visitor intake could be raised by 1975 to 70,000 from within Australia and 50,000 from overseas; and these 120,000 would spend between, roundly, $14 million and $20 million. By 1980 there would be a potential of some 200,000 tourists, spending around $40 million—which is double what the pastoral industry contributed to

v

the economy of the Territory in 1968-69. Pastoralism's rate of increase was unlikely to match that projected for tourism—which *could* (but not necessarily would)—become, from the Centre's earnings alone, the Territory's second biggest industry, topped only by mining.

"Tourists," Elspeth Huxley remarked, "yield better profits than beef; they do not need to be dipped or inoculated, are much more readily mustered, and pay for their keep."[4]

In this territory of the New Australia, the mining scene is mainly in the Top End, from Tennant Creek (a veteran copper-gold producer) north, with newer development of iron and uranium mines towards Darwin. In Arnhem Land the "world's richest uranium mine" at Nabarlek near Oenpelli was announced in September 1970. East of this, at Gove, a huge bauxite enterprise had come into production; manganese was being mined on Groote Eylandt; and a vast lead-zinc deposit was under study at the McArthur River on the north-east corner of the Gulf of Carpentaria.

The Centre has some oil, at Mereenie west of Alice Springs, and large reserves of natural gas. The strike of natural gas near Palm Valley in 1970 was the biggest yet made in Australia. It flowed 76 million cubic feet a day.

ALICE NOT IN WONDERLAND

I FLEW up to Alice Springs from Adelaide in two hours. I had no wish to take two days getting to the Centre by the train, still called the Ghan (in tribute to the early Afghan camel-drivers), or three days in one of the tourist coaches that come up through such places as the Coober Pedy opalfield I'd flown to in 1935. Nor would I have wanted to drive myself, even if the unsealed road up from Port Augusta had had a few graders over it since its 1968 description as "for most of the way atrocious".[1] Of course you could always put your car on the Ghan—or hire a Land Rover at Alice Springs. From the air you see best the spread and pattern and contours of this mainly South Australian country; and the desert stretches in particular can be fascinating.

There is not nearly as much desert in Australia as is commonly believed. ("Desert may be described as a region which from lack of water is uninhabitable".[2]) But there are a few regions it would be absurd to call anything else. None of these deserves the name more than does the desert that occupies much of the north-east corner of South Australia and extends most of its 30,000 square miles into the Northern Territory and was named for A. A. Simpson who financed expeditions into it. The Simpson Desert has Sahara-like ridges of sand, red sand. The ridges run north-south from horizon to horizon, like waves of a sea, often over a hundred feet high, and the wind that moulds them drifts them. North of Oodnadatta you see some of the red sand-drift country, sparsely dotted with spinifex (or what I propose to call spinifex even though there is no *true* spinifex in inland Australia, only on the coast).[3]

Sometimes the outcropping rocky hills sweep in parallel curves, like seats in a vast amphitheatre. But approaching Alice Springs you see ahead the long east-west line of the MacDonnell Ranges, nicked with Heavitree Gap.

Through this gap is the oasis of Alice Springs—with eucalypts growing forty feet high in its streets. It gets only ten inches of rain in an average year, but there is underground water less than twenty feet down.

ALICE SPRINGS is not nowadays called "the Alice" as much as it used to be. Increasingly, the name is shortened to just "Alice". This is not only a result of Nevil Shute's making the place known world-wide with his novel *A Town Like Alice*. A certain gaucherie is beginning to attach to the "the"—like going into a newsagent's and asking for *The Pix* magazine.

Until two years before I first saw it in 1935 the town was called Stuart, after the redoubtable explorer John McDouall Stuart who made the first crossing of Australia from north to south in 1862. The trail thus blazed, the Overland Telegraph Line was put through from Adelaide to the northern outpost that became Darwin, so that Australia's isolation of ship-only communication with Europe and Asia could be ended by linking the overland line with the submarine cable that had reached Java. The place of the midway telegraph station in 1871 was called—after Alice Todd, wife of Charles Heavitree Todd, South Australia's then Postmaster-General—The Alice Springs. Actually the "springs" are part of the Todd River that flows (when it flows) through the town that became Alice Springs in 1933.

Pastoralists opened up the country by moving cattle in and the Alice Springs I knew was a cattle town with a rowdy weatherboard pub called the Stuart Arms where the only beds we could get were on the veranda. Now entirely rebuilt, the Stuart Arms had a plushy, low-lit, carpeted "Bull Bar" designed to make jet-setters feel at home. There were three other hotels and seven motels.

The town that is no longer even like A Town Like Alice was going to end up as a small city with traffic lights in Todd Street— where the American tourism surveyors reported traffic congestion in 1969. They were critical of Alice's northside "unattractive light industrial area", with ugly junkyards, its "unsightly overhead utility poles and wires" and "unimaginative architectural style". They said that Todd Street "could be a main street anywhere in the Western world", and that "Alice should develop a physical character that reflects the environment and will give the town a definite sense of identity."[4]

The town-planner and architect of the team had prepared what looks to me an excellent re-plan of Alice with a characterful "Visitor Centre" of local stone and wood, designed to blend with the environment, and even street benches that had a natural rugged unfussy look, and simple non-jazzy signwriting. As the consultants said, "The greatest asset of Alice is its dramatic natural setting in the MacDonnell Ranges." Commercialism and "feature"-happy builders should not be allowed to detract from this.

The town has, though, more Australian character than most. Wide-hatted Aboriginal and white stockmen in the streets and, quite a few bearded oil-drillers, give it the air of belonging to the Australian Outback. The eucalypts and athel-trees (a kind of tamarisk) and other street trees are good (though some had been hideously lopped because of overhead wires). The John Flynn Memorial Church connects the town with a distinctive Australian pioneering development, the Flying Doctor Service. And there is a good deal of "Australiana" about, much of it in the form of watercolour paintings by Aranda artists in galleries and shops.

When I got off the bus from the airport the Ansett office ordered a taxi for me to go to the Mount Gillen Hotel-Motel. I went out to wait for it, and a big, sombrero'd, atypically fat Aboriginal who looked about forty lurched up, breathing wine, and started to talk. "You jes' come Alice Springs, eh? Where you comin' from . . .?" The taxi arrived when I'd said no more than "Sydney" and, excusing myself, I got in and said to the driver, "Who was that character?"

"Just a savage." The voice was gritty. "All right, but in his place." I decided not to start an argument.

"What would he have wanted?" I said and got the answer I expected: "A dollar to drink with."

But the Aboriginal situation we'll come to, later on and here and there.

ALICE'S PLACE in the scheme of the Centre's tourism will vary with the individual tourist. Some women, and a few men, appear to travel mainly to shop. Especially if they are Americans, they will send boomerangs from Central Australia to their friends, which is generous of them and good for business, even if the boomerangs are garish in a way no Aboriginal ever decorated them. However, the returning boomerang—a functionally beautiful object, though a toy, a sport-thing not a weapon—was never used by the Aborigines of Central Australia.[5] They used the hooked boomerang, which *is* a weapon, for striking and throwing; but it does not come back.

Alice Springs I regard as little more than a base for Centre-seeing, and I spent the least possible time there. Alice, in short, is not in wonderland, which is miles and more miles away, most of it to the west or south-west, where Ayers Rock is 285 miles by road, 210 by air.

The places tourists usually go to in and near Alice Springs are: The historic Old Telegraph Station (two miles north); the John Flynn (founder of the Flying Doctor Service) Memorial Church, in Todd Street; the Flying Doctor Base and School of the Air (both are here conducted much as I wrote of them in connection with Broken Hill, N.S.W.); the Tmara-Mara Art Gallery run by the painter Rex Battarbee, who taught the famed Aboriginal artist Albert Namatjira to paint, and who has the best collection anywhere of Namatjira's watercolour landscapes (and who told me that he considered Albert's son Ewald "a great artist", as good as his father, and that another son, Oskar Namatjira, "paints better ghost-gums than Albert did" and, of the younger Aranda painters, he thought Keith Morris had "great potential"); Pichi Richi, two miles out, a native birds/plants sanctuary, with pioneering relics and sculptures of Aborigines by the Victorian sculptor William Ricketts (written of in the Dandenongs chapter); Anzac Hill for the panoramic view; and to see Mrs E. M. Jenkyns's collection of opal.

The biggest thing at Alice Springs you cannot go to see. Its location is not marked on any maps, though everyone knows it is along a road that turns off right when you go south through Heavitree Gap. It is not mentioned in brochures and booklets about the place. You cannot look down on it from the air: flying within two and a half miles of it is prohibited. It cost $225 million to establish—nearly a third the cost of our Snowy Mountains Scheme. The Americans began building it in 1967. They have also built 250 houses in Alice Springs for its staff and their families. It is usually referred to, by its location, as "Pine Gap", or the "Space Base".

That, of course, doesn't tell us what it really is. Neither does its official description: Joint Defence Space Research Facility. Guesses at its top-secret function usually suggest that it is part of the United States early warning system in case the Russians or the Chinese were mad enough to start launching intercontinental ballistic missiles with atomic warheads, or that it is to do with missile control if the U.S. did, or retaliated.

Such a function, it has been suggested in the Press, would make Alice a high-priority target for an I.C.B.M. in order to knock out the J.D.S.R.F. Some Alice-ites have worried about this. Others say, "Alice has ceased to wonder what might be going on behind those sealed doors. . . . It's no business of hers at all, so she happily clasped to her bosom the free-spending American servicemen stationed there", and, "even in the first year the Base contributed millions of dollars to the town's economy". And they tell you what fun it was at the 1969 Bangtail Muster carnival when the Americans at Pine Gap entered a float in the procession with pretty girls and a white-coated "scientist" working a Heath Robinson rig-up and with cases branded CORN LIKKER and a sign saying "Trespassers will be Intoxicated" and another that made it plain to laughing all that J.D.S.R.F. stood for "Jim Dandy's Still and Refreshment Factory". But this book is not supposed to be about what a mad world we live in.

As to climate, the best time to go to the Centre is between May and September. Alice is at its liveliest in the first week of May with its carnival Bangtail Muster (stock, when mustered and being counted for sale, used to have the ends of their tails cut straight) and early in September there is a hilarious Henley-on-Todd Regatta, a race of mock-up boats on the waterless river.

Summer heat rises to an average maximum of 95 degrees in January, but it is dry heat and the nights are not sweaty. Such rain as this semi-arid region gets usually falls mostly between November and March, but there is no "Wet". Summer months average four days when rain falls, winter months three days.

Americans can regard the region as Phoenix, Arizona, but not quite so hot, and with air even drier. Tourists from Europe can look forward to a lot more sunshine than they get in sunny Spain —Alice has only 35 days of the average year when any rain falls, as against 90 in Madrid. Australians from Melbourne can expect 9.7 hours of sunshine a day as against an average 5.6 hours at home.

But—some people expect a tropical-inland climate: it isn't. Also, though the plain the mountains rise from looks like sea-level, it is really a plateau nearly 2,000 feet up. So, although winter days are bright and warm, they aren't really hot (June's average maximum is 67) and early mornings and nights can be *cold*. Away from Alice Springs there is no room-heating (though Ross River resort fits beds with electric blankets). I didn't take a topcoat, only because I did not want to lug it to hotter places I was going on to. Woollies, such as pullovers, you definitely need and, on tour, most women wear slacks. When dressing for the day, put on to peel off as the day warms up. Don't forget a wind-cheater and scarf. Take a torch: lighting is likely to be switched off by midnight at some lodges.

AYERS ROCK AND THE OLGAS

To HAVE BEEN to Alice Springs and not gone out to see Ayers Rock sounded so discreditable that I could not wait longer than overnight before setting out for it.

My excuse for not going to Ayers Rock in 1935 is that the Rock had very few white visitors before 1936, when a party led by the famous old bushman Bob Buck, and including a Mrs Foy, not only got to the Rock but climbed it (not that they were the first to do so). It was 1950 or thereabouts before the first tourist parties began jouncing out there in Len Tuit's bus, with camping gear. There was still no accommodation when Bill Harney became the first Ranger of the Ayers Rock-Mount Olga National Park in 1957. In the year he left, 1961, there were 4,000 visitors. In the 1969-70 year there were 27,000.

The Pioneer coach I joined at 8.30 a.m. on this crisp and cloud-less early August morning would go through to Adelaide, but you could use it for a three-day tour that returned you to Alice by air. Except for two Americans, the party consisted of Australians, from all States except Tasmania and Queensland. Along the road, the driver-commentator ("My name's Phil") used the microphone to ask everybody, somewhat to my surprise, "What do you all do?" As to occupation, at least half the passengers replied, "Retired". The woman who answered cryptically, "You wouldn't understand", turned out to be a psychiatrist. Her comely companion, with a figure like a model's, was a barrister.

We go out through Heavitree Gap and past the turn-off to the Pine Gap "mystery", eight miles out. The road will be part-bitumen for the first sixty miles. On either side the flat land stretches away, tan, tufted with mulga grass, sparsely treed with the casuarinas called desert-oaks. Branches—and, on roadside trees, even the sparse long needle foliage—are sharply etched on the hard blue sky. The light is brilliant as a diamond, the shadows are cut-outs in jet-black. People rave of the light in Greece, but here, with the nearest sea haze six hundred miles away and no forests of eucalypts to exude into the air, the light on any undusty day is brighter than Hellas ever knew. Half an hour out, there is a low range to the north, sculpturing the horizon with what are like crowns carved in red ochre.

The trees turn to mulga, the small spready acacia, and what Phil calls desert-mallee. The stony earth between is humped with spiked green cushions of spinifex (*Triodia*). But, more than anything else, there is a pale grass that is exactly peroxide-blonde colour. The first ghost gums appear—white as the gloves Italian policemen wear, chalk-white, immaculate, so immaculate you fear they will get dirty; but they never do. The Hugh River is where the bitumen ends, and the bed of the river is as dry as the dirt road that takes us past the end of the James Range. Twenty miles farther down the plain is the Finke River (how much better than Finke is the Aboriginal name, Larapinta!). The Finke is as dry as the Hugh was. We've been going two hours. That means a coach stop. There are no structures of any kind at the Finke.

"Ladies to the left. Gentlemen to the right." It is to become a kind of refrain to outback coach touring. Vegetation takes on a new value. It thickens beside river-beds; and for the left-goers there is no needly spinifex just here.

None of this country, east to the Simpson Desert and west to the Aboriginal reserves, is considered wasteland. We are running through cattle-station properties all the way to the National Park the Rock is in. We are on Henbury now, 1,700 square miles. A notice board at a road going off to the west says TEMPE DOWNS 66/ANGUS [Angas] DOWNS 80. *Warning—50 Miles Loose Sandy Road.* NO WATER. *Travellers to Ayres* [Ayers] *Rock are Advised to use Main Road via Erldunda and Mount Ebenezer.*

Then another road turns off, a shorter route to Angas Downs Station—and to Ayers Rock, thirty miles shorter. But it, too, is bad with sand (as I was to find later). It is about time this more-direct route was made trafficable: 286 miles is longer than people want to travel by coach to get to the great tors. The Stuart Highway we stay on for another forty miles becomes Vibration Highway, with a great chattering of windows in their frames; and this road turns into red sand.

This is the Red Centre—with green balls of paddy-melons growing at the road verge. Phil says that they are split open for the cattle to eat in drought time. The last two seasons have been good, and the country has "recovered wonderfully" from the five drought years to 1966. But the drought left a lot of very dead mulgas.

We turn off west on to the Petermann "Highway"—it's no highway—that runs to the Petermann Ranges no tourists get to. Erldunda's homestead doesn't look as lonely as the next homestead on Staines. Then we are on Mt Ebenezer station and there are three or four hundred cattle in a mob, and Phil says, "Ebenezer's been doing some mustering. Best mob of cattle I've seen in years." There is a log-cabin style roadhouse where we lunch. It is bright with Aboriginal décor, right down to WATTY (Men) and GOONA (Women) on the loos.

When we leave, a westerly wind is hurling dust before it, and Phil thinks it could blow up rain. I am reading, as well as the corrugated road permits, Bill Harney's book, *To Ayers Rock and Beyond*.[1] And how I wish him still alive and custodian at the Rock, my old tent-mate of the Arnhem Land Expedition (1948) whose guide he was: I made the first radio recordings of his wonderful yarns of the Aborigines he knew so well (he even married one, but she died, and their son was accidentally killed). To the dark people his name was, I found, one word—*Billarni*.

Just past the Angas Downs turn-off the small Basedow Range rises. Bill writes that, to the natives, a part of this is *Wilbia*, and there is a ridge with a circle of cleared earth, a sacred and taboo place, where there is the Wilbia Stone, anointed with emu fat and blood. And although the "grand and awe-inspiring spots such as Ayers Rock, Mount Olga and King's Canyon are also invested with sacred significance . . . the Wilbia Stone holds precedence, for it is to that area the initiates go to pass into a sacred way of life."[2]

The red-sand road was aimed, like a long spearpoint, at a mountain standing solitary on the plain. Scarp-sided and with a very long flat top—or so it looks, remarkably level—this was Mount Conner. Now the road has turned away from this great mesa that is eleven hundred feet above the plain. Bill Harney's book says, "Bushmen who have climbed on to its summit have told me that mulga trees of giant size flourish up there in a little world of their own."

Conner is an arresting mountain, almost as high as Ayers Rock, though not as high as Mt Olga, and not so remarkable in form and colour as either—a coronet beside two crowns. I half wished I had not seen so many pictures of the Rock and the Olgas: I felt I knew what I was coming to, knew how they would look.

Should I, then, try to see Ayers Rock in another dimension—in terms of what it was to the Aborigines? Bill Harney had written: "The Rock of *Uluru* [the native name] was sacred . . . but it was never secret or taboo." What does *Uluru* mean? He doesn't say, precisely: nobody does. Harney says it must be "regarded as one complete ritual-stone because it is the abiding place of the all-knowing Wanambi-serpent who lives in the valley of *Uluru*." What valley? In another publication[3] he says it "lives forever at the Ngati [rock-hole] of Uluru".

What does Mountford say? (C. P. Mountford, the anthropologist, who led the Arnhem Land Expedition I joined, to document it for the A.B.C., and with whom I later worked on the Aboriginal sequences of a film.) I have his book with me, too, *Ayers Rock*.[4] It says: "This wanambi, which is regarded as the most dangerous and unfriendly in the country, has its home in huge caverns under, not in, the waters of Uluru. The snake is many hundreds of yards long, has an enormous head, long projecting teeth and beard, and a skin which old Balinga said had the same colours as the rainbow." And Balinga would not let Monty (as I know him) go near the rock-hole because "Balinga fully believed the wanambi would have trans-formed himself into a rainbow, and killed us both." So it's the old Rainbow Snake myth—which Stanner[5] cuts down to size by calling it a "rite-less myth"; and Mountford agrees that it is—but Bill Harney has the rock as a "ritual-stone"....

What does Mountford on Ayers Rock think of Harney on Ayers Rock? Monty gives Bill the soft footnote crunch: "As the majority of Mr Harney's statements do not agree with my research, I will not refer to them in later descriptions."[6]

Mountford is also at odds with Strehlow. (Top authority on the Aranda people, T. G. H. Strehlow, born at Hermannsburg, son of a pioneer Centre missionary, speaks the language like a native. He is Reader in Australian Linguistics at the University of Adelaide.)

And when we arrive at Curtin Springs Station—it's the afternoon-tea stop—Peter Severin, the owner, who was a friend of Harney's, says to me: "I see that Strehlow is having a shot at Bill in the latest *Inland Review*."[7] Yes, he can let me have a copy. In this magazine, following an article by Strehlow, is reproduced a letter from Bill Harney to a friend, saying that he sits there at Ayers Rock fascina-ted by the *Uluru* that symbolizes the great Earth Mother and also symbolizes "the phallic serpent that lives in an inaccessible rock-hole within it".

Comment on this from Strehlow: "Bill Harney did not know any of the Centralian languages. . . . His preoccupation with the Earth Mother and the phallic serpent (his version of the Rainbow Serpent of the Northern Australian cults) is also responsible for his distortions of the Ayers Rock traditions." Strehlow in his article deplores the "wholesale production of worthless mythological accounts [of Ayers Rock], written by the uninformed for the ignorant".

Strehlow implies that *he* knows the whole story. But—"The few trusted outsiders who have been granted glimpses of this sacred world have invariably been put under a solemn obligation to divulge only a minimal amount of their religious information. . . . For the present the Aboriginal traditions should be respected by the few white men who know anything about them. Hence, it is not possible, at this stage, to write at any length on the myths or songs of Ayers Rock or of any of the other striking geographical features of Central Australia except in scientific publications."[8] Which leaves book-author Mountford where? Doesn't really know, or, if he does, shouldn't really say?

On one anthropological expedition into Aboriginal country the eminent professor leading it showed his colleagues a wooden object brought in by an old man of the tribe. It was so sacred, the professor said, that they were very privileged white men to set eyes on it. Later, one of the party (who told me the story) saw Bill Harney (who was that expedition's guide also) walk by with this so-sacred object dangling from his hand, and spluttered, "How did you get hold of—that?", and Bill said, "Good one, isn't it? Got it from that old bloke for six sticks of t'bacca."

At least Strehlow and Mountford agree that the Central Australian Aborigines believed that the earth is eternal, not created, and that it was once all a flat, featureless plain. Strehlow is said by Mountford to maintain that local belief was that the natural features were created by totemic ancestors—who rose out of the ground in the forms of animals or humans—as they moved across the plain. Mountford says the Pitjandjara (whose territory the rock of Uluru is in) told him that these ancestors moved about the plain without raising anything, just living on it, and there was "no change in the topography until the close of the creation period".[9] Then, Ayers Rock, their great *Uluru*, rose miraculously out of a large flat sandhill.

But, broadly, they are in agreement here. "Where one or another of the heroes had performed any task, a mountain range, an isolated hill, a valley, a watercourse, or some other natural feature was created"—Mountford. "Mountains, sandhills, plains, saltlakes, swamps, river courses, springs and soakages, all came into being to mark the travels and exploits of roving totemic ancestors and ancestresses"—Strehlow,[10] who makes the point that the *whole* countryside, not just prominent features in it, was sacred, in validation of the myths. Some places were more sacred than others, and spectacular appearance had nothing to do with their ranking. Strehlow gives a photograph of a humdrum piece of landscape about 150 miles south-west, called Wapirka (near Victory Downs Station) that, "considered as a major totemic centre, outranked by far Ayers Rock."

On how the topography, the features of Uluru rock, were formed, the myths as given by Strehlow, Mountford and Harney *substantially* agree. Harney was less informed (about this area, not the north) than Strehlow or Mountford; but he was not "uninformed". To summarize a summary by Strehlow:[11]

The southern side of the Rock is associated with the Carpet Snake (*Kunia*) ancestors of the Pitjandjara people. These non-poisonous snakes were attacked by a horde of Venomous Snakes (*Liru*). There was a battle to the death at Mutitjilda waterhole (which has become "Maggie Springs" to tourists). Blood from the

snakes stained some of the rock surfaces red. Many rock forms and
boulders are dead snakes turned to stone.

The northern side of Uluru is associated with Hare-Wallaby (or
Rat-Kangaroo) ancestors, *Mala*. A hunting-initiation party of *Mala*-
totem men came from the south. At Uluru a *Mala* man was incensed
at seeing a Willy Wagtail totem woman sitting by the track leading
to the cave where the young men were to be initiated. He killed this
woman. Subsequently, an ancestral Kingfisher tried to warn the
sleeping *Mala* men of the approach of a man-eating monster, an
enormous dingo. Two were ripped to pieces and the others fled.
(Mountford says the monstrous dog killed most of the *Mala* men,
and their families. He also brings in Linga the Lizard Man, who
couldn't get enough honey-ants to eat, so he slaughtered and cooked
and ate a young woman.)

These Ayers Rock myths are harsh with the burden of blood and
violence that is the bane of so much mythology. There is little of
story-appeal in them and less still of anything that translates as
poetry. Aboriginal myths, nevertheless, show the First Australians
to have been a highly imaginative people.

I decide not to try to interpret the Rock, but just look at it.

WHAT CAME IN SIGHT before Ayers Rock did was the dome of Mt
Olga. It is 3,419 feet above sea-level, 549 feet higher than the
Rock's 2,870, of which 1,143 feet is above ground level.

"Ayers Rock" and "Mt Olga" instead of *Uluru* and *Katajuta*.
Why? The explorer Giles who in 1872 saw the highest head of
Katajuta (which means "many heads") saw it from fifty miles north,
tried to get closer, but his horses could not cross the salt swamp of
Lake Amadeus, and he did not see the Rock. He wanted to call the
dome Mount von Mueller, after the great botanist and sometime
explorer who was one of the financial backers of his expedition.
Baron von Mueller had been honoured with the Order of St Isabella
of Spain, so he said the mount's name should be that of Spain's
Queen Olga.

Giles returned in 1874 for a closer look, and this time came to
the Rock—where there was a tree cut with "G" (it is still there)
by another explorer, 31-year-old William Gosse, who had come in
the previous year. The first white man to set eyes on Uluru named it
after the premier of South Australia, Sir Henry Ayers. Gosse and
his Afghan camel-driver, Kamran, were the first non-Aborigines to
climb the Rock, on 20th July 1873.[12]

It is claimed in the *Guinness Book of Records*[13] that Mount
Augustus, 200 miles east of Carnarvon in Western Australia, and not
Ayers Rock, is the world's greatest monolith. Mount Augustus is

not monolithic in the sense of being a single block of one kind of stone: "it is composed of very hard gritty conglomerates"[14] whereas Ayers Rock is one glorious block of arkose (containing mica) sandstone. Mt Augustus is larger, about five miles by two, broken and undistinguished in shape and, in a good season, low vegetation grows over most of it. Ayers Rock is, in miles, $1\frac{3}{5}$ long from east to west, $\frac{7}{8}$ wide, $5\frac{1}{2}$ round.

Its dome appeared for us about five o'clock against a sky so darkened with clouds that Phil the driver said, "Bring your raincoats?" Its colour was not apparent then; it was an almost black silhouette against the horizon where the sun was going down behind cloud. As it loomed larger it became a dark ochre-brown. Then its colour did not seem to matter, only its size and form. It was enormous. None of the photographs I had seen prepared me for its bigness. Almost as impressive as its size were the forms within its shape.

I had not envisaged the Rock as being such a marvellously sculptural thing. Its naked body of stone had ribs and groins and shoulders, it had mouths and navels of caveholes, and, high on the side towards the north, the smooth sheer surface was incised with a strange complex of shallow erosion carvings that have been given the name of the "Brain" (PLATE 31).

When we had off-loaded at the Ansett Lodge I came out of the lounge and stood, beer in hand, gazing at it—this wonder mounded on the plain, losing its ochre colour, purpling in the dusk. It towered so near—its huge presence seeming to press it closer than the mile away it was—yet it remained so aloof, a stone monarch to the shifting sand, so venerably bald above the flat of grass and dotted mulga, and so implacably *old*, ancient beyond the count of years.

The sky above was clear now. The clouds at one end of the Rock had gone to put out the fire of the sun—I hoped they would stay in the west, or go away. Sunrise I wanted to see light the face of *Uluru*.

IT DIDN'T SEEM TO MATTER much then what the Ansett Lodge was like as accommodation; but, for the record, it was less than first-rate, partly because it was built at the "primitive" stage of Centre tourism, partly because of staff difficulties. And because of proposals to change the whole accommodation set-up in the Rock-Olgas area there wasn't much point in up-dating accommodation that could be phased out and cleared away from this eastern end of the Rock.

Two newer motels had rooms with "private facilities", and there were some at the Ayers Rock Hotel; but the Ansett Lodge didn't. It was licensed, yet it didn't serve wines, owing to "staff problems", the manageress said.

At night there was so little to do that the old yardman, Ossie

Andrews, showed his colour slides. He kept his camera up at the rubbish tip, which he was constantly visiting in the course of his job. Seeing the Rock under all conditions, year in, year out, he had wonderful opportunities for registering its changes of colour.

Ossie was a bushman-true "character", who put on a somewhat hilarious show that was much enjoyed, even if a few slides were upside down or he didn't focus too well. His commentary went something like this: " 'Nother one of the Rock from the Rub-bisheap. Like a great big slug, ain't it? . . . My mum came up here from Port Lincoln by donkey team . . . . That's another very pretty daisy. I like takin' flowers. I call 'em all daisies . . . . I had Curtin Springs for ten years, but the drought beat me. . There's that dog of mine. Always waggin' his tail, but you wouldn't know that from the picture. . . . That's another one of the Rock from the Rubbisheap. It's the atmospheric conditions make the colour. . . . Course, it's not only drought that gets yer cattle, some'll eat poison weed and keel over, and then you lose a few to some other station. They'll kill the bullocks they nick off with, and put their brand on the calves. Only way to get equal is to go and round up a few o' theirs. They all do it. . . . That's some more daisies. The picture's a bit muzzy, but they're very pretty. . . . That's another one I took from —strike a light, upside down again!—but you won't see the Rock that real, deep-purply colour, 'cause yez is only here for a coupla days. I always reckon it's like a big slug or something. . . . That's the west side before they put the chain in so you can climb up easy, 1964 they put the chain. I reckon I'd have climbed the Rock about two hundred and fifty times. Course, I've been to the Rubbisheap a lot more times than that. . . . Now you see in this one how it's all silvery-coloured. That's the way it looks after rain . . . . There's another. After a hailstorm. Think it had snow on it, eh? Never seen snow. Never been east or west. . . . Now look at that one—real dark purply-black. I been wonderin' when these good ones was going to turn up. . . . You wouldn't think it'd ever be *this* colour now, pale yellowy, like a cut-in-half damper. . . . And this one, half red, black on top . . . . Now here's a *real red* one. Got to be some clouds in the sky for it to get as red as that . . . You'll see it pretty red, but yez are only here for a coupla days . . . . Still, you get the best sun-rises in the tourist time. . . ."

Ossie Andrews had a few quite remarkable shots, and many people bought duplicates of them, which, of course, he had available.

The lighting plant switched off at 11.20. The night was very cold. The walls of the rooms (twin-bedded) were single-sheet fibro. I woke before dawn, aware that I'd been snoring—but not, I hoped, as loudly as the man next door on the right. Maybe I *had* wakened the couple in the room on the left. Through that wall came voices, so plainly. She: *What time is it?* He: *Five o'clock. Cold, isn't it?* (Pause.) She: *I'm—lonely. . . .* He: *Ah . . . I should have brought me bedsocks!*

She stayed lonely. If he had barefooted it across the chilly lino to the other bed in the next room I should certainly have known about it.

AT SIX-THIRTY next morning it could hardly have been said that all the world at the Ansett Lodge was waiting for the sunrise. Three other people had got up to see it light the Rock.

The sky was clear, the air bitterly cold, a small, marrow-biting wind brushing the blond grass. The three waiting men, hands in pockets, envied the lone woman her gloves. If a girl with a tray had appeared saying, "Morning tea, a dollar a cup!" she would have had customers. There was no morning tea, then or later; nor any electric jugs in the rooms to make it.

The sun didn't rise until seven. When I had looked out at picca-ninny daylight the Rock had had a strange darkling glow. As the light increased it became bright ochre. When the sun lit first its head and then its eastern face it changed radiantly towards red. Then the sun was on the ground, too, and the few mulgas' long shadows crept towards it, pointing their lengthening fingers at the vast red-jasper gemstone on the plain's flat palm.

To see Earth's greatest stone thus aglow made "Worth getting out of a warm bed for" one of those understatements. Cold fingers clicked and clicked. Yet sunrise on the Rock doesn't make quite such vivid pictures as sunset does (PLATE 3).

After breakfast the coach took us to the western side, past what is called the Brain (probably because Finlayson in 1931 described the high sculpturings of erosion as "somewhat like the sagittal section of a human skull with mandible attached").[15] (PLATE 31). To the Pitjandjara it was the "camping place of old *Mala* men and initiates"[16] who were attacked by the man-eating dingo. The nearby holes in the Rock are said to be the monster dingo's footmarks.

The extraordinary formation now known as the Kangaroo Tail is a thin slab of rock, aslant and perhaps two hundred feet long, that is only partly attached: you see a long slit of sky between it and the face. To the Aborigines it was their sacred pole turned to stone.

We get to the western extremity and "Who's for climbing Ayers Rock?" Those who don't want to will get shown more of it at ground level now; those who do, later. Fifteen of the forty people in the coach get out to climb. Three look again at the steepness of the side—the least steep side, but still very steep, about 45 degrees—

and get back in. Twelve start, six give up on the way, six of us make it to the cairn on top. (I think I was the eldest.)

A woman of eighty-four is supposed to have done the climb (perhaps the one Bill Harney referred to[17] as having been helped and carried by the coach-captain most of the way), and a man with a crutch, which I find hard to credit. Coming down, I was appalled to see a spastic young man who had struggled, so gamely, up the first hundred feet, almost crawling. I tried to dissuade him from going farther by saying it was a long way (which, indeed, it seems to be) and the climb had nearly killed me. Which it hadn't, but it was far from easy, very testing, the side-ascent part: after that it is not strenuous.

The chains slung between iron poles (PLATE 31) are regarded by some as a disfigurement of the Rock. I think they are to be excused, on the grounds of safety: after all, three climbers have been killed. The chains are low-slung and not the help a hand-rail would be to an adult; but grasping them can save people who get faint and may fall. Rubber soles are essential. I wore sandshoes, and would again. Nobody with a heart condition, or fear of heights, or who has been drinking should undertake the climb. They can take comfort from the fact that that sturdy bushman Bill Harney never made it to the top when he was the Ranger: "About seven hundred feet up I begin to conk out from the height which gives me a dizzy feeling as though I am about to fall."[18] He was then about sixty.

The record time—for 700 feet of slope and then about a quarter-mile of summit—was fifteen minutes, and twenty-four minutes up and back. Most people take, as I did, about an hour to reach the cairn; and come down in half that time. Some say the descent is harder; I didn't find that so at all. But in coming down one is likelier to slip.

The surface gives good rubber-grip because much of Ayers Rock is rough like stucco. Thin flakes of sandstone have cracked off in the heat and the sand-driving winds that are said to have even hollowed out the caves. A curious effect of the stucco look is that, in close-up as you clamber, the Rock seems less ancient. The flaking gives an effect of newness—almost as though the plasterers finished their mammoth job only last week.

At lung-taxing last I got to where the great summit stretched undulant to the east, the track across it marked in a broken line of white paint. The ascent had been in almost still air from the Rock's sheltered side. On top it was bitterly cold, with a wild wind tearing in from the south-east. From that side a great fissure cuts in. Looking across to its other side you see, vividly, that the stratification is vertical. The sedimentary rock that had been laid down horizontally

Ayers Rock, Earth's greatest monolithic stone, mounding its shape on the Central Australian plain. This aerial view is from the east.

Sculptured by the elements, this Rock form is called the "Brain".

Climbing Ayers Rock. The chain is a safety measure and some help.

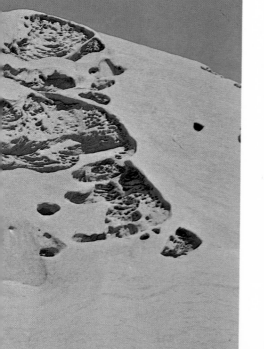

Sunrise strikes fantastic forms that are companions of Mt Olga, twenty miles west of Ayers Rock. This early morning flight was unforgettable.

King's Canyon is another great sight in the Red Centre. Access isn't easy, and tourists not so many yet; but I rate it next to Ayers Rock and the Olgas.

had, in some convulsion, been turned completely on its side. This, says Laseron, is "very puzzling".[19] All that section is furrowed vertically as well.

On the horizon of one's Rock-world the cairn appears like a small pile of crumbs, with ants going to and from it—not many, perhaps a dozen cold ants, some teetering in the strong wind. You go up and down depressions that must hold, or run off, a lot of water in times of heavy rain—which the Rock gets rather more of than the surrounding country because its bulk creates its own local storms. The tremendous run-off is why there is green growth round the base of the Rock.

You walk with your back to the Olgas, and only when you get to the cairn do you see how fine they look in the distance. Dressed in a purple haze, they are a wonderfully strange mass of mounds, a congress of camel-humps, a jumble of dome-heads, Mt Olga the tallest. There were a few bushes growing on top of the Rock, in crevices and where depressions had collected an earth deposit from blown dust and sand. After rain there are pools.

Sign the cairn's Visitor's Book, in a box there, with cold fingers that write badly. Rest awhile. Look about and savour the scene. That night at Ansett Lodge dinner we six mini-mountaineers get badges from Pioneer with the wording, "I Climbed Ayers Rock."

THE CAVES in the base of the Rock are more fascinating as caves than as repositories of Aboriginal art. The Pitjandjaras' best art-form was making elaborate ceremonial patterns on the ground, with ochres and feather-down, white and dipped red in blood. As cave painters they are almost child-like in comparison with the Arnhem Land tribes whose strong, active and remarkable art we shall be seeing at Obiri and Oenpelli.

These paintings are secular, not sacred, Mountford says: he found no evidence that they were part of the ceremonial life.[20] His native informants didn't know the meanings of most of the cave art. Harney wrote that a thin crude drawing of a snake, "symbolizing the Rainbow-Serpent God" was "the most important design on the mountain".[21]

Interpretation of the Rock to visitors was very bad. Under the circumstances of anthropological disagreement and taboo it would be difficult for it to be very good: but it could surely be better. Phil, our driver, had some story he said he got from a quarter-caste in Alice Springs that a figure with a hole in its head represents a boy with "no brains" (the Aborigines did not associate the brain with intelligence) who then learns hunting and tracking (there are track symbols) and emerges as a man (figure with big penis).

w

These paintings are not very old (one tries to depict a horseman) and photographs taken by Michael Terry when he went through motor-exploring in 1940 show them to have changed considerably since then, Mountford says.

The colouring of the Initiation Cave back wall, with sparse designs on it, is a rather lovely, pastel-ish mixture of yellow-pink-brown-heliotrope. Some of the pinkness may be from long-faded blood that spurted from the men's pricked arm veins as part of the initiation rituals which (if Harney is correct) were last held there about 1910. Certainly none are nowadays. At the Rock there was not a single Aboriginal.

The so-called Fertility Cave is usually said by guides to be where women who wanted to bear a child came to be "fertilized" with the spirit of one. (The Aborigines did not associate intercourse with procreation.) According to Mountford and Harney, this cave was a place pregnant women came to in the belief that Bulari, an ancestor woman whose cave it was, would assist them to give birth more easily.

A cave with curiously eroded sandstone forms hanging from the roof has become, to the guides, the Organ Cave, since it was found that striking the pendant stones produced an echoing sound. Now it is, with some drivers, the Cathedral Cave, in which they do a xylophonic act they call "playing the organ". Bill Harney said these pendant stones represented the fallen-out entrails of Linga the Lizard Man; to Mountford each point is the clitoris of a *Mala* woman—both making it an Organ Cave in quite another sense.

The Cathedral nonsense should be stopped before Ayers Rock is vulgarized into a cheapjack Jenolan. A guide pointed to one interesting formation and said, "That's the Duck's Head." Bill Harney was disgusted by such other white-given names as Napoleon's Hat, the Bell, the Sound Shell, the Wine-glass and the Porthole.

All this is hardly to the credit of the Northern Territory Reserves Board that controls the area. People who visit Ayers Rock and the Olgas should be able to buy a good guide booklet about the area. The publication of Harney's material as *The Significance of Ayers Rock for Aborigines* represents no more than a valiant try on Bill Harney's part to interpret an area that was new to him. But even if it were regarded as accurate, it would still be much less than adequate—and, in any case, it was not available at the Rock when I was there.

"THE OLGAS" seems to be the only way to refer to the remarkable group of mountains that lie twenty miles west of Ayers Rock. It is essentially a group, a plurality of naked domes of ochre-red rock—

"many-headed" as the Aboriginal name *Katajuta* means—and hardly to be indicated in the singular by the name of just one of the heads that to the white man is Mount Olga. (And to the black man? Harney gives both *Malakata* and *Ghee*).[22]

However, the Aboriginal name from *kata*—heads, *juta*—many, applied, apparently, only to the main western group, not the eastern, lower heads of the complex. The best Aboriginal-derived name for the whole group could be the Katas (pronounced *kartas*). Yet, inappropriate as it may be that a Queen of Spain's name should be given to this Central Australia wonder, the name Olgas, curiously enough, sounds rather like these domed mountains and hills look, if I may put it like that: "Olgas" has a rounded hardness to it. And any such name, whatever its origin, that is onomatopoeic and easy to say is likely to remain.

To some people the Olgas are more fascinating than the Rock. Arthur Groom, in his book,[23] headed his chapter about the Olgas *The First Wonder of Australia*, and described sunrise on their domes as "an unforgettable sight, transcending by far the grandeur of Ayers Rock, or anything else I have witnessed in my lifetime".[24] Finlayson, describing the complex he calls "Mount Olga" against the western sky at evening, wrote: "In the finished symmetry of its domes it is beautiful at all times; but now the sunset works upon it a miracle of colour, and it glows a luminous blue against an orange field, like some great mosque lit up from within. Five times I saw the sun set beyond Mount Olga, but in five hundred times it would not pall. It is the most delicate sight in all the land."[25]

A much more recent viewer, J. A. C. Dunn, a Sydney journalist who travelled Australia in 1970, wrote: "Why are the Olgas billed as an afterthought to Ayers? They are much more interesting, much more of a *sight*, mammoth stone globes, some rarely climbed by anybody, with valleys and gorges writhing among them."[26]

I would agree with Groom that sunrise on the Olgas (particularly if seen, as I saw it, from the air) is a greater sight than sunrise on the Rock; and with Finlayson that the Olgas against the sunset are superb; and with Dunn that the Olgas are far more interesting than they are announced to the tourist as being.

But—I think Ayers Rock still has to be considered the No. 1 attraction of inland Australia. We are not billing our sights to Australian travellers only, but to travellers world wide, and the fact that some Australians may think the Olgas a greater sight than the Rock is beside the point, which is that Ayers Rock is the greatest monolith on earth: it is unique. And the Olgas-type rock formation is not. Quite comparable naked rock forms tower up from the Thessalian plain at Meteora in northern Greece. Meteora's are even more extraordinary in their near-vertical contours. (Added to their natural strangeness are the monasteries perched on top of some of them. Meteora I have written of in another book.)[27] The Olgas are infinitely more colourful than the iron-grey monoliths of Meteora and they are, happily, nature-pure and free of habitation. But they are not incomparable, not "on their own", as Ayers Rock is.

When you go west from the Rock across the plain to the Olgas, the impression of them at a distance can be below expectations, especially in the early afternoon when tourists are usually taken there, so they can photograph the sunset on the Rock on the return journey. The Olgas' biggest domes don't jut from the plain on this side: they are set behind the eastern group, called the Minggari which, except for one bulbous mount, appear rather like foothills to the *Katajuta* group. From the north-east they are clumped unspectacularly. A much better view would be from the west, but the tour doesn't go to that side. It goes from the north *into* the Olgas, into one part of them now called the Valley of the Winds. This is strange and wonderful.

The valley becomes a chasm between four domed mountains that Giles compared to enormous haystacks leaning towards each other. There were ghost gums and corkwoods along the track—and a surprising profusion of winter wildflowers in this green place that was well watered from the run-off down the great walls that confronted us. Other walls towered darker on either side. Some are almost sheer. Much of the Olgas is the same red sandstone Ayers Rock is—but much is a rougher "pudding stone" conglomerate.

As we wandered towards the head of the valley I had the impression (as, I was to find, Finlayson[28] had) that all this might at one time have been one long monolithic "loaf" of rock that was somehow sliced into hunks, split into parts by some unimaginable upheaval—and the elements had done their work; widening the gaps between; rounding the tops to domes and cupolas; sloping the straight-cut sides, and gnawing them into caves and holes.

The westering sun was full on the walls ahead and they glowed golden-ochre up to the bluest sky; except that one monstrous corner-tower with a pitted dome was purple-brown and darkly streaked with the run of what in time of heavy rain must be a waterfall.

The path leads left towards a deep V made by two rockwalls. When you climb up to this there is a fine view of the "other" Olgas, mounding to the east. Aboriginal legend (according to Harney) calls the highest dome over there *Pungalung*—who was a myth-man so big he strode with killed kangaroos dangling from his hair-belt, and was such a lecher that he deflowered all the *Minggari* (Mouse totem) women, who are represented in stone by the smaller domed hills. We went back to the coach, where the billy (dixie, rather) was boiled for afternoon tea.

Groom camped in this chasm and wrote that the wind howled all night.[29] A native who was with him, Talkaljeri ("Tiger", whom I was to meet at Hermannsburg), knew the place from boyhood and said it was usually like that; but on this day the air was still. I felt I could spend a week at the Olgas—this was like being shown one room of a palace and then whisked away. Where I should like to camp is on the western side, and do some exploratory walks from there and come back in the evenings to watch the sunset on the Olgas.

We went off to view what the sunset does to Ayers Rock.

SEVERAL COACHES were pulled up a mile or two west of the Rock. The place where the chief natural wonder of Australia's Centre takes on its greatest splendour could, surely, have been spared association with Hollywood-TV. But no, it has become "Sunset Strip".

Everybody piles out to the tune of, "We leave in fifteen minutes, soon as you've all got your pictures." I take off to get the best possible, most-elevated, least-interrupted view from this part of a plain that has a lot of young trees on it. The spot I find is about 250 yards from the coach stop, 45 degrees right towards the Rock.

The Rock is already brilliant ochre-red. From here you can see the whole base, without treetops intervening. I take an Ektachrome every thirty seconds or so as the Rock grows still brighter and redder. The western face is more fissured than the eastern, the dome less pronounced, the Rock looks longer. And more beautiful than it did at sunrise. It is magnificent.

The shadows creep towards it as the sun goes down, darkening the green of the good-season scrub and the spindly desert poplars. There will come a moment when the whole foreground is darkened —and the blazing-red Rock will be mounted on this shadow-base, giving greatest contrast to its luminous glory. This, as I expect, turns out the best of all the colour shots. (PLATE 3).

Now the shadow band begins to make the colour at the base subtly duskier. I am taking this and looking forward to the colour-fading changes, when one of the three people who have followed me to this vantage point says, "The coach is going!" What I say is not printable.

The Olgas are also well in view from here (but the distance requires, for them, a telephoto lens). Several times I turn to register their changing from grey-violet to deepest-purple silhouettes against an horizon fired to burnt-orange with the flare of the sunken sun.

Last man to rejoin the coach, having raced down and picked it up along the road, I say to Phil that he didn't even stay the full fifteen minutes, and he says other people had got their pictures and were back in the coach ready to go. "We don't muck about once the sun goes down."

But, but. . . . What's the use of trying to explain? Everybody else is happy, singing *Ten green bottles, hanging on the wall* . . . .

NEXT MORNING I have, in half an hour, one of the scenic experiences of a well-travelled lifetime. At two minutes before sunrise the Cessna takes off from the strip beside where the "Brain" is on the Rock.

The pilot is Harry Purvis: I have been so glad to see him again. The last time Harry flew me was to search for the crashed Stinson on the Lamington Plateau back in 1937. He still looks great, though his hair is nearly white. With his fitness and good-flying record of so many years, I am not surprised that D.C.A. lets him still hold his licence at an age when others have had to turn theirs in.

Of these scenic flights, the one to get on, if you can, is the sunrise one. Harry's Cessna had the window that flips up ideally for the photographer: you don't have to shoot through glass. An icy slipstream comes in with the window up. That didn't matter. The plane takes three passengers.

Soon after take-off the Rock becomes a glowing *cabochon* of red-jasper on the dun-olive plain with its string of ochre road. Higher, you begin to see—still from the east with the sun's brilliance on it—what shape the Rock really is (PLATE 31). Then, as you circle, see how much more deeply it is folded on the western-southern sides that are bayed with shadow as black as the sandstone is red. Beyond its furrowed red-ochre roof the distance is bulbed with the purple outline of the Olgas.

The Olgas, as we thrum through the cloudless morning towards them, are clearly going to be the sight of sights. They soon begin to be a hundred times more impressive from the air than they are at ground level. You can see them *all*.

When they are reached, in this early sunlight, the ochre-orange baldheads of *Katajuta* are fantastic (PLATE 32). These shapes are not really describable. "Domes" becomes so regular and ordinary as to be silly. They are—if one must try—the knees-up of some vast subterranean Earth-Mother-Brown; or the stubby toes, spread canyon-wide, projecting from some gigantic buried statue of red-rubbed gold. And they throw black shadows of themselves on the sides of other formations just as bizarre.

NO ROOM AT THE ROCK?

A SITUATION was building up in 1970-71 that could mean that many tourists, Australians and from overseas, who might want to go to the Centre and stay for a few days at the Ayers Rock–Mount Olga National Park would not be able to.

There simply would not be the accommodation for the numbers who were likely to want to go there, in the winter months at any rate. In off-season, summer, they might get in; but shouldn't bank on it.

What had happened (and not happened) was this:

The number of visitors to the Rock increased between 1960 and 1968 at the high average annual rate of 27 per cent, and to about 30,000 in 1970. Four out of five of these tourists were Australians. The Australian Tourist Commission (an organization set up by the Commonwealth Government to "sell" Australia's tourist attractions abroad) aimed at augmenting the inflow to the Centre with a great many overseas tourists. Sensibly, it wanted the increase properly planned for.

The Commission had a *Tourism Plan for Central Australia* prepared by the team of American experts—travel consultants, architects, engineers, accommodation advisers—already referred to in connection with this team's proposals for Alice Springs. A second, more detailed report, called the *Ayers Rock–Mt Olga National Park Development Plan*[1] was prepared for the administering authority, the Northern Territory Reserves Board. Both reports, which I have studied, are dated 30th June 1969. They seem to me good plans indeed for coping with the tourist increase.

The N.T. Reserves Board has adopted its report "in principle". The Board can do nothing about implementing it until and unless the Commonwealth Government approves the recommendations and provides the money.

Let us waste no time at all on the contention that a tourist "invasion" of the Rock-Olgas area is going to "spoil the place". More and more people will go there because more and more are being told that it is a wonderful place to go to. To try to keep them away would be as futile as playing a turned-round Canute trying to keep surfers off Bondi Beach. Large numbers of tourists are inevitable, and must be provided for. Of course, the place *could* be spoiled by tourism. The plan is for tourist development of a kind that would *prevent* the environment's being spoiled.

The American study team considered that the environs of the Rock were being spoiled already. The existing accommodation (two lodges, two motels, one hotel), located near the Rock's easterly end, was much too close to it, they said, and added, "The general quality of development at Ayers is unattractive . . . and greatly depreciates the Rock's handsome natural setting." Moreover, existing accommodation "did not meet standards acceptable to overseas as well as many domestic visitors".[2] Of the 112 rooms only 53 had "private facilities".

They recommended that this accommodation be phased out, and that all new hotels, etc., be built at a new location. This recommended new location is about ten miles west of Ayers Rock, midway between it and the Olgas—not in line of sight between them but to the north of that line. From where the accommodation is now the Olgas is not visible at all: the Rock is in the way. From the new location both wonders are visible. This makes more sense.

Therefore, it is against the whole spirit of the proposed development that any more accommodation should be built at the present location. If more was, more compensation would have to be paid when the area was cleared.

The American experts' recommendations were based on a projected 100,000+ tourists in 1975 and 150,000 in 1980, requiring 200 rooms of accommodation, stepping up to 400 rooms. There would also need to be: shops, a caravan park, camping places, a Visitor Information Centre, a museum of things geological and Aboriginal, a small theatre where talks could be given, a recreation area with public swimming-pool, a fauna park—and a residential section for the estimated 400 employees who would have to live there to service the tourists. All this would be in what was termed a Resort Village.

The biggest building would be a 150-room luxury-level hotel, followed by a 50-room resort inn, and then, by 1980, two 100-room hotels, all part of the Village complex. Away from this there would be no development, except shelter-places, lavatories, picnic facilities at the base of the Rock and at the Olgas.

The airport, it was recommended, should be re-located 3½ miles north-east of the Resort Village. At present (1971) there is a small-plane strip, right beside the Rock. It is so subject to flooding that sometimes Alice Springs is loud with the wails of irate tourists who have arranged to fly to the Rock and can't because the airstrip is unusable. The new airport would have a longer runway to take larger aircraft.

A plan of the Resort Village was made and an architect's impression of how the major hotel should look (reproduced from the report, top of opposite page) if it was to blend with the landscape. Use of natural materials, such as the local red sandstone, was recommended.

American architect's concept of a proposed main tourist hotel between Ayers Rock and the Olgas.

Was there sufficient water available for all those expected tourists —potable water, and saline water from bores to flush all those toilets?

A year later the indications were that enough saline bore-water would be found. This, the Americans suggested, could be desalinated and made potable (at a cost they worked out). But potable bore water had been located ninety miles away, near Mereenie, and this raised hopes that there might be nearer supplies of the same. The drilling operations had hardly been the "crash program" the Americans were doubtless expecting to be undertaken.

But if a thousand million gallons of fresh water had been tapped on the site immediately it would not have meant that any part of the rest of the American time-table would have been achieved. They had scheduled the new airport to open in July 1970; the 150-room destination resort hotel to open in July 1971; the Resort Village to be "substantially under way" by July 1972.

That sort of programming is doubtless based on the speed with which things get done, sometimes, in Hawaii or some other American tourist area. It was wildly optimistic to assume that it could happen in Australia.

However, the most erroneous assumption the American experts made was a very natural one to make. They assumed that—because they had been called in to make proposals on how Australia could earn a great sum of dollars from overseas tourists coming to the Centre—the Commonwealth Government, if it considered the plan a good one and not unreasonably high in cost or likely to be uneconomic, would be prepared to finance it and implement it. Of course, the Government would have to consider the plan fully. But it was naturally assumed that this consideration would be expedited and this plan, or some other plan, got under way fairly rapidly.

IN JULY 1971 all of two years had passed since the two development reports were received from Harris, Kerr, Forster & Company, and the situation was like this:

—The plan was still being considered by an inter-departmental committee in Canberra, of representatives of all Commonwealth departments likely to be concerned.

—Cost had still not been worked out, even approximately. For the overall scheme, involving Alice Springs improvements as well, and sealing the road to the Rock. One heard figures as varying as $7 million to $10 million and $10 million to $20 million.

—No money was likely to be forthcoming in the near future, because Treasury was not at all convinced that tourism would generate the revenue that the advisers said it would. Treasury is likely to have convincing proof placed before it that this would be so—but this statistical evidence probably would not be prepared before 1972.

—Tourism had become the Ministerial concern of a junior Commonwealth Minister whose grab-bag ministry also included Arts, Aboriginal Affairs and Environment.

—Unless the whole policy and procedure changed radically, there was not likely to be a Resort Village between Ayers Rock and Mount Olga before 1974, if then.

—Even if tourists who could not be accommodated at the National Park were prepared to settle for a (less than satisfactory) flying one-day visit to Ayers Rock and the Olgas, from Alice Springs, they were likely to have accommodation trouble at Alice.

—The N.T. Reserves Board told me in 1970 it was already contemplating the prospect that "tourist numbers will have to be restricted". (So intending tourists should book early.)

"THE CENTRE is being promoted beyond its capacity to serve tourists. We should stop 'selling' it until we have the service facilities." That was said to me by Mr E. J. Connellan, managing director of Connellan Airways, at his station, Narwietooma, west of Alice Springs, in August 1969.

Since then the Centre has been "sold" more than ever before— by international airlines flying to Australia. American Airlines has been beating the "Go to Australia" drum particularly hard. The Great Barrier Reef and the Great Outback are promoted by all airlines as the two major attractions for tourists from the United States, Europe and Japan—and from New Zealand, still the country from which most of Australia's overseas tourists come. Who, if not tourists, are going to fill all those seats—in the 350-passenger jumbo-jet

Boeing 747s that Pan-American Airways are flying to Sydney; in 350-passenger 747Bs that Qantas will begin to operate in 1971; in Air New Zealand's 245-passenger DC10s coming in 1973, and in the big planes of eight other airlines? None of these carriers can afford to stop "selling" Australia in order to get tourist passengers to it. And where will those overseas tourists be able to go when they get to Australia? To the Ayers Rock–Olgas National Park? Still with 112 rooms, 53 with toilets?

The pressure of people who want to go there and can't get anywhere to stay is likely to create pressure from private enterprise to extend accommodation at the present location. That *could* end up with the Rock's being ringed with motels (and shops and cool-drink stands and souvenir shops and gas stations). Or the pressure could be for new accommodation to be erected at the new location—but higgledy-piggledy and not to the plan and standards the American study-team laid down. Such pressures would (I was told) be resisted. So, not even accommodation development that would "ruin" the area was likely to take place within the Ayers Rock–Olgas National Park. And, although two big concerns were known to be planning to build big motels at Alice Springs, they could do so only when the recommended zoning re-plan for Alice was approved, or abandoned and an alternative plan prepared—unless, of course, Alice was to go on being a Topsy and allowed to grow without any plan.

THIS SITUATION is not simply an instance of governmental inertia. Australia's prosperous condition is in part responsible: it inclines the country to think that it doesn't have to hustle after the tourist dollar, or even to measure the size of it. Mainly, though, the laggardliness stems from lack of understanding of tourism as an *industry*.

Because tourism doesn't grow, graze, manufacture, mine or export anything, Australian governments pay relatively little heed to it—even though tourism is already a higher earner of foreign exchange than sugar or dairy products. Particularly was this so at Country Party level in the coalition Federal Government—where the Minister for Works had been, as his minor function, also the Minister in Charge of Tourist Activities *under the Country Party's leader*.

Australian Governments, Federal or State, are reluctant to get financially involved with tourism. They tend to regard it as self-generating through private enterprise development, in the Surfers Paradise manner. Domestic tourism, given roads and essential services, can operate at that level, after a fashion, though it may play havoc with the environment in the process. International tourism, the kind that spins new money into the economy, requires government involvement as to investment, control, incentives and loan-finance. Or so it has been found in other countries. In Greece the government has built scores of *Xenia* (tourist) hotels; in Italy hotel developers can borrow money at three per cent; in Britain the builder of a tourist hotel could get government subsidy up to £1,250 a room;[3] in Tahiti, government would lend the hotel builder half the cost and exempt him from income tax for eight years.

The American experts' *Tourism Plan for Central Australia* listed incentives given by twenty-three other countries to develop tourism for foreign visitors. "Without sufficient long-term financing, destination resorts and motor hotels of the quality necessary to attract overseas visitors cannot be provided," their report said.

Unless the Commonwealth Government begins to act boldly and imaginatively in regard to tourism, Australia will lose not only revenue it could be gaining, but lose goodwill. Travellers who have been inadequately serviced in a country carry home a poor opinion of that country. A couple of powerful American airlines yakking in Washington that they are losing traffic because "those Aussies are taking a hell of a time to get off their asses and do something about tourist accommodation in Central Australia" could have repercussions beyond Canberra. It would hardly help, for instance, the Australian argument that the United States should not restrict its buying of Australian beef.

The hard-pressed rural sector that opposes spending on tourism needs to look at it again. It could be the revenue earner that provides the extra money the countryman says he needs in subsidies.

CHASM, GORGE AND CANYON

THE CENTRE is not just Ayers Rock and the Olgas. These are the dominant marvels, yes, but they were not the only reasons why the American team of travel experts rated Central Australia as a region of "outstanding tourist attraction, unique to Australia and of world-wide appeal". After travelling in thirty-odd other countries, I think it is, too.

What else the Centre has, as to places, I am going to list in the order that I found them scenically rewarding: King's Canyon, Glen Helen, Palm Valley and what is called the Amphitheatre, Standley Chasm, Ormiston Gorge, Serpentine Gorge, Ross River's Valley of the Eagles and Trephina Gorge, and Simpson's Gap. All of these places can be reached by coach tours; but only motorists with four-wheel-drive vehicles can get to King's Canyon and Palm Valley. None could be reached by air (in mid-1971) but an airstrip near King's Canyon was expected to be restored to use.

A Department of the Interior tourist publication, in its recommendations on what to see outside of Alice Springs, did not even mention King's Canyon. The Northern Terrritory Tourist Bureau's booklet and leaflet mentioned this most spectacular of the places I toured to, but located it "140 miles west of Alice Springs". King's Canyon is over 200 miles south of west.

Being poorly informed about the Centre, many tourists did not realize how much there was to see, and so did not allow sufficient time for their stay. They went to it—usually seeing Ayers Rock and the Olgas, Standley Chasm and Simpson's Gap and spending more time in officially boosted Alice Springs than Alice was worth, relatively—but they did not tour it. And the Centre is well worth touring. To tour it as I did, using regular operators' transport, took two weeks.

SIMPSON's GAP (14 miles west) is the nearest to Alice of the scenic highlights. Vividly red rugged bluffs tower beside a permanent waterhole at this break in the Chewings Range. It was named for the same A. A. Simpson the Simpson Desert was.

A day-tour (Pioneer) that went to Standley Chasm returned by way of Simpson's Gap at about three thirty in the afternoon. The light conditions in winter are better in mid-morning. Bob Darkin, owner of Simpson's Gap station and Ranger of what was part of the cattle property until it was made a reserve, said, "The black-fellers wouldn't go near the Gap. You couldn't get a stockman to bring a bullock from that waterhole. They say it's where one half of a tribe wiped the other half right out—men, lubras, piccaninnies and all." I asked if the Aborigines still feared the place as haunted, and Bob Darkin said, "Now they'll go anywhere to get money to buy liquor. Mistake to let them drink."

That could have been the start of an interesting discussion, but the coach was waiting. On this tour you got a barbecue lunch at Jay Creek Aboriginal Settlement. This place and Hermannsburg Mission (visited on the Palm Valley–Glen Helen Tour) had best, I think, come into a following chapter about the Aborigines.

STANDLEY CHASM (32 miles west) is much more of a "must" for the tourist than Simpson's Gap is. The full-page colour-photo (PLATE 33) shows better than words can say why the chasm is spectacular.

Midday is the time to be there. When the sun is overhead and shining down into the cleft, it gives maximum colour to the red walls that tower more than two hundred feet. The average width of the fissure is only about fifteen feet. Many people walk through to the far end and wait there for the sun to be right. A much better position for the photographer is at the approach end when you walk from the bus: it was from there that I took the Ektachrome reproduced. The chasm is named for a Mrs Ida Standley who was an early schoolteacher at Alice Springs.

Ross RIVER (about 50 miles east) is a particularly well-run resort on what was part of a cattle station. The river is usually dry.

Although three red-rock gorges are in the vicinity, Ross River's main attraction is not its scenery: it appeals to tourists who want to experience something of the Australian outback way of life—without the discomforts. The brothers Gilbert and Douglas Green who operate it have concentrated on providing accommodation that is comfortable and at the same time characterful. Wooden cabins with stone floors had private facilities, hot-water service, electric blankets on the beds in winter, 240-volt current for electric shavers. In the old (1896) homestead there was a cosy bar and good evening atmosphere round the log fire under the chimney arch made from the iron tire of a bullock wagon. Sixty per cent of the guests Ross River was getting were Americans.

As part of its Australian character the resort had Max Bloomfield, who was almost as dark of skin as a full-blood Aboriginal (Max was a grandson of pioneer station-owner Bloomfield), and looked the part of the well-set-up stockman. He demonstrated to guests how to throw a boomerang, crack a stockwhip and, if they wanted instruction, how to ride a horse well. He also made the best damper I have ever eaten. Max always met the sightseeing bus on the dry bed of the Trephina River, where he mixed his damper and cooked it in an iron camp-oven dish sunk in the sand.

Doug Green, wide-hatted and bearded, drove the resort bus out from Alice Springs and conducted the sightseeing tours, and was the most intelligent and best-informed guide on the trees, plants and animals that I came across in Central Australia.

Corroboree Rock, seen on the run out to Ross River, was interesting as a former Aboriginal ritual place, where the initiates passed through a hole in the back of a ledge cave to be "reborn" as full members of the tribe.

Trephina Gorge has rockwalls with Aboriginal incising, though only of elementary designs that marked a gathering place. The Valley of the Eagles, when it was so named by the Australian photographer Frank Hurley, had many wedgetails nesting on its cliff ledges. The shooters went in, and few eagles soar there now. We shall come to more spectacular gorges farther out; but not to a better-managed place to stay—though I would not endorse the practice of some Americans who put comfort before scenery to the extent that they settle in at Ross River and do not go to see anything else, not even Ayers Rock.

When we came back for lunch, on the second day, Max Bloomfield brought some witchetty grubs—fat white caterpillars the Aborigines regard as a delicacy—that he had dug out of a rotting tree. He presented them to the pretty English girl who was on a working holiday and waitressing at Ross River. She had tried witchetties and, although she baulked at eating them raw, had come to relish them cooked in a smear of butter on a hotplate. I tried one: it had a nutty flavour.

The pretty English girl was Virginia Ovenden-Rogers from Maidstone, Kent, who was hitch-hiking round Australia.

PALM VALLEY and Glen Helen (81 miles west) were reached by a three-day Pioneer tour that returned by way of Ormiston and other gorges. This is a recommended trip with a splendid variety of Centre scenery. You go into country that does not provide smooth riding all the way, but the roads and the accommodation were better than I expected.

Central Australian Tours did the same tour as a two-day "safari" with a camp-out night in two-bed tents at Glen Helen, where Ansett-Pioneer had the only lodge.

Our coach was a smallish four-wheel-drive one with a cheerfully competent and obliging driver-commentator, Mick Leahy. The crisp morning warmed into another brilliant August day of cloudless blue as we ran out from Alice and past the grave (topped with an eight-ton globular rock, one of the "Devil's Marbles" brought from farther north) of the founder of the Flying Doctor Service, the Reverend John Flynn.

A pink-and-grey swirl of galahs rose from the pale grass near two beautiful ghost-gums that figured in watercolours by the Aboriginal painter Albert Namatjira. Farther on, about thirty miles this side of Hermannsburg Mission, there is a Namatjira monument, a tall stone pillar that says only that this was the landscape that inspired the artist. It might be truer to say that Namatjira was "inspired" to paint his country, which he found that he could do quite well in the white man's fashion after Battarbee had shown him how, because it enabled him to earn money without having to work on a cattle station, and more money than any Aboriginal had ever earned before. That a blackfellow could master perspective and use a full palette skilfully to depict landscape was considered amazing.

At Hermannsburg we turn onto the road that runs twelve miles to Palm Valley, and the ride gets rough beyond the Finke River, where we stop for a picnic lunch. The men collect firewood to boil the tea-dixie, the prepared salad is handed round on cardboard plates, you find a fallen tree in the shade to squat on or a hump of earth that isn't an ants' nest. The hillside seems to regard us, from under brows of red-ochre rock, with the blank stare of a timeless land, a landscape hardly man-marked at all now that the road has disappeared into the Finke's silent river of sand.

Then Mick Leahy is saying, "Near here a drilling rig of the Magellan company made a good strike of natural gas."

Palm Valley 2 well in February 1970 brought in what was described as Australia's largest strike of natural gas, with a daily flow estimated at 70 million cubic feet.

Could this gas be piped some 700 miles north to the Gulf of Carpentaria where a LNG (liqufied natural gas) plant could, economically, liquefy it for shipment to Japan? A Japanese consortium was studying the feasibility of this in July 1971, when another plan was announced—to pipe Palm Valley gas 1200 miles to Perth. The Premier of fuel-hungry Western Australia (Mr Tonkin) announced that the feasibility of this was being studied. However, in the same month it appeared that Western Australia might have all the natural gas it needed, offshore on what is called the North-West Shelf, where the Woodside oil drilling company had tapped what appeared to be a huge undersea gasfield.

A ROADSIDE SIGN warns the motorist FOUR-WHEEL-DRIVE ONLY. We need this extra traction to cross the sandy bed of the Finke, and thereafter on the few miles of the rough track that climbs from the river. Soon, at the top of a rise, there is spread before us not Palm Valley itself but a broad annexe to it called the Amphitheatre. It doesn't really resemble an amphitheatre, for the walls of vivid rock that rise beyond the spinifex-dotted "stage" are cliffs not tiers; but the place is certainly theatrical. From the stage-floor rise such strange outcropping formations as one called Initiation Rock. Sandstone the colour of dried blood has been eroded into a platform with something so like a head that Arthur Groom[1] refers to it as a sphinx. Another form, a much bigger one, rears up with a high frontal cave that must have suggested a Gothic-arched entrance to whoever dubbed it Cathedral Rock; and a splendid long stacked escarpment has become Battleship Rock. Such names dissipate the primal mood.

From Palm Valley Lodge, which is in the Amphitheatre area, some of us went out when the sun was setting. The eastern rock-walls were a burning red.

In the afternoon we had gone into what Giles, its discoverer, called the Glen of Palms. It is long and narrow, red-cliffed on either

33/NORTHERN TERRITORY   Standley Chasm at midday, lit by the overhead sun.▶

Katherine Gorge. The tourist launches go to Aboriginal rock-paintings and beyond to a separated stretch of water. There are freshwater crocodiles.

Dreaming Water it was called, this place we came to on the coach tour to the edge of Arnhem Land. Patterns of pandanus-palm "made" the picture.

side, and not only the pristine white nakedness of ghost-gums is raised against the harsh red-ochre sandstone. The valley's distinction is the green luxuriance of its ancient cycad palms. Tall and slender, *Livistonia mariae* is one of the very few Australian inland palms, and their only occurrence, so far as we know, is along the Finke River. To see the palms' plenitude you need to go to where the gorge bends and, climbing up the rocks there, look back along the defile.

Palm Valley Lodge was ordinary, adequate accommodation. After dinner we went out to a campfire entertainment. A young Aboriginal man, Graham Ebatarinja, from Hermannsburg Mission where he worked in the carpenter's shop, who had been to Melbourne with a singing group, played his guitar and sang Western folk songs —until a godly woman in the party got him onto hymns. Then two shabbily clad younger Aborigines of about fourteen moved their lips to the Aranda words of what they had been taught at the Mission; but their heads hung down in shyness and they never raised their eyes. Afterwards an old man named Cornelius—inured to getting crumbs from the white-boss table—removed his stockman's sombrero and took up a collection. Hardly a joyous evening—but a beginning to Aboriginal participation in the Centre's tourism, at entertainment level.

GLEN HELEN, farther up the Finke, is only 35 miles north of Palm Valley by the direct road, but we took a roundabout route. The westward run of this brought us close to Gosse's Bluff, a circular massif rising a thousand feet, its pinkish-red rockwalls enclosing a valley miles across.

The motorist needs to be wary of this country. On this particular tour we passed eight abandoned cars. They break down and when the stranded occupants—sometimes after distressing experiences if they haven't had the forethought to carry enough water and food— are taken to Alice Springs they find that the cost of towing the car in for repair is more than its value justifies.

We came to an oil drillers' camp. Nobody was there: A notice said: HANDS OFF IT!

Then we side-tracked on foot to Roma Gorge where there were Aboriginal rock peckings, simple motifs such as concentric circles and a fishbone series of straight lines. They could have been a hundred or a thousand or ten thousand years old. Nobody knows, and you can't carbon-date rock engravings.

An hour later we were at Glen Helen Lodge. On the way we had seen a dingo, several emus and a couple of kangaroos. Emus are scarce in this area and Mick Leahy said it was only the second

x

time he had seen any on this run. But it was not uncommon to see wild donkeys. There were wild camels, too.

The Glen Helen country was first taken up as a cattle run in 1880, and it was twice abandoned after deaths caused by the attacks of hostile Aborigines. Frederick Raggatt took it over in 1902 and named it after his niece Helen Wakefield.

Now Glen Helen is one of three properties belonging to Bryan Bowman, who married an Aboriginal girl; he was by no means the first Territorian cattleman to do so, although it is still unusual for the white man to do more than cohabit. He had built a new homestead, and the old one, converted into a tourist lodge in 1957 and later taken over by Ansett, was where we stayed. It is a place of character with bullock traces and other gear hanging decoratively on the thick old whitewashed walls.

The lodge is set beside the Finke, and the river's other side is walled with rugged cliffs. The sunset fired these rocks to a glowing red and the water's mirror doubled their image to make the picture that is PLATE 30 and also on the back of the book jacket. Farther down, the Finke bends into the beauty of Glen Helen Gorge, where broader water reflects striking formations of vertical rocks.

Next morning I found three Aborigines sitting in the sand opposite the gorge entrance, one of them at work on a watercolour painting. He was Kenneth Undata from Hermannsburg, who sells his work through Rex Battarbee's gallery in Alice Springs. Early rising was rewarded by a glorious view, just after sun-up, of Mount Sonder (which has been much painted by the followers of Namatjira, as it was by Albert himself). Sonder thrusts its long and splendid contours several thousand feet above the northern horizon. When it was burnished by the rising sun all the shadows of its slopes were purple.

"I never get tired of looking at this country," an English girl, Anne Sills, who was working at Glen Helen Lodge, said. "It makes what we are used to at home seem no more than—dainty. This is the Australia I was expecting, not the Australia of poor-looking, crammed-together houses you see when you get off the plane at Sydney. I love this wide, rugged open-hearted Australia with its nights of brilliant stars and days full of beautiful sun."

Did nothing about Australia trouble her? Anne Sills thought, and then said, "Only that the Australian men in the outback drink so much."

ORMISTON GORGE appears to be 86 miles west of Alice Springs on the N.T. Reserves Board's road map, which isn't much of a map, but is more reliable than a Department of the Interior publication that has it "about 100 miles west" and says that Ormiston Gorge has been described by world travellers as "more impressive than the Grand Canyon".

This is an overstatement one can hardly imagine being made by anybody who had seen Arizona's Grand Canyon, or even a photograph of it. The two places are no more comparable than little Ormiston Creek is with the mighty Colorado River that courses a canyon a mile deep, an average eleven miles wide and more than a hundred miles long. Ormiston Gorge is not a canyon (even though the Pioneer Tours leaflet describes it as a "huge" one). Australia has some grand sights to show, but it has nothing like the Grand Canyon.

What some American traveller possibly said of Ormiston Gorge was that the *colour* of the rocks—not their extent or their formation —was more vivid than the hues in the vast Grand Canyon. The painter Rex Battarbee has rhapsodized about the variety of coloration there, both bright and subtle—but my personal preference is for Glen Helen, and King's Canyon is scenically ten times better. Ormiston Gorge had been "oversold" as a scenic highlight of the Centre, and was none the better for some results of its induced popularity. Beer-cans littered the edges of pools that reflected the rocks' brilliance, and the tourist authorities had installed a prefabricated lavatory block walled with fibreglass of a colour so alien to the landscape that it jumped at the eye.

SERPENTINE GORGE has a waterhole that blocks the narrow entrance. Two of us decided to explore the gorge while the rest of the party picnic-lunched (we could eat later, on the road). After donning trunks to swim across the waterhole, we found that, against the western bluff, it was only knee-deep.

We walked along a stony creek-bed for half a mile or so. Scarps of bright-red rock rose on either side. At the foot of the cliffs a lot of cycads made low green fountains of palm-like growth: this *Macrozamia macdonnellii* species is peculiar to the MacDonnell Ranges.

We came to a wall of red sandstone, cleft straight down in the manner of Standley Chasm, but the slit was much narrower, only a few feet across. It obviously went right through, for we could see sky higher up, but at the base the passage had a bend in it—and it was full of water. What we needed, said my companion, who was a Rover Scout type, was an inflatable rubber dinghy. It was frustrating not to be able to go through this dim tunnel-like passage to whatever lay on the other side. But at least we had seen more of Serpentine Gorge than tourists ordinarily do. There was no track and we didn't see a single drink can or cigarette packet.

ELLERY GORGE had a longer and wider pool between bluffs that were not very high. The pool invited swimming and, as we still had our trunks on under our shorts, we went in. I have never come out of water so fast: it was freezing. In the hot sun of midday it was easy to forget that the night temperature had been down in the thirties. With its grey herons and dabchicks, Ellery Gorge's waterhole had more birds than we had seen in Ormiston Gorge where many dotterels pipe at the edges of the pools.

On the run back to Alice we stopped to watch a pair of Major Mitchell Parrots courting. The male is somewhat like a glorified galah, and when he deigns to raise the scarlet crest that lies on his pink head he is particularly handsome.

It had been a good tour, and there hadn't been a cloud in the sky for three days.

KING'S CANYON is 60 road miles west from a tourist lodge called Wallara Ranch that is 145 miles south-west of Alice Springs. Tourists should be able to fly to Wallara or fly back: one way along the sand-wallow of a road that turns off the Stuart Highway is enough. There was an airstrip at Wallara and another at King's Canyon. Neither strip was serviceable.

However, Connellan Airways landed at Tempe Downs station 40 miles from Wallara. Could Wallara send a car across and pick me up from Tempe Downs? Wallara said it could.

The first landing, half an hour after 8.15 a.m. take-off, was at Narwietooma station. Its owner who came down to meet the Connellan Airways plane was E. J. Connellan (pronounced *Conn*ellan, not Conn*ell*an). Nearing sixty now, he started the service when he was twenty-seven, in the year World War II began. It is an extraordinary and distinctively Australian service that began with ex-schoolteacher Connellan touring the Territory first in an old Spartan biplane and then in a 1922 Rolls-Royce and getting station owners to put in airfields he could fly to. Now Connellan Airways flew to a hundred stations, settlements and towns in the Northern Territory, Western Australia, Queensland and South Australia; and its safety record was such that in thirty years of flying it had never injured a passenger.

Tourists sometimes took the flight I was doing. At Narwietooma, a modern homestead, morning tea was always served to passengers. Outsize oranges and grapefruit grew in the bore-watered red soil of the garden. Next stop was Papunya Aboriginal Settlement with about a thousand native people. I saw only two of the thirty staff members, who come down to the airstrip to collect the mail and freight—young people, zesty with the sense of doing a worthwhile job. The girl was a Canadian.

Fifteen minutes later—it was still only ten o'clock—I was talking to the manager of Haast Bluff station that runs 5,000 Shorthorns. Haast Bluff itself and another mountainhead had made fine photographs as we came in. On this run you get a low-altitude look at not only the highest mountain in the Territory (Mt Ziel, 4,955 ft) and the colourful MacDonnell Ranges, but at strange rhythmic landforms such as those of the Krichauff Range, where lines of crests run parallel in a scalloped, or what might even be thought of as a "sea serpent", formation.

The pilot obligingly veered east to show me what lay inside that ring of rugged pale-red heights that is Gosse's Bluff. Its walls were caved, its valley floor grassed, and there was a pattern of vehicular road-tracks. The drillers for oil had been in.

Although not only the Pioneer tour driver but the American report on Centre tourism spoke of Gosse's Bluff as an "enormous meteorite crater", it does not appear to be one—any more than Wilpena Pound in South Australia is regarded as other than a formation resulting from complex geological pressures. Gosse's Bluff is not mentioned in the article on meteorite craters in *The Australian Encyclopaedia*. There is quite a fair road past this remarkable and picturesque formation, but the N.T. Tourist Bureau booklet had not a word about it for the touring motorist.

When we landed at Tempe Downs station, John Cotterill, son of the owner of Wallara Ranch (who is known as Jack Cotterill) was there to pick me up. Tempe Downs runs about 5,000 head of cattle on red soil country with a lot of coolibah-trees. Its owner did not think much of tourists since one of them had washed her hair in a cattle trough and left the water polluted with frothy shampoo.

The Connellan flight went on to Hermannsburg Mission and returned to Alice Springs about 12.30. Although one scrapes only meagre acquaintance with the places landed at, it still seemed to me well worth the round-trip fare of $21.

WALLARA RANCH wasn't a ranch, and the accommodation it provided was not in the same class as at Ross River. No American tourists emerged from the ten pastel-painted doors of two-bed rooms in corrugated-iron structures without heating or "private facilities": there was hot water, though, and electric-shaver points, in the washrooms. The dining-recreation room décor was kitschy and, outside, the surroundings were unenchanting. A home-made sign in front said *"Welcome to Wallara Road-House"*. One soon returned to the bar. The one good—indeed, great—reason for the place's existence lay sixty miles away.

Jack Cotterill, a big-hearted "battler", could hardly have built his place closer to King's Canyon because there was no normally trafficable road west of where he had set up to accommodate as many tourists as his four-wheel-drive bus could carry, which was about twenty. In the off season he worked on the road, grading it. He and his wife were triers: the cheese board at dinner, for instance—I couldn't get even mousetrap cheese at the Mt Gillen Motel in Alice.

A competent, forward-looking N.T. Tourist Authority (if such a much-needed organization existed) would have upgraded the road, restored the washed-out airstrip and loan-financed Cotterill or somebody to set up a characterful tourist lodge right at King's Canyon. As things were, only by taking the Cotterill three-day King's Canyon tour and staying at Wallara for two nights could tourists (unless they came in four-wheel-drive vehicles) get to what is unquestionably the Centre's grandest scenic place after Ayers Rock and the Olgas.

That I should thus rank it, above Glen Helen and Palm Valley, Ormiston Gorge and the rest, would surprise the three English girls who called in at Wallara for a drink just after I arrived. They had come up from Adelaide in a Land Rover and gone out to King's Canyon, and camped the night there. I asked them what they thought of it, and was disturbed to hear, "We didn't think it was so much."

It turned out that they had been only to where the canyon *begins*. From there the spectacular section is not in view, because the canyon turns east. Moreover, lacking local knowledge or such information as was nowhere in print for motorists, they did not know that you have to walk up a hillside and along the plateau on the southern side for about two miles to get the breathtaking views of the canyon's great north wall.

Several women of the party I went with decided that the walk was too strenuous for them—it looks formidable at the start, but only about a quarter-mile is rocky track climbing—and they, alas, gained no more from going to Central Australia's largest canyon than the girls in the Land Rover did.

Before the road, such as it is, was made Jack Cotterill used to bring out visitors in a Land Rover that took six hours to cover the last eighteen miles and was a wreck at the end of a year. The road follows the track of the explorer Ernest Giles who named the George Gill Range after a friend and the canyon in it after another, Fielden King. To the Aborigines it was *Watarka*, from the acacia-trees that grow there. *Wallara* is a native word meaning "joyous", Jack Cotterill said. On the sixty-mile trip out he stops for lunch at a place called Reedy Rockhole, and you begin the walk about two o'clock.

THE PLATEAU riven by King's Canyon is, in part, a pattern of rough domes, and John Cotterill, the guide, said, "We call this the Ruined City."

Imagination might see it as a worn-down Angkor Wat; but in ruddy-golden rock so alien to Cambodia's wet jungles that not even a lichen could live unshrivelled by the sun. Some of the domes were agape with caves, and all shaped themselves with startling vividness against the naked blue sky.

More curious still was a small massed formation, not much bigger than an army of larger-sized lead soldiers, that had been dubbed the "Sculptures", though "Figurines" might have been better, if such christenings are obligatory. But these oddities were only the fringe benefits of coming to King's Canyon.

PLATE 32 shows something of the east-facing wall of the canyon. It rises about nine hundred feet above the creek that courses through. It looks sheer from where I took the picture, but other photographs show a slight inward slant. This Ektachrome shows the deep splendour of the rock's ochre-redness, and how a great part of the wall is cleanly cut as if by a gigantic knife.

Canyons are not just for looking down into: that magnificent red wall deserved to be looked up to, so I asked John Cotterill if there was any way of going down into the canyon. He said there was. A young schoolteacher in the party came down with me.

Getting down was, at the start, dicey. Then we were in the "Garden of Eden": it is called that. A narrow gorge beyond the canyon's end, it has cycad palms like green fountains over pools of water beside beautiful walls of coloured rocks you expect to be covered with Aboriginal paintings. John Cotterill said the reason there are none is that the Aborigines were scared stiff of the place: the Rainbow Snake owned it.

We came to a (dry) waterfall at a level about half-way up the nine-hundred-foot rockwall. It swooped away in a marvellous parabola. If an extra-wide-angle lens could have photographed what my eye encompassed, the picture would have shown, on the left, this towering and seemingly endless sheer cliff of ochre; and on the right, inward-leaning cliffs Nature-painted pale beige to pink, horizontally and vertically streaked with black. It is maddening not to be able to reproduce more than one colourphoto of this wonderful place.

A skilful rock climber could have got down the side of the waterfall and proceeded back along the floor of the canyon. John Cotterill came down to show us a more direct way up to a point the party had returned to, and there was one ledge that had to be crawled along that I could not have reached unaided. In future years I suppose iron ladders will be installed in such spots, so that more people can get down to the marvellous vista at the waterfall.

The plateau atop the canyon is mainly bare, but in places we came across fine ghost-gums, and the delicate pink desert rose that is the Centre's floral emblem.

When we got back to the bus it was near sunset, and Jack Cotterill said that when the sun got right down to the horizon a part of the range near the entrance to the canyon would be lit to glory— and it was, a blazing vermilion. Then a crescent moon came up while we were eating our barbecue steaks, the trees silhouetted beautifully against the afterglow. The colour burned to blackness and the sky that seems wider in the Centre than anywhere else filled with a brilliance of stars as we began the long chug back to Wallara.

Next morning I went back on the coach to Alice Springs. We came on a car stuck fast in the sand, and then a big tourist coach similarly sand-bogged. Jack Cotterill got his towropes and pulled them out, cheerfully performing what he said was a regular chore.

Near where this stretch of road joins the Stuart Highway we lunched beside the Henbury Craters. There is no question about these being made by meteorites. There are thirteen depressions, some hardly noticeable, but the largest is more than 200 yards across and perhaps fifty feet deep. Apparently the meteorite exploded into at least thirteen big pieces just before it hit ground. You can find bits of a brownish rock known as "impact glass"—sandstone that was melted by the meteorite's heat. An American scientist who had been studying these craters on Henbury Station had estimated that the meteorite fell about two thousand years ago, Jack Cotterill said, and added, "I'd like to find a nice big hunk of meteorite. They can be very rich in nickel."

On the seventy-five-mile run from there to Alice Springs we saw close to a dozen emus but only a couple of kangaroos.

"We are Black Australians"

"NEW AUSTRALIANS" has been the term for migrants fresh from Europe, but it is no less what the Aborigines are. Only since 1967 have Aboriginal people been included officially in the Australian population. Their numbers, of full-bloods particularly, are still imprecise because there has not been a census since the 1967 referendum changed the Constitution to give them Australian status. The mid-1971 census should tell us exactly how many Black Australians there are in White Australia.

All now have voting rights (though not all exercise them). In Queensland the full franchise was granted only as recently as 1965. Some remaining discriminatory State legislation is to be off the Statute books by 1972—or 1973.

Tourists in Central Australia who went to such places as Jay Creek Aboriginal Settlement or Hermannsburg Mission got very little understanding of the Aborigines. But at least they saw some. The average Australian, who dwells urbanly, has never seen a full-blood Aboriginal (not Aborigine unless you disagree with Fowler,[1] who says Aboriginal is better as the singular noun).

There are far more full-blood Aborigines in the Northern Territory (21,000 was the 1966 estimate) than in any other part of Australia. But there are a greater number of part-Aboriginal people in Queensland (30,000) and in New South Wales (23,000), where there are only about a hundred full-bloods left, and there are no full-bloods in Victoria. Of people classed as Aborigines some 80,000 out of 130,000 are only partly so. Only in the Northern Territory are mixed-bloods the minority, about 5,000. The Territory, then, is where the Aboriginal "problem" is at its most Aboriginal.

The Territory is the one sector of Australia where Aboriginal advancement is entirely the Commonwealth's, not any State's, concern. And the Commonwealth is spending proportionately more on its Aborigines of the Territory than the States are spending on theirs. So, if the problem of Aboriginal advancement is not being solved in the Territory—where the most resources are being brought to bear on what is most Aboriginal about it—then it isn't likely to be nearer solution anywhere else. If what is being done in the Territory still isn't good enough, then the failure is not just regional, but national.

Such failure on Australia's part to improve the Aboriginal condition adequately was pointed out in 1970 in what is called the Montgomery Report.[2] This was made, after a tour of inspection in the Northern Territory, by Colonel Patrick Montgomery, the secretary in London of the Anti-Slavery Society for the Protection of Human Rights.

He reported that: "Many Aborigines today live in dependent poverty that is extreme by world standards. Illiteracy, malnutrition, disease, infant mortality, broken families, parental deprivation, emotional disturbance, institutional living, unemployment, drunkenness, gambling, idleness and crime are at a high level among non-nomadic Aborigines."

He went on to say: *"The Commonwealth Government is not at*

present disposed to give such financial and political priority to Aboriginal affairs as could prevent deterioration of the present situation."

This trenchant criticism was of an Australian government that had (i) budgeted 27 per cent more money for Aboriginal advancement than the previous government had done, (ii) had well-qualified experts to advise it on Aboriginal policy, (iii) instituted such aid schemes as capital loans for Aborigines to start commercial enterprises, and Aboriginal scholarships, and study grants, (iv) created a new portfolio that made its Minister for Social Services also Minister in Charge of Aboriginal Affairs. Australian reaction, especially at political level, could well be: Surely the situation is not as bad as Colonel Montgomery says it is and the blame has been laid on too thick!

Unhappily, what the Montgomery Report said was true, though not new. Nothing it said about the high incidence of Aboriginal disease, infant mortality and malnutrition and emotional disturbance had not been said already[3] by Dr H. C. Coombs, chairman of the Council of Aboriginal Affairs, which was set up within the Prime Minister's Department to advise the government on Aboriginal policy. Nothing Colonel Montgomery said about the pauperization of the Aborigines was more than putting into other words what had already been said about the Aboriginal condition of "homelessness, powerlessness, poverty and confusion" by Professor W. E. H. Stanner,[4] the anthropologist, who was also a member of the three-man Council specially created to inform the government on what needed to be done.

Creating a Minister in Charge of Aboriginal Affairs (Mr W. C. Wentworth) meant less than the title said. The Minister had no direct control of staff engaged on Aboriginal work in the only Commonwealth-administered region, the Northern Territory. "This anomalous position [said the Montgomery Report] gives the public a false impression and is unfair to the Minister."

It was manifestly unfair to the Aborigines to have the conditions of their employment on cattle stations policed by officers of a department whose Minister was of the Country Party that represents the interests of pastoralists. Clearly the Ministry of the Interior administration had tolerated conditions of pay, food and housing such as caused Aboriginal stockmen of the Gurindji tribe to strike and walk off Wave Hill, a Vestey's cattle station, in 1966.

It was the Gurindjis' fight to gain land of their own—they "squatted" on a part of the Vestey lease called Wattie Creek—that, more than anything else, prompted the Anti-Slavery Society to have the Aboriginal condition investigated by its secretary when he was in

Australia. Lord Vestey in London had not only agreed to Colonel Montgomery's visiting Wave Hill and another Vestey cattle station, but offered to place the firm's aircraft at his disposal and pay his travelling expenses within Australia. This assistance was accepted on the condition that nothing less than an objective and frank report was to be expected from Colonel Montgomery.

WHEN a civilized protagonist for human rights and freedoms—Colonel Montgomery in this case—looks at the Aboriginal condition in Australia he sees something different from, and worse than, what Australians and their governments see. They have lived long with the Aboriginal problem, and are inured to its being, "like the poor, always with us". Australians see the Aborigines as problem people. The Montgomerys see them as poor people. And, in what is an affluent country, they see their poverty as stark and inexcusable.

There tends to be an Australian proposition that the Aborigines are poor because they are a problem people, a difficult people to help. This runs counter to enlightened opinion that they are not temperamentally or congenitally feckless, lazy, stupid, dirty, dissipation-prone, without concern or willingness to help themselves; but appear so only because they have been demoralized and debilitated by poverty, lack of education and lack of opportunity.

The Montgomery Report says that white employers who disregarded the need for giving their Aboriginal stockmen a balanced diet (not just salt beef, flour, tea, sugar) had mistaken for laziness the lethargy produced by malnutrition. It does not mention such recent findings on Aboriginal health as these:

—At two N.T. Aboriginal Settlements, Papunya and Maningrida, 69 per cent of the children had a history of repeated ear-nose-and-throat problems, 68 per cent of gastro-enteritis, 83 per cent of respiratory infections.[5]

—In the Kimberleys district of Western Australia the "estimated" number of Aborigines with leprosy was 600—close to one-tenth of the Aboriginal population![6]

—In New South Wales a survey report on one South Coast town said that 66 per cent of Aboriginal children registered died before they were four years old.[7] And, at Bourke, of 51 cases of syphilis reported 47 were Aboriginal.[8]

Of such shocking Aboriginal health conditions Dr H. C. Coombs said, "There is nothing insoluble about them. Existing knowledge, determination and resources could transform this scene in a decade and eliminate the problem within a generation."[9]

The States had "faced an impossible task" because of lack of "human and financial resources" to deal with the health situation, Dr Coombs said. "Last year [1968] for the first time Commonwealth funds were made available in modest proportions." The States had been given $500,000 between them for Aboriginal health.

In 1944 the total spending of States and Commonwealth on the Aboriginal population was only $500,000. In 1969 it was $27 million, over fifty times as much—and yet, clearly, still not enough. In addition, over $13 million was paid to Aborigines in Social Services endowments and pensions. Yet, in Colonel Montgomery's view, Australia was not even holding the line, and the situation would deteriorate unless Aboriginal advancement got higher priority.

That the then Prime Minister, Mr Gorton, did not see the situation like that was evident from what he said in 1968 to a conference of Commonwealth and State Ministers responsible for Aboriginal affairs. He congratulated the States on "the vigour of their approach to the question of Aboriginal welfare. . . ." To give effect to a new policy of Aboriginal advancement he enunciated, he was prepared to increase spending from $21 to $27 million. But he said he expected this sort of increase to be essentially a "short term" measure and added, "In proportion as our policy succeeds, outlay will diminish."

(A claim that the cost of housing Aborigines throughout Australia would be "at least $141 million" was made in April 1971 by the Secretary of the Western Australian Aboriginal Association.)

The new policy's primary aim, Mr Gorton said, would be ". . . to make our Aboriginals self supporting as fully and as quickly as possible. Effective assimilation is dependent upon Aboriginal citizens being able to stand on their own feet."

The new policy sounds admirable in principle, but it seems to me to raise several questions:

Why have the Aboriginal people, who for at least 20,000 years before we expropriated their country stood on their own feet in it, become such a dependent people? With so many of them ill-housed, badly schooled, poorly skilled and ravaged by diseases we introduced (e.g., tuberculosis, leprosy, syphilis, measles), can it be assumed that they are able to stand on their own feet without a much more massive programme of support than the Government appears to envisage as necessary or contemplates providing funds for? And if they are to stand on their own feet, what are their own feet to stand on? Land? Land that we have taken all title to, or land they can regard as their own?

"LAND RIGHTS FOR ABORIGINES". These words lettered on a rock are central to a cartoon by Tanner that appeared in the Melbourne *Age*. Politicians of Federal Cabinet are fleeing away, and a young Aboriginal is saying to an older one, *They're a lazy shiftless lot who go walkabout when it suits them.*

The matter of Aboriginal land rights cannot be run away from or for much longer ignored at Commonwealth level; but that does not mean the matter is a simple one. Professor Stanner of the Council for Aboriginal Affairs has said, of the lands rights question, "I discuss it with trepidation, because it is full of difficulties for both sides...."[10]

Colonel Patrick Montgomery could not be expected to soft pedal his criticism because rendering land justice to the Aborigines raises a problem for white Australians. Our problem is, after all, a molehill to the mountain of a problem we imposed on the Aborigines when we dispossessed them of their tribal lands.

The Montgomery Report declares: "The Commonwealth Government's refusal to grant to Aboriginals the unrestricted title to any part of their tribal lands, the excision from so-called Aboriginal reserves of such parts as are found to contain mineral wealth and the (inadvertent) destruction of sacred sites are violations of human rights and in the opinion of some historians constitute a continuance of the violation of the most basic international law."

This report to the Anti-Slavery Society suggested to that body: "*A warning of impending publicity at the United Nations, particularly on the denial of land rights, appears to constitute the best hope of securing reform.*"

As an Australian I naturally do not want to see my country castigated at the United Nations, branded as shamefully withholding rights and freedoms from the Aborigines, and represented to the world as being in its racial attitudes a sort of second South Africa. In truth, Australian attitudes are not at all those of *apartheid*.

South Australia's (Labour) Government in 1966 enacted legislation to pass into the control of an all-Aboriginal Lands Trust ten reserves in that State. Transfer of mineral rights on these lands was blocked by the Upper House, and these remain reserved to the Government, which has, however, undertaken to pay to the Trust mining royalties from Aboriginal lands equal to what the Crown receives.

The Victorian (non-Labour) Government decided in 1970 to give to an all-Aboriginal trust, representing the 5,000 mixed-blood Aborigines in Victoria, full land rights to two reserves (Lake Tyers, 4,000 acres, and Framlington, 582 acres). The Aborigines Advancement League in Melbourne contended that other reserves should also be handed over and compensation payment of $600,000 made for "land taken from us".

The general assembly of the Presbyterian Church of Australia in

September 1970 called upon Commonwealth and State governments to give Aborigines corporate ownership of all Aboriginal reserves in Australia (350 totalling nearly 190,000 square miles—equal to half the area of South Australia). The church also supported the Gurindjis' request for Wave Hill land at Wattie Creek. A clergyman of the Australian Board of Missions said of the Aboriginal on a reserve, "He has as many rights on the land he occupies as a koala bear on a koala reserve."

Although there is much talk of Aboriginal land rights now, very little was being said in 1962 when I wrote: "Might not we have to return to the ownership of the aboriginal people, communally, either the reserve lands they are on or other lands sufficient for their needs, and assist them to develop these lands, in order to provide a base for any respectable and acceptable policy for their future?"[11] At the same time I questioned whether the assimilation policy—adopted as government policy nationally in 1951 (and reaffirmed in 1965)—was what the Aboriginal people wanted.

Today (1971) the Aborigines' radical voice, an organization called the National Tribal Council, speaks out loud in these terms: "Government must abandon the failed policy of assimilation which amounts to cultural genocide, and encourage the growing desire for bi-culturalism in a genuine and voluntary plural society."[12]

The N.T.C. manifesto went on to say: "We want the Federal Government immediately to adopt a policy of full recognition of the right of Aborigines and [Torres Strait] Islanders to the ownership of their traditional land, of just compensation for all land taken from them, and for royalties to be paid to those communities which are affected by mining, forestry, or other outside exploitation."

The mind reels at the implications of the compensation demand; and it could be contended that the Aboriginal people on Groote Eylandt have never lived better, materially, than since they were "affected" by B.H.P.'s "exploitation" of the manganese deposits that underlay their hunting grounds. However, I should not think that semantics much concern the new Aboriginal breed of young, angry, educated spokesmen like Bruce McGuinness of the Aboriginal Advancement League in Victoria. He does not attempt to disguise the bellicose accents of Black Power when he says: "*Do-gooderism went out with Ned Kelly pin-ups as far as the Darkies are concerned. We are sick and fed up of being told that we are being helped by The Man and that The Man is being very generous in giving us this and giving us that. We know this is a whole lot of Toro Excreta. All The Man is doing is appeasing his conscience. He is trying to con himself that he is a good guy. Well, he is only kidding himself, because us Black Boys ain't buying any of his con.*"[13]

Notice that the word Aborigines is nowhere used. "Aborigines" is an "out" word with the new-generation militants, even with those who are less militant than the McGuinnesses. They prefer to call themselves Black Australians.

One must agree that "Aborigines" is a general term that identifies poorly a particular people. For the same reason Negroes is, in the United States, "out" with the militants who say they are Black Americans. It is for this particular Australian people to say (not for us to say) what they shall be called. When I talked to an intelligent young man of the Foundation for Aboriginal Affairs, in Sydney, he said they rejected "Aborigines" as non-descriptive; "Black Australians" was the name now favoured; but discussion about what they should call themselves and prefer others to call them was still going on. I asked what he thought of *Abstralians*. The *Ab* does not only abbreviate *Aboriginal*; as a prefix *ab* connoted, perhaps, the separateness or apartness some seemed to want in a bi-cultural Australia. No, he didn't like my "Abstralians". It wasn't black enough, apparently. The young man said, "We are proud of being black."

We must expect the Black Australians to become much more assertive than they have been in the past, especially in the matter of land rights, or what they claim are their rights of ownership to some of the land that was either taken from their people by our people and put to our people's use, or alienated by being vested in the Crown. Particularly will they be concerned with gaining full title (mineral rights included) to Crown lands that Aboriginal groups have been living on in areas we proclaimed Aboriginal reserves for their "use and benefit", but to which they hold no title whatsoever, freehold or leasehold.

Whatever Australian courts have decided on the validity of Aboriginal claims, there seems to me little doubt that if the matter were taken to the United Nations the basic claim to entitlement would be upheld. Article 11 of Convention 107 of the International Labour Organization, which is a U.N. agency, reads: *"The right of ownership, collective or individual, of the members of the populations concerned over the lands which these populations traditionally occupy shall be recognized."*

The I.L.O. Article says *occupy*, not *occupied*. Assuming its accordance with international law, it would be in support of the Yirrkala people's claim to land rights on the Gove Peninsula of Arnhem Land where Nabalco is mining bauxite on land leased to them by the Commonwealth Government; but not in support of a claim, say, by an Aranda group to own the land the Americans built their Space Base on at Alice Springs because it was where they lived when they were living tribally.

More needs to be said on this "hot" issue of Aboriginal land rights; but it can be said in the Arnhem Land section.

EXCEPT at Ross River, where Max Bloomfield represents intelligent involvement of the Aboriginal in tourism, what the Centre tourist sees of these people is likely to prove dull, depressing and discreditable.

Jay Creek Aboriginal Settlement (run by the N.T. Administration) was visited mainly because tourists have to eat and the tour operators had come to an arrangement with Jay Creek to provide a barbecue steak lunch in between sightseeing at Standley Chasm and Simpson's Gap. No explanation of the settlement's working was given. By asking questions of one of the pleasant white staff women who served the lunch I learnt that the number of Aborigines there varied from 200 to 250; the men mainly worked a small herd of cattle; women helped in the orange grove or in the kitchen. ("Some are very good—intelligent. But nearly all need to work under white supervision.") Some lived in houses, others in the camp across the creek. ("If they can appreciate a house they get a house.") Some in the camp were visiting Pintubis who still lived tribally. ("We try to help them, not change them all at once.")

The camp was out of bounds to tourists. Glimpsed from the coach on the road out, it looked rubbishy and ugly with sheets of iron set up as windbreaks. It was in no way transitional to the house-occupancy stage. A simple open-front barracks with an ablutions block and sanitation could be.

On the settlement the only Aborigines seen were three young girls playing in the dirt who, when their photographs were taken, said, "Two bob", meaning that they wanted twenty cents. The party was taken to see dingo pups in a wire-netting enclosure. On a rock-face were painted in white some kangaroos and emus. Of no significance as Aboriginal art, these could have been the work of half-skilled whites. The Aranda had no figurative painting worth a damn —but they made marvellous ground patterns, which it would have been interesting to see recreated on the floor of a settlement museum. Jay Creek was a dull place with an air of unimaginative do-gooding.

Outside the entrance a few men and women sat in the dirt whittling wooden things such as clap sticks which they decorated, not well, with pokerwork designs and sold to tourists. One man turned out to have spent a lot of time at Ayers Rock with my old mate Bill Harney. He was known as Harry Bigfoot: such white-man namings for a physical peculiarity or deformity are not uncommon. An old man, Mick, was leading a camel round, giving rides on it for twenty cents. Mick, I learnt, was a Pitjandjara who in his tribal days was a big *kurdaitja* man. Greatly feared for his bone-pointing sorcery, the *kurdaitja* man wore shoes made of emu feathers so that he left no identifiable footprints, and he took the role of avenger against men who had broken tribal law.

HERMANNSBURG MISSION was founded by Lutheran Germans in 1875. More than any secular institution, it pioneered Aboriginal welfare work in the Centre, with Pastor Karl Strehlow, and his son T. G. H. Strehlow after him, making notable contributions to understanding of the Aranda people and their language. Reverend F. W. Albrecht encouraged the development of the Namatjira school of watercolour painters. These are still painting, in exactly the same manner as Namatjira did, and their watercolours are displayed and sold to tourists visiting Hermannsburg, as are other Aboriginal artefacts, few of which are of much artistic merit, although the copies of sacred *tjuringa* stones are interesting.

The old church, its pink stucco dappled with tree shadows, makes a charming photograph. The new church is modern A-line architecture. Some other buildings are ugly. So, when I was there, was the Aboriginal scene.

Women and children were squatted in the dust beside a fence topped with barbed wire in front of the church, across from the Mission store where the people shop. Skinny dogs lay with them or nosed about. Tourists were requested to "respect the people's privacy" by not descending on them with cameras, and to ask their permission before taking photographs. Fair enough; but I had the feeling that the Mission wanted to minimize picturing of women in dirty second-hand clothing, which can hardly be otherwise than dirty when the ground is all there is to sit on.

I took a number of black-and-white photographs that the people did not know were being taken because I took them from a distance, using a telephoto lens. There were also the usual Aboriginal children with snot running from their noses: they could doubtless be taught to use a handkerchief, if they had a handkerchief. That a few people sat on the steps of a hideous flat-iron shed suggested that they did not squat in the dust from choice, but because there was nowhere else to sit while they waited for whatever they were waiting for. Benches or seats could easily have been provided, if not from the Mission's funds or the subsidy money it gets from the Administration, then by the Welfare Department of the Administration.

An Aboriginal named Nandjiwara Amagula, speaking at a Summer School on Aboriginal advancement at the University of Western Australia in 1969 said: "We want our children to live in a proper home where they can be happy to live, rather than going back to

Y

their old humpies and live with the dust. What about *your* children? Do you want them to live on the dust? I don't think so."[14]

I did not see where these people lived. The only inspection conducted was of the church. No booklet was on sale detailing and illustrating what the Mission did, and nobody told the tourists about the place. One got the impression that tourists were welcomed, if that's the word, only for what they might buy in the way of Aranda watercolours or artefacts or leave in the donation box.

There was a kind of Aboriginal major-domo who had a military uniform and cap. The cap had on it a metal badge in the shape of a map of Australia inscribed with TIGER, *No. 1 Boss of* PALM VALLEY. His tunic front was stuck all over with badges given him by people—including young mods who, without thought for his dignity, had contributed buttons that said *Down with Everything*, *Stamp Out Good Sportsmanship* and *Handle with Care*. All the tourists took Tiger's photograph and a couple gave him twenty cents. He was, everybody said, quite a "character". Twenty-two years ago Talkaljeri (Tiger) was Arthur Groom's guide on a camel trip from Hermannsburg to Ayers Rock, and Groom's book paid him tribute. Now, though he doubtless felt important in his uniform with all the absurd badges, he was a figure of fun.

If I had any say in the running of Central Australian tourism I should close Hermannsburg to tourists until the Aboriginal indignity there—and the same goes for Jay Creek settlement—is got rid of. Before expecting these people to "stand on their own feet" we need to get them up out of the dust.

PINE CREEK, about 150 miles south of Darwin, is not a place where tourists usually stop for more than a meal. I was there overnight. It was long enough to see as bad a place for Aboriginal degradation as exists (I hope) in the Territory.

Gun Alley is the local name for what is referred to as the blacks' camp on the outskirts of the town, stony red earth and spindly gums. About thirty Aboriginal people usually lived there. The camp was, in part, the old police station. In one room of a derelict corrugated-iron structure there remained, attached to a ringbolt in the cement floor, a chain that was used to tether prisoners. There was also an old sheet-iron prison bed; bedding indicated that it was still in use. The other structures were humpies made of sheet iron. One family had mattresses on the ground and a kitchen-table arrangement on two oil drums, out in the open. It hadn't rained since May and probably wouldn't before October.

In front of the main group of humpies was a large heap of rubbish. Most of it was bottles, and wine flagons, some still with the red label *Penfold PORT*. An old man was sitting motionless as a corpse on a box in the litter-free space between the huts. A painfully thin young man, who looked ill, moved about slowly. Two youngish women in bright cotton frocks came out of one humpy and went across to another.

"Those two lubras—you should see them drink!" Peter Cooper said. Peter was the local publican. He added, "The drink transforms these women worse than it does white women. One night, when the Pioneer coach was there for dinner, a gin came screaming into the pub stark naked. Chased her out, and she came back wearing a pair of bloke's underpants she'd got off the clothesline. She flew at her husband and swiped him off a chair."

I asked if there was a lot of prostitution.

"Yes, a good bit. Bottle of port or a dollar. Ringers in from the stations—never drunk port in their lives—will say, 'Think I'll take a bottle of port to the room. Man might get thirsty in the night. Yeah, you better wrap it up.' They bring it down here, silly buggers. Any woman living at Gun Alley's likely to be loaded with V.D. Or the women go up to the hotel—not into the rooms, mind you, but I've tripped over them out at the back."

Of the local male Aborigines only one, Peter Cooper said, had a job. He was assistant to the local P.M.G. linesman, and he lived in a house not a humpy.

Katherine Gorge

NORTH of Alice Springs the Stuart Highway runs 934 miles to Darwin. That is a lot of road, with not much either side of it and, according to tourists who had been over the route, some pretty sub-standard overnight accommodation. I decided I could bear to miss seeing those big round rocks called the Devil's Marbles—there was a nice one on Flynn's grave, anyway—and bypass Tennant Creek, where they mined those Old Australia minerals copper and gold; and Elliott, Newcastle Waters, Daly Waters and Mataranka. But not Katherine. I had to see the Katherine Gorge.

So I got on to Eddie Connellan's air service and flew to Mt Isa (already written of in the Queensland section) and from Mt Isa to Katherine, by way of McArthur River and Borroloola, and Roper River Mission in the corner of Arnhem Land, where this Connellan flight sometimes stops for the night. It didn't even land at the Roper but went on to make Katherine just after the molten-red ball of the sun went down west of the great rangy wilderness that stretches for two hundred miles with only a couple of cattle stations and Beswick Aboriginal Reserve in it, south of the Arnhem Land border.

Katherine (pop. about 1,500) had a tourist future but not much of a tourist present. It had two hotels and two motels, one of which, the Corroboree, was recommendable. I had somehow been booked into the other one, which had a notice saying *It is requested that clients pay for motel accommodation in advance*. This motel did not serve lunch or dinner, which could be taken handily at a restaurant known locally as the Greasy Spoon, which had a notice to patrons saying "PLEASE BE DRESSED AND BEHAVE". There was a better place called the Dynasty.

Katherine also had a meatworks, which had upped the values of surrounding cattle properties considerably, but was hardly a civic enchantment. Land was expensive in Katherine town. Crown land could not be sold until it was serviced with electricity and water, and such servicing was not happening at anything like the demand rate.

Three miles out of Katherine was a C.S.I.R.O. Research Station I had heard about. I telephoned and the officer in charge, L. J. (known as Flip) Phillips came in and picked me up. He was very good value. What his station had been experimenting at length with was Townsville lucerne, which is a legume but not a lucerne, and is now called Townsville *stylo*. Accidentally introduced from South America, it is a weed full of protein. Pastures sown with it had dramatically increased the weight of cattle. The calving rate of cows running on natural bush feed was 7: on pastures improved with *Stylosanthes humilis*, alias Townsville lucerne, the rate was 14—double.

Agronomist Phillips, who was a realist, thought it would take a decade at least for the benefits of Townsville stylo to permeate the Territory's cattle industry so that it realized its potential. Distance from market was a problem, and cattle were bringing much better prices at Townsville in Queensland.

KATHERINE GORGE I went to by courtesy of Len Smith who operated the Corroboree Motel and was the kind of man Northern Territory tourism needed more of. He sent me down in his truck with some Aborigines, in case I wanted them in photographs of the rock paintings one comes to on the Gorge cruise. However, there can be only one photograph (PLATE 34).

The picture describes only one section of the stretch of Katherine River's gorge the tourist sees: there are two sections, separated by a rock bar at a pleasant swimming place near the Aboriginal paintings on the cliff walls. Changing here from one of the excellent sightseeing launches to another, you go on round a turn in the river to where the bluffs are higher—what is called Jedda Rock rises 210 feet sheer from water that was very blue on this cloudless day.

A young freshwater crocodile about two feet long was sun-basking on a rock and plopped into the water only when the launch was a few feet from it. These Johnstone River crocs, as they are called, are harmless to man and are now protected. I can vouch for them being harmless, having watched shooters near Normanton in Queensland dive naked repeatedly into a waterhole they took forty from, retrieving them in that fashion after they had shot them.

Some of the Aboriginal rock paintings are weathered to indistinctness. Two human figures in red ochre (one of them headless) and a brolga are well defined. To the right of this group were six oval shapes. These were emu eggs, said Marapunya, the man Len Smith had sent with me. Marapunya's two sons, Samuel, aged fourteen and Joseph, five, had come with him. The boys could look at these paintings but not at others higher up on the rockface, because they had not been initiated. The higher paintings were less clear, but Marapunya pointed out the figure of a man with a crocodile's head, a kangaroo, and a faded figure of a man with what he said were flying-foxes. In another place was a figure of a "spirit man" who, Marapunya said, had come from the sea. The boys could look at that one, too. Samuel, his father said, would be initiated next year; and then he would tell him the legend of the higher-up figures—which could only have been painted when there was a platform of rock that had fallen away from the face. Marapunya said they were painted before his grandfather was born, and perhaps two hundred years ago. This was still a sacred place to his people, and Samuel would be brought here to be initiated, with circumcision as part of the ritual.

Dr Marie Reay, an anthropologist of the Australian National University, has written of these paintings[1] (she was able to find out little about them) and others she describes as "lively and interesting" at the entrance to limestone caves sixteen miles south of Katherine. These caves, she says, are comparable to those at Jenolan in New South Wales. I did not go to the Cutta Cutta Caves, which are open to tourists. I had contracted a feverish misery called the "four-day flu" that half the population of Katherine seemed to have or to be recovering from. I had two days of it, there and at Pine Creek, where it was also rampant.

PINE CREEK I reached by the Pioneer express bus that ate up the sixty-four miles of bitumen in an hour and a quarter. A missionary on her way to Darwin said the country was now more interesting—

less flat and with more trees and grass to it—than it had been south of Katherine.

"Magnetic" termite hills, some taller than a man, proclaimed that this was the Top End, as the country is called north of Katherine. Only this species of "white ants" builds its mud nests so that the narrow ends point north and south. Why, so far as I know, has not been satisfactorily explained; but the orientation is said to have to do with maintaining humidity within the labyrinth of the nest. If the soft-bodied white ants become desiccated they die.

Because Pine Creek, unlike Katherine, with its gorge and caves, had no attractions for tourists and was not an overnight stop for the coaches, it had no motels with modern amenities, just the Pine Creek Hotel that Peter Cooper and his wife ran. The downstairs rooms were usually taken by cattle station ringers, or miners, who came to "blow their cheques" by getting drunk.

In the eighties the Chinese labourers who built the railway line down from Darwin to Pine Creek mined a lot of gold from around Pine Creek, which had had its first rush in the early seventies. Their diggings can still be seen; but now the mining interest in the area is in its deposits of iron, uranium and wolfram. The Frances Creek Iron Mining Co. had a contract to deliver three million tons of ore to Japan.

About thirty Frances Creek workers came into town the day I was there and stayed until after midnight, drinking and singing to the guitar one of them had. They were all Torres Strait Islanders, mostly from Badu; and if the wolfram mining development on Moa Island turns out well they will probably have jobs much nearer home, which they would like. They were a merry crowd. These Islanders are a heartier-spirited, more extroverted people than the Aborigines.

Edges of Arnhem Land

ARNHEM LAND takes its name from the Dutch ship *Arnhem* that coasted this big northern "head" of New Holland in 1623. The name used to be applied right across what is now known as the Top End of the Territory, but nowadays it signifies only the Arnhem Land Aboriginal Reserve. No tours may enter the reserve, and what Pioneer calls the "Arnhemlander" tour goes only to its border, at a point where this is formed by the East Alligator River.

The tour is, nevertheless, an interesting one into country fairly typical of the Arnhem Land I had seen with the scientific Australian-

American expedition in 1948 when it was based at Oenpelli. It is a five-day tour that starts at Darwin, comes down the Stuart Highway to where I joined it after lunch at Pine Creek, and eventually returns to Darwin by a different route.

About thirty miles in from Pine Creek we come to Moline, a treatment plant for silver-lead; and then, about sixty miles along the all-weather road, glimpse the abandoned workings of the El Sherana uranium mine. This produced in 1955 the largest piece of pitch-blende uranium ore found anywhere in the world, weighing 1,875 pounds. Four hundred men were working at El Sherana until there were no more contracts for uranium oxide because Britain and the United States had adequate supplies. Rum Jungle, farther north, also suspended operations, but most of its deposits had been worked out. New discoveries were to establish the Territory as richer in uranium than any State and probably the richest uranium province in the world.

Hundreds of small pinnacles of termite nests intersperse the spotted gums in country that grows greener by the Mary River, rises to sandstone escarpments, spouts a waterfall from a cliffside, and then flattens out again. The earth changes colour, from brown to red, pointed with red anthills. We are on Goodparla cattle station, American owned.

American owned is what fifty per cent of the leased pastoral land in the Top End is today (1971). It is what between fifteen and twenty per cent of all the pastoral leases in the Northern Territory are. An article in the *Wall Street Journal* early in 1970 headed "The Great American Land Grab" suggested that Americans held two-thirds of the leased Top End pastoral properties: the N.T. Director of Lands said it was only half.

With English interests holding fifteen per cent of leases, and some Hong Kong investment, Australian equity in the Top End pastoralism was only about thirty per cent. Americans had acquired twenty-seven properties in the Territory, giving them 43,000 square miles of Top End country on leases, which are for 99 years with the right to renew after 60 years.

That a hunk of the Northern Territory about half the size of Victoria is leased to Americans does not disturb me to the degree it disturbs some other Australians. After all, we want the country developed, and Australians haven't developed it to the extent that is desirable, for the reason that a country of only twelve million people simply cannot generate the kind of money to develop a continent of this size pastorally or agriculturally any more than it can develop its mineral resources without taking in overseas capital.

(Australia could, however, do without the type of American

cattleman managing Ban-Ban Springs station for the son of Nelson Bunker Hunt of Texas, the one who told TV interviewer Alan Whicker that if Aboriginal stockmen bothered his daughters, "they would be dead men just like that", and added, "You would get away with it here, too." You wouldn't get away with it.)

Personally, I would not invest a dollar in the Northern Territory cattle industry. If Americans are prepared to invest millions of dollars in it, then I think there are good reasons for letting them do so. It can hardly be said that, by their Territory acquisitions, they are taking over the Australian cattle business. The big cattle State is Queensland. Even small Victoria has more cattle than the Territory, and produces more, and much better, beef. Although Queensland runs more beef cattle than all other States do in the southern half of Australia, the south still produces twice as much beef as the northern half. It does not export twice as much, for the southern beef is the good beef most Australians eat. Territory beef is for hamburgers and smallgoods.

Primitive is what the Territory cattle industry has been, and exploitation has been the name of the game—exploitation of the land, of the Aboriginal workers, and of the beasts to a degree calculated to raise the hackles of any half-way humanitarian. Indeed, one Australian agronomist writing in 1966 said ". . . the standards of animal husbandry in the north were amongst the most primitive in the world. Even today, in some of the more remote areas, management consisted of two operations only—branding and turning off those cattle which can be mustered."[1] It was much less a cattle-raising industry than one based on cattle hunting—and still is on some stations, except that, instead of bulldogging the wild steers from horseback, Land Rovers and Toyota vehicles are now used to knock them over with what is called a "bull bar" mounted in front.

The system of running cattle on the open range with (as Davidson[2] puts it) fencing practically non-existent, breeding uncontrolled, water points mainly natural ones supplemented by some bores and dams: this paid off because the lease cost of land was so low, so little was spent on improvements, and Aboriginal labour was so cheap—and much of it casual labour that was laid off in the Wet. That was all right for the pastoralist. But ". . . uncontrolled grazing and indiscriminate stocking have resulted in thousands of square miles of good cattle country being rendered almost useless. . . . The problems of erosion and pasture regeneration will eventually cost government millions of dollars."[3]

Now there are changes, with the Americans leading the way in controlled breeding, pasture improvement, tick control and fencing. Properties are tending to be reduced to more manageable size: Victoria River Downs (owned by Bovril) is no longer the 13,000 square miles that made it larger than Belgium. The largest Territory station now is Alexandria, 6,290 square miles. The largest American-owned N.T. property is Brunette Downs, its three million acres bought by the King Ranch organization of Texas.

Goodparla, the station our road ran through, was 1,300 square miles. It had fenced paddocks with horses in them, plenty of scrub and grass growth, and was particularly good country near the South Alligator River.

Just before this river we saw the first of many buffaloes, its black hide mud-caked from the wallow it had been in. The water buffalo, the placid workbeast of the Asian ricefields, is an animal with a spread of horns that look formidable, but it is most unlikely to charge unless it is wounded. Originally they were brought in from Timor to be meat for the garrison settlements that preceded Darwin, and when these failed they went wild and bred plentifully on the swamp edges of the billabong-and-plain country, particularly between the two Alligator rivers. Twenty years ago they used to be shot extensively for their tough hides that went to Egypt to make the long-wearing sandals of the fellaheen, but now the hides are worth little and they are shot for their meat. Much of it is used in pet foods and smallgoods; but prime buffalo steak was prized (and priced) in Darwin above the best beef fillet.

As typical of this country as the termite nests is the screw-palm, the pandanus, its slim trunk hoisted on a high bundle of broomstick roots, its crooked arms ending in very long pointed leaves. There are occasional cabbage palms, too, among the paperbarks and eucalypts, and shrubs that may have their leaves stitched together to make the nests of the stinging green tailor-ants. The road turns to bulldust in places.

Along the sides of the road trees were cut down. This was to widen it to bring in on wide-loaders the instant housing that Tom Opitz has set up as tourist accommodation beside Jim Jim Creek, a tributary of the South Alligator. Four miles this side of it, at the head of a creek arm, you come to Opitz's store, where you can buy beer and other drinks, even whisky, to take down to the Motel Jim Jim. There were brolgas on the plain, and more buffaloes, and kangaroos came out to feed when the sun went down.

The accommodation, built in Adelaide, consisted of six multi-units, each as long as a railway carriage and containing three sleek bedroom units with shower and toilet, reading lights and electric fan. Set apart was a dining-recreation hall. Jim Jim Creek, belying its name and looking wide as a river, was a couple of hundred yards away.

All this Territory-top country parches through a winter as warm as a Sydney summer. Between November and March about sixty-five inches of rain falls, and a lot of this water stays through the year, not only in rivers and creeks but in billabongs alive with birds. We went on the Jim Jim next morning in motor boats. The water was very blue and thickly banked with trees. Clive the driver hooked a big barramundi.

In the evening I went up-creek again with Ted Opitz, Tom's brother. There was a reach where the big trees were alive with thousands of flying-foxes, hanging upside down like black fruit from the branches, or flying and squabbling and filling the air with a din of squeaking. Coming back in the evening light, Jim Jim was beautiful.

DREAMING WATER is another beautiful place. There is a picture of it, with a pandanus-palm pattern in the foreground (PLATE 34). Swimming was not advisable here, the driver said. Crocodiles.

"You won't get a native to come within a mile of Dreaming Water," Clive said, and told us what he had been told was the Aboriginal legend of the place. A "chief" (the Aborigines had no chiefs, only elders) had gone off on a hunting trip, and when he didn't return a party was sent to look for him. When that party didn't return either another party went to search. They found a message stick from the first party, which had been drowned in a great flood, saying that the chief had been taken by an enormous crocodile.

Aboriginal message sticks did not convey messages. How could they when these people had no form of writing? The message stick was no more than a baton that was handed to the message bearer with nicks in it to remind him that he had to deliver verbally so many messages (the Aborigines in Arnhem Land knew numbers up to the count of four) and a tribal design served to identify the bearer as being of a certain tribe or clan.

Another fiction is that the Aborigines could send messages by smoke signals. Interrupting the smoke column served to differentiate it from a cooking fire, and the puffs signalled "We are here"; but that is all.

Ted Opitz knew the blacks, from walking about in Arnhem Land, looking for gold, and living off the country, with Aborigines of the Gunavidgi tribe from round Maningrida on the north coast. When you were hunting kangaroos and saw one you never pointed with your hand—to make the movement of doing so was the height of foolishness. You pointed by pursing your lips.

He said, "The Kunudpa tribe, they were very cheeky—lit a bushfire upwind of our camp and churned up a well so we couldn't drink the water. But I like the blackfellas. They've never let me down once. And they can do extraordinary things. Once we had to cross a deep creek and this fella Horace puts a swag on his head and walks into the water and bloody disappears. He walked across on the bottom.

"This mob I'm a brother with were having an initiation and gave me this small boy to hold. He's been kept awake for three nights, being sung, so he barely knows what's happening, but with me holding him across my knees it still hurts when they cut his cock. They presented me with the foreskin. I had a jar of metho with a snake and a big scorpion in it, so I popped it in there. Couple of nights later we came on a plant operator, so I naturally put up at his camp. The night after that I find him roaring drunk and yelling, 'Come an' 'ave a cocktail!' Damned if he hadn't drained my jar of metho and mixed it with powdered milk!

"They've got wonderful corroboree, this mob I'm brothers with, the best I've ever seen. But you can have too much of it, and one night I couldn't get to sleep for them, so I walked up to where they're singing and said, motioning towards the darkness, 'Who's that out there with a torch?'

" 'No torch, boss,' they said.

" 'Yes,' I told them. 'Look. You can see man with light!'

"They *saw* the light that wasn't there. They were scared stiff and huddled close to my camp all night. Next morning two were sick and had to be taken back to Maningrida. They believed that the light signified a debbil-debbil man who, while they slept, cut them open and put a stone inside them."

(The most authoritative Australian anthropologist, Professor A. P. Elkin, substantiates in his writings[4] that belief in supernatural introduction of stones into the body was common to a number of tribes. Some believed that organs, or kidney fat, were magically excised and replaced by stones.)

JIM JIM remained the base, but each day the coach took us somewhere else. The afternoon of Day 2 was devoted to fishing in a shadeless muddy waterhole that Clive believed to be alive with barramundi, and nobody got even a nibble.

No fisherman, I wandered off to a shady reach and watched the bright blue kingfishers swooping for water insects. A larger kind of kingfisher, with blue wings, is the Northern Territory kookaburra. It does not "laugh" but has a loud discordant cry.

One of the sights of this region is the abundant bird life of the billabongs. We picnic-lunched beside one on Day 3. It had white herons, egrets, a multitude of magpie geese and some pygmy geese (which look nothing like geese), Burdekin duck and black duck, and plovers piping at the edges. On another billabong a fleet of pelicans sailed. As I went towards the billabong to take photographs, the pelicans all took off, big wings beating the air.

"They're touchy. They've been shot at lately," Clive said. He went on to say that on a recent trip he had passed six dead buffaloes lying beside the road. "These Army types in Darwin get week-end leave, hop in a Land Rover with their guns and shoot at anything that moves."

The NO ADMITTANCE sign at the gate to Muirella station was riddled with bullet holes. There was no ranger in the area and, according to Tom Opitz (who had offered to be an honorary ranger), netters had come in and, illegally, taken two thousand pounds of fish out of Jim Jim Creek and sold the fillets in Katherine. The police were also required to do duty as rangers; but as one of them from Pine Creek said to me, "Two of us are supposed to cover an area of twenty thousand square miles. It can't be done."

The N.T. Tourist Bureau puts out a booklet saying "Shooting in the Territory is, of necessity, strictly controlled. . . . Some species have been seriously depleted by uncontrolled destruction. We have to protect our wildlife." The booklet has on the cover a comical figure with a gun under its arm. Anywhere north of Mataranka the Agile Wallaby could be shot, year round, and the Red Kangaroo in season. Only partly protected—"They may be taken or killed only under a licence issued by the Chief Inspector of Wildlife"— were all the cockatoos, corellas, galahs, budgerigars, and thirteen varieties of finches. On ducks there was a July-October open season, and an August-December one on magpie geese (which the English writer Elspeth Huxley predicts will be shot out in this region). A tourist booklet says, "Buffaloes are only protected in the area of the Top End where they are used for meat production."

The Administration's tourist bureau was wooing hunters to make a quick tourist dollar—even though it had no adequate means of policing its all-too-permissive regulations. The hunters would further deplete the region of the wildlife that was a prime attraction for the much more numerous tourists who did not want to shoot with anything but cameras.

Gun vandals who killed roadside buffaloes and blasted billabong birds with shotguns were not the only kind on the rampage. Near Nourlangie there was the ruination of a cave of Aboriginal paintings. Sump oil had been thrown over them and set alight. A tour operator who discovered the damage, Douglas Banks, said, "I bloody near cried." He added, "There were beer cans everywhere."

ABORIGINAL ART in its two most interesting forms—painting on rockfaces and painting on sheets of bark—is nowhere else in Australia as good as it is in and around Arnhem Land. The best cave paintings are found in the west of this region, and the best bark paintings come from the north-east.

The two outstanding areas for rock paintings are Oenpelli and its vicinity, east of the East Alligator River, and Obiri/Cannon Hill /Nourlangie area which is on the west side, outside the Aboriginal Reserve. The first I had seen with the Arnhem Land Expedition in 1948, and was to revisit. Nourlangie I have not been to, but the Obiri galleries were visited on this Pioneer tour (and it was the only tour that went to them).

In the *Australia* volume of the UNESCO series on world art, *Aboriginal Paintings—Arnhem Land*,[5] six of the sixteen large-format reproductions of rock paintings are from Cannon Hill or Obiri, and ten are from the Oenpelli region. These proportions, I think, fairly represent the relative importance of the two major sites. Oenpelli, being within the Reserve, is not ordinarily accessible to tourists; but Obiri has paintings that are comparable and they are the work of the same tribal groups that painted at Oenpelli. The places are only about fifteen miles apart.

In classing Oenpelli's as the outstanding galleries of Aboriginal cave paintings I am not unmindful of the caves in the Kimberley district of Western Australia with what are called *Wandjina* painting. These haloed and mouthless faces are unique and very strange, but it is their strangeness and size that impress, rather than their artistic vitality. On Cape York Peninsula in Queensland many caves of paintings have been found (notably by the Ansett pilot Captain Percy Trezise[6]), but artistically they are not up to those of western Arnhem Land.

By "cave" paintings is meant, in Australia, paintings on the backwalls and roofs of shelters formed by overhangs of rocks, ledge caves—not underground caverns such as have been found in Spain and France wonderfully muralled with paintings of bison and deer by paleolithic artists who lived perhaps 20,000 years ago. Aboriginal art, even the Arnhem Land best of it, is a more primitive form of art; but it is nonetheless art, and firmly establishes itself as such (as Sir Herbert Read points out[7]) because of its strength of design and its sensuous quality.

Although the Top End has the best Australian galleries of Aboriginal cave paintings tourists can see, the Territory tourist literature does not mention them. The driver-guide on this tour knew nothing of the paintings' meaning and did not even know the name of the first place he took us to.

If this place was not Cannon Hill, which is three miles north of Obiri according to C. P. Mountford, at least it had paintings of the "dangerous Namarakain spirits" he has reproduced from Cannon Hill.[8] We were there only about five minutes—which I spent mainly on my back taking photographs, for the best paintings were on the cave roof—and then Clive led off back to the bus to go to Obiri, which is admittedly the major site, with many more paintings in two much larger ledge-caved outcrops. Obiri is a fine place where I could easily have spent half a day.

There are, broadly speaking, five kinds of Aboriginal cave paintings common to the Obiri-Oenpelli areas either side of the East Alligator River. They are:

(i) X-RAY PAINTINGS of fish and animals. Parts of the anatomy, such as the vertebrae, the swim bladder of a fish, the main organs, are patterned within the outline of barramundi, kangaroo, crocodile, turtle. The Aborigines living did none of these paintings. Probably they were painted with a magical purpose, in the belief that depicting kangaroos or barramundis or turtles led to their increase.

(ii) MIMI FIGURES, usually running or fighting. These stick-thin drawings on the rock are believed by the present Aborigines (who don't know who did them or how long ago) to have been done by, and to represent, Mimis. These they describe as a fairy-like people so thin the wind could blow them over, who lived inside the rocks.

Mimi figures from a frieze of running hunters at Obiri. Triangular objects are goose-wing fans. (Drawing done from a photograph.)

(iii) DANGEROUS SPIRITS called Namarakain or Mamandi. Sometimes these are portrayed in Mimi style, but mostly they are depicted in a highly designist manner. The depiction of hands, feet, and sex organs in rhythmically conventionalized style is remarkable.

(iv) SORCERY PAINTINGS, in which the artist may depict an enemy, or a woman who has refused to have sexual intercourse with him, suffering some horrid fate.

(v) RECENT PAINTINGS, such as one at Obiri that depicts a white man in shirt and trousers with his hands in his pockets. The Aborigines told Mountford they painted a white man like this because he seldom did anything else but give orders.[9] Photographs of cave art at Nourlangie show, as well as the traditional forms, paintings of ships. Blue (from Reckitts washing blue) has been added to these paintings, which were previously confined to a palette of red ochre, yellow ochre, pipeclay white and charcoal black.

The notable frieze of running Mimi figures at Obiri is in pipeclay white on a reddish wall. Superimposed on the last two of four figures are two drawings in red ochre, stylishly done with a sure line, representing Namarakain women, very tall and thin-bodied with ominously outcurving arms and strings stretched between the hands. "By means of the string they are able to travel from place to place in their search for human victims."[10]

Paintings were commonly done on top of other paintings, which is somewhat confusing to the viewer. Moreover, guide interpretation —and without interpretation they don't mean very much—was practically nil on this tour. What I have written should aid understanding, but the best pocket guide for the tourist would be *Aboriginal Paintings* in the Fontana Unesco Art Books series, with text by C. P. Mountford (priced at about a dollar).

In the presence of Arnhem Land cave art one may feel an emanation of beliefs and fears that remain for us darkly mysterious. At the same time, there is an almost exultant expression of themselves by the people who, grinding their ochre colours in depressions worn in the rock through centuries, applied their paints with a twig's chewed end for a brush. They left behind a vital as well as a primal essence of the human mind making its mark on this ancient Australian land.

FROM THE TOP of the main Obiri outcrop there was a fine panoramic view across the East Alligator floodplain that stretched flat like a sea between capes of treed land and rugged coasts of sandstone. Hundreds of black buffaloes could be seen grazing.

On the way back to Jim Jim we drove through Mudginberri station. Half a dozen men were hacking at buffalo carcasses on a hoist in an iron-shed butchery. The shooter, Merv Parker, had just come in. He wore only shorts and was brown with the sun and the dust from the plain. He showed us his Magnum .375 rifle fitted with a powerful telescopic sight, and the long heavy-calibre bullets. "You go for a neck shot or between the horns," he said.

Over at Oenpelli Mission they were using the same rifle but, increasingly, their buffalo hunters were using tranquillizer darts. So I learnt from Don Kinslow, a young American who was taking a refrigerator truck of buffalo meat into Darwin from Oenpelli and stayed overnight at Jim Jim on the way. His sister had married one of the missionaries and he was visiting from Texas and helping out with the shooting, too.

"Shooting from horseback is out," he said. "The place is a pattern of roads and tracks now and we shoot from jeep-type vehicles. You aim to hit in the head and kill with one bullet. Or tranquillize. It's still nearly all bullet shooting, but next year I guess it could be fifty-fifty tranquillizing. The regulations on meat are strict and you can't have any shot buffaloes running—muscle deterioration sets in—and the meat inspectors won't pass the meat unless it's butchered within an hour. That limits your range. So you tranquillize, load them live and bring 'em in to slaughter. It's expensive—three dollars a dart. And difficult, because you don't shoot a dart straight but on a trajectory. And you have to leave them twenty-four hours for the tranquillizer to dissipate—it's a poison—before killing. By that time they're up and cranky wild."

One plan being considered at Oenpelli was to "farm" buffaloes, tame them and raise them like beef cattle. Mudginberri station had the same idea, and so did Marrakai and Mount Bundey. Buffalo domesticate easily, they do better than beef cattle on this country, and they are heavier and produce more meat.

Don Kinslow considered a prime buffalo fillet was as good as the best Texas beef. This surprised me, and he said, "You ate buffalo steak for dinner. Wasn't it good?" As a matter of fact, it wasn't, although it was tender enough. It was cooked through, and I think it was too fresh to have much flavour. But it was bringing 80 cents a pound in Darwin.

WHEN I was at Oenpelli in 1948 buffaloes were killed, to augment the funds of the Church Missionary Society, very differently. The Mission's white shooter and his Aboriginal helpers shot from horseback, with sawn-off rifles. I watched as they galloped in on the lumbering buffaloes and, using the rifle with one hand, shot them in the base of the spine.

They did not shoot to kill but to paralyse. They did this in the late afternoon when the buffaloes left the wallows and came out on to the plain to feed. Then the shooters went home. In the morning they came out (I came with them) and there were the para-

Aboriginal bark painting can show a high level of design. This one done at Groote Eylandt was purchased by the Native Welfare officer holding it.

35/NORTHERN TERRITORY

Gove's bauxite treatment plant, from the air, as it looked under construction for Nabalco in November 1970. The plant will produce alumina.

Painted cave at Oenpelli in Arnhem Land shows the "x-ray" type of
Aboriginal art that patterns the anatomy of fish and other creatures.

36/NORTHERN TERRITORY

A boy for initiation at Yirrkala (near Gove in Arnhem Land) has his chest
painted with totemic designs and is being "sung" by the man with the clap-sticks.

lysed buffaloes, down by the hindquarters, eyes full of flies, agonized by thirst as well as the pain of a shattered spinal column they had endured for some sixteen hours before deliverance came with a revolver bullet between the eyes.

Economically, it made sense. The shooters could shoot until dark and skin next day. Left alive all night, the buffaloes were easier to skin.

I wrote about this cruelty in a chapter of *Adam in Ochre*[11] titled "The Buffalo Dies Next Day". Before that I did a radio documentary called "The Buffalo Shooters" for the Australian Broadcasting Commission, for whom I was then writing on contract. This was recorded and ready to go on the air when I got a telegram from the A.B.C.'s then Director of Drama and Features, Neil Hutchinson, saying TODAY BOYER REMOVED BUFFALO SHOOTERS FROM PROGRAMME.

The late Sir Richard Boyer, a godly man who was then the Commission's chairman, had said, "The A.B.C. is not *Smith's Weekly*", meaning that the A.B.C. did not go in for *exposés* as that paper did. So they got a staff man to restructure "The Buffalo Shooters" (I was not prepared to change it), and the part about leaving the shot beasts alive overnight was not excised entirely, but it got minimal mention in the feature as it went on the air. Ironically enough, the editor of *Smith's Weekly*, Eddie Dunstan, happened to hear it —and he wrote a piece that ripped into the A.B.C. for its "callousness" in passing over this cruelty.

The publicity helped to get the practice stopped. When, a few years ago, an A.B.C. "Four Corners" television team got a Marrakai shooter to demonstrate how the buffalo industry used to operate, there was a public outcry. But I am not suggesting that spine shooting stopped because it was exposed as being abominably cruel so much as because it was no longer a practical method when the basis of the industry changed from hides to meat.

Buffalo-shooting is a business, but it can never be a sport. Racing up on them in a jeep and pumping bullets into a bull with a big set of horns to mount on the wall as a trophy has no more validity as hunting than going into a paddock and shooting a dairy cow.

On DAY 4 the tour had its picnic lunch by the East Alligator River at the crossing where the road goes on ten miles to Oenpelli Mission, and where a notice board says YOU ARE ABOUT TO ENTER AN ABORIGINAL RESERVE and then says that if you do, without authorization, the first-offence penalty is a fine of $200 or six months jail or both.

Back at Jim Jim we found a swimming place, one that was apparently croc-free, near Tom Opitz's store, and afterwards felt refreshed and in good appetite for the final-night barbecue dinner of grilled buffalo steak and roast barramundi. The nights were so still at Jim Jim, and the Milky Way so bright, and if you got up early in the morning you disturbed wallabies feeding right beside the cabins.

We left at nine o'clock for Darwin, heading west through paper-bark country with red-earth termite hills and here and there the yellow-flowered wild kapok. Beyond the South Alligator there was a billabong white with birds and, after crossing the dusty bed of the Mary River, the vast and treeless Marrakai plain. Dun-coloured in this dry season, it would be bright green in the Wet when it turns into a quagmire, with such depth to the mud that the builders of a bridge had to sink ninety-five feet to get a base on rock. Buffalo herds grazed on the plain and buffaloes lay up in the midday heat among the paperbarks round the billabongs. We had lunch beside one that was loud with the sound of magpie geese, all talking about our intrusion, and black cockatoos screeched from the trees. Clive the driver pointed out a fruit like a miniature orange. It was *Strychnos nux-vomica* that yields the poisonous drug strychnine.

A larger river than we had seen, the Adelaide, looped its way across the plain of Humpty Doo. That name (a corruption of what the Aborigines called Umdudu) is not likely to be forgotten by the Americans and others who invested a lot of money there in a rice-growing project that began in 1955. Territory Rice Ltd was the brainchild of an American millionaire, Allen T. Chase. Another heavy investor was Art Linkletter, the television showman and author. He has written that Australia's late Prime Minister, Harold Holt ("an old friend of Allen's and mine") said at Chase's Bel Air home in California, in 1954 when Holt was Federal Treasurer, "As the western United States was perhaps a hundred years ago, so Australia is today—on the verge of a rich expansion. Nowhere else in the world is there a place where money invested will pay such high dividends."[12] Which proved to be true enough in the case of Esso's investment in oil search in Bass Strait (with B.H.P.), but when the Territory Rice investors eventually abandoned their project, in Linkletter's words "more than two million dollars had gone down the drain".[13]

Unquestionably rice can be grown on these flood plains, and the Humpty Doo enterprise grew it. But, although it had Sir William Gunn, the Australian wool industry chief, as its adviser, mistakes were made on a massive scale as to the kind of rice planted, the methods of planting and the flood engineering with dikes and pumps that did not cope with the Wet season deluge. Moreover, the magpie geese flocked in. Chase, according to Douglas Lockwood,[14] sent a telegram to his Darwin manager, "SHOOT EVERY GODDAM GOOSE IN

THE NORTHERN TERRITORY" and Linkletter writes, "We must have killed a million of these birds."

The C.S.I.R.O. Chief of Wildlife Research, Dr H. J. Frith, made a study of the magpie geese's habits. It was then pointed out that the geese were ". . . not digging for rice at all but for the sedge bulbs *Eleocharis*. It was true that, when the rice plants came up, the birds did graze the young shoots and poach the ground, and may have done some damage, but they also did good by encouraging the roots to tiller [put up shoots]. . . . The conclusion was that both the number of magpie geese involved, and the extent of the damage, had been greatly exaggerated."[15]

Some of the rice was, in the Wet, five feet under water. A Los Angeles millionaire, Robert McCullough, who was induced to take up 800,000 shares to carry on the project after its first season's failure, ended up by selling his holding for a token two dollars.

Humpty Doo's failure did surprisingly little to discourage American investment in the Territory. Witness the Tipperary Project, a hundred miles south of Darwin on the flats of the Daly River. Here the Tipperary Land Corporation in 1967 took up 192,000 acres to plant it with grain sorghum. The proposal to spend $20 million of mainly American money in developing this land by 1972 envisaged its being cut up into farms and Australian farmers being financed onto them, with a Daly River community growing to 12,000 people. The sorghum was not being grown as grain food for cattle but for export to Japan at the rate of 300,000 tons a year. Huge agricultural equipment had been brought in. The first season's crop was below expectations. There were fears then that Tipperary sorghum would be added to the Territory's long list of agricultural failures that began with sugar back in the 1880s. It was a relief to find that sorghum-growing had not been specifically foredoomed in Dr Bruce Davidson's devastating book *The Northern Myth*, in which this agricultural economist contends that any crop grown in the Territory "could be produced at lower cost south of the tropic". In 1971 Tipperary was reported a failure.

Davidson has declared, "Northern development is proceeding at the expense of the Australian standard of living."[16] Where no government subsidies are involved or any costly dams for irrigation, it is hard to see why that should be so, particularly when the finance comes from overseas. Admittedly, in the case of Humpty Doo, the Federal Government did spend a million dollars on a dead-loss area by putting in power lines and a sealed road to it. However, this road also serves the productive Mount Bundey iron mine.

So now we are back on the bitumen, and this soon joins the Stuart Highway. The termite mounds we stop to see are dark grey and slim, like very old eroded tombstones. These, up to twelve feet high and seldom more than a foot through their width of about three feet, are the true "magnetic" anthills, their ends orientated north-south.

The trees are greener now, and there are no more water-buffaloes. Houses appear, perched high on piles for coolness, with garden flamboyance of the magenta bougainvillea. The sou'-east breeze streams seaward through the fronds of the first coconut-palms. We are coming into Darwin.

The Darwin Evolution

DARWIN, with a population of 30,000, was a hundred years old in 1969, but didn't look it. The fastest growing capital looked new, and it was virtually a new city that had been built on the ruins of the only place in Australia that was extensively bombed in World War II: and what the Japanese bombers didn't destroy the Australian Army in occupation did. After the war "the designers of the New Darwin envisaged the site as vacant land".[1]

The Old Darwin was, by all accounts, a disreputable back door to Australia that appalled not a few air travellers. I first saw the new place in 1948 when the rebuilding was half-heartedly under way. What I liked most about it then was the lush growth and colour of its tropical trees and shrubs—the glorious *Poinciana regia* was in vermilion bloom—and the airy louvred houses hoisted in gardens full of frangipani and crotons. I liked, too, the palmy edges of Darwin's sea-girt situation on the head of a peninsula.

Twenty-one years later I found myself liking the same things about a Darwin whose population had increased tenfold; and so many new buildings had burgeoned, including an impressive Post Office and a couple of churches of rather formidable modernity. Darwin's growth had been too much for its peninsula to contain. What I had known as Darwin was now but the comet-head to a broad tail of suburbs, each with its own shopping centre and with big regional schools breaking the rectilinear pattern of brick bungalows. On wide raw acres of newly-bulldozed land more houses were rising in a sprawl of neighbourhoods miles from the sea and without a hub. This centreless Darwin was hard to define civically—but a Department of the Interior booklet defined it in other terms as *Darwin . . . A Way of Life*.

Meaning what? Climatically, complete escape from winter: the July average minimum was 67.8 degrees as against 50 in Melbourne

—with a November-March wet season when about 68 inches of rain fell, temperatures went into the nineties, and the humidity discomfort was high. Women could wear cotton frocks year round, and men could go to the office in shorts and tieless. For semi-formal wear what was called "Darwin Rig" consisted of long-sleeved white shirt, tie, long trousers and dark shoes. This was even all right on some Government House occasions that did not call for "Darwin Formal" with black bow tie and cummerbund, white jacket optional.

Commercially, it was a place where Sydney or Melbourne head office was apt to forget that Darwin branch had more work to do than staff to do it with. Governmentally, the same was said of Canberra's attitude to Darwin. The Director of Welfare could often be found in his office at night.

Recreationally, Darwin dealt a full hand on clubs—from "service" clubs like Rotary and Apex to the R.S.L., the Royal and Ancient Order of Buffaloes, and the Workers Club where beer went with indoor bowls, which also flourished outdoors, as golf did and night-lit basketball. Of sport there was so much that playing fields had to be rostered for the football that was played in the sweaty "summer" and the cricket in what would have been the winter months if there had been any winter. In competition sport there was no colour bar at all. In cosmopolitan Darwin, sport, like beer, was very much part of life. At weekends there was also the beckoning of a fascinating hinterland, as well as the bookmakers calling the odds at Fannie Bay racecourse every Saturday.

Culturally, sports-mad Darwin was pretty arid. It didn't get a bookshop until 1969 (and television till August 1971). However, there were occasional falls of manna and one resident said, "Where else could you sit on the lawn, beer in the Esky beside you, and watch the Australian Ballet?" The ballet had performed in what is called the sound shell in the Darwin Botanic Gardens.

What, though, did Darwin have for the tourist, the visitor?

It was certainly much improved on what it used to be. In 1948 at the Hotel Darwin, then the best place, I had asked for a pink gin. The waiter brought a dark brown concoction that tasted sweet, and I asked the barman what on earth he had given me. He bridled: "The waiter says you want a pink gin, and I say, 'What's that?' and he says he asked you and you said it was gin and angostura bitters, and I say, 'What's he want with it?' and the waiter says, 'I dunno', so I say, 'Give him lemonade'. . . . How much bitters did I put in it? Only a teaspoon, that's all. And I've mixed drinks for better bloody men than you!"

I felt sure that the Hotel Darwin now knew what a pink gin

was, and the staff I found very mannerly. However, the brewery that owns the place appeared to have spent little on the rooms in twenty years, and the refrigerator lacked an ice-cube tray or water jug. I much preferred the Koala Motel, which was fully licensed and, although it had better rooms and better meals, was no more expensive. (Accommodation rates in Darwin run high.)

"Darwin should concentrate on becoming a city noted for its flowers and gardens," the American travel consultants said in their 1965 report.[2] Having walked through the Botanic Gardens and seen the Aboriginal Museum within its precincts, what else did the tourist in Darwin do? See the Chinese joss house, still a going concern, open fronted and very Kodachromatic for the photographer. Visit Mindil Beach. Have a drink at the palmy Fannie Bay Hotel. Watch the sun go down from the Nightcliff. In the evening there were dine-and-dance places as well as the welcoming clubs; and the visitor was likely to be shown "local colour" in terms of the nightly rort at the Don Hotel, where a concrete dance floor was open to the street and Aboriginal women danced and got drunk with the only kind of white men who would dance and drink and perhaps go off with them. In short, there was nothing very much in Darwin itself worth travelling a thousand miles to see. Rather was it a tourist base.

Of hinterland tours there was the "Arnhemlander" I had been on to Jim Jim and there were others dubbed "safaris". These safari camps provided for the hunter, although one of the operators, Alan Stewart, an old acquaintance met in Darwin, said that nowadays most of the people he was getting were not concerned with shooting; but they liked hooking a twenty-pound barramundi out of a waterhole at Nourlangie.

Nearer Darwin there were, for the excursionist, such places as the Yarrawonga fauna park complete with crocodiles (13 miles), Howard Springs (16 m.), Fogg Dam bird sanctuary (18 m.), Berry Springs (30 m.), Manton Dam (42 m.) and one-day "safari" runs to see buffalo and birds on the Marrakai Plain. And there were excursions across Darwin's harbour.

Mandorah is an hour's ferry run and the tourist attraction was Aboriginal corroboree dances. Normally there were eight dancers, the resort proprietor said, "But today's pay day and two of them are drunk. You have to give them the booze. If you withhold it they won't come to dance." They were Waugeits and I had seen this tribe's dancing at Delissaville Aboriginal Settlement. It was ranked by the American dance authority Ted Shawn as the best primitive dancing he had seen anywhere in the world. The dancer Mosek (who died of cancer in 1950) Shawn described as "a great dance artist, in world class". These Waugeits at Mandorah were much less than Moseks, but the dance quality was still there, the quick authority of movement of their lithe bodies and lean legs. This, though, was hardly the way to present Aboriginal dancing to tourists.

There was need, I felt, for what might be called a Directorate of Aboriginal Arts that would be concerned with the preservation of the dance forms to a high standard and their presentation with dignity and artistic discipline, the performers having the status and rewards of dance artists. These distinctive Australian art forms— Aboriginal dance and bark painting and some carving (which is only good in Arnhem Land)—merited being nurtured at a level of appreciation the tourist industry was not showing it, although tourism had much to gain from it. (Aboriginal art forms now come within the concern of the Australian Council for the Arts.)

MICA BEACH was the other place I went to across the harbour. A lusty Dane, Axel Sindholt, and his wife had worked very hard to build up a restaurant and attract tourists, and Axel's dream was that one day it would be the "Tivoli of the north—all pretty".

The best idea he had was taking people for a walk of about a mile, a bushcraft *wonga*, with three Aborigines. These Waugeits, who had put on their tribal markings in white pipeclay and brought along their spears, pointed out such plants as the wild passionfruit and the "strychnine bush" that yielded a native medicine from its roots, and a red-flowering tree with a seedpod they said was "good tucker", but the juice was blinding if you got it in your eye.

They made fire by twirling a stick in another holed stick and blowing up the spark in grass tinder. They cooked a fish and, while it was baking, one of them, Minita, did a dance while Jardad played the didjeridoo and Mulloch beat rhythm and was the songman. The fish we were invited to share tasted very good. Then they demonstrated spear-throwing, and showed us how to hold the spear against the throwing-stick, the *woomera*. None of us could hurl a spear straight or nearly as far as they could.

Not much of the tourist potential of the Darwin region had been developed. Melville Island, about fifty miles north, has the vital Tiwi tribe whose corroboree, called *yoi*, is the most spectacular I have ever seen, or heard, with the singing rising to a remarkable crescendo. Cruises to Melville's Aboriginal settlement at Snake Bay were supposed to be developed back in 1966 by the N.T. Tourist Board. Connellan Airways flew there and to adjoining Bathurst Island where there is a Roman Catholic Mission. Its founder, Father Francis Xavier Gsell, who became Bishop of Darwin, was known as

the "bishop with 150 wives". He had bought the Aboriginal girls—
the price was usually some calico, a tomahawk, sugar and tobacco
—when such girls of puberty age had shown reluctance to become
the wives of polygamous old men of the tribe. They grew up as
wards of the Mission to marry younger men of their own choice.

The Aboriginal custom of betrothing girl children to old men,
who claimed them as brides when they reached puberty, has two
social justifications in the eyes of the tribe, or at least of its elders:
(i) Young men could not marry before they were initiated and dis-
ciplined and, as Elkin puts it, "The early marriage of the girls to
the old men means that the former are protected, whereas if this
form of marriage be stopped, loose living results between these girls
and the youths",[3] (ii) "It ensures an efficient provider of food in
the old age of the man and his old wife if he has one."[4]

The situation had changed. Of nearly 21,000 full-blood Aborigines
in the Territory only 300 or so were still living in a state of tribal
nomadism: the rest comprised 6,300 on Aboriginal settlements,
6,000 on Missions, 4,200 on pastoral properties, 2,500 in township
areas, 1,000 in small mining communities—and all the aged and in-
digent were entitled to receive social service payments on the same
basis as other Australians.

The Director of Welfare, who gave me those figures, was very
much against this old-man/young-girl marriage. "Such girls may
bear four or five children before they are twenty-one," he said.
"At Maningrida settlement we have girls of fourteen or fifteen with
babies, girls still going to school. The young women are beginning
to object. If a girl appeals to us that she doesn't want to be the
second or third wife of some old man, we'll back her up. We'll
invoke the under-sixteen age of consent law."

THE ABORIGINAL EVOLUTION

THE DIRECTOR, Harry (H. C.) Giese, was an impressive Civil
Servant, physically tall, good in looks and personality, intelligent
and articulate. In the matter of Aboriginal advancement, he said, he
was dealing largely with a young population. At some settlements
more than half were under the age of sixteen.

When Harry Giese came to the Welfare post in 1954 fewer than
five hundred Aboriginal children were getting any education in
government, as apart from mission, schools. Now six thousand were.
It was progress in which he could feel pride; but he was inclined
to give the credit to Paul Hasluck (now Sir Paul, Australia's Governor-General) who, in 1951 when he became Minister for Territories, instituted a New Deal for Aborigines: not that it gave them
much or recognized any land rights.

Before 1950 the Aborigines were considered to be dying out, and the policy was one of "pillow-smoothing" their passing. I think I was the first to write that they were *not* dying out (*Adam in Ochre*, 1951). Dr W. E. H. Stanner substantiated this from the Port Keats (N.T.) area in 1952, and in 1953 Professor A. P. Elkin said that they had "turned the corner". The increase in the number of full-bloods in the Northern Territory since 1950 has been close to fifty per cent, and Mr Giese said he expected that today's 21,000 would become double that number in the 1990s.

In any assessment of what White Australia is doing government- ally for Black Australians, and what it is possible to do for them, or reasonable to reproach Australia for not doing, three things have to be considered. Firstly, our forbears did take away from them their tribal lands, in order to pasture sheep and cattle and grow crops, and by this dispossession made continuance of their tribal life impracticable. Secondly, white retaliation against Aboriginal resistance to our invasion was, in many cases, extremely brutal. There are many evidences that this was so, including this one from Alfred Searcy's book:[5] "I had a letter from a man who was attacked by niggers in the Gulf country: 'I shoot on sight. Have killed thirty-seven to date.' Another man boasted that he inflicted his punishment with a stockwhip and a wirecracker. To be particularly severe he sharpened a piece of sapling and drove it through both hands of the offender. He assured me that he was ceasing to have trouble with the niggers." Thirdly, in relation to the Northern Territory, not until eighty years after the settlement of Darwin was any attempt made by the government to begin educating these people in a way that would fit them to become Australian citizens. In 1950 twelve mission schools were teaching nearly 600 children, after a fashion, and the Commonwealth had taken some steps to teach half-castes, but for fully Aboriginal children it had done nothing.

If it had not been for the work of the missions, the Aboriginal full-bloods in the Territory would probably have died down to a much smaller number than the 14,000 there were when the New Deal came in 1951. Missions taught the black people little that was not about God and Jesus, but at least they gave them protection and sustenance and there was communication with them and under- standing of them. Their languages, and through their languages their customs, were studied, notably by such missionaries as Streh- low (and his son T. G. H. Strehlow) in the Centre and Fr. Ernest Worms in the West.

That 6,000 children now got government-provided pre-schooling or primary schooling; that Kormilda College in Darwin had about

130 Aboriginal students (it was for them entirely, and residential) gaining an education with a stress on manual and domestic science skills; that 28 Aborigines were pupils in Darwin High School in 1969 (and Harry Giese expected that there would be 200 high-schoolers by 1975): this was all very creditable and the Director and his staff were entitled to a sense of educational achievement. But it did not mean that what the Welfare Branch of the Administration was doing was adequate to the so-long-neglected needs of the Aborigines in education, health, housing and employment opportunities and conditions.

The Welfare Branch could work only within what the Commonwealth Government laid down as policy and with the finance it provided. The policy's key word was "assimilation" and the way this was being put into effect was called "gradualism".

Unless the transition from one way of life to another is made gradually, Harry Giese said, the native people become confused. There is validity to this "gradualism", up to a point; but it can also become the basis of much government rationalizing and the great excuse for not doing enough soon enough and not spending enough. It has been abandoned as the policy in New Guinea, where Australia has had to do more and do it faster to prepare the people for independence, and spend proportionately more than is being spent on native advancement within Australia, because New Guinea is a Trust Territory under the inspecting eye of the United Nations.

What the Commonwealth is spending on Aboriginal advancement in the Territory now looks big ($6 million in 1970) because what it used to spend was so little ($400,000 when Giese began in 1954). And money, up there, does not go very far. A house for a school-teacher that could be built "down south" for $10,000 cost $28,000 to build at Maningrida Aboriginal Settlement on the north coast of Arnhem Land. It seems incredible, even taking into consideration the freight on the materials and the high wages of the white workers who do the building and their having to be accommodated. But that is what the Director of Welfare said a house cost. Why could not Aboriginal workers build the houses? Because we hadn't taught them how to. Kormilda College is doing something about remedying that ignorance, and an Aboriginal building team had recently been developed.

SETTLEMENTS as isolated as Maningrida are wrong in the opinion of such critics of Commonwealth policy and the Welfare Branch of the Administration as Frank Stevens. When he was a Research Fellow in the Economic History department at the Australian National University, Stevens wrote that at such places the Aborigines are "removed from the centres of exposure, experience and workforce absorption"; such settlements were "a major obstacle to assimilating Aborigines into the broader Australian community" and—here he speaks with the authority of one who has worked with Negro, Mexican and Indian rural labour in the United States and also worked for the United Nations in the Middle East—he charged that the Administration "persists in their operation in defiance of world-wide experience in the process of readjustment of detribalised native people".[6]

Frank Stevens also wrote, in 1968, "Although the Northern Territory European workforce has multiplied by nearly 400 per cent since the Second World War, there are, today, fewer Aborigines employed in the general community than there were during the War."

The Montgomery Report[7] said in 1970: "Today only one in fourteen school-leavers in the Northern Territory can be placed in employment."

Not only is unemployment demoralizing and lack of employment unjust in terms of opportunity, but the conditions of Aboriginal employment have been discreditable, as the Montgomery Report pointed out. One of Stevens's criticisms of the Welfare Branch was: "Not one employer of Aboriginal labour has been prosecuted for failure to meet the legal conditions of employment established some twenty years ago. . . ."[8] A 1965 survey found that on one property the value of rations other than meat amounted to less than five shillings (fifty cents) per person per week.[9]

Health services in the early sixties were so inadequate that Aboriginal mortality in the Centre was 250 deaths per thousand births, ten times higher than for white Australia, "probably the highest in the world."[10]

Director Giese said that up to 1956 infant Aboriginal deaths were not recorded. The 1969 rate he gave as ninety per thousand births, which he described as "still extremely high". The principal killer was gastro-enteritis.

Although the Commonwealth grants to the States for Aboriginal advancement increased forty per cent in 1970 to a total $7 million, of which $4.8 million was to be spent on housing, the Aboriginal situation could still remain so deplorable that, as Dr Desmond Crowley[11] has said, "Australia will face charges of inhumanity by world opinion which will not be easy to answer."

IN DARWIN it was a Saturday when Mick Fryer, the helpful manager of the Koala Motel, telephoned Harry Giese, whom I had not met, and said I wanted to talk to him. I did not expect that the Director of Welfare would be available until Monday, but he came round that night, picked me up and took me to his office, where we talked until nearly half past eleven. Then he drove me out to Bagot Native Settlement where about five hundred Aborigines live in Darwin.

Bagot used to be a hospital before the big new one was built and much of the accommodation was converted from the old wards, but there was some much better-looking new housing. Most of the people were asleep, but I talked to Davis Daniels, vice-president of the Bagot Council. The Aboriginal Councillors act as overseers of the settlement. They could have had a wet canteen, but had decided that there were nearby hotels where people could drink, and they didn't have to drink on the settlement.

"Maybe when we get our co-op store, which will sell liquor, we can set up a social club," Davis Daniels said.

The Council president had just come from his job at the airport —he was an aircraft cleaner for TAA—and was sitting out in front of his house on the lawn that he had planted with a border of crotons. Inside I could see such furnishings as a refrigerator. George was a very reliable worker, the Director said. One of the street lights shone into a window sufficiently to show some of the ceramic pots of the woman who was running a pottery class on the settlement. The place was as still as the pots. Bagot was probably the quietest part of Darwin at midnight on that Saturday night.

Harry Giese drove me back to the motel and came in to have the drink he had declined earlier. I had a bottle of whisky and Mick Fryer joined us and we drank it slowly and talked until 2 a.m. I didn't make any further notes but recall the Director of Welfare saying, "I'd like to bring more pressure against plural marriages. But how to do that without vitiating something else? You need to have the wisdom of Solomon in this job."

And he had a nice story of a bright Aboriginal young man who had been sent south on some study project and who had written to say, "Better get me back home soon. These Sydney sheilas get blacker every day."

The Pregnant "Eldorado"

A PREDICTION was made in 1885 that, "The peninsula of Arnhem Land will yet become one of the greatest mining centres in Australia",[1] and three years later: "I doubt that any province will be found in any country so singularly favoured as Arnhem Land in respect of mineral riches."[2]

Both predictions were made by a remarkable man of Australian science, Julian Tenison-Woods, who came under the Newman influence at Oxford, joined the Roman Catholic Church and took holy orders. This did not prevent his steeping himself in geology, palaeontology, zoology and botany. As geological adviser to the South Australian government on mining and railway developments he made

Northern Territory journeys that broke his health and he died in 1889, the year after he prophesied that Arnhem Land would become, in the eyes of the world, a sort of Eldorado.

Nearly a century after Tenison-Woods's first prediction the Arnhem Land Aboriginal Reserve is, indeed, becoming "one of the greatest mining centres in Australia" although not in terms of the minerals the geologist-priest was thinking of—gold, silver, copper and lead. This region of 35,000 square miles, bigger than Austria, has been until recent years a kind of sanctuary for about 4,000 Aborigines, sequestered and virginal. Today it is pregnant and about to give birth to:

1. The largest mining enterprise and third largest town in the Northern Territory, Nhulunbuy on the bauxite-rich Gove Peninsula.

2. A controversial but still very rich uranium mine, at Nabarlek (pron. Narbalek), east of Oenpelli.

3. A new concept of the Reserve, with consideration of the Aboriginal Australian's right to share in the mineral wealth being found in his tribal lands.

What else I think will happen—and predict that this will happen within ten years—is that Arnhem Land will cease to be an Aboriginal Reserve. This will come about, it is hoped, not because the region has been thrown open to greedy exploitation, but because parts of it will have passed into the hands of Aborigines who, living on their own land, will have no need to live on a reservation. One can also hope that large areas of it will, within a decade, be gazetted as National Parkland.

The concept of Arnhem Land as an inviolable Aboriginal reserve, proclaimed in 1931, was modified in 1952 by this provision: "If any part of a native reserve has ceased to be necessary for the use and benefit of the natives it may be severed from the reserve and, if mining takes place on the severed portion, royalties will be paid into a special fund to be applied to the welfare of the natives."

This modification was to allow the mining of the first deposits of high-grade bauxite that had been found in 1950 at Marchinbar (one of the Wessel Islands) off the north-east tip. Further deposits were found in 1955 at Gove, the name given to the north-east peninsula when it was an air base during World War II.

Manganese, essential in steel making, was another mineral Australia had felt the lack of during that war. The largest deposits in Australia, and high-grade manganese at that, were discovered in 1960 on Groote Eylandt. Although in the Gulf of Carpentaria, this "Great Island" of the Dutch discoverers is, like many a lesser island, part of the Arnhem Land Reserve, B.H.P. moved in and mining began in 1966.

The "richest uranium mine in the world", not yet a mine, will be based on a discovery made in June 1970. It happened thus: A retired hospital matron in Adelaide, Mrs Gwendoline Stevens, who knew nothing about mining and had never been to the Northern Territory, thought she would like to prospect, and some friends at the Bureau of Mineralogy said not to overlook uranium. On their advice she picked a claim area of 1,282 square miles in the Aboriginal Reserve, near Oenpelli. Unable to prospect herself, she optioned the claim to Queensland Mines Ltd who commissioned an aerial survey. When the survey plane was over a point eighteen miles east of Oenpelli its gamma-ray spectrometer gear set up a furious chattering.

Ground prospecting revealed, only four feet below the surface, a thick core of uranite (pitchblende). Drilling then intersected an occurrence of pitchblende so rich that it assayed an unprecedented 1,300 pounds of U308 (uranium oxide) to the ton. (*Three* pounds to the ton is regarded as payable. One gramme of uranium can produce as much heat as three tons of average coal, and one ton of uranium as much as 30,000 tons of coal.)

There were "indicated reserves of 55,000 short tons of uranium oxide" it was announced by Queensland Mines in September 1970. The average grade was given as a phenomenal 540 pounds to the metric (2,000 lbs) ton. At the ruling price of, say, $6 a pound, such reserves would have been worth $660 million. Nabarlek was proclaimed "the richest uranium mine in the world".

Consternation in investment circles followed a statement that issued in mid-August 1971 from the Queensland Mines board (from which a director representing Noranda Mines Ltd, a big Canadian uranium producer, dramatically resigned). This statement downgraded the Nabarlek reserves of U308 from 55,000 metric tons to 8976. It said drilling had outlined reserves of (a) 400,000 m-tons of ore averaging 16 pounds of uranium oxide, a total of 3,200 m-tons, and (b) 48,000 m-tons of high-grade ore averaging 240 pounds, a total of 5,760 m-tons of U308. This gave an overall average of 40 pounds to the m-ton, as against the earlier indication of 540 pounds. Valued at $6 a pound, the uranium oxide in these lodes would be worth under $108 million, less than a sixth of the originally-inferred value of $660 million.

The shares of Queensland Mines and its half owner, Kathleen Investments (Australia) Ltd, were temporarily suspended. An inquiry began and adjourned (and this edition had to be finalized).

It was truly a bad, confidence-shaking situation; and it could turn out to be complex in its causes. A power struggle within the company could have had a bearing on the downgrading statement being issued *before the drilling programme was completed.* The drilling of other Nabarlek orebodies was unlikely to be completed before the end of the year. My information was that such drilling could result in a significant re-assessment of Nabarlek's potential.

The fact remained that, at an average 40 pounds of uranium oxide to the metric ton, Nabarlek was still very rich as uranium mines go. (Mary Kathleen averaged only two-to-five pounds.)

A HUGE DEPOSIT that appeared to be Australia's largest uranium lode (though it was not of Nabarlek's grade-richness) was reported in October 1970 by Peko-Wallsend Ltd. This Ranger 1 prospect was on the western side of the East Alligator, outside the Arnhem Land Reserve. Drilling reports given by the company in August 1971 indicated 71,000 metric tons of uranium oxide. The grade was given as approximately 7 pounds of U308 to the metric ton.

Still another deposit had been found near Jim Jim Creek by Noranda Australia Ltd, the Canadian backed company that had bought an interest in Queensland Mines and in Kathleen Investments. (This gave Noranda about a seven and a half per cent holding in Q.M. It had been decreed from Canberra that foreign holdings in either could not exceed fifteen per cent.)

The Peko prospect is only about 30 miles from Nabarlek. One township and road system could possibly serve both enterprises. Within eight miles of Nabarlek there was ample water for a town.

There are interesting rock formations near Nabarlek, including a sacred one (PLATE 35), and many Aboriginal paintings of the area.

THE BEST GALLERY of cave paintings in Australia is in the hill called Unbalanja (or Inyaluk) about a mile from the Oenpelli Mission. Bill Harney had taken me to them when I was at Oenpelli with the Arnhem Land Expedition. I wanted to see them again. The only way I could do so—having got a permit to enter the Reserve and a telegraphed O.K. from the mission—was to get off the Connellan plane that went on to Maningrida and have a rushed look before the plane came back in an hour. The mission had a jeep waiting and an old Aboriginal named Jacob to accompany me to Unbalanja hill.

There they were—the Mimi women running, the best x-ray kangaroo I've ever seen, the shoal of ochre barramundi swimming across the cave roof, the grotesque sorcery drawings, the whole marvellous collection I had written of in *Adam in Ochre* twenty years before. I took photographs (PLATE 36), and all too soon it was time to go.

The great billabong lagoon below Unbalanja was alive with birds, though not so many as I remembered. The mission superintendent, the Reverend Alf Wilson, admitted that there were fewer magpie geese and said he was trying to restrict the taking of eggs for tucker.

I asked Mr Wilson how much longer he thought the great Aboriginal art gallery could remain closed to tourists. He said he was against tourists coming in, though the mission did occasionally have such visitors.

"The tourists I've seen I haven't much respect for," he said. "They come and they gawp and have little appreciation of the paintings. Tomorrow they will have forgotten what they saw."

37/NORTHERN TERRITORY *Corroboree dance at Yirrkala (near Gove) of Aborigines smeared with pipeclay. Man at rear right is blowing the wooden dronetube, the didjeridoo, while man at left beats rhythm with sticks.*

At Gove peninsula in Arnhem Land what will be the Territory's third largest town, Nhulunbuy, was being built behind this beach, preserving the foreshore.

Near Nabarlek in Arnhem Land, where a particularly rich uranium deposit was found in June 1970, is this rock formation Aborigines hold sacred.

The missionary said that the Aboriginal people did not want tourists. I could not accept that the people knew what they wanted in this matter. Tourism would enable them to earn more money; and there are much worse jobs than being a tourist guide.

The notable uranium find at Nabarlek was not made until some months after I was at Oenpelli, so there was no discussion of what it would mean to the Aborigines in terms of employment and what else they would get out of it. In the matter of land rights, none was living tribally on the Nabarlek lease area (which Queensland Mines has extended to 3,000 square miles), nor was any of it part of the mission's lease.

It can be argued that, left in the possession of the blacks without white intrusion or left inviolate as Aboriginal Reserve land for their "use and benefit", such areas of Arnhem Land would have produced nothing for them except kangaroos to hunt, yams to dig, and other subsistence; and if the Aborigines got no more than employment opportunities to work for the mining companies, digging out the ore and driving trucks, supplying the buffalo steaks and growing vegetables, they were still better off—as a result of the development of the area by white technology and enterprise. Moreover, they were now Australian citizens and as such would share the general benefits that accrued nationally from the discovery and exploitation of such mineral riches.

However, the Aborigines had been for so long a disadvantaged people. Whereas a white Mrs Stevens of Adelaide could take out a prospecting lease, a black Australian of Oenpelli was hardly in the position to do so. (The Croker Island people in 1970 applied for a prospecting lease that was disallowed on the score that the application was "not properly worded".)

Where the Aborigines were at a major disadvantage was that their tribal lands had been taken into the ownership of the Crown, i.e. the nation; and, although this land had been reserved for their "use and benefit" they owned none of it, nor did they hold any part of it on lease.

It would have been against the policy of Australian mining law—which is, broadly, "to make all of the mineral wealth of the nation accessible to persons who are able and willing to conduct mining operations, regardless of questions of abstract ownership"[3]—for the Commonwealth to have made over land to the Aborigines which gave them ownership of the minerals in the land. With few exceptions, white Australian land owners have no such entitlement to mineral rights, and their lands can be prospected even without their consent if the mining warden grants an "authority to enter". Crown Lands

AA

can, in general, be prospected by anyone—or anyone with the requisite permits to enter such places as the Arnhem Land Reserve.

If the area where the Nabarlek uranium was found had happened to be land that had been granted, mineral rights inclusive, to an Oenpelli Aborigines co-operative called Gunwinngu Buffalo Raisers, they could have set any figure they liked on its value, in cash or royalties. If it had been on lease to them they could have negotiated the best figure the mining warden's court would agree to. Since they have no such entitlement and the land is Crown Land, the Government will get royalties on the value of the uranium mined.

Of such royalties, the Commonwealth Government's intention is, I understand, to pay a substantial part, probably the major part, into a trust fund for the benefit of Aborigines of the Northern Territory. Nobody can say, at this stage, how much this will be. However, if it be assumed that Queensland Mines can get contracts to sell its uranium, and if the price is still $7 a pound when production starts (as is proposed) in 1973, it could be as much as 1,000 tons in the first year, yielding a gross $14 million.

Suppose the royalty were $2\frac{1}{2}$ per cent on the gross and the Commonwealth paid into the Aboriginal Trust fund 2 per cent. This could amount to over $250,000.

Lest it be thought that an over-generous proportion of the revenue accruing to the Commonwealth from such mineral riches in the Territory is being given back to the Territory blacks, it is to be remembered that, as J. G. Gorton said when he was Prime Minister, "From any such discovery, we [the Commonwealth Government as the taxation authority] get half."

The profits tax is $47\frac{1}{2}$ per cent, and royalties make up the rest.

THE "GODSEND" AT GROOTE

AFTER the Dutch navigator Abel Tasman named the large (*groote*) island he sighted in 1644 no other European came near it until 1803, when Matthew Flinders and his artist William Westall landed on rugged Chasm Island just off Groote's north coast and recorded the first Aboriginal cave paintings found in Australia.

On Groote itself—the island is about forty miles long and nearly as wide as that in the south—there are many cave paintings. Some depict Indonesian praus from Macassar. These had been coming to this northern coast before the Dutch appeared and dubbed it Arnhem Land: the Berndts[1] refer to the "first visits of the Macassan traders in the sixteenth century", and the traders continued to come until 1907. They came to gather trepang (*bêche-de-mer*) to sell to the Chinese. From the Macassarmen these Aborigines learnt how to make dugout canoes and to carve wooden images, such as the formalized head of a man to set up on his gravepost. From the Malay trepangers they first got steel, cloth, tobacco, alcohol and the tamarisk-tree. Intercourse left a slight tincture of Indonesian blood in these Arnhemlanders, and it widened their horizons in a way that happened to Aborigines only on the north and north-west coasts. Some sailed on the praus to Macassar and Java and east to New Guinea.

When the first missionaries set foot on Groote in 1907 the natives they met spoke no word of English but could hold some converse in Malay. The Church Missionary Society didn't establish itself there until 1921. The early years produced "continual dissension between the Aborigines and the missionaries"[2] who at one stage built a stockade against an expected attack.

On the near mainland there were, in the early 1930s, the killings of five white men and at least as many Japanese, whose trepanging and pearling luggers were landing, illegally, on the coasts of the Arnhem Land Reserve right up until World War II. Some killings appear to have been provoked by misuse of Aboriginal women (although women were frequently prostituted to luggermen by their Aboriginal husbands) and some were motivated by greed for loot. The Groote Eylandt missionary of the day, the Reverend A. J. Dyer, said in court that " . . . if he were dictator he would drive all the abos into Liberty Square and give them all a good flogging. . . . Then he would let them see a bayonet charge and have the soldiers up to show them a volley and then tell them if there was any more killing they would all be shot down on the beach. He was not speaking as a missionary or as a protector but as a dictator. He knew his mission friends would not agree with his utterances."[3]

Then the wind of change began to blow in the Arnhem Land the distraught Mr Dyer said had been for so long "neglected". Darwin talk of punitive expeditions to "teach the niggers a lesson" was abashed by a rising demand in the south for more enlightened policies. An anthropologist went in to find out why the native mood was so hostile. Alien contact had disrupted their tribal life, said Dr Donald Thomson. He prescribed "absolute segregation"—which was neither practicable nor what the Aborigines wanted. World War II came and maximized contact, particularly on the Gove Peninsula with its big Army-Air Force base. When the Servicemen withdrew the Aborigines were a people between two worlds and there could be no return to the tribal *status quo*. In the Gove region they clustered round Yirrkala Mission; on Groote round the mission and government settlement that had been established there at Umbakumba. The wind of change had dropped to a breeze.

Then the drills went down and showed the great deposits of bauxite at Gove and of manganese on Groote, where the discovery was made in 1960. Gemco (Groote Eylandt Mining Company, a subsidiary of B.H.P.) shipped out its first ore in 1966.

"IT WAS A GODSEND," the C.M.S. missionary, the Reverend Jim Taylor, said when I asked him what he thought about B.H.P.'s coming to Groote.

"We were civilizing these people but our great problem was, 'What do they do now?' Along comes the company and they've got employment."

Paul Jeans, Gemco's then manager, was young and vigorous, as the missionary was, and they couldn't have got along better: "Jim Taylor's a remarkable man. I've talked to him by the hour, and the company has had every assistance from him. As for the Aborigines, they've got plenty of pride left—still settle problems with the spear on occasions. About forty are working for us, and there's quite a bit of prestige attached to some of the jobs they've shown they can do."

I came to know as "Carl" the Czech boss of the crusher plant. He lived in the six-bedroomed house where I was quartered, and I had never met a miner who had such pride in being a miner. Carl had mined in half a dozen countries: mining and its challenges were his life. Give him a record to break and he'd sweat satisfaction in breaking it. It followed that, as a boss, the expert and prodigious worker Carl was about as easy to please as he was soft in the biceps or narrow in the chest.

When I went down to the crusher with him I was surprised to see that the young man in charge of the section where the hunks of rock go in was black. He had an array of buttons before him up there in the Meccano set. Not only did he have to stop the crushing every fifteen minutes to take ore samples, but sometimes a very big boulder would stick and jam the works. He had to stop the crusher quickly then and clear the hunk, manoeuvring it so that the steel jaw could get it at the right angle to crack it.

"This is John Mujiji," Carl said. The eyes under the yellow hard-hat blinked and the wide thick lips parted in a nervous grin. How old are you, John? *Twenty*. You're a Groote man? *No, from Rose River, the mission on the mainland.* Why is your English so good? Embarrassment and then, *I was a religious instructor at the mission.* You like this job better? *Yes.*

When we had left John Mujiji pressing his array of coloured buttons and doing the right thing about clearing recalcitrant rock I asked Carl, "How long did it take to teach him that job?"

"Two weeks. I gave him the job of a white man who had been doing it for eight months, and was still no bloody good."

Stuart Buckle, ex-Darwin, was the Aboriginal driver of a Cat 988 front-end loader. He lived in a company house and his four kids going to the Groote Eylandt school were looked up to because their father drove this roaring machine. Six days a week it moved about a thousand tons of reddish ore in a ten-and-a-half-hour shift. That was what everybody worked, and Stuart Buckle got the same as a white man for working it. With the overtime it was likely to be $170 a week. The white workers wanted the long hours for the big pay. Many came to "cash up" and were gone after six months. Not so the Aboriginal worker: ninety per cent could be relied on to work for a year, Paul Jeans said. And if they went off they were more likely to come back.

"Staffers" couldn't come and go like that, but Alan Wright, the personnel man who ran me round, seemed happy. His wife Kay liked the climate, liked the house—up on stilts, spacious, all mod. cons.—and baby Peter was thriving. Kay Wright missed her parents who missed seeing their only grandchild, but she liked the "social life".

There was far more social life at this township named Alyangula on remote Groote Eylandt than in towns of comparable population (which doubled to 450 by the middle of 1971) within a hundred miles of Sydney. The company actively promoted it to keep the workers happy. Ordinarily, towns of two, four, six hundred or even a thousand people do not have a swimming-pool. There was a beauty just down the road from the Wright's house. The satiny sea just outside it was bluer and lovelier, but not very safe swimming. The shoreline here had been landscaped by a gardener who placed a big boulder of manganese rock decoratively.

Away from the town's forty houses that were to be eighty by mid-1971 the bulldozers cleared off the timber and the huge scrapers removed the overburden. The ore was drilled and blasted and the loaders such as Stuart Buckle drove moved in. Production of manganese ore for the 1970 year was over 600,000 tons.

The company paid a royalty to the government. It also paid a royalty to the Groote Eylandt Trust Fund for the local Aborigines at a rate of $10,000 for the first 100,000 tons and thereafter one and a half per cent of the value of all ore shipped. The Trust was headed by Mr Nandjiwara Amagula, who in the 1970 honours list got an M.B.E.

Royalty payments into this Trust were expected to total $2.5 million by 1975.

Such royalty payments, made directly for the benefit of the local Aborigines from the mining company, had been negotiated at Groote (but not, as we shall see, at Gove) because the manganese had been discovered by a government geologist of the Bureau of Mineral

Resources and the N.T. Administration, as a Commonwealth agency, had given the C.M.S. mission at Groote the opportunity to take out a prospecting lease over the deposits. This, primarily, was why the Aborigines at Groote were happy with B.H.P.; and why the mission which was getting improvements made out of the lease-royalty arrangement, was no less happy.

UMBAKUMBA is on the other side of the island from the mission, forty miles by road from the company town. When you turn off the blacktop the road is bad and the dust is as red as the anthills between the eucalypts in the bush that is mounded in places with rugged outcrops of granite. There are enough hills on Groote to give rise to several rivers, and water is no problem. Of wildlife I saw little— not even a wallaby. About 350 of the 850 black population (which is increasing) live on the government settlement at Umbakumba. Here a community hall was being built. The framework was up and the roof was going on.

Attached to the community hall would be a kitchen and, in the refreshment area, a soda fountain with refrigeration. Near by a big showers-lavatory block was ready for fitting. The contract price was $70,000. Down south it could have been built for about $35,000. But Territory building costs were like that, what with freights and high-wage workmen. All the carpenters I saw were white, if that is the word for men with sun-darkened bare torsoes and faces lost in beards.

The money came from the royalties the mining company paid into the Groote Eylandt Trust Fund. The Trust's eleven directors included the Native Welfare Officer, Michael Casey, who had driven me to Umbakumba, the settlement superintendent, and two representatives of the C.M.S.: the other seven directors were Aboriginal.

The Mission at Angarugu was where even more of the native people lived, over 500 of them. More than half were under the age of sixteen, 120 under the age of five. In contrast to the appalling Aboriginal infant mortality in many parts of Australia, only one baby of the thirty-six born in the previous year had died. These were probably the healthiest, and the wealthiest, Aborigines in Australia, and in the opinion of one academic who knows the social situation there particularly well, "Groote Eylandt has perhaps a better chance than any other similar area on northern Australia of seeing the growth of a really successful integrated society."[4]

"It isn't fair to say that the Aboriginal won't work," Jim Taylor said. "Only about fifteen per cent of our men aren't holding some job, and most of those are earning money from making carvings and bark paintings. That leaves only five per cent who are unwilling to work—and it has to be realized that 'work', as we define it, is still a new concept for some of these people who have grown up as hunters and with a Stone Age technology. Because they were never agriculturalists, it is difficult to get a man to work in the gardens, where we grow such things as bananas and limes. They regard that as too much like yam digging—women's work."

There was still some polygamy, but not much. The days when the old men used to get all the young girls as wives were gone, or going fast, with the young women speaking up against marrying "in line". On the other hand, the elders complained that the young girls were "running about" too much.

There has only been one case the missionary knew about of sex between white employees of the company and Aboriginal girls. Four men were meeting four girls up behind the water tanks. Aboriginal men at the mission got to know of it and it was reported to the company.

"B.H.P. sacked the four men and told them to pack up and be on the next plane out. That's their invariable rule—even though two of those chaps were very good plant operators." (And even though, I was told from another source, it was the girls who did the soliciting.)

Jim Taylor added: "The people here don't like half-castes. They have a real aversion to milk-chocolate babies."

Fourteen Aboriginal women, mostly young, worked in the prawn factory that had been set up to process Gulf prawns by Michael Kailis from Western Australia. They earned sixty cents an hour and they did the work of heading and tailing the prawns for snap freezing very well, according to Mel Pach who was the factory manager until, the week after I left, it was burnt down.

Before I left Groote to fly to Gove I went with Michael Casey to a place about three miles east of the mission where a bouldered hill rose to a big-ledge cave of paintings in ochres. Red predominated, though yellow was used very boldly, as for a whole fish, not patterned in the x-ray style: little use was made of white or black. Most of the paintings were on the roof of the cave, which was thick with them—a vivid gallery of fish, crocodiles, turtles, a few bird-forms, and men fishing from a large bark canoe.

THE DRAMA AT GOVE

To FLY from Groote Eylandt to the Gove Peninsula was to come to a very different situation, Aboriginally and industrially.

Fly to Gove one must: there is no road to this eastern tip of Arnhem Land. MacRobertson-Miller Airlines flew between Darwin, Gove and Groote daily; and you can fly in from Mt Isa or Cairns in Queensland. If the MMA plane from Groote had made for the coast and followed it all the way up there would have been no sign of habitation whatever along the lonely mangroved shores until Gove Peninsula came in sight. Then, suddenly, the natural face of the country was transformed. What was being constructed at this Ultima Thule of the continent is the biggest single private enterprise project ever built in Australia.

The reason for its being sited here was made plain by the clawed acres of bare red earth. It was the place of 250 million tons of bauxite. Getting the ore out, and converting much of it into the alumina that makes aluminium, would involve the spending of over three hundred million dollars ($310 million was the precise figure the company, Nabalco, gave).

The parties to this enterprise, which is being managed by Nabalco, are Swiss Aluminium (70 per cent) and the Australian-equity Gove Alumina (30 per cent) with such partner companies as Colonial Sugar, two big insurance firms, two big banks, Peko-Wallsend mining and the pastoral company Elder Smith–Goldsbrough Mort.

Nabalco was building a town, which would be permanent and fully air-conditioned, to accommodate 4,000 people in 1972 and 5,000 or more in 1974—a town called Nhulunbuy (pron. Newlunboy) because the Aborigines said that was the proper name of the place, and they didn't want it called Gove. Port installations were going in on the fine natural harbour that is Melville Bay, named by Matthew Flinders when he sailed in in 1803. On the bared earth behind it would rise the plant to process bauxite into alumina, beginning in 1972. In 1973 Nabalco expected to be shipping out a million tons of alumina a year plus two million tons of bauxite.

That would generate royalty revenue of about $850,000 in that year. Even by mid-1972 the royalty should amount to $650,000. Additionally, nearly half whatever profit Gove Alumina made would accrue to the Commonwealth in tax. (Swiss Aluminium would not aim to make a profit from the mining: it wanted alumina for its smelters overseas where the profit would be made on aluminium; nor would its subsidiary Nabalco be concerned with profits from Gove). There was also rent of the leased land, the Crown land excised from the Arnhem Land Aboriginal Reserve.

The company, Nabalco, has been the meat in the sandwich of dissension between the Commonwealth and the local Aborigines.

The Aborigines were claiming that the land was theirs, had been theirs from time immemorial. They had put their case to the Supreme Court sitting in Darwin, and the hearing began in May 1969 before Mr Justice Blackburn. (The Commonwealth Government, although co-defendant with Nabalco Pty Ltd, would pay the Aborigines' legal costs.) In April 1971 he delivered his 262-page reserved judgement.

THE JUDGE dismissed the Aborigines' claim to their tribal land on the Gove Peninsula. He did so mainly because he found that, in terms of English law, when Captain Arthur Phillip laid claim to Australia at Sydney Cove in 1788 "every square inch of territory in the colony became the property of the Crown". The natives' claim that they had communal title to the land their clans had lived on for centuries, and which they said they had derived from their "spirit ancestors", could not be held valid in terms of what we consider law, the judge said.

Mr Justice Blackburn held that the human race had "a right and duty to develop the earth's resources. The more advanced peoples were therefore justified in dispossessing, if necessary, the less advanced. Related to this was the doctrine that discovery was the root of title in international law."

By thus giving judgement strictly in terms of the law, unswayed by any considerations of personal compassion, Mr Justice Blackburn may well have opened up the whole matter to the light of justice. What we see is a legal situation that is less than a just situation. As the law stands (and the anthropologist T. G. H. Strehlow of the University of Adelaide has said this[1]) the Australian Aborigines are "the only human race in the world which owns no land".

Surely the law must be changed to remedy a legal condition that does not equate with justice.

THE PLANE landed on a red airstrip of solid bauxite. The strip was built in 1940 and the place named after a Flying Officer W. J. H. Gove who was killed while flying in the area on active service. None of the thousands of Australians who were there in wartime appear to have known what bauxite was. When, at the end of the war, Australia decided to make aluminium, we imported bauxite from Malaya.

The Marchinbar Island deposits of bauxite were discovered by the captain and mate of an Administration vessel, who received a reward that would appear to relate to the Gove deposits also; but those, according to the late Sir Harold Raggatt, were found in 1955 by a geologist of his Commonwealth Bureau of Mineral Resources.[2] Either way, it was a government not a private enterprise discovery, and the Methodist mission at Yirrkala would have been just as entitled as the C.M.S. mission at Groote Eylandt to take out a lease on behalf of the Aborigines.

Yirrkala Mission didn't do that. The missionary then in charge, the Reverend Edgar Wells, considered that the Aborigines were not ready for the change that bauxite mining would bring. According to what the Director of Social Welfare told me in Darwin, Mr Wells took the view that the bauxite would still be in the ground and it would be better to wait ten or twenty years. The Director, Mr Giese, said, "In purely human terms this dedicated missionary had a case. In terms of the national economy, no."

The anthropologist considered most authoritative on the area, Professor R. M. Berndt, had written in 1954, "Arnhem Land must remain a country for the Arnhem Landers alone." They were bound to the country, he said, by "traditional and spiritual ties". (Actually many of them had left their traditional country in the Caledon Bay area to live round the Yirrkala Mission.) Professor Berndt was thinking in terms of a fishing industry when he added, ". . . and they must exploit its natural resources themselves".[3] They could hardly exploit its bauxite themselves.

Giving evidence for the Aborigines in the court case, Professor Berndt said, "A large scale intrusion of Europeans into the area and the projected establishment of a township close to them will inevitably lead to the destruction not only of their society but of their culture." He added that these relatively unsophisticated people were ". . . disillusioned and bewildered in the face of what appears to them to be—and in fact is—the more or less deliberate destruction of their way of life, their values and aspirations."

If this sort of bone-pointing by wicked capitalist exploiters with nothing better to do was, in fact, going on, it could be assumed that the Aborigines knew it was, didn't want it, and fervently wished that Nabalco would go away.

That, I found, was not the situation.

As soon as I got to Gove I sought to prospect the Aboriginal situation, first with the company. Leigh French, an intelligent Californian who could discuss architecture or music as readily as mining engineering, was then in charge. He expressed the company's viewpoint thus: "We negotiate with governments. It is for the government to negotiate with the native people. We make a deal in good faith for the lease of certain lands from the government. If anybody is taking away land from the Aborigines the government is. It is not our job to know what their land entitlements are. It is, frankly, not our job to deal with the Aborigines, except as employers when we employ them or when they supply goods and services. But we are dealing with them on other matters—we meet with them once a month. Our attitude towards them is one of goodwill and we'll help them in any way we can."

I asked about the destruction by bulldozing of one of their sacred sites.

"That wasn't done by Nabalco but by one of our contractors," Leigh French said. "When the contractor's man tore that great hole in the hill at Mt Saunders he acted against my instructions to the contractor. I had talked to the contractor and written a letter to him— but that guy just didn't pass the instruction on.

"The contractor was very sorry about it and he did his best to rehabilitate the place—it was a place where a clan forefather named Wuyal sat down. The mission thinks he's done an excellent job. And the people are happy about it now."

Why did they have to bulldoze that particular area anyway? I asked the Industrial Officer about that. He said the matter of placing a water tank on top of this hill had been discussed with the tribal elders, and they had agreed that it was the only place with the height for a water reticulation scheme. But the elders, apparently, didn't ask the *people* if it was O.K. When the damage was made good they accepted that mistakes had been rectified and they were pleased at what was done. Only *after that* did the matter hit the Press headlines.

It was an odd situation. You go to a place to find out what a $300 million development is all about in a remote corner of Australia, and the most important thing you feel you have to do is to talk to the only people you can't talk to, the Aborigines. Their spokesman, Roy Marika, is away in Darwin on the court case. However, you soon gather that, on this matter of land rights, the mission and the Aborigines think alike. But the head of the mission is away, too. So you talk to the acting superintendent, the young man who is in charge, Rob Waters. He is slight and earnest, and copes valiantly with your questions:

Why is the situation here so different from that at Groote Eylandt? —"I don't know how the mission on Groote managed to hold a mineral lease without working it."

Does the Methodist Church regard the Aborigines as the rightful owners of the land leased to Nabalco?—"The Church recognizes that the people have always thought of the land as being theirs. Yes, the Church supports their land claims."

Are the land rights the Aborigines are claiming confined to the 140 acres leased to Nabalco?—"They are also claiming rights to land that is outside the Nabalco lease."

Is this, in fact, the tribal land of the 600 people living here?—"Only about half are concerned with land rights as their traditional entitlement. The rest of the people here come from outside this area." (It was reported in December 1970 that 200 of the people at Yirrkala were planning to move back to their "own country", which is around Caledon Bay. A company was proposing to mine in this area.)

Does the mission want Nabalco to go away and not mine the bauxite?—"No. The general feeling among the Aborigines and ourselves is that we want the company here."

You would agree that there are benefits to the Aborigines, through employment with the company and through supplying the company with bricks you are making here with the brick-making plant, and supplying such other things as vegetables?—"Yes, but we don't think these fringe benefits are enough."

What will happen if the Aborigines win their case at Court?—"They will have established that they own the land."

And that they own the mineral rights?—"No."

So what is the main real difference it will make to them?—"It would make a difference to the royalty for a start. These people are looking to Groote, where a percentage of the royalty is paid directly to the local people—as we think it should be here."

THE DRAMA at Gove was more than an Aboriginal land rights drama. Gove was dramatic in terms of its construction. (PLATE 38.)

—Down near the port you stand up on the steel frame of a building and watch the earth explode into the sky. The big blast is to clear a rocky outcrop to site the alumina plant. The rain of rock fragments falls short of a big banyan-tree that grows in the foreground. It is roped right round and notices say KEEP OFF. Nabalco is taking no chances that this sacred banyan of the Aborigines will be destroyed as another one was at Mt Saunders by the contractor. A fire truck appears and hoses water onto the roots of the precious banyan.

—You drive along a dirt road beside a clearing that goes up to the crest of a low hill. A yellow dingo lopes away into the silent bush. Beyond the low crest the clearing goes on straight for miles. Right along it would be reared the conveyor belt that would carry the ore overland from the mining area to the plant at the port. It would run for eighteen miles, the longest conveyor in Australia. (It cost $13 million and began operating in mid-1971. The first shipment of Gove bauxite went to Rotterdam in July 1971.)

—Alongside another dirt road a board nailed to a stringybark-tree says HOSPITAL. Farther along another board on another tree says NURSES QUARTERS. (In mid-1971 both were under construction.)

—The town plan shows such buildings as Post Office, Telephone Exchange, Fire Station, Library, Dental Clinic. Blocks of family flats and bachelor housing will be three-storeys high: Nhulunbuy will be the first multi-storey company town; and more than a company town, a regional centre, with government offices. The town of Nhulunbuy will cost $45 million, of which the Commonwealth Government is putting in $10 million for the school (primary and secondary for 600 pupils), the post office, hospital, police station and housing for its employees.

The climate is, like Darwin's, winterless and two-seasonal, Wet and Dry; but rather better in the Dry because the south-east tradewind comes water-cooled off the Gulf of Carpentaria. It is 60 to 80 degrees in the cooler months, and up in the nineties in November-December. Rainfall averages 53½ inches, with June-November very dry.

A booklet *Living at Nhulunbuy*, issued by the company to all employees, says that the local Aborigines are "a people of dignity, independence and pride" and they should be treated with courtesy; "Give them a smile or a wave, say hello to them, never make it a practice to walk past in silence." The sacred sites are enumerated and their significances explained. "When buying artefacts it is preferable to make purchases through the store at Yirrkala Mission. This safeguards the buyer against unintentionally obtaining some sacred object whose acquisition is prohibited by law."

BARK PAINTINGS were a big thing at the Yirrkala Mission, and a good thing. The best bark paintings come from Yirrkala, and sales had risen to $28,000 a year.

Probably the most accomplished of bark artists was Mawalan, who died in 1968. Wanjuk, aged about fifty, was now regarded by Rob Waters as No. 1: there were others who thought Narratjin was. Prices ranged, at Yirrkala, from $10 up to about $100. (Ten years ago the best bark painting I have ever seen, in a Sydney exhibition, sold for seventy guineas—nearly $150—and would probably fetch $2,000 or more in New York today.)

One of Village Council president Roy Marika's complaints had been that company work on the water scheme had bulldozed an area where orchids used to be gathered for their sap that acts as a fixative for the paints used on bark. Roy Marika was the carver of a painted wooden brolga I bought: his wife had done the painting. Such other artefacts as didjeridoos are painted and decorated. Sales were increasing all the time as Nabalco employees grew in number, and there was a wide market in Australian cities in the south.

The brickworks at the mission was set up with a $90,000 loan negotiated with the Commonwealth Government under its loans-aid-for-Aborigines programme. In mid-1970 the plant was supplying Nabalco and its contractors with 4,000 bricks a day. Only the foreman was a white man. Aborigines' experience in the working of fork-lift trucks would fit them for similar jobs with the company.

Aborigines are now doing all the laundry for the 2,000-plus workers at Gove, using a modern plant that was purchased by the company and, I should think, will be handed over to the Yirrkala people. They are also supplying the growing town with a lot of vegetables and fruits. About twenty Aboriginal men were directly employed by the company. They got the same pay and conditions as whites, and could drink in the same canteen. (But when the hotel being built at Gove was completed, the Village Council decided, it wanted the hotel to be out of bounds for Aborigines.)

One young man I talked to was working on house construction and making $123 including overtime for a sixty-hour week. The houses were of white sheet steel and very modernly equipped, as were the single-men's quarters: all were air-conditioned.

Roy Marika had said he had reason to believe that some Aboriginal women had cohabited with white company workers, and this had to stop: the people did not want there to be any half-caste children. (In pre-war days "yella-fella" babies were done away with.) Marika suggested that white prostitutes be brought in. The then Minister for the Interior (Mr P. Nixon) declared tersely, "Prostitution is not on."

The Aborigines were speaking up as never before, and confrontation of the Federal Government was largely in terms of confrontation of Mr Nixon. The Secretary of the Yirrkala Village Council, J. Galarrwuy Yunupingu, wrote in a letter to the *Australian*:[4] "Mr Nixon, the Minister for the Interior, has no rights at all to have authority to say about Aboriginal tribal land in the Northern Territory. . . . Nobody thinks that Mr Nixon is the head of our land, and we as Aborigines don't believe that he has the power to sell lands that are not his. . . . Who told him that Aboriginals should gain the land the same as others? Aboriginal people always had land of their own. . . . We are not Europeans that we should buy lands."

Were they, in Professor Berndt's words, faced with "the destruction not only of their society but of their culture", these Aborigines who were standing up and talking out so boldly; these people who had withstood, since it was founded in 1934, a mission that tried to make Christians of them; this tribal group who had come through the wartime occupation of Gove by 5,000 servicemen? I found it less than credible that this was what the bauxite mining enterprise was doing to them.

Land rights apart, their main problem seemed to be the old one of how to have their cake and eat it. A tribal elder I talked to—after a fashion, for his English was only rudimentary—said, "Bulldozer shifts my kangaroo", meaning that the mining operations interfered with his hunting: not that there were many kangaroos on the peninsula, and most Yirrkala people now live on white-man tucker plus fish-turtle-dugong from the sea.

"This land Nabalco got—you want it back?" I asked.

"Land Nabalco got O.K.," the old man said. "Nabalco good. Trouble finish."

"Roy Marika, he doesn't say that."

"Roy come back, I talk to Roy."

I didn't think anything the old man said to Roy Marika would cut much ice with the articulate young spokesman for a people whose spokesmen were no longer the old men. Their society was changing—and not so much because the white man was changing it as because they were using what they had learnt from the white man to change it themselves. Civilization is change.

Many well-intentioned whites may want the Aboriginal *status quo* preserved. But it is not for *us* to say that it should be, or to say what they should preserve of their old way of life and what they should change. If they want to discard elders' rights in marriage, or ordeals of initiation, or to question superstitions and their old beliefs, it is not for us to say they should not. It is for them to say whether they want to become Nowtime people instead of Dreamtime people.

While I was at the mission I heard singing. Not hymn-singing, which of course is to be heard there, too, but Aboriginal singing with the click of the rhythm sticks. I asked about it and Rob Waters said a boy was being prepared for initiation. The main ceremony would be that afternoon. So the old culture was alive and well and living right on the Methodist mission station.

Could I see the ceremony? Rob Waters said it was not for him to say. He would ask the people. He asked them and said they had no objection. When I returned in the afternoon the scene was as in PLATE 36. They didn't at all mind my taking photographs.

The boy, aged seven, whose name was Ulungo, was being "sung" while his torso was being painted with totemic designs. The painter, Bob Malinyan, was very skilful. The quiet boy lay there in the dappled shade, in the centre of a group of his relations and clanfolk. Afterwards he would be circumcised.

THE TOWN BEACH, as it is called, is an attractive one: PLATE 38 shows it. Lovelier still is a sweep of white sand edging the bright blue Arafura Sea and backed by an equally blue lagoon at what is called Woody Point.

This place was not easy of access: the four-wheel-drive vehicle of the then personnel manager, Ian Maze, ploughed through a track of deep sand to get to it, and, as I walked along it with him and his wife and another young woman, I thought what a beautifully pristine place it was—trackless sand and not a beer can in sight. That evening Mrs Leigh French told me that the French family had picnicked there recently. Leigh had had the children help him collect seventy drink cans and put them in the car.

David Griffin, chairman of Nabalco, had shown me a colour picture of this beach before I left Sydney and had said, smiling as he pointed to a spot, "I think about *there* is the site for the Gove Hilton."

Hardly anything was then built at Gove and it seemed fantastic to talk of an international tourist hotel. Yet in August 1971 the $1.3 million Gove Walkabout hotel-motel was opened in the town of Nhulunbuy.

Gove would move on to the tourist map as well as loom large on the industrial map of the New Australia—larger, perhaps, than as a producer in 1972 of alumina that will go to, among other places, Iceland to be turned into aluminium. A feasibility study in progress would determine, by the end of 1971, whether Gove would also be, as Weipa on Cape York may, the place for another big Australian aluminium smelter.

THE "DUCK" FLIGHT

FLYING from Darwin to Gove, or vice versa, the MMA Fokker Friendship goes over a lot of the Arafura Sea edge of Arnhem Land. Flatworm rivers of *café-au-lait* crawl in mangroved curves through mudflats to the light-bright blue. There are no cliff coasts, no hard edges of what is land and what is sea. Much of the land is marooned as islands, such as the ones where Millingimbi Mission sits on what are called, with *Boys' Own Paper* overtones, the Crocodile Islands.

Another way to see the north coast of Arnhem Land, although only as far as Elcho Island, is to get on the Short Skyvan of Connellan Airways. A Skyvan looks like it sounds—a van with wings. It is squat and squared-off and loads from the back into a wide box of a cabin that takes eighteen passengers and a heap of freight: it is noisy and goes through the air at the snail speed of 150 m.p.h. Not an elegant aircraft, it is called the "Pregnant Duck".

The big gingery type I take to be the Duck's captain isn't. The slim young woman in slacks with her khaki sleeves rolled up is not only the pilot but Connellan's chief pilot who trains all the other pilots. She also happens to be the Christine Davy who represented Australia in the Olympic Games ski teams in 1956 and 1960.

Our first stop on the morning flight out of Darwin at six-thirty is Maningrida Aboriginal Settlement. Here the Duck has a drink of petrol and while it is doing that we whizz into the settlement. The truck takes five minutes each way, which gives only five minutes there, spent in a big store full of bark paintings and carvings. Some of the barks are good and I buy one for $17. A piece of paper pasted on the back gives the name of the artist, his age (29), his tribal moiety and what the painting is about: "Seven echidnas they live in the rocks but during afternoon they all comes out and feeding around the ants beds . . . also two snakes . . . they all looking for many legs to eat in the hillside." *Legs* to eat? He must mean *eggs*. The design is so good, with a swinging rhythm, and the brushwork is good too—and the English is pathetic.

On the plane I talk to a Methodist mission teacher who is going back to Elcho Island where, he says, next year he will be teaching adults. Teaching them what? "Literacy—you see, the young ones have been getting a lot of education but the older ones have hardly any." So there is a generation gap?

"Yes, there is," the teacher says. "But it would be wider if they did not live so closely together."

Thinking of the space, or lack of it, in most Aboriginal housing—not that it looked too bad at Maningrida but it is, generally, sub-standard—I say that this close living must make problems for the school-agers with homework to do.

"They return at night to the school to do their homework. In five years, I think, I hope, they'll be able to do their homework at home."

Elcho Island where we will land next is twenty miles long and two or three wide, the bright-eyed mission teacher says. It had only a small population before the Methodists came. The Wessel Islands were well populated, he says, but the people there killed each other off. Aborigines, being territorially unambitious, weren't supposed to kill each other off like that. But the bright-eyed mission teacher is probably right. You acknowledge the dedication of his much-criticized kind for what they did in bringing about the time when the killing had to stop in Aboriginal Australia.

There are more bright frocks and clean black skins on the strip at Elcho Island. White teeth are showing everywhere over Teacher's return. He greets this one and that and says how the baby has grown and they welcome him with what looks like love.

In 1925 an oil company drilled here, but didn't find any oil. However, there is a sedimentary basin that covers this area of the Arafura's edge. Who knows, other drills may go down and bring up enough royalties to build houses where the kids can do their homework at home, and leave the schools for the night-time teaching of semi-literate adults like the bark painter.

Isn't Australia making enough out of the Bass Strait oil for us to afford to do this now? It is a question you ask yourself as the Skyvan, the Duck that is now noticeably less pregnant with passengers, throbs back to Darwin over the strangely ugly-beautiful coast of Arnhem Land.

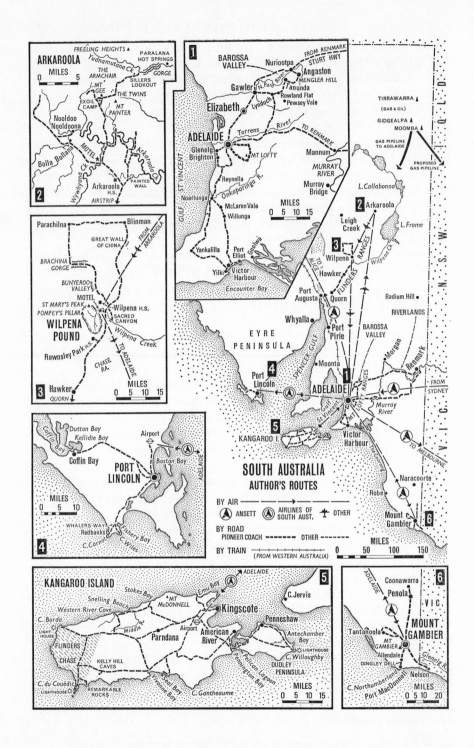

ARKAROOLA

MILES
0   5

FREELING HEIGHTS ▲
PARALANA HOT SPRINGS
Yudnamutana Ck
THE ARMCHAIR
GORGE
SILLERS LOOKOUT
MT GEE
THE TWINS
EXOIL CAMP
MT PAINTER
Nooldoo Nooldoona
Bolla Bollana
MOTEL
Wywhyana Ck
Arkaroola Ck
Arkaroola H.S.
PAINTED WALL
AIRSTRIP

2

Parachilna
Blinman
GREAT WALL OF CHINA
FROM ARKAROOLA
BRACHINA GORGE
BUNYEROO VALLEY
MOTEL
ST MARY'S PEAK
POMPEY'S PILLAR
Wilpena H.S.
SACRED CANYON
WILPENA POUND
Wilpena Creek
Rawnsley Park H.S.
CHASE RA.
TO ADELAIDE

3 Hawker
QUORN

MILES
0   5   10   15

1
BAROSSA VALLEY
FROM RENMARK
STURT HWY
Nuriootpa
Angaston
MENGLER HILL
Gawler
N. Para
Tanunda
Rowland Flat
Pewsey Vale
Lyndoch
Elizabeth
TO RENMARK
ADELAIDE
Torrens   River
Glenelg
Brighton
MT LOFTY
Mannum
Reynella
MURRAY RIVER
Onkaparinga R.
Murray Bridge
Noarlunga
McLaren Vale
Willunga
TO ALICE
Yankalilla
Port Elliot
Goolwa
Yilki
Victor Harbour
Encounter Bay

MILES
0 5 10 15

TIRRAWARRA ▲
(GAS & OIL)
GIDGEALPA ▲
MOOMBA ▲
GAS PIPELINE TO ADELAIDE
PROPOSED GAS PIPELINE

2 Arkaroola
L. Callabonna
L. Frome
Leigh Creek
3
Wilpena
FLINDERS   RANGES
Hawker
Wilpena Ck
Radium Hill
RIVERLANDS
Port Augusta
Quorn
Whyalla
Port Pirie
BAROSSA VALLEY
Morgan
Renmark
EYRE PENINSULA
SPENCER   GULF
Moonta
FROM SYDNEY
4 Port Lincoln
MT LOFTY RANGES
1 ADELAIDE
St Vincent   Gulf
Murray River
5 KANGAROO I.
Victor Harbour
TO MELBOURNE
SOUTH AUSTRALIA
AUTHOR'S ROUTES
Naracoorte
Robe
Mount Gambier
6

BY AIR ━━▶ ANSETT   AIRLINES OF SOUTH AUST.   ✈ OTHER
BY ROAD
PIONEER COACH ━━━━━   OTHER ─────
BY TRAIN ━━━━━ (FROM WESTERN AUSTRALIA)

MILES
0   50   100   150

Dutton Bay
Kellidie Bay
Airport
Coffin Bay
Coffin Bay
PORT LINCOLN
Boston Bay
ADELAIDE

MILES
0   5   10

WHALERS WAY
Redbanks
Fishery Bay
C. Carnot
C. Wiles

4

KANGAROO ISLAND
ADELAIDE
Stokes Bay
Emu Bay
MT McDONNELL
Snelling Beach
C. Jervis
Western River Cove
C. Borda
Kingscote
LIGHT HOUSE
Middle
Airport
Penneshaw
FLINDERS
Parndana
American River
Antechamber Bay
CHASE
KELLY HILL CAVES
Pelican Lagoon
Pennington Bay
LIGHTHOUSE
C. Willoughby
DUDLEY PENINSULA
C. du Couedic
LIGHTHOUSE
REMARKABLE ROCKS
Vivonne Bay
Seal Bay
C. Gantheaume

MILES
0 5 10 15

5

6
ADELAIDE
Coonawarra
Penola
V I C.
MOUNT GAMBIER
Tantanoola
MT GAMBIER
Allendale
DINGLEY DELL
Glenelg R.
Nelson
C. Northumberland
Port MacDonnell

MILES
0 5 10   20

Q'LD
N.S.W.
VIC.

SOUTH AUSTRALIA

The Arts at Adelaide

SOUTH AUSTRALIA conforms, in a way, to what might well be the image of an Australian State in the mind of an intending migrant.

In prospering huddles of urban industrialism and enclaves of picture-book verdure and vineland nearly all the State's million and a quarter people live with a hinterland that fits the conception of Australia as "two-thirds desert".

Historically, South Australia is atypical. It had no convicts, no gold-rushes, barely a bushranger, and few rumbustious characters. While the rest of Australia attracted so many Irish and other adherents of Roman Catholicism that by the turn of the century twenty-one per cent of Australians were of that faith, in South Australia the percentage was only fourteen. And of Anglicans it had only a ratio of three out of ten when the national average was four. Wesleyan Methodists, Baptists, Congregationalists and German Lutherans had come in such numbers as to make it the dissenters' State—with a high level of what the author of the book *Paradise of Dissent* called "nobly depressing rectitude".[1]

Adelaide has long been looked upon by other-Staters as the capital with the clergyman's collar, the "City of Churches". The Lutherans in the Barossa Valley might grow a great deal of wine but swilling Sydney remained convinced that it was virtually impossible to get a glass of it to drink in Adelaide after six o'clock in the evening (and they weren't too far wrong, before ten o'clock closing came: even nowadays some puritan prejudice lingers). Old Cornishmen from the copper town of Moonta used to stump about in *Bulletin* cartoons in the 1940s, calling each other "thee", and the Adelaidian Establishment maintained an aura of social righteousness as solemn as the editorials used to be in the *Advertiser*.

Today (1971) South Australia is the only State where abortion is legal, and, until recently it was the only State where an adult Australian could legally buy a copy of *Portnoy's Complaint*. And, although a night-time walk down King William Street, or any street either side of it, might appear to confirm an Adelaide writer's statement that in no other city of its size have prostitutes been "harried as near to extinction",[2] Adelaide had "escort services" openly advertised, of young women who performed the call-girl function. It was the only Australian capital where sex was on the telephone.

Even several such swallows do not make a summertime of permissiveness. Babylon-on-Torrens Adelaide is not, or likely to become. What it began to see itself as, though, in the 1960s was the "Athens of Australia". This was too much, even if one were willing to discern lineaments of a Pericles in Mr Don Dunstan, the State's enlightened young Labour premier, and make an Australian Aristophanes of the ebullient Max Harris.

The Edinburgh of Australia, yes. Complete with an almost John Knox-ish religious background in dissenter terms; characteristic stone buildings; North Terrace doing duty for Princes Street; and a roughly comparable population—though Adelaide had surged ahead of Edinburgh's half million to 800,000—when, in 1960, Adelaide began its Festival of Arts that has come to be quite worthy of being spoken of in the same breath as the Edinburgh Festival.

What is virtually the only major festival of its kind in the Southern Hemisphere was sparked by the enthusiasm of Professor John Bishop, Director of the Elder Conservatorium of Music at Adelaide's university, and gained solid support of moneyed citizenry led by the *Advertiser's* chairman, Sir Lloyd Dumas. For the first Festival of Arts, masterpieces of Turner were brought from London's Tate Gallery and Mexican paintings from San Francisco's Museum of Art, and four Australian symphony orchestras performed. Musically, it moved up a notch nearer Edinburgh standard at the second festival which had the London Philharmonic Orchestra, Yehudi Menuhin and his sister Hephzibah. The third festival (1964) saw world premières of Robert Helpmann's ballet *The Display* and Patrick White's play *Night on Bald Mountain*, first Australian performances of works by Benjamin Britten and Sir William Walton, and a showing of contemporary American paintings as well as exhibitions by such top Australian artists as Nolan, Drysdale and Arthur Boyd. With the fourth festival it became no longer possible to list in a few lines the imported attractions—drama from Athens, Swiss and Tyrolean music, dances from India, the New Zealand Opera Company doing *Porgy and Bess*, and the Mertz collection of Australian paintings among the art exhibits. The fifth had such performers as Marlene Dietrich, Tito Gobbi, the Salzburg Marionette Theatre, a national dance troupe from the Philippines, Spanish and Hungarian instrumentalists, and Acker Bilk's jazzmen. The back-up of Australian-performed music and drama was more than make-weight. While the purpose of Adelaide's festival is to achieve international-standard attractions, its function is also to be "guided in the long term towards an increase in the Australian content . . . with the purpose of presenting from time to time a festival Australian in character".

The 1970 Festival of the Arts was a feast I was able to enjoy in March for two of its three weeks, but this Adelaide enjoyment was not confined to the festival; so let us come to its highlights within the context of the amiable city that created it.

AMIABLE is what Adelaide is. Few cities are, and perhaps amiability is not a quality to be expected of cities. But when it does occur it can be very pleasant.

Most cities spread themselves beyond the possibility of their being amiable. Adelaide can't. The sea constricts it to the west and the Mount Lofty Ranges to the east. Expand though it does north and south of the Torrens, it is still a city where ninety per cent of the people live within eight miles of its centre—if it can be said to have a centre in the truly metropolitan sense. For Adelaide's "heart" is green, is parkland, with the Torrens meandering, blue and broad enough, between the main part of the city and North Adelaide, which is not a suburb but the other half of a specially "knowable" city. Adelaide is a congregation, in the secular sense. Too much is made of its being a "City of Churches": the cliché is not only a bore but a bit of a lie. There is nothing dominantly ecclesiastical about its architectural aspect. Nor is there, really, enough architectural felicity to sustain the often-applied adjective "elegant". Civic elegance one associates with British cities founded earlier than 1836 when Adelaide was—too late for the benison of Georgian architecture.

The best laid out of Australian capitals, Adelaide owes its plan to Colonel William Light, who well deserves his monument on a North Adelaide hill overlooking the city—and his being honoured with the agreeable custom of an annual toast to his memory drunk in Australian wine. Light's plan flanked and bisected the city with parklands, a green belt in a form "like a square-cornered 8".[3] In contrast to this, and the drives that wind through the central park area, is the formal grid pattern of the city either side of wide King William Street. This principal thoroughfare is nicely interrupted by Victoria Square, which is fountained and, on Festival occasions, given special illuminations.

Light bounded his city proper with four boulevards that are the North, South, East and West Terraces. The prospect from South Terrace I have enjoyed on several occasions from excellent accommodation on the upper floors of the Parkroyal motel. East Terrace is stepped, not straight as the others are, but, as West Terrace does, it looks out across parkland, and then over the principal racecourse that, characteristically, is of the city, not out in the suburbs. But North Terrace is Adelaide's finest ornament and, as no other thoroughfare in an Australian capital does, evidences the city's character—compact, gracious, companionable.

North Terrace parades not only Adelaide's principal hotel—the South Australian, its Victorian dignity still supported with very-Australian veranda posts—and the granite-and-marble Parliament building and the railway station: that is only its beginning. North Terrace is where Government House is only lawns' breadth away from the traffic at the King William Street intersection. It is where the University of Adelaide merges gown with town. It is where the Public Library is and the Art Gallery is and the Museum displays through a glass wall the marvellous bones of a monster that roamed prehistoric southern Australia. This admirable boulevard flows on to the Botanic Gardens, one side a green bank of fine trees that in Festival time are baubled with coloured lights.

THE 1972 FESTIVAL, to be held from 3rd to 25th March, is being programmed with emphasis on attractions of a national or regional character from the Pacific and South-East Asia. Representation from Japan, Singapore, Philippines, India, the United States of America, Mexico, Thailand, New Zealand and New Guinea was expected, according to a preliminary announcement in July 1971. Other attractions would include the Royal Philharmonic Orchestra, the Academy of St. Martin-in-the-Fields Chamber Orchestra, a 120 strong folkloric group from Russia, and a play commissioned by the Festival. It was also expected that there would be strong representation of pop music groups, a staging of *Jesus Christ Superstar*, and invited writers would include the American *avant-garde* poets Alan Ginsberg and Lawrence Ferlinghetti.

To those who have not been to an Adelaide Festival let me say briefly what made the 1970 occasion so memorable: The Royal Shakespeare Company from Stratford and London presented the best Shakespeare I have ever seen, vitally acted and exciting in décor, an unforgettable *Twelfth Night* and *Winter's Tale*. Nureyev danced the Basilio role in *Don Quixote* of his own superb production and choreography, with the Australian Ballet and Sir Robert Helpmann as the Don. The English Opera Group performed, as well as *Curlew River*, two other Benjamin Britten church parables, *The Burning Fiery Furnace* and *The Prodigal Son*. Also from abroad were the Warsaw Philharmonic Orchestra, the Russian violinist Nelli Shkolnikova, the Georgian Dancers, the Balinese Dance Company and the

Royal Thai Ballet. Local offerings that stood up very well in this high company were the South Australian Symphony Orchestra, the *Sound and Image* presentation by Stan Ostoja-Kotkowski, who is a genius (but one could have done without Elizabeth Dalman's dancers), and Richard Meale's exciting recital of contemporary music. Chekov's *The Seagull* wasn't Russian enough in mood, but such "fringe" theatre as Genet's *The Maids* was remarkably well done.

The visual arts were offered in a wide rich range, from contemporary British paintings of the Peter Stuyvesant collection to Mexican art (pre-Colombian to modern) to a magnificent retrospective exhibition of the art of Leonard French. There were other exhibitions in no less than twenty galleries in Adelaide and North Adelaide.

In connection with Writers' Week the American playwright Edward Albee was expected, and didn't come; but British novelists of note did, the exuberant Anthony Burgess and a decorative Edna O'Brien. Writers' Week I found very good value—but then so was the whole Festival: all that one needed was a rustproof constitution to keep up with the hospitable plying and the ability to be in several places at once and get along without much sleep. In such greenswards as Elder Park a lot went on out of doors, including music.

For two of the three weeks (while Claire was with me) we stayed at a small, well-regarded hotel, the Earl of Zetland, which provided the pleasant company of the painters Leonard French and Fred Williams, Rudy Komon, the Sydney art dealer and wine buff, and a poet and critic or two. Mostly we ate out. The best places we found:

For sea-food dining, Swains in Glen Osmond Road, Frewville; for a mid-city lunch, with wine, the Chesser Cellar; for relaxed eating beside the river, Ernest's; good Italian food at Asio's; the Copper Kettle in Hindley Street; savoury French fodder at the Château Fort at Unley. The Alpine, charmingly set in the park by South Terrace, didn't live up to its looks. The Parkroyal's restaurant was good. "George's Exclusive Seafood Restaurant", so advertised, in Gouger Street, was about as exclusive as a Formica tabletop, but had good fresh fish: however, it was not only unlicensed but the proprietor said we could not drink our bottle of white on the premises. (We did, after telling him to send for the gendarmes.)

Our favourite, though, was Decca's Place at North Adelaide (shown in PLATE 40). This is a creation of a pace-setting personality and fortyish bachelor named Derek E. Jolly, who is in other ways changing the face of Melbourne Street where Decca's Place is in this pleasant part of Adelaide that approximates to Sydney's Paddington. One was not surprised to hear that Derek Jolly, a merchant's son who went to the right schools (important in Adelaide) used to be a motor racing driver and had even hurled a Lotus round the Le Mans course.

He told me he had no office or files, just a small notebook in which he entered all the dealings of what are called the Derek E. Jolly Group of Companies. These engage in motion picture production, have sound recording studies, do commercial photography and offset printing, and can make available the Moog. The Moog Synthesizer Mark III is described in the Jolly literature as "the greatest revolution in the field of music since David wrote the Book of Psalms". I have met the Moog very briefly and find it a quite incomprehensible monster; but that excellent Adelaide musician Peter Tahourdin, who did some electronic music for one of the Festival offerings, thinks very highly of it. Mr Jolly has since leased Decca's Place, but purveys excellent food at another restaurant near by, the Magic Flute.

In 1971 he was enthusiastically producing pop-music records, dabbling in books and still thinking about a five-storey project that would further change the face of North Adelaide and cost two million dollars.

The Jollification of the North Adelaide environment looks fine so far; but I shouldn't want to see it changed too much. Between the art galleries there are old cottages with bluestone faces that have considerable charm.

Some of the stone churches that Adelaide is supposed to be stacked with have been converted into warehouses. The South Australian brown stone is also very good, though not as distinctive as the blue. The region's lack of timber led to great use of stone, as well as bricks, in the building of Adelaide. Wooden houses are relatively rare, even in the suburbs, though oiled pine is becoming vogueish.

Nothing has done more to invigorate Adelaide, broaden its horizons and increase its amiability, than its biennial Festival. It is also good for a city to have people like Sir Robert Helpmann in residence and saying controversial things as Festival director.

The 1972 Festival's preparation would appear to be in highly capable hands with Louis van Eyssen, who was last time the Festival's administrator, as the director.

Tours out of Adelaide

"YES, BUT . . . ." said the daughter I had been telling about Adelaide's festival. "Suppose I go to South Australia in an odd-number year when the Festival of Arts isn't on."

"In that case," I said, "you still get a festival, if you go in April.

You get the Barossa Valley Vintage Festival, the wine one. It's biennial, too."

She said the Barossa Valley festival sounded good, but doubted if she'd get to South Australia in autumn. What else was there within, say, fifty miles of Adelaide? (The Barossa is about thirty miles.)

Like Melbourne with its Dandenongs, the city of Adelaide is backed by hills, rounded hills that are not as high as their name suggests, the Mount Lofty Ranges. Their average height is about fifteen hundred feet—enough to increase the rainfall to forty inches in some places and give rise to the rivers that water the coastal plains, notably the Torrens and the Onkaparinga, and to deposit between the hills such fecund silts as we find in the Barossa Valley, which we'll come to.

The first half-day tour I took went into these near ranges to Belair National Park, which is only seven miles from Adelaide. It struck me as being, with its picnic tables and asphalt tennis courts, a recreation place for the local citizenry rather than of much sight-seeing interest to tourists.

Cleland National Park, also reached on an afternoon tour, was better. The fauna reserve here is one of the newest in Australia (1967) and one of the best-planned. Kangaroos, wallabies and emus are running free in a wide acreage of enclosures, not cooped behind wire. The wombat enclosure has the Hairy-Nosed Wombat, which Adelaidians have been commendably zealous in saving from extinction.

An engaging animal I have never seen, and thought might be here, is the numbat. Photographs show it to be rather like a small bandicoot, with a long bushy tail. It is the "most beautifully coloured of the marsupials",[1] with its dark brown pelt banded across the back and rump with white. An alert little creature, it lives on termites, feeding by day among ant-eaten trees, licking up the ants with a long thin tongue. The numbat used to occur as far east as western New South Wales, where an extinct species had white bands on a body that was "a kind of rich brick red".[2] The South Australian species has also quite gone, according to the naturalist David Fleay, "leaving only the south-western corner of the continent as the last home of the little Westralian pointy-nosed *Myrmecobius*".[3]

In the lizard enclosure at Cleland National Park one sees the perenty, a desert goanna that grows up to eight feet long and is Australia's largest; and the Painted Dragon lizard of semi-arid South Australia, which in the breeding season develops vivid colouring. I have seen one that was bright orange.

This tour also goes to Mount Lofty (2,334 feet) with a sweeping panorama of the plain where Adelaide sits, and the sun-sparkled Gulf of St Vincent beyond. The coach returns through the Piccadilly Valley, picturesque with market gardens. Near the little town of Norton Summit is the home of Sir Thomas Playford, who was premier of the State for twenty-six years, living in delightfully rural surroundings only eight miles from Parliament House (where he reigned for so long that it was known to South Australians as Uncle Tom's Cabin).

As we descend from these pleasant hills with their rich-soiled farms, a shining whiteness can be seen in the northern distance. These are the Dry Creek salt flats. The gullies turn silvery with olive-trees, many of them self sown and growing wild like eucalypts. Pockets of deep chocolate earth nurture celery, which comes to Sydney and Melbourne mainly from South Australia, which also grows about half Australia's barley.

The paradox of South Australia is that, although it is so preponderantly arid, with the western half and the northern half virtually useless agriculturally, it developed as a farmers' rather than a pastoralists' state. Fifty years after it was founded (nearly fifty years later than Sydney was) its south-eastern corner was not only the granary of the continent but had nearly half the farmed land in all Australia.

WHERE South Australia was proclaimed a province, in the name of His Majesty King William IV in 1836, we saw on the first tour. The Old Gum Tree, synthetically preserved, is arched right over to the ground, at Glenelg, where Captain John Hindmarsh landed on a very hot 28th December. Glenelg is by way of being Adelaide's Bondi, except that it is surfless, as are the other beaches along the Gulf of St Vincent; but they are good as beaches.

Victor Harbour I also toured to. It is the State's principal seaside resort but, although the town is usually overrun in summer with bowlers and fishermen from as far afield as Broken Hill (N.S.W.), if you go a few miles along this scallop of Encounter Bay it is charmingly restful. Here at Yilki a fine old house called Yelki (which I am assured is properly the place's name) gazes out across the bay that, on this day, was bluer than azure and brighter than cobalt. Yelki began as a whaler's inn soon after the ship *Victor* anchored there in 1837, and the inn portion—the house was enlarged by a renowned Congregationalist, James Jefferis, who died there in 1917—is the oldest stone building south of Adelaide. Encounter Bay has its name from Matthew Flinders' encountering the French sea explorer Nicolas Baudin there in 1802.

Beyond Yilki is a small bay where a whaling station was, back in 1837, and now, overlooking Rosetta Bay, is "Whaler's Haven". This is more than the usual privately run tourist museum with old harpoons and flensing knives and some outsize whale bones. An early settler's cottage has been reconstructed, and furnished very well. A blacksmith shop and a saddlery shop adjoin it, and there is Whaler's Inn with a large dining-room decorated with a painting by Ainslie Roberts, the South Australian artist who renders Aboriginal mythology—in this case a myth about a huge whale called Kondole—so strikingly.

Port Elliot, also visited, was the original port but it proved too dangerous. From it the first public railway in Australia ran to Goolwa, seven miles east. Goolwa is developing fast as a holiday resort.

FROM ADELAIDE we had come down the 52 miles to Victor Harbour through vineyard country.

"Undoubtedly, for fine dry reds the Southern Vales and Langthorne Creek are the specialist districts," said a South Australian friend who knows his State's wines particularly well. Reynella, Seaview, Tintara, Glenloth and Potts are notable wineries hereabouts.

Almonds are widely grown in this area where the rainfall is little more than twenty inches a year: the almond is not a thirsty tree and can be a particularly profitable one.

Stone houses, so characteristic of the South Australian scene, are especially interesting at Willunga, where they are roofed with slate. The old courthouse, restored by the National Trust, even has slate guttering.

The rolling hills, so dried off at summer's end that dairying needs irrigation, are tawny, the colour of old lions whose flanks are subtly variegated within a range of dun-ish hues.

WINE VALLEY, VIA ELIZABETH

THE SON of a British trader and a Malayan princess of Kedah—such was Colonel William Light—gazed on a fair valley in the ranges behind the Adelaide he was planning and named it from a battlefield in Andalusian Spain, where he had served with the Duke of Wellington: but the place in Spain is Barrosa, not Barossa.

An Englishman from Newcastle-on-Tyne, George Fife Angas, a rich and kindly man who felt for the plight of German Lutherans suffering religious persecution in Prussia and Silesia, brought six hundred of them, largely at his own expense, to South Australia in 1838 when the colony was only two years old.

A German geologist named Johann Menge—not one of the migrants but brought out by the South Australian Company to prospect for minerals—wrote in 1840: "I am quite certain that we shall see flourishing vineyards . . . throughout all New Silesia" (which was what the Lutherans called their new home, but it has remained the

Barossa Valley). The first vines were soon planted, and the first wine pressed from them in 1850.

Today the Barossa Valley is the greatest wine-producing area in Australia.

The valley is about twenty-five miles long by five miles wide. If you drive north-east from Adelaide along the Sturt Highway and turn off at Gawler you come to Lyndoch, where Light first admired it, after thirty-four miles. Exactly half-way is the city of Elizabeth. Fifteen years ago it wasn't there. What has happened, so recently, where there was only a treeless plain does not captivate the tourist as much as what has been going on in the Barossa Valley for well over a century—and there is no good reason why it should. But Elizabeth is more significant on the New Australia scene than the wine valley is.

ELIZABETH ("so named by gracious permission of Her Majesty the Queen") is an interesting example of the State at work in South Australia, which had three problems, (i) not enough manufacturing industries, (ii) not enough workforce to staff them if it got them, and (iii) an over-centralized population with 60 per cent of its people living in Adelaide.

Now that 50,000 people live in Elizabeth, the population of Adelaide and this satellite city only seventeen miles away, and separated from it by only eight miles of open space, amounts to 70 per cent: the urban imbalance is worse not better. However, decentralization was not the major purpose of the Elizabeth exercise, which has been highly successful in attracting both industries and people.

Seven out of ten of South Australia's Elizabethans are (or were: the proportion seems to have diminished somewhat) new Australians who migrated from Britain. Nor is this to be wondered at: a Mersey-sider with the glossy colour brochure saying "At home, work or play, life is good in Elizabeth" could well believe it and start asking when the next ship left for the South Australia that offered him "a home of your own . . . a place to grow . . . high standard schooling" with plenty of job opportunities. Nor would he feel a stranger—there is a local Merseyside Association, and pubs called the Red Lion and the Rose and Crown.

What would he work at? Making some of the 30,000+ Holden cars that roll off the assembly line at the Elizabeth plant of General Motors—Holden's, which employs 5,000 people. Perhaps making the "instant housing" I saw so much of in the new mining towns, turned out by WOWIC (for World Wide Camps) Industries at Elizabeth, the biggest makers of transportable workforce housing in the Southern Hemisphere. Or with one of the fifty-odd other industires that make anything from forklift trucks to men's suits, asbestos pipes, sewing machines and plastics. Should our Merseysider feel a bit strange working for a far-flung subsidiary of some multi-national cor-poration—Caterpillar Tractors or N.V. Nederlandsche Linoleum-fabrik or L'Air Liquide of France—he could always apply to Wm. Shakespeare (A/asia) Ltd, who are in the boat building and light engineering business.

Elizabeth, with some 12,000 houses (and about 300 flats), all of brick, is divided into eleven neighbourhoods each with its own shop-ping centre. There is a Town Centre as well.

The city is the creation of the South Australian Housing Trust which calls itself a "statutory body", not a State government agency. The houses it has built—and was selling in 1969 for $10,000 to $12,000 (about half the price of similar housing in Sydney with its high land values) were of forty-five designs. None was likely to win a Sulman Prize for architecture, but they were nevertheless the kind of houses that most people would build for themselves.

Hindsightedly, Elizabeth could have been more imaginatively New Australian, but it works. It is claimed to be the fastest growing place in Australia and should reach the stated limit population of 70,000 before the mid-seventies. The Adelaide academic who damned it as an "English ghetto" is likely to be dismissed by the glad-he-migrated Merseysider with a curt, "The man's daft", as he downs his glass of cold West End beer before going home to the best house he's ever had in the first car he's ever owned.

I WENT TWICE to the Barossa Valley, the first time on a coach tour for the regular tourist experience and the second time on a private car jaunt that was unalloyed pleasure.

March was a good time to go. The grape harvest (PLATE 43) be-gins in February and continues into April. The Barossa Vintage Festival is held in odd-numbered years, and the valley is *en fête*. It is usually only a two-day festival, its highlights the Weingarten dinner in a park pavilion at Tanunda with traditional food and the *Liedertafel* (male choir) leading the folk singing, the afternoon Vin-tage Carnival with grape treading contests and other entertainment, and at night the crowning of the Vintage Queen.

The other good time of the year is spring. The valley is not by any means given over entirely to vineyards. It has many orchards—called locally, and rather delightfully, "fruit gardens"—which are then blossoming. There is also a good deal of wheat, and in March, with the rolling hills dried off and sheep in the stubbled fields, the Barossa was a chequerboard of blond and green.

The coach tour I took (it wasn't Pioneer, either, but the driver-commentator, Len Pfeiffer, was good) went to only one winery, the big one at Seppeltsfield, founded by Joseph Ernest Seppelt from Germany in 1851. The winery buildings are interestingly Colonial with Germanic accents. The wine-making processes are explained by guides (and have already been explained in connection with Seppelt's Great Western winery in Victoria).

Towns with German names are surprisingly few. Aboriginal are Tanunda (plenty of wildfowl), Nuriootpa (a meeting place) and Yalumba (the country around). Lyndoch was named by Light for his friend Lord Lynedoch (the "e" got lost). Kaiser Stühl has resumed its old place on the map, as a winery: during World War I the German "King's Seat" was changed to Mt Kitchener.

The towns themselves are redolent of the German settlers, and each has a stone Lutheran church—indeed, Tanunda has three, and one of these, the Langmeil, is the most picturesque in the valley. Tanunda is the most characterful of the towns, with its tree-shady main street and air of cleanly reticence. The custom of taking a plough to church to be blessed is still carried on. In Tanunda's historical museum is many a relic that came from Prussia or Silesia, or was made here in the German mould. There is not only a 1706 German Bible but a copy of the Book of *Die Propheten* (The Prophets) printed at Wittenberg in 1564.

ON TOP of Mengler Hill, with the Barossa Valley spread below, was where I had lunch a few days later. It was the best picnic lunch I have ever eaten, and some worthy wine went with it. Rudy Komon, the Sydney art dealer who is also a wine buff, saw to that.

The lunch had been prepared by Dr Earle Hackett, who was chairman of Trustees of the Art Gallery of South Australia, and his wife. We had come in a car and the Hackett station-wagon, the tailboard of which was soon laden with the choicest cold beef, sausage, salad vegetables and relishes to be had in the city of Adelaide. The gourmet Komon was suitably impressed. Fred Williams, the notable painter, who has a slight weight problem, groaned at the array of temptations, and then happily fell to. Also in the party were Leonard French, whose splendid retrospective exhibition was mounted in the State gallery as a Festival attraction, and David Bailie of the Royal Shakespeare Company, who played Florizel in *The Winter's Tale*. The fruit basket Mrs Hackett had prepared was like a work of art in itself, grape bunches nesting among perfect peaches, plums and strawberries, and decorative with vineleaves.

In this excellent company I had spent most of the morning at the Yalumba winery. No German was its founder but a "patient, God-fearing brewer from Wareham in Dorset", Samuel Smith, who settled in the valley in 1847 and two years later forgot about beer and planted his first grapes. The winery is near Angaston, but one of the Yalumba vineyards is at Pewsey Vale, which was originally planted by a man named Gilbert in 1847. The Rhine Riesling grapes of Pewsey Vale produced in 1969 a white wine that the Royal Sydney Show judges (Rudy Komon was one of them) gave a gold medal to, and it won other gold medals in Melbourne and Adelaide. It was this beautifully fruity riesling that we drank in the house of the present Yalumba proprietor, Wyndham ("Windy") Hill-Smith, whose forebear was the brewer Smith from Dorset.

Having lunched superbly, we made a leisurely visit to the Orlando winery at Rowland Flat. As at Yalumba, trucks of grapes were coming in, for the harvest was at its height. Here we tasted a number of wines, all of them good and two of them particularly memorable. A very fine robust dry red was the Orlando Barossa Cabernet, 1963. The other was a rosé which even the connoisseur Komon pronounced very good although he was not, he said, a rosé man. It was (and I quote another expert, Ian Mackay[1]) ". . . made from a patch of grapes planted in one corner of their large Barossa Valley property back in 1912 or so by Gustav Gramp, son of Johann, the company's founder. No one knew what kind of grape it was—but it produced a rosé of brilliant colour and a dry, full flavour, and with typical Gramp honesty the label bore the legend 'made from grapes unknown'." Samples were sent to France for identification and Orlando's impressive young winemaker, Mark Tummel, now knew what the grape was—the variety called *grec*. I hoped they would plant more of it because it made a superb rosé.

This (1970) was a particularly good wine year in South Australia, and a claret Gramps entered at the Adelaide show, although it was so young, gained a gold medal and the highest points on record.

The Man for Arkaroola

ARKAROOLA means the place of Arkaroo, and Arkaroo was the local Aborigines' name for the great snake that coils and arches and slithers through the myths of their Dreamtime. Arkaroo, as they tell it, drank Lake Frome dry. His enormous body carved out Arkaroola Creek and he made water in it as he went through the ancient hills of what the white man calls the North Flinders Ranges.

Geologists tell it differently and stress that the Arkaroola region is of much greater antiquity than men or serpents. They point to massive cores of red and white granite they date as old as 1,650 million years. They say that at one time the central part of Australia sank so that the sea came flooding in from the north and cut the continent into two great islands. Sediments covered the seabed rocks and formed sandstones, quartzites, slates and limestones. "At the end of the Cambrian Period [perhaps 500 million years ago] a great change took place. The newly formed rocks were subjected to enormous lateral pressure. By this they were squeezed from east and west and pushed upwards into a series of great folds. . . . In the Flinders Ranges the folding was more complicated, and pressure came from the north and south also, resulting in the formation of large domes and basins."[1] The basins are called pounds, and the chief of these amphitheatres like craters or mountain-walled corrals is Wilpena Pound, which we'll come to.

A million years ago there was no desert here. "The interior of Australia was green and teemed with life. There were great herds of the giant wombat-like creature the Diprotodon, and the giant kangaroo and other extinct marsupials."[2] Between five and ten thousand years ago the rainfall began to diminish. Aridity overtook the land and the sea shrank to muddy saline lakes. Of these, Lake Callabonna was one of the last refuges of the prehistoric animals, and white salt shining under a pitiless sun surfaces a graveyard where we find their bones. The earth that was once so well-fleshed is brown and bony, and the ancient spine of ranges is marrowed with minerals (uranium among them), and kaleidoscopic with the kind of rock specimens that shine in the collector's eye. Such is the geological background, briefly, of the region we are going to, in the wake of the man who has opened it to the traveller.

R. C. (REG) SPRIGG is a geologist. He also graduated in zoology and has a M.Sc. among his degrees. His mentor was Sir Douglas Mawson. As senior geologist of the Mines Department of South Australia he explored geologically the top end of the Flinders Ranges, where Arkaroola was a sheep station. Radium, the only valuable constituent of uranium ores in those days, was discovered in this area back in 1910. When, during World War II, the Americans were seeking uranium supply, Sprigg was sent out to re-open the radium mine. In the atomic bomb that was dropped on Hiroshima there was Flinders Ranges uranium.

In the course of walking over the craggy, red-brown face of Arkaroola, Reg Sprigg found its harsh and arid countenance beautiful. He fell in love with what had become a sheep property only because brothers named Greenwood had been given the least favoured ends

Near Port Lincoln there is striking variety of scenic coast, including cliffs 500 feet high, at Cape Wiles, reached through "Whalers' Way".

Kangaroo Island has some beautiful beaches as undeveloped as this one, Pennington Bay. Another has a colony of quite approachable seals.

The Blue Lake at Mount Gambier becomes intensely blue between November and February. Scientists are still trying to explain why this occurs.

Decca's Place is an attractive restaurant in North Adelaide that serves good food and wine in a viney courtyard. Taken when we lunched there.

of three stations to make into one, as their fee for eradicating the "vermin" of the area, wild camels, donkeys, dingoes, goats. Sprigg saw Arkaroola as a precious segment of wild Australia, an area geologically unique and uncommonly interesting in its fauna; and he saw it as being vandalized. It disturbed him that the wartime uranium miners shot those rare Yellow-Footed Wallabies that sat up and looked at them. Mineral man though he was, he became alarmed at what the miners were doing to the region by, as he puts it, "the seemingly endless need to bulldoze into magnificent cliff faces to provide temporary drilling sites".

At the same time he was excited, as a geologist, at what had begun to happen in the New Australia and, soon after oil was discovered in the West at Rough Range in 1953, Reg Sprigg left the Government service and set up his own consultant company, Geosurveys of Australia. Although he moved as consulting geologist into areas much farther afield, in exploration for oil and nickel, he did not forget Arkaroola. He tried hard to get the South Australian Government to acquire it as National Parkland. When he heard, in January 1968, that the property might be purchased, he got on the telephone and bought it, although he had not seen Arkaroola's homestead in fourteen years.

I had wanted to meet Reg Sprigg, and he and his wife came to have morning coffee with me when I was staying at the Parkroyal in Adelaide. He was fiftyish, clean-featured, vital but not at all pretentious, and his wife, Griselda, was impressive, too. She was from Scotland and shared his love of the arid Australian inland to the extent that she had gone with him on journeys that included a crossing of the Simpson Desert in 1964. On a trip five years before that, with their two young children with them, the strangest thing happened.

The map of the desert area they were travelling through north of Lake Frome showed, near Coonana gas bore, a notation *Ruins*. As Reg Sprigg wrote,[3] "Not having seen a sign of human habitation for two days of hard going, this intrigued us. As we neared the position at high noon we peered round each sand dune expecting to see a ruin. Suddenly we did. . . . Our children were asleep but Griselda and I both saw it at the same moment.

"There it was, a little old gable-roofed and stone-walled building, with a galvanized iron veranda facing south. Behind it were some taller gums, and on the south-west corner nearest us a green pepper-tree grew to veranda roof height. We were now only 100 feet or so away so I continued on, intending to round the bushy green pepper-tree from the south and draw up at the veranda.

"Great was our surprise when, upon rounding the tree, there was

cc

no house, or anything to suggest former human occupation. More-over, the tree was not a pepper-tree—merely a sapling gum."

Both described seeing the same thing. They sat down back to back and made drawings of what had appeared to them, and their sketches of the house with the pepper-tree were identical. They wished they had wakened the children: would they have seen the same thing?

Subsequently they revisited the area and explored it thoroughly, finding remnants of a stockyard, but no building such as might have appeared near to them through the effect of mirage. The Spriggs are convinced that what they saw was not a mirage. (Nor, if there was no such building at a distance, could it have been.) It must then, they admit, have been an hallucination. Yet a mutually experienced hallucinatory experience is surely a very odd psychological pheno-menon. Hallucinations can be induced by great fatigue: they say they were certainly tired after two days hard travelling, but they were by no means exhausted. A state of anticipation can also pro-duce a hallucination of seeing something that is expected. Reg Sprigg concedes that they were in a keyed-up anticipatory frame of mind. But what he had expected to see, he says, was "a ruin without a roof, and with collapsed walls—not a roofed old cottage, merely deserted, as this appeared". And appeared to both of them at the same moment and in the same form as they described to each other in identical detail.

What nobody seems to know is what was there or what was seen by whoever caused the notation *Ruins* to be placed on the map.

ARKAROOLA has been developed by Reg Sprigg as a tourist resort. It lies 420 road miles north of Adelaide, with bitumen most of the way and the rest graded. Tourist coaches are making weekend express trips to it via Leigh Creek, the big open-cut coal mine eighty miles west. The most scenic road route would be via Wilpena Pound and Chambers Gorge. Or you can fly direct from Adelaide (325 air miles) by a twice-weekly air service.

The Flinders Ranges stretch nearly three hundred miles north from Spencer Gulf. The North Flinders is the more continuous sec-tion and reaches its highest point, St Mary's Peak (3,900 feet) near Wilpena Pound. Some ranges' hills are as rounded and bare as an elephant's back—and hardly more colourful—and rhythmic lines of outcropping rock are common. Others are sharply ridged and clad with more than spinifex. Colour increases to rusty red as you come over the northern end of the range, where the country changes to granites, and this is where Arkaroola Village is. (PLATE 41 shows the lodge.)

The whole 225 square miles is now a wildlife sanctuary. Reg

Sprigg and his partner-manager, Dennis Walter, want to reintroduce to the area the brush-tailed possum and the wombat. Manna gums have been planted that will be feed for koalas. Tortoises, too, they wanted to introduce. A Painted Dragon lizard not recorded elsewhere had been found. Dennis Walter's parents have helped establish the fauna park.

Sheep were still on the station, but were being phased out as it is poor sheep country, and will not support cattle either. Rainfall is only eight inches in an average year and in 1969 only two and a half inches fell.

Tourists who come on the coaches or fly up, and so are without cars of their own, are taken round in four-wheel-drive vehicles, and it was in one of these that I spent most of my time with the lodge guide, a bright-minded young man, Dale Palomountain. You can also, in such a Toyota vehicle, traverse "roads" the ordinary car cannot negotiate. More than sixty miles of road had been developed by Arkaroola Pty Ltd and, in what is scenically the best part of the region, these roads linked with those put in by a uranium-prospecting company, Exoil (PLATE 42).

One can understand a geologist's enthusiasm for the Arkaroola country, even without knowing what the tumbles of rocks, the soaring stratifications and dramatic outcrops mean. Some understanding of geology (my own is minimal) helps appreciation of it, and to be a "rock hound" is reason to rummage its stony flanks and creek beds with passionate enthusiasm. Detailed directions tell you where to collect magnetite crystals or white feldspar or the orange albite feldspar gem cutters love. If you are after fibrous tremolite, barite crystals or glistening black hematite, they are there, too, on the run to places called Bolla Bollana and Nooldoo Nooldoona.

At Bolla Bollana there is an old smelter from a copper mine of the 1890s. The kiln looks like a big stone beehive and was so well built that it still stands intact on what has been declared a historic site. There is a splendid view from a hilltop we reached by the simple expedient of Dale Palomountain's pointing the Toyota at a slope covered with rocks and spinifex and, dodging the bigger boulders and the odd mulga, up it went. We walked to a waterhole where, from the rocks above it, I was able to photograph a euro and a wallaby drinking. At another place in another direction, Barraranna Gorge, we must have seen between fifteen to twenty kangaroos or wallabies.

Wywhyana Creek, not far from the motel, is lined with big red river-gums and a few miles south-east is the vivid Painted Wall. This is a deposit of ochres stratified in brilliant colours from yellow through to purple-brown.

The trip I most enjoyed was out to the Mt Painter area and beyond, where Exoil had done a lot of drilling for uranium. According to the company's 1970 report, they have found more than their geologist on the spot, Eric Streitberg, told me of. On the low land near Lake Frome, what the company called its Beverley prospect indicated 900,000 tons of ore containing 5½ million pounds of uranium oxide—six pounds to the ton. This was regarded as likely to prove "a large deposit of commercial significance" in a "major sedimentary uranium province".

We had lunch at the Exoil camp, sited in rugged terrain cut with the red roads of the drillers. Thirty-five men were living in transportable "instant housing" that must be somewhere else now. As to food, they lived well. The previous night's dinner menu was still up on the wall where the chef, Peter Walkley, had written it, and I almost said to him, "You're joking!" It read: *Chicken Bouillon/ Oysters Kilpatrick/Turkey, Ham & Pineapple/Roast Pork & Apple Sauce/Escallop of Veal* followed by a choice of four desserts, *Blackberry Float* to *Marshmallow Surprise*.

Exoil, in the course of spending well over a million dollars in exploring this area, had put in a hundred miles of roads for the drilling plants to move along. PLATE 42 shows the principal road that goes on past the rugged side of Mt Painter (2,850 feet).

The whole Mt Painter region is, Reg Sprigg points out, an area of instability in the earth's crust. Movements continue along the "fault" lines and, from time to time, earth tremors set up rumbling noises the Aborigines identified with the great snake Arkaroo turning over in his sleep.

From Siller's Lookout you gaze west to a magnificent jumble of angular mountains, and east across the plain to the heat-hazed salt whiteness of Lake Frome, north of which is Callabonna, the graveyard of Diprotodons. The eye is caught by a group of trees, oasis-green in the dry land. Behind these are reddish cliffs, and from their base water issues almost boiling hot.

Paralana Hot Springs are, according to the knowledgeable Dennis Walter, the only active residue of Australia's volcanic era. The water, he says, is weakly radio-active. Small amounts of helium and radon in it testify to the origin of the springs being deep within the earth. These and other mineral elements were regarded as being so curative of such ailments as rheumatism that, in 1924, Paralana was developed as a health spa by a Dr Fenton. Owing to the place's remoteness and the hard travel to get to it, the enterprise failed. Today, with planes and any amount of level land in the vicinity for them to alight, these hot springs of a kind unique in Australia might be developed successfully.

But Reg Sprigg was not thinking in terms of exploiting the hot springs, Dennis Walter said. All they wanted to do was to protect and preserve them. They had offered their adjoining land to the State government if it wanted to establish an Aboriginal community there, because it was a sacred place of the local Andjnamutana tribe.

The geologist was also concerned with protecting Yudnamutana Gorge, which he said was the deepest and longest known gorge in Australia, from mining companies' bulldozers. It seemed to me that it was a good day for conservation in South Australia when Reg Sprigg fell in love with Arkaroola.

Wilpena Pound Plus

IN CONTRAST to Arkaroola, which was the kind of place that bristled with problems of tourist development, Wilpena Pound "had it made": a natural wonder near the north-south highway and just a good day's drive from Adelaide, 260 miles. You could fly, but most people came in their own cars to what was an excellent base for touring the northern Flinders Ranges.

The two places complemented each other. About eighty per cent of the people who went to Arkaroola had been to or would go to Wilpena Pound; and about half who went to Wilpena went also to Arkaroola, which was a much newer resort and not nearly so well known, as well as being relatively off-track. They were about 150 miles apart by road. I flew across in Arkaroola's Cessna, leaving at four-thirty in the afternoon when the shadows were beginning to cut deeply into the red-brown ruggedness round Mt Painter and the Armchair. You fly on across ranges less truculent, less like a mailed fist thrusting at the sky its red knuckles of granite, ranges that have a more recumbent look. Then the mountains are on guard again, crags bristling from the long formation known as the Great Wall of China and, south of that, you begin to make out the bastion range that runs right round to enclose Wilpena Pound. The plane lands close to where the motel sits at the foot of the only break in the wall, the one way in.

As Charles Laseron has said,[1] before we had aeroplanes such curious formations as Wilpena Pound could be examined only piecemeal from the ground, and it took long, patient geological survey to reveal their general structure. Only within the past fifty years has our vision of the country expanded from the groundling animal's to the soaring bird's. Wilpena Pound I wanted a good look at from the air. Kevin Rasheed, proprietor of the excellent Wilpena Pound Motel, said there was no problem about that. A former R.A.A.F. pilot in World War II, he flew his own Cessna. We took off at 7 a.m. and ascended into a perfect morning.

Wilpena Pound's mountain walls rise up in runnelled slopes from a tree-clad base and turn to tiers of rock, rugged and commanding. On the inside they slope gently down in a dished formation, like some sunken cake that failed sadly in the oven, though the usual description is that it resembles, as it does, the crater of some vast volcano.

The pound—so called because it would be a great natural corral to impound animals in—is about twelve miles long by five wide. These dimensions suggest that it is a narrower ovoid shape than it appears from a plane flying at about seven thousand feet outside it, as I was when I took photographs (PLATE 41). The highest peak to the wall is St Mary's (3,900 feet). Pompey's Pillar is 3,850, and a high saddle between these closes the north-western end of the pound. The other end's outer side is of formidable cliffs, deeply riven with ravines. Yet, at the one break in the bastion wall access to the pound, along Wilpena Creek, could hardly be easier.

I went in the following morning with the pleasant girl from the motel's office, Maureen Murphy, who drove about a mile and then we walked half that distance. We came to a small stone homestead: a farmer named John Hill brought his family to live there at the turn of the century and grew wheat for a few years. Then he was beaten by a disaster it is always difficult to associate with this dry country— flood.

The country within the pound and outside it looked, after the harsh broken hills of Arkaroola, park-like. Wilpena gets about eighteen inches of rain a year, double Arkaroola's average, and the country is fairly well grazed. We went to Wilpena Station, which has a particularly charming stone homestead built in 1868 and added to since. Here and at another nearby sheep station, Rawnsley Park, tourists are shown sheep-dog drafting and shearing of sheep.

In this March the weather was perfect, the days brilliantly blue and hot, although it was autumn. It comes as a surprise to be told that Wilpena means "bent fingers", from the Aborigines finding winter mornings so cold that they could hardly open their hands. But the winter days soon warm. The most popular time is mid-August to mid-October, when Spring decks the Flinders Ranges country with such wildflowers as the brilliant red Sturt's Desert Pea, the salmon-pink wild hops and the purple spread of Salvation Jane, known as Paterson's Curse in the eastern States.

NOTEBOOK: Wilpena Pound Motel, fully licensed, has pleasant bar where I talked with Kevin Rasheed's friend Fred Teague who's been studying Aboriginal rock carvings for forty years and says you find them at creek junctions that allow three ways of escape. Bird-track markings, he says, point the direction tribe was going so, having found some carvings, he knows where to look for more. Fred also says, "In 1870 half the population of South Australia was in the Flinders Ranges looking for copper."

Rich lode of copper was found by a wooden-legged shepherd called "Peg Leg" Blinman, at what became the town of Blinman. Kevin drove me over there and we wandered round the defunct copper mine. Talk is, as always in old mining towns, that Blinman will be revived. Somebody seems to have a lease on the workings because lettered large on an old boiler is KEEP OUT. THIS MEANS YOU. Blinman started in 1860. Concentrate used to be hauled out by bullock wagons, then steam traction engines: 2,000 to 3,000 people there then—now twenty. Yet pub somehow keeps going, with tourists dropping in. One of the oldest pubs in S.A. (1861). Its man-of-all-work used to be executive with motor firm. Blinman's only future probably is as a tourist "museum" town. Someone from Adelaide has bought and restored admirably old mine manager's house. Cemetery has grave of William Kekwick who was McDouall Stuart's second in command on expeditions through centre: died here in 1872.

West about 20 miles is Parachilna, railway line hamlet with even fewer houses than Blinman, but it has a pub. Kept by Angus Donald McKenzie who used to truck frozen rabbits from Innamincka, which I hadn't thought of as country that could feed a rabbit. Angus says, "The drier the country the better their meat," and says that Innamincka bunnies often have yellowish fur, as protective coloration against their main predator, the dingo.

Pull up under some gums on the Parachilna Plain, with Aroona Range decorating the horizon, and boil the billy for lunch. Then Kevin says, "Just along here I'll show you some fossils called Archaeocyathinae." And we pick up—they are on the ground as thick as gibbers almost—stone sponges. About 500 million years ago they were soft sponges, on a seabed.

Brachina Gorge we go on to. This is in very broken, rusty red, Arkaroola-type country, with rugged rockwalls and fine big river red-gums beside running water (which Brachina means, Aboriginally). K. Rasheed (his name is from Lebanon) says that once he was driving through here and he saw a big wedge-tailed eagle sitting on a fallen tree. It didn't move as he approached it: he knew it must be sick. When he returned through the gorge an hour or two later it was still there. "I went up and looked closely at it. I could see where it had been shot in the breast. It looked at me and its eyes said, 'Do the right thing, old man. Don't leave me to die slowly from the bullet.' I don't carry a gun. So I found a lump of wood and its head didn't even flinch as it saw the blow coming."

You go on a little and look back at the remarkable diagonal stratification of the red rocks jutting out of slopes candlewicked with clumps of spinifex. There are flocks of galahs and some bounding kangaroos as we head back to Wilpena via the Bunyeroo Valley. The sierra of mountains standing at the end of this valley as dark-blue heights above a foreground of rolling dry-grassed country bright as copper in the sun, this, from the lookout point we stop at, is one of the best sights the Flinders Ranges have to show.

I HAD BEEN TOLD, by Max Harris in Adelaide, not to miss seeing Quorn: its old buildings were special. I have news for Max about Quorn, but that can wait till we get there, by way of Hawker.

Kevin Rasheed drove me down, and we called in at Hawker Motors which is run by the Aboriginal-carvings enthusiast, Fred Teague, and it is the only service station I know that has a museum of Aboriginal artefacts, with mineral specimens and fossils, behind the petrol pumps.

In the forty miles down the sheep-and-wheat plain between Hawker and Quorn the R.A.A. map shows four townships marked *Deserted* and has a notation saying *Ruins*, just off the highway. Substantial ruins they are, too, of Kanyaka, a century ago a populous sheep station. Seventy families lived on it and Kanyaka ran 40,000 sheep. The woolshed, huge and of solid stone, still stands, as do other buildings including the station-hands' quarters, which were in process of restoration by the Naturalists' Society of S.A. who were doing the job very well.

Quorn. This town of about 600 people that calls itself the "Gateway to the Flinders Ranges" indeed has some characterful old buildings. There is the unexpected half-Italianate elegance of the Town Hall; the veranda-posted Victoriana of the railway station that was by-passed by the north-south line when it went standard gauge in 1956; and the old flour mill that has had its face painted and been turned, attractively enough, into The Mill motel-museum. But, for the rest, main-street Quorn has been ruined by the brush of the painter and signwriter. Three of the four hotels bash the tourist across the eye with their names in letters feet high and one yells ICE from a sidewall. The smoke from the barytes treatment plant (barytes makes the mud oil-drillers use) is hardly an allurement, either. Some State authority should give guidance to towns like Quorn that, needing tourism to sustain them, go so hamhandedly about trying to attract it that they only drive it away. And the potential is there, in the wide main street that has so much Australian character that it was where some of the film *The Sundowners* was made.

On the way back to Wilpena the sun was going down, setting fire to the Chase Range and lighting to glory the eastern walls of the Pound. One could well understand why Hans Heysen was so fond of painting the Flinders Ranges.

Next day Kevin Rasheed flew me down to Adelaide.

Zest at Port Lincoln

THE PLACE that was almost Adelaide. Such was the port Flinders sailed into in 1802, giving it the name of his native English province and writing of it as "a second Port Jackson in the south". The whole British Fleet could ride snugly in Port Lincoln proper, and as many ships again in adjoining Boston Bay.

However, when South Australia was founded and Colonel Light as Surveyor-General came to look at the great southern harbour, he found its environs short of water and somewhat barren of aspect. So the capital was sited on the Torrens River with its port on the Gulf of St Vincent.

Port Lincoln was left to work out its own destiny at the tip of the big tongue of land called the Eyre Peninsula. It lived mainly by shipping out the wheat grown on the peninsula and by fishing, which grew into a big industry based on the catching and canning of blue-fin tuna. Now a third development is prospering the town that sits beside sheltered blue water for sailers and anglers and is central to other bays and beaches. Tourism has been latched onto so avidly at Port Lincoln that visitors outnumber its 10,000 inhabitants each year at the end of January.

That is when Port Lincoln holds what it calls its Tunarama Festival, with processions of floats and boats, bevies of bikini girls, and much else that does little more than suggest that P.L. is becoming the Surfers Paradise of S.A.—except that there are literary and art contests as well as sporty ones. However, other towns have festivals in which culture gets its corner, even if they have not had as English master at the local high school such a literary light as Colin Thiele,

who has published volumes of poetry and written such highly regarded verse plays as *Burke and Wills*. One of his poems appears in
the tourist brochure and begins:

> *Port Lincoln's heritage is shine and dapple—*
> *The winter's gold transmuted from a cloud,*
> *The summer's haze a-shimmer on a mirror*
> *Of still, blue glass.*

The broad blue mirror of Boston Bay the poet praises reflects at
night the lights of wheat ships and tuna boats at its jetties more
brightly than the stars; the eye of the tourist perambulating bayside
Tasman Terrace is taken with the Chinese junk, an exotic importa-
tion from Hong Kong; what bulks in the vista from the bald top of
Winter's Hill are the silos; and one is conscious of the industrial whiff
of fish and fertilizer, the "smell of money", rather than of any aura
that might be called, at a stretch, Athenian. Even though PLATO
is here. And even though PLATO (Port Lincoln Advancement Trust
Organization) is the brainchild of a solicitor and adept money-
maker with the poetic-painterly name of Tennyson Turner.

It was to accommodation owned, as much else in Port Lincoln
was, by Mr Tennyson Turner that the Airlines of South Australia
plane brought me, in just one hour's early-morning flight, from
Adelaide. At least, the plane brought me to Port Lincoln's airport
and the young man I had been sitting beside (who lived there and
was always glad to come home for weekends from Adelaide, where
he worked, because P.L. was "such a wonderful place for water-
skiing") said his parents were meeting him and they would drop me
off at Boston House.

The car turned off the road to what appeared to be a large two-
storeyed residence of stone with iron-lace balconies: one might describe it as a mansion. The furnishings were lushly elegant and suites
had such names as Jasper, Turquoise and Onyx. The grounds were
vast and the verandas gave sweeping views of Boston Bay.

Had I come a year earlier it would have been not to Boston House
but to, as it was then called, the Renaissance Motel Spa—and nothing
indicates better the freewheeling imagination of the zestful Port
Lincoln promoters, Tennyson Turner in particular, than this establishment that offered, in the words of its brochure, "Rejuvenating
sauna and mineral spa baths with spa water from a spring on the
property", along with beauty treatment, hair care, reducing equipment, exercise apparatus, sun lamps and—should some dowager feel
like having the full Cleopatran treatment—milk baths. There having
been rather a South Australian shortage of dowagers and other rich

ladies who patronize such places at Harrogate in England and Continental spas, Mr Turner conceded that the Renaissance Motel Spa was somewhat ahead of its time. It had not been a "goer", but when it had become known as the elegant Boston House motel it would, he thought, revert to being a luxury spa.

Tennyson Turner, a very personable and suave man in his middle forties, seemed quite unworried about having dropped some money on the spa project: he had so many other profitable interests. He was in mining, in Southern Concrete Masonry and in other motels (the ones called Hilton, rather surprisingly, since they have no connection with the chain of prestige American hotels of that name): there was a Hilton Motor Inn at Port Lincoln. He was also in the process of creating Holidayland. This large project he did not expect to complete until 1972, but it already had twenty holiday "villas"— all identical and each one looking like a giant-sized television set. They were TV shaped in fibreglass—Transtar Villas was their trade name, and they were made in South Australia at Blair Athol—and for about $5,000 you could get one delivered on site fully equipped with electrical wiring, plumbing, wall-to-wall carpet and air-conditioning. They were spankingly furnished in the modern manner and, since the land Tennyson Turner owned 350 acres of was inexpensive, he was able to offer Holidayland accommodation at relatively low rentals. He had put in a restaurant-shop and a squash court; gaily coloured beach buggies were on hire, and a large swimming-pool was in the making.

While I was still wondering how Robin Boyd would have reacted to rows of TV-shaped fibreglass villas—described by the makers as being of "futuristic design, so pleasing to the eye!"—and inwardly deploring their lack of Australian character, Mr Turner whisked me in his Mercedes to his First Landing Motel, which was so Colonial in character that it had veranda posts, four-poster beds and Australian historical prints framed on the unit walls.

And before I could recollect what Senator Murphy, the Labour Leader in the Senate, had said, in very trouncing fashion, about some share deal that Tennyson Turner was involved in, he was showing me Ravendale House. This admirable stone building with its graceful French doors was built in 1842 as the Government Residency. Since the Vice-Regal representative was also the magistrate, it served as the courtroom as well. It is finely constructed of local limestone, but by 1965 was badly in need of restoration. It had been restored, and very well furnished—much of the furniture was originally in Boston House—and this had been done not by the National Trust but at the expense of Tennyson Turner.

However, it would be wrong to suggest that this surprising solicitor and promoter bestrode Port Lincoln's tourism as Gulliver did Lilliput—which small-peopled kingdom, incidentally, was located by Swift in his *Gulliver's Travels* "north-west of Van Diemen's . . . in the Latitude of 30 Degrees 2 Minutes South", about 200 air miles away in the region of Ceduna. The zest of Tennyson Turner was abetted by that of such others as Port Lincoln's sheepfarmer mayor, its newspaper editor, and Peter O'Brien who brought the junk from Hong Kong, owned holiday flats, and could have been described as a "live wire" if he had not been in the electrical business.

COFFIN BAY is not the most alluringly named of seaside resorts: the discovering Flinders paid tribute here to an eminent friend Vice-Admiral Sir Isaac Coffin. But there was nothing funereal about the place or the pace it was developing at. Coffin Bay lies across on the other side of the peninsula tip, about thirty miles from Port Lincoln.

"It's a booming 1970 resort where, five years ago, you could hardly give land away," said Peter O'Brien who drove me there. Flats had sprung up that were letting for $65 a week in the Christmas holidays.

The fishing village atmosphere lived on in jetties that spindled out into the broad blue expanses of two inner sheltered waterways, Kellidie Bay and Dutton Bay. The first is too shallow for centreboard sailing but fine for motor-boating and water skiing, and so good for fishing, Peter O'Brien said, that some friends of his had recently brought home from their holiday 200 pounds of whiting they had sold to the Safcol cannery in Port Lincoln for $50.

It is a sanctuary area for wildlife, and a swamp that dries out in summer has, in winter, a multitude of birds.

In another direction, a good conservationist-developer was Bob Theakstone. It was possibly some kind of record in this trigger-happy country that he owned and lived on 12,000 acres of land and didn't own a gun. Several thousand of the Theakstone acres, which Bob's grandfather took up in 1889, comprised a bold headland twenty miles south-west of Port Lincoln. This nature area is caped and bayed so scenically that Bob Theakstone had put in roads and opened it to the public for a fee and, because there was a whaling station here when Port Lincoln was born, he called it Whalers Way.

You go through his gate and down to Cape Wiles where the sea has carved from the limestone two spectacular islet formations. Then there is Cape Carnot where the seaspray cascades over beautiful rocks. Farther on is Redbank where the cliffs are so red they look like bauxite. From Black's Lookout there is a panoramic view forty miles in each direction. A curious formation called Theakstone's Crevasse cuts straight as a ruler through the rocky land to an edge of the rugged coast.

The whaling station that was set up in 1837 was where you enter Whalers Way, on Fishery Bay which has a splendid beach of white sand and good surfing. This area seemed certain to develop, but Bob Theakstone said he would keep any building off his private reserve. He wanted to see as its only inhabitants kangaroos and emus and the birds that had been abundant before farming and the introduced fox came. They included the distinctive ring-necked Port Lincoln Parrot.

Industrially, Port Lincoln claims to be the biggest fishing port in Australia, with its tuna, crayfish and whiting catches. The bayside wheat silos *look* the largest, even if they aren't. Mineralogically, this region could be heard from. B.H.P. was getting limestone sand from Coffin Bay, and near Port Lincoln had a large fenced-in lease area it would drill. Offshore drilling for oil was talked about, and the Noranda company of Canada was reportedly interested in a uranium prospect in the Port Lincoln area.

Of course, the biggest industrial accomplishment in the Eyre Peninsula region has been at the top of this inverted triangle, on the Spencer Gulf side, at Whyalla. This is Australia's biggest shipbuilding yard and, after Newcastle and Port Kembla in New South Wales, the country's third iron and steel centre. But its shipbuilding was a World War II development and the steel industry was set up in 1958: Whyalla is hardly *New* Australia. Nor is this highly industrialized city, set in unenchanting terrain, of much interest to the traveller. Hundreds of Whyalla workers, in their holiday time, take off for Port Lincoln and its purlieus of Mediterranean-blue water, where the climate is rather like that of the Greek islands and less than an inch of average rain falls in any month of summer.

Kangaroo Island

QUIZ QUESTION for Australian travel agents: Of what part of Australia was it once written, *circa* 1910, that it "can lay claim to undisputed sovereignty as the fairest of all the queenly seaside resorts of the Commonwealth"?

I'd be surprised if, outside of South Australia, one in a hundred gave the right answer, which is—Kangaroo Island.

South Australians know it is a good place to holiday, even if they do not claim it as the fairest in the land. But many a travel agent in the other States has yet to make his first tourist booking to what is, Tasmania excepted, the second largest island off the Australian coast (Melville Island, north of Darwin, is a bit bigger). However, it should not be long before Kangaroo Island looms larger on the tourist map.

What has inhibited development of the big island's potential has been access to it, unless you flew. By air from Adelaide to Kingscote, the "capital", takes only forty minutes, (or you can leave Sydney after breakfast and be on the island in good time for lunch). But air fares cost rather much for families going on holiday. True, they could get there from Port Adelaide, car and all, by the vehicular ferry *Troubridge*, but this was a six-hour crossing and only twice a week.

Scheduled to come into service in July 1972 is a new ferry service from Cape Jervis on the mainland to Penneshaw on the island: this is only twelve miles. "We believe," says the S.A. Government Tourist Bureau, "this will open up Kangaroo Island to tourism on a fairly grand scale."

Historically, K.I. (as the locals call it) might have been described in the old hymn's words as the place where "every prospect pleases and only man is vile". The plentiful kangaroos were so tame when Flinders, on his way out from England in the *Investigator*, discovered the island in 1802 that his men were able to walk up to the animals and club them, for the first fresh meat they had had since Capetown. There were no Aborigines on the island then, although relics show that they had lived there; and they were probably Tasmanoid, not mainland, types.

The seals on the beaches were almost as abundant and as tame as the kangaroos, so sealers soon came to the island. It acquired as its first settlers men who were described thus: *They are a complete set of Pirates . . . having their chief Resort or Den at Kangaroo Island, making occasional descents on the main Land to carry off by force native women. When resisted they make use of the Firearms with which they are provided. Amongst themselves they rob each other, the weak being obliged to give way to the stronger. At Kangaroo Island a great scene of villainy is going on where, to use their own words, there are many graves, and numbers of desperate Characters, runaway Prisoners from Sydney and Van Diemen's Land.*[1]

Other contemporary accounts speak of the brutality with which they used the Aboriginal women who were virtually enslaved and made to kill and skin seals and kangaroos. The sealers traded sealskins and seal oil for rum and tobacco, dressed in clothing made from kangaroo hides, and had little use for money, except gold sovereigns which they fashioned into ear-rings—for themselves, not their women. A remnant of the wild sealers, living more orderly lives, was on the island when the first shipload of respectable settlers arrived direct from England in 1836.

Few of South Australia's first immigrants stayed long on Kangaroo Island. They found it too infertile. Looking at today's sheep and cattle pastures and fields of barley, one might wonder why. The soil needed trace elements and superphosphate fertilizer. Given those, it has turned into good farming land. But, with the market for wool gone sour, the island has become increasingly dependent on getting more tourists than the several tens of thousands it gets already.

FROM THE AIR Kangaroo Island looked, at the end of summer with its sheep pastures tawny and barley fields fallow brown, less interesting than it was to prove, particularly along its shores that run for over 300 miles. It is an island ninety miles long and up to about forty wide. It had a thousand miles of roads. Only about seventy miles of these were sealed in 1970, but it could be expected that more would be with the coming of the new ferry from the mainland that is so plainly in view from Penneshaw, and only eighty car miles from Adelaide. It could also be expected that motels and holiday flats and caravan parks—particularly caravan parks—would proliferate.

There were ten motels or hotels already. I was to stay, very comfortably, at two of these, and be shown round by the people who ran them and by another motel operator. The Kangaroo Islanders have a reputation for being solicitous about their visitors. There are about 3,500 islanders, of whom some 1,200 live at Kingscote. The other two tourist centres are Penneshaw and American River, which is not a river but an inlet of the sea. It got its name because back in the years 1803-4 some American sealers built a 35-ton schooner there. The cove runs into marshy Pelican Lagoon and, but for a mile or two of isthmus land, Dudley Peninsula, the head to the island's body, would be a separate island.

I went from the plane to Linnett's motel guest-house at American River. Within the hour, with the younger of the Linnett brothers, Gordon, I was on a beautiful beach. Pennington Bay, on the south side of the island, sweeps away to the stretch of blond-cliffed headland (PLATE 39). Points of picturesquely eroded limestone divide its arc of clean pale sand into several beaches. The water was a deep turquoise—I haven't seen it bluer in the Greek islands—and a surf of the longest waves hilled and turned over into white shoots that looked quite irresistible. The beach was utterly deserted, the dunes behind it and the cliffs beyond empty of any sign of human presence. There was only, if you looked back to the road's end, our parked car; not even a dressing-shed. The day was warm without being hot, a summer's-end one: it was the first of April. I stripped in mid-beach —I had swim-trunks with me—and went into the blue-glass water.

After taking a couple of small shoots I came out and told Gordon Linnett how good it was.

"It looks good," he agreed. "All right for you, you brought your bathers." These were off and I was drying myself. I said I supposed we could be awful April Fools if another car appeared and added, "I'll risk it with you." He laughed and pulled off his pants. By the end of 1972 there is pretty sure to be a caravan park there, at least, and nobody will be able to swim naked in a Pennington Bay of such solitude.

Fishing used to be what brought just about all its tourists to Kangaroo Island. Now Linnett's was getting, Gordon said, an increasing number of visitors who came for the scenery and the island peacefulness. Fishing remained, though, the biggest attraction, whether it was line dangling from a jetty, dinghy fishing in sheltered bays, sea angling for twenty-pound snapper, or the momentous pursuit of great sharks as long as twenty feet that had drawn to the island in the past such big-game hunters of the sea as Zane Grey, Bob Dyer and Jack Davey. Leon Linnett remembered the late Jack Davey being there and how he had found a baby seal and brought it back to the guest-house. It had been taken to Pennington Bay and let go there. The next morning it was back at the guest-house. It must have made its way nearly a mile overland—the skin was off its flippers—to get into American River. Nobody could understand why the pup seal—like some abandoned cat or dog making its way home—should have returned, having lost its own kind, to human company.

The best places for fishing are given, along with other tourist information, in a useful booklet, *Portrait of an Island* by Neville Cordes, locally available and worth the visitor's dollar. It says, "Registered firearms and licensed shooters are permitted on Kangaroo Island, but generally not welcomed." There are no foxes and, oddly for a part of Australia, no rabbits. K.I. is blessedly conservation conscious: there are a number of fauna sanctuaries, and the fish as well as the birds are protected in Pelican Lagoon, where there are black swans among the bird life.

PENNESHAW, the small township that will grow when the new ferry service comes to it, sits picturesquely beside a good safe beach, at one end of which is Frenchman's Rock. The French navigator Baudin landed here soon after Flinders had discovered the island, and while the *Géographe* was filling its water casks an officer scratched on a rock: *Expédition de découverte par le Commandant Baudin sur le Géographe 1803.* The historic rock has been removed to the South Australian Art Gallery, but an exact replica of it is here under a protective white dome. That a number of capes and

Wilpena Pound is a remarkable crater-like feature of the Flinders Ranges. The Pound can be entered easily from near Wilpena Pound motel.

At Arkaroola, in the red-brown northern Flinders Ranges, a tourist lodge-motel was developed in 1970. Here sunset lights the face of Mt Griselda.

Uranium prospecting by the Exoil company in the Mt Painter region entailed building 100 miles of roads. One uranium lode found was high-grade.

Moving a drill to another location for further exploration for uranium in the northern Flinders Ranges. The market for uranium was expected to improve.

bays on the island have French names is due to Baudin.

I had lunch at Penneshaw at the Sorrento Lodge Motel and after-wards its proprietor, German-born Bill Franke, drove me to another first-rate beach, Antechamber Bay. The small Chapman River runs into it through a thicket of tea-tree and we wandered along the quiet grassy banks of a still reach beloved of bream fishermen. We drove on to the lighthouse, the first erected in South Australia, on the island's eastern tip, Cape Willoughby. To one side of this is a gulch where the inrushing sea must put on a spectacular show in rough weather. The top of the precipice near the lighthouse was littered with rubbish and so were the rocks below, some of it build-ers' debris. Surely the Commonwealth Lighthouse Service should re-frain from such litterbuggery.

As to climate, Kangaroo Island is, according to Bill Franke, an average seven degrees warmer than Adelaide in winter and seven degrees cooler in summer, at its eastern end. Kingscote's rainfall is about twenty inches a year and most of it falls in the May-August winter. Spring brings out a wealth of wildflowers, beginning with "forests of wattles" in golden display, according to Neville Cordes, who adds that a number of wildflower species are exclusive to the island.

There was drizzling rain next morning as the tour minibus, with its driver-guide, Myrtle, set off from Linnett's—such tours are in-clusive in a moderate tariff—for the western end of the island. Its third town is Parndana, centred on a successful soldiers' settlement scheme. After World War II a quarter-million acres of gum-scrub land was opened up and made fertile by the use of trace elements, mainly copper. As well as sheep and barley, some beef is raised. K.I. also produced gypsum, basalt rock, fish and (though not much of it nowadays) yacca gum, from the grass-tree that is a feature of the landscape. It yields picric acid, used in the making of paints and explosives. Vivonne Bay, a big one, was not on at its best on this grey day, and we soon went on to Kelly Hill Caves, which are hardly a must for people who have seen limestone caves elsewhere. But the fresh fish served for lunch outdoors was excellent.

Flinders Chase, at the western end of the island where the rainfall is about five inches more and the vegetation taller and more abund-ant, is a fauna-flora sanctuary of 220 square miles. Kangaroos come to the visitor's hand. A pleasant walk showed some of the biggest koalas I have ever seen—introduced from Victoria—perched in the forks of high manna gums. Myrtle, who was very knowledgeable on vegetation, said that there were no less than thirty-seven varieties of orchids in the Chase.

Two of the finest natural formations on the island are just down

DD

on the south coast. At Cape du Couëdic, beyond the (automatic) lighthouse, the track descends to where the sea has tunnelled right through a high point of land to form a great open-ended cave, called Admiral's Arch.

Not far along the coast from here—and a fine, rugged, sombre-cliffed coast it is—you come to what are called, and are indeed, the Remarkable Rocks. They stand, as though set up as exhibits, on the platform of a granite headland so high above the sea that the elements of rain and wind have done most of the sculpturing of their fantastic forms—at least in the last hundred million years or so. One great caved boulder, perhaps twenty feet high, suggests by the hooked end to its prong of stone its name, the Eagle's Beak. Less malignant and superbly abstract—though it may suggest the petrifaction of some prehistoric monster's skull—is the one that is perhaps the most strikingly formed boulder on the whole Australian scene. Photographically, I had a good time here; but reluctantly decided that Pennington Bay (PLATE 39) was perhaps more representative of Kangaroo Island.

PETER ELLSON's grandmother started a guest-house at Kingscote in 1924 and it has been extended by his father to become Ellson's Seaview Motel, its units well-equipped with refrigerators, sinks, TV. I moved over from Linnett's, missing only the liquor licence and wine service with meals that it had and Ellson's didn't. Next day Peter Ellson devoted to showing me more of the island. We went first to Seal Bay on the south coast.

Seal Bay has a long beach that runs back into shrubby-grassy dunes pocketed with places where the seals lay, mostly sleeping, as well as on the open beach. The first one we came to was a young seal, utterly unafraid and something of a comedian, or so it appeared from its antics of scratching itself with its flippers and rolling over.

Eight kinds of seals (including the seal-leopard and seal-elephant, often called sea-leopard and sea-lion) are found in Australian waters. The ones hunted for their skins used to be, principally, the fur-seals. These at K.I. are hair-seals. They were not spared by the sealers who, between 1800 and 1830, killed the fur-seals almost to extinction: hair-seals and other kinds were clubbed and stabbed on these beaches and rendered down for seal-oil.

Bull hair-seals can be up to six feet long and, as well as being more massive than the females, are darker in colour, nigger-brown to the cows' fawny-grey, and both are lighter-coloured on their undersides. Despite the name hair-seal they are not hairy but very smooth. As we went along the high verge of the beach there were seals in the sand hollows between the growth, scores of them, usually in groups of mother and child or a family of three or four, sluggishly opening an eye at our coming or simply remaining comatose. It was good to find them so without fear. And, of course, it was a photographer's boon.

Down on the beach there was a bit of action. Two young males near a big bull with his harem reared their powerful necks and, open-jawed, snapped at each other, barking. But they soon subsided. Seals are often inquisitive, and a young one with round girlish eyes came lolloping across the sand to us on its flippers, halting only when it was within inches of our empty hands. Others were disporting in the water: you could see them riding in, not on the wave but within it as though encased in glass, slipping through and shining in their element.

We went on to Cape Borda where a square-towered white light-house, the Flinders Light, has stood since 1858 on the edge of cliffs that drop five hundred feet into a wild sea, the graveyard of six ships off this end of an island that has known more than thirty recorded shipwrecks. You can go up into the lighthouse and see the glittering reflectors that send the beam thirty-five miles to sea. Cape Borda is probably the coldest, windiest spot in South Australia.

We ate our lunch above Scott's Cove, where there is an impressive view along the cliffed coast. Far below, five crayfishing boats bobbed on the cobalt sea.

Along the central north of the island the land is hilled as high as Mt McDonnell (850 feet) and it gives rise to several rivers. To the mouth of one of these, the Western, the road descends steeply to a picturesque cove, its popularity with bathers and fishermen attested by one of those "toilet blocks" that councils always seem to build as obtrusively as possible, as though they were prideful civic monuments and not necessities to be merged into the landscape. Kangaroo Island, which is really only on the verge of realizing its tourist potential, has the chance to develop the island to aesthetic guidelines laid down by a first-class architect and planner.

The landscape is, for the most part, comely still, and mercifully free of signboards, outside the towns. Nowhere does the island look better, with its gentle contours rolling down to the coast, than from the top of what is called Constitution Hill, where you look down on the Middle River entering the sea and forming small blue lagoons behind the white dunes of a beach that deserves a better name than Snellings and where the only habitation is, as yet, a farmhouse. One almost regrets the caravan parks that are so inevitably coming, with the new car ferry, into the picture here; but it is surely selfish not to share such places.

If I were asked what part of Kangaroo Island appealed to me most

I should have to toss a coin to decide between Pennington Bay and Stokes Bay—which hasn't the scenic sweep but has the advantage of being on the sheltered side of the island. Where you drive down to Stokes Bay it is nothing much, and none the better for the four or five fishermen's shacks that have gone up there. You must go through the high rocks at one end, wind through them as through a narrow sort of tunnel. You emerge onto a delight of a beach with firm silver sand, clean as the water frilling in from the run of a gentle surf. The beach is backed by limestone cliffs that mingle the colours of pewter and honeycomb. On top of the cliffs a tourist hotel will surely rear before very long. I hope it is not an angular paint-box of a place but designed to merge with the cliffs and beach of what must be one of the loveliest locations on the coasts of southern Australia.

To the Murray at Renmark

SOUTH AUSTRALIA is ahead of the other States in the control of advertising billboards that uglify roadsides and railsides and are particularly obnoxious in New South Wales and Queensland. It has had a Control of Advertisements Act for many years, but this began to work effectively only when the State Planning Authority was established in 1967 and the Director of Planning made responsible for administering the Act. In Adelaide I talked to the director, an intelligent man named Stuart B. Hart.

"We are attempting to cut out all advertising signs along rural roads and confine them to town areas," he said. He was getting co-operation from the Outdoor Advertising Association and, at last, from the South Australian Railways.

I asked Mr Hart if he had photographs of a rural roadside showing how it looked before billboards went up and how it looked now. No, but he had something better. He had photographs, taken at the approach to the town of Murray Bridge, showing how the landscape looked when there were seven billboards at a road junction, and the same roadside looking so much better *after the signs had been taken down.*

Sixty-one signs had been removed from the Princes Highway in the vicinity of Murray Bridge, and the State Planning Director's latest report said, "There is now a prospect that the tourist highway to Adelaide from the Victorian border will soon be cleared of these disfigurements." (And now this highway has been so cleared.) The authority has been able to remove 350 signs in rural areas.

THE MURRAY, or that part of it that goes on into South Australia and then bends south to empty into the sea east of Victor Harbour, is the only river of size the State has. How much it depends on the Murray waters was apparent on a car trip of 350 miles I did with the deputy director of the S.A. Government Tourist Bureau, E. G. (Ted) Correll.

When we were still forty miles from the Murray there was a roadside pipeline that brought its water from Mannum, salty water that was also limey, so that many households ran it over beds of marble chips to soften it.

Mannum, a port town in the days of the Murray riverboats, still has a fine old paddlewheeler, the *Marion*, moored and fitted out as a museum. The river here is very pleasant with green parkland along its banks.

Soon we were in the mallee country that has broken many a wheatfarmer's heart in years when most of the sparse twelve-to-fourteen inches of rain stayed in the sky that arches so wide over the flat land, and drifts of sand moved in and buried half the crop. Yet, here and there, where the sand turns red and hillocks of it are top-ped with the spindly scrub, the mallee country has its own odd beauty. The road bores through it dead straight for twenty miles to Halidon. We turn north towards the Murrayside where ninety years ago a boundary-rider named Loxton had his hut, and there is now a town named after him with 6,500 people living in and round it. Most are fruitgrowers, thanks to irrigation from the Murray.

Loxton is the town of the biggest war service settlement scheme in Australia: 270 ex-servicemen are on blocks of about twenty-five acres. Citrus, stone fruits and grapes are irrigated: the non-irrigated farms grow mainly wheat—and the hungry limestone mallee coun-try produces wheat of the highest protein. Many of the hardy pioneers were Lutheran Germans. Over lunch at the amiably modern Loxton Hotel-Motel I asked the District Clerk, David Crocker, who had been there twenty-two years, what he regarded as the out-standing characteristic of the people of this farming community. He said without hesitation, "The calibre of the women."

The town has uncommon civic calibre, even for a region where co-operative enterprise thrives. Wide landscaped gardens lead down to the Murray with its parkland and riverside drive. The Loxton Club of 1,400 members had raised $14,000 towards the town beauti-fication scheme. The hotel, set about with lawns and rockpools, was community owned.

The hotel had, as well as its large dining-room, a steak bar: so did the club. Steak bars are a South Australian institution, and a good one. For little more than a dollar you could have a grilled steak, or fish or smörgasbord, self-served, with drinks at bar prices.

Beyond Loxton the country changes dramatically from the dry mallee, for the road is never far from the river and the river lets the arid land put on a deep green dress of orange orchards and the vineyards. Between the orange trees they plant peaches, which bear sooner than the six or seven years oranges take. Most of the oranges we buy in Sydney seem to bear the stamp RIVERLAND: they come from the irrigated farms along the Murray between Morgan and Renmark, where we stayed two nights and spent the Sunday delightfully, on the river.

IAN SHOWELL is a rosy big man with a grey moustache, an engineering background and a number of inventions to his credit. An idea of his has given holidaying at Renmark a new dimension—the paddle-wheel houseboat.

He calls his type of houseboat the *Liba-Liba* (pronounced Libba-Libba) from an Aboriginal word meaning two canoes. He designed it specially for the Murray, with a draft of only eighteen inches, catamaran-type twin unsinkable hulls, and a Holden car engine drives the two paddlewheels astern. He had a dozen of these Liba-Libas, five-, six- and eight-berthers, fitted out with everything from hot-water service to flush toilet and equipped right down to linen.

Anyone who had driven a car could manage one, Ian said. He gave his mobile tenants an introductory run and sent them off with such detailed maps that they hardly ever got stranded; and, anyway, there was two-way radio aboard. Liba-Libas churn along at a leisurely six miles an hour. (PLATE 43 shows one we passed on the river.) They rented (April 1970) for $50 a weekend, $126 a week, which could work out as low as $3 a person a day, plus petrol, which averaged $9 a week: most people booked for a week. They went upstream to Wentworth and Mildura and downriver as far as Murray Bridge. Ian Showell said he was fully booked from December to May, and he aimed to build his Liba-Liba fleet to fifty.

On the river, it was like boating in a house, cruising in a sort of motel unit with a wheel in the dining-room where you played captain to the five-knot churn astern. Or sat in deckchairs on what was less like a deck than a back veranda—unless you sat up on top like the three people on the Liba-Liba we passed, who were peacefully Murray-gazing.

The Murray was more interesting here than I had found it at Mildura. Backwaters were best of all—glassily still, full of the skeletons of trees and their reflections. And birds, ducks by the hundred swimming, and some swans. A tourist pamphlet I was handed at the Renmark Hotel with my room key said, "Good duck shooting is always to be had in season." Gain two duckshooters and lose ten tourists who are not only on the side of the ducks they like to see, but don't like the idea of the peace of the river being shattered with shotgun blasts.

Not far up the river is where an old village community at the 1890 settlement of Murtho attempted irrigation farming, but the cost of lifting the water beat them. Renmark (not Mildura) is where it all began, the Murray irrigation scheme of the Canadian brothers Chaffey (as detailed in the Victorian section). Red cliffs appear, at a bend of the river that has been eucalypt-green along its banks. "Renmark" means, I am told, "red mud"—mud in a region of ten-inch rainfall. Somebody puts a glass in my hand—and I feel like drinking to the prohibitionist Chaffeys who showed how to turn the arid Murrayside into (as they say in the Barossa Valley) fruit gardens. And vineyards. Then Ian Showell says, "Here they come. Wine ahoy!"

The river flurries with a speedboat's wake. From it step two amiable men I am introduced to as Bill Crowe and Tom Bodroghy, a Hungarian name. They come from Angove's, the oldest-established winery on the South Australian Murray and the distillers of St Agnes brandy. They come bearing a flor sherry that is relished all round before lunch and a Bookmark riesling (Bookmark is a local placename) and what proves, with lunch, to be a highly agreeable Tregrehan '65 claret. Tregrehan is a Cornish name: the original Dr Angove came from Cornwall, to Tea Tree Gully near Adelaide, where he planted vines "for the benefit that could be given to his patients". (Medicos used to be keen on prescribing a glass or a dram: whisky bottles often bore back-labels with testimonials from the *Lancet*). Tregrehan is not a brand I was familiar with—it is always inhibiting in asking for a wine to be unsure of the pronunciation, which in this case is near enough to *tree-grain*. It is a claret blended from Cabernet Sauvignon grapes grown on the Murray River and at the original Tea Tree Gully. The name is not, any more than other brand names are, a guarantee of year-to-year quality; but I have come by two vintage Tregrehans that were admirable—indeed one of them ranked with the best clarets I've ever enjoyed.

The point here is that there is a widespread belief that irrigated vineyards produce inferior wines. This seems to be a fallacy. There is no evidence that it is true, according to Walter James,[1] who probably knows as much about Australian wines as anyone. He says that scientists who made prolonged tests of grapes from irrigated and non-irrigated vineyards found that ". . . beyond the well-known tendency of irrigated grapes to be deficient in acid (which can be remedied) they could define no real difference in the factors making for quality."

Good watering at the right time so greatly increases the grape yield that a Murray grower may get twice the harvest off the same acreage as a Barossa River grower dependent on natural rainfall—which along parts of the South Australian Murray is only about ten inches, and without irrigation grapes could not be grown at all.

The Murray is a very big wine-producing area—Tom Bodroghy said that Angove's had the biggest planting of Rhine Riesling and Cabernet grapes in Australia—and wine production at Berri farther down the river is huge. In many Australian wines we drink there is the juice of Murray grapes. On the way back to Adelaide we went via Nuriootpa and passed, along the highway, grape-laden truck after truck, all from the Murray and all heading for wineries that would label their bottles and flagons as products of the Barossa Valley, which indeed they were, but all the grapes in them were not necessarily grown in that famous district.

AT RENMARK we stayed at what was the first community-run hotel in the British Commonwealth when it was built in 1897. When, ten years earlier, the Chaffeys founded the town they had it enacted that no hotelkeeper could have a liquor licence. Finally, the community rebelled and got one. The hotel is still community owned and operated, and run better than many a private or brewery hostelry. Moreover, the money stays in the town and from the Hotel Renmark's profits about $250,000 had gone into civic improvement and to local charities.

Renmark was soon to have a showplace motel. Ian Showell would build it on some of the riverside land he owned, near what was called the Jane Eliza Landing. The plans he showed me looked good. The Jane Eliza Motel was to open in late 1971.

Few men with ideas have Ian Showell's resources to put them into practice: his father who came from England took up land and combined farming with engineering, stockbroking and zoology.

An enterprising migrant without money, Joe Bredl, has developed a fauna park on the outskirts of Renmark. Much more could be made of it as a tourist attraction; but long-term loan finance for such projects is much harder to get in Australia than it is in other more tourist-minded countries. Up to a point, this disability is overcome along the Murray by community enterprise.

Industrially, the town of Berri, which we soon came to after leaving Renmark to return to Adelaide via the Sturt Highway, is about as communal as a place can get. The winery and distillery (which crushes ten per cent of the whole Australian grape harvest, more grapes than any other place in the Southern Hemisphere) is a co-operative. So is the big cannery of orange, tomato, grapefruit, apricot juices. So are the main packing sheds. Again, the hotel-motel is community owned, as it also is at the next place we stop at Barmera.

Community enterprise has created at Barmera not only holiday cabins of particularly good design but the best caravan park on the Upper Murray, where caravanning—from as far away as Broken Hill in New South Wales—is a big part of tourism. In this case the holiday-makers come not to the riverside but the lakeside. Barmera is on Lake Bonney, an effluent of the Murray and connected to it by a creek.

Lake Bonney is where Donald Campbell tried to break his own water-speed world record in the *Bluebird*. It is four miles long and fourteen miles round, the safest of waters for swimming, very good for water-skiing, and it has a considerable population of birds—pelicans, swans, ducks, shags, ibis and coot. Although, I was told, a pelican's belly can hold seventy small fish, there seem to be plenty left for the fishermen. Away from the caravan park, the verges of the lake were rather bare; but the District Council was aware of that and had tree-planting well in mind.

From Barmera we headed along the Sturt Highway and through Waikerie, another irrigation town and mainly remarkable for its spindly forest of television aerials reaching high for reception—which in the Riverlands, as the region calls itself, is not very good. Then through flat she-oak and sheep country, darkening in the evening light that flared into a gorgeous sunset as we came into the foothills of the Mount Lofty Ranges and, crossing these, descended into the Barossa Valley, to dine at Nuriootpa.

Ted Correll knew a first-rate restaurant, *Die Wein Stube* (The Wine Room). He said the dinner was his: I said the wine was mine. With an excellent steak and a fine cheese afterwards, we had a 1964 Penfold Grange Hermitage.

"Grange Hermitage is probably the most sought-after red wine in Australia," says a well-known cellarmaster and writer on wine, Len Evans.[2] Good reds of the Hermitage/Shiraz grape are matured in small hogsheads of new oak, a Bordeaux idea that Penfolds introduced to Australia in 1952. Answering the question, "What is Grange character?" the authoritative Evans writes, "To me it is the full marriage of fruit and wood, depth of flavour on the palate, a perfumed nose often quite voluminous, a balance and completeness and a clean finish with a fair amount of soft tannin." He considers the gold-medal-winning '64 a bit light in oak character and body, but it tasted very good to me. With the buffs paying $5 to $9 a bottle for these Granges at wine auctions, one doesn't get much chance to make comparison with those of other years, of which Len Evans considers '52, '53, '55, '56, '60, '62 and '63 the best, with the '53 topping them all, "a magnificent Australian wine".

Lake-and-Legend Corner

THE TOURIST in South Australia—until he comes to the south-east of the State—may well feel that he is outside the Australian locale of legend. Nowhere has he crossed the path, as in Victoria, of anyone like a valiant Peter Lalor or a villainous Ned Kelly, or a Jorgen Jorgensen of Tasmania, or a Lasseter with a fabulous gold reef, as in the Centre.

But in the south-east corner legend lives: indeed the liveliest of the South Australian *literati*, Max Harris, would have us believe that here legend lives uniquely, as "a historical dimension not to be found in the rest of Australia", in what he calls "this land of black soil and dead volcanoes" and the tragic poet-on-horseback Adam Lindsay Gordon—and, of course, the Tantanoola Tiger.

Dismissing out of hand the more typical South Australia of the Flinders Ranges, Max Harris, in an article in the *Australian*[1] about Mount Gambier (his home town) had a poke at "our national obsession with Drysdalian outbackery" and said the tourist would "probably do better by concentrating on the south-east, using Mount Gambier as his operational headquarters". That part made gratifying reading at "The Mount's" tourist office, but I met local citizens who were still shaking their heads worriedly over his article. He had hardly mentioned what Mount Gambier considers its greatest tourist attraction, the Blue Lake. This giving to legend priority over the famous lake was viewed as akin to a reporter from the *Bethlehem Times* in the Christian calendar year 1 doing an interview with Mary the wife of Joseph in terms of, "Now, apart from the matter of your Child...."

I FLEW IN on an Ansett Airlines flight that left Adelaide at 9.30 a.m. on a heavily overcast day. When, an hour later, the plane came down out of the clouds we had been above all the way, the country was like no other part of South Australia I had seen. It was so much greener and it had big dark stands of pine forest—alien pine, Californian *radiata*, growing in such abundance in the State that built in stone because it used to have so little timber. These were the largest pine forests in Australia, growing in the driest State, in this corner of it that got thirty-one inches of rain a year. Moreover, the dairyfarmer could keep his pastures verdant year round with underground water that was only ten feet down.

A good-looking city sat at the foot of the mount that was Gambier, but the airport was well this side of it, and only later did it become apparent that the mount was an extinct volcano that held four lakes including the famous blue one.

A car took me in to what its founder christened Gambier Town, but people would call it nothing but Mount Gambier. Now it has 18,000 citizens and an air of prosperity imbues a main street dignified with an Institute of graciously Italianate architecture, a Town Hall more soberly in keeping with the strong Scottish traditions of the place—both of these in soft-hued local limestone—and what is surely one of the best-looking old pubs in Australia, the Jens Town Hall Hotel, its balconies graced with superb iron lace that looked so good in olive-grey against the white walls that you found yourself forgiving this painting of stonework. Behind the Town Hall the city centre is prettily hollowed with a Cave Garden, where roses bloom above a yawning cavern that hints of mysterious subterranean regions at the same time as it conveniently takes care of the stormwater drainage.

In Mount Gambier you mount—I like hilly cities and towns—and what the black ribbon of road winds up to is a sight that, in season, is nonetheless remarkable because it has taken on a certain cliché character in tourist postcards.

THE BLUE LAKE, cupped in a crater bowl with pale steep limestone sides, gets as blue as it appears in the PLATE 40 Ektachrome, but only between November and February. When I saw it in April it was still very blue, but not the ultra-bright blue that begins to fade perceptibly by March. By June the lake is grey, and stays grey until November when, quite suddenly, it resumes its intense blueness.

Why this colour change should occur scientists from Flinders University were still investigating. Mount Gambier's Town Clerk, Douglas Roeger, said, "The accepted theory is that the blueness is due to precipitation of calcium carbonate. But there is no satisfactory explanation of why the precipitation occurs." He added, "My own theory is that the colour has something to do with the sun's trajectory." Others have said that winter's cold and rain make the water denser and more disturbed; in summer the mud settles, only fine particles are left, and these diffuse the sunlight. Surely this must commonly happen in lakes throughout the southerly latitudes—yet only this one turns a spectacular turquoise. Mount Gambier doesn't really *want* to find out what causes the colour change. The Blue Lake is all the better as a tourist attraction if its blueness remains a mystery.

Legend used to have the lake as "bottomless". Measurements have given depths ranging from 180 feet to 672 feet in what is called the "Bung Hole", which is thought to connect with a subterranean storage basin where an underground river flows. Mount Gambier draws its water supply from the Blue Lake, yet the level remains almost stable, except in times of heavy rain or drought. The crater bowl that holds the lake is three miles round the rim.

You look down on three other lakes adjacent to the blue one, and much more accessible. The one called Leg of Mutton Lake had been dry for two years. The others, Valley and Browne's, are part of the inner prospect of the cratered mountain that walls out all view of the city and leaves the eye to plushy green slopes with coppices of pines and woodsy waterside.

On the highest point is a lookout tower that extends the view to a wide panorama of prosperous-looking farmland, its soil enriched by the ancient outpourings of basaltic lava and ash from the last line of Australian volcanoes: Mount Gambier has more in common with the country over the Victorian border (where we looked, near Port Fairy, at the extinct volcano of Tower Hill) than it has with any other part of South Australia. Similarly, it grows potatoes and raises fat lambs and cattle.

The trudge up the steep path to the lookout, though well rewarded when you get there, is too much for many visitors and there have been suggestions about putting in a chair-lift.

An obelisk near the Blue Lake marks the (approximate) spot of Gordon's Leap. Adam Lindsay Gordon who, as the rather "wild" young scion of an English family was induced to go to Australia in 1853, when he was twenty, jumped his horse over the fence by the lakeside cliffs onto an eight-foot ledge, and then jumped it back again. This and other feats of horsemanship Gordon performed—he once won three steeplechase events in the same afternoon at Flemington racecourse, Melbourne—were the more remarkable because the poet, as he became (after being a policeman at Mount Gambier and Penola) had defective vision: he was very short-sighted.

I went to his house called Dingley Dell, now restored as a museum with relics of his riding and his writing. He bought it in 1864, having come into a legacy of £7,000 and married seventeen-year-old Maggie Park, and the few years he lived there were probably his happiest. His first published verse appeared, at his own expense. With no talent for business, he failed in a livery stable venture, moved to Melbourne, was hailed by Marcus Clarke as a great Australian poet, and published two more volumes of verse; and his not having the money to pay the printer had bearing on his suicide when he was thirty-seven: he shot himself. Gordon's verse is out of fashion now, with its simple values, *Life is mostly froth and bubble,/Two things stand like stone:/Kind-*

ness *in another's trouble,*/Courage *in your own.*[2] However, his ballad *The Sick Stockrider* is memorable, and he is not to be begrudged his bust in the Poets' Corner of Westminster Abbey.

A more felicitous poet was Australian-born at Penola, 32 miles north of Mount Gambier, in 1872. There, and in the Wimmera district of Victoria his family moved to when he was eight, Shaw Nielson had less than three years' schooling. The books he loved he could not always read because his eyesight was even worse than Gordon's. He worked on farms, shovelled earth on the roads, chopped rock in quarries. And he wrote poems delicate as thistledown, such as the one that begins:

> *Quietly as rosebuds*
> *Talk to the thin air,*
> *Love came so lightly*
> *I knew not he was there.*[3]

The Dingley Dell of Adam Lindsay Gordon—it is a pleasant, white cottage with a garden where the visitor can picnic—is near Cape Northumberland. Here the sea acts its drama on splendid rocks of eroded limestone—and here the local crayfishing industry empties the carapace husks of the lobsters that have had their tails twisted off while still alive, for export of frozen cray-tails.

This is near Port MacDonnell, a charmless place where the local pub served no meals at all and the second-rate fish café we lunched at had crayfish "only at the weekends". I felt sorry for the nubile schoolager who, looking like jail-bait and ripe to take off with the first truckie who asked her, said, "I don' wanna spend the rest of me life in this place."

On the 18-mile run down to Port MacDonnell the road, at Allendale, skirts a fenced-off spot where the earth has caved in. The story is that a man, and the horse and buggy he was driving, disappeared underground: legend even had his body carried by a subterranean river to Robe, which is eighty miles away.

COONAWARRA is forty-odd miles north, past Penola and the great stands of pine where (said Peter Davey, the tourist officer who was driving me) some of the timber workers were mighty men who could wield an axe in one hand and a chain-saw in the other.

Here are the most southerly vineyards in South Australia. The biggest wine-growing property is the "estate" of Wynn's, with 326 acres of it under grapes. As well as two clarets and a riesling, the Wynn's winery here makes sherries and vermouths. It is a fine old place built in 1890 of the local limestone, beamed with oregon and having many big oval-ended casks of French oak in its cool underground cellars.

The soil is reddish over a layer of limestone that is broken up so that the planted vines can sink their roots into softer limestone that is for ever moist with the underground water. The harvest, the latest in Australia, was still going on in April. Italian and Yugoslav women were snipping the bunches.

For those who are interested, Wynn's 1969 Hermitage claret, which would market about the end of 1971, was expected to be as good as or better than their 1954 that won the championship in Adelaide in 1961. Great hopes were also held for the 1969 Cabernet. Such wines, put down, can improve in value as much as in bottle age. On the way back we called in at the Penola Hotel, where the young publican, John Hayward, caters for buffs from a couple of boxes he keeps upstairs. Coonawarra Estate Cabernet '62 was four dollars. A moderately priced ($1.65 a bottle now in 1971) Wynn's red I am partial to is their Ovens Valley Shiraz burgundy, from their Victorian vineyards.

IN LIMESTONE COUNTRY you expect caves. The district has them aplenty, and some that a rabbit-hunter discovered have been lighted and developed as a tourist attraction called the Tantanoola Caves—which description is likely to make the motoring tourist take the Tantanoola turn-off: he should keep right on towards Mount Gambier. But people take the Tantanoola turn-off, anyway, because of the Tiger.

The Tantanoola Tiger story originated with a young man of the village saying that when he was returning from a dance in the dawn-light of a morning in 1889 he "saw what he supposed to be a tiger spring over a fence with a small sheep in its mouth".[4] The animal was hunted without avail and sheep continued to be taken—although not so numerously after one Robert Edmondson, a great spreader of stories about the "Tiger's" depredations, was sentenced in 1911 to six years' jail for stealing and killing seventy-six sheep and selling their skins.

At the Tiger Hotel at Tantanoola a glass case displays what I regard as a stuffed dog. The *Australian Encyclopaedia*, which is usually authoritative, makes the general statement that "lions" and "tigers" reported in country districts have proved to be large crossbred dogs. The animal in the glass case at Tantanoola is a mean-muzzled creature that looks as if it had Alsatian in its ancestry. It is fawn with a blackish back, and a goitrous neck that is possibly the taxidermist's doing. It is not even a huge dog: it measures five-feet-one from nose to tail tip. It is nothing like a tiger, and nothing like a wolf, either, despite Max Harris's giving credence, in his poem "Tantanoola Tiger", to the story that it was a Siberian wolf that swam ashore from a foundered ship, the *Helena*. The typical Siberian wolf is nearly white and much larger than this animal. The hotelkeepers say it is an "Assyrian wolf" and "presumed to have escaped from a shipwreck off the coast". (There hasn't been an Assyrian nation since about 600 B.C.: Assyria is now part of northern Iraq, and its fauna includes hyenas and jackals, but not wolves.)

A story said to have been "verified from early South Australian records"[5] is that a nonagenarian named Alf Warman, when he clapped eyes on the stuffed animal at the Tantanoola hotel in 1957, exclaimed, "That's my dawg!" He gave a circumstantial account of how, in the 1890s, he had given away this dog he couldn't afford to keep at his home in the Adelaide suburb of Norwood, and it had been sent to the south-west to help kill wild dogs there, and had gone wild itself. The sheep-killing animal in the glass case was shot by a farmer named Donovan in August 1895.

What is interesting is the persistence of reports of "tigers" being sighted in the district, with the sighters always insistent that the animal was striped. Descriptions tally with that of the thylacine, the so-called Tasmanian "tiger" or "wolf" now said to be extinct in Tasmania. Unlikely as it may be that the thylacine survives on the mainland, a photograph that appeared in *Walkabout* in June 1968 (said to have been taken near the South Australian-Victorian border about the end of 1965) shows a striped animal that looks remarkably like the Tasmanian "tiger". So do sketches based on what some children said they saw in the Coorong region and on what a Naracoorte train driver says he sighted on two occasions. So there may yet prove to be more substance to the "tiger" legend than one sees in the glass case at the pub at Tantanoola.

WHAT IS "NEW AUSTRALIA" about Mount Gambier is an industry that happened unexpectedly. The Alliance Oil Development company was drilling for oil about ten miles out of the city in 1966 when it penetrated a vast underground storage of carbon dioxide. Reserves of the gas were given as 75 million cubic feet of it to the acre.

Since early 1969 the lessees of the area, Carba (Australia) Ltd, have been working the first commercial CO_2 development in Australia. The gas is liquefied and six big tankers a day take the roads. It is used in refrigeration, carbonization of beverages and to make dry ice.

Touristically, a particularly charming place to drive to, about twenty miles from Mount Gambier, is the Glenelg River that takes a small bend over the South Australian border to the little fishing town of Nelson, which is in Victoria.

(References to discoveries of oil and natural gas in South Australia are on page 572. Locations are on map facing page 403.)

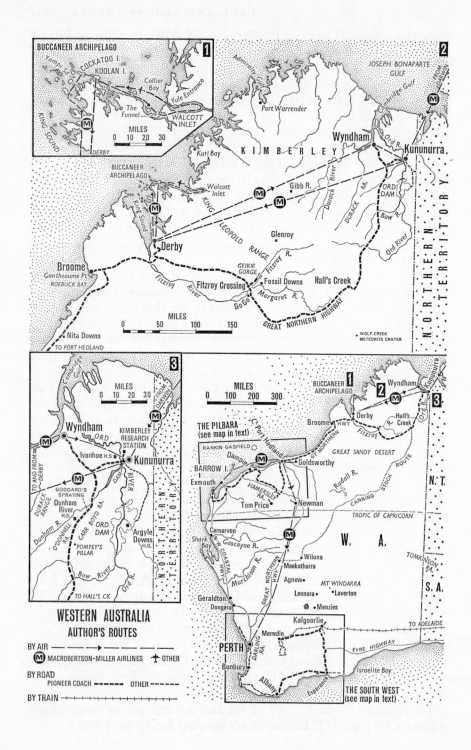

1

BUCCANEER ARCHIPELAGO

Yampi Sd.
COCKATOO I.
KOOLAN I.
Collier Bay
Yule Entrance
The Funnel
WALCOTT INLET
KING SOUND

MILES
0   10   20   30

DERBY

2

JOSEPH BONAPARTE GULF
FROM DARWIN
Cambridge Gulf
Admiralty Gulf
Port Warrender
Kuri Bay
KIMBERLEY
Wyndham
Kununurra
Ord R.
ORD DAM
DURACK RA.
Bow R.
Durack River
Ord River

BUCCANEER ARCHIPELAGO
Walcott Inlet
King Sound
KING LEOPOLD RANGE
Gibb R.
Glenroy
Fitzroy R.
Derby
Broome
Gantheaume Pt.
ROEBUCK BAY
Fitzroy River
GEIKIE GORGE
Fitzroy Crossing
Go Go
Margaret R.
Fossil Downs
Hall's Creek
GREAT NORTHERN HIGHWAY

MILES
0   50   100   150

Nita Downs
TO PORT HEDLAND

• WOLF CREEK METEORITE CRATER

NORTHERN TERRITORY

3

Cambridge Gulf
MILES
0   10   20   30
FROM DARWIN

Wyndham
ORD
Ivanhoe H.S.
KIMBERLEY RESEARCH STATION
Kununurra
TO AND FROM DERBY
GODDARD'S SPRAYING
DURACK RANGE
Dunham River H.S.
O'DONNELL RA.
CARR BOYD RA.
ORD DAM
DAM
RIVER
POMPEY'S PILLAR
Argyle Downs H.S.
Dunham R.
Bow River
Ord R.
TO HALL'S CK.

NORTHERN TERRITORY

WESTERN AUSTRALIA
AUTHOR'S ROUTES

BY AIR ————————
Ⓜ MACROBERTSON-MILLER AIRLINES   ✈ OTHER
BY ROAD
PIONEER COACH ━━━━━   OTHER ─────
BY TRAIN ┼┼┼┼┼┼┼┼

1

BUCCANEER ARCHIPELAGO

MILES
0   100   200   300

THE PILBARA
(see map in text)

RANKIN GASFIELD
Dampier
BARROW I.
Exmouth
HAMERSLEY RA.
Tom Price
Newman
Goldsworthy
Pt. Hedland
GT. NORTHERN
Broome
Derby
Fitzroy
R.

2 Wyndham
Ⓜ
Hall's Creek
3
ORD R.
Kununurra

GREAT SANDY DESERT
Rudall R.
CANNING STOCK ROUTE
TROPIC OF CAPRICORN

N.T.

W.   A.

Carnarvon
Shark Bay
N.W. COASTAL HWY
Gascoyne R.
Murchison R.
GREAT NORTHERN HWY
Wiluna
Meekatharra
Agnew
Leonora
MT WINDARRA
Laverton
Menzies

S. A.
TOMKINSON RA.

Geraldton
Dongara
Kalgoorlie
Merredin
PERTH
DARLING RA.
Bunbury
Albany
Esperance
EYRE HIGHWAY
Israelite Bay
TO ADELAIDE
TO PERTH

THE SOUTH WEST
(see map in text)

WESTERN AUSTRALIA

New Pioneers on the Ord

Where does the West, the West begin?
The land that was "sand, sore eyes and sin".
The State with the iron-ore mountains in
And more darn nickel than Tassie has tin—
Tell me, where does the West begin?

THE WEST began for me, on this trip, at its farthest north. Mine was hardly the route a young man would take if he wanted to go to explosively progressive Western Australia at the urging of its Minister for Industrial Development, Mr Charles Court,* who was by way of being the Australian Horace ("Go West, young man") Greeley.

However, Mr Court's main concern was with getting big corporations to invest another thousand million dollars in mining and processing the wealth in the earth of what used to be called the Cinderella, or mendicant, Australian State.

The Minister had made a couple of points about Western Australia that are worth keeping in mind when we look at this million-square-mile State, a third of Australia, with only a million people in it. References to Western Australia as the "boom State" pained Mr Court.

"We are not," he said, "having a 'boom'. A boom is something that eventually goes bust, and this isn't going to happen here. We have the natural resources—the Pilbara is probably the biggest high-grade iron ore zone in the world, and there are such reserves of nickel and bauxite that by 1980 our minerals and metals should be worth about $2,000 million a year and be the biggest single force in the Australian economy. This is capital and enterprise intensively at work to a plan. Don't call it just a 'boom'."

Mr Court had no patience at all with the charge that mining development is turning his State into a vast "quarry" for the benefit of

* Elections in Western Australia in February 1971 removed the Liberal Party government from office. Under Labour, the Ministry that was Mr Court's has been re-named Industrial Development and Decentralization and the deputy-leader of the Labour Government, Mr Herbert Graham, became its new Minister.

EF

Japanese steelmakers. "We are building a human environment," he said, "not destroying one."

KUNUNURRA is the New West, the first of the new towns of the North-West, born in 1960. It is up in that corner of the Kimberley country where the Ord River flooded into Cambridge Gulf each Wet season a wealth of water that was soon to be dammed. Kununurra means, Aboriginally, "big water". The Kimberley can be regarded as the top of the State north of latitude 20° and the Pilbara region as between 20° and 26°. All the area north of the twenty-sixth parallel is the North-West.

The people who met me at the airport said that after dinner I might like to meet some other Kununurrans—and another guest who was also a writer, Mary Durack. She was visiting what used to be Durack country. The Duracks brought the first cattle to the Ord, in 1885, overlanding them from Queensland on an epic trek that took two and a half years. As well as the Durack River and the Durack Range, the map showed half a dozen cattle stations that grew out of the Duracks' pioneering. Mary's father lived most of his life here and was parliamentary member for the Kimberley. Of the first two white women in the region, one was a Durack. The life was hard and often cruel. In her book *Kings in Grass Castles*[1] Mary Durack writes of her grandfather Patrick's youngest brother, "Twice, in the fever epidemics of 1898, Galway Jerry had the heartbreaking task of digging a child's grave at the Dunham River station . . . three years later Jerry himself was shot by a native stockboy on his homestead veranda."

In the Depression years of the 1930s Mary and her artist sister Elizabeth, with the aid of the Aboriginal stockmen, managed Ivanhoe station. If there was a "capital" to the cattle kingdom of Patrick Durack's founding—a kingdom where "all the grass castles were blown away on the winds of drought, depression and change"— Argyle was it. And Argyle's homestead was soon to disappear, under the waters of the great Ord Dam.

Tomorrow I'd see the site of the dam that would be bigger than Lake Eucumbene of the Snowy River Scheme. And, when I got to Broome, "Horrie and I will be there," said Mary Durack who is Mrs H. C. Miller, the Miller of MacRobertson-Miller Airways, now owned by Ansett.

The new MMA Fokker Fellowship 530-m.p.h. jet had made Kununurra little more than four hours flight from Perth: it was already flying Darwin-Derby-Perth in five hours. In September 1969 it had become possible to jet right round Australia.

THE NEW PIONEERS of East Kimberley were growing mainly cotton.

Since 1963 a diversion dam on the Ord had provided the water, a $17-million scheme. The main dam would have three hundred times the storage and cost $21 million, and the whole new irrigation project $48 million.

There were some thirty cotton farms, averaging 600 acres. To put one into production cost about $80,000; and the average income a year was $150 an acre or a gross $90,000. The Kununurra bank manager who gave me figures didn't look like a worried man. The failure rate among Ord cotton-growers had been low. But it had to be remembered that they were sustained by a government bounty, without which all growers would have shown a loss.

The climate was the testing thing. In September, when I was there, the days were hot—the days are *never* cool. Nights were no more than warm: in May-July they could be bracing. But from October through to March—"Last year we had sixty-two consecutive days when the temperature didn't go below 100!"

"Too hot to play any sport, I suppose."

"Oh, no. We have our golf—at half-past-five in the morning, when you can't hear yourself swear for the screeching of the galahs and white cockatoos."

Air-conditioning is the big boon the Durack-era pioneers never knew. Mary Durack's grandfather, that great-hearted Irishman, would not have believed that such comfort could come to the Kimberley as the traveller now enjoys at the Hotel Kununurra with its excellent air-conditioned rooms and its courtyard swimming-pool. He wouldn't have believed the food and drink prices, either.

Costs in the North-West can be the killer, if there isn't constant prosperity to offset them. The economist who wrote *Australia's North-West*,[2] Dr Alex Kerr, said in 1966 that out at Halls Creek the electricity charges were at a level where operating an air-conditioner in one room for one night cost two dollars, and cement that was $24 a ton in Perth was, up there, $72; and beer was twice the Perth price.

Kununurra is, nevertheless, a town with its houses well-equipped with such modern amenities as hot water (solar heated), washing machines and septic sewerage. The town grew straight out of bushland to a Housing Commission plan and had streets with good Australian names like Coolabah. Its 1,200 people were expected to increase to 6,000 by 1975. Houses were provided in the town for the cotton-growers, who commuted by car to their farms.

Average rainfall is nearly thirty inches, and December-March is the Wet. Then the Ord River roars out of the ranges gorged with a brown flood that swells what was a twenty-foot stream at the end of the Dry to a torrent a hundred yards wide, a Niagara of a river hurtling a million cubic feet a second towards the sea.

That kind of water was what the main Ord Dam was being built to conserve—and, put that way, the Ord project seemed utter sense. Yet the scheme is highly controversial, with one economist, Dr Bruce Davidson (*The Northern Myth*), saying that it is a grave misuse of public money, because nothing that can be grown north of the Tropic of Capricorn cannot be grown better and cheaper south of it; and we have Dr Alex Kerr rebutting Davidson's figures on cotton yield, and quoting yields as much as 65 per cent higher. Dr Millington at the Kimberley Research Station near Kununurra told me that Ord cotton-growers had an advantage over those on the Namoi River in New South Wales in that they had virtually a year-round growing season. But they also had a bigger problem with insect pests.

THE MAIN ORD DAM was building fifty miles south of Kununurra. The plains it would irrigate—150,000 acres—were to the north, west and east, where one area was over the border in the Northern Territory.

Gregor McQuie, who operated tours from Kununurra, drove me down to the dam site. On the way he turned off the road six miles to the Territory border, where the bitumen ended. By the end of 1971, he said, a sealed road would extend right across to Katherine on the Stuart Highway. A new beef road (for the road transport of cattle) would link Halls Creek with Tanami, where there would be a desert motel. Tourists would come to it from Alice Springs in air-conditioned coaches with heat-proof glass, then travel on west to Hall's Creek and up to see the Ord Dam, where a motel was already planned.

As we neared the dam site the country to the west rose massively into the rugged Carr Boyd Range, and when we reached the valley of the Ord one side of it was walled with great red bluffs. Before we came in sight of the dam there was the construction camp set up by Dravo Australia, a branch of the big American concern that had won the dam-building contract. It had 480 workers billeted in what Gregor McQuie described as ". . . the best construction camp I was ever in. The food is marvellous."

The main job was to build a damwall that would create the biggest water storage in Australia. The Ord Dam would impound 4.6 million acre-feet of water as against 3.9 million in Lake Eucumbene of the Snowy Mountains Scheme. The Ord would lose its primacy in 1975 when Stage I of the Gordon River development in Tasmania dammed over twice as much water, 9.6 million acre-feet. But the *surface* area of the Ord's great lake would still be bigger than that of the Gordon's two lakes, each of about 100 square miles. The Ord waters would spread over 285 square miles: Eucumbene's covered only 56. The area of Sydney Harbour is 21 square miles. So the Ord's will be a stretch of water as big as thirteen and a half Sydney Harbours, and the dam will hold nine times Sydney Harbour's volume.

From a rocky eminence that was one side of a ravine the Ord runs through, we could look up the valley that was to be drowned—the valley where much of Argyle station of the Duracks would go under —and down into the cleft where the dam would rise 220 feet, and be 1,100 feet across its crest to the opposite mountainside. The scene, with the pale blue Ord looking peaceful as a pond, is shown in PLATE 45.

Dust hazed the hard glare of the sunlight, rising from where the earth-movers were at work on the dam below. From this height they didn't look very big, but one of them was the biggest front-end loader in Australia. It lifted fifteen cubic yards at a bite and its tires were so big it took a tall man to reach the top of one: the tires cost $4,000 each.

What would happen in December when the Wet began and the Ord flooded down in million-cusecs volume, bringing enough water at its peak to fill Sydney Harbour in half an hour? It would be diverted through two tunnels in the dam abutments, and some would go over the section that was built and would be shielded with rock. The dam would have an impervious core flanked either side by a couple of million tons of rockfill.

How to get the rock was no great problem to the project boss, Guy Reid of Phoenix, Arizona. He was already figuring out what he called a "coyote" blast.

That biggest non-nuclear explosion in Australia took place, after two 300-foot tunnels had been crammed with 500 tons of ammonium nitrate, on 21st June 1970. The mountainside I had been looking across at crumbled into the ravine, and Dravo had its two million tons of rockfill.

The wall of the dam was to be complete before the end-of-1971 Wet—and even if twice the greatest recorded flood came down the Ord it would not overtop the wall but would go over a spillway five miles to the north. The mud would settle and the water turn blue. The tops of the rocky hills in the valley would be islands. The water would be up the sides of those great bluffs to the east, and they would reflect their rusty-ochre colour in it. Lake Ord, I thought, was going to look mighty impressive.

AND YET, according to Dr Bruce Davidson, it was all an economic mistake and a great waste of money. It was a "most illogical decision", he wrote, for the Western Australian Government to proceed with the Ord irrigation scheme, and "irrational" for the Commonwealth Government to provide $48.18 million in grants and loans for Stage

II. It would not "people the North" in any considerable sense, for the 150,000 irrigated acres would support, he estimated, only 9,500 population. Its farmers would have to be subsidized, and there was no guarantee that they could sell what they grew. As for the argument that if Australians didn't develop these great open spaces there were crowded, hungry millions of Asians who would want to, Dr Davidson maintained that, "While northern Australia is undeveloped it is not attractive to our northern neighbours: once it is developed it might be."[3]

One recognizes an Australian need for questioning realists of Dr Davidson's kind: we are more inclined to applaud the man who says we must "think big" on development than the one who says we must think our problems through. Action is what we like, not accountancy. At the same time, I have the feeling that that perceptive analyst of the Australian condition, Professor O. H. K. Spate[4], may be quite right when he speaks of the "brute negativism of Bruce Davidson's balance sheets, technically correct enough (though this has been questioned) but making no allowance at all for the intangibles in a nation's life."

The main intangible Professor Spate was thinking of was the "White Australia ring-fence". As he says, we simply cannot people the north so that it looks peopled by Asian standards. Nor could we, by admitting Asians to it, give any real relief to Asia's population pressures. But by developing the north in some measure we at least "make it a little easier to fend off the accusation of being mere dogs in the manger".[5]

It seems to me that a couple of tangibles weren't fed into Dr Davidson's computer-like mind when he programmed it with all the facts and figures of the Ord Dam question and got the answer that it didn't make sense. Quality-of-life in such a region is surely to be regarded as a tangible thing, and Lake Ord can contribute to this, and not only in terms of weekend pleasure boating and swimming and water skiing. Abundant water is such a dry-season boon in so hot a climate, and can turn a harsh brown environment into a kindlier green one. Then there is tourism. The continent's largest man-made lake—indeed, its largest lake with permanent water—will surely draw tourists; and not only to gaze at the Ord "achievement". Lake Ord can become a winter place for southern Australians to vacation in a dramatic landscape with sun-filled days. Already, tourist cruises on the Diversion Dam were popular and Gregor McQuie was about to launch a new 54-passenger boat.

Surely, too, the Ord irrigation scheme could be of more benefit to the cattle industry than Dr Davidson seemed prepared to concede. He sees beef production as the one system of land use that has proved

economic in the north, and he would clearly like to have seen money
spent on beef roads instead of on irrigation.

Yet an American named Goddard had introduced spray irrigation
on his Kimberleys cattle property. He obviously didn't agree with Dr
Davidson that irrigation is uneconomic because he had dammed the
Dunham River at his own expense, and I saw water from it spraying
onto paddocks of pasture he was growing to feed his cattle. This
seemed to me to make more sense than running them on unfenced
ranges and hunting them like wild beasts, which in fact they become.

One likes to think that, by such methods, the cattle industry in
tropical Australia could become less primitive and more humane.
According to Dr Davidson its considerable achievement has been that
it has been able to rear north of Capricorn a third of Australia's cattle
"despite formidable difficulties—for instance, owing to the intense
heat and consequent dehydration, a calf born at any time between
dawn and late afternoon has very little chance of surviving the first
day".[6] This need not happen with cattle in paddocks of irrigated
pasture with shade and stockmen handy.

Sorghum, which is good grain feed for cattle, is already being
grown for that purpose under irrigation on Ivanhoe station, a one-
time Durack property now in the hands of the L. J. Hooker pastoral
company. There is also cattle feed in the residues of cotton and the
oilseed crops, safflower, rape and linseed. One cotton-grower said
that there was more future in safflower than in cotton. However, Dr
Davidson thinks that even if the overheads are shared by rotating
these two crops, costs will still beat the Ord grower.

It may be hopeful, rather than just wishful, thinking to believe that
the factors this relentless critic cites against the Ord scheme are not
necessarily constants that cannot change. Against subsidized farming
in the north Dr Davidson argued in 1966 that Australia's rural mainstay, wool, was completely unsubsidized and that wheat had been
subsidized only for short periods. In 1971 the wool industry was being
heavily subsidized, and crying out for more.

Other crops under investigation at the Kimberley Research Station
were rice (which is already being grown), wheat, oats, barley, sugarcane, soybeans and peanuts. Much of the plain that will be opened up
by the big Ord irrigation project will be suitable for rice-growing.

Stage III of the Ord project will be the generation of hydro-electricity. As the power needs of the area grow so will generators be
installed up to a capacity of 30 megawatts. And if the whole Ord
irrigation project confounds its critics and proves successful it is
planned that a similar dam will be constructed on the Fitzroy River
that runs into King Sound at Derby.

As to minerals, the Kimberley region has not been explored to the extent the Pilbara, the great iron province to the south of it, has. There was talk of a large lead-silver deposit in the Kununurra region; there is iron in the Carr Boyd Range, and one Kununurran said, "The Kimberley is swarming with geologists and buzzing with helicopters."

The big find has been bauxite, proven reserves of about 200 million tons of it, on Admiralty Gulf. At Port Warrender there has been nothing on the map, not even a mission station as at Weipa and Gove, the other big bauxite developments. There will be a town of about 3,000 people, a mining complex, a plant to turn the bauxite into alumina—another Gove, more or less, and costing about as much—$300 million. Amax, a subsidiary of American Metal Climax, is the managing operator for an international consortium, and the project will be wholly overseas-owned.

When the estimated cost was $100 million it was thought that Australian interests would have a 25 per cent equity in it. When the costing went up to $300 million, and projected production up to 1.2 million tons of alumina by 1975, no Australian interests with $75 million were forthcoming. Which does not mean that there will not be the usual wail later on that another hunk of the Australian mineral heritage is being "exploited by foreign interests". We had the opportunity to participate but not the initiative—or, perhaps, just not the kind of money such developments require.

As to oil, it is quite possible at this early stage of exploration along the Kimberley coast that this remote region of Australia could produce a bigger strike than has been made at Barrow Island.

As to natural gas, Woodside Oil was officially reported in July 1971 to have tapped a "major gas field" with its Rankin 1 well 80 miles off the coast between Dampier and Port Hedland, on what is called the North-West Shelf.

I JOINED at Kununurra a Pioneer coach tour called the "Nor'wester" that had started at Darwin and gone from there to the Katherine Gorge, where I had already been. This is (on the 1971 schedule) a seventeen-day tour through to Perth—it also runs Perth-Darwin. It goes into the back country of the North-West, then down the coast, where I was to leave it at Exmouth to go to Barrow Island.

From Kununurra the coach did not make the 100-mile run to the main Ord Dam and back, but went to the Diversion Dam at Bandicoot Bar, which is worth seeing. From there it went to the cottonfields (PLATE 45), the Kimberley Research Station and the cotton ginnery where the crop was being treated and baled. Some of the seed the ginning removes was crushed for cattle feed; some went to Japan where the "fuzz" from it was used for stuffing toys and the husks in the making of firecrackers. Nothing was wasted.

The only vacant seat in the coach when I got on was next to an old man who, when he was young, had been a pugilist and was known then as "Basher" Smith (let us say). I have never thought highly of the fight game, and thought even less of it after a week alongside poor old Basher. He had been hit about the head so much in his fights that he was somewhat punch drunk, as well as having little faculty of hearing left behind his cauliflower ears. He was a likeable old man who spoke seldom and slept most of the time the coach was on the road. The other passengers felt compassion for him and hardly anybody laughed when he asked the only question I heard him ask, of the local guide who joined the coach at Kununurra. He blinked out at the field of snow-white cotton awaiting the harvester and said, "Where do they grow the black cotton?"

The Buccaneer (and Iron) Islands

THE YEAR IS 1980. In Melbourne two wives of young executives who get their annual holidays in winter are discussing where they will be going this year.

"For us, it'll be back to the Barrier Reef. We love it so."

"No, this is going to be our year for the Buccaneer Archipelago. I believe it's marvellous. And the weather's so much more reliable."

"Yes, the Atkinsons went last year and Phoebe got *such* a suntan. But isn't it rather far?"

"An extra hour's flight, that's all, now that you jet directly through Alice Springs to Derby."

It could happen. Even though, I'd wager, ninety-five out of a hundred Australians today would not be able to point to where the islands with the swashbuckling name of the Buccaneer Archipelago are on the map.

They lie off King Sound, which the average easterner could not pinpoint either. It might be fairer to say they are off Yampi Sound. Then perhaps, the penny drops and you hear the reaction, "That's where Cockatoo Island is, the iron mine. Not one of the West's new ones, though." No, it isn't. An iron mining operation that started shipping out ore back in 1951 is now regarded as old-hat, certainly not New Australia—and, what with its being a company workplace, hardly the spot to spend a holiday.

However, Cockatoo is not the island that comes immediately to mind when I think "Buccaneer Archipelago", which consists of four groups of small islands. Not that Cockatoo isn't an eyeworthy island, rising in chromatic cliffs from a cerulean sea. There is Koolan, bigger and rather better, and also given over to iron mining. Best of all, there are the small islands, some with no names to them, including what are called the Ballast Group, because how iron came to be discovered here, back in 1880, was that luggermen used to take on heavy rocks from the island shores as ballast.

It is this whole area, not just spots of it, that I find as fascinating as any in Australia. In fact, I had been fascinated with it for twenty years, especially King Sound. Once, on paper, I navigated a pearling lugger through Whirlpool Pass and into King Sound and into the grim lagoon-like bay called the Graveyard, and out through the roaring tide rips of Hell's Gate because a hurricane was coming. I did it all in a novel, with the aid of Admiralty charts. I had never seen King Sound. On this trip I was determined to see it, at least from the air. Which I did, flying from Derby to Cockatoo Island, and flying back to Derby from Koolan.

The King of King Sound was Captain Phillip Parker King, one of the earliest surveyors of this coast. He named the Buccaneer Archipelago because William Dampier was a buccaneer. Dampier came in January 1688, in a piratical ship from Mexico called the *Cygnet*, exactly a hundred years before the First Fleet reached the east coast and nearly a century before Cook set foot on it. While the *Cygnet* was being careened, probably in a bay of King Sound, Dampier had a look at the hinterland, which he described as a poor sort of place and its Aborigines as "the miserablest people in the world". However, he was to return to the New Holland of the Dutch in 1699 as captain of the *Roebuck*.

Yampi Sound is from Stokes of *H.M.S. Beagle* hearing the natives call freshwater *yampee*. Derby is one of those ubiquitous christenings after the Colonial Secretary of the day, who was Lord Derby. Australians pronounce the town as spelt, although they are aware that the great English horse-race is the *Darby*.

DERBY I flew to from Darwin, via Kununurra, to which I returned. So, between these places, I had two flights over the Kimberley country—and strange and formidable country it is.

Its mountains are sculptural, but so ancient and worn; as Laseron says, "another of those old land surfaces which have survived for incredible ages",[1] much of it a plateau of ancient rocks deeply dissected by gorges the rivers have cut through—gorges, some of them, where no white man has ever been. The only road east through the rugged Leopold Ranges peters out into a four-wheel-drive track beyond Gibb River station and there are few other points of station habitation on the flight route of 370 miles from Kununurra to Derby.

The Kimberley's earliest explorer—in 1838, nearly fifty years before there was any permanent settlement—was a remarkable man who, as Sir George Grey, was to govern South Australia, South Africa and New Zealand. Grey found the extraordinary Aboriginal cave paintings that, we know now, represent spirit beings called *Wandjina*: for many years they were fancifully attributed to Asiatics and even Arabs. There are Wandjina paintings on Gibb River station we fly over, and in many other parts of the West Kimberley; but none, as yet, is on the tourist track.

The uplands, dead-brown in this dry season, fall away to coastal plain that merges in a haze with saltpans and the sea. The tide is out, and when the tide goes out at Derby it leaves a quarter-mile of sand between the jetty and the sea. The Western Australian State Shipping Service builds its ships so they can sit on the bottom when the water deserts their keels at the rate of ten feet an hour at top-springs, when the difference between rise and fall is 35 feet.

I had landed at Derby's airport before, a good twenty years ago. Derby I remembered in terms of boab-trees, the boab being a memorable tree that looks less like a tree than a bottle—out of which an obese genie with upflung skinny, crooked arms is trying to escape. The branches have this frantic look, in contrast to the static corpulence of the trunks. In colour boabs are on the silvery side of elephant-grey. They bear nuts as big as emu eggs, and these are carved for sale to tourists.

Incidentally, no West Australian would ever call a boab by its right name, which is baobab, and not even an Australian name, but an African one. The Australian species is distinct.

THE FAMOUS BOAB at Derby is less like a bottle than a misshapen flagon, and when MMA's Fokker Friendship landed at 5.10 p.m., and Graham Whitford of the North-West Administration met me and said there was still plenty of light for a run-round, he drove me to what is called the Prison Tree.

This boab (PLATE 49) is of huge girth and, although it is hollow as a Halloween pumpkin, it is still very much alive. Tourists are always told that in the hollow of this one Aboriginal prisoners were incarcerated by police troopers.

Why should a policeman halt only five miles from the town he would have wanted to get back to? Prisoners were customarily brought in linked with chains round their necks and would not have had to be stuffed into the boab's suffocating lock-up to prevent escape. Graham Whitford did not believe that the tree was so used, though he thought prisoners had, on occasions, been chained to it.

But the "Prison Tree" it will continue to be. It could, of course, be viewed as just the Big Boab.

Big it is, and almost husky enough to defeat the vandals. They had hacked their initials into its trunk, but the old boab had continued to fatten and, in doing so, filled in many scars. This has left the trunk with the texture of a warty pachyderm. However, the "I-was-here" oafs take a lot of beating. They now climb up and slash the insignia of their stupidity into the branches.

Through the sparse-leaved branches of the boabs (someone once said that they were like trees planted upside down with their roots in the air) the angry sun that had been glaring at us slipped like a molten penny into the slot of the horizon, and we went into town to the Spinifex Hotel. This proved to be all right as to accommodation, but, then and later, very poor as to service. When you are thirsty and fancy a glass of beer while waiting for your dinner you hardly expect the waitress at a Swan Brewery hotel to say, "We're very busy. I can only serve you wine."

Derby has been the North-West's administrative centre, a position it is losing to upsurging Port Hedland; but it has handsome modern shire offices. And, in what had long been regarded as a rather rough-necked meatworkers'-stockmen's town, has burgeoned a good-looking civic and cultural centre.

The Air Beef scheme that flew in beef from abattoirs on Glenroy station—and was more publicized than profitable—was discontinued in 1962 and now the development is of beef roads for road-trains of cattle, or beef in chiller trucks.

NEXT MORNING at six forty I took off for Cockatoo Island in the MMA Twin Otter plane that was under charter to B.H.P. or, rather, its subsidiary, the Dampier Mining Company.

It was low tide again. Derby's long, long jetty stood in sand and mud that stretched beyond the end of it. In King Sound the water had retreated from the cliffs and mangroves of headlands, bays and islands. At its mouth the big inlet is a fragmented mixture of land and sea, the navigator's nightmare. However, I could pick out fairly easily the Graveyard (where my novel's divers fought on the treacherous seabed) and identify Whirlpool Pass. Then we were over a maze of islands and long rock-ribbed landspits channelled with that lightest-brightest blue of tropical seas. A break of open water formed Yampi Sound and beyond it the only habitation sighted since Derby appeared. Cockatoo Island humps high out of the sea and tails away to a length of three miles or so. There wasn't much room for an airstrip on top, but Twin Otters are good at these short ones.

Mining the iron, open-cut fashion, has terraced one side of the island with ferric-red cliffs that are all the more vivid in a setting of sea so beautifully blue. I go with Laurie James, the young manager, to watch the electric shovels claw out from the explosives-shattered rockwalls the great scoops of ore they dump into the Haulpak trucks. The Haulpaks race off, huge tires spurning deep-red dust, and tip their loads to the crusher beside the wharf where the ore ships come in to take it to the steelworks at Newcastle and Port Kembla. No long rail haul, as from the newer mines of the Pilbara—but there the deposits are so much vaster.

Cockatoo has high-grade hematite ore, up to 69 per cent iron. About 1.5 million tons a year are being mined from a lode that is known to go deep below sea-level. Koolan Island's iron is considered to be a continuation of the same deposit and enough to last past the end of this century, perhaps forty years. Cockatoo's mining could cut out before then, if the below-sea-level ore imposes cost problems. I heard speculation that, if that happened, it might be turned into a tourist village.

Water was a problem: the ore ships had to bring it as backloading. Houses were not as modern as in the new company towns, but were rather more commodious. They rented for less than five dollars a week to the workforce of 180 men: with wives and children Cockatoo had 350 people. The sea-tempered climate is cooler than the mainland's, and over-the-century heat is rare. There is an eight-months' Dry.

Thirsts were being slaked comfortably at the airy hilltop club that served barbecue steak dinners at weekends. A Dutchman presided pleasantly over the bar. A disgruntled German said *Ach!* to the place and that he was going soon back to Hamburg. An abstemious Swiss confided that he was banking $150 a fortnight. A husky Haulpak driver let his eyes covet for a moment the pretty wife of a plant engineer and said the money was all right but, "Gawd, a man misses his sex life." His mate said it was a good idea to play basketball.

When the club closed we took some beer to Vic Cox's house. Vic liked crocodiles. He had two Johnstone River types, eleven-foot Henry and nine-foot Savage, living under the veranda. He used to have thirty-two crocs, but the big ones ate the little ones. At times Henry wouldn't eat for weeks, Vic said. He also had a turtle and a snake-necked tortoise.

A SPEEDBOAT made of fibreglass and belonging to the young English assayer, Peter Brown, zips through the water that is bluer than the cloudless morning sky. We go past the Piccaninnies, islets where white cockatoos breed in thousands, and across to the mainland's rocky shore.

We go up Silver Gull Creek, where there is a spring that Cockatoo Island used to draw its water from, by barge. The place of the spring is called (cross my heart) Cleopatra's Pool. The creek is walled with salmon-red rockfaces so fractured vertically that they are masses of points and pinnacles. Indeed, as we go on farther up the coast the whole area proves to be full of remarkable rock formations, in colours ranging from bright red to cinder black. And what would have been a mangrove mudflat at low tide was now, at noon, a canal-like water-way with the half-submerged mangroves lining it like shrubberies. Koolan Island I'd be going to later. A long black ore carrier was berthed against the island's red-rock shore. We went on to see some of the smaller islands of the Buccaneers.

One island we landed on I am not going to identify by name because Peter Brown had been asked by the Aboriginal who showed him what was on it not to make it generally known. In a cave you climb up to, on a ledge, were three bundles of bones wrapped in bark. The one that was open showed not a full set of human bones, just a jawbone and some others. The largest bark "coffin" was only about eighteen inches long. One was much smaller and may have contained a child's bones (we did not undo its binding of string made from hair).

Subsequently, in Derby, I asked a knowledgeable Aboriginal called Wattie, the head gardener at the school, about the bones on the island, which he had been to. He said that up to about fifty years ago tree burial was widely practised by the local tribes. The bones would have been taken from a tree, carried about for a few months by a female relative, and then placed on the island.

PLATE 44 shows one of the islands. There are others with beaches as secluded, water as translucently jade-blue, rocks even more curious. Physically they are more striking than the islands of the Great Barrier Reef, though they lack the coralled edges—and the up-to-35-feet tide rise and fall makes their charm variable and creates problems of access.

However, I do think we are going to hear more of the Buccaneer Archipelago as a tourist area.

IF I WERE ASKED to nominate the most beautiful views I have ever seen—and they would include sunrise on the Himalayas, a sunlit armada of icebergs off the Greenland coast, Fujiyama across Lake Hakone and other prospects as memorable—I think I should have to include the view from Koolan Island's rubbish tip.

Koolan Island (PLATE 47) is the only place where I have been taken to see the local rubbish dump. On the way to it there is a notice-board: TO THE WORLD'S MOST SCENIC RUBBISH TIP. Well . . . you think of other waggish, gimmicky notices. You come to where a truck is in the act of tipping a load of rubbish, dowsing it with sump oil and lighting it so that a sheet of red flame and black smoke goes up in an iron-clad box arrangement on the edge of a cliff. When this is over you approach—and the view of cerulean sea set with a host of islands is breath-taking. Yes, it must be the most scenic rubbish tip in the world.

I just think that Koolan should burn its rubbish somewhere else and set up a nice little rotunda there for the local contemplatives, if any.

If you live by iron mining, or your husband does, on a place like sea-girt Koolan I suppose you get accustomed to the surrounding scene, and the most important places in your life become the club or the golf course, which on Koolan has red fairways and the greens are of sand, but a golf course is a golf course. The swimming-pool also becomes pretty important. The houses are more modern than on Cockatoo, because Koolan is much more recently developed: it began producing in 1965. Koolan had about 400 people.

POWER generation requires coal—which Western Australia is notably short of—unless it is nuclear power or hydro-electric power such as the Ord Dam can generate, or oil or natural gas. Another way to generate hydro-electricity could be by using the tides.

A thirty-foot rise and fall of tides could generate an enormous amount of electricity. Where could this terrific tide-run best be harnessed? Experts looked and indicated a place called Funnel or, next door to that, Yule Entrance to Walcott Inlet.

This project is unlikely to come in the next ten, or even twenty years. It would cost a great deal of money and the regional industries that would need such power are hardly in prospect. But the West's at-that-time Minister for Industrial Development (Mr Court) thought it would come eventually.

So I decided to have a look at Walcott Inlet. The only way to do so was to charter a plane, and a Cessna that was on Koolan's airstrip happened to be available. Also, I had been told that the flight to Walcott Inlet was very special, scenically.

It was, too. The scene from the air is of a glorious litter of islands, including islands with beaches in coves one yearns to explore, but most of them standing up straight with cliff shores that forbid a landing, rockbound islands in fascinating formations and of many colours.

Walcott Inlet, where mangroves stretch to the foot of rock-browed heights, we came over at the turn of the tide. "Lower," I said to the pilot, and he took the Cessna down to within fifty feet of the most vicious water I have ever seen. It spun, it whirlpooled, it vortexed like something out of Edgar Allan Poe's *The Maelstrom*. Froth outlined a fury of water patterns across the narrow entrance.

Near the Funnel the people who came to prospect its potential as a power source had left a Land Rover we flew over, apparently because they couldn't get it out.

This whole region seems to me to have great potential for tourism of the more adventurous kind, particularly if helicopters are used for passenger transport, as they already are on the Barrier Reef Islands. There would be cruises from resort points, of course—necessarily with skilled boatmen of the calibre of Alf Brown who runs the workboat I went to Koolan on from Cockatoo and who is said to be able to navigate any channel of King Sound at any tide and even at night.

Outback and Pearlers' Broome

WYNDHAM was the first place the Pioneer "Nor'wester" tour went to after leaving Kununurra. It is the State's most northerly port, though it won't be when Port Warrender on Admiralty Gulf gets going with Amax bauxite development.

The 65 miles of blacktop beef road leads to a town that lives mainly on its meatworks. Its 1,200 population swells to 1,600, mostly men, in the killing season. Wyndham claims to have Australia's biggest beer thirst for a town of its size and the roughest golf-course; some say it has the worst climate—excessively hot and humid. Beside the unenchanting tidal flats of Cambridge Gulf, it is a strung-out sort of town that shows signs of coagulating at what is called its Three Mile.

At the cemetery on a ridge, Keith the driver says, the ground is so rocky graves can't be dug with picks and shovels: they use gelignite. By the roadside is a great stack of cotton seed in sacks, unprotected; but it isn't likely to rain before November. Despite the heat, there is a football ground. And a shameful rubbish-heap of a blacks' camp.

Back along the beef road we turn off onto the Great Northern Highway and run down it between the O'Donnell Ranges and the red-brown ramparts of the Carr Boyds. At Dunham River station we stop to see the spray irrigation the American pastoralist Goddard is doing on the greenest land we'll see this day. Sprays like firehoses are throwing water a hundred yards across the fodder crop beyond the boab-trees.

The bitumen ends, the road becomes corrugated, and out of the

Grape picking in the Barossa Valley, north of Adelaide, where some of Australia's best wines are made. Grape harvest is in March-April.

43/SOUTH AUSTRALIA

On the Murray River near Renmark, where vacationers hire modernly equipped, drive-yourself paddlewheel houseboats, called here Liba-Libas.

dry-grassed country with white-trunked trees rises a big thumb of rock called Pompey's Pillar. Here there is a known iron deposit; but, although about ten million tons of it is reckoned high-grade hematite, the average grade is between 40 and 50 per cent and, in view of the great 64 per cent deposits farther south, nobody is bothering to mine at Pompey's Pillar.

We stop by the Bow River ("Ladies to the left, gentlemen to the right") which has very little water in it, boil the dixie for tea, and eat a chicken-salad lunch from cardboard boxes.

Then the road goes on through stony spinifex country. Old Basher, my seat mate, suddenly exclaims, "All y'see on this trip is *land*. Nothing but damn *land*!"

Much more enthusiastic about the tour is Mrs Vene Drury from Glen Osmond, South Australia, who is a big woman and, I should think, in her sixties. She has done this Nor'wester tour before, but in the opposite direction. I doubt if there is a Pioneer tour to anywhere Mrs Drury has not done at least once. She started her Pioneering in 1950 (when she had never been out of South Australia except for one air trip to Sydney) and, by mid-1971, she had done 268 tours with 186 coach captains, whose names she knew, and she had kept a diary of each trip.

All this is cattle country and although there are a couple of station homesteads near the highway we see no sign of cattle until we are approaching Halls Creek. Thousands of reddish anthills (termite nests) appear between the white ghost-gums, and then we are in better-looking country, though it is still clumped with spinifex. The day's run has been 300 miles and the sun is blazing low on the horizon when we pull up at the welcome, though primitive, hotel.

HALLS CREEK is not the town that throbbed to the first Westralian gold rush in 1885: the original settlement is ruins ten miles farther on.

Now there are about 130 whites there and in the Wet, when the stations lay off most of their Aboriginal labour, up to 600 black people come in. In the hotel bar, called the Bullring, a notice says ALL RIGHTS MUST BE PRODUCED BEFORE LIQUOR IS SERVED.

This was for the Aborigines, who had to apply to the local police or the Welfare Officer to be given the right to drink. (Discriminatory legislation against Aborigines in Western Australia's north-west remained until June 1971.)

The publican said he was a bit shocked when he took the hotel over last year and white men would say to him, "Don't serve that black bastard. He hasn't got his rights." But he's used to it now.

The young Welfare Officer said the rights did more harm than good. Aborigines who have their rights, if asked to get liquor for

◀ 44/WESTERN AUSTRALIA Islands of the Buccaneer Archipelago north of King Sound are, as yet, off the tourist track. Some are beautiful.

kinsmen who haven't, get it, because they couldn't refuse: it would be disgraceful, tribally, to do so. They were constantly being arrested for doing this. They never denied it, always pleaded guilty, served a month's jail, came out and did it again. The illicit drinking was usually of cheap port wine, whereas in the bar they were likely to drink beer.

The schoolteacher says he has only six white children out of 187 in the school. Between the full-bloods and the mixed-bloods there is no difference in school performance, he finds; but the coloured children start far behind the white ones, and they don't feel the same incentive to learn. What are they going to do with book-learning, anyway, when they grow up to work on a cattle station? A father will bring his son to the hostel, where fifty Aboriginal children stay, and say he would like his boy to be able to read and write. "Then when I want some part for my car, he can write away to get it." But some who learn to read and write will, when they leave school, still endorse their pay cheques with a cross or thumbprint, so as not to appear "superior" to their friends.

After dinner I was sitting out at the tables of what might be called the beer-garden with a couple of people from the coach including an American young woman whose first name was Joyce and who came from Washington, D.C. Drinking at the next table was a building inspector from the State Housing Commission and he was saying loudly to a contractor that the Aborigines were the "most hopeless bloody people on the face of the earth".

I said they were undoubtedly a problem people and suggested that the problem was of our making and asked how he would solve it.

"You can't solve it!" the B.I. said, and then, "Stop them breeding for three generations!"

I said, "You can hardly do that."

"Then shoot the bloody lot of them—the men, anyway!"

Somewhat taken aback, I said I had thought that sort of thinking went out sixty years ago with a Western Australian squatter named Mason who wrote that male Aborigines should all be castrated.

The B.I. said, "Well, that's what I meant, really. But I didn't like to say it with a lady present."

After that indication of what the B.I. regarded as being obscene, Joyce from Washington said, "Why don't you just let them be happy living their natural tribal lives?"

It had to be explained that their land was gone, their tribal organization was gone, there was no tribal life left to live. Also, the Aborigines had come to want tobacco and liquor and motor-cars, just as we did.

You can't argue with B.I.-types, so I went to bed. This was easier said than done, because there were four beds in a room big enough for two and in order to get to mine I had to climb across old Basher's. There was no other furniture in the room, there being space for none, and not even a mirror. This was the only really bad accommodation on the tour, and it was the only accommodation Halls Creek offered. The next town was 200 miles farther on, so it had to be an overnight stop. There was nothing to see there.

What there is to see in the Halls Creek region lies 65 miles south of it—the Wolf Creek meteorite crater. This is the second-largest known meteorite crater in the world, 2,800 feet in diameter (one in Arizona is about 3,300 feet), symmetrically round and 160 feet deep from the top of the rim, which is raised high above the surrounding desert.

Only as recently as 1947 was this remarkable formation identified as caused by a great meteorite plunging into the earth, and brought to public notice. There is a reasonable road to it (in the Dry, flooded in the Wet).

NEXT MORNING we headed for Fitzroy Crossing through much the same sort of dry-grassed country with more multitudes of pointed anthills and then isolated flat-topped hills rising from the plain.

Here was truly the "wide brown land", the "sunburnt country" under the "pitiless blue sky" of Dorothea Mackellar's *My Country*. After watching it for an hour or two the coach passengers began singing, everything from *Waltzing Matilda* and *People Will Think We're in Love* back to World War I songs like *Roses in Picardy*.

The homesteads of the cattle stations were out of sight, nothing striking in the way of vegetation appeared, nor any animal life—not a kangaroo or an emu or even a scuttling rabbit. Old Basher beside me was fast asleep, the singing had stopped and others were dozing when the coach slowed at a station gate with the improbable name of GOGO on it—and standing beside the gate were *three large elephants*.

The reason lay a hundred yards ahead—a cavalcade of motor wagons lettered SOLE BROS. CIRCUS. The rear wagon, painted bright red, also had DANGER! AFRICAN JUNGLE LIONS. And all the vehicles were as halted as the elephants were, just this side of big gums lining the Fitzroy River, blocking the road. Several of us got out.

"Please get back in the coach!" An agitated man from the circus came up. "Our three lions have escaped—gate on their cage must have jumped its lock when we crossed the creek back there. The big lion and two lionesses. They're lying up just over in that grass area."

This bit of excitement went on for about half an hour, by which time a helicopter called in by radio was buzzing overhead, reportedly bringing tranquillizer guns. I climbed on top of the coach with camera and telephoto lens, but when I did see a lioness break the grass her appearance was too momentary to photograph. Then we heard she was back in her cage, and so were the other two. The coach made its way round the cavalcade and went on to Fitzroy Crossing ahead of Sole Bros' "45 Units of Rolling Stock, 54 Animals, 24 Star Acts from All Parts of the World—the First Real Circus to Circumnavigate Australia."

It was the first circus ever seen at Fitzroy Crossing. Ray Kilroy, the publicity man (he also appeared in the ring and his daughter did the dog act and drove one of the station wagons) was still excited about the lions' escape when I talked to him that night.

"Very serious thing to happen, you know," he said. "But it's an ill wind . . . I phoned the Sydney Press soon as we got in. Tomorrow it'll be in just about every newspaper in Australia!"

GEIKE GORGE (pron. Geekie) we went to that afternoon. This gorge of the Fitzroy River, fifteen miles from the Crossing is, I think, even better than Katherine Gorge.

The river is rather wider than at Katherine and perhaps the walls of rock are not so high, but they are more variegated in their colouring. The Fitzroy has the second-largest volume of water, next to the Ord, of all the West's rivers and up the limestone walls to the gorge you can see how high it floods. Up to flood level the rock is white, and undercut and honeycombed by the water's erosion with a beautiful sculptured effect. PLATE 50 shows some of this.

A crocodile plumped into the river at one point and, as we were returning up the gorge towards evening, thousands of flying-foxes swarmed in the bright green trees that grew on the banks against a background of multi-coloured cliffs that assumed the strangest shapes, like piled turrets. And there were the reflections of the white-to-black-to-red cliffs in the still blue water.

Fitzroy Crossing's population is given in several references as 33. I'll swear there were 500 people in it the night we were there, and most of them were black. The first-ever circus had brought in all the Aboriginal ringers from the cattle stations, and their families.

I went to the circus, and didn't see much of it. I was looking at the audience, and the kids were marvellous, loving every minute of what they saw with shining eyes and white teeth glistening. And a better behaved audience I have never seen.

Back at the pub—and it's a good pub, the Crossing Inn, with some air-conditioned motel-type units added to cater for tourists, and an attractive garden—I had a drink with the local police sergeant. He was a young sergeant, thirty-four, who had been there two years. He had come from a southern district where most of the Aborigines were mixed-bloods, and he hadn't liked them much.

"These people," he said, "are all right. They don't give trouble—most of the trouble I get comes from the whites, though there are fewer of them. They're a simple people, and I like them, and I try to do what I can for them. I get called all sorts of names for taking their side. But that doesn't worry me."

When the admirable policeman had gone and I was alone at the bar a white ringer asked (the usual introduction), "Where you from?" I said Sydney and asked where he was from. Sydney. He had been been up here a couple of years on a cattle station. ("Ringer", incidentally, derives from riding round the cattle, "ringing" them.)

I asked him to join me in a drink and suggested we go outside and sit down. At a nearby table a couple of whites were drinking. A black stockman came up and, pointing to two vacant chairs, asked politely, "These taken?" A white man answered, "Yes. They're taken." Then a white woman with two women friends came and asked if the chairs were available. "Sure. Go ahead. Take them."

The ringer said that on his station a lot of the cattle were wild and I asked him how they mustered. He said they used Land Rovers with bull-bars.

"You get a cow and take the calf away. She bellows like hell and that brings the wild cattle out of the scrub. Or you light a fire and burn 'em out. Anyway, bull-catchers get twenty dollars a head for what they knock down with the bull-bar and hog-tie and get on the truck. They're bruised, but you've got 'em."

We leave Fitzroy Crossing next morning after a breakfast that begins with luscious paw-paw, or papaya, grown in what Americans might regard as "desert" Australia.

The morning is spent running 170 miles through similar country, mostly blond-grassed plains with mesa hills, to Derby, where I've been. The only thing there we are shown that I haven't already seen is the Myall's Bore, an artesian-water drinking-trough for cattle that are shipped south. Three hundred feet long, it is said to be the longest trough in the Southern Hemisphere: it is also one of the most forgettable tourist sights in the wide world.

Leaving Derby, coach-captain Keith says that the afternoon run is going to be rather monotonous; but at the end of it we get Broome. He talks a little about how the Fitzroy comes down in the Wet with a flood of three quarters of a million cubic feet a second, and we stop for photographs at another great spread of anthills. Then most of the passengers have their window blinds down and are snoozing.

I think about the place where we'll spend the next two nights, and wonder how much it will have changed.

BROOME, 1948, November, just before the pearling season lay-up for

the Wet. A white-red-and-blue place; the buildings white-painted
and many of them corrugated iron, the earth ochre-red, the sea bright
tropical blue, with the town stretched along the shores of Roebuck
Bay, found in 1699 by Dampier, who noted the presence of pearlshell.

Broome with the full moon laying across the bay the glistening
path of light the locals really did call the "Golden Staircase". They
cherished the idea that Broome was "romantic"—at least the whites
did. The Malays, who post-war took the place of the Japanese divers,
had got themselves guitars and used to sing the haunting *Trang Bulan*
("Clear Moon"), or some did. They also got themselves the bends,
the diver's paralysis; but none had died of it the year I was there
(several had at Thursday Island). Twenty luggers were working and
pearlshell was high, £600 a ton. Good Malay divers could afford to
shack up with white girls who preferred the Broome life to the
brothels in Perth's Roe Street. Their hotel haunt was the Roebuck,
at what was called Chinatown. The meat-workers drank at the Governor Broome, and the prime pub was the Continental where the
black handyman, Old Con, was even more of a character than the
white cockatoo that swore so volubly.

Colourful was the word for it, but there was a lot of death and
disaster in the Broome canvas, much of it attested by the decorative
gravestones in the Japanese cemetery. Old-timers were still alive then
who remembered the terrible willy-willies (cyclones) of 1908 and
1910 as well as the 1935 one that caught the luggers at sea and took
142 lives. Still there was Bernie Bardwell, who had lost three luggers
and twice cheated the sea himself by being a powerful swimmer: once
he was in the water for thirteen hours before he got ashore. And
Tudor Owen who rode out a willy-willy on his father's lugger, lashed
to one of the masts: his mother was lashed to the other one. And
"Long" Mackenzie who stayed on through the war when the town
was evacuated and saw the fourteen flying-boats full of refugees from
the Dutch East Indies arrive—and they were like sitting ducks on the
water when the six Jap. Zeros swooped in, machine-guns blazing.
There was a cemetery of the victims by the old jetty where the
Koolinda used to sit on the mud when the water dropped thirty feet
at what are called king tides.

The old-timers all agreed that pearls were not what they used to
be. There didn't seem to be any more stones (they always called a
pearl a stone) like the rosy beauty Elles the pearl cleaner skinned for
the Bardwell brothers, and it brought £4,000. Of course, the greatest
from Broome waters was the "Star of the West", fished by one of the
luggers of Clarke, the "Pearl King", in 1917. The big buyers used
to come then from Europe, the Frenchmen, the Romanian Jews, the

Germans, and Sussman offered £10,000 for the "Star", but it brought
£14,000 in London. There were no more prices like that after Mikimoto developed cultured pearls. But shell was doing all right. Pearl
buttons hadn't turned into plastic ones.

WE CAME INTO BROOME at what is still called Chinatown, though
there is hardly a Chinese there. Tropicana Lodge, the accommodation, was less than modern, but hibiscus and frangipani nudged its
verandas nicely.

After dinner I collect Mary Durack from her Broome house and
we go down to see the transformation at the old "Connie" that has
become the Continental Motor Hotel. It has thrown out a wing of
twenty-three motel rooms round a mosaic-tiled swimming-pool that
has steps up to it and looks as if it is waiting for an Indian rajah to
bathe. Broome of the pearling past obviously believes that its future
lies in tourism; and that tourists want air-conditioned comfort and are
prepared to pay for it.

Not that pearling is dead, but it is pearling of a different kind. Some
luggers still work out of Broome. They take the pearl oysters the
divers gather to Kuri Bay 250 miles up the coast, where Japanese
experts introduce the nuclei that grow cultured pearls (as explained
at Thursday Island in the Queensland section).

The sorting of pearlshell can still be seen, though in nothing like
the quantities there used to be, in the packing sheds of Streeter and
Male. According to Osmar White in his 1969 book on the North
West,[1] "Last year three million dollars of cultured pearls were produced in North Australian waters—twice the value of all the beef
shipped from the Kimberley meatworks."

Next morning we looked at Dampier's concrete monument shaped
as a sea chest, and at the fine old Court House building, and at derelict luggers lying in the mangroves along the foreshore, and then
went to the Japanese cemetery.

The hundreds of gravestones attest more than the Japanese population Broome used to have. The price of pearlshell was so high in terms
of lives that many of the Japanese buried here must have been washed
up drowned after cyclones or been divers who died of paralysis or
other accidents of their perilous calling. The reason the cemetery
has become a prime tourist attraction is that the gravestones reflect
the Japanese love of natural stone and, though cut in slabs, these are
not straight-edged as is our fashion, but retain the contours of the
broken stone. It is this, in combination with the calligraphy of Japanese characters that we see purely in terms of design, that makes them
so decorative.

The cemetery is well cared for now—in contrast to when I had last seen it, when bitter feelings towards the ex-enemy were still upper-most. The previous year, for the first time since before the war, the *Bon Mitsuri* ceremony had been held in the cemetery. The five sons of a Japanese diver buried there had sent lanterns from Japan to deck his grave, Buddhist rites were performed, the Japanese consul came, and fruit was distributed and *sake* offered not only to the departed spirit but to Europeans who attended. In the old days, when there were over a thousand Japanese at Broome, there used to be held in August the *Tsuki Miro* ceremony. After food and rice wine was placed in the lantern-decorated graveyard the Japanese would launch on the bay little model luggers, laden with rice and flowers. As these went out on the tide the spirit of a dead diver was supposed to sail with each one.

Then to Cable Beach, which is white sand stretching for fourteen miles, and its gentle surf looked so enticing that some of us swam: beaches as good as this one are rare in the north. Gantheaume Point is highly picturesque with tumbled rocks of vivid red.

The new jetty on Roebuck Bay is 2,000 feet long, and ships can remain afloat at it even at the lowest tide.

MARY DURACK asked me to dinner at their house that used to be "Long" Mackenzie's. Horrie Miller, her husband, was there. He said that during the war a famous K.L.M. pilot, Smirnoff, badly wounded from an attack by Japanese fighter planes, crash-landed in the shallows of Carnot Bay, north of Broome, when he was bringing out of Indonesia for the Dutch authorities a fortune in diamonds. The natives found some, and one of the mission fathers collected a tin can full. He buried the can, but became confused about where, and could never find the spot again. "There's a very rich piece of ground up there somewhere."

Mary I wanted to hear talk about the Aborigines, for few people know the station blacks as well as she does. And none has written of them so well, not anthropologically but humanly. She begins her book *The Rock and the Sand*:[2] "The people of the dream watched the people of the clock come out of the sea and strike their flagstaff firmly into the sand."

No one has expressed more perceptively the character of the people the white man found so unpredictable: "Expected to flourish under improved conditions, the people would lie down and die; lamented as a dying race they would unaccountably revive. Encouraged into the new economy they would languish for loss of their tribal ways; given reserves they would withdraw to the amenities of civilization; withheld citizenship and social benefits, the injustice of their situation would strike at the white man's self-esteem, but let them be granted equality in all material respects and the white man would stand condemned by their spiritual deprivation and lack of incentive. Let Welfare Departments declare a policy of assimilation and the dark people would discover their pride of race; recognize their right to a separate identity and they would suspect a move towards segregation . . . attempt to grade their needs according to colour and it would appear that the degenerate near-white could be more dependent than the robust black."

When she talked of them it was with the warmth of a mature woman's love for the black people's capacity to—*love*, saying, "They are more Christian than we are, more sincere. They really live by the rule: he who has two coats *does* give one away. I remember old Albert saying to one of the mission Sisters. 'Well, Sister, we not got the education you people got. You got everything, but one thing we can teach the white people about—love.' They see us as being so competitive, trying to gain status over each other, and they don't understand why we should want to assert ourselves so. With sport in the schools, it was found that children who could run faster than others, didn't. They didn't want to lick the other kids, it seemed wrong to them to demonstrate their superiority. They are a very sensitive, civilized people."

I asked about their alleged cruelty to stockhorses, and Mary Durack said, "The horse to them is a tool for doing their work with. They are not going to say to the boss, 'I can't ride this horse today because it has saddle sores.' "

I asked why so many drank so much. The figures on Aboriginal arrests for drunkenness were out of all proportion to the number of blacks in the population.

"They tell me they drink because, '*It make the glad come up.*' "

She had been, Mary said, one of those who fought for the Aborigines to be given drinking rights. They'd been drinking themselves to death with "plonk" and methylated spirits. Now most had their "rights" and, she added, "I watch from this veranda the results, and it breaks my heart. But they are beginning to learn. They are beginning to cope. They have to do it for themselves, we can't do it for them. Old Albert—my house is his home when he comes to Perth—says, 'We don't want to get into that town. I want to tell that big man, that Minister, we don't want to get mixed up with the town. The young boys only start drinking if we go to live in houses in that town. We want our own separate place.' "

Sometimes I think that Australia has to invent a respectable synonym for *apartheid*, which South Africa says means separate and parallel development, but it doesn't because there is nothing parallel about it. Yet, that would be wrong: we have to stop telling the

Aborigines what is good for them, and let them tell us. Naturally they are not going to speak with one voice, any more than we would. But at least the voices are theirs—though we have to listen hard and try to recognize which voices are really representative of what are probably the most egalitarian people on the face of the earth, and therefore the people least given to having leaders to speak for them.

Agreed that their complexity of character and our lack of understanding of this, as well as the white man's inbuilt prejudice and high-and-mightiness, made it difficult to give them an equitable deal. But the deal they have had has been disgraceful.

They are entitled to a greater share of the wealth of what was *their* country; even though the wealth is of *our* developing.

The main wealth in the West we are coming to.

The Big, Big Bonanza

THE ROAD from Broome down to Port Hedland, following the line of the coast for 375 miles, is the only road connection between two regions divided for the most part by the no-man's-land of the Great Sandy Desert. The road takes us from the Kimberley to the Pilbara— and the Pilbara (pron. *Pill*bera) is, industrially, the most dramatic region of the New Australia.

This is the great iron province of the State that, until 1960, was still supposed to have high-grade ore reserves of only about 260 million tons, not enough to allow export—and where, in 1970, it was known that the reserves of exportably rich iron ore were 20,000 million tons.

As to reserves of lower-grade ore in the Pilbara, estimate figures had become astronomical; and, as mentioned much earlier, Hamersley Iron's managing director, Russel T. Madigan, figured that, in the 30-per-cent-iron category, the region had something like 100,000,000,000,000 (one hundred million million tons) as against 200,000 million in North America. Lang Hancock, who was instrumental in much of it being discovered, believes there is even more than that and has given the figure of 125,000,000 million tons. Even in terms of the second-commonest metal on earth, bonanzas don't come any bigger than that.

However, grade is very important, and this is where the Pilbara scores high. When we got to Mt Tom Price a Hamersley engineer I talked to quoted an American expert from Kaiser Steel as saying to him, "What you are using here for road metal we in the States call high-grade hematite." The American iron-miners have to be satisfied with ore yielding 51 per cent iron. What Hamersley has contracted to supply in hundreds of millions of tons to Japan is 64 per cent.

Much of North America's iron has to be mined underground, which is more expensive extraction than the open-cut mining that is the rule in the Pilbara. Certainly the principal North American deposits, round Lake Superior in the United States and Canada, are mined open cut; but it has been said of what was the most productive iron ore region in the world before the Pilbara opened up that "the virtual extinction of the open-pit mines could be foreseen in the latter half of the 20th century".[1]

Hamersley's Mr Madigan has been quoted as saying that the Pilbara has enough iron to supply the world's needs, at the present rate of usage, for 140,000 years. Mr Hancock makes an even more astonishing statement: "The Suez Canal took ten years to build, but if the same tonnage as was moved to build the Suez Canal were removed from the Pilbara iron deposits every single year, it would take a million years to exhaust them."

The late Mr Tom Price, who was a vice-president of the Kaiser Steel Corporation, said in 1962 when he came to Australia to look at the area, "There are mountains of iron ore here. . . . It is just staggering. It is like trying to calculate how much air there is." The mine at the iron mountain named after Tom Price has been producing only since 1966. But in this year of 1971 it is expected to become a bigger producer than Sweden's L.K.A.B. mine at Kiruna in Lappland. Which would make Tom Price the biggest iron mine in the world.

Mt Newman commenced production in April 1969. It is expected to be mining 25 million tons a year in 1972, when Hamersley may mine 37 million tons. Mt Goldsworthy, which was the first Pilbara producer in April 1966, also has very high-grade deposits. And no less than eight new iron mines are regarded as being on the way.

BETWEEN the Kimberley and the Pilbara we stopped and ate our lunch in the bough-shed by the homestead on Nita Downs sheep station. To the east, along the 19th line of latitude, the big aeronautical chart I had showed nothing except indications of sand ridges for 200 miles, and for 300 miles there wasn't a track, and then only the marking of the Canning Stock Route.

Edging the Great Sandy Desert is this coastal band the road traverses. It is what is called pindan scrub, with low acacia and clumps of grass and spinifex. It supports seven sheep stations. The 375-mile stretch of red-dusty mostly corrugated road runs through flat country all the way; there wasn't even sight of a kangaroo, and the road crossed only one river and that was bone dry. But before we reached the De Grey River down near Port Hedland, we were within a dozen miles or so of Cape Keraudren. Here the scheme (now shelved) was to blast out a harbour with a nuclear explosion.

Cape Keraudren's port would have been nearer than Port Hedland to Mt Goldsworthy, which can be seen in the distance from the road. Soon we were running parallel with the company-built railway that carries Goldsworthy's ore to Port Hedland, where the ore from Mt Newman's mine is also shipped out. Hamersley's port is Dampier.

A welcome sight to the traveller is the white-walled Walkabout Motel by the roadside six miles out of Port Hedland. With this attractive Walkabout and another at Newman, Graeme Robertson, a builder who used to run the bus service between Perth and Port Hedland, has shown that motels don't have to be the characterless places most of them are.

In the fast-changing town of Port Hedland I was to spend a few days later, and from there go to Newman and Goldsworthy, where the tour did not go. But it went to Mt Tom Price, via Wittenoom.

Near Wittenoom was another big deposit of iron ore, and there was a proposal to mine this by setting off a nuclear explosion. The proposal came from Mr Lang Hancock.

LANGLEY GEORGE HANCOCK (b. 1909), who must now be the richest man in Australia, was a pastoralist. His sheep station, Mulga Downs, is just north of Wittenoom. Back in the thirties he had discovered seams of blue asbestos in Wittenoom Gorge, pegged the area and begun mining it. He sold his mine to the Colonial Sugar Refining Company which formed Australian Blue Asbestos Limited and built the township of Wittenoom Gorge; but high costs made the enterprise uneconomic and in the mid-sixties the asbestos mine was closed down. In 1966, Hancock bought it, and part of the town, for $1.8 million. He had that kind of money then, and he saw Wittenoom as an iron mine, because of what happened in 1952, when he and his wife were living at his asbestos mine farther north at Nunyerry in the winter, and coming south to Perth for the summer. He flew his own plane between his three homes.

In 1952 he left it rather late to fly to Perth, and storm clouds of the coming Wet forced him to fly low down a gorge. He thought the dark-red walls of the gorge looked like iron. Next winter he took another look from the air and traced the iron for seventy miles. So he knew he had found a huge deposit, and he landed in the spinifex and took samples. He didn't expect the grades to be good, but they were. The discovery was of no use to him then because there was a blanket embargo on iron ore export and all deposits were reserved to the Crown: individuals or companies couldn't peg them. In 1958 it became evident that the embargo would be lifted, as it was in 1960. So Hancock wrote off to a number of large mining companies round the world inviting their participation—and got an answer from only one of them, Rio Tinto of Britain (which was to merge, in 1962 with Consolidated Zinc and become the Rio Tinto Zinc Corporation, R.T.Z., and set up Conzinc Riotinto of Australia, C.R.A.).

Rio Tinto's geologists were not greatly impressed with the deposits of limonite iron ore Lang Hancock pointed out. However, Hancock had found a hematite deposit near his station homestead. The geologists stayed in the area for over a year, mapping and sampling massive Hancock-discovered occurrences of limonitic ore that were shown to contain 1,000 million tons of 50 to 57 per cent iron. Then they turned to a mountain Hancock had spotted from the air in 1958, and shown to Rio Tinto's top geologist from a plane in 1961.

On 11th September 1962 two of the geologists landed from a helicopter separately, four miles apart. They found themselves sampling the limits of a great deposit of high-grade hematite. Subsequent drilling showed an ore-body of about 500 million tons averaging 64 per cent iron. This was to become known as Mt Tom Price, and on it the big Hamersley mine was based.

Lang Hancock went to London and saw Rio Tinto's chairman, Sir Val Duncan, who, as Hancock tells it, said, "I think I'll ring Edgar Kaiser" (head of the giant U.S. group of companies), and, "Of course, Billy Muggins from the bush didn't think he could ring up a bloke on the other side of the world and say, 'Look, Edgar, I want to dob you in for forty million', but that's what he did."

So, in 1962, Hamersley Iron was formed. (It is owned by Hamersley Holdings, in which C.R.A. has a 54 per cent interest, Kaiser Steel of the U.S.A., 34·5 per cent and public shareholders, 11·5 per cent directly, and indirectly, through holdings in C.R.A., 21·9 per cent.) Two years later it had letters of intent from Japanese steel mills to take 65·5 million tons of ore and 17·9 million tons of iron pellets. In another two years, the mine, the town of Tom Price, the 182-mile railway line to Dampier, and the port of Dampier, were all constructed and the first ore was shipped in August 1966.

For leases Lang Hancock and his partner E. A. Wright transferred to Hamersley Iron (also covering the huge Paraburdoo deposit to be developed south of Mt Tom Price) they receive in royalties two-and-a-half per cent of what Hamersley gets for its ore. Mr Hancock's share was reported in June 1971 to be $30,000 a day, which is over ten million dollars a year!

Lang Hancock has gone on prospecting. In fact the Hanwright company has spent (to mid-1971) $4·4 million in outlining other large iron-ore bodies. One called Rhodes Ridge, north-west of

Newman, was estimated to contain 3,700 million tons of iron ore. One closely drilled section is said to have 270 million tons of high-grade ore. Rhodes Ridge was under option, for drilling, to Texas Gulf Sulphur, an American company that is the world's biggest producer of lead and silver. Another Hanwright-discovered deposit in the same region, called McCamey's Monster (of which more later) was even larger. Hanwright claimed other deposits, called the Angelas, that could suit Armco, the American concern that proposed to set up steel making in opposition to B.H.P. at Jervis Bay (N.S.W.). (An announcement by Conzinc Riotinto of Australia in March 1971 that it had withdrawn from the consortium did not necessarily mean that Armco would not set up as a steel-maker.)

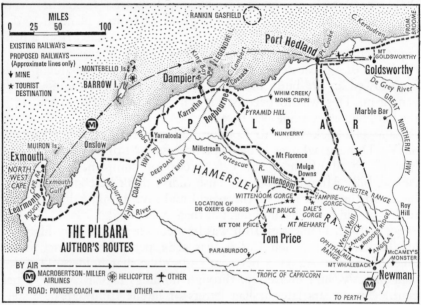

The formidable Mr Hancock (who, with partner Peter Wright, owns a Perth newspaper, the *Independent*) is linking his fortunes with powerful companies for the development of Hanwright's more recent iron ore discoveries. The new (February 1971) Labour Government in Western Australia is not "socialistic" and Mr Hancock's claims to reserves were faring better under it than they were likely to under the Liberal Government in which Mr Court was Minister for Industrial Development, and was not well disposed toward Mr Hancock and some of his big schemes.

Lang Hancock's big thinking gets as big as his saying that north-west Australia could be the iron-mining, steel-making "Ruhr of South-east Asia". He has also said, "I believe that, given the right conditions, a Japan-like growth is possible for Western Australia."

In a profile of "Hancock: King of the Pilbara", Colin Chapman wrote: "Hancock's importance to Australia overshadows by far that of any contemporary politician or business leader."[2]

Lang Hancock believes in White Australia, fears a "trade union dictatorship" under the militant A.C.T.U. leader R. J. Hawke as prime minister, has little time for politicians or public servants.

Tom Price, and Dr Oxer's Gorges

THE GORGES are what bring tourists to Wittenoom. At present the coach tourist sees some good gorges but does not see the best gorge scenery the region has to offer. I was fortunate in being able to see some off-track gorges.

After leaving Port Hedland for Wittenoom we ran through red plain country outcropped with stony hills; saw two emus that were the first wildlife seen since Kununurra; and, after lunch, entered the Hamersley Range country and stopped to look at Dale's Gorge (PLATE 50). A number of gorges have this stepped, terrace-like formation; but the sides of the most spectacular ones drop sheer. The rock is commonly redder than it is at Dale's Gorge.

Dale's Gorge is a long one and a road goes right into it. The brows of ochre rock frown down on a narrow valley picturesque with ghost-gums. Here and there you see signs of asbestos mining, which is particularly arduous and also hard on the miner's lungs.

The veins of asbestos in Yampire Gorge show as thin bluish stripes in the red-brown rock. This is crocidolite, known as blue asbestos. There is no such mineral as asbestos, which is a general name covering a number of fibrous minerals, including the long-fibred chrysotile that Mr Hancock had been mining at Nunyerry. The big asbestos treatment plant in Wittenoom Gorge is still there, above the town of Wittenoom, with an old-style hotel, where we spent two nights.

When we got to the hotel there was a message for me: "Please call Dr Oxer", who was the only medical practitioner at Wittenoom and, as it turned out, an extraordinary man. I asked him to have dinner with me. The figure that entered the dining-room was very tall and spare, the lined face dark from the sun—not at all a surgery doctor's complexion—and if there is such a thing as an "explorer's nose", Dr Gordon Oxer has it. His age (I was told) was seventy. If this was true he was the spryest septuagenarian I have ever met. His hobby was discovering gorges.

I said we had been to Yampire and Dale's Gorges and, while they were pretty good, they were hardly a match for a place like King's Canyon or the Valley of the Winds in the Centre.

"Come out with me tomorrow," Dr Oxer said. "I'll show you *gorges.*"

Of course I wanted to, I said. But I had to see Mt Tom Price, the great Hamersley iron-ore mine.

Dr Oxer sighed. "All right, we'll go there first." I said I could go on the coach, but Dr Oxer shrugged the coach aside and said, "My vehicle will be outside at eight o'clock."

It was; and it was a vehicle as extraordinary as its owner. Dr Oxer, clad in khakis and a vintage sombrero with a very wide brim, was leaning on the bonnet of a four-wheel-drive Austin Champ powered with a Rolls-Royce engine. He called his vehicle the Camel, possibly because he felt that it could go anywhere a camel could go. The thirstiest of four-wheeled camels, it drank a gallon of petrol every twelve miles. It was a real workbeast of a vehicle with such fitments as a small crane, shovels clamped to its sides, enough tools to build a house with, and jerrycans of petrol and water. It also had a canopy that Austin would hardly have fitted it with, made of flat galvanized iron.

We took off for Mt Tom Price, three of us: Dr Oxer had also invited Mrs Henrietta Steinhardt, a Viennese-Australian who was of the coach party. The red road disappeared very fast under the Camel's tires on the sixty-seven-mile run to Tom Price, and we arrived well ahead of the coach.

DR OXER whizzed into the town. A minibus drove us up the mountain on the *right* of the road. In Australia we drive on the left, but at Mt Tom Price the local rule is that you allow the big ore trucks with their heavy loads the inside of the road for extra safety.

From the top, the view of the mining operations was impressive, if somewhat hazed by the dust that rises as the side of the mountain is torn apart. You look down on Marion electric shovels scooping out twenty-five tons of ore at one bite. Then there is the dust from the 100-ton trucks that race their loads away at the rate of 5,000 tons an hour. Hamersley pays its open-cut workers "dust money". But the prevailing winds keep most of the mining dust out of the town.

We went to another point where you look down on what happens to the ore that has been mined. A great arm of webbed steel, the conveyor, runs out from the crushers to what is like a crater of a volcano, except that it is not erupting but swallowing. Down the centre-hole of this enormous stockpile the crushed ore flows incessantly, to be pulverized further and screened.

Then the ore goes down into railway trucks that are gravity-filled

The Ord River—which in wet-season flood carries more water than the Rhine, Rhone and Thames—is being dammed to irrigate 150,000 acres of cropland.

45/WESTERN AUSTRALIA

Cotton was already growing on farms watered by a diversion dam at Kununurra, 26 miles north of the big dam. This crop was almost ready for harvesting.

Mining the iron mountain of Whaleback with electric shovels. The Mount Newman company held contracts for ore worth $1,500 million.

Iron ore from Mt Goldsworthy mine stockpiled at Port Hedland. Loaders shown scoop it on to conveyors that run to the ore ships that carry it to Japan.

with a hundred tons in a matter of seconds. The train that is about to take off for Dampier 182 miles away is 152 trucks long. At Dampier do not imagine that hundreds of shovelling workers laboriously unload it. There is a mechanical enormity called a "rotary dumper", a cylopean cylinder that takes the ore trucks, two at a time, and turns them upside down, empties out the 200-ton load and sets the trucks right side up again, all in 45 seconds.

The mind boggles at the technological efficiency of it all. When the operations are viewed at a distance, everything seems to happen automatically, as with a wind-up toy. One has almost to be reminded that each electric shovel is worked, each lorry is driven, each crusher or conveyor is superintended by a human operative. Tom Price has now (1971) over 3,000 people. How do they live?

They live, most of them, in houses that cost $29,000 to build and service; rented for $6 a week. The houses are part-furnished and are air-conditioned, and the average cost to the company of air-conditioning a house is $25 a week. They are brick-veneer houses with tile roofs, and they look like the houses people live in in capital-city suburbs—or would like to live in if they could afford one. They can, and still have more money left in the pay packet, if they go to Tom Price to live. The standard of house is one of the lures, as well as the fatter pay packet. Electricity is free; the company supplies plants and grass seed for your garden and lawn; there is an Olympic-size swimming-pool, a bowling green, a nine-hole golf course, movies, a library, a supermarket, even a yoga club. Still, Australians, for all their overseas image as big-country types, are the most suburban-living people in the world, and not enough can be tempted out of the cities and into the "outback". Half the workforce at Tom Price are migrants, mainly from Britain.

HAMERSLEY IRON, in 1970, produced from Mt Tom Price 16·9 million tons of ore and shipped (including pellets) 16·2 millions tons of product. Its sales revenue was over $128 million.

What would Australia get out of this—apart from the "fringe" benefits of employment, construction, servicing, etc., and benefits to Australian shareholders? I asked the company, early in 1971, about royalties and taxation, and this was the reply: "Royalties are paid to the Western Australian Government and the current rates are, per ton, on lump ore, 7½ per cent (of the price received) or 60 cents, whichever is the greater, and on pellets 17 cents a ton. The Western Australian Government will receive $7·7 million from Hamersley in royalties in respect of 1970."

What about Commonwealth taxation on Hamersley's profits? "Hamersley Iron will pay taxation at the rate of 47½ per cent on the profits of the company over the whole life of the venture. During the construction stage, however, there are numerous items that are allowable as tax deductions. These are not 'exemptions' but 'deferments'. In the early years of the operation the tax payable to the Commonwealth Government is nil or very small. These deferred taxes will, however, have to be paid later on, and the company is making provision for future taxation." Hamersley's 1970 balance sheet showed current tax as only $1,000. It showed provision for future taxation as $21,816,000. Consolidated profit, after provision for depreciation and taxation, was $28,102,000. Net value of the company's assets was approximately $400 million.

In 1973, according to announced plans, production is to be lifted to 37·5 million tons (more than twice what was produced in 1970). By 1973 the company's second mining town, at Paraburdoo, is expected to have 2,500 people.

WITH DR OXER we sped back along the red road that had here and there a dead kangaroo lying beside it; they had been hit by cars at night. The doctor stopped at a turn-off to adjust a signpost, and swore at a couple of bullet holes shooters had made in it. This signpost, and a number of others in the region, had been lettered and made and erected by Dr Oxer. He was a kind of one-man Tourist Promotion Council, who went out and found the tourist attractions of the region and then indicated where they were. His long-fingered hands were less like a doctor's than a tradesman's. One of the placenames on the sign pointers he had erected on a steel post read: MT BRUCE.

Mount Bruce, he said, had long been considered Western Australia's highest mountain (4,024 feet). Recently surveyors had landed by helicopter on top of another Hamersley Range mountain named Meharry, and found that it was higher. Nobody had ascended Mt Meharry: so Dr Oxer had aimed the Camel at it and up the Camel went, right to the top. However, it could still be said that nobody had *climbed* Meharry: so, only a few days before, he had returned to Mt Meharry, left the Camel at the foot, and climbed it.

We turned off the road, and as we ran along what was at first quite a good track, Dr Oxer said happily, "Now this is better, isn't it? I hate main roads, hate those bloody corrugations." A few moments later the Camel ploughed into foot-deep bulldust. The dust wrapped us in a pink-brown cloud. It was fine as talc powder, but still gritty on the eyeballs. I stuffed my cameras into plastic bags. There was a lot more bulldust to come. When we stopped for lunch I noticed that Henny Steinhardt's complexion was several shades darker. The dust was so pervasive that the filter of the cigarette I lit after lunch was pink. We had boiled the billy hung from a hook on a tripod of steel rods that folded together—an invention of Dr Oxer's.

We went on across a stony plateau with ghost-gums (PLATE 49) and ochre-red anthills that rose in every strange shape from beehives to bulbous forms reminiscent of elephant gods seen in India. Then there was a canyon that dropped sheer at one rounded end, over which flowed (on occasions when enough of the fifteen-inch rainfall occurred) Joffre Falls. We also came to a Bismarck Creek, and I remarked, "That's a fine old Aboriginal name"—and found, to my embarrassment, that Dr Oxer not only discovered these gorges but he named them. There was also Rio Tinto Gorge and Red Gorge, which had a beautiful big pool of water at the bottom.

As the afternoon wore on the travelling got rougher, for we had run out of road of any kind and the Camel was now doing its cross-country canter, and we got dirtier and dirtier. Henny Steinhardt's face had turned the colour of Hiawatha's girl-friend, Minnehaha, and she told me I now had red hair. We came to a ridge's rocky spine leading downward. This baulked the Camel and Dr Oxer said, "Here we have to walk." Mrs Steinhardt, who had taken the rough ride with sterling spirit, smiled her defeat and said she would stay with the Camel. The doctor led the way nimbly down the stony spine between two narrow gorges that were so deep the bottom of either could not be seen until the lookout was reached.

The lookout was a platform of rock, a point to a precipice, and you looked down at what was the junction of not two gorges but three. The one directly in front was the much deeper end of the Red Gorge we had seen earlier. To one side was Hancock Gorge and coming in on the other side was Weano Gorge (Weano was an Aboriginal henchman of Lang Hancock's). The setting sun lit the eastern top of Red Gorge to fiery glory. The other two were sunk in shadow. Another gorge came into Hancock Gorge at right angles and there was a stretch of water in it. I thought, "What a place to be in a boat, looking *up* at those towering cliffs. What a place this whole place is—what a marvel of a lookout!"

I should mention that, along the edge of the rock platform—where if an unwary visitor's foot had slipped he would have fallen hundreds of feet to certain death—a rough wooden railing had been erected between two steel fence-posts sunk into the rock and cemented in. This had been done, right on the precipice edge, by Dr Oxer. He hadn't got round to signposting as yet.

Then, in that remote spot, we suddenly had company. The man coming down the ridge turned out to be a Hanwright man from Wittenoom. He had come out to decide the best places to bring to, next day, a movie crew who were shooting a film of Western Australia's scenic highlights.

"You'd naturally bring them here," I said. "The gorge scene is really spectacular from this lookout that doesn't seem to have a name."

"Oh, yes it has," said the Hanwright man. "We call it Oxer's Lookout."

BECAUSE THE VIEW is in three directions it is not possible to take from Oxer's Lookout a photograph that shows this confluence of gorges: it would need to be taken from the air. However, I did take a number of Ektachromes and should have liked to have reproduced at least one of them. But—in the course of travel for this book, I sent off from various parts of Australia nearly a hundred rolls of colour film for processing, to Kodak in Melbourne, from whom came a note that one film envelope arrived empty. The roll lost in the mails was the one taken at Dr Oxer's gorges and Oxer's Lookout.

I don't think I have exaggerated the spectacular quality of this place. Subsequently, a survey team organized by the Australian National Travel Association was taken there by Dr Gordon Oxer. In the team's report on the tourist potential of the Pilbara, released in March 1971, it says that it was "particularly impressed" with the gorge scene from the lookout and believes ". . . the natural attraction of this area could warrant the establishment of a tourist hotel. This would enable tourist coaches to terminate in the area and would facilitate inspection of the gorges on foot and by floodlighting at night."

Whaleback to Weeli Wolli

FROM WITTENOOM the coach goes back to the coast. The biggest of the iron-ore mountains being mined, the one that is being cut down by the Mt Newman Mining Company, lies in the other direction, south-east. I didn't go to it until later, but I think we might look at it now.

There is a Mt Newman and, since 1968, the town of Newman, but the mountain that is being mined is Mt Whaleback. The range it is in is called the Ophthalmia Range, a curious christening that supports the last part of the old derisory description of Western Australia as the land of "sin, sand, sorrow and sore eyes".

Stan (A.S.) Hilditch was a prospector who came to the area looking for manganese. In 1957 he found, on the then-nameless long hump of a mountain that became Mt Whaleback, what looked like promising samples of hematite iron. He sent them to his partner in Sydney, C. H. Warman, an engineer, who had the specimens assayed. Some were 68.8 per cent iron. Hematite's maximum is 70 per cent.

That myopic thirty-year embargo as to not only the export of iron ore but the pegging and exploitation of deposits was still on. Hilditch went off copper mining until 1960 when, with the lifting of the embargo, he and Warman were able to peg Mt Whaleback. During the next two years other big deposits were prospected by Stan Hilditch, who found by his own efforts much more Pilbara iron than had Lang Hancock, whose name is much better known. Hancock, though, made his initial discovery earlier, and has gone on to find other major deposits in recent years.

Executives of Amax (American Metal Climax) were on a world tour seeking new mining prospects. Hearing about Mt Whaleback from Warman, they optioned the lease, and made a geological survey that showed a very large deposit of high-grade ore. Amax invited the Colonial Sugar Refining Company to participate in the development, which became a sixty per cent Australian venture with Pilbara Iron (which is 68 per cent C.S.R's) and B.H.P. each holding 30 per cent, Amax 25 per cent, Japanese companies, Mitsui-C. Itoh, 10 per cent, and a British mining finance house, Selection Trust, 5 per cent. Bringing in B.H.P. gained not only an Australian partner with iron-mining expertise but a customer who signed up to take 70 million tons of ore. This, with the 100 million tons Japanese steelmakers contracted to take, made economically feasible a $200 million enterprise. The Mt Newman Mining Company, by 1970, had spent the $200 million, and was in process of spending almost as much again. B.H.P. manages the enterprise.

Port Hedland, where the Goldsworthy Mining Company already had installations, was selected as the port. The required further dredging and land reclamation was done by American and Japanese contractors and new harbour works installed. The longest privately owned railway line in Australia (265 miles) was built, in fourteen months, by an American contractor using enormous line- and sleeper-laying machinery (a world-record 4.35 miles of line was laid in one day). In just under two years from construction's beginning, the Japanese carrier *Osumi Maru* loaded ore from Newman at Port Hedland on 1st April 1969.

In 1971 Newman was producing iron ore at a rate of 20 million tons a year: this was to be lifted to 30 million tons by 1973. Two-thirds of it would go into the blast furnaces of Japanese steelmakers, who had placed orders with the Mt Newman company for 305 million tons.

An aerial photograph taken a year before production began shows the town site with what look like large cubes dumped in rows. These were rooms of houses, with everything from refrigerators to mattresses packed inside them. The rooms had been assembled in six different designs.

The white, metal-walled houses have wide eaves supported by stanchions of steel, not so much because of the termites whose ochre-red nests stand up across the spinifex country, or because B.H.P. makes steel, but because the whole Pilbara region is subject to cyclones and the houses have to be strongly attached to the red earth.

They are all air-conditioned, and not only because the heat frequently goes over the century and has hit 118 degrees. Air-conditioning draws out dust. The only accommodation at Newman that is not air-conditioned is in the police station's jail cells—quite a crime deterrent. What with the provision of housing, lawns, trees, a supermarket that sells goods at Perth prices, and such amenities as the open-air cinema, swimming-pool and golf-courses, the company estimated it cost $60,000 to "establish a married man on site". The Newman houses, like those at Tom Price, rent for $6 a week. The average tradesman was, in 1970, earning close to $100 a week.

I FLEW to Newman in a small plane from Port Hedland in exactly an hour. At first the land is flat as your hand, then it begins to be knuckled with hills, then the ranges start and Mt Newman (3,700 ft) appears, looming large in the distance. This side of it Whaleback comes into view, and you see how it is being cut down. Mt Whaleback rises 750 feet above the plain, or it used to. From extensive drilling, geologists have mapped its structure, and the high-grade ore is down to about plain level at the eastern end where the mining is.

Close-up, these mountains being mined are pictures of ravaged earth. But, seen from the air in the context of thousands of square miles of Never Never country, the excavations, like the towns, look insignificant. A good deal of nonsense has been talked about "overseas mining interests turning Australia into a great quarry, taking out huge profits and leaving us just holes in the ground". At Newman most of a mountain will disappear, as will happen at Tom Price, but there are no great holes in the ground nor is it likely that there will be. The Hamersley-Ophthalmia Ranges run for about three hundred miles and a few mountains that are much less than scenic treasures will hardly be missed. The biggest holes in the ground I saw on this trip were at Queenstown in Tasmania and flying over Mount Morgan in Queensland. Nobody ever raised any fuss about them, because they were regarded as Australian enterprises. For that matter, the non-hole at Newman is sixty per cent Australian.

Hindsightedly, it is easy to contend that there could and should have been a big, brave, broad-visioned comprehension of our country's mineral resources and a great national initiative, spurred by government action, for their all-Australian development. The record as to prospecting in the thirty years to 1960 hardly suggests that Commonwealth governments, or State ones, had that kind of capability—apart from such governments' commitment to development through private enterprise. Democratic countries get the governments of their people's choice, and socialist countries (at least in my experience in the Soviet Union) have shown themselves less efficient than capitalist ones. There is no good reason to believe that Australian companies, even if they had shown the same initiative as multi-national corporations, would have had the same access to capital and expertise. It is most improbable that they could have paralleled what is being done, with overseas interests mainly involved, at such places as Weipa, Gove, Tom Price and Savage River and—with a higher proportion of Australian equity—at Newman.

At the same time, it is easy to underestimate the extent of the actual Australian contribution, not only of local investment in mining enterprises—which has been unprecedentedly large and widely spread—but of expertise. B.H.P. managed the whole construction—in which Australian contractors played a large, although not the major, part—that brought into production at Newman an iron mine that could possibly outstrip Tom Price and become the biggest single iron mine in the world, if only because it is mining a bigger mountain of ore.

The fringe benefits of such enterprises, whoever capitalizes them, Australians are inclined to underestimate. The Mt Newman Mining Co. says that in 1969 it spent, on this project, $150 million, of which $110 million was spent in Western Australia. Hamersley Iron says in its 1970 report that it has spent $435 million in Australia. These enterprises are in a State of only one million people, with the greatest acreage of wheat and the second-greatest number of sheep, more sheep-to-population than any other State.

The Western Australia that was so rurally dependent would not be—with wheat in some glut trouble and wool in such prices-costs trouble—as prosperous as it is if Australia had embargoed the import of overseas capital to develop the West's mineral resources.

Where mining companies, not the State, build towns and railways, the money-flow into the economy is, initially at any rate, considerably more than the State receives in the way of royalties.

Moreover, the Eastern States now have, according to Hamersley Iron's managing director, R. T. Madigan, ". . . a market in Western Australia running at about $600 million annually. Most of this would have arisen from the mining industry."

IN NEWMAN, where more than 3,000 people are living, the new houses being built had changed from the earlier steel-stanchioned type to mod. sub. bungs. of brick construction.

Of this type the Senior Lecturer in Architecture at the University of Western Australia had written, critically, "The typical suburban ambience of temperate Australia looks as out of place in the tropical north as a typically English house looks in suburban Perth."[1] Is it that what people are used to is what they want if they are to be induced to work in the north-west? Or is it that not enough thought has yet been given to the design of more suitable houses that, although less conventional, would have obvious advantages that would make them acceptable?

Single men lived in big two-storeyed blocks of bachelor quarters that radiated from a central court and showed up from the air as two big white crosses in the town plan. The best-looking building was the white-painted-brick Walkabout Motel. The colonnades that enclosed its swimming-pool were loosely roofed with tea-tree branches that cast delightful shadow-patterns on the walls. Here I stayed comfortably, and ate very well.

In Newman's workforce there were people of many nationalities. Only thirty per cent were Australians. Most of the rest were English, Irish or Scots; there also were quite a number of Jugoslavs and other Europeans, a few Indians, an Arab and a Seychelles Islander.

The iron-mining operations were of the same pattern as elsewhere, but beginning with blasting on such a scale that one twenty-hole firing (using nine tons of ammonium nitrate explosive mixed with dieselene) could bring down as much as 100,000 tons of rock (PLATE 2). Nobody was allowed to be nearer than 800 feet when a blast went off. After the explosion I watched, a vast dust cloud rolled down in the vicinity of the crushers, but it did not trouble the town that is four miles from the mine.

Three electric shovels, made in Japan and costing half a million dollars each, scooped up fifteen tons of ore at a time. Shovel operators are required to load a 75-ton Haulpak truck in two and a half minutes: there were thirteen of those and four bigger 120-tonners. The trucks tipped their ore into the maw of a crusher 48 feet wide at the top, and it needed to receive 20,000 tons of ore a day.

The crusher, its great head clad with toughest manganese steel, could break boulders as big as five feet across into lumps no bigger than about eight inches, and mostly it crushed the rock much smaller. Lumps bigger than four inches were "scalped off" mechanically and went to a secondary crusher. Then they joined the under-four-inch stuff on a conveyor that ran for 525 yards to where the ore was sampled. Transferred to a stacker, this fed it onto the huge stockpile the ore trains were loaded from, in a very long and dusty concrete tunnel where fifty rucks were loaded in forty minutes. The ore went into the trucks, 180 tons at a time, through pneumatically operated chutes in the roof of the loadout tunnel.

In about eleven hours the train of 150 trucks, drawn by three big locos on a line that was downhill most of the way, delivered 15,000 tons at Port Hedland. There, a huge rotary dumper (such as was described in connection with Hamersley's unloading at Dampier) swung the trucks upside down and emptied them.

CHARLIE SNELL, grey eyes glinting in a sun-browned face, looked very fit and under forty. He was an ex-dogger who had become Newman's horticulturalist. As a dogger (dingo destroyer) Charlie had shot or trapped as many as 275 dingoes in one year, earning $60 a week plus $4 a "scalp" (ears and tail).

Two people who were long-time inlanders had told me they considered the all-out war on the dingo unjustified. One said dingoes kept the kangaroos down. The other said that any calves dingoes got were weaklings that would probably die anyway.

"Ah," said Charlie Snell, "he'd be a cattle country man who said that." (He was.) "This is sheep country."

Where were the sheep?

"Forty thousand on Roy Hill station to the north a bit. I've gone into a paddock and seen five sheep dead and six more with their legs or noses chewed. A dingo'll kill just for the hell of killing, they don't just kill to eat. I admit that, in this area, doggers are taking dingoes that aren't doing any harm. But if you let 'em breed up in numbers here they'll move south into the sheep country and do big damage. So they have to be shot. Like wild donkeys and camels. I've counted forty-seven cattle dying of thirst beside a waterhole because eleven donkeys were keeping 'em off it. Camels are worst of all. Cattle can't stand the smell of them, and camels'll take the water off donkeys, even."

Did dingoes keep down the number of kangaroos?

"Oh, yes. I've walked up a gorge at a place called Pipe Spring and seen forty or fifty dead 'roos the dogs had pulled down."

There were a lot of kangaroos in the area?

"Feller out at Weerlarana station, fifty-six mile from here, shot seven thousand kangaroos in three months. He was running three thousand sheep, or trying to."

The 'roos were eating all the grass?

"Grass? Sheep don't feed on grass in this country, in a bad season.

There isn't any, unless you call spinifex grass. They feed on the scrub, the trees—saltbush, acacia, mulga—it's all feed. The sheep can only reach up about three feet, and the kangaroos eat it off to four feet and then the sheep get nothing. And the donkeys'll outreach the 'roos. So they've all got to be shot."

Now Charlie's trigger finger had turned into a green finger. He was raising thousands of seedling trees. Planting trees along the streets, in the fenceless precincts of the new houses, handing them out to anyone else who would plant them. Shrubs, too, and flowers, native ones: Charlie had a nice clump of the scarlet Sturt's Desert Pea on the footpath garden of his own green-lawned house. And vegetables in the nursery plots and, in his own backyard, plump-hearted cabbages, silver beet flourishing.

"We could grow all the vegetables the town needs—even supply Tom Price! The big boss wants me to plant vines. 'Plant a vineyard', he says."

With only thirteen-inch rainfall?

"Water's no problem. It's only a hundred feet down, plenty of it. Just sink a bore."

And the desert shall bloom . . . .

WEELI WOLLI is the name of a creek and a spring north-west of Newman, maybe fifty miles as the geologists' helicopter flies. The way we went, with Charlie Snell in a four-wheel-drive Toyota, the return trip was close to 200 miles.

Near Weeli Wolli is a big iron deposit. It is hematite, too, not quite as rich as what is being mined at Whaleback, but 60 per cent iron. This deposit is on a Mt Newman Company lease. It is certain to be mined in the future. But the company reckons on 1,100 million tons of high-grade ore in Mt Whaleback (the largest proved deposit of rich ore in Australia). It took out 14.5 million tons the first year, 17.7 million in 1970 and expects to be producing 25 million tons in 1972, 37 million in the mid-seventies. Such high production still leaves many years of mining at Whaleback. There is no urgency about developing Weeli Wolli.

I went to Weeli Wolli because Charlie Snell said there were a lot of Aboriginal rock carvings there. A good man on things Aboriginal, he said, "I won't take anyone out unless they're genuinely interested in studying 'em."

I am glad I qualified, if only to be able to say: Along a couple of hundred yards of Weeli Wolli Creek is the most interesting gallery of Aboriginal rock carvings I have seen anywhere. Better than in the Hawkesbury River region near Sydney (which F. D. McCarthy,[2] the top authority, considers the best of the known repositories of carvings). According to J. B. Wright of the Institute of Aboriginal Studies the Pilbara region has the "richest concentration of Aboriginal rock engravings".

Not many people have been to Weeli Wolli. Enough have, though, to leave beer cans and one set of chalked initials on a rockface. I fear that, in the next chapter of *The Vandal's Progress* that is being written right across the Australian landscape, some oaf will come along with a chisel and think it smart to enlarge the penis on one of the carved Aboriginal culture heroes, and chip in initials. It is the responsibility of State-Commonwealth authorities, and primarily of the mining company and its B.H.P. management, to see that these Weeli Wolli carvings are protected. For the time being, until a ranger is stationed there, the place had best be put out of bounds to all but company geologists and planners, anthropologists, and students of such art.

I don't propose to describe the carvings in detail; and economics prevent their illustration. But nowhere else have I seen Aboriginal delineation of wallabies so well done (one has its tail curled concentrically), or of copulating kangaroos; nor have I seen such a complex scene as is pecked into one rockface, or quite such vigorously figured culture heroes. Many Aboriginal rock carvings are, let us face it, pretty crude art forms. Some of those at Weeli Wolli may be so regarded. But here exceptional and imaginative rock engravers have been at work, and their work must be preserved.

A spring feeds Weeli Wolli Creek and so it would always have been a gathering place for the tribesmen. I picked up a good specimen of a flint knife. The place was picturesque with the ghost-gums that are in such contrast to the red-rocked countryside clumped with spinifex like cushions with spikes. At one place we picked the red fruit of the wild quandong: Charlie Snell would plant the seeds and grow them into trees for Newman. We gathered big sheets of paperbark he needed, and collected coloured stones such as make rockhounds jubilant. It was a good day.

True, Jock Ritchie, the company's P.R. man, remarked at one stage, "We might travel with a bit less speed and a bit more comfort", Charlie was racing the Toyota along a sandtrack at fifty miles an hour. But Jock, too, had to admire what Charlie's grey eyes could see, even at speed—the mark where a snake had crossed the road, dingo tracks at the side of it, the print of a fox. The Aborigines, of course, can read the ground like a book; but Charlie Snell was remarkable for a white man and had a lot of bushlore.

Once an emu pounded along in front of us and Charlie had to ease off the accelerator to thirty miles an hour. He said he had once clocked an emu doing close to forty.

"Port Happening"

PORT HEDLAND. So much was/is happening there in the way of expansion that anything written about its present can be out of date by the time it is published. Nowhere else in Australia does Today swallow Yesterday, and get swallowed by Tomorrow, quite so fast.

The hotel I stayed at, the Esplanade, was a big old-style country pub, its drinkers mostly hairy young men with their shirts open down chests dark from working on some outdoor construction that paid wages high enough to provide plenty of beer money at the end of each hot day. The bars and the big cement-floored beer court did a literally roaring trade and a jazzband played nightly. The morning I slept through the breakfast hour I went across the road to the Port Hedland Café, which was full of hearty breakfasters on steak 'n' eggs.

"We don't get any call for boiled eggs," the waitress said when she brought mine, rolling on a plate. "So we got no eggcups."

It wouldn't surprise me if this café is now a restaurant with a silk-corded menu listing eight egg dishes, situated on the top floor of a new multi-storey building: or maybe I'm thinking of the dining-room of the new motel that was about to rise. There was already a Swan Brewery motel that cost a million dollars, as well as the excellent Walkabout Motel mentioned earlier.

Peter Hedland, master of the exploring 16-foot cutter *Mystery*, had his name given to the port in 1863. If he could have seen the town in 1963 he would not have been greatly impressed—a sleepy, cyclone-battered place, still edged with mud and mangroves, its population only about 800, and not a wharf that a big ship could tie up to. But Port Hedland 1971!

The biggest ship ever to tie up in an Australian port loaded 120,383 tons of Newman ore at Port Hedland in April 1971, and sailed with the biggest cargo shipment ever made from an Australian port. This huge Japanese ore carrier *Yachiyosan Maru* was by no means the first over-100,000-tons super carrier to berth there.

Moreover, this port was ready to take the 160,000-ton carrier *Universe Aztec*, which only two other ports in the world could take. Port Hedland, from being a no-account Nor'-West coastal service port, had become the country's biggest export outlet, moving out a larger tonnage than Sydney or any other port in Australia.

JOHN TOZER, who trained as a municipal engineer, became Administrator of the North-West towards the end of 1969. A lot of capability was evident behind his pleasant manner as, with his white shirt sensibly open at the neck, he talked to me in his office before showing me some of what was happening at Port Hedland.

"The growth pattern has been phenomenal," he said. "And the growth is only starting. This whole area north of the twenty-sixth parallel half a million square miles, had a population in 1965 of only twenty thousand people. I expect to live to see it have a quarter-million.

"As to Port Hedland, it isn't going to be able to hold all the industry and all the people who'll come here. Nor is Finucane Island over there where Goldsworthy Mining operates—I expect that, by 1975, the old island town will reach saturation point with seven thousand people. The new suburban development at Point Cooke won't take care of the growth either. We have had to plan a new inland town, seven miles away, South Hedland. Where there was nothing but spinifex plain twelve months ago I expect that another six or seven thousand people will be living by 1975 and, eventually, forty thousand."

I didn't see how the iron-ore industry could create this growth of people. New mines would start up but their ore would go to new ports; and everything was so mechanized.

"It isn't just iron," John Tozer said. "I thought as you did, and only after I came down from Derby in 1967 did I realize how much more than the iron industry there is in the growth picture. Or you could call it a snowball, with iron at the core. The growth here is largely due to what we call the service industries. Everything from building materials' suppliers to firms that buy in groceries in 500-ton lots. The big contractors used to have to discard their worn tyres—the ones on those huge trucks and earth-movers they use—or send them to Sydney to get them re-lugged. Now it's done here."

By 1971 more than a hundred 'service' companies had moved into Port Hedland to support the major industries and the community created by them. The new hospital was already too small. High schools were going up. The coaxial cable, laid from Perth, would mean television, and being able to dial London direct.

The Administrator added, "Iron plus service industries don't make up the whole picture, either. One major industry can breed another. Go out and have a look at Leslie Salt. It cost ten million dollars to establish and could form the basis of a complex chemical industry."

SALT piles up in conical mountains at Port Hedland, as it does at Shark Bay, and will at a number of other places along the coast of the North-West. High evaporation and big tides on a flat coast make solar salt-producing conditions ideal. In San Francisco Bay it took five years from when the seawater was pumped into the saltpans to when the harvesting machines scraped off the salt crop; in Spencer Gulf of South Australia it took three years; on this coast only twenty-one months.

A ton of salt sold for only about four dollars. So it wasn't an industry that could stand such infrastructure costs as building big port installations to ship it out. The new general purpose wharf at Hedland cost a million dollars more than the $1,200,000 Leslie Salt put in to build it; Mt Newman Mining and the State ($400,000) put in the rest.

Only a very small percentage of salt produced ends up on the table. Industry uses enormous quantities of salt derivatives, in making of everything from paper, plastics and soap, to aluminium and insecticide. Japan takes most of Leslie Salt's production.

The works manager of this American company was extraordinarily close-mouthed. No, he couldn't tell me how much salt was produced in a year and what it was worth, or let me take photographs closer than from the roadway of what was going on round the white stockpile mountain (PLATE 51): they didn't want competitors to know too much about their business and their processes. I could see bulldozers pushing salt about in a glistening white scene like something from Antarctica.

The Westralian economist Dr Alex Kerr[1] wrote that Leslie Salt's production target for 1970 was around 500,000 tons; and "by 1975 annual production may be raised to two million tons". That would be worth to Western Australia, in royalties rising to 7.25 cents a ton, $128,500. The evaporating ponds would grow to cover nearly 20,000 acres of tidal flats. You see their gleaming geometry from the air.

THE ADMINISTRATOR drove me past where houses for three thousand people were going up on the last available residential land. These were conventional brick houses in conventional suburban rows.

The new inland Port Hedland, John Tozer considered, would be much more imaginative and built to a modern cellular plan that separated pedestrian from vehicular area. He talked of "Moroccan concept" dwellings that would have under one roof eight units separated by small courtyards (the first of them were ready in 1971), and of "inward looking houses" and multi-storey housing that provided more shade and "collectively screen each other."

Thousands of trees had been and were being planted in the bare red earth, along new footpaths and median strips, and in what would be caravan parks and other parks and playing fields—a shire council activity the North West Admin. was ardently encouraging.

"It all looks a bit of a mess now," the Administrator said as we drove past the commercial area. "But if people can put up with the growing pains of the next ten years they are going to have a pretty good environment."

THE IRON MINERS who shipped from Port Hedland, the Mt Newman and Mt Goldsworthy companies, both have very big installations there, for unloading the ore, crushing it smaller, stockpiling it into hills that look purple against the red ground and the hard blue sky.

Mt Newman had an enormous stockpile, perhaps two million tons, at Nelson Point where there was another of those "instant housing" villages where workmen lived transiently. But, out in the residential area, big new blocks of two-storey bachelor quarters were replacing the trailer-style accommodation.

About a mile and a half beyond Mt Newman's offices—past where mangroves grew in blood-red water, coloured from the earth that filled a reclaimed area—there was a spread of flattish limestone rock. A notice said: ABORIGINAL SACRED TRIBAL AREA—KEEP OUT. The rock was engraved with hundreds of carvings—turtles, figures with hair standing out like rays such as I had seen at Weeli Wolli, a crocodile, a shark, boomerangs, shields and many markings I could not interpret.

Goldsworthy Mining has its portside operation over on Finucane Island. Enormous bucket-loaders were scooping into the stockpile to get the ore onto the conveyors to the ships. The dust that used to be cursed in the town had been controlled by spraying the hills of ore with water pumped from the sea. Goldsworthy's ore is particularly rich, much of it 67 per cent iron, and it is markedly purple in colour.

The Goldsworthy Mining Company was first off the mark as an iron ore producer, in 1966. It is one-third owned by Consolidated Gold Fields of Australia. Two American companies, Utah Construction & Mining Co. and Cyprus Mines Corporation, both of California, each own a third. Australian shareholders have only about eight per cent of the C.G.F.A. holding. Goldsworthy's ore is shipped to Japan, where steelmakers had contracted to take 88·6 million tons worth about $657 million. Although it mines much less ore than Mt Newman or Hamersley, Goldsworthy's profit rate per ton has been the highest.

I went up to Mt Goldsworthy, briefly. By bus it was seventy miles, across a plain outcropped with strange isolated knobby-topped hills. Parched, dry-grassed country waited for the meagre Wet. Rainfall is only eleven inches.

Sitting next to me was a young woman whose husband was a train controller on the line that carried Goldsworthy's ore to Port Hedland. She was English, from Manchester, and had been in Australia less than a year.

"Yes, I'm very glad we came out. The people here are so much more interesting."

Did she like the housing at Goldsworthy?

"Oh, yes, the houses are nice. We haven't got one yet—still in the caravan we came up from Perth in. But we'll be getting a house soon.

Only nine dollars a week fully furnished."

Did her husband like it there?

"He often says, 'If only it'd *rain* sometimes.' But I don't miss the Manchester rain the way he does. Then, I'm in the air-conditioned caravan while he's out in the heat and the dust."

Was the dust a big problem?

"You must wash the clothes in cold water—if you use hot it sets the colour like a dye. I wash the bed sheets every second day. Still, I'd rather be here than in Perth in spite of the lack of greenness. There's a good supermarket for shopping, at Perth prices. And the people are wonderful."

When we got to Goldsworthy I was taken to the mine and up on a steel tower of the crusher to watch the afternoon firing. The sun was low and reddening the purple-dark hills of ore stockpiled in the front of a low mountainside that was cut away in benches. The tower we were on shuddered when the blast went off. The black fountain of exploded rock swelled up and dispersed itself into a pale red cloud of dust.

Mt Goldsworthy held reserves of about 49 million tons of high-grade ore. It was no Whaleback or Tom Price, but when it was mined out the company would develop similar deposits at Shay Gap, 50 miles inland and Kennedy Gap about 25 miles farther east, a place that was said to be scenically spectacular. Goldsworthy, too, has leases in the Weeli Wolli region.

The workforce was mainly English migrants and Australians at first; but now there were Irish, Scots, Welsh, Slavs, Greeks, Italians, Hungarians, Rumanians, a few Turks and one Egyptian.

After dinner I talked, over drinks in the community club, with some Goldsworthy people including an English couple who had been there three years. The wife said, "We're quite happy here, for ourselves. But there's only a primary school and we don't want to send the children down to Geraldton to high school—there should have been by now a five-year high school at Port Hedland. It's a wonderful country but the great disappointment of Australia has been the education system."

They talked about, but tolerated, the heat. Marble Bar has long been regarded as the hottest place in Australia, but Goldsworthy's average, I was told there, was higher by about one degree. One day in 1967 the temperature in the open-cut rose to 152 degrees. Mining had to stop. The men couldn't work.

Sometimes in summer the wind was quite burning, the English wife said. And there was the dust. There were no white or black-and-white cats at Goldsworthy; but there were pink cats and black-and-pink ones.

47/WESTERN AUSTRALIA *Koolan Island in Yampi Sound is, with nearby Cockatoo Island, an older B.H.P. iron-mining operation. Aerial shot shows the town and, beyond, the mainland.* BELOW: *Iron-bearing rock in the foreground, an ore-carrier comes in to Koolan to load.*

Jubilee offshore drilling rig, from the helicopter that flew me onto it from Barrow Island's producing oilfield. The rig was drilling for Wapet.

Kambalda is where Australia's big nickel producer, Western Mining Corporation, mines and treats in this concentrator plant over a million tons of ore a year.

An Irishman there, one with a soft spot for the Aborigines, told a good story: Paddy returns to Ireland from Australia and his old cronies in the pub in Dublin ask him what Australia was like.

"A wonderful country," says Paddy, "and a wonderful people, the Australians. If yer hungry, they'll give ye a feed. If yer thirsty, they'll buy ye a drink. If yer broke and they've got any money, they'll lend it to ye. If you want a woman, they'll even provide a woman for ye. A wonderful people!"

"Then why, Paddy," his cronies ask, "if the Australians are such a wonderful people—why did you come back to Ireland?"

"Ah," says Paddy, "I couldn't get on at all at all with those white bastards!"

More Mountains of Iron

CONTINUING the "Nor' wester" tour, the Pioneer coach had left Wittenoom and run through Mulga Downs station owned by Lang Hancock. We were trailing a dust cloud down the red road near Mt Florance when there was the uncommon sight of another vehicle. It was not on the road but off it, in the spinifex.

It was a VW Kombi van and, as the coach stopped, a boy came running. Lancashire spoke in his voice: " 'Ave you anyone who knoos abart first-aid. Me mother's 'urt."

What had happened was that the man of this English family had been seeking work at Wittenoom, and was coming away from there when a truck had struck his van and damaged its steering. The truck was towing him back to Wittenoom when the tow-rope snapped, the van careered off the road and, as the boy put it, "Mum was chucked about pretty bad."

On our coach was a man who looked like a cartoon tourist, Hawaiian shirt and all, and who had worked with the St John Ambulance Brigade. He confirmed that the woman had a back injury and should not be moved until the ambulance came out from Wittenoom, where the truck had gone to get it. He made her as comfortable as he could, a tarpaulin was rigged to shade her, and we were able to rustle up some analgesic tablets for her pain. The van had food and water. There was nothing else we could do for the unfortunate migrant who, in contrast to others met in the North-West, must have been ruing the day she left Lancashire.

By a lovely oasis in this harsh, though fascinating, country we stopped to boil the billy and have lunch. Its name, and the name of the station it is on, seems excessively English—Millstream. But a stream there is, year round, a wide blue water that is part of the Fortescue River, black swans on the blueness and parrots shooting through the big paperbarks that shade its banks in the company of occasional palms as well as eucalypts. (It goes without saying that, at this popular spot with wayfarers, the biggest gum-trees have had initials cut into their trunks, and there is a rubbish pile high with drink cans.)

In mid-afternoon we start to descend from the Pilbara plateau that is so loded with iron, and on the way down stop to view the coastal plain. It still retains isolated mounts and mesas, and one that we'll be passing is called Pyramid Hill (PLATE 52). In the distance these hard-core hills, residuals of millions of years of erosion, are hazed and heliotrope, absurdly and beautifully soft in contrast to the rough, red-rocked foreground with its stubble of dry spinifex.

A roadside cross marks the spot where an Afghan camel driver was buried where he died, back in the days when people talked of Pilbara goldfields, not ironfields. Not that iron's being omnipresent would have surprised the Westralian government geologist H. P. Woodward who wrote in 1894 of "immense lodes . . . enough to supply the whole world should the present sources be worked out".[1]

But Woodward did not pinpoint any large deposits or say anything about grades or reserves. And Woodward never explored in the Hamersley Range, where Lang Hancock made his discoveries a life-span of years later.

We stop again and walk to what is called the Python Pool. The plain has hunched up again into rock that is split with a creek that falls into a deep pool at the foot of a semicircle of vertical cliffs. The rock walls are spectacularly vivid, vermilion to purple, rising out of the green water.

We have been seeing kangaroos, but dead ones, beside the road, at intervals all the way from Wittenoom. They lie up in shades and caves during the heat of the day, come out when the sun goes down, and feed into the night. Headlights coming along the road confuse them so that they leap, more often than not, across the road, and too late. Beside a doe's corpse was her joey's. One hears in outback bars learnedly technical discussions on how much damage hitting a 'roo at speed can do to a Holden's bonnet. In this context kangaroos or wallabies are regarded only as night-drivers' menaces, which of course they are. But I sometimes get the impression that the only nature-loving Australians are the city-bound types, and that the ones who live closest to nature are indifferent to it.

ROEBOURNE we came to for the night stop. There was an ugly "blacks' camp" at the edge of the town, usual for this part of Australia.

We stayed at the old-style Victoria Hotel. There was only the one, and it had added some motel-style units for the tourist trade. Not more than a couple of hundred people live at once-prosperous Roebourne that declined when the pastoral boom diminished, the main pearling fleet moved north from its port of Cossack to Broome, and the Pilbara goldfields gave out, as did the copper mine to eastward at Whim Creek. This mine, which was a rich producer, was re-opened in 1963, but closed again the year after. Japanese prospectors weren't satisfied with it; but American-Canadian companies have taken up the leases and the W.A. Department of Industrial Development clearly thinks Whim Creek will be a "goer" again and projects for it a population of 1,500 in 1975.

Farther east there are known deposits of manganese. Out in the Great Sandy Desert there was an early 1971 report of indications of a major occurrence of platinum.

However, the main activity that could rub off on and revive Roebourne somewhat is the development at Cape Lambert.

AT CAPE LAMBERT, twenty miles from Roebourne, construction has begun of a port, and a town to be called Wickham, and the biggest pelletizing plant outside of North America.

This is all, primarily, in connection with the $257-million development of Robe River iron ore. The mine is being based on limonite deposits estimated to contain 3,000 million tons of 55-per-cent iron round Mount Enid, near where the Robe River comes out of the western end of the Hamersley Ranges 70 miles east of Onslow.

For Robe River iron there were contracts for 158 million tons of pellets and sinter fines valued at $1,260 million. These would go to six principal Japanese steelmakers through Mitsui & Co. Mitsui had a thirty per cent interest in the project. So did Cleveland Cliffs Iron Co., of Ohio. Of the remainder, in the 35 per cent the Australian company (Robe River Limited) held, the major interest had been acquired by Mineral Securities of Australia (Minsec), the company that was revealed in February 1971 as having overreached itself and was put into liquidation. This complication was not expected to affect the Robe River development vitally. With Garrick Agnew of Perth holding five per cent, the equity in the hands of Australian shareholders looked like being about 25 per cent, before the collapse of Minsec. The managing company is Cliffs Western Australian Mining, which is American owned.

At Cape Lambert the main ore jetty was due to be finished in August 1972. It will be built a mile and a half into the sea, and strong enough to withstand cyclonic winds of 130 miles an hour and waves up to 45 feet high. In early 1971 construction of the town of Pannawonica, near Mt Enid, had begun, and work had started on the railway line that will be 104 miles long. The company expected to begin exporting from Cape Lambert in the latter part of 1972, and to have production up to 23 million tons a year by 1975.

The Robe River development had been expedited by a B.H.P. agreement with Cleveland Cliffs to let the company have 150 million tons of ore from deposits B.H.P. holds west of Mt Enid, at Deepdale. Robe River, in return, would let B.H.P. share port facilities at Cape Lambert and the railway line and the pelletizing plant. This arrangement was also expected to result in earlier development of the Deepdale deposits.

Another iron ore project that could use Cape Lambert to ship from was likely to develop from the Hanwright leases at Wittenoom, possibly in conjunction with Texas Gulf Sulphur. Further, there was a report that a railway route had been surveyed to Cape Lambert from the Hanwright orebody at Rhodes Ridge, which lies between Newman and Weeli Wolli. Here again Texas Gulf Sulphur was the talked-of partner. Logistically, though, Rhodes Ridge would appear to be most easily developed by an extension of the Port Hedland-Newman railway.

Another big Hanwright find is called McCamey's Monster. A 1970 report that B.H.P. was "secretly drilling"[2] this was incorrect.

Ken McCamey, Hanwright's exploration manager, and "boss" of its company-town Wittenoom, was born at Roebourne. A six-foot-three former fitter-and-turner who is at home in the outback, McCamey had been schooled by Lang Hancock in identifying (by indicators that included the vegetation) iron ore deposits from the air.

The location of his Monster—"I was staggered by the size of it, sixteen miles long. It probably contains more than a thousand million tons of ore. . . . I flew round it several times rubbing my eyes," McCamey was reported as saying[3]—has been given as "350 miles inland from Learmonth".[4] McCamey's Monster is twenty miles east of Newman. It has been test-drilled by Hanwright and Mt Isa Mines.

A joint venture agreement to develop this enormous lode was signed in June 1971 by Mount Isa Mines Holdings Ltd and Consolidated Goldfields of Australia (controlling the Mount Goldsworthy mining company) in conjunction with Hanwright Minerals Ltd.

As we were leaving Roebourne in the morning I noticed a shirt-sleeved solid-looking man standing beside a Holden utility. The coach driver said, "That was Lang Hancock." It would have been interesting to talk then and there with the multi-millionaire partner in Hanwright that ". . . holds the rights to or draws royalties from at least 75 per cent of the known ore deposits in the immensely rich Hamersley iron province."[5]

We did not go to the "ghost town" port of Cossack. It is only five miles from Roebourne, but the road was described as worse than I understand it is, except in the Wet. Roebourne itself has some of the interest Cossack holds, but Cosssack evidently has more old buildings of solid stone, the variegated stone of the region nineteenth-century masons crafted so well.

Stone the buildings needed to be: cyclones many times tried to blow both Cossack and Roebourne off the map, and corrugated iron roofs—if they weren't tethered to the ground with steel hawsers stretched over the top—have gone flying in such willy-willies as sank fleets of pearling luggers. At Roebourne the post-office, court-house and police station and the monumental jail are interesting stone indestructibles. But Cossack, I am told by Mrs Marjorie Finch of the Australian National Travel Association which is praiseworthily interested in the place, is an old gem. Doubtless it will be re-cut and polished by tourism.

This highly mineralized region is, naturally enough, very good gemstone country. In Roebourne we went to the shop where Cyril Leak, an expert cutter and polisher with a pointed beard, had excellent specimens, including the very showy striped zebra-stone.

DAMPIER, forty-six miles down the coast from Roebourne, is an industrial town that has sprung up from nothing since 1965 when Hamersley Iron came to a piece of coast that the buccaneering William Dampier might justly have described, with the adjective he wrongly applied to the Aborigines, as the "miserablest".

If it hadn't been for the port King Bay afforded, nobody would have set a town where Dampier is. There were so many hunks of rock that the constructionists couldn't clear them—so they filled the spaces between them with earth to get level surfaces to build houses. There was little fresh water. Dampier is the only town in Australia where the water that comes out of the household tap is sea-water—desalinated. The desalination plant works off waste gases from the most powerful diesel electric power station in the Southern Hemisphere. This was necessary to power the plant that makes the iron pellets from the Mt Tom Price ore. The Japanese steel makers contracted to take 18 million tons of these. So Dampier was born.

The mile-long trains come in and the ore from their upended trucks is crushed smaller at Dampier. Some of it goes to the pelletizing plant, from which the 64-per-cent iron marbles rain into the Japanese ships with names that always ended in *Maru* until a 55,000 tonner with the Westernized name of *Japan Cedar* arrived in April 1969. Now Dampier can take carriers of 100,000 tons.

But Dampier isn't big enough to cope with Hamersley expansion into mining the Paraburdoo deposits as well as Mt Tom Price, and into turning iron ore into "HImet" as well as ordinary pellets. The company was building a new port on an island in King Bay with the odd name of East Intercourse Island (which is possibly appropriate when one thinks of who Australia has gone to bed with, industrially). This will take Japanese ore carriers of 150,000 tons. And East Intercourse Island is where the HImet plant will be built and is due to commence production in 1973. (HImet is defined in the next section.)

Ports and plants also mean people. The company town of Dampier had 3,000 of them, living in superior mod. sub. brick bungs. with lawns. Many more thousands would be needed within this decade.

A new town called Karratha is rising twelve miles from Dampier. Karratha's first residents moved in in August 1970. Construction of houses for about 1,500 Hamersley Iron employees were to be completed in 1971. Karratha was expected to grow to 6,000 people and eventually to 20,000. A high school has been built there. The Administrator of the North-West, when I talked to him in Port Hedland, felt sure that Karratha (which is not a company town as Dampier is) would become an important administrative centre.

So Karratha was slated to become a second Port Hedland; and Port Hedland itself to expand off its island into a Karratha-like second town; and the port of Cape Lambert with its town of Wickham was about to come to birth; and there was talk of a third port development in the Dampier area, at Legendre Island, that would take 300,000-ton ore carriers; and there would be 2,500 people at Paraburdoo in a couple of years; and probably more at Robe River's new town Pannawonica; and up on Admiralty Gulf there would be bauxite's Port Warrender.

I could not understand the critics of the mining companies' developments (because they were largely foreign-capitalised) who declared that these were making no significant contribution to peopling the North-West. There was every indication that minerals would put more people in the region in the seventies than pastoralism had put there in a century.

MAKE STEEL IN THE NORTH-WEST?

WHEN a visionary like Lang Hancock—who is none the less a visionary because he happens to be big and aggressive and doesn't look like one—talks of North-West Australia's becoming the "Ruhr of South-East Asia" a lot of heads get shaken dubiously.

The realists point out that the Ruhr which supplied 90 per cent of Western Germany's steel had, for a start, the world's second largest coalfield; and in Western Australia coal is as short as iron ore is abundant. The only considerable known coal deposit is at Collie down in the south-west corner, a thousand sea miles away. Thin seams have been found in the Kimberley, but not a deposit worth a damn so far.

No coal is no worry to Mr Hancock, who points to the water-energy of the Ord and Fitzroy and says these rivers could generate enormous hydro-electric power. Water-power, though, doesn't appear to have priority in the thinking of the extraordinary multi-millionaire from Mulga Downs, who is very nuclear-minded. He says that the big iron miners, all with their own power plants at present, could jointly consume, "in the foreseeable future", the 200 megawatts that is the minimum justification for a nuclear plant.

Even the realists concede, on the power front, that if enough natural gas or oil were discovered in the North-West, this could provide the steel-making power. And, what with Barrow Island flowing oil and Dongara established as a gas field, a sufficiency of such fuels is much more than a remote possibility—especially since Woodside tapped oil and a massive flow of gas on the North-West Shelf in mid-1971.

But—given all the power to do so, would it make economic sense to make steel in the Pilbara?

It wouldn't if the market were the eastern States, which is the big steel market in Australia. Not only, at Newcastle and Port Kembla, is abundant coal practically under the floors of the steel mills, but Sydney is just about as far from the Pilbara ports as Tokyo is.

So Pilbara steel would have to be exported. To where? Hardly to Europe, in view of the even greater distances involved. To where "two-thirds of the world's population" lives, says Lang Hancock, who appears to have included China in the South-East Asia he sees North-West Australia as the Ruhr of. As geographer and arithmetician Mr Hancock may be imprecise; but, even if the area he is thinking of embraced only Indonesia and Malaysia, it is still likely to be a considerable steel market and a growing one.

But it is, already, Japan's market. And the Japanese are our big customers for Pilbara iron ore. W.A.'s former Minister for Industrial Development, Mr Charles Court, put the position thus: "Beyond certain points of processing in the Pilbara we defeat our own ends and are in head-on collision with our customers."[1]

However, that does not rule out a Pilbara steel industry.

It might suit Japanese steel-makers—or one of them—to make steel in North-West Australia for the South-East Asia market, instead of shipping ore or pellets all the way to Japan and shipping the steel all the way back to, say, Indonesia. My information is that Kobe Steel has expressed interest in doing this. Indeed, one iron man I talked to, who named which Japanese steel executive said what, expected to see Kobe Steel established at Port Hedland within ten or fifteen years. I said that no Japanese steel-maker would be allowed to set up in Australia—or not without an Australian partner, and, even then, we had to protect our own steel industry. The iron man said, "Of course, there'd be an Australian partner. How about Mt Newman Mining? That would make the partner, in effect, B.H.P." This may have been only talk. But it rang like significant talk.

Some Western Australians believe that a steel industry *has* to come to the North-West because the major mining companies are committed, by their agreements with the W.A. Government, to go into steel-making eventually. This is not quite so. The agreements say that certain major companies must "process" ore within nine years (as Hamersley Iron is already doing, way ahead of time, by pelletizing ore); and, within nineteen years, they must "manufacture a steel product"—which could be only a raw steel product, semi-finished steel. But, if they don't, all that really happens is that they lose their right to do so, and have to move over and let some other company do what they are not prepared to. Excluded from the "steel product" part of this obligation are Goldsworthy Mining —which was first in, before this commitment was operative—and B.H.P., in relation to its Deepdale deposits, because it is already a steel producer at Kwinana. No company is bound to make a "steel product" in the North-West: it can be elsewhere, so long as it is in Western Australia.

When the agreement is read in conjunction with the incontrovertible statement that Pilbara steel-making could collide with the interests of the Pilbara's iron-ore customer, Japan, there is clearly no reason to think that the Labour Government that has come into office is likely to insist that the iron miners turn their ore into anything the Japanese steelmaking customers would object to.

Even if Japanese enterprise-capital were involved—as it has been suggested it could be in the case of Kobe Steel—such a project would still be subject to the pressures of industrial power politics. Suppose Kobe Steel did want to come in. Suppose B.H.P. wasn't resistant and was prepared to partner Kobe. Other Japanese steel-makers might say, "If you let Kobe make steel in Australia, we'll buy less of your iron ore." Or they might want to come in, too, in order to compete on equal terms for South-East Asian markets. And so there might be not only one steel mill but several in the Pilbara where good reasons can be adduced for there not being any.

Among reasons why there might be a steel project, one that had never occurred to me was given by a well-placed official who said that, because of air pollution in highly industrialized and densely populated cities, Japanese steel-makers might want to move some of their befouling blast furnaces from the vicinities of smoggy Tokyo or Osaka down into the empty air of north-west Australia. They could continue to make steel in Japan by using much cleaner electric furnaces.

HOWEVER, the blast furnace that is fed ore or pellets and turns out pig-iron is being supplanted in much modern steel-making by the electric furnace that makes steel directly. Electric furnaces are not fed ore or pellets: they take mainly scrap steel. (Nearly half the steel made in North America and Europe is produced from scrap.) Excellent supplementary feed for these furnaces is iron ore processed into a much more up-graded form than pellets of 63 per cent iron. What Hamersley proposes to produce it calls by the registered trade name HImet. This product will be up to 93 per cent iron.

Hamersley Iron's managing director R. T. Madigan foresees, as a result of increasing use of steel-making electric furnaces, an eventual lowering of the demand for blast-furnace feed materials—iron ore, and pellets such as Hamersley is making at Dampier. Moreover, Mr Madigan has said, "The production of pellets for export is not really justified by existing price levels."[2]

Yet other companies are committed, under their agreements with the W.A. Government, to proceed to the processing of millions of tons of pellets: Goldsworthy by 1976 and Mt Newman by 1982, Robe River in four years after it commences production of ore, and Hanwright in five years from commencement. Mr Madigan thinks that "more pellet plants will undoubtedly be established in the Pilbara, but not everyone would agree that pelletizing on this scale is economically desirable".[3] Whereas a metallized product, he believes, "could prove of greater importance to the development of this country than would the development of another steel industry".[4]

Mr Madigan also says that, by producing iron material of the HImet kind that lets the steel-maker by-pass the blast furnace, Australian iron could "gain access to a new market area". He could be thinking not only in terms of Europe. Steel-making in South-East Asia is more likely to use the relatively cheaper method of the electric furnace, which can take what is also called "pre-reduced iron ore" of the HImet kind.

This iron product will be made by a process developed by the big German steel company Lurgi in conjunction with the Steel Company of Canada (Stelco), and Republic Steel and National Lead, both of U.S.A. In December 1970 it was officially announced that these four companies and Marubeni-Iida and Mitsubishi of Japan would join with Hamersley Iron in the construction of a plant at East Intercourse Island off Dampier capable of producing 1.4 million tons of HImet a year. In announcing the undertaking, the then Minister, Mr

Court, hailed it as a "major break-through in advanced forms of processing in the north of the State".

Mt Newman Mining, which has an obligation to begin pelletizing in 1982 and produce two million tons a year by 1985, might decide to by-pass pellets and match Hamersley's HImet with a similarly high-grade ore product suitable for electric furnaces. The Government was expected to be only too ready to alter the agreement to allow of this. I heard speculation that Mt Newman would possibly do this kind of processing at Port Hedland, and in conjunction with Goldsworthy Mining, which also rails its ore to Hedland and which had to start processing in 1976.

STEEL the world *needs* in greater quantity than is being made, but the peoples who most need steel-girdered buildings, cars, tractors, refrigerators, washing machines and so on cannot afford to buy a sufficiency. So, as Hamersley's Russel Madigan says, "The world has currently an excess of steel-making capacity."[5]

Therefore, he sees schemes like Lang Hancock's to establish a "super steel plant" in which major overseas steel companies join together to produce steel, even in semi-finished form, as probably "more idealistic than realistic".[6]

But, if the problems of high costs in the Pilbara (high because it is necessary to provide supporting facilities such as power, housing and water), and of confrontation with the Japanese customer, could be overcome and cheap power was available—then, Mr Madigan thinks, there would be enhanced prospects of making steel in the Pilbara "by the electric route".

Despite all his realistic provisos, Mr Madigan can still sound a little like Mr Hancock at times, as when he says: "It is staggering to calculate the quantities of steel which our close neighbours such as Indonesia and Malaya and the Philippines could assimilate as their standard of living rises. Perhaps this is where our real opportunity lies."[7]

However, he recognized that the Japanese "see this region as their largest market in the years to come". Japan, he added, was assisting the development of local steel industries in South-East Asia: Australia would need to give similar assistance.

ON PILBARA IRON ORE the Australian economy is likely to depend to the extent that it used to depend on wool.

So an Australian could be forgiven for thinking he heard alarm bells ringing when someone as authoritative as the managing director of the Commonwealth Banking Corporation, Mr Bede Callaghan (a former director of the International Monetary Fund and the International Finance Corporation of Washington) said, "There is a real danger that at any time in this decade there could be an over-supply of some minerals and ores."[8]

An impression might be gained that Australia had discovered so much iron ore it had created a glut. That certainly was not the position in 1970. Australia's production in that year was only about 40 million tons out of a world total of 700 million, less than 6 per cent.

In a world situation of over-supply of iron ore Australia could be expected to fare better than just about any other country, because it has such large deposits of ore that is *high-grade*—easier to sell as ore, easier to pelletize, easier to turn into feed for electric furnaces. And, for the seventies at any rate, the country appears to be sitting pretty because its producers of iron ore have such long-term contracts.

It would be hard to overstate the Australian economy's present degree of dependence on Japan. It is estimated that in 1975 Japanese steel-makers will require 177 million tons of iron ore. Australia had already contracted to supply 68·5 million tons. That is 40 per cent.

If the Japanese *boomu* went bust Australia could be, economically, a disaster area. Fortunately, there is no evident reason why that Japanese situation should occur. Japan serves an enormous, and growing, market. Its economic graph can be expected to show dips as well as rises, just as the United States's graph does; but if any country looks like sustaining economic growth it is surely Japan.

The economy-watcher at the head of the Commonwealth Banking Corporation had no apparent fears of an economic let-down in Japan bringing about an Australian let-down. "In ten years or less," Mr Callaghan said, "Japan will be an industrial giant." Where problems for Australia could arise was not from any Japanese weakness but from Japanese powerfulness.

As Mr Callaghan put it, "The growing dependence of Australia on Japan, unless we are very careful and widely spread our trade nets, could produce growing Japanese pressure on Australia's political and trade policies."

For their iron-ore supply Japanese steel-makers do not like to rely overmuch on one source. They are currently getting about 70 per cent of their furnace material from South America, India, Africa, Malaysia, Canada, the United States and the Philippines. Whereas, on the latest available figures (1970), Australia exported some 35·5 million tons to Japan and only 4·8 million to Europe and U.S.A. We were thus 88 per cent dependent on Japan.

The Japanese dependence on our ore could increase to beyond 40 per cent; but not to an extent that would make much difference to the powerful position Japan was in to exert pressure on Australia's political and trade policies.

So, at the same time as the Japanese market for the Pilbara's product was an enormous boon to the Australian economy, it had produced a situation in which the question "Make steel in the North-West?" might have to be replied to with, "Ask them in Tokyo."

Or so it seemed until April 1971 when the W.A. Premier announced that Mr Lang Hancock had presented him with proposals to set up a steel mill at Cape Lambert. The Hanwright Company planned to do this in conjunction with the American steel giant Armco. The plant would draw its iron ore from the Angelas deposits —if Hanwright got title to these.

At the time of writing (August 1971) a question mark hangs over the whole deal, with Armco still eyeing Jervis Bay in New South Wales and not acting the part of the Pilbara bedmate happy in the arms of Hanwright. However, Lang Hancock, with his vision of an Australian Ruhr in the North-West, is not easily jilted.

Exmouth Talks to Fish

THE ROAD TO ONSLOW is, for most of the 167 miles from Dampier, the North-West Coastal Highway. It does not hug the coast, which is mainly saltmarsh; nor are we yet on the bitumen that had been extended nearly a thousand miles north of Perth. The other road, the inland Northern Highway, became blacktop as far as Meekatharra in 1970 and provided a faster route to Port Hedland.

Not that this stretch—spinifex plain mostly—was very eyeworthy. Now and again somebody would say, "Look! Emus", or the coach-captain, on sighting an infrequent vehicle coming up the road, would announce "Dust!" whereat we slid closed the driver's-side windows to keep out the gritty red-brown cloud.

There is enough tussocky grass between the spinifex to support four sheep stations in this ten-inch-rainfall country: a statement with which the poor-looking sheep would not necessarily agree. However, 30 per cent of our sheep and 35 per cent of our cattle are grazed on the native pastures of the arid or semi-arid land that makes up 74 per cent of Australia. And what is happening to tracts of this land has lately become the acute concern of C.S.I.R.O. scientists.

The leader of the C.S.I.R.O.'s Rangelands Research Programme has said that on the country that carries a third of Australia's flocks and herds the pastoral industry is, in the absence of scientifically based management methods, *an exploitative mining venture steadily depleting the land and vegetation resources*.[1] He says the Murchison district, farther south, is "severely degraded".

Native grasses are eaten to the point where they do not regenerate. Erosion sets in. Rivers and watercourses silt up. The land is no longer productive—"and the resultant dust bowl will affect the living conditions of even our urban populations". Much of the desert or semi-desert of the Middle East was reduced to that condition, 2,000 years or more ago, by uncontrolled grazing, mainly with sheep.

If, owing to the use of synthetics and the fall in wool prices, the number of sheep (47 million) running on this kind of country is reduced, it could be an economic ill-wind that blows good to physical Australia.

Not that we saw many sheep. Some on Yarraloola station were being mustered by an Aboriginal on a motor-cycle. On a station farther back the Ab. station-workers' quarters were like a row of corrugated-iron boxes and must have been hellishly hot.

The Robe River flows through Yarraloola, and 25 miles up a road that runs inland is B.H.P.'s Deepdale iron-ore deposit; and, beyond that, the Robe River company's ore bodies in the river's gorge and mesa hills that are capped with iron.

It was late September, a month when the average rain is a scant six points. Yet it was spring, and so the baked red-sandy earth by the roadside offered up wildflowers, most commonly the mauve-headed mullamullas that can carpet whole sections of the plain but weren't doing that here. Nor did we see, in the region of the Ashburton River that runs into the sea near Onslow, any specimens of the Ashburton Pea, "a giant herb up to eight feet tall . . . the flowers varying from pink to bronze or violet".[2] This coastal plain is not very good wildflower country by the standards of Western Australia, the "Wildflower State" that was to put on a fine October show of native flora when I got to the southern districts.

Onslow, where we stayed that night at the wide-veranda'd old Beadon Arms Hotel, has only about 350 people, many of them Black Australians. It is the kind of place where you never feel sure whether the oldest inhabitant should be pitied for not having had the initiative or the wherewithal to move out long ago, or clapped on the back and given some kind of medal for his fortitude in staying there. Possibly the latter in view of Onslow's history.

The original Onslow, founded in 1885 as a wool port, was so hammered and torn by cyclones that in 1926 the town was moved to where it stands on Beadon Bay. Here, more willy-willies hit it devastatingly in 1934, 1961 and 1963. All the corrugated-iron roofs are stoutly reinforced with battens. The Ashburton Race Club marks its racetrack with white-painted 44-gallon oil drums filled with earth.

Cyclones apart, about the last time Onslow got its name in the overseas newspapers was when it was the mainland base for the British scientists who exploded a nuclear weapon in an atomic test in October 1952 at the Montebello Islands. Since then it has had a smear of relative prosperity from the oil discovery on Barrow Island, to which I was to go from Exmouth.

Gum-trees grew down Onslow's somnolent main street. Some Aboriginal sheepmen lounged outside the general store that sold everything behind a windowless façade: in cyclonic Onslow shops don't favour plate-glass.

The battered jetty spindled out across dirty sand tidal flats that, by day, could not have been less enchanting. By night, when we walked out along the jetty in the light of a round tropical moon (we were still north of Capricorn), it was wonderful what moonlight's transformation could do.

WE GO ON TO EXMOUTH next morning, through much the same sort of sandy red country, not a mountain in sight for two hundred miles. Then, as we are rounding the bottom of Exmouth Gulf there is Rough Range, where a sensational oil discovery was made in 1953; and to the north of that rises the Cape Range.

Near the top of the great prong called North-West Cape is the town of Exmouth. This has not arisen because of the oil strike (which fizzled out) or because of anything to do with mineral development, but because of what is on twenty-nine square miles of land there that is leased to the United States.

The Americans spent 80 million dollars in erecting a United States Naval Communications Station. In fact, there are three stations (and three Prohibited Areas marked on the local maps). Two are for high-frequency radio transmitting/receiving, but more important is the VLF (Very Low Frequency) one. As part of the U.S. defence network, there are about a hundred other VLF stations scattered round the globe. Unique it is not, this great U.S. Navy installation that has been named the Harold E. Holt Base, for the late Australian Prime Minister, who was never thought of by Australians as having a middle initial. But few other VLF stations have the importance of this one.

"Importance" in this connection has to be spelt out: The Western Civilization part of our divided world (whose division makes it basically uncivilized) has as its pre-eminent defender the United States, which has submarines carrying Polaris nuclear missiles. This VLF station is so powerful that it can communicate with these atomic-weaponed submarines wherever they are on or under the oceans of the world. This is necessary because the Communist Civilization (which is no more civilized than ours and often appears even less so) also has nuclear-missile submarines, which it also has to spend vast sums to keep in radio touch with. Both sides have to manifest a deterrent state of readiness to wreak atomic slaughter if the other side does, or if they think it is about to.

On the day the base was opened, 1st September 1967, the then U.S. president, Lyndon B. Johnson said that it "reflected the warm ties between our two nations", and, "Today is a happy one for both our countries."

For Australia the "happiness" must lie in being under the American defence umbrella. This particular Exmouth umbrella has thirteen spokes in the form of slim steel-latticed towers, each higher than the Eiffel Tower. It may or may not be, as the notation on the Australian Tourist Commission's tourist map of Australia asserts, the "biggest defence installation in the Southern Hemisphere"; but its highest tower, the 1,271-foot Tower Zero, is the tallest thing in this hemisphere.

"The power is terrific," I was told. "In certain parts of that central blockhouse building, if you stand with a neon tube in your hand it will light."

Tourists are not allowed in, so I did not have that luminous experience, or find out whether the crew-cuts of the 400 U.S. Navy staffers at the base crackle when they are combed. About 130 American families were living in the town of Exmouth in air-conditioned, cyclone-proofed houses. Of the rest of Exmouth's 3,000 population (some 900 were Americans) not more than a couple of hundred were Australian-born. A lot were English and there were thirty-four other nationalities. Some were itinerants who lived in caravans.

Exmouth had known American servicemen before. During World War II it was a base for U.S. submarines. Then it was code-named Potshot, and the modern motel we stayed at was called the Potshot Inn. It was rather stylish in its décor, though it surely could have tried for some regional character instead of having Fragonard-type prints on the wall; and it might well have served more of the seafood that is so abundant in Exmouth Gulf. Still, it did put carafes of wine on the table at dinner.

Colonel J. K. Murdoch (retd), the Civil Commissioner, said Exmouth had a better climate than Perth for eight months of the year and, although it did get "stinking hot" in January-March, he preferred the dry heat of 110 degrees there to a humid 96 in Perth. In June-July it could be cool enough for a pullover. Hardly any rain fell from September to the end of the year, but twenty-five bores provided sufficient water. Given water and some trace elements it was deficient in, the soil would grow most things.

One wondered what would happen to Exmouth if the Powers came to their senses and achieved nuclear disarmament, if the Harold E. Holt Base was sold off as scrap metal and the U.S. Navy personnel all went home. The Commissioner thought Exmouth had a tourist future, particularly for fishing. There had been world-record catches of sailfish, marlin were plentiful, and so were Spanish mackerel, sharks, and all sorts of smaller fish, such as coral trout. Yes, there was coral on this North-West coast, too. An Exmouth Fishing Gala began as an annual event in September 1969.

Oysters and big mudcrabs were abundant and there were so many prawns that, farther down Exmouth Gulf, M. G. (Mick) Kailis had based an industry on them and was exporting about a million pounds a year to Japan.

Safe swimming was a problem, the Commissioner conceded. There were many bities in the beautifully blue sea, including sea-snakes. But sea-water pools could be built, and there were other attractions. Turtles, for instance.

"Turtles we have in such numbers that on one of the Muiron Islands off the end of the Cape, where there's a beach about two hundred yards long, a twelve-year-old boy—his name is Stephen Newton—walked the length of it without touching the sand, stepping from turtle-back to turtle-back."

Then there was the scenery of the Cape Range, which was a National Park; and Colonel Murdoch wanted the whole of the western side of the cape declared a fauna preserve.

"We've just about banned shooting on the cape," he said.

THE CAPE RANGE we went to in the coach. The land along the excellent gulf-side road is as dry and as flat as a biscuit, but there were quite a lot of wildflowers beside the bitumen. Mullamulla was the commonest, but there were also scarlet patches of the lovely Sturt's Desert Pea. And despite notices saying, AS YOU TRAVEL, DON'T LITTER THE GRAVEL, lots of drink cans and stubby bottles.

The coach turned off and went into the Cape Range along the Charles Knife Road. I happened to know Charlie Knife and had written about how that road came to be built.[3] He was an accountant and Ampol Petroleum's treasurer at the time that Ampol's chief, W. G. (now Sir William) Walkley was spearheading the search for oil in the West, where Australia's top geologist, Raggatt, said a range on North-West Cape was the likeliest place to find it. Knife went there and said there'd have to be a road made to get the drill in, but the country was extremely rugged. Walkley agreed that a road must be made and told Knife to go back and mark one.

The accountant said, "Don't you think we should get a surveyor?"

Ghost gums, so immaculately white in the red country of the Pilbara. These were in the Wittenoom region beside one of the gorges visited with Dr Oxer.

49/WESTERN AUSTRALIA

Boab (or baobab or bottle) tree at Derby, hollow inside and said to have been used as a temporary "jail" for Aboriginal prisoners in the early days.

Dales Gorge, not far from Wittenoom, typifies the terraced-cliffs formation of much of the iron-bearing country of the Pilbara region.

Geike Gorge, near Fitzroy Crossing, is walled with wonderfully "sculptural" limestone cliffs. I thought it even better than Katherine Gorge, N.T.

and Walkley replied, "No. A surveyor'll only say it can't be done."
Charlie Knife and Jack King marked the road, using many rolls of
toilet paper, which they tied to vegetation, and then building stone
cairns they daubed with aluminium paint. W.A. Main Roads Board
surveyors reported: *Mr Knife's proposed road is definitely impracticable*. They suggested another route that was ten miles longer and
would cost £75,000 to build. The Perth contractors, Bell Brothers,
built the road for £50,000 along Charles Knife's seven-mile route.
The drilling rig went in, but the Cape Range produced no oil for
WAPET (West Australian Petroleum Company, in which Ampol was
a partner). We came to the abandoned well, with a notice board
that says it was drilled to 15,187 feet, and NO SMOKING.

Rough Range, farther south, is where the first drill went down—
and struck oil that in December 1953 sent the Australian Stock Ex-
changes into a frenzy of trading scarcely matched since goldrush
days. With Rough Range flowing 20,000 gallons a day—Australia's
first flow oil—and geologists of the American partners saying that the
Australian find was "on a par with the Saudi Arabia oil discovery",
Ampol Exploration's shares shot up from shillings to £8 each.

The sensational first-hole flow did not last, and other Rough Range
wells proved dry. But Ampol's initiative had shown that there *was*
oil in the West, and the Rough Range find, though non-commercial,
gave the greatest impetus to further exploration, and not only in
Western Australia, where WAPET went on to find the Barrow Island
oilfield.

Rugged scenery flanks Charlie Knife's road. There is the impressive Charles Knife Canyon. This isn't country as spectacular in its
formations or as vivid in colour as the Red Centre's or Dr Oxer's
Wittenoom gorges, but it is interestingly broken and honeycombed
with caves, and it would attract walkers in the mid-year months that
aren't too hot. Much of it is sharply eroded limestone that can wear
out a pair of boots in a week. Commissioner Murdoch had the idea
of getting in about twenty donkeys tourists could hire to explore
the ranges.

Colonel Murdoch recognized the existence of, and was concerned
to cater for, tourists who did not think of North-West Cape only in
terms of fishing, and having barbecues of sea mullet: "You put them
in whole, as caught, no cleaning. When they're cooked you peel off
the skin, thumb off the flesh, leaving the stomach intact." If you
preferred crayfish, garfish, whiting, tuna, Exmouth Gulf had plenty
of those, too.

My colleague Osmar White writes in his latest book[4] that he considered Colonel Murdoch was being "euphoric" when he pro-
pounded his proposition that Exmouth had a tourist future; but,

after he looked round, Osmar changed his mind. He rates the fishing in Exmouth Gulf as "probably the best in Australia".[5]

What I should like to see hauled from the waters of the world and barbecued in the nearest blast furnace are those monstrous metal fish, the nuclear-weaponed submarines of the U.S.A. and, of course, the U.S.S.R. What a happier day it would be for civilization if radio-towered Exmouth spoke to them: "You are to surface, jettison your missiles and return to your bases. The nuclear confrontation has ended. It has been jointly agreed that War is the dirtiest word, and in future our only enemies will be Poverty and Ignorance."

Oil Island + Montebellos

I SAID GOOD-BYE at Exmouth to the people on the "Nor' wester" tour that would go on south and reach Perth in another three days. I was heading back north to Barrow Island.

The coach would, that afternoon, reach Carnarvon, where I had memories of seeing luxuriant plantations of bananas and other tropical fruits, and the biggest beans I'd ever set eyes on, all grown with water pumped out of the sands of a Gascoyne River that looked bone-dry. Pioneer's tourists would go to see Carnarvon's latter-day wonder, the Space Vehicle Tracking Station that was set up in connection with the Apollo project for landings on the moon and is Australian-operated for the U.S. National Space Administration.

Next day the coach would run down past Shark Bay, where there was only fishing and salt-making. What I should most like to have seen in this region to the south was off the highway and even off the road that runs off it, about sixty miles north of Geraldton. From a place called The Loop, off the Kalbarri Road, the view of the vividly coloured Murchison River Gorge was said to be wonderful.

Then the tour would overnight at Geraldton. Here Australia's biggest single fishery exported millions of dollars' worth of lobster (crayfish) tails to the United States. Prosperous Geraldton, the most populous Westralian port north of Perth, was only a mini-Hedland in its shipments of iron ore (from inland Koolanooka) but much more diversified industrially. It still had a lot of tourists.

The coach would continue south through Dongara. Here, and even as close to Perth as Gingin, Wapet (West Australian Petroleum Pty Ltd) had found oil and natural gas. Not enough oil to proclaim the area a commercial field as yet, but enough natural gas to justify the building of a 253-mile pipeline that would take supply not only to Perth but south of it to the industrial centre of Kwinana. (In March

1971 there was another good gas strike, 107 miles north of Perth.)

THE STATE'S FIRST OILFIELD, its only producer so far, was where I was going. Barrow Island was proven commercial in 1966, after the smaller Moonie-Alton field in Queensland and just before the bigger B.H.P.-Esso field in Bass Strait. It produced as high as 50,000+ barrels a day in 1970, and 1971 production was expected to be about 18 million barrels.

Barrow Island is quite off the tourist track. Not that it is difficult to get to: I was to fly there from Learmonth on North-West Cape on a regular MMA service. But there is no motel or any other facility for tourists on the island. Moreover, it is all-male. Barrow Island is as womanless as the Benedictine monastery at New Norcia my erstwhile coach companions would be seeing on their way south (and where the monks proved quite lively drinking companions when I was there some twenty years ago). If I had been a female author I doubt if I could have got company permission to go to Barrow, even though I knew top people at Ampol Petroleum, the Australian company that pioneered the search for oil in Western Australia. Ampol's Walkley got Wapet, the operating company, going. He persuaded Caltex (short for California Texas, formed by Standard Oil of California and Texaco) to back oil search in Australia with the kind of money Ampol didn't have and Australians showed no eagerness to contribute. Today Ampol Exploration has a one-seventh interest in Wapet, Caltex has four-sevenths and Shell two-sevenths.

Wapet's backers had put about $70 million into oil exploration in the West when, eleven years and nine months after their non-commercial strike at Rough Range in 1953, they got a flow of oil and gas from a Barrow Island well in July 1964. Fifteen years from exploration's start, after 240 wells had been drilled and close to $100 million spent, Wapet shipped its first oil from Barrow Island in 1967.

It might well have happened earlier but, for a whole decade, Barrow Island—which was included in Ampol's original exploration permit in 1949—was "out of bounds". It was excluded from the permit in 1952 because it was within a forty-five miles' radius of the Montebello Islands, where Britain made a test explosion of an atomic weapon in October of that year; and, because of radiation precautions, it was not reinstated as a Wapet area until 1963.

At the stage when Barrow Island was proven as an oilfield about $370 million had been spent on oil exploration in Australia by private enterprise: of this Wapet had spent nearly a quarter. Commonwealth Government subsidy, to all oil explorers, then amounted to about $60 million—and the Commonwealth will get more than its money back in royalties on the oil produced and taxes on the successful companies' profits and on the profits of the contractors and suppliers to all companies. In effect, Australia gets the oil at no eventual cost to the taxpayer, and the benefits are immense. If the Bass Strait oilfield produces its expected 325,000 barrels a day for the financial year ending June 1972 it will save Australia spending about $250 million abroad to buy oil. Barrow Island's production could save, in foreign exchange, $40 million.

However, the way Australian oil consumption is rising and is expected to go on rising, if Australia is to maintain its present situation of producing 60 per cent of its oil requirements then it may need to find (according to a petroleum expert in the Department of National Development[1]) 10,000 million barrels of oil in the next twenty years. Barrow Island's producible reserves are estimated at 220 million barrels. In other words, we need to find the equivalent of forty-five Barrow Islands in the next twenty years, one every five to six months.

Yet the search for oil was losing impetus, from lack of private investment and not enough encouragement at Commonwealth Government level—even though the return to the Commonwealth (if not to share-buyers who had lost money in companies that had failed to find oil) had been highly profitable, even when that return was calculated only on oil yield, apart from the immensely valuable "bonus" of natural gas finds.

In the region already proved oil-bearing north of Barrow Island intensive exploration needed to be encouraged. Major finds of more oil, or of natural gas, in this area could greatly enhance the Pilbara iron ore province's potential for industrial development.

BARROW ISLAND is a flat brown place, but it proclaims itself by flying flags of flame here and there at ground level. Waving fiercely in the breeze, the vivid orange-pink flames shoot out horizontally in flare pits where excess gas that comes up with the oil burns continuously.

The MMA Fokker that flies from Learmonth in less than an hour landed me there in the middle of the day. It must look specially dramatic from the air at night.

"Barren Island" would have been excusable naming for what was christened "Barrow" in 1836 when it was charted by H.M.S. *Beagle*, with the great Charles Darwin aboard. A long pancake of an island —about twenty miles by up to eight—lying fifty miles offshore from a point south of Dampier, it has soil that is largely pale-red sand tethered with spinifex and a lowly acacia scrub. Yet, oil apart, it has an interest for us now that it could hardly have held then for the author of *The Origin of Species*. No Aboriginal, or his dingo dog, or any of the animals introduced to the Australian continent—fox, rabbit, domestic cat or dog—has ever upset the ecology of Barrow Island. We may well think that the oilmen with their drills and bulldozers and the vehicle-tracks that pattern the landscape would have been more destructive than any animal predators the island was spared—and what about the radiation from the Montebello atomic tests? Yet the island fauna, some of it distinctive, seems fairly well preserved.

There were about three hundred men on Barrow. They were there, as is always the case, because of what a few men had done earlier. Geologists had plotted the island as an anticline structure, *possibly* oil-bearing. Geophysical surveyors, with instruments in air-craft and seismic gear, had built up a picture of the rock structure that suggested it was *probably* oil bearing. The first well drilled produced gas, and then oil from a depth of 6,700 feet. Subsequently most of the oil came from sands at about 2,300 feet.

More than 340 wells have been drilled and nearly all have produced oil. Three drilling contractors' rigs were drilling more, full time—which meant three shifts a day, seven days a week. If you were on a contractor's four-man drilling crew, after seven weeks you got a week off, air fare paid to Perth. If you were on Wapet staff you got a week off after every four weeks, company-paid to Perth. Nobody earned less than $100 a week, with no-cost accommodation. When the Barrow Islanders flew to Perth they were in good fettle financially as well as physically.

"Gushers" seem to be unknown on Australian oilfields. Some wells flow to the surface; others need to be pumped. A well that flowed only two barrels a day had been pumped to produce five hundred. One method was to "flood" up the oil by injecting water. From a reservoir estimated to have 120 million barrels, Wapet could expect to get over 200 million barrels by using water injection. The water came out of the ground, too.

What were called horse-head pumps—they looked to me more like enormous birds' heads in perpetual pecking motion—brought up oil from other wells. The oil went to one of the "separator stations". Some of the separated gas came back to drive the pumps. So much was automated that you seldom saw a man in attendance on any part of the cycle of production. Even the roaring blowtorches of fifty-foot flame in the shallow flare pits seemed to be self-regulating—and in the wildest wind they could hardly start a bushfire on an island without a tree on it.

Having got their 50,000 barrels of oil a day (you never, of course, saw a *barrel*, which is just a unitary measure equal to 35 imperial gallons) they had to get rid of it. The oil was pumped into five great squat cylinders of tanks, each able to hold seven million gallons, near the shore. But there wasn't a semblance of a wharf an oil tanker could berth at. A 20-inch pipeline that took a very shallow dive into the water at high tide was bare for about a mile when I saw it again at low tide. Way out, in the direction the big steel snake was taking, was the tanker. It wasn't only that the water was shallow: the sandy bottom was of the kind that wouldn't hold a tanker's anchor. A diver had taken three months to find an anchorage, and then it was six miles offshore. So that was how long the pipeline through which the oil was pumped out to the tanker had to be—six miles.

THE MEN at Barrow lived well at the mess Wapet subsidized. Turkey was on the dinner menu. Drilling crewmen, even though most of the operation is mechanized, still have heavy work to do because the equipment is so weighty, and they come in with enormous appetites. For dessert, the driller sitting opposite me had added to his plate of stewed fruit eight scoops of ice-cream.

They get mighty thirsts, too: it's hot, though not as hot as some inland places. Beer they could buy, and at Perth prices. Spirits, no. Gambling was not allowed, either: it could lead to men losing their wages at poker or two-up and becoming disgruntled because they couldn't then afford to go to Perth for the break they needed. Fire-arms were also banned, and domestic cats and dogs, in order to protect the fauna.

There were wallabies and possums and a kind of kangaroo-rat that had no apparent tail. Some came round the kitchen and fed from the hands of the staff. A large lizard of the goanna type, called a *bungarra*, grew up to five feet long. A black bungarra named Charlie lived under the kitchen.

Wapet, priding itself on its conservation image, indignantly denied a newspaper report in 1970 that Barrow Island wallabies were being shot and their meat used for shark-fishing bait. The only wallaby meat that might have been so used, the company said, was from wallabies accidentally killed by vehicles on the roads. Shooting was strictly prohibited.

The average young oilfield worker, called a "roustabout", needed to have more than muscles. Technical competence was also called for and most, I was told, had had five years of secondary education. Oil-mining, if you could call it that, was a young man's industry. Barrow Island did not require to build up a settled community based on married people, as was the aim at the iron-ore towns, Tom Price, Newman, Goldsworthy. The industry was conditioned to a high labour turnover, although it tried to minimize that by keeping the workforce happy. There were such amenities as a swimming-pool.

The one night I spent there was far from dull. The men live in transportable, air-conditioned "instant housing" units set in rows near the Mess Hall that is built like a fortress against cyclones; and in the unit of the Field Superintendent, Bevan Cook, was a party. Big Davy played his guitar, somebody else a piano-accordion, and there was a lot of lusty singing—interrupted by beer and a first-rate supper that came over from the kitchen. Not all of the sung ballads were as bawdy as *Poor Little Angeline*, led by a vocally gifted Taffy-the-Welshman.

NEXT MORNING a helicopter flew me over to the Jubilee offshore rig that was drilling about fifty miles to the north. It was the jack-up type of rig that is square-shaped and carries its steel "legs" jacked up high at its corners when it is floating, and lets them down to stand firmly on the seabed where it has to drill. It can thus anchor itself in depths up to 200 feet.

The Jubilee rig, worth about $7 million, was towed out from the United States for its owners, the Offshore Drilling Company, which was drilling for Wapet under contract. Oil search is a great money-eater and a rig like the Jubilee costs the explorer about $22,000 a day. It had been at this location for twenty-seven days, so the well it was drilling had cost well over half a million dollars so far. (Government subsidy for offshore drilling approved for Wapet in May 1971 was $22,365—enough for one day's drilling.)

The helicopter whirled me round where the rig was standing in the sea, to take pictures (PLATE 48); then we came in and sat down on the heliport apron that projected from one side. Aboard, the rig had some look and feel of a ship, with companionways and a lot of white-painted steel and radio antennae and cabins; but no motion, just the vibrant thrumming of the powerful motors at the end where the drilling tower was. On the decking stood several new bits. Each had three cutting heads and was thicker through than I was.

"We're drilling now at six thousand three hundred feet and making about thirty feet an hour," said Ted Ingram who was Wapet's field supervisor. He and a geologist were the only Wapet men aboard. Offshore Drilling's rig complement was forty-nine men.

The drilling crew, three young men and one who was senior (the driller), had hard hats and long trousers tucked into heavy boots and they got very dirty at the work of fitting yet another length of drill pipe, winding round it the chain that was used for the motor-man to screw it tight, and throwing their weight against a great clamp-like thing. Perspiration gleamed on their arm muscles.

"You need to be husky," I said, watching them.

"They get husky," Ted Ingram said. "Young Curly there was working in the cookhouse—the flabby type. Look at him now—all muscle. You wouldn't want to pick a fight."

They took me to the "geology department". Offshore's geologist was examining drill-core samples in a spectroscope under ultra-violet light. On the wall was a pin-up of a bosomy nude. Kidding the geologist, somebody said that what he would much rather look at was fluorescence in the sand samples. That meant hydro-carbons, oil.

"No indications yet?"

"Not of oil," the Wapet geologist said. "But four days ago we had a show of gas. When we get that sort of encouragement, we start feeling keyed up about the prospects, a bit excited."

You find yourself immediately involved, sharing the rigmen's state of anticipation. You feel let down when, weeks later, you read on some financial page that all that $22,000-a-day drilling was for nothing, the hole has been abandoned and Jubilee has moved to another location—from just where? It had seemed important, at the time of raised hopes, to ask, "What's the rig's position?"

"Five miles east of the Montebello Islands."

So it was hardly out of the way at all for the helicopter to take a swing over the Montebellos on the way back to Barrow.

THE MONTEBELLO ISLANDS (named for a French duke whose title was Montebello, not the Monte Bello that appears in Australian encyclopaedias and maps) are always spoken of as "uninhabited", and so they are. Yet it is a fact of our history that one of these islands was the first Australian land ever to be inhabited by Europeans—for a week in the year 1622, nearly a century and a half before Cook.

The first known English ship to sight an Australian coast was the *Tryal*, belonging to the East India Company, which was on its way to Java when it got off course, and became the first English ship to be wrecked in Australian waters, on what are now called Tryal Rocks, in May 1622. Ninety-two people were lost (along with "considerable treasure") but a boat with thirty-six of the survivors landed at an island "five leagues south-east", which is where the Montebellos are, and there they spent a week before setting out for Batavia, which their boat eventually reached. We don't know which of the islands their sojourn was on. Probably Trimouille, the main one of three northern islands: it looked from the air to be about five miles long and easy for a boat to land on. The largest, called Hermite, is so fragmented it is more like a group of islets. Some of the smaller Montebellos and parts of the larger ones are platformed on rock that has been undercut by the sea. Signs of the atomic tests were principally on Trimouille.

The first A-test Britain carried out in October 1952, involving Australian scientists as well and a task force of sixteen Navy ships, eleven of them Australian, was mainly to find out what would happen if a nuclear weapon exploded aboard a ship in a port. The frigate H.M.S. *Plym* ended its days in this experiment. Two other "atomic devices" were later exploded at the Montebellos in 1956. About those tests no information was released.

Flying over, I had an excellent low-level view from the chopper of what there was to see; but no way of knowing what effects I was seeing of which blast of what kind. Nor did I know how the islands had looked before the blasts, as to vegetation, or afterwards; so I did not know whether the spinifex that covered a good deal of Trimouille had regenerated since 1952-56 or had survived anyway. The only sign of trees on the island was at one place where there was a disarray of dead, white broken trunks and limbs.

There was no picture of overall devastation, but plenty of what we might call "relics" of the atomic occupation. I took photographs that show concrete blockhouses; a rusting vehicle like a car's trailer (still rubber-tired) and a good deal of metal litter in the vicinity of that; objects whose technical purposes I had no comprehension of, such as cylindrical something in a kind of cage of steel bars that went into a concrete slab; sheets of twisted galvanized iron; smaller cylinders sticking out of the ground on pipes; perforated steel sheeting buckled and half buried in the sand round a notice that said WARNING and that the enclosed section should not be entered because the ground was contaminated by radiation. A tattered flag of faded red still waved.

The 'copter pilot, David Eckersley, said that overflying the WARNING-notice area at less than a hundred feet used to be prohibited; and that some of the materials left behind had been taken away by fishermen and others. One rather wished they had taken more. The atomic tests had certainly littered the landscape.

I had no wish to land there. There was something repellent about the debris, the WARNING sign on the steel plate, the torn rag of red flag. However harmless the atomic visitation here had been, the visitor was nevertheless the abominable A-weapon, the Doomsday thing.

I should have liked to have explored the other islands. On one of them a family party had landed from a boat, and waved up to us from the enjoyment of their picnic.

THE WATER was very beautiful, of a colour between turquoise and jade-green, translucent to a bottom of white sand in the shallows, with the sun brilliant overhead, visibility perfect. And we looked down as though into a great natural aquarium.

Turtles flippered along and now and again broke the surface with their shining brown carapaces. Sharks were there, huge ones. And, best spectacle of all, the rays. The big, horned rays that are black as the devil and are called devil-rays and can be twenty-feet across. The ones we saw were not of that size, but big, and moving with a marvellous motion of their black batwings—more like underwater flying than swimming.

When we came off the northern end of Barrow Island there were some more rays there—and more sharks than I have ever seen anywhere.

"Look at that school of them—there must be thirty sharks in it!" David, the pilot, said. I got a picture and afterwards counted them. There were nearer forty.

I had intended to stay three days on Barrow but MMA had changed its timetable and it was a case of leaving that afternoon for Port Hedland or staying five days, more time than was warranted or I could afford. From Port Hedland I was to fly to Newman and from there direct to Perth.

Perth: Lucky Black Swan

PERTH has been rather like the swans the Dutch voyager Willem de Vlamingh discovered on its river in 1696—black swans with scarlet bills, beautiful birds but very confusing for Europeans, to whom swans were proverbially white and "black swan" a contradiction in terms.

Just as swans were expected to be white, a twentieth-century capital was expected to look and act like a capital city. The largest State of Australia's capital, now with 650,000 of Western Australia's million people, didn't conform. With an engaging sort of immaturity, it had gone on looking and acting like—Perth. One of its most perceptive writers and academics, Peter Cowan, wrote in 1966 that Perth was, still, "a capital in the process of becoming a city".[1]

Even in the sixties, little of the metropolitan look, which is coming so fast now, had come to Hay Street, the main shopping thoroughfare. When, in 1963, the Perth City Council housed itself in the international-modern box on St George's Terrace, this thirteen-storey structure was pridefully referred to as a "skyscraper" and the Council House was added to the city's architectural sights. These had heretofore been thought of as mainly the old Town Hall, modelled on a seventeenth-century English market hall in Jacobean style; the 1863 Barracks, crenellated and with a Crusaders' Gothic look (now demolished, except the archway) and the shopping block and arcade called London Court, built in 1937. London Court is Tudoresqueplus, with enough "magpie" wood-strapping, shingles, shutters, gables, shields and diamond-pane windows to bring tears of nostalgia to the eyes of a migrant from Chester or Shropshire's Ludlow. The pointed roofs above the Olde English lettering lack only a rooks' nest and snow.

In Australia's sunniest capital (Perth averages about eight hours of sunshine a day) with temperatures averaging 64°F. and never known to go down to freezing point, mock-seventeenth-century London Court might be considered out of place, out of step, out of time; but Perth has never regarded it other than affectionately. "Un-Australian" it could be called but never "alien"—because of ties of sentiment with England, ties of blood and a share in Shakespeare. Perth, in its isolation—it has been called the most isolated city of its size in the world—felt the need for a bit of hand-holding across the seas. Sydney, Melbourne, even Adelaide (closer but still 1,377 air miles away) were hardly regarded as Australian sister cities; more like distant cousins. Virtually neighbourless, Perth could hardly have become other than self-regardful and inward-looking. Also, there was not much point to any ambition to branch out and do big things civically because, until the late sixties, Perth didn't have much money in its pocket.

One thing it did—or such benefactors as Sir J. Winthrop Hackett, who, from being editor of the *West Australian* became its proprietor, did for it—was to set up a free university that charged no lecture fees. (It does now.) The buildings of the University of Western Australia, finely sited beside the Swan and with delightful grounds and a Sunken Garden outdoor theatre, are attractive and harmonious. At least the building style recognizes that the climate is of the Mediterranean type. The architecture, with its Roman-arched colonnades and clock-tower and rounded terracotta tiles, is Mediterranean-derived and would look at home on an Italian, or a Spanish-influenced Californian, shore.

THE ODD THING about the capital thus given to European borrowing, where so little had the look of being indigenous, was that Perth gave the impression, at least to other Australians, of being *more* Australian than any other capital.

Visitors from Sydney and Melbourne found the Swansiders the friendly, easy-going types Australians were supposed to be; more so than the visitors themselves were and even more outdoor-oriented and sport-loving—and at the participant, not just the spectator, level; more open-natured, and their speech less spiced with Americanisms and the jargon of the commercial rat-race. The reaction of the "Easterners", as Perth still calls them, was seldom the patronizing attitude that Perth expected, but a warm liking for this ultra-Australian character. The Perth clerk who went to the office in summer without a coat and wearing neat shorts and long socks (as they did a couple of years before this practice came, and then only half-heartedly, to Sydney) was admired as "sensible". Business execs came home saying, "You don't see so many worried faces over in Perth. They don't let the job get them down the way we do."

The Easterners liked the Perth climate. Even in the winter, when most of the city's 35 inches of rain fell, it wasn't cold by Melbourne-Sydney standards. When you got to Perth airport, which was so pleasant with its Westralian shrubs and flowers, the air smelt fresh and clean ("not like stinky Mascot") and it stayed clean right in the city: when you took off your shirt it didn't have that grimy collar-edge. The visitor was not always aware of why the Perth air was like that, why the city had a higher proportion of "white-collar" workers than his own, or why it was virtually slumless—but he liked it for being so. He also liked there still being space to park a car; no jostle of pedestrians when he walked down St George's Terrace; the Swan Beer and the leisurely drinking of it. His kind were invariably surprised and impressed to find that Perth had at Cottesloe and Scarborough beaches (PLATE 53) comparable with what Sydney had at Bondi and Manly. True, the hotel wasn't good, and the nights were very tame. Nevertheless, these visitors returned to the Pacific side to tell their wives, "Perth's a good place" or "Perth's very pleasant". Some even went so far as to add, "I wouldn't mind pulling up stakes and going over there to *live*."

They had stories of what a place of opportunity it was. No wonder there was a statue of Dick Whittington in that London Court! Look at "Tom the Cheap Grocer", tipped to become the next mayor—as he did, in 1969, become the Right Honourable T. E. (now Sir Thomas) Wardle, Lord Mayor of Perth.

The shrewd ones, the high-salaried executives who flew cross-continent from time to time to inject a bit more sales-mindedness into Perth Branch, saw the shape of things to come. They noted that any eight-storey block of home units could get its picture in the paper as a symbol of "soaring" Perth, heard the locals marvel that housing developments were starting as far as *twelve miles* out (which was no distance by Sydney standards), and cocked a valuator's eye at single-storey milk bars on precious beachfronts. They invested in Perth real estate.

"In the mid-sixties, even later," one such investor told me, "Perth was a lift you could get into on the ground floor knowing that it could go in only one direction, *up*. How far up? With all that new mineral wealth about to explode into iron money in the north, and with nickel and oil finds, there just had to be floors added."

This lucrative situation had been sighted from eight thousand miles away as the jet flies, by the new breed of metropolis makers. Big London-based corporations started figuring out Perth potential for ten years ahead while the shopkeeper doing well in Hay Street was still wondering whether he should add a third storey to his premises next year. The capital-D Developers moved in.

Taylor Woodrow International, whose cranes swing high on the skylines of a dozen countries, presented the Perth of olde-worlde London Court with what advertisements announced as: "CITY ARCADE. The 20th Century Market Place", which was to bring to the retail centre of the city, ". . . the colour of an eastern bazaar. The hustle and bustle of a town square. The peace of a traffic-free mall", along with ". . . a breathtaking concept—a beautiful, soaring lantern, a shaft that will rise from a garden fountain in the middle of the Murray Street Arcade." Perth got this "city within a city" for Christmas 1970.

However, City Arcade was to be over-topped by CITY CENTRE, a development revolution being wrought by St Martins Properties, also London-based. Its February 1971 advertisement announced: "A spectacular new business environment right where the action is. . . . Three glorious office towers. A picturesque pedestrian plaza. A two-level shopping arcade linking St George's Terrace with Hay Street." Those who had known the Perth-that-was must have blinked to behold, in prospect, this "vital new hub of Perth's bustling business world" that was ". . . happening now. Already National Bank House and C.B.A. House are thrusting up on the Terrace . . . to be followed by the central tower. The arcade. The cinema." One of the "three glorious office towers" was to be topped by a "unique revolving restaurant". This was to be Perth's New Year's gift for 1972.

It sounded like the end of the world of the pleasant, slow-paced, leisurely-liveable, non-metropolitan, city-in-process Perth. Yet mourners of its passing could well find themselves a lonely few. Perth people (as Peter Cowan says) never much liked the old-look city; and indeed there wasn't much to like about its three-storey architectural Victoriana. "They are proud of their new skyline, of the reflected lights across the wide expanse of Perth Water at night, of the view of the city from King's Park."[2] They also like it that the towers of new apartment blocks within the city have given it some population that doesn't withdraw at the end of the business day, so the place is less "dead" than it used to be at night. Most would like it even more when the developers were through. And those British migrants coming to what some still thought of as an Australian wild west, with the occasional kangaroo in the streets, would doubtless be delighted to find that they had arrived in antipodean international-style Metropolis.

For THREE REASONS Perth was likely to remain a good place to live, whatever the developers and the new prosperity did to it. Only some unlikely act of civic lunacy could alter what was best about the city, the things that made Perth triply fortunate.

ONE. Industry such as uglifies and smogs up a city Perth is virtually free of: hence its clean, bright, unpolluted air. Heavy industry, newly come to the West, is down at Kwinana, twenty-six miles away. No part of the city's waterway, the Swan, is taken up with a clutter of docks; nor is there any of the smoke, noise, oil-oozing and heavy haulage associated with cargo-shipping. All that goes on twelve miles away at the Port of Fremantle. And Fremantle's environs, not Perth's, bear such essential but hardly salubrious industries as tanning, wool-scouring, fertilizer-making, oil-refining, milling, meat-chilling and fish-freezing.

TWO is the Swan waterway. This is Perth's pride and joy as Sydney's is its harbour. At Perth it is less a river than an estuary, fronting the city as the lake-like basin called Perth Water. Beyond the neck of the Narrows, which is gracefully bridged, it opens out into miles of a fine broad reach with bays and beaches, ideal for boating and swimming, and giving long suburban shorelines with delightful water views from either side, before it narrows again and dwindles down to Fremantle Harbour.

THREE is King's Park. Perth has a thousand-acre height that is mostly bushland within about a mile of the city's centre. This not only gives fine panoramic views of the city and the water (PLATE 53) but is, uniquely, a glorious preserve of non-city within the city, perfectly a recreation area year round, and in spring a nature-garden of Westralian wildflowers. So it is a tourist attraction of the first magnitude, as well as a blessedness for the citizenry.

The last time I was in King's Park was in the month of October. It is showiest of all in September, but the kangaroo-paws were still everywhere in bloom. The distinctive Western Australian emblem flower, the kangaroo-paw is strangely unfloral and like no other. One striking variety has a scarlet, furry, long stem that thickens and sprouts a crest of what look like miniature kangaroo's paws, feel like felt, and are green. Another kind is all-green, stem and anthers; another is black, breaking into yellow-green. A variety that grows near the coast north of Perth is entirely golden. The "paws" in King's Park are mainly the red-and-green.

Spring also brings out the enamel orchids and donkey orchids, the little purple fringed lilies, buttercups and native violets. The pink

Swan River myrtle blooms from July, and the burnt-orange banksia even earlier. In October a stretch of grass under the gums had turned white and pink with daisies.

The restaurant in King's Park is a pleasant place to lunch or dine. Beyond it, the viewing eminence of Mount Eliza gets rather "busy" with war memorials and such, and then botanic gardens edge the bushland that is intersected with car drives and walking tracks. There is an imaginative children's playground where what are provided for climbing on and playing in are not the usual things of steel-pipe and concrete, but big tree trunks laid out on the ground, and other arrangements of natural wood.

Perth has, of course, other parks and gardens, and good ones. Its historical museums reflect the early circumstances of a West where the Dutch touched early and the convicts came late, to alleviate the work of hard pioneering. Its Art Gallery can hardly be expected to have a collection comparable with Melbourne's European art or Sydney's array of Australian canvases. But the arts in Perth are looking up. The impetus has come largely from the University, where in 1953 open-air concerts for students were the small beginnings of the Festival of Perth.

Perth's annual festival—which had been a diffident affair, unsure of its aims, spread over too long a period (six to eight weeks), and lacking the business-community support Adelaide gets for its biennial Festival of Arts—moved up several notches nearer the Adelaide standard with the 1971 occasion. Its five-week Festival program from 1st February included Sir Tyrone Guthrie productions of *King Oedipus* and Shakespeare, the pianist Rosalyn Tureck, Count Basie's jazz orchestra, Boston Pops conductor Arthur Fiedler, guitarist Alirio Diaz, the American organist Marilyn Mason and bass-baritone Simon Estes, dancers from Singapore, plus a lot of local and interstate performers; exhibitions of Mexican art and Leonard French; and enough "art" cinema for a Film Festival.

A three-million-dollar concert hall being built on St George's Terrace might be ready before the 1972 Festival of Perth. It would seat 2,000.

Perth had people like John Joseph Jones, met at a party Mary Durack gave, and described in the *West Australian* as "playwright, poet, composer and visionary". Although he lacked money, he was building a large open-air theatre, of stone in the Greek amphitheatre style, in bushland twenty-three miles out. J. J. Jones, a passionately concerned, plump, youngish man, had begun the back-breaking task single handed and carried it on for three years. Then, in 1969, he got twenty-five enthusiastic workers who came promptly on the job at eight o'clock each morning in a truck that, each afternoon, took them back to Bartons Mill, a medium-security prison. Also enthusiastic was the W.A. Comptroller of Prisons, who said the work had an "uplifting effect" on the prisoners working on this antipodean Glynebourne, where John Joseph Jones began in 1971 to stage a new kind of Australian drama in a natural Australian setting.

THE ACCOMMODATION situation has altered very much for the better since American surveyors of our tourism reported in the mid-sixties: "The lack of adequate first-class hotel accommodation can seriously deter the growth of travel to Perth."[3] Not only was what used to be the top hotel, the demolished Adelphi, less than first-class, but it and another principal hotel charged higher room rates for double occupancy than the best hotels in Sydney.

The Parmelia Hotel (named for the ship that brought the first settlers to the Swan River Colony in 1829) which rose in 1968 in Mill Street, just down from where the old Adelphi stood, is a jewel among Australian hostelries. It is without doubt the most luxuriously decorated hotel in the country, particularly in the dining-room, where the elegant chairs are covered in a fabric that cost $U.S.25 a yard, and the paintings on the wall include two by Sidney Nolan, a Judy Cassab and a Ray Crooke. These are part of the Parmelia's collection of works by leading Australian artists—a collection such as many an art gallery might covet, and one that must be increasing in value to an extent that could repay handsomely the outlay of the management that made such an admirable purchase. The hotel's foyer has an art-gallery look and the acquisitions extend into the bedrooms. I understand that there is a Sidney Nolan on a wall of the principal suite, but couldn't inspect this because it was occupied, by the then Prime Minister, Mr Gorton.

So there had been created, by Australian art of high quality, an atmosphere of a distinguished *Australian* hotel, which is something more than a hotel of international standard in Australia.

The five-star Parmelia is, expectedly, in the expensive bracket; but the 1970 rate of from $20.50 for a double (single from $14.50) was actually only 50 cents more than the Adelphi used to charge for double occupancy five years earlier.

Parmelia service was good. The dining-room was, in my limited experience, variable; but a top-class dish the Parmelia had on its own was the cold *smoked* turkey. I spent only a couple of nights there, having moved in from the Riverside Lodge Motel (which has since been enlarged and become the Riverside Hotel).

BACK IN PERTH in mid-1971 I was very comfortably accommodated amid the plushy European-baronial décor of the Chateau Commodore

Salt, mountains of it, is now being produced along the west coast. This pile was
at the solar salt plant at Port Hedland of the Leslie Salt Co.

51/WESTERN AUSTRALIA

Giant karri and jarrah logs are sawn to planks in this modern mill at Pemberton
in the big-timber country of the south-west corner of the State.

*Along the red road to Roebourne appeared this not-uncommon Pilbara forma-
tion of a pyramid hill topped with a cone of solid rock, probably containing iron.*

*At Cape Le Grande, near Esperance on the south coast, strange forms of rock
flank a blue cove. Few tourists from other States yet visit this region.*

Motel; and liked very much the look of another new one, Transit Inn in Pier Street. Under construction was the five-star Sheraton Hotel, to open in 1973 on St George's Terrace—where six banks were building in a stretch of about three hundred yards. There were many such symbols of the New Perth, where the black swan was less of a reality than the skeletal arms of constructors' cranes pointing and swinging against the sky.

However, it was from a Parmelia room window that the best thing about Perth, the thing that made the City of the Black Swan such a lucky capital, was manifest—its evironment of bright, unpolluted air and water, and the bushland breathing so close by in King's Park.

Strangest Sight in the West

NORTH OF PERTH about ninety miles is a place that is quite extra-ordinary. Nature has here sculptured an assemblage of forms so strange that they could constitute a major tourist attraction, of Western Australia or anywhere.

No provision whatever has been made for tourists to go to this place, which is in Nambung National Park and is known, by a name that describes it poorly, as the Pinnacles. Nor was it likely to be "opened up" (I was informed from the W.A. Tourist Develop-ment Authority early in 1971) for "some considerable time". The National Parks Board, which controls the area, was apparently un-able to house a Ranger there and provide tourist facilities and access roads because it couldn't get the finance to do so from a State Government that seems to have a low level of understanding of tourism and the responsibilities that go with it.

So a rare natural treasure was being left unprotected. The authori-ties take the view that it *is* being protected—by its being well away from any main road and difficult of access; and that if they don't "promote" the Pinnacles hardly anybody will know that the place exists or be encouraged to go there, and the few who do go won't include any vandals; and they think everything will be all right for a few more years—at least for the place, if not for tourists in Western Australia who are being denied the opportunity to see it by tour coach or by car along a reasonable road.

The authorities concerned are deluding themselves, and not only because the place has already been well publicized. The Sculptures (as I prefer to call the Pinnacles) have, to my own knowledge, been pictured and written about in *Walkabout* magazine,[1] featured on the jacket and in eight pages of the photographer Ivan O'Riley's big book about Western Australia;[2] they appear in Vincent Serventy's *Landforms of Australia*,[3] and were the subject of the main picture-story in a Perth newspaper's coloured supplement. In any case, a place as outstandingly interesting as this one soon gets talked about, and its whereabouts and how-to-get-there spread by word of mouth.

Bad though the road-track is, the Sculptures could be reached without a four-wheel-drive vehicle if the driver was skilful enough (and didn't get lost). I got there in the Holden utility of the Ranger from Yanchep National Park, which is about sixty miles south, via the "coast road" that was both rugged and sand-trappy. There is another easier way in from the east.

When we arrived the place was not at all desertedly awaiting the day when Nambung's Ranger would be protectively present and there would be a LADIES and a GENTS and a kiosk selling Coke and coloured postcards. In fact there was a whole busload of people, camping-tour types, who were gathering wood to make a nice big fire (until Yanchep's Ranger, Ken Gibbs, pounced on them). Their bus was sand-bogged, but an attendant Land Rover was pulling it out. One could hardly blame the tour operator for being there: he knew of this remarkable, off-track scene and how to get to it, and was showing it to his appreciative customers. They would surely tell their friends what a wonderful place it was, and so the growing traffic to the unprotected "Pinnacles" would continue to grow.

THE SETTING is a patch of desert that suddenly occurs amid coastal scrubland. The sand is a reddish-gold colour and mostly hard, or it appears to be. It has a curious "binding"—thin verticals that look like petrified tree-roots and everywhere protrude as little spikes that crunch underfoot as we (unwitting vandals, already destroying the precious sand-binding) approach the Sculptures.

Rising out of this mini-desert is a scattered congregation—a group here and a hundred or so over there—of stone shapes up to about twelve feet high. The stone is limestone, golden to grey in colour, and though some of the shapes may look only like anthills turned to stone, many are far from being as ordinary as that. Rockforms have been hewn and abraded by the sand-hurling wind, and eroded by the rain, into shapes that are wonderfully strange.

Anyone familiar with non-classical or contemporary art in three-dimensional form will feel as though he or she is viewing a vast out-door sculpture exhibit. Amorphous or "abstract" forms—there are plenty of these; but often the accidental modelling by mindless natural forces takes on the guise of impressionistically sculptured images: a surprising number are semi-figurative. Here a tapered rock-form's raddling suggests a bearded face beneath baroque high headgear, atop a Rodinesque rough-cut of the cloaked figure of an ancient king, a Nebuchadnezzar nine feet high. Over there three or four figures stand together as if in converse, elongated patricians or cowled ones with a medieval look. A great fretted form takes on, from another angle, the fragmentary head of a monstrous cat. Other shapes impinge on the imagination as semblances of ruined idols, anything from the theatrical to the phallic, the hobgoblin to the absurd. The squat Cretan Earth Mother is here and the ten-foot-tall Grand Inquisitor, and something very close to Rodin's famous *Balzac*. Other forms look as though Henry Moore or Giacometti could have had a hand in their shaping. It is a place that would have excited Yves Tanguy, who took some of the forms in his surrealist paintings from the menhirs of Britanny and other standing stones he saw in North Africa.

PLATE 54 seems quite inadequate depiction of where I took nearly a hundred photographs in colour and many in black-and-white. (A colourphoto with human figures in it—they are the Yanchep Ranger and John Starcevich of the W.A. Tourist Development Authority —was selected to give scale to the rockforms.)

How WERE THEY FORMED, the Sculptures that are more than Pinnacles and that Ivan O'Riley calls by a name that seems to me to do them even less justice, the "Tombstones"?

"Trees Into Tombstones", the heading to an article Mr O'Riley wrote,[4] suggests that the forms are trunks of large trees that have turned into stone: but the geologist he quotes does not say they are petrified wood. Dr W. N. MacLeod of the W.A. Mines Department says they are deposits of lime and silica that have hardened into pipe-like forms, akin in formation to the cores of hard basaltic lava that are built up in the necks of volcanoes and left as residual pillars.

The Sculptures' only connection with trees would appear to be the embossed patterns of the root systems that appear on the sides of some of them in petrified outline.

The small protuberances—most only inches high, but some a foot or more—that stud the sand so thickly round many of the pillar-like formations are (according to Vincent Serventy)[5] the results of "lime [and silica?] being deposited along plant roots and increased in amount after the plant died". These, as mentioned earlier, bind the sand. If these delicate things—they crunch underfoot like a soft sort of glass with every step every visitor takes in approaching the Sculptures—are trodden away, not only will the little desert have lost one of its strangenesses, but the top layer of sand will have lost its binding. Then, it seems to me, the sand must become, as the sand along the car track in the area already is, drift sand such as blows away, or moves, in a strong wind. In blowing or moving, the sand could reveal more of these glassy "roots", to be trodden down and so loosen further sand. More of some of the Sculptures on the higher ground may be revealed in this way. But others, in areas where the rockforms are shorter and stand in non-rooted drift sand, may be completely buried.

One wonders how far the stones go down. Ivan O'Riley writes that they are like icebergs, showing only their tips. Dr MacLeod the geologist said he had seen similar formations in the Sahara as pinnacles up to 2,000 feet, in what has become a notable centre of tourism in southern Algeria.

WHAT I should like to see happen is this:

1. The Tourist Development Authority, the National Parks Board and the Perth newspapers press the State Government to grant finance to develop the Pinnacles/Sculptures area *now*. The authorities need to rid themselves of the illusion that the area is being "protected": this simply arises from an attitude that is slothful, short-sighted and, as to money, cent-wise and dollar-foolish. To recoup expenses, they can charge tourists an admission fee. The place is well worth it.

2. The area be developed on the advice of an expert panel of advisers —a conservationist, a geologist, a landscape-planner, a top architect for the buildings which, unless they are aesthetically unobtrusive, could ruin the overall look of the place. I think it will be necessary to have a fence or barrier along a road winding through the area, though not blatant fencing. People simply cannot be allowed to trample the fossilized roots to get pictures such as I got—much less a photograph of Mum and little Darlene standing in front of a rock-form.

3. W.A. be the first State in Australia to declare something a "Natural Treasure" (as the Japanese declare their finest old artists-performers-craftsmen National Treasures, and have even gazetted as a "treasure" an old mud wall: incidentally, the Japanese, who have great feeling for natural stone, would, as the tourists they increasingly are in Australia, be "crazy" about this place). The National Trust of Australia has recommended the Pinnacles for classification "A", meaning "to be preserved at all costs".

THE SHADOWS of the Sculptures were long across the sand when I had finished taking more photographs than I have taken at any one place in Australia except Ayers Rock.

The location, incidentally, is north of Lancelin. I do not feel that

I should give exact directions on how to get there, even if I could, to Tom, Dick and their friend Harry who always carves his initials on things. The carting away, by university students, of a stone slab with Aboriginal carvings from Mootwingee near Broken Hill (N.S.W.) showed that even the better educated are not always to be trusted.

On the way out by the eastward road we came to other rock forms, away from the sand and looming out of vegetated land. These were more massive: some looked twenty-five feet high, and had the company of trees as tall. They were darker, and the hoary stones wore lichens such as could not grow on the ones standing in the desert patch, because of the wind's sand-blasting.

The last of the sun lit huge slabs standing to one side of the road, and here the foreground heath was rich with the scarlet of kangaroo-paws, the red-and-green ones, a host of them. On the western side, great shapes on a low ridge silhouetted against the flushed sky. Some were oddly like the tops of men or monsters, as though they were heads from some fantastic procession halted stock-still on the ridge's other side.

The Kwinana Reaction

"KWINANA" was an Aboriginal word for a maiden. *Kwinana* was the name of a ship that in 1920 was damaged by fire and moored in a cove of long Garden Island that breakwaters Cockburn Sound and makes it such a fine big harbour. The *Kwinana* broke its moorings in a storm that drove it ashore on a beach: the beach, though only twenty-odd miles from Perth, was still a lonely place of sand dunes, lifeless and nameless. Kwinana came to be the name of the area where the *Kwinana's* hulk lay rusting. Weekend cottages went up and the place grew into a small holiday resort.

In 1950 that was all Kwinana was—except in the mind's-eye of Sir Russell Dumas, then W.A.'s State Co-ordinator of Works. He saw it as a place where a great tract of available and level land fronted miles of shoreline to a deepwater harbour and where, being only twelve miles south of Fremantle, industry would have no trouble getting workforce. But even Sir Russell would hardly have dared to prophesy:

"In twenty years, in 1970, Kwinana will be the biggest industrial complex in the State. There will be smokestacks and oil tanks and power stations, and railway marshalling yards. There will be a blast furnace disgorging pig iron and great plant structures making everything from fertilizer to alumina and nickel. There will be a dozen jetties thrusting out into Cockburn Sound and big ships unloading raw materials and taking away manufactures. At Kwinana twenty companies will have invested nearly 350 million dollars by 1971.

"Kwinana will be in process of becoming an industrial city such as New South Wales has at Wollongong—another Newcastle even. Western Australia will be a different kind of State largely because of Kwinana."

How different it could be was not apparent until 1971 when B.H.P. announced completion of a feasibility study for a giant new steel industry at Kwinana—a steelworks that would produce four million tons of semi-finished steel products by 1978, and go on to produce ten million tons. *Which is half as much steel again as Australia was producing in 1970 and more than a third of the total output of the entire British steel industry.*

Such a huge project would probably need foreign partners.

TODAY's KWINANA was conceived in 1951, from Western Australia's wooing of British Petroleum. When B.P. decided in that year that the Kwinana shore of Cockburn Sound was, indeed, the right place to put its refinery, the West got an $80-million industry that was greater in value than all industrial plant in the whole of the State.

Big deal though this was for the West, it was only the big beginning. B.P.'s coming to Kwinana set off an industrial chain reaction.

B.H.P. set up in a modest way at Kwinana in 1954, with its Australian Iron and Steel subsidiary making steel fence posts. By 1956 it had a rolling mill. In 1960 it undertook to develop an integrated iron and steel industry there, providing it got leases of the iron-ore deposits at Koolyanobbing, about 300 miles east—and providing the government undertook to build, before the end of 1968, a standard-gauge railway to bring the ore to Kwinana, with the company as the line's big freight-paying customer. This sparked action on the long-talked-of plan to standardize the narrow-gauge line to Kalgoorlie. With the Commonwealth Government induced by Kwinana development to help foot the $156-million bill, this was done.

Few Easterners who were, from March 1970, able to get on a train in Sydney and get off the same train in Perth, knew that they could do so because of happenings at Kwinana, where Australian Iron and Steel had blown in the West's first blast furnace in 1968. This blast furnace would aid supply of $6·5 million worth of iron to China, which placed an order with B.H.P. for this in May 1971.

The chain-reaction process was re-activated by the mineral developments from 1960. In that year Western Aluminium—now Alcoa of Australia (W.A.)—announced that it had proved 37 million tons of good-grade bauxite at Jarrahdale in the Darling Range, only 28 miles from Kwinana. The company is a subsidiary of Alcoa of Australia, 51 per cent owned by the Aluminum Company of America, biggest aluminium producer in the world. Kwinana got what has grown into one of the biggest bauxite-into-alumina refineries in the world. By early 1971 Alcoa's Kwinana operation was exporting alumina at the rate of over a million tons a year.

Industry, of course, needs power. So the State Electricity Commission has set up at Kwinana the State's biggest powerhouse. B.P. draws its electricity from this plant that is oil-fired with B.P. oil. Some of this oil now comes from Barrow Island to the huge refinery that is still the big wheel of the Westralian industrial gear-box: it covers 1,000 acres and has increased from an $80-million investment to $102-million. Not only does every gallon of every brand of petrol that goes into every car or truck in Western Australia come from B.P. Kwinana, but nearly all the other industries there draw oil from it. Commonwealth Industrial Gases (C.I.G.) draws gases from it to make hydrogen. And B.P. has set up the Kwinana Nitrogen Company. But who at Kwinana needs hydrogen and nitrogen?

The new (1970) nickel refinery of Western Mining Corporation needs both. Kwinana's industrial growth has been not so much explosive as like a process of molecules coming together, one industry attracting and needing others. W.M.C.'s refinery not only turns the nickel concentrates that come from Kambalda into nickel metal. It also produces, as a by-product, nearly ten times as much ammonium sulphate as it does nickel. This feeds into the C.S.B.P.-Farmers Ltd plant that makes fertilizer and is the State's major producer of superphosphate the Westralian farmer needs, and now doesn't have to pay freight-cost on from the Eastern States.

With so much structural work going on, four big construction companies have established themselves at Kwinana (including the admirable organization behind the Transfield Prizes for Australian painting and book design). Also established at Kwinana in 1971 were makers of pipes, concrete, furnace bricks, a bulk handler of grain and makers of starches and weedicides.

A contributor to Kwinana's further growth will be, unfortunately, the Soviet Union. The Russians have, as the Americans have, some ships of war and submarines in the Indian Ocean. Because of this Soviet "presence" the Commonwealth Government is likely to set up a considerable naval base at Cockburn Sound. Whether it is necessary to spend tens of millions of dollars on such a base is highly debatable. However, this would be another big customer for the industrialist suppliers and servicers at Kwinana.

I WENT DOWN THERE with Nick (F.B.N.) Hodges, an officer of W.A.'s Department of Industrial Development who had trained as an economist and was an Australian who had a couple of years earlier been a Welshman.

I got an idea of Kwinana's rapid growth from Nick's saying, as we came to a metalled road, "This was dirt a few weeks ago", and, when we crossed a railway line, "Good Lord! This wasn't here a month ago!"

Kwinana is people as well as plant. It has contributed significantly to the record Nick Hodges claimed for the Perth area—"the highest urban building rate in the world". The holiday resort that grew up near the wreck of the *Kwinana* had, before there was a hint of industry, about a thousand people. By 1972 the Kwinana area is to have 25,000. As to what happens after that, one gets varying estimates. There are those who look at the planning boards and see a City of Greater Kwinana with 100,000 people. Others say, "No, no. There will be *employment* for 100,000. The population will rise to well over 200,000."

Beyond the spanking Shire of Kwinana council building housing developments were arising everywhere in towns or suburbs called Medina and Calista and Orelia. Nick Hodges jerked a thumb at a lot of scrubland and said, "That will be another new suburb, Parmelia." Then we were back in the region of a hundred fringe industries near Fremantle, many of them there because of Kwinana.

The name had begun to sound like a new word in the language, a new plural. Just as we speak of a swarm of bees, a gaggle of geese, a pack of hounds or a pride of lions, so could we say, "a Kwinana of industries".

Too Good a Corner to Cut

IF YOU TRAVEL east from Perth the Aboriginal names of towns commonly end with *in* (Cunderdin, Kellerberrin, Merredin) or *ing* (Mundaring, Quairading), but if you take the South-Western Highway you are soon down in the *-up* country.

Cardup is the farthest up, on the railway line that meets the road at North Dandalup and goes on to Coolup, Wagerup, Cookernup, Wokalup, Burekup and (if you don't take the turn off to Bunbury as we did) you come to Dardanup and Boyanup. The suffix *-up* signified a place where there was water. The suffix *-in* signified rock.

Of course, not all placenames along the highway are native. Like a breath from the British Isles come Argyle, and potato-growing, peaceful Donnybrook, followed by Brookhampton. Then the road map gets the hiccups again with, successively, Yornup, Palgarup and Balbarrup on the way to Manjimup.

That last twenty-mile stretch of -up towns may turn out to be the heart of a new Westralian nickel province. Drilling in 1970 yielded some good nickel values in the Yornup area—where five companies had taken up leases—but prospecting is necessarily protracted in an area so thickly timbered. If nickel-rich ore is found here there will be no problem, as there is out in the semi-desert areas, of transport. Hard by runs the railway line to the port of Bunbury.

However, it was not this region that interested me so much as the far south-west corner of the State and from there east to Albany, where I would pick up a Pioneer coach and go on to Esperance and up to Kalgoorlie-Kambalda. But you could not get to Albany via the corner route by tour coach: you could only return to Perth that way from Albany, which the coach went to directly by an inland highway. I should have to go down the Albany Highway and back to Perth and down the same highway again—or cut the corner. The W.A. Tourist Development Authority agreed that it was too good a corner to cut.

THE CAR driven by an amiable officer of the tourist organization, John Starcevich, left Perth on an October Sunday morning and soon ate up fifty-odd miles of pleasant pasture country, with flowering gums and a vineyard or two. We were at Pinjarra.

Pinjarra is changing its shape. Western Aluminium, the Alcoa of Australia subsidiary, is building there a second alumina refinery that is expected to become even bigger than the one at Kwinana. By mid-1973 it is to start treating Darling Range bauxite with a plant worth $30 million. Pinjarra, with about 1,200 people, was predicted to grow in fifteen years to a place with a population of 23,000.

The known bauxite deposits in the Darling Range are bigger than those at Gove in the Northern Territory, although not as great as those at Weipa (estimated at 2,200 million tons) on Cape York peninsula, where other huge deposits may soon be mined by Alcan and by a consortium of American-Australian-Dutch interests. Near Jarrahdale in the ranges that lie only thirty-odd railway miles from Pinjarra, Alcoa of Australia has bauxite reserves estimated at 500 million tons. Other bauxite leases in the Darling Range are held by a Hanwright-C.S.R. partnership and still others by Alwest Ltd, a subsidiary of Mr Rupert Murdoch's News Ltd, which proposes development in partnership with B.H.P. Both partnerships are expected to set up alumina refineries.

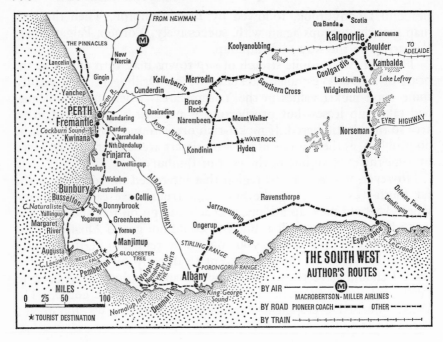

Farther down the South-Western Highway, John Starcevich turned off to the coast to show me Australind. It has the smallest church in Australia. Once a workman's cottage, the little weatherboard, cross-topped (Anglican) structure can seat only about thirty people. Ironically, Australind was planned, in 1839, to be a city, with a thousand acres reserved for public buildings, colleges, hospitals, parks and quays; but the ambitious Western Australian Land Settlement Scheme, which was to centre on Australind, collapsed.

Along this coast the so called "beach sands"—which are usually inland where the highway runs and are the sands of one-time beaches not the present ones—are particularly rich in granular minerals. La-porte Titanium has at Australind a $10 million plant that processes a black substance (ilmenite) and turns it into titanium dioxide that makes paint white. Farther down, near Capel, what was said to be the biggest beach minerals plant in the world was operated by Western Titanium. Near by at Yoganup another big miner was Westralian Sands. Zircon and monazite were produced as well as ilmenite, of which Western Australia produces at least 90 per cent of the Australian production—but very little rutile.

Bunbury is a Tidy Town. Don't be a Litterbug, said a sign we passed at noon. The place that won the State's first "Tidy Towns" award in 1969 is the third-largest town in Western Australia and, with nearly 20,000 people, close to being a city. Bunbury is the port of a hinterland that produces everything from Collie coal and Green-bushes tin to timber, beef and pork, potatoes, apples and hops. From Boulter's Heights, the flower-bright local scenic eminence we went to, Bunbury looks a cleanly town, despite its increasing industrialization. New harbour works to cost $20 million would provide for the shipping of alumina from the Pinjarra refinery.

Busselton, farther down, is a seaside resort with no bustle, with peaceful grassy banks to its Vasse River, and the longest jetty: it goes out from the beach for a mile and a quarter. The highway we are on now, named after pioneer Bussell, goes on through forest and cattle pasture, crosses rivers called Buayanyup and Carbunup and, 177 miles from Perth, comes to the town of Margaret River. Here and at two other places along the coast between Cape Naturaliste and Cape Leeuwin are spectacular limestone caves. No less than 120 caves are known, including the Mammoth Cave fourteen miles south of Margaret River and the Lake Cave which John S. thinks is even more beautiful than the renowned Jewel Cave at Augusta, which is huge and was not fully explored until 1958. Like the Lake Cave's, its lighting effects are enhanced by reflections in water.

We are to eat our belated picnic lunch at the Australian Land's End that is called the Leeuwin. The roadside is wreathed in wild-flowers. The distinctive Westralian brown boronia is thickest near a place called Boranup. Violet *hovea* decorates stems with prickly leaves like holly. There is a pink-and-white loveliness the farmer curses because it is poisonous to cattle.

So we come to Cape Leeuwin, which is as far as anyone can come in Australia from where this book began, off Cape York—about two thousand five hundred miles across the map from there to here, but to get here I've travelled a distance greater than round the world at the Equator. Such a big country, requiring such a big book.

From the Ultima Thule of Australia the next land due south—not a speck of it in between—is Antarctica; and the next land-mass due west would be Africa near its southern tip, over five thousand miles away.

The lighthouse, beyond the keepers' white houses, towers from the low cape. We go down to the point where a dark slope of bare rock has been licked smooth by the rough white tongue of the sea. From that green immensity under a dour sky, a tearing wind sends us back to eat lunch inside the parked car. A salty fury lashes the blue-flowering heath.

An hour later wind, salt and sea are walled away behind a forest getting taller and taller as we speed down the inland Brockman Highway. We leave this for a dirt road that cuts miles from the route and, soon after rejoining the bitumen, go down into a tree-darkened valley to see the cascades of Beedelup Falls.

What is outstanding is the bush itself. It is pillared with enormous trees. A roadside notice says *Welcome to Pemberton and the Kingdom of the Karri.*

WE ARE IN one of the great forest areas of the world. Only the Californian forests of redwood (*Sequoia*) have trees more massive. The forests in Victoria of mountain ash (*Eucalyptus regnans*) have trees that are taller than any existing karri; but the karri is of greater girth; the Westralian forests of karri and jarrah are more extensive and, in their density round Pemberton, more impressive.

Karri, a eucalypt, is not to be confused with *kauri*, a pine, usually thought of as a New Zealand timber, although kauri grows biggest in parts of Queensland. Karri is a bigger tree than kauri and, in bulk, the biggest tree in Australia.

As to height, there are stories of karris attaining 400 feet, but no record of any that ever matched the authenticated 375 feet of a mountain ash measured in Victoria in 1880. This was taller than the world's tallest living tree, the 364-foot "Founders Redwood" Sequoia in California: the magnificent Victorian eucalypt was, soon after it was measured, cut down. The tallest Australian tree living is said to be a mountain ash near Maydena in southern Tasmania that was 322 feet in 1957.

The tallest karri the visitor sees is the one we went to next morning in Warren National Park just out of Pemberton. It was 265 feet. The trunk soared from a base nearly seven feet through to 158 feet before the first limb projected. The notice board said its value as sawn timber would be $2,830.

"It would have taken four hundred years to grow to that size," said Ralph Kelly, the local authority on timber and tourist attractions. "And a faller with a power saw could have it down in twenty minutes."

That would have been a sad happening I thought as I peered up the straight grey bole, to which perspective gave much more taper than a karri actually has. The crown to the towering trunk looked sparse, patterned against the blue sky. There were many other big karris along the National Park road worth peering up at. Oddly enough, the Aboriginal name for the place where the district's first pioneer, Thomas Muir, took up land in 1856 was—Peerup. A pity it wasn't retained as the name of the National Park—even though Warren was actually the name of the tribe whose word was *Peerup*. "Pemberton" is from another pioneer, Pemberton Walcott.

Tourists can climb a 212-foot karri. It is called the Gloucester Tree, after the Duke who was Australia's Governor-General when he visited here in 1946. A sturdy forester named Reynolds who had climbed to the top, using spiked boots and safety belt, to lop the crown, was inserting wooden pegs in the trunk. When Reynolds came down, the Duke picked up the forester's auger, did a few turns with it, and said it seemed easy. "Course it's easy," said Reynolds. "You're not through the bloody bark."

A spiral ladder winds round the tree trunk, up which you haul yourself by grasping the metal and wooden (good, strong karri) rungs, inside a protective wire lacing. (No climber had ever been injured.) You emerge into a boxy tree-top room, which is a lookout for bushfires, the world's highest. Ten thousand people had climbed the Gloucester Tree that year, said Ralph Kelly, who, when I came down, handed me the printed slip of paper that certifies that one has not only performed this not-uncommon feat but also done it "with courage and dignity"!

This lookout tree has branches lower down the trunk than most big ones, because it grows in a clearing and the sun gets to it. No sunlight ever activates the buds to shoot on the giants that grow close in a forest, and so they remain clean-boled.

Jarrah, another massive eucalypt, shares this forest with karri. It commonly grows to 120 feet, and is spread over a wider area than karri. Jarrah, not karri, is Western Australia's most useful timber, and about three-quarters of the State's production is jarrah. Karri may be even stronger and tougher, but jarrah is more resistant to weather and the worm. The two timbers look alike—reddish-brown, solid hardwoods. Burn a splinter of karri and it turns to white ash: jarrah, slowly, becomes a black charcoal.

New railways to the iron-ore mines of the North-West brought the South-West's timber industry orders worth $9 million for sleepers (railroad ties to Americans). Jarrah is unbeatable for these. The sleepers of the London Underground are jarrah, and so are those of lines in New Zealand and South Africa. It does not expand when wet as karri does and is a superb timber for flooring and better than karri for furniture making.

Karri blossoms every four years, and when it does the beekeepers move in and the honeyflow is the world's biggest. An apiarist with 380 hives had averaged a record 785 pounds of honey a hive. It is very good blending honey, and almost white.

The great menace is the bushfire—an Australian term that covers everything from a fire snaking through plainland grass to a terrible wall of flame advancing at tree-height to high-forest fire exploding from treetop to treetop without touching the ground. The Pemberton region gets about forty inches of rain a year, but hardly a drop in January-February-March, the danger months. Planes drop fire-bombs evolved by the C.S.I.R.O. for the controlled burning of firebreaks through semi-cleared areas.

Australia's Most Modern Timber Mill says the sign outside the mill operated by the Hawker Siddeley organization at Pemberton (PLATE 51). Logs of jarrah and karri up to five feet in diameter were going through. A man moved a lever that tipped a log down a ramp, pressed a button that set it moving to the roaring bandsaw that chewed through the hardwood like cheese. Soon the slices were automated into planks that were further reduced into long three-by-three billets that would be cross members on telephone poles. (So now when I look up at the overhead ugliness in urban Australia I not only wish the wires were underground but think, "For this a mighty karri died in Western Australia.")

The mill could saw up twenty-five to thirty trees a day. Of the two hundred men working for it, only two were fallers (the industry's name, not fellers). One faller, in fact, could keep the mill going. The days when axemen, high on their precarious perches, slogged away at a trunk or laboured at each end of a crosscut saw, are gone: the powered chain-saw put an end to that, as the tractor had to the bullock-team and road haulage to the puffing timber train.

The tourist has no chance nowadays of seeing a falling. That afternoon, a falling of a big karri had been arranged for delegates from a timber merchants' conference. I'd heard an enormous tree, in a forest on the east coast, "talk" and then give its screaming cracks, and watched the plunging diagonal of its death, and felt the earth shudder as it crashed. I didn't particularly want to see King Karri die. In any case, we had an appointment with Albany.

Pemberton, where we had stayed at Karriholm guest-house, very reasonably, is a picturesque town of about 1,500 people, a forest clearing big enough to have lush green cattle paddocks set with homesteads that all seem to have roofs of the brightest red, some stone-fruit orchards and potato fields. It also has trout hatcheries and good streams. Tourists, understandably, like Pemberton and coach tours make it an overnight stop.

South Coast Surprises

FORTY MILES east of Pemberton we come on to Highway 1. In Sydney, 2,600 road miles away, I live within a mile of it, this highway that runs right round Australia with many a change of name. As the Eyre Highway it goes across the Nullarbor Plain and into Western Australia to end at Norseman. There, most motorists turn north to

Coolgardie and go directly along the Eastern Highway to Perth. To get to Perth via Highway 1 that goes down to the south coast takes twice as long; but it is considered to be twice as interesting.

After leaving Pemberton, the forests of karri and jarrah were still with us. Along the coast beyond Walpole, one can turn off to the Valley of the Giants. Here a karri relative grows large, the tingle-tree or tinglewood, the red tingle and the yellow. One towering red tingle has a splayed butt that is hollowed and is of such girth (64 feet at axe-handle height) that a car can drive through it. This is in Nornalup National Park.

Denmark, a town with a pretty river, had something more tourist-attracting, a natural phenomenon that so impressed one writer that he described it as "spellbinding"[1]—a petrified forest, meaning a lot of remains of trees that had been calcified. This Denmark *had*. Sand had covered the stone trees, to the extent that so many tourists were disappointed at seeing so little that, in early 1971, Denmark's tourist bureau stopped advertising its "petrified forest" as an attraction.

The road leaves the coast. In this October there is countryside spread with a purple shrub-like gorse, and the verges of green-pastured sheep and cattle paddocks are bright with wildflowers.

ALBANY is pronounced *Al-* not *Aul-*bany. With no more than 13,000 people it is the biggest town and port on the south coast of W.A. Its surroundings are so impressive that Thomas Wood[2] wrote that just the sight of its harbour could "nearly repay a voyage to Australia". Up on Mt Clarence that overlooks King George Sound, the local tourist manager, Joe Wiggins, said, "The best harbour in Western Australia, going to waste."

There is no doubt about Princess Royal Harbour, which is so commodious and almost landlocked, being the best harbour in the West and one of the very best in Australia. But the last time it had a lot of ships to accommodate was during World War II, when it was a United States Navy base. The time before that was in World War I, when it was the fleet assembly harbour for the first A.I.F. and New Zealand troops going to Egypt. Which could explain why there is, on Mt Clarence, a dramatic war memorial to the Anzac Desert Mounted Corps—except that the memorial was re-sculptured and re-erected here in 1964 because the original monument in Port Said was irreparably damaged by anti-British Egyptian rioters during the Suez crisis of 1956.

Albany is the oldest town in the West. It was established in 1826 with a garrison and convicts as a British foothold to forestall the French. Captain George Vancouver, an aide of Cook's, had discovered this "very excellent harbour" as he called it, in 1791, the year before he discovered Burrard Inlet on the Pacific coast of Canada, where the city grew up that bears his name.

So Albany had a head start on the Swan River settlement, and it became a whaling station and a coaling station for ships, and all the mailboats from England made Albany their first Australian port of call until 1900, when Fremantle took away the mailboats. Then ships got oil and didn't coal there any more.

Not all was lost, and much was added. Albany is still a whaling station, the only whaling station left on an Australian shore. So I was whisked out to the Cheynes Beach Whaling Company's operation. There wasn't a whale in. The place smelt to high heaven without one, and I didn't want to watch all that bloody flensing, anyway.

There is no aroma of New Australia about Albany. It rates, though, as a "new" place for the interstate tourist. Its attraction is not, primarily, that Albany is redolent of Westralian history—which eastern Australians aren't much interested in, but they could neverthe-less be charmed by the Old Farm (the oldest in the West) on Straw-berry Hill or the Patrick Taylor museum cottage.

Nature has been kind to Albany, and not only in giving it such a scenic setting. It has endowed it with remarkable rocks, not all of them at the seashore. One near the middle of the town is called Dog Rock. Imagine (since we can't have a picture) a stone dog so big that from its neck to its nose is about twenty feet. It has sunk into the ground and only its head shows. The nose of this Labrador-type rock dog is upthrust, as though sniffing the air.

What does Rock Dog smell, in the way of Albany-and-hinterland sustenance? Eight million sheep for a start—or that was the number before the price of wool went sour and more and more sheep were ending up as frozen mutton for Japan. Albany's woollen mills, turning some of the fleece into travel rugs. Beef cattle, in increasing numbers, for the local processors of boned meat. More wheat, from the drier areas to the north, than the keenest-nosed dog could sniff a market for. Whales, salmon, herrings; apples and pears; potatoes and peas; and, oddly enough in Australia, the sweet smell of that ancient Celtic hooch made from honey, mead. A whiff of superphosphate from the big fertilizer works at the head of the harbour. But nothing at all of that "new money" smell that derives from minerals.

Albany's magnificent harbour may yet end up as a shipper of what is mined from the earth as well as what the good earth of its hinter-land grows. Western Mining Corporation disclosed in March 1971 that it had pegged a 200-square-mile area, where preliminary drilling had shown commercial grades of lateritic nickel, "close to deep water near Albany". Near the Fitzgerald River, about 140 road miles north-east, it was announced in 1970 that there had been found an estimated

Perth, the capital, from King's Park, a thousand acres of bushland so close to the city. In early October it was glorious with wildflowers.

Good beaches are by no means confined to the eastern States. Scarborough, nine miles from the city's centre, is one of the beaches near Perth.

Wave Rock, spectacularly curved like a breaking wave, is at Hyden, out in the wheatlands 218 miles east of Perth. From Kalgoorlie I reached it via Merredin.

54/WESTERN AUSTRALIA

Like sculptures are these extraordinary rockforms, called the Pinnacles. They rise in a small desert area about ninety miles north of Perth.

40 million tons of brown coal, not commercial in itself but containing valuable montan wax, perhaps enough of it to be worth $1,000 million, according to the company that was fighting conservationists for the right to mine it, Newmetal Mines, which had bought an 80 per cent interest in Jupiter Minerals, the company that was to exploit the wax.

Albany's rocks are yielding tourist dollars, not only Dog Rock and a couple of other weather-and-wind sculptures called Helmet Rock and Nigger Head Rock, but mainly the rocks across the peninsula on the ocean side. The sea lashes with a fine white fury against vertical cliffs of granite at a place called the Gap. Near by the waves rush in under a great rock arch, the Natural Bridge.

Unhappily, the scene here is marred by about the worst name-writing vandalism I saw anywhere in Australia; and there was no lack of it at many other places. MAC and MIKE brought white paint and left their names in foot-high letters on the Natural Bridge, with the date 1.4.67 (appropriately, April Fools' Day). DENNIS is a menace who has inscribed himself in several places. A cliff face bears ugly witness that ELDER DON HONE was here and, although an execrable letterer with the white-paint brush, managed to leave his full address in UTAH, U.S.A. An "elder" being an officer of the (miscalled Mormon) Church of Jesus Christ of Latter-Day Saints, Elder Hone's stupid exhibitionism is also a pretty bad advertisement for that Church: perhaps some Australian co-religionist will get up there and remove it, since Albany Shire Council appeared singularly unconcerned about a major tourist attraction remaining so blemished.

I LEFT ALBANY on the Pioneer tour coach that had come down from Perth via the Albany Highway. Soon, on the 308-mile run to Esperance, we headed off Highway 1 for a while and took the more picturesque northerly road that crosses two mountain ranges, the Porongurups and the Stirling Range.

Rain misted the bald-headed granites of the Porongurup Range, doubtless to the joy of the pastoralists who run nearly a million sheep in a shire with the very unAustralian name of Plantagenet. The sun returned to light the contours of the higher, more extensive Stirling mountains. Bluff Knoll, the highest peak, is 3,640 feet and looks higher because the range rises, about forty miles from the sea, straight up from the coastal plain.

In spring the whole region richly proclaims the West as the "Wild-flower State", and no part of it is richer than Stirling National Park which is said to have 500 varieties of flowering plants, of which about a hundred are distinctive to the area. Among its glories are the beautiful Cranbrook Bells that grow at the eastern end of the range, another *darwinia* bell that grows nowhere else, the *isopogon* shrub that fringes its glowing orange heart with pink, and the Showy Dryandra, something like a great orange thistle, that appears on the jacket of M. K. Morcombe's *Australia's Western Wildflowers*.[3] This is a book with superb colour photographs of not only the flowers but the pollinators —the birds, the insects and such tiny marsupials as the enchanting honey possum that is no bigger than a mouse and sips nectar from the scarlet *hakea* and the lovely *Eucalyptus rhodantha* that emerges as a big tassel of crimson in a pale grey cup. It blooms between January and May. The Westralian bush doesn't put away its palette when Spring ends with October. It has a number of summer-flowering beauties, not least the glowing Christmas-tree that decorates itself with masses of burnt-orange bloom.

Some tour-coach drivers are able to identify few of the landscape's flowers and trees. Laurie Campbell, who was on this Pioneer run, was quite exceptional. Some others were good, but he was the most knowledgeable coach captain I travelled with anywhere in Australia. He knew nearly every roadside flower by name, and if there was one he didn't know he looked it up in a reference book he carried. Sharp-eyed for an unusual bloom or a colourful patch, he'd stop for his passengers to get out and take photographs—and I was surprised at how many others did so. Before we reached the Stirling Range he had pointed out the Albany Pitcher Plant that catches insects in its little red-green jugs with striped lids, and the Painted Lady orchid, and identified for us as Smokebush a grey-blue shrub of the region. He knew that the characteristic grass-tree called the Blackboy (*Xanthorrhoea*) with its tall spear that covers in tiny cream flowers, belongs to the lily family. Usually a dweller in poor soil, it grows very slowly, perhaps no more than an eighth of an inch a year. A specimen ten feet high could be a thousand years old.[4]

The country got flatter and drier-looking. The ring-necked parrots called "twenty-eights", from their call, were flashes of green above wheatfields. Ongerup is one of those wheat-country towns where the concrete cylinders of the silos tower over nothing-much-else, and a dog is the only thing moving in the gap-toothed main street. The plain stretches without limit on either side as, now back on Highway 1, we go on through Needilup and then yet another -*up*, Jerramungup, which is a new town, with a very modern-looking church to pray for rain in. "The drought has hit them," Laurie Campbell says.

Twenty miles east of here is where the montan wax occurs in the brown coal seams. Copper and lead are mined at Ravensthorpe, reached after fifty miles more of wheatland interspersed with belts of the mallee scrub that was cleared by pulling it down with a heavy chain drawn between tractors. A lorry laden with mallee roots is standing outside the big old Ravensthorpe hotel that proclaims itself built in 1907.

After lunch here we stop at Bandalup Creek where copper has been found, but what they are mining is magnesite. This very hard white substance—we pick up pieces from a mined hill of whiteish earth—is used mainly to make the firebricks that line steel-furnaces. (A nickel find at Bandalup Hill, a large deposit of lateritic ore, was reported by the big American concern Pickands Mather in February 1971.)

The country is, thereafter, for a while, remarkable only for the wildflowers putting on their October show by the roadside—the brilliant bottlebrushes (banksias) and native pomegranate, the red as well as the much-more-common blue leschenaultia, tea-tree and boronia and a blue eriostemon and a handsome stand of the rich all-red kangaroo-paws near the Rabbit-Proof Fence. The capitals seem appropriate to a fence 641 miles long—and which used to stretch for 1,139 miles, from the south coast near Esperance to the Eighty Mile Beach beyond Port Hedland up in the North-West.

Although some rabbits came to Australia with the First Fleet (1788) these never went wild. It was the progeny of two dozen English rabbits introduced in 1859 to a property near Geelong in Victoria that spread westward (as well as north and east) at the astonishing rate of seventy miles a year. Having crossed the southern desert, they appeared in Western Australia in 1894. The "No. 1 fence" took five years and a great deal of money to build. In 1950 Western Australia decided that it would no longer maintain the northernmost 500 miles of it. Such fences are now regarded as not much of a deterrent to the burrowing bunny, but they control migration of dingoes (which kill rabbits but also kill sheep) and emus, which trample crops. However—and the observation may not be worth much—the only rabbits I saw in Western Australia were just east of the Rabbit-Proof Fence. They were literally in clover—on land where there used to be only mallee scrub, the heath called chittick, and banksias and Christmas-trees.

"The big change happened here when the Americans came, headed by Allen Chase," Laurie Campbell said. "On country that was supposed to be worthless you're seeing cattle—look at those Polled Herefords over there, in beautiful condition—and sheep on clover, and crops." And, farther on, "Now this farmer has what we call a 'shandy', a mixture of wheat and oats, for hay. That crop with the pretty blue flower, that's linseed. The Americans went for this land because there was a lot of it, and no big timber on it, so it was easily cleared. Of course, they used a lot of trace elements and fertilizer. The best fertilizer they used was the one Australians wouldn't have put into it. Money."

We were coming into Esperance then, its bay a sight of brilliant blue ahead, and Laurie added, "Esperance has gone ahead out of all recognition in the last few years."

EBULLIENT ESPERANCE was in 1954 the run-down town of a district that supported only thirty-six farmers working some 20,000 acres. In 1971 there are about six hundred farmers on nearly a million acres.

The idea of making the land productive with trace elements plus fertilizer came from Australian agronomists at the Esperance Downs Research Station of the W.A. Department of Agriculture. The initiative and money came from Americans. Undeterred by the failure of the Humpty Doo rice-growing project in the Northern Territory, Allen Chase, the Californian friend of the late Prime Minister Harold Holt, formed a new syndicate, the Esperance Plains Company. In 1956 it got an option to buy from the Western Australian Government a million and a half acres of land at 55 (US) cents an acre.

The original Chase development project failed. Its advisers ignored the findings of the research station agriculturalists that a fallow period was essential, and they tried to bring the land straight into production; the company got a very raw deal of inadequate clearing, ploughing and sowing by Australian contractors; and the planting was done in the (1957-58) driest season in fifty-one years. However, after costly initial setbacks, several properties began to prosper—notably the ten thousand acres taken up by Art Linkletter, the television personality. Largely on the strength of this, Chase got the Chase Manhattan Bank (no connection) and the big agricultural combine American Factors to back a new company to take over the land in 1961. The Esperance Land and Development Company put a lot more money in and, as Art Linkletter says in his book, "What we had flamboyantly promised when we first arrived at Esperance began slowly to become a reality."[5]

Among other well-known Americans still involved in Esperance land development are: David Rockefeller (president, Chase Manhattan Bank), Benno C. Schmidt (managing partner, J. H. Whitney and Co, New York investors), the film stars Robert Cummings and Rhonda Fleming.

Britain, however, is in the picture. The family of Earl Mountbatten of Burma, former Viceroy of India, owns a 10,000-acre property, Shamba, 60 miles east of Esperance, raising cattle and sheep, with wheat and barley. Lord Mountbatten visited it in March 1971.

What the other Pioneer coach tourists did the day after we arrived was, according to the itinerary, "Launch cruise on beautiful Esperance Bay. Afternoon scenic drive to Four Mile Beach, Pink Lake."

I had thought the most interesting property to see would be Art

Linkletter's. Over the front gate is LINKLETTER'S PLACE. A notice saying "*STOP. Private Property. No Through Road*" is hardly welcoming, but doubtless a visit could have been arranged. However, the people who drove me round, Mrs Jean Stuart and Mr Duncan Stewart of the local tourist bureau, thought I should find it more interesting to visit Orleans Farms, in the same area, about sixty miles east of Esperance.

I did, though, get a general view of the wide Linkletter acres from Condingup Hill, and the property looked as impressive as the new homestead and cottages were white. The foreground scrub showed what the land was like before it was cleared and became the comely green pastures that stretched for miles across the plain. The property was running mainly sheep, about ten times as many, then, as cattle, and it was growing wheat, barley, oats and linseed. The young Australian manager, John Hagon, who has been most successful, was quoted as saying in 1967 that Linkletter's Place was valued at "not less than $1 million" and a less-developed Linkletter property at $300,000; and Art Linkletter himself wrote that he was making "better than 15 per cent per year on my investment at Esperance".[6]

Orleans Farms is the 16,000-acre property jointly owned by the American millionaires Benno Schmidt and David Rockefeller. It has an intelligent and efficient young Australian manager, A. M. (Tony) Moore, who doesn't mind tourists looking over the property if they apply through the Esperance Tourist Bureau. Orleans Farms was running 52,000 sheep and 1,000 breeder cattle. The plan was to phase out the sheep, except stud sheep, and build up the herd of Santa Gertrudis cattle. It was already a leading Santa Gertrudis stud.

This breed was developed at the famous King Ranch in Texas about fifty years ago as a cross between the humped Brahman cattle of India and the Shorthorn; and King Ranch (Australia) brought the first Santa Gertrudis to Australia in 1952. The name is from King Ranch land the Spanish called Santa Gertrudis in honour of St Gertrude. As beef cattle Santa Gertrudis are more meat on the hoof (bigger, longer, heavier), they are hardy and do well in Australia.

There had been a tragedy at Orleans Farms: one could hardly call it less. The previous Sunday had been exceptionally hot and the stud cattle had drunk thirstily from their trough—into which, by sheer mis-adventure, dip solution had seeped and poisoned the water. Dead was the prize bull, King Ranch Jacobean, that had been bought for $17,500 four years before and had grown to be worth $50,000; dead were eight prize cows, all in calf, each worth $4,000. So highly was the bull regarded by King Ranch (Australia) that its representative had been due to arrive on the next Sunday to buy a quarter share in Jacobean's semen for insemination. The loss was all of $100,000.

Tony Moore asked to be excused from showing us round the property personally. He was understandably distressed and did not want to see what was seen when we showed ourselves round. Beyond the paddocks where fine-looking, bright-brown Santa Gertrudis grazed, smoke was rising: the carcasses of the poisoned beasts were still being burnt. The auction hall with its tiered seats, where the stud cattle were sold at a big annual occasion, was almost like a corrugated-iron theatre. (Orleans Farms must have recovered from the blow to its stud quality, for, at its 1970 sale, buyers in its auction hall paid $92,000 for breeders, including a record Western Australia price of $9,200 for a Santa Gertrudis bull, Orleans Farms' Bernard.)

Of the land that was part of the original Allen Chase purchase for about 50 (Australian) cents an acre, Tony Moore said, "It cost exactly $32.70 an acre to get it cleared, pastured and fenced. Total spending has been about $45 an acre." (For 16,000 acres that is $720,000.) He expected that the investment would "break even" in 1970. It was more money than Australian investors were likely to have put into the land.

Trace elements of copper and zinc had been added, in the first year, in the ratio of only a quarter ounce to a ton of superphosphate fertilizer. In the sixth year the land was carrying five sheep to the acre, which is high. Proximity to a port, obviating freight costs, was important; and now there was a superphosphate plant at Esperance.

THE MANAGER'S HOUSE at Orleans Farms was the unlikely repository of something that interested me more than Santa Gertrudis cattle. The house was not at all the station-homestead type: indeed, it looked like the larger sort of fibro mod. sub. bung. in an outer Sydney suburb. The people who took me there hadn't mentioned what it contained. This came as a splendid surprise.

I walked through the fancy-gauze-wire front door into a house hung with a million dollars worth of Australian art. Most of our best-known, front-rank painters were represented. It was Benno Schmidt's collection, and must rate as one of the very best private collections of Australian paintings anywhere. Mr Schmidt was interested in acquiring top-quality works only of the most highly regarded artists, and he had the money to pay big prices to get them.

I had a fine time wandering from room to room, amazed at what was on the walls. A list of what there was will suffice for those who know the names and work of leading Australian painters:

—Six Drysdales (including "The Drover's Wife", valued at $150,000); five Donald Friends; four Arthur Boyds; three each of Nolan (including his "Daisy Bates"), Dobell, Blackman, Herman;

two each of Conder, Heysen, (Margaret) Preston, Dickenson, Fair-weather, Pugh, (Godfrey) Miller, (Peter) Macintyre; one each of (Tom) Roberts, Streeton, French, (Fred) Williams, Perceval, Daws, Tucker, Passmore, Juniper, Crooke, Strutt and (Pro) Hart.

I asked Tony and Phyllis Moore how they liked living in a house with these paintings, not one of which they owned or was of their own choosing, and which hardly fitted in with Tony's background as the former manager of a sheep station north of Kalgoorlie.

"We love them," they said. "We think it's wonderful to have them in the house."

Benno Schmidt has bought extremely well. If the Art Gallery of Western Australia inherits the collection, as I think it may, it will have a lot to thank "one of those rich Yanks who invest in Australia as a tax deduction" for.

Esperance had no doubts about the American investment being a Good Thing. In 1954 its population was 706, and falling. In 1970 it was over 7,000 and rising. Apart from the American-originated land development revitalizing the place, little else had happened to bring about such increase, except that tourism was prospering.

For the tourist from interstate the Esperance area is almost untrodden ground, though it has long been a popular holiday place with Western Australians from its hinterland. In its depressed period the town was living largely off miners' families coming down from Kalgoorlie to the nearest seaside. Their holiday shacks, built when land was dirt cheap, were in 1970 being pulled down on allotments that were selling for $4,000.

Esperance's appeal was not to be judged from its tourist literature, which was very dull. Scenically, the best things it had were its undeveloped areas.

Orleans Bay, where there was not even a kiosk, is beautiful. At Thistle Cove near Cape le Grande the rocks are strange and dramatic (Plate 52). Wherever I went by the seashore, wildflowers and heaths in bloom were in the foreground of every view; and much of the landscape must be spectacularly coloured when, in December, the gorgeous Christmas-trees burst out.

Grass-tree "blackboys" grow thick and tall at the base of the mountain called Frenchman's Peak that rises eleven hundred feet from sea level. It wears, like a Phrygian cap, a great rock on its summit, hollowed with a big cave. Jean Stuart's agile aunt aged sixty-eight had climbed up to this, and I should have liked to have had the time to do the same.

As to accommodation, the Pier Hotel was rated first and the Travellers' Inn motel, where we stayed, third. Few places in Western

Australia have more tourist potential than Esperance in the summer season (average maximum temperature is in the high seventies, annual rainfall only 26 inches). Off its bay there are islands with seals and Fairy Penguins; but no way for the visitor to get to them. One could almost hope for some enterprising, dollar-laden American to come along and develop the place touristically as well.

Esperance is, after all, a French word for "hope". It was named for an exploring French ship, *L'Espérance*, that entered its bay in 1792. Its sister ship was *La Recherche*. So there is the Recherche Archipelago off Esperance, the islands with seals and penguins. The extent of their development can be gauged from the *Australian Encyclopaedia*'s saying, "About 58 of the larger islands have been named".

Industrially, Esperance will gain new importance by the mid-seventies as a shipper of nickel (it already ships nickel concentrates) from the $30-million nickel smelter that Western Mining undertook in November 1970 to establish near Kalgoorlie. A standard-gauge railway from Kalgoorlie-Kambalda is to be built to Esperance. W.M.C. has agreed to contribute $9 million towards the cost of this.

Indefinite but interesting was the prospective development of what appeared to be a huge deposit of mineral-rich sands about 150 miles east of Esperance at lonely Israelite Bay. Preliminary testing by the exploring company, Comstock Minerals Ltd, was reported in December 1970 to indicate unusually high percentages of ilmenite, leucoxene and zircon. Much more drilling was required to substantiate that the deposit was of the estimated 500 million tons and that the indicated values were such that Israelite Bay could become the biggest sand-minerals development in Australia.

Gold Was and Nickel Is

OUT OF ESPERANCE about twenty miles the Kalgoorlie-bound Pioneer tour stopped at the Research Station. The manager got on the coach and talked to us as we ran past the paddocks of experimental agriculture and stock raising. One of the things he said was that, out of the station's flock of 5,000+ sheep, about forty died every week. (That's 2,000 a year!) Sheep, he said, were not as good a proposition as cattle. Cattle were not so disease-prone, less trouble and more profitable.

In Western Australia nearly half the State's 14,200 farmers on sheep properties were in financial difficulties in 1970, according to a survey made by the Bureau of Agricultural Economics. The B.A.E. predicted that Australian income from wool, which had been

$1,245 million in 1968-69, would fall further to $860 million in 1974-75. The Golden Fleece wasn't golden any more.

What was not so well known as the sheepmen's plight was the extent of the increase in cattle raising. When the sixties began 118,600 Australian rural holdings had flocks of sheep and 85,900 had beef herds. In 1966 the position reversed: there were *more beef herds than flocks of sheep*, (118,900 as against 112,600).[1] Dairy cattle have decreased, and there are still seven or eight sheep for every one of Australia's twenty million cattle. But beef cattle had become more profitable than sheep.

The Bureau of Agricultural Economics forecast in January 1971 that beef would, in this year, displace wool as Australia's most valuable rural product. Beef would be worth $681 million—$63 million more than the estimate for wool, although wool would remain the most valuable rural *export*.

Whether the export market for beef would hold up any better than the overseas markets had for wool, wheat and dairy products was the big question. One danger was that, with more and more sheep-raisers turning cattle-raisers, we could get another over-production situation. The unfortunate man on the land who had fallen off the sheep's back might fall off the bull's back as well.

Hardly amusing to Australia's 300,000 farmers of all kinds (of whom it was being gloomily said that 100,000 might have to leave their uneconomic farms) was the blithe heading to an article in the Sydney *Bulletin* towards the end of 1970,[2] HOW TO FALL OFF THE SHEEP'S BACK WITHOUT REALLY NOTICING IT. The writer said that the 1970 wool-exports cheque could drop by $150 million; Britain could move into the Common Market and buy less meat, wheat and condensed milk from Australia; China could buy from Canada all the wheat its "green revolution" didn't produce; Australia's rural exports *in toto* could be cut back by as much as $500 million over the next three or four years, a whopping 25 per cent fall on 1969 figures, but— "Unless there is some extraordinary setback in other markets, Australia will survive this drop without noticing it, because other exports [minerals and manufactures] are expected to rise correspondingly or better." As, in fact, they had done in 1969 when, although wool declined 15 per cent in price, "overall exports went up by a gigantic 24 per cent".

A cheerful prognostication, or at least one that could sound so to the 83 per cent of Australians who didn't live in rural areas. It could also sound almost too good or too smug to be true—the kind of thing one might hear voiced by the traditional careless-minded Aussie optimist as, "She'll be right. If you can't grow it, you can always gouge it. Hey, cop this for a gag, mate—this is *Ore*stralia!"

Yet, it could be well-founded optimism and perfectly true. The State hardest hit by wool price decline and wheat glut, Western Australia, was still the State with the highest prosperity growth, because of its so-opportune new mineral wealth. Its wellbeing was certainly being braked by the rural crisis, but not as much as it was being accelerated by the bonanzas of iron ore, bauxite, oil, natural gas, sand minerals and nickel.

The big nickel area, Kambalda, we were on our way to.

ON THE WAY to Kambalda we were to pass through Coolgardie, the gold town that once meant so much and now means so little. The tour also went to Kanowna. Twelve miles north-east of Kalgoorlie, this was at the turn of the century a town of 17,000 people. It had fourteen hotels and three trains a day ran to Kalgoorlie. Kanowna is now a spot on a red-earth plain where signboards beside some brick rubble say COURT HOUSE and POST OFFICE, there are discernible remains of a railway station platform, and the population consists of three old pensioners, one of whom, Scotty Henderson, 68, remembered when the last mine closed in '28 and the last pub in '52.

You wonder if history could repeat itself. Then, when you find out how the meaning of mining has changed, you don't see why it should. Of course, the meaning of metals can change in terms of demand for them; but it appears unlikely that the new metal, nickel, will lose its commercial lustre the way the old metal has.

Gold, the metal that generated all the excitement in this area originally, is no longer exciting, commercially. Gold's price stayed pegged at $31.25 an ounce from 1935 until 1967. After that its free market price rose above $40 but has since declined. The costs of mining it had risen all that time and were still rising.

At Norseman, where we stop for lunch, there is a huge grey dump of mine tailings, shaped like the base of a stepped pyramid or an Aztec tomb. It is said to contain two million dollars' worth of gold the old mining processes couldn't extract. It could be extracted by modern methods, but not economically.

The company called Norseman Gold Mines hasn't mined gold since 1948. It mines magnesite near Ravensthorpe and has an interest in copper there and, over near Busselton, in sand minerals; it harvests salt from Lake Lefroy in conjunction with a Japanese company; it was drilling in 1970, north of Norseman, what were said to be good values of nickel. Some gold was still mined at Norseman by the Central Norseman Gold Corporation, a subsidiary of Western Mining, whose 1970 report said output and income were down (despite government subsidy on gold produced of $8 an ounce). In mid-1971 the Central Norseman mines ceased gold production and were put "in moth-balls" on a care-and-maintenance basis.

Norseman's wide main street is flanked with veranda-posted shops that go back to 1901, when the Princess Royal reef was found and proved marvellously rich. The town, named after a prospector's horse, looked like a sleepy, sun-bitten setting for an Australian-type "Western" film. About the only shop that wasn't closed for lunch hour was one where you could buy specimens of stones and minerals attached to a card. The area is a rockhounds' paradise, yielding beryl, chalcedony, rock-crystal, tourmaline, along with platinum, silver, lead, zinc, molybdenum, scheelite, tantalite—and such other -ites as amblygonite.

The country grew more timber—mainly the eucalypts called gimlet and salmon-gum—than I had expected of the goldfields region. Past the Eyre Highway signpost that says ADELAIDE 1249 MILES, the road goes on towards Coolgardie.

We stop again at Widgiemooltha, where there are big containers for salt that comes in on the new railway branch line from Lake Lefroy, and there are trucks of nickel concentrate going down the line to the port of Esperance. In the new one-storeyed hotel the bar-room talk is of nickel. "Plenty of it about here," says the publican. Anaconda's find, they tell you, looks the best bet (Anaconda Mining Co., of U.S.A., with whom C.R.A. is one of two partners in the areas being drilled down the road at Higginsville). B.H.P. in conjunction with International Nickel (Inco) had reported nickel values of up to four per cent on their prospects near Widgiemooltha; and in January 1971 began sinking an exploration shaft into an orebody that may be even bigger than Anaconda-C.R.A.'s reputed six million tons.

Beside the road runs the water pipeline. It is the 100-mile branch pipe to Norseman; there is another new branch to Kambalda, as there is from Southern Cross to the new iron-mining at Koolya-nobbing. This was, and is, one of the great water supply schemes of the world. Before the pipeline reached Kalgoorlie in 1903, bringing the water 350 miles across the arid land from a reservoir near Perth, water was selling for up to two shillings (equivalent to nearly $1.50 today) a gallon. Miners had to dry-blow the crushed quartz they could not wash and belt their clothes with sticks to "clean" them. The pipeline watered the dusty gold towns and let them grow; it brought into being the wheatbelt towns along its route.

The engineer who schemed it all, that great man Charles Yelverton O'Connor from County Meath in Ireland, was called a fool whose pipes would "either rust or bust", a mad dreamer and scandalous waster of public money. Driven to despair by the years-long barrage of bitter criticism, O'Connor went down to a beach of Fremantle

Harbour—which he had created, as engineer—and shot himself. Six months later, in October 1902, the pipeline water reached Coolgardie.

A few miles up from Widgiemooltha is a little place called Larkinville. It produced Western Australia's greatest nugget, the Golden Eagle, so called because it was shaped like an eagle with outspread wings. Amid great excitement, it was weighed in a Kalgoorlie bank and tipped the scales at 1,136 ounces, worth £5,500 (about $44,000 at today's gold price).

That was in 1931, and the Golden Eagle started another Westralian gold rush that was to bring a bright gleam of prosperity into the dross of the Depression years. "The Denver City Hotel in Coolgardie had its best year in 1933, the worst year of depression in Australia."[3]

Gold had, nearly fifty years ago, done for Western Australia what it had done in the 1850s for New South Wales and Victoria. In 1880 that western third of Australia, of nearly a million square miles, had only 29,000 people in it (Perth had been declared a city, because it got a bishop, before the population was 3,000). It looked as though poor little Cinderella would never get a golden slipper. But the discoveries that began in the Kimberley with Halls Creek spread south and then east again—involving hardship beyond measure and leaving a trail of diggers' and would-be diggers' graves—until it reached Southern Cross and, from there, the fields of Coolgardie in 1892 and Kalgoorlie in 1893.

Of gold discoverers, most Australians know the name of Kalgoorlie's Paddy Hannan, but a more extraordinary one was, as Professor Blainey calls him, a "dapper camel-rider" named Leslie Robert Menzies, who left his name to the gone-down town of Menzies eighty miles north of Kalgoorlie: "He recalled how in October 1894 he jumped from his camel, crushed his heels into a pile of nuggets, gathered £750,000 of gold in two hours, carried it a hundred miles to Coolgardie, shouted 4000 dollars-worth of champagne, and triumphantly wheeled the gold in a barrow from his hotel to the bank. A strong man, a strong barrow, his six tons of gold equalled the recorded yield of the entire colony for 1894!"[4]

COOLGARDIE is unreal. I suppose any town where you can park a car at any hour outside the Town Hall is, nowadays, unreal. Coolgardie's colonnaded Town Hall of splendid stone is three storeys high in the middle, and stands against the hard blue sky with a vivid dignity. Yet this "noble edifice" is as an exhibit in a museum, which Coolgardie has become, although six hundred or so people still live where more than 20,000 used to.

It is the most famous ghost-town in Australia—and, for a ghost-

town, the fine wide bitumen highway makes an unreal-looking main
street. On one side there is an admirable stone police station and
other good stone buildings as well as the outstanding Town Hall.
On the other side of the road are such "exhibits" as the Denver City
Hotel—a genuine, 18-carat Australian exoticism—and the outdoor
Pioneers' Exhibition with old vehicles and the like. There is also the
Ghost Inn, which is a slapdash gimmick and quite unworthy. Notices
under glass, some with old photographs, have been erected to tell
the visitor such snippets of Coolgardie's history as that, in its hey-
day, it had seven newspapers, three of them dailies.

This was the goldfield where the discovering prospectors Bayley
and Ford got about $150,000 worth (at today's value) in three
months. But Coolgardie was no more than the golden step-stone to
the richest of all Australian fields—richer by nine million ounces of
gold than the next best, Victoria's Bendigo. East Coolgardie it was
called, the field where the two towns of Kalgoorlie and Boulder City
grew up like Siamese twins. At first Kalgoorlie (the name is a
corruption of Aboriginal *Kalgurli* or *Galgurli* or *Colgoola*) was
known as Hannan's.

Patrick Hannan—a bronze statue of the stringy, bearded prospector
holding his waterbag sits in Kalgoorlie's main street, Hannan Street
—was one of three Irishmen who discovered gold there in 1893. The
spot where the first gold is said to have been found, by Hannan, is
now fenced and hallowed and planted with Paddy Hannan's Tree.
One of Hannan's two mates, Tom Flanagan, said he was the one
who found the first gold, at another spot, while looking for a strayed
horse, and the third Irishman, Dan Shea, is said to have confirmed
that (and later in life said that *he* found it). Hannan was the most
experienced prospector and the one who went in to register the
claim at Coolgardie, with a hundred ounces of gold that started a
rush to the new field.

The gold the Irishmen found did not maintain its richness, and it
did not make them wealthy men—it was on a pension from the
Government that Hannan retired from prospecting. They did not
find the Golden Mile.

The Golden Mile lies between Kalgoorlie and Boulder and is an
extraordinarily rich auriferous reef area that is actually about two
miles long and a third of a mile wide and has been mined to thousands
of feet. The outcropping reefs that led to it were found about three
miles from the Irishmen's strike, at what is now Boulder, by two
prospectors named Brookman and Pearce sent out by an Adelaide
syndicate of investors.

On this tour we were shown over surface operations at one of the
mines on the Golden Mile, which have produced gold that would be

worth today a thousand million dollars, and they still produce about half Australia's gold. The mine of Gold Mines of Kalgoorlie (G.M.K. locally) was an unprepossessing place of ore treatment in old corrugated-iron buildings—doubtless for economy's sake. In 1970 this Western Mining Corporation subsidiary earned little more than half the profit of the previous year, when costs beat profitability in another mine, one that used to be Australia's largest producer, Lake View and Star. This once-great gold mine has now (1971) been taken over by the nickel-mining company that performed so sensationally on the Stock Exchange, Poseidon N.L. Lake View and Star's gold treatment plant would be converted to treat Poseidon's nickel ore. And in mid-1971 the once-great G.M.K. gold mine closed.

The switch to nickel has already happened with Great Boulder, a mining company with a mine that has produced in its seventy years gold worth more than $200 million. Great Boulder, in conjunction with the North Kalgurli company, is working nickel deposits north of Kalgoorlie, notably at Scotia.

Not all the rich gold mines of the region were on the Golden Mile. North of Kalgoorlie about 150 miles was one called the Sons of Gwalia. It was examined, recommended, opened and excellently managed in 1898 by a young American mining engineer named Herbert C. Hoover. He later got a bigger job as president of the United States.

KALGOORLIE has something of the same Old Australian character as Broken Hill. Both are mining-dependent and highly unionized places isolated out in the dry country well away from coast or capital city.

There is the same maleness and mateship and back-country friendliness—Kalgoorlie says "G'day" to strangers—and the same independent reluctance to toe the line of the law. So the hotels stay open later, and the police turn a blind eye towards that very-Australian illegality known as the Game (two-up: two pennies are spun into the air from a small piece of flat wood called a kip, and you bet on their coming down two heads or two tails: one of each doesn't count). The Game goes on at a place off the Menzies Road nightly except Friday, which is pay night: it is agreed that men should not be encouraged to gamble away all their wages.

Kalgoorlie is the only town in Australia where prostitution is carried on openly in tolerated brothels. These are in Hay Street, and some look ruggedly Australian with gateless entrances through high fences of corrugated-iron painted red or green: others are a bit more modern and inviting. There were six of them, with such names as Nancy's, Mona's, Louise's. The dozen or so girls were praised by the old taxi-driver called Snowy who drove me round the area:

"Nice girls they are, mainly come from Sydney, well-spoken. Have 'em in the cab you'll seldom hear 'em swear. They aren't allowed to go to hotels, but sometimes they'll call a cab to go to the pictures. Doing a very necessary job, those girls, in a town with a lot of young men. I'll bet if it was put to a vote the mothers in the town would want the brothels to stay—they feel that, with these places here, their teenage daughters are safer." Although the girls are registered with the police and have regular medical examinations, the medical officer at Boulder was reported as saying in 1970 that he regarded Hay Street as the major reason why the local ratio of gonorrhoea infection was extremely high.

The environs of Kalgoorlie are fairly hideous where mining has bared and scarred the earth and left great grey slime-heap mesas. The townscape's harshness has been softened in side-streets planted with shade trees. The main street has an imposing Post Office, a Town Hall that doesn't begin to match Coolgardie's, and some other buildings that could have a Victorian sort of distinction if they were not so cluttered and plastered with a blatant plethora of bad sign-writing such as makes the top end of Hannan Street an eye-searing mess.

The most agreeable building in Kalgoorlie is a small one on Outridge Terrace that used to be the British Arms Hotel and is now the well-displayed Golden Mile Museum. This is a "must" for the visitor.

The best place to eat was the Grill in the old Palace Hotel, but the rest of the hotel made me feel glad that I was staying out at the Highway Motel, which was just a motel, but at least all the rooms had telephones. As a sign of Kalgoorlie's revival, the Swan Brewery was putting up a large new modern hotel.

Boulder looks like a seedier sort of Kalgoorlie, though there is some character and charm to be found in at least one side street. Boulder still had about five thousand people.

Population figures for the twin towns of Kalgoorlie and Boulder are usually joined. They peaked to about 30,000 just after the turn of the century. With the decline in gold, population had dropped to 20,000 by 1965. Land was becoming unsaleable, shops were closing, and there were many who said that Kalgoorlie would end up as another Coolgardie ghost town.

Then the reviver came, as it had with the Golden Eagle in the depression year of 1931, from down near Lake Lefroy. This time the eagle was made of nickel.

KAMBALDA, thirty-seven miles south of Kalgoorlie, is thought of as a shiningly new name on the map. Actually, there was a town site named Kambalda there in 1900.

In 1898 a wonderfully rich, but shallow, shoot of gold that developed into the Red Hill mine had been found. It soon petered out, and the barely-born town died. The builders of the new Kambalda (Western Mining Corporation) had the problem of finding out who owned land covered with gimlet-trees and salmon-gums in what were once the streets of old Kambalda.

In 1947 two prospectors named Morgan and Cowcill were poking round where the old Red Hill mine was, looking, of course, for gold. They found outcrops of gossan (a minerals indicator, usually rust-coloured) that proved goldless, but they took specimens home. In 1954, hearing of the high demand for uranium, they wondered if their gossan was radio-active, and took it to the School of Mines at Kalgoorlie. Analysis showed no uranium, but traces of nickel. Ten years went by. Then Morgan, hearing that W.M.C. was looking for nickel, brought his samples to the company's assistant chief geologist, whose assays showed the values to be unpayable—but he thought the area worth looking at. Two geology students from university got holiday jobs looking for more gossans. They found plenty. But the nickel values were still not commercial, about one per cent. Convinced that the area was a nickel environment, W.M.C.'s geologists started a full-scale reconnaissance with follow-up drilling.

In January 1966 the drillers intersected rock showing eight per cent nickel, which is wonderful. The orebody proved to be massive —more than two million tons of ore with overall indications of 4·35 per cent nickel. Other orebodies were soon found, one of which was even richer. The prospectors Morgan and Cowcill got a reward of $50,000 from W.M.C.

That was the start of the Australian nickel rush. It was utterly unlike a gold rush with men looking for a mineral that glittered on the ground or in the dish or out of a knapped reef outcrop. Nobody picks up nuggets of nickel. It lurks in host minerals only geologists are likely to recognize, most commonly in pentlandite, millerite, garnierite; or the indicator may be weathered serpentine rock, a deposit of white magnesite, or cobalt that often keeps nickel company. Nickel sulphides are the rich ores; nickel oxides (laterites) the low-grade.

All that most of the so-called prospectors knew enough to do was to peg leases near to where somebody had found nickel or was rumoured to have found it. Any ground with a "good address" could be sold to company promoters. Some companies were floated on leases without so much as a drillhole in the ground. Of course, an intensive drilling programme to test a lease is an expensive project, requiring funds that could come only from share investors. Nickel became the glamour metal and there was a proliferation of companies whose shares were to make the fortunes or burn the fingers of Stock Exchange punters from Sydney to London.

Poseidon N.L. sent the market soaring like helium gas in a balloon, and any company having nickel leases was regarded as a potential "second Poseidon", the investor's dream. One Kalgoorlie citizen bought 2,000 Poseidon shares at 14 cents and sold them for 95 cents and felt pleased with himself. At 95 cents 5,000 Poseidon were bought, with borrowed money, by a young man named John Young who had hitchhiked from Melbourne and arrived in Kalgoorlie with three cents in his pocket. He sold most of his holding at $30 and, having invested the proceeds profitably in other stocks, was soon worth $400,000. Had he hung on to his Poseidon and sold when they peaked at $280 he would have been more than a millionaire. Anyone who had the money and daring to buy 5,000 Poseidon at that price (and at least one Sydney investment counsellor told his clients that the shares would go to $400) and hung on to them and sold at the $37 they are as I write, would have lost $1,125,000, plus brokerage.

However, Poseidon does have nickel. (It is not to be bracketed with a company like Tasminex whose shares shot up to $9 after its chairman was reported to have said it could be "bigger than Poseidon": its shares had gone down, in July 1971, to 57 cents). The then Financial Editor of the *Sydney Morning Herald* wrote of Poseidon's drilling report that came out in December 1969: "It is a fine achievement to have 'positively indicated' the existence of four million tons of nickel-bearing ore barely three months after the first inkling of any nickel occurrences at Windarra." (Mt Windarra is about fifteen miles north-west of Laverton, which is 225 road miles north of Kalgoorlie.) However, T. M. Fitzgerald pointed out that the market was valuing Poseidon's 96,000 tons of indicated nickel at nearly one-third of Western Mining Corporation's 575,000 tons, although W.M.C. had six times as much. Poseidon shares were then $130.

A sharp and important distinction must be made between the Australian share market boom-that-bust in highly speculative nickel stocks and the Australian nickel bonanza. That the five-cent shares of I.M.C. (International Mining Corporation) ran up to $9 and are now (July 1971) selling at 47 cents reflects only what the share market thought then and thinks now of that stock. It has nothing whatsoever to do with the value of the nickel W.M.C. has in the ground, or Great Boulder has at Scotia or Carr Boyd Rocks, or Anaconda-C.R.A. has, or B.H.P.-Inco has, or Poseidon has, or, even, I.M.C. has.

Western Mining Corporation is in process of taking out of the ground at Kambalda, nickel that was valued at $1,500 million in 1969 when the reserves were estimated at 15·5 million tons. The reserves in 1970 were increased to 17·1 million—and that figure is for *proved* reserves only. W.M.C. is a conservative company headed by Sir Lindesay Clark, one of the four great figures of the Australian mining decade (the other three are C.R.A.'s Sir Maurice Mawby, Mount Isa's Sir George Fisher and B.H.P.'s Sir Ian McLennan).

The producers' price of refined nickel increased in late 1969 by nearly a quarter, to $2,600 a ton. W.M.C. has long-term contracts for both its nickel concentrates and the nickel coming from its Kwinana refinery. It shipped almost 138,000 long tons of concentrate for the year ended June 1970, mostly to Japan. W.M.C.'s profit for that year, over $14 million, was nearly five times the previous year's profit.

The company's fast-rising productivity in nickel (it has, of course, many other interests) would be further increased by its purchasing and treating ore from other producers, Metal Exploration and Freeport of Australia, and nickel concentrates from Great Boulder's mine at Scotia.

Western Mining almost doubled its nickel concentrates production in the year ended June 1971, and boosted its net profit 50 per cent to $22 million. Its record and potential did not, however, make any difference to the predictions of those computer-minded gurus of the stock market, the chartists, who plot every crisis of confidence and upsurge of optimism on the part of investors. One of them headed his chart on W.M.C. shares "IN GRADUAL DOWNTREND". (The shares rose more than a dollar, thirty per cent, in the following three weeks. Chartists can make astrologers look respectable.)

W.M.C. signed an agreement with the W.A. Government in November 1970 to establish a $30-million nickel smelter ten miles south of Kalgoorlie.

Kambalda nickel has clearly saved Kalgoorlie from decline. Kalgoorlie, while nickel lasts—and that could be as long as gold that has lasted almost eighty years, and might last another eighty if the price went up (but why should it?)—won't become a museum town. But neither is it likely to become a metropolis. Its Town Clerk, D. R. Morrison, quoted to me W.M.C.'s executive director for W.A. (Mr L. C. Brodie Hall) as saying, "The mineral potential of the area between Wiluna and Esperance will give this part of the State a new life that will last for ever." But, the Town Clerk added, "Scotia and Carr Boyd Rocks could be of more benefit than Kambalda to Kalgoorlie." Clearly he shared the Mayor's view that Kalgoorlie might not remain the supply base for Kambalda, which could grow up to self-sufficiency.

KAMBALDA is already two towns, Kambalda and West Kambalda. The latter, the newer town, is impressive. But the whole operation is impressive in a much quieter way than the iron-mining or the bauxite-mining places, because there is none of the open-cut drama: all the mining goes on underground.

You speed down a perfect road from Kalgoorlie (past the spot where two detectives named Pitman and Walsh were murdered and their cut-up bodies dumped down shafts by the men they had caught smelting stolen gold) and between the blackbutts and gimlet-trees the view turns white—Lake Lefroy, glistening with salt. The nickel mine goes under the lake.

The mine-top is mainly remarkable for a plaque that reminds one that this pioneering nickel mine was begun as recently as 15th September 1967. There is of course the view of that strange salt-white plain called Lake Lefroy and, from another eminence, the concentrator plant (PLATE 48) that is treating nearly a million tons of ore in 1971, and the town of Kambalda.

We go down into the town. Away from the modern supermarket, the swimming-pool, the tennis courts, the medical centre, the school, it has brick-and-tile houses that suggest a newly-sprung metropolitan suburb. Although the New Australia's company towns look alike, they are good-looking and the most liveable, though not the most characterful, towns in the continent. They could be better, but the companies with money and imagination have done much to achieve standards that shire councils with no imagination would not have achieved, even if they had had the money. Such as keeping the trees.

West Kambalda is particularly good. Not a tree has been cut down that could be left when the houses were built. A third nickel mine was to be opened adjacent to this town, and the fact that the canny and so-commercial Swan Brewery had moved in with a hotel was sufficient indicator that this was to be *the* Kambalda town. The hotel had to conform to W.M.C.'s town-landscaping plan.

Sir Lindesay Clark's company, W.M.C., is not limiting its nickel operation to Kambalda. Though it had assayed values as high as 10·16 per cent in Kambalda shoots it was not uninterested in vast (estimated 120 million tons) deposits of lateritic nickel assaying only one per cent, to the north of Kalgoorlie about thirty miles, near Ora Banda. It was interested to the extent of coming to an agreement with the State Government in November 1970 on the company's right to build a railway to Ora Banda. That one-per-cent nickel, if it can be economically treated, could be worth about three thousand million dollars, if nickel holds its price.

W.M.C.'s executive director in Western Australia was quoted as saying, in November 1970, that it was reasonable to expect that a nickel belt would be developed with a great many more orebodies, including a few more big deposits with a long life such as Kambalda's.

But what if the price of nickel slumped, or froze the way the price of gold did? Canada is the world's top producer, with big deposits of the rich nickel sulphides. The French island of New Caledonia (with nickel oxides or laterites) is considered to have the largest reserves—but it could be that Australia has. There was a 1970 report from New York that a nickel glut was foreseeable and would force the price down. As against that, an authoritative paper presented to the American Institute of Mining, Metallurgical and Petroleum Engineers at the end of February 1971 forecast demand for nickel increasing by 200 per cent by the year 2000. The only higher-increase forecasts were for copper and aluminium. New uses for nickel alloys are being found all the time. It is no longer something thought of in terms of stainless steel cutlery and coins. In the structure of every Boeing 707 plane there is a 4,000-pound content of nickel.

Australia is more than likely to come up with other big nickel deposits. In the five years since Western Mining Corporation proved its Kambalda deposits the country's surface has been no more than scratched for this metal that involves such complex prospecting: you can't spot it from the air as Lang Hancock did Pilbara iron or register its presence with a geiger counter. For the small companies, adequate testing of their lease areas is often beyond their capacity geologically and financially, the more so since the share market soured.

Nickel does not occur only in Western Australia—in Queensland deposits at Greenvale are being developed—and it occurs in the West not only in the region of the eastern goldfields of a State so big that Kalgoorlie is in its western half. We still don't know what lies in a great deal of it, including the northern edges of the Great Victoria Desert, except that there is a huge laterite-nickel area in the Tomkinson Ranges on the border. This is remote and regarded as uncommercial; but a new Canadian (Sherritt Gordon) process for the treatment of low-grade nickel ores, being tested in New Caledonia, looks like working. Hence the interest of W.M.C., which proposes to use this process, in the lateritic lodes at Ora Banda.

A major nickel strike eleven miles south of Kambalda was announced by W.M.C. in July 1971. What is called the Foster Shoot in the St Ives area showed extensive nickel occurrence in values up to 7·32 nickel, which is very high.

Another nickel area of high promise was at Agnew, about 100 miles to the north of Kalgoorlie.

It is more than conceivable that there may yet be found the nickel equivalent of the Golden Mile. And if such a find depressed the price of nickel, then Australia would cry all the way to the bank.

Wave Rock and the Wailing Wall

WAVE ROCK it is called, and you would hardly expect it to be called anything else. It is a long concave wall of granite curved over like a wave, a wave fifty feet high that was just about to break when it turned into stone.

There is something else remarkable. This improbable natural sculpture of a wave looks as if the stone has been painted. PLATE 54's top photograph may suggest that it has been touched up with a brush to accentuate the striped colour effect: it hasn't. The rock is really like that. The formation is longer than the picture shows, several hundred feet.

This curiosity attracts tourists, but not as many as would go there if it were more conveniently situated than it is, 218 miles east of Perth out in the middle of the wheatlands, at Hyden. I reached it by getting off the Pioneer coach that was returning from Kalgoorlie to Perth via the Great Eastern Highway, at Merredin. From Merredin it is 106 road miles south to Hyden. Merredin Shire's president, J. M. Brown, drove me down.

Hyden had been getting 12,000 visitors' cars a year because of Wave Rock, a couple of miles east, where a caravan park had been set up. The people of Hyden asked a brewery to build a tourist hotel in the town; and when the brewery said no they built one themselves. It was making a profit of $20,000 a year and was being enlarged.

The W.A. Tourist Development Authority has managed to make information about Wave Rock incomprehensible to the layman in a leaflet that gives details supplied by geologists. These turn it into a *monadnock* with such fascinating features as varying *phenocrysts* in the *facies* which are, in patches, *pegmatitic*. Motorists who may wish they had popped the *Concise Oxford Dictionary* in the glove-box should not worry: those terms aren't in it, anyway. With the aid of a ten-pound dictionary, translation into laymanese is possible, though difficult. Wave Rock is a hill left on a plain and its granite shows crystals of quartz and feldspar. One gathers that it is the shape it is because of erosion by water and weathering. Some of the granite crystallized 2,700 million years ago.

The stripes of colour were caused by water "charged with carbonates and iron hydroxide" trickling down, the geologists say. A shrewd local farmer and shire councillor, R. B. (Ben) Mouritz, told me he thought the orange colour, at least, came from acids in cement used on a wall on top of the rock. He pointed out where cement had been mixed, and the rock was bright orange.

The low wall on top of Wave Rock—it tends to jut unaesthetically into photographs if one isn't careful—is to channel water from this catchment area into the local reservoir. Near the western end of the formation the granite was, until a few years ago, being *quarried*—and by a W.A. Government body, the Country Water Supply people.

There is a clump of less remarkable rocks in the area. The one called the Hippo's Yawn has part of its cave painted white to cover up the defacing names and initials that had been written by visitors —who now leave their names or initials on the defacing white surface so mistakenly provided. The young visitors—the young do nearly all the damage—haven't spared the outside either. There is no point in going to these rocks: they are ruined. Bates Cave, at another formation called the Humps, must have looked much better before the arrival of MARG, VIC, GLEN, REN, BARB and MAL who deserve to be rounded up, fined and set to work with paint remover. The cave has Aboriginal hand stencils.

Wave Rock, which is well worth seeing, had so far escaped moronic vandalism.

Near the Humps are good examples of what the Aborigines called *gnamma* holes and valued for the water these contain. They may be only eighteen inches across at the top, but what you see is like the neck to a flagon that widens out below to provide substantial storage of water. "How these form is something of a mystery," Vincent Serventy writes of gnamma holes,[1] and gives the theory that a natural break in the hard stone surface allowed the softer material below to be hollowed out by rain and wind and the scratching of thirsty animals. Councillor Ben Mouritz's theory was that the Aborigines made them. They would drop a diorite boulder on the rock and listen for a hollow sound indicating there was water below, he believed. Then they would sink through to the soak by lighting a fire on the rock and, when it was very hot, throwing water on it, causing the granite to chip off and so gradually deepening a hole until it reached the natural tank.

MERREDIN is wheat; wool, too, and pigs, but mainly wheat. Within seventy miles of Merredin two-fifths of all Western Australia's wheat was grown. At Merredin was the biggest wheat storage in the West —an enormous shed that held eight million bushels. Big trucks were tipping their loads of grain and it was being sprayed, as from an outsize firehose, onto a long hill of wheat.

In the previous season Australia had grown an all-time record 540 million bushels of wheat. Drought and quotas cut that back to 358 bushels for the 1969-70 season. Further reduction, to save the industry from growing more wheat than it could sell or even store, would cut that back to an estimated 253 million bushels for the season ending in April 1971. "Wheat", in the cityman's vocabulary, had become synonymous with "glut".

There were 265 million unsold bushels on 1st December 1970. With the 253 million due in the new season, the Wheat Board would have 518 million bushels to sell. And China, which had been buying from Canada—which has recognized "Red" China as Australia has not—hadn't ordered any Australian wheat at all. The man in the street was thinking "Woe is wheat" in early 1971.

In March 1971 it turned out that the wheat crisis was being over-stated. Export sales (without China, which favoured Canada and did not order) would take care of 249 million bushels. With domestic demand, this would leave a carryover of 193 million bushels—less than last year's surplus. That was still a lot of wheat, but the position wasn't worse: it was better.

This was good news, good for the country, and good for towns like Merredin—and, although the country didn't need any more wheat towns as such, it needed more towns like Merredin. It wasn't a big town (only 4,500 people in it, 6,000 in the shire) and, being flat on a plain, it wasn't scenically blessed. But Merredin was a town of un-common calibre. It had spirit and, in the best sense of the term, pride.

Merredin's houses looked better than most country-town houses do. Its schools and hospitals looked better. Such buildings as the Women's Rest Centre were a credit to it. Merredin's streets were good, sealed surfaces and very clean: it was top of its town-class in the "Tidy Town" contest; and it had planted 3,000 trees. It was the first town to treat sewage to irrigate its parks and gardens and play-ing fields. Only much-bigger Kalgoorlie in the rural West was ahead of Merredin in providing a public swimming-pool, and of Olympic dimensions at that. Merredin had the best-looking and best-stocked library of any town of its size in the State.

Two miles out there was a State forest, originally set aside for the town's firewood in pre-electricity days. As the wheat farms spread, this 3,000 acres became the only virgin land left in the area. One applicant to buy it, clear it, plant it got a member of parliament to back him up. The Road Board said no, and persuaded the Lands Department to declare the forest an A-class reserve. Even then, yet another applicant got a Minister of the Crown to back his contention that the land was not required for public use and that the enact-ment as a reserve should be annulled. Merredin dug its heels in and said "No!" The Merredin National Forest stayed a reserve.

Australia needs, particularly with wool's decline, its new-money mining towns. But it also needs, very much, its Merredins. This kind of rural community, this kind of sterling countryman character at its best—prevailing over the greedy, philistine, farming-is-all attitude and building up the quality of country life with civic graces and amenities and things like a good local library—this is not expendable.

The Australian cityman is quick to say that, as a taxpayer, he doesn't owe the farmer a living: nor does he. However, when the cityman says, "If too much wheat is being grown, why don't they have the sense to plant less!" he over-simplifies the wheatgrower's problem. As the Professor of Agricultural Economics at the University of Sydney[2] has pointed out, it is the weather the farmer gets rather than the area he plants that determines the size of the crop and, "In many areas, he does not know whether the acreage he plants will yield 30 bushels to the acre or 15 bushels or even no wheat at all." Drought is not predictable, nor is rain at the wrong time. Australia is not, overall, a kindly country to those who live off its land. Its rural nature has been typified as a man beating out a bush-fire with a flood-warning notice. Even dry-country Merredin (13-inch rainfall) has had its floods, and storms that flattened crops with hailstones "as big as tennis balls".[3]

Coping with adversities, whether elemental or economic, has made the average Australian farmer more efficient, more resistant and more resilient—readier to change his methods or his product—than he is usually given credit for being by the cityman who habitually says, "The farmers are always crying." As minority Australians they have to be highly vocal to get heard—especially now when their importance has been down-graded by the new wealth the miners are producing.

However, it does not appear that there is any present need for the wheatfarmers of Merredin to use Wave Rock as a Wailing Wall. They are unlikely to be doing as well as in the four or five years to 1969, when they were doing particularly well. But grain growers have been getting "satisfactory financial returns, despite the frequently over-estimated cost-price squeeze", according to the lecturer in Economic Geography at the University of Melbourne, E. J. Donath, writing in February 1971.[4]

"Has everyone exaggerated the size of the rural crisis?" was the heading to Mr Donath's article. The sheep industry, he conceded, was "in dire straits". But wheat growers were getting by; beef producers were doing well; so were sugar growers; even the dairy farmers, "in spite of the perpetual poverty claims", didn't really have much to complain about.

Mr Donath said that even if his assessment erred on the optimistic side—and trade figures for 1971 supported his optimism—the gloomy predictions being made were still "quite unjustified".

IT APPEARED in early 1971 that the blue sky of the Australian economy was being polluted by inflation. It wasn't inflation to anything like the degree that had been experienced in Europe or North America, but it was viewed with considerable alarm.

After reading the statements of ten economists on how bad Australia's inflation was likely to get and what should be done to check it, I felt none the wiser. There was a notable lack of consensus even among the economists of the august Institute of Social Research and Applied Economics. If politicians didn't know what to do it was possibly because they didn't know which economist to believe. The then Prime Minister (Mr J. G. Gorton was deposed from that office by the Liberal Party parliamentarians on 10th March 1971, and Mr William McMahon became Prime Minister) ordered that a costly Air Force exercise be called off, which seemed a good idea: then he decreed that Canberra's street lawns should be mown less frequently and that the water jet of the Captain Cook fountain in the lake should not play daily but only on Sunday afternoons. That, I think, was where I gave up the study of inflation—or it may have been at the point where one grouping of economists at the Institute of S.R. and A.E. said that Australia could be heading for another Depression like the dreadful one in 1931, and thought that measures such as were adopted then (salaries and pensions were cut by twenty per cent and taxation steeply increased) were needed now.[5]

The possibility of such a catastrophe seems not to have occurred to the Foreign Editor of the *Economist*, London, when, in a review of Australia's economic prospects in 1971, Mr Brian Beedham said that the outlook was bright even if Britain did enter the European Economic Community. Earlier, in August 1970, Mr Beedham had written a survey of Australia saying that it reminded him of the United States in 1955. Australia was trying to do much the same kind of things—and it might run into the same kind of crisis that the United States had in the 1960's, with the same disappointments and heartburnings. "But I don't think so," he added.

Brian Beedham considered Australia to be ". . . a much more stable society than the United States; indeed it is probably one of the most stable societies in the world." And, with its mineral discoveries, it had had one of those strokes of good fortune that can come to one country in a dozen once in a hundred years, he said.

He thought overseas investors were putting more into the country than they were taking out of it, and concluded:

"By the usual check list of what a successful economy needs—labour, capital, natural resources—Australia is sitting pretty."[6]

Reflections on a Treeless Plain

THE TRAIN pulls out from a Kalgoorlie station platform that is a third of a mile long. Two mornings earlier I was on a night train that pulled into it, from Merredin. This time it is the homeward journey, to the end of the line.

The line will end 1,108 miles east at Port Pirie in South Australia, in twenty-nine hours. For the first two hundred miles the country will be lightly timbered. Then it will be plain—and such very plain-looking plain—with next-to-nothing on it. Although there is so much of it, it need add little to the narrative.

When the scenery outside is nothing much you can always look inside your head and try to see what the Australia you have already seen *means*. You can take the reflection process a step further and try to see where the New Australia is going.

There is plenty of reflection time on this train ride that begins at 7.15 a.m. from this long Kalgoorlie platform where women lug their own heavy suitcases because there are no porters. The Australian railways, although it is "the biggest single employer of labour [122,000 people] . . . one in every hundred Australians works for the railways"[1]–is still as under-staffed as it is debt-burdened with interest on loans, some of which have to do with platforms that are two platforms long because they have to serve two different railways. Western Australia laid its rails 3 ft 6 in. apart, as Queensland did. The track I am on is 4 ft 8½ in., known as "standard" gauge, which New South Wales has. Poor South Australia has some of this, some of the narrow three-foot-six, and a number of lines that are the wide-track 5 ft 3 in. Victoria adopted. This foolishness goes back to before Federation when the States weren't States but separate British colonies. To rectify all the problems that arise from break-of-gauge would be enormously expensive.

However, you can now travel standard-gauge for 3,074 miles from Brisbane in Queensland to Fremantle in Western Australia. And, since March 1970, you can step into an Indian-Pacific Express (named for the two oceans it links) in Sydney and step out of the same train 2,461 miles and sixty-five hours later in Perth.

I did not travel on the Indian-Pacific, which runs twice weekly in each direction and is, by all reports, an excellently appointed train (or trains), noise-insulated, air-conditioned, with stylish "twinette" accommodation, club car, ice water. It's Australia's best train, though not particularly fast (65 m.p.h.). I was on the Trans-Australian Railways train that does the seven-days-a-week service. It is quite a good train. The service could be better; but, then, train staff can't service you with such things as information booklets and route maps and Perth newspapers if nobody has put these things on board. A dollar tip to the car conductor early in the journey proved a good investment.

There is a town or two along the Eyre Highway that runs well south of the line, along the top of the Great Australian Bight. By the railway, until you reach Tarcoola, nearly 800 miles from Kalgoorlie, you pass thirty-two "stations" (without platforms). These usually consist of three or four houses in which fettlers (men who maintain the track) and their families live. If you've seen one fettler's house you've seen the lot: they are identically wooden, iron-roofed and wide-veranda'd.

I had flown this route a couple of times and, although there was really nothing in the view from a jet at 30,000 feet to encourage belief in the Nullarbor Plain's being, as a Commonwealth Railways brochure terms it, "fascinating", I expected it to be more interesting and less drear than it was.

From a combination of the Latin words *nulla* and *arbor*, Nullarbor means "no tree". This isn't strictly true—there are belts of myall, mulga and mallee—but great expanses of the plain have little growth except clumps of saltbush and grass. This grass, when I saw it, was two years old: there had been no rain at all that winter or so far that spring. ("I've seen it *green*," the old conductor said.) It only gets about six and a half inches of rain in an average year, anyway. It looks all the more arid because the Nullarbor is a limestone plain. Limestone being porous, the water seeps away, and beneath the plain forms limestone caves. Subsidences on the plain have revealed some of these. A great cavern near Koonalda on the Eyre Highway is about 300 feet long by 150 feet high and wide. Incidentally, road travellers do not cross the true Nullarbor (treeless) plain. They glimpse only one section of it, at a place called Nullarbor.

How wide is the Nullarbor Plain? is a good question. One answer: "The limits of the plain have never been strictly defined, but it is generally taken to extend about 200 miles west and 150 miles east from the Western Australian border"[2]—about 350 miles. A Commonwealth Railways booklet says "extending for 420 miles"; but its route map has the limits near places called Naretha, 250 miles inside W.A. and Lyons, 300 miles inside South Australia—550 miles apart.

What the railway is very proud of is that across 297 miles of the Nullarbor is the longest straight—dead straight, not a bend—stretch of railway track in the world. I suppose they are also grateful: you can't get easier track-laying than that—or drier, more desolate country to lay it across. The sleepers for the desert section were carried in on camel-back during the 1913-17 building of the line.

The country turns into sandhills near the Aboriginal settlement of Ooldea, 484 miles from line's end. But that was passed in the night.

If you don't put your watch back one and a half hours when, after 450 miles of the far-east West, you cross into South Australia, you are likely to think—after the welcome sight of wheatlands—that you have arrived at Port Pirie ninety minutes later than the scheduled 1 p.m. (S.A. time).

Now that we are back in South Australia a development should be mentioned that came too late for inclusion in the S.A. section. If I am still living in Sydney in, say, late 1973, my breakfast will be cooked with South Australian natural gas.

An agreement was signed in March 1971 for New South Wales to draw its natural gas, by a pipeline about 850 miles long, from the Gidgealpa field in desert country of north-east South Australia.

North of the Moomba-Gidgealpa gasfield, Tirrawarra 1 well flowed 600 barrels a day of oil in July 1970, the first major strike on the mainland since 1964. Tirrawarra 2, in August 1971, gave 1,500 barrels a day, the largest oilflow recorded on the Australian mainland and indicative of a field as big as Barrow Island (W.A.). South Australia was in the oil business as well as gas (of which Tirrawarra 2 also gave a substantial flow).

WHAT IS DISTINCTIVE about the Australian scene, one might reflect after travelling through 35,000 miles of it, is that so much of what is most eyeworthy is Nature-made, not Man-made. The historical is not superimposed on the geophysical as it is in Europe where so many hilltops are surmounted by the ruins of fortresses or, in Greece, temples. It would be absurd, of course, to suggest that the Acropolis at Athens would be the better for not having the Parthenon on it. However, there is something to be said for the Australian difference of naked naturalness. If Ayers Rock were in Greece the Christian era would have resulted in its having a clutch of monasteries on top: I much prefer the Rock the way it is. Nor would I want an island of the Great Barrier Reef to have the stone ruins of a shoreside bath-house built by some emperor of an early Australian civilization.

It must be an odd experience for a European or a Japanese tourist to travel a country where *nothing*, absolutely nothing, was built by Man until less than two hundred years ago. Although Man had been here for thousands of years he made virtually no mark on the country except some incising of rocks and painting in caves.

The other thing distinctive is that parts of this prehistorically old Australian landscape have suddenly been set with Man-makings that are so remarkably *new*. The tourist can find himself in a town that wasn't there a year ago and is not yet on any map of Australia.

Millions of dollars were being spent at Robe River (W.A.) on building a mining town the company had not decided on a name for. This could only happen in Australia, and the Japanese, who are 35 per cent partners in Robe River's iron ore enterprise, must think it very curious. Not that the Japanese—who have produced three translations of James Joyce's *Ulysses*, which is not translatable—don't do some curious things themselves.

But what the Japanese are doing now vis-à-vis Australia isn't curious: it is, though, momentous.

ON A CLEAR DAY or night (I am speaking reflectively and the clearness has to be in the head) from Australia you can see Japan. It is a small country, but it looks larger. From anywhere in Australia, Japan is beginning to look very large indeed.

It depends, of course, on who is looking—and most Australians aren't, or not very hard, yet. Also it is difficult to see Japan 1971 clearly because Japan 1941 gets in the way. What do *I* see?

There is Japan. It doesn't much matter that I have been there four times. It does matter that I know about what Japanese did to Australians in World War II. (Just after the war I walked over the infamous Death March trail in North Borneo and documented Australia's worst prisoner-of-war tragedy, and what happened was cruel and ghastly.) It may matter that I think Japanese attitudes to war have changed greatly. It does not matter that I have some good Japanese friends, or that there are things about Japan that I dislike and things about Japan that I admire. What really matters is this:

Australia's future—its economy, its standard of living, its almost-everything—depends on Japan. We are not in the position that if the Japanese economy sneezed the Australian economy would catch cold; but we are certainly in the position that if Japan got economic influenza Australia would catch it as well.

The growth rate of the Japanese economy (it had been 10·14 per cent in recent years compared with Australia's 5·5) was certainly prejudiced by the United States' drastic dollar-rescuing measures announced in August 1971. The American 10 per cent surcharge on many imports would affect about US$5,000 million worth of Japanese exports (but not affect Australia's U.S. market very much). The Japanese challenge to the United States' world-leading economy was manifest in the prediction: "The Japanese Gross National Product (the third highest in the world now) could surpass that of the Soviet Union before the end of the 1970s."[3]

Japan, which builds half the world's ships, expects to overtake the

United States in about 1976 as the world's leading steel-maker. Japanese per capita income is expected to exceed that of Britain by 1974, the United States by 1984 and Sweden by 1988, if those countries' present growth rate does not change. If the average Australian is still more prosperous then (as he is now) than the average Japanese, it will be because of Japan's boosting the Australian economy by buying so much of what Australia has to sell. Or, it may well be, in part at least, because of Japanese investment in Australia and Japanese establishment of industries in Australia, particularly heavy industries processing mineral ores.

It is expected that Japan will, before the end of the seventies, be taking 40 per cent of all our exports, about three times as much as Britain or America will take. Already Australia supplies 30 per cent of Japan's iron and coal, more than half its bauxite, a lot of its alumina, copper and nickel; and at the wool sales in Sydney during the month of January 1971 Japanese buyers bought 74·4 per cent of the wool. Japan is buying more and more manufactured goods from Australia, as well as raw materials. Our exports to Japan, which in 1970 had risen to $1,114 million, are expected to rise by 1980 to a staggering $4,000 million—as much as all our exports to all countries are today.

Australia's imports from Japan have been running, in value, less than half, but not much less, of what Japan buys from us. However, as a buyer of $504 million worth (in 1970) of what Japan makes, Australia was a useful customer. As Europe and America withdraw more and more into their own economic blocs and restrict imports, Japan must become increasingly dependent on its other markets. South-East Asia, the Japan Economic Research Centre calculates, will take as high as 42 per cent of its imports from Japan by 1975— if Japan increases its own imports from S.E. Asia and gives countries there aids to economic growth. In short, the "South-East Asia Co-Prosperity Sphere" that Japan tried to bring about by force of arms in World War II Japan is now trying to create by economic means.

Japan obviously thinks of Australia as being in such a sphere. But Australia's place in it is special. Australia is the one country in this region that Japan buys more from than it sells to. And what Japan buys from Australia—raw materials—is vital to the Japanese economy. Without our raw materials Japan's heavy industry—the economic core—would be insecure, even though there are other sources of supply. It is as important to Japan to be able to buy our iron-coal-alumina-nickel as it is to Australia to be able to sell it. The Japanese wish we would find enough oil to be able to sell them some of that, too. The Middle East oil producers' threat in early 1971 to stop supplies unless customers paid more—that worried the Japanese.

So the dependence is mutual. However hard we try to minimize our export dependence on Japan (and, of course, we should try) we can hardly hope to sell our raw materials in anything like the same quantities to Europe or America, which have supplies of their own and other supplies in countries nearer than Australia is. The Japanese know this, and they know we shall try to gain other markets. They are going to do their utmost, as they must do, to see that their raw-material supply from Australia is assured. The best way to do that, of course, is to become part-owners of the mines—as Japanese firms already are in the case of Mt Newman (10 per cent), Savage River iron ore, and Dampier Salt, and will be in Robe River iron ore and Admiralty Gulf alumina. Japanese interests wanted to be involved in Australian oil-gas exploration, too.

These are only the first freshets of what can be expected to come in the way of Japanese investment in Australia. The Yen River should really start to flow, in all the volume Australia will allow, in 1972. This can be expected in consequence of the visit (March 1971) of a most potent group of Japanese big-business men, including bankers, and a visit from the Japanese Minister for Trade and Industry.

Not only has the Japanese Ambassador in Canberra forecast a big increase in Japanese investment here, but their Finance Ministry has, for Japan's 1971 Budget, recommended a 30 per cent increase in funds that can be invested overseas. Existing tax concessions for Japanese investors in overseas oil projects are likely to be extended to investors in overseas nickel, copper and uranium. Japan's nuclear-power programme gives such uranium discoveries as the one at Nabarlek in the Northern Territory special importance in Japanese eyes.

Moreover, an upsurge in Japanese portfolio investment in Australian stocks is likely in the near future.

Donald Horne, the author of *The Lucky Country*[4] and *The Next Australia*,[5] has shown the most acute Australian awareness of the coming Japanese-Australian relationship, particularly in what he has written in February-March 1971 as editor of the Sydney *Bulletin*. He has come right out and asked, *"Are we smart enough to work for the Japanese?"*[6] Horne has slated Australian naïveté in not recognizing that Japanese technocracy and Japanese executive training in decision-making are much superior to and more sophisticated than our own, and he is irked by the Australian slowness to adjust to a new view of the Japanese and see that there is a new geopolitical environment that embraces Australia and South-East Asia.

Earlier I wrote, in a Pilbara chapter, that Kobe Steel, the Japanese steel-maker, might set up at Port Hedland and export steel to South-East Asian countries from there. Donald Horne has gone so far as to say, "It makes economic nonsense for the Japanese to ship Australian ores and coal 5,000 miles to produce basic iron and steel. They could produce it much better and deliver it cheaper if they located their basic steel plants in Australia."[7]

The Australian National University's expert on economic relations with Japan (Peter Drysdale) has argued that Australia and Japan could institute a species of free trade in certain goods, such as types of motor vehicles that could then be sold by as much as 30 per cent cheaper in Australia.

Sir Robert Menzies, when he was Australia's Prime Minister, said about ten years after World War II ended, "Whatever our thoughts about the past . . . we have to live in the same world as Japan." I added, in the preface to a book I wrote on Japan,[8] ". . . not only in the same world, but in the same eastern hemisphere, on the same side of Pacific Street, in the same democratic block, in the same regional House of Asia, where Australia is on the ground floor and Japan is the country upstairs." Nobody would have foreseen, when I wrote that in 1961, the extent to which Japan would be coming downstairs.

The implications for Australia are mind-shaking. One reads that "Japan's Ministry of International Trade and Finance has rushed completion of a university near Tokyo to train the people needed to staff the mines and refineries it hopes Japan will build in foreign countries",[9] such countries as Brazil, Liberia and, of course, Australia.

There goes the White Australia Policy. . . ? (There are many Australians, now, who would say good riddance to it.) One could wonder how many years it will be before as many Australian secondary schools as now teach French are teaching Japanese.

One could even wonder whether the Power that Australia has been fighting alongside in the horrible war in Vietnam would be the Power that Australia would look to if Communist China, a decade from now, went on the warpath south.

Such a contingency is, surely, just this side of unthinkable. Yet the thought squeezes in, and it comes of thinking how far the still-turning wheel of Australia's fortune in relation to Japan has turned since, in World War II, an Australian Prime Minister, the late John Curtin, said, "Australia looks to America"—to save Australia from the Japanese, which the United States did.

I don't want to believe that our world could be stark-mad enough to produce a situation where a belligerent China could produce a nuclear-armed Japan; and that situation produce one that would go beyond irony, with an Australian Prime Minister saying, "Australia looks to Japan."

Reference Notes

PAGE AND
NOTE NO.

PROLOGUE

2/ 1   R. Logan Jack was a Queensland Government Geologist. *Northmost Australia* (2 vols) details the exploration of Cape York Peninsula. (Simpkin, Marshall, Hamilton & Kent, London, 1921).

5/ 2   Evans's report is quoted in *Mountains of Ore* by the former Director of the Commonwealth Bureau of Mineral Resources, Sir Harold Raggatt. (Lansdowne Press, Melbourne, 1968).

THE NEW AUSTRALIA

6/ 1   Henry Lawson in "The Roaring Days" (Lawson's *Poetical Works*, Angus & Robertson, Sydney, 1947).
                    *Their shining Eldorado
                    Beneath the southern skies. . . .*

7/ 2   The Australian dollar is currently (March 1971) worth 46 new pence U.K., or $1.13U.S.

7/ 3   R. T. Madigan, managing director of Hamersley Holdings Ltd.

7/ 4   The only place where nickel ore had been produced in Australia (about 600 tons of it) was near Zeehan on Tasmania's west coast, from a mine abandoned in 1938.

8/ 5   Financial Editor, *Sydney Morning Herald* (T. M. Fitzgerald, who resigned from this position in August 1970).

11/ 6   Charles Mitchell, an Australian businessman, writing in the fortnightly periodical *Nation*, 18th October 1969.

12/ 7   W. D. Borrie, in a paper presented to the Australian and New Zealand Association for the Advancement of Science in Brisbane in 1961, "How Many People can Australia Support?"

20/ 8   Published in 1968 by Heinemann (Melbourne and London).

QUEENSLAND

23/ 1   Comalco Ltd is the parent company of Commonwealth Aluminium Corporation Ltd (bauxite mining at Weipa), Comalco Aluminium (Bell Bay) Ltd (primary aluminium production at Bell Bay, Tasmania) and Comalco Products Pty Ltd (which makes sheet and rod aluminium at Sydney, Perth, Brisbane, Adelaide). Comalco is jointly owned by Conzinc Riotinto of Australia Ltd and Kaiser Aluminium and Chemical Corporation of Oakland, California (45 per cent each, public shareholders 10 per cent).

23/ 2   Commonwealth Scientific and Industrial Research Organization.

30/ 1   In *A Year on the Great Barrier Reef* (Putnam, London and New York, 1930). Dr Yonge led the Great Barrier Reef Expedition of 1928-29.

31/ 2   *Come Away, Pearler* (Angus & Robertson, Sydney, 1952). Paperbacked in Pacific Books (same publisher, 1962): now out of print.

33/ 1   Dr Thomas Wood in *Cobbers* (Oxford University Press, 1935).

35/ 2   Elspeth Huxley in *Their Shining Eldorado: A Journey through Australia* (Chatto & Windus, London, 1967).

36/ 3   Frederick D. McCarthy in *Australia's Aborigines: Their Life and Culture* (Colorgravure Publications, Melbourne, 1957).

44/ 1   *Australian Encyclopaedia*.

PAGE AND
NOTE NO.

45/ 2   From "Five Visions of Captain Cook" first published in *Trio*, poems by Kenneth Slessor, Harley Matthews and Colin Simpson. (Sunnybrook Press, Sydney, 1931).

47/ 3   Angus & Robertson, Sydney, 1968.

58/ 4   *Wonders of the Great Barrier Reef* by T. C. Roughley (Angus & Robertson, Sydney). First published in 1936, it has been many times reprinted.

66/ 5   *A Year on the Great Barrier Reef* by C. M. Yonge (Putnam, London and New York, 1930).

68/ 6   In *The Great Barrier Reef and Adjacent Isles* by Keith Gillett and Frank McNeill (Coral Press, Sydney, 1959).

69/ 7   See 68/ 6.

70/ 1   Elspeth Huxley in *Their Shining Eldorado* (Chatto & Windus, London, 1967).

73/ 2   In *The Rush That Never Ended: A History of Australian Mining* (Melbourne University Press, 1963).

74/ 3   *The Rush That Never Ended* (see 73/ 2).

78/ 1   See 73/ 2.

84/ 1   Vincent Smith in *The National Times*, 5-10 July 1971.

85/ 2   *Australia's Travel and Tourist Industry*, prepared by Harris, Kerr, Forster & Company and Stanton Robbins & Company Inc., New York, for the Australian National Travel Association, 1965.

91/ 1   Penguin Books in association with F. W. Cheshire (Melbourne, 1963).

92/ 2   In a booklet, *Enjoy Australia on a Budget*, distributed overseas by the Australian Tourist Commission and available from its offices in London, New York, San Francisco, Los Angeles, Tokyo and Auckland.

98/ 1   Published in 1940 by W. R. Smith & Paterson, Brisbane.

NEW SOUTH WALES

109/ 1   By John Yeomans (Longmans, London, 1967).

110/ 2   First published by Ure Smith, Sydney, 1957.

112/ 3   Issued by the Australian Tourist Commission.

112/ 4   Issued by the Australian Tourist Commission and available from its overseas offices (see 92/ 2).

124/ 1   *The Australian Encyclopaedia* and Harry Hodge in *The Hill End Story* (2 vols, published by the author at Adamstown Heights, N.S.W.) both say the first stamper battery in Australia operated at Hill End in 1857: Geoffrey Blainey in *The Peaks of Lyell* (Melbourne University Press, 1954) says the first such battery operated at Clunes, Victoria, in 1857.

126/ 2   *Hillendiana* (Ure Smith, Sydney, 1956).

128/ 3   *Guide to Historic Hill End and its Environs* (Hill End Publications, Adamstown Heights, N.S.W.).

129/ 1   Lines from the lyric of the song version, reprinted by arrangement with Allan & Co. Pty Ltd, Sydney.

143/ 1   *Their Shining Eldorado* (Chatto & Windus, London, 1967).

147/ 2   *Adam in Ochre*. First published by Angus & Robertson, Sydney and London, 1951; since paperbacked in Pacific Books (A. & R.). A United States edition (Praeger, New York) is out of print.

151/ 1   First published in the United States by Prentice-Hall; revised edition available in Walkabout Pocketbooks (Ure Smith, Sydney/Horwitz Group Books, London).

154/ 1   *They Struck Opal!* (Associated General Publications, Sydney, undated but 1948).

160/ 1   *The Lightning Ridge Book* by Stuart Lloyd (privately published by the author, 1967).

164/ 1   From *The Snowy—An Appraisal*, Current Affairs Bulletin, vol. 31, no. 13, May 1963 (Department of Tutorial Classes, University of Sydney). The author, "an Australian economic geographer", was not named.

PAGE AND
NOTE NO.

CANBERRA, A.C.T.

187/ 1 In *The Australian Ugliness* (F. W. Cheshire, Melbourne, 1960; Penguin Books Australia, 1963).

187/ 2 In his book entitled *Australia* (Ernest Benn, London, published 1930).

189/ 3 From *The Work of Bunning & Madden, Architects and Town Planners* (privately printed, Sydney, 1970).

194/ 4 Donald Horne's *The Lucky Country* has been an Australian best-seller. (Penguin Books paperback 1964; Angus & Robertson hardback edition 1965).

VICTORIA

203/ 1 In the document written by Kelly at Jerilderie, as a justification of his crimes and as a warning to informers. Known as the Jerilderie Letter, it appears as an appendix to Max Brown's *Australian Son: The Story of Ned Kelly* (Georgian House, Melbourne, 1948). However, the Jerilderie Letter was not, as claimed by the publishers, "a piece of Kellyana which had lain in dust for over sixty years" and was "published for the first time". According to *The Australian Encyclopaedia* it had been published in the *Melbourne Herald* in November 1930. Nevertheless, it is valuable to have it accessible in Max Brown's book.

203/ 2 See 203/ 1.

203/ 3 Max Brown (see 203/ 1).

204/ 4 From the Jerilderie Letter (see 203/ 1).

208/ 1 Sub-titled *The Decay of a Visual Environment*, a study by the Royal Australian Institute of Architects, edited by Donald Gazzard, with many photographs, mainly by David Potts (Ure Smith, Sydney, 1966).

208/ 2 Sub-titled *Considering the Australian Environment*, edited by John Button (F. W. Cheshire, Melbourne, 1968). The text is contributed by an impressive list of architects, planners, designers and authors, and there are excellent photographs.

210/ 3 So described was the not-named writer of *Wildlife Conservation or Carnage?* Current Affairs Bulletin, vol. 37, no. 3, 20th December 1965 (Department of Tutorial Classes, University of Sydney). This C.A.B. was written by Dr A. J. Marshall.

211/ 4 C.S.I.R.O. "experts" were reported as holding this view in an article "Farming—One Way to Save the Kangaroo" by Michael Richardson in *Walkabout*, February 1970.

213/ 1 In the *Australian*, 4th March 1969.

215/ 2 The not-named writer (described as a "well-known and well-considered poet, critic and academic teacher") of *Melbourne*, Current Affairs Bulletin, vol. 32, no. 11, 14th October 1963 (Department of Tutorial Classes, University of Sydney).

215/ 3 *Australian Encyclopaedia.*

216/ 4 Published by Hill of Content, Melbourne, 1968, with photographs by Gordon De'Lisle.

216/ 5 Published by Joey Books, Melbourne, 1969.

217/ 6 In *Melbourne* (see 216/ 4).

221/ 7 "The Year of Anti-Football Protest" by Keith Dunstan in *Walkabout* magazine, April 1968.

222/ 1 In *Lyrebirds Calling from Australia* (Robertson & Mullens), an extract from which appears in *Land of Wonder: The Best Australian Nature Writing* selected by Alec H. Chisholm (Angus & Robertson, Sydney, 1964).

222/ 2 *Australian Encyclopaedia.*

223/ 3 *Australian Encyclopaedia.*

223/ 4 *Guide to Australia* by Osmar White (Heinemann, Melbourne and London, 1968).

224/ 1 *Australian Encyclopaedia.*

224/ 2 *Guide to Australia* (see 223/ 4).

232/ 1 *Australian Encyclopaedia.*

232/ 2 *Modern Encyclopaedia of Australia and New Zealand* (Horwitz-Grahame, Sydney, 1964).

PAGE AND
NOTE NO.

232/ 3   Issue of 11th July 1970.
235/ 1   In the *Melbourne Herald*, 11th March 1969.
235/ 2   E. Crosbie Morrison did in *Phillip Island in Picture and Story* compiled by Joshua Gliddon (published by the Cowes Bush Nursing Hospital Trust Committee, Phillip Island, 1968).
236/ 1   In an article "Three Yanks Down Under" in *Walkabout* magazine, July 1970.
238/ 2   Charles F. Laseron in *The Face of Australia* (Angus & Robertson, Sydney, 1953).
239/ 3   Edited by Geoffrey Dutton, quoted from "Australian Fiction Since 1920" by Harry Heseltine (a Pelican Original, Penguin Books, Ringwood, Vic., 1964).
240/ 4   *Australian Dictionary of Dates and Men of the Time* by J. H. Heaton (George Robertson, Sydney, 1879).
241/ 5   *Australian Encyclopaedia.*
242/ 1   *The Face of Australia* (see 238/ 2).
245/ 1   In an article in *Walkabout*, March 1968. (*The Wines of Australia* was published by Hodder & Stoughton, London and Sydney, in 1967.)
246/ 2   In *Walkabout*, March 1968.

TASMANIA

261/ 1   Michael Sharland in *Tasmania* in the "Around Australia Program" series of booklets (Nelson Doubleday, Sydney, 1966).
261/ 2   The same.
267/ 1   *Australian Encyclopaedia.*
269/ 2   Quoted in *The New World of the South* by W. H. Fitchett (Bell, London, 1913).
269/ 3   The same.
270/ 4   *Australia: Her Story* by Kylie Tennant (Macmillan, London, 1956).
274/ 1   Self-published, apparently, in 1941 in Hobart. Sub-titled *For the First Time—The Truth about the State's Convict History*, with a foreword by the then Premier of Tasmania, Robert Cosgrove.
274/ 2   *Australian Encyclopaedia.*
274/ 3   W. H. Fitchett, *The New World of the South* (see 269/ 2).
274/ 4   Kylie Tennant, *Australia* (see 270/ 4).
274/ 5   Quoted by Lorraine Cazalar in an article "Charles O'Hara Booth: Benevolent Martinet" in *Walkabout*, June 1969.
279/ 1   The issue of *Angry Penguins* (Reed & Harris Publications, Melbourne) was the "1944 Autumn Number to Commemorate the Australian poet, Ern Malley". A cover painting, illustrating lines of Malley verse, was by Sidney Nolan. The exposé appeared in two issues of *Fact* supplement to Sydney *Sunday Sun*, 18th and 25th June 1944.
279/ 2   In *Hobart*, Current Affairs Bulletin, vol. 33, no. 11 (Department of Tutorial Classes, University of Sydney, April 1964). The author, James McAuley, described as "a poet and teacher", was not named, in accordance with C.A.B. practice until 1970.
282/ 3   *Wake Up in Europe* by Colin Simpson (Angus & Robertson, Sydney and London, 1959).
285/ 1   Harris, Kerr, Forster Report, 1965 (see 85/ 1).
289/ 2   Published by Melbourne University Press, 1954.
290/ 3   Geoffrey Blainey in *The Rush That Never Ended* (Melbourne University Press, 1963; 2nd ed. 1969).
290/ 4   See 290/ 3.
290/ 5   See 290/ 3.
292/ 6   In *Narrative of a Visit to the Australian Colonies* (1843) by James Backhouse.
292/ 7   Thomas Dunbabin in *Sailing the World's Edge* (Cape, London, 1931).
292/ 8   *Western Tasmania* by Charles Whitham (published by the Robert Steht Memorial Library, Queenstown, 1949).
294/ 1   In *The Peaks of Lyell* (Melbourne University Press, 1954).
295/ 2   Blainey, *The Peaks of Lyell.*
298/ 3   See 294/ 1.

PAGE AND
NOTE NO.

NORTHERN TERRITORY

304/ 1   Quoted by Ernestine Hill in *The Northern Territory* (Angus & Robertson, Sydney and London, 1951).

304/ 2   *The Tyranny of Distance* by Geoffrey Blainey (Sun Books, Melbourne, 1966).

305/ 3   In *Tourism Plan for Central Australia*, prepared for the Australian Tourist Commission by the American experts Harris, Kerr, Forster & Company, in conjunction with Belt, Collins and Associates Ltd and Wilson, Bishop, Bowes & Craig, June 1969.

306/ 4   In *Their Shining Eldorado* (Chatto & Windus, London, 1967).

306/ 1   *Guide to Australia*, Osmar White (Heinemann, Melbourne & London, 1968).

306/ 2   Charles Laseron in *The Face of Australia* (Angus & Robertson, Sydney, 1953).

307/ 3   The true spinifex occurs on the east and south coasts as *Spinifex hirsutus* growing in sand—a creeping, thorny silvery grass sometimes called rolling grass—and on northern and southern seafronts as *S. longifolius* (according to the *Australian Encyclopaedia*). The green hummocks with long needle-like points that are so widespread inland are of a distinctively Australian genus, *Triodia*, of which there are thirty species. Although in Central and South Australia it is sometimes called porcupine-grass it is generally referred to as spinifex. Such authors as Charles Laseron, Professor O. H. K. Spate ("a grass as spiky as its name"), Geoffrey Blainey (*Mines in the Spinifex*), Charles Mountford, Jeff Carter and other writers about the inland use "spinifex", and I think it would be pedantic and pretentious for me not to.

308/ 4   *Tourism Plan for Central Australia*. Report from Harris, Kerr, Forster & Company to the Australian Tourist Commission (30th June 1969).

309/ 5   F. D. McCarthy, the Australian anthropologist who is the world authority on Aboriginal material culture, writing in the *Australian Encyclopaedia*.

313/ 1   First published in 1963 by Rigby of Adelaide, then in 1969 as a Seal Books paperback.

313/ 2   Same source as above.

313/ 3   *The Significance of Ayers Rock for Aborigines* (Commonwealth Government Printer, Darwin, 1968).

313/ 4   Published in 1965 by Angus & Robertson, Sydney and London.

314/ 5   Professor W. E. H. Stanner, anthropologist, of the Australian National University.

314/ 6   In his *Ayers Rock* (see note 4, above).

314/ 7   Issue of June-August 1969.

314/ 8   Same source as 314/ 7.

315/ 9   C. P. Mountford, *Ayers Rock* (note 4, above).

315/10   *Inland Review*, issue of June-August 1969.

315/11   Same source as note 10.

316/12   According to Arthur Groom in *I Saw a Strange Land* (Angus & Robertson, Sydney and London, 1950).

316/13   Published by Guinness Superlatives Ltd, London, 1968.

317/14   Charles F. Laseron in *The Face of Australia* (Angus & Robertson, Sydney and London, 1953).

319/15   *The Red Centre* by H. H. Finlayson (Angus & Robertson, Sydney, 1935).

319/16   C. P. Mountford in *Ayers Rock* (Angus & Robertson, Sydney and London, 1965).

320/17   In *To Ayers Rock and Beyond* (see 313/ 1).

320/18   Same source as note 17.

321/19   Charles F. Laseron, *The Face of Australia* (Angus & Robertson, Sydney and London, 1953).

321/20   *Ayers Rock* (see 319/16).

321/21   *To Ayers Rock and Beyond* (see 313/ 1).

323/22   Same source as note 21 above.

323/23   *I Saw a Strange Land* (Angus & Robertson, Sydney and London, 1950).

323/24   In the above.

582   REFERENCE NOTES

PAGE AND
NOTE NO.

323/25   H. H. Finlayson, *The Red Centre* (Angus & Robertson, Sydney, 1935).
323/26   In *The Sydney Morning Herald*, 11th July 1970.
324/27   *Greece: The Unclouded Eye* (Angus & Robertson, Sydney, 1968; Hodder & Stoughton, London, 1969; Fielding Publications/Morrow, New York, 1969).
324/28   In *The Red Centre* (see 323/25).
325/29   *I Saw a Strange Land* (see 323/23).
327/ 1   Both plans were prepared by a team representing: Belt, Collins & Associates Ltd, engineers, planners and landscape architects; Harris, Kerr, Forster & Company, hotel and travel consultants and accountants; Wilson, Bishop, Bowes & Craig, accountants. All three are United States organizations. The two reports were submitted from the Honolulu office of Harris, Kerr, Forster & Company.
328/ 2   In the report *Ayers Rock—Mt Olga National Park Development Plan*, June 1969 (see 327/ 1).
332/ 3   According to the report *Tourism Plan for Central Australia* (see 305/ 3, 327/ 1).
336/ 1   In *I Saw a Strange Land* (Angus & Robertson, Sydney and London, 1950).
345/ 1   *Modern English Usage*, Oxford University Press.
345/ 2   My copy from the Anti-Slavery Society, Denison House, 296 Vauxhall Bridge, London, S.W.1.
346/ 3   In an address on Aboriginal health to the Australasian College of Physicians, 5th June 1969.
346/ 4   Professor of Anthropology and Sociology at the Institute of Advanced Studies at the Australian National University, Canberra, in the Boyer Lectures 1968, delivered over A.B.C. radio and published as a booklet, *After the Dreaming* (Australian Broadcasting Commission, Sydney, 1969).
347/ 5   "Respiratory Infections in Australian Aboriginal Children", by Professor G. M. Maxwell and R. B. Elliott, *Medical Journal of Australia*, 30th November 1968.
347/ 6   Statistics issued by the Commonwealth Department of Health, Canberra, 1968.
347/ 7   *Report from the Joint Committee of the Legislative Council and Legislative Assembly (N.S.W.) upon Aborigines Welfare*, September 1967.
347/ 8   Commonwealth Department of Health statistics, 1968.
347/ 9   See 346/ 3.
349/10   See 346/ 4.
350/11   In the revised edition of *Adam in Ochre* (Angus & Robertson, Sydney and London, 1962).
350/12   As reported in the *Bulletin*, Sydney, in an article "What Do the Aborigines Want", which contained the manifesto from which I have quoted, issue of 24th October 1970.
350/13   See 350/12. The term "The Man" does not necessarily mean the white man, although it does in this context. Today's White American revolutionaries, as well as Black Power ones, use "The Man" to signify the authorities or the Establishment.
354/14   Amagula's talk is published, along with other addresses at the Seminar, in a book *Aboriginal Progress: A New Era* (University of Western Australia Press, 1969).
357/ 1   In the Australian anthropological journal *Mankind*, vol. 5, no. 12, November 1962.
360/ 1   *Beef Cattle in the North*, Current Affairs Bulletin, vol. 38, no. 9, 19th September 1966 (Department of Tutorial Classes, University of Sydney). The author is described as having "an academic background of agricultural economics and wide professional experience in the areas concerned".
360/ 2   B. R. Davidson, Senior Lecturer in Agricultural Economics, University of Sydney, in *The Northern Myth* (Melbourne University Press, 1965).
360/ 3   *Beef Cattle in the North* (see 360/ 1).
363/ 4   Particularly in his book *Aboriginal Men of High Degree* (Australasian Publishing Co., Sydney 1945).

PAGE AND
NOTE NO.

365/ 5   Published by the New York Graphic Society by arrangement with UNESCO, with a preface by Sir Herbert Read and text by Charles P. Mountford.

365/ 6   Percy Trezise has written a lively and excellently illustrated book about his cave finds, *Quinkan Country* (A. H. & A. W. Reed, Sydney and Auckland, 1969).

365/ 7   In the preface referred to in 365/ 5.

366/ 8   Charles P. Mountford, *Aboriginal Paintings from Australia* (Fontana Unesco Art Books/Collins, 1964). See also 365/ 5.

367/ 9   *Records of the American-Australian Expedition to Arnhem Land, 1948*, vol. 1, "Art & Mythology", by Charles P. Mountford (Melbourne University Press, 1956).

367/10   Mountford (see 365/ 8).

369/11   First published by Angus & Robertson in 1951. Revised edition 1962.

370/12   *Linkletter Down Under* by Art Linkletter (Ure Smith, Sydney; Prentice-Hall, Englewood Cliffs, New Jersey, 1968).

370/13   See 369/11.

370/14   In *The Front Door: Darwin 1869-1969* (Rigby, Adelaide, 1968).

371/15   Elspeth Huxley in *Their Shining Eldorado* (Chatto & Windus, London, 1967).

371/16   In *The Northern Myth* (see 360/ 2).

372/ 1   Douglas Lockwood in *The Front Door: Darwin 1869-1969* (Rigby, Adelaide, 1968).

374/ 2   *Australia's Travel and Tourist Industry*, report by Harris, Kerr, Forster & Company and Stanton Robbins & Company Inc. (for the Australian National Travel Association, 1965).

376/ 3   Professor A. P. Elkin in *The Australian Aborigines: How to Understand Them*, 3rd ed. (Angus & Robertson, 1954).

376/ 4   Elkin (see 376/ 3).

377/ 5   *In Northern Seas*, published in Adelaide, 1905.

379/ 6   Frank Stevens, "Territory Welfare—A 'Myth'?" in *Aboriginal Quarterly*, vol. 1, no. 1, March 1968 (published by Abschol, Aboriginal Affairs Department of N.U.A.U.S., Australian National University, Canberra).

379/ 7   Written by Colonel Patrick Montgomery, Secretary of the Anti-Slavery Society for the Protection of Human Rights, and published in London in 1970.

379/ 8   In the article in *Aboriginal Quarterly* (see 379/ 6).

379/ 9   From a booklet by Frank Stevens called *Equal Wages for Aborigines* (Aura Press, Sydney, 1968).

379/10   F. Lancaster Jones in *A Demographic Survey of the Aboriginal Population of the Northern Territory* (Australian Institute of Aboriginal Affairs, Canberra, 1963).

379/11   Director of Adult Education, University of Sydney, in an article on inadequacies in Aboriginal policy, *Sydney Morning Herald*, 17th November 1970).

380/ 1   As quoted by Ernestine Hill in *The Territory* (Angus & Robertson, Sydney, 1951).

381/ 2   *Proceedings of the Royal Society of New South Wales, 1888*.

385/ 3   *Australian Encyclopaedia*.

386/ 1   Ronald M. and Catherine H. Berndt in *Arnhem Land: Its History and People* (Cheshire, Melbourne, 1954).

387/ 2   See 386/ 1.

387/ 3   See 386/ 1.

390/ 4   C. C. Macknight, Lecturer in History at the School of General Studies, Australian National University, Canberra, in an article, "Groote Eylandt Interpreted" in the *B.H.P. Journal*, May 1970.

393/ 1   In *Australian Book Review*, August 1970.

393/ 2   In *Mountains of Ore* by H. G. Raggatt (Lansdowne Press, Melb., 1968).

394/ 3   In *Arnhem Land* (Cheshire, Melbourne, 1954).

398/ 4   Issue of 6th October 1970.

PAGE AND
NOTE NO.

SOUTH AUSTRALIA

403/ 1   D. F. Pike, *Paradise of Dissent* (Longmans, London, 1957).
404/ 2   *Adelaide*, Current Affairs Bulletin, vol. 36, no. 1, May 1965 (Department of Tutorial Classes, University of Sydney).
405/ 3   *Australian Encyclopaedia.*
409/ 1   J. H. Calaby writing on "The Numbat of South-Western Australia" in *A Treasury of Australian Wildlife* edited by D. F. McMichael (Ure Smith, Sydney, 1967).
409/ 2   The same.
409/ 3   From *Land of Wonder: The Best Australian Nature Writing* selected by Alec H. Chisholm (Angus & Robertson, Sydney, 1964).
415/ 1   Writing in the Sydney *Bulletin*, 28th November 1970.
416/ 1   Charles F. Laseron in *The Face of Australia* (Angus & Robertson, Sydney, 1953).
416/ 2   The same.
417/ 3   In the *Australian Amateur Mineralogist*, September 1960.
421/ 1   See 416/ 1.
430/ 1   Major Edmund Lockyer, founder of Albany, W.A., quoted by Thomas Dunbabin in his *Sailing the World's Edge* (Cape, London, 1931).
439/ 1   Author of *Wine in Australia, A Word-book of Wine*, etc., writing in *Winegrowers' Diary 1969* (published by S. Wynn & Co., winegrowers at Modbury, Magill and Coonawarra in South Australia and Yenda in New South Wales).
441/ 2   In his "Cellarmaster" column in the *Bulletin*, Sydney, 30th May 1970.
442/ 1   Issue of 16th January 1970.
445/ 2   From his poem "Ye Weary Wayfarer", in *An Anthology of Australian Verse* chosen by George Mackaness (Angus & Robertson, Sydney, 1952).
445/ 3   "Love's Coming", in *The Penguin Book of Modern Australian Verse* edited by John Thompson, Kenneth Slessor and R. G. Howarth (Penguin Books, 1961).
446/ 4   *Australian Encyclopaedia.*
447/ 5   According to Pamela Harris in an article "Hold That Tiger!" in *Walkabout*, June 1968.

WESTERN AUSTRALIA

450/ 1   Published by Constable, London, 1959 (also available as a Corgi paperback).
451/ 2   Published by the University of Western Australia Press, Nedlands, W.A., 1967.
454/ 3   In *The Northern Myth* (Melbourne University Press, 1965).
454/ 4   Director of the Research School of Pacific Studies, Australian National University, in *Australia* (Ernest Benn, London; T. C. Lothian, Melbourne, 1968).
454/ 5   O. H. K. Spate, *Australia* (see 454/ 4).
455/ 6   In *The Northern Myth* (see 454/ 3).
458/ 1   *The Face of Australia* by Charles F. Laseron (Angus & Robertson, Sydney and London, 1953).
471/ 1   *Under the Iron Rainbow* (Heinemann, Melbourne and London).
472/ 2   The story of Roman Catholic Missions in the Kimberley (Constable, London, 1969).
475/ 1   *Encyclopaedia Britannica.*
479/ 2   In *The Sunday Australian*, 27th June 1971.
488/ 1   P. Middleton, in a paper "Comfort in Dwellings in Towns" delivered at a Symposium on Northern Development/Pilbara Prospects in the 1970s.
490/ 2   Director of the Australian Institute of Aboriginal Studies, Canberra.
491/ 3   "Pilbara Rock Galleries", *B.H.P. Journal*, Autumn 1971.
494/ 1   In his book *Australia's North-West* (University of Western Australia Press, Perth, 1967).
498/ 1   *Mining Handbook to the Colony of Western Australia*, 1894.
500/ 2   *Jobson's Investment Digest*, 19th March 1970.

PAGE AND
NOTE NO.

500/ 3   In the *Bulletin*, 7th November 1970.
500/ 4   The same.
500/ 5   See 500/ 2.
503/ 1   *Symposium on Northern Development: Pilbara Prospects in the 1970's* under the auspices of the Institution of Engineers, Australia (Perth Division), May 1968, University of Western Australia, (Government Printer, W.A.).
505/ 2-4 Same source; Mr Madigan's paper, "Mineral Development in the Pilbara".
506/ 5-7 Same source.
507/ 8   Report of Mr Callaghan's talk on "Perils and Pitfalls of the Seventies" to the American Chamber of Commerce in Australia, *The Australian*, 8th July 1970.
508/ 1   *C.S.I.R.O. Rangelands Research Programme*, by R. A. Perry (Canberra, 1968).
509/ 2   *Wildflowers of the Northwest*, booklet by J. S. Beard (Westviews, Perth, undated).
512/ 3   In *Show Me A Mountain*, The Rise of an Australian Company, Ampol (Angus & Robertson, Sydney, 1961).
513/ 4   *Under the Iron Rainbow*: Northwest Australia Today (Heinemann, Melbourne and London, 1969).
514/ 5   *Guide to Australia* (Heinemann, Melbourne and London, 1968).
516/ 1   Mr W. L. Williams, assistant director, petroleum exploration, in the Department's Bureau of Mineral Resources, quoted by Mr J. M. Flower, director of the Petroleum Information Bureau (Australia) in *The Sydney Morning Herald*, 20th July 1970.
522/ 1   Peter Cowan, Perth-born author and senior lecturer in English at the University of Western Australia, was the writer of *Perth*, Current Affairs Bulletin, vol. 37, no. 7, 21st February 1966. (Department of Tutorial Classes, University of Sydney.)
525/ 2   Same source.
528/ 3   *Australia's Travel and Tourist Industry*, a report by Harris, Kerr, Forster & Company/Stanton Robbins & Co. Inc., New York, 1965.
529/ 1   Issue of August 1968.
530/ 2   *Giant in the Sun* (published by the author, Perth, 1968).
530/ 3   Published by Angus & Robertson, Sydney and London, 1967.
531/ 4   In *Walkabout* (see 529/ 1).
531/ 5   In *Landforms of Australia* (see 530/ 3).
543/ 1   Ivan O'Riley in *Walkabout* magazine, August 1968.
543/ 2   Author of *Cobbers* (Oxford University Press, 1935).
546/ 3   Published by Landfall Press, Perth, 1968.
546/ 4   According to *The Australian Encyclopaedia*.
548/ 5   *Linkletter Down Under* (Prentice-Hall, Englewood Cliffs, N.J., U.S.A./ Ure Smith, Sydney, 1968).
549/ 6   Same source.
553/ 1   The *Bulletin*, Sydney, 16th January 1971.
553/ 2   Issue of 7th November 1970.
556/ 3   Geoffrey Blainey, *The Rush That Never Ended* (Melbourne University Press, 1963, 2nd ed. 1969).
556/ 4   Same source.
566/ 1   In *Landforms of Australia* (Angus & Robertson, Sydney and London, 1967).
568/ 2   Professor Keith Campbell in *Wheat*, Current Affairs Bulletin, vol. 45, no. 1, December 1969 (Department of Tutorial Classes, University of Sydney).
568/ 3   *The History of the Merredin District of Western Australia* by F. A. Law (Merredin Road Board, 1961).
568/ 4   In the *National Times* (a Sydney weekly review) issue of February 8-13, 1971.

PAGE AND
NOTE NO.

569/ 5   The *Australian Economic Review*, December 1970. Responsibility for the
          views expressed were taken by University Professors R. F. Henderson,
          R. Downing, J. O. N. Perkins, A. G. Lloyd, and Dr D. S. Ironmonger
          (Editor of the *Review*). Published by the Institute of Social Research
          and Applied Economics, Melbourne.

569/ 6   Mr Brian Beedham's review in *The Economist*, London, of August 22-8,
          1970, headed "Australia, She'll be Right" was restructured by him and
          published under the title "Australia—1980?" in the Current Affairs
          Bulletin, vol. 47, no. 6, February 1971. (Department of Tutorial Classes,
          University of Sydney.)

570/ 1   N. McCusker, Commissioner of Railways, New South Wales, writing in
          Nat/Dev, journal of the Department of National Development, Canberra,
          issue of June 1970.

571/ 2   *The Australian Encyclopaedia* (Angus & Robertson, Sydney and London,
          1958).

573/ 3   Arthur Stockwin, an Australian National University historian on study
          leave in Japan, in *Japan and Asia*, Current Affairs Bulletin, vol. 47, no. 7,
          22nd February 1971. (Department of Tutorial Classes, University of
          Sydney.)

575/ 4   Subtitled *Australia in the Sixties* (Penguin Books, Ringwood, Victoria,
          1964).

575/ 5   Published by Angus & Robertson, Sydney and London, 1970).

575/ 6   *The Bulletin*, Sydney, issue of 27th February 1971.

576/ 7   *The Bulletin*, 13th March 1971.

576/ 8   *The Country Upstairs*, Aust. ed. title (Angus & Robertson, Sydney and
          London, 1956, 2nd revised-enlarged ed. 1969); U.K. ed., *Picture of Japan*
          (Hodder & Stoughton, London, 1966); U.S.A. ed., *Japan: An Intimate
          View* (A. S. Barnes, New York 1959, revised-enlarged ed. 1969).

576/ 9   *The Australian*, issue of 4th November 1970, from its Tokyo correspon-
          dent, Gregory Clark.

INDEX

INDEX

Aborigines, 344-55, 376-86, 472-4; art of, 140, 147, 244, 321-2, 334, 337, 353, 357, 365-7, 384, 386, 397, 423, 459, 490, 491, 495; burial customs of, 462; dances of, 374-5; and drink, 80, 465, 473; education of, 346, 376, 377, 378, 401, 466; employment problems, 346, 370-1, 379, 509; government policy on, 344-50, 377, 378-9, 390 (*see also* land rights); grants to States for, 379; health of, 346, 347-8, 379, 390; land rights, 346-7, 348-50, 385-8, 392-9; legends and beliefs, 313-16, 334, 343, 362, 363, 415; marriage customs, 338, 376, 391; missions, *see* Missions; Montgomery Report on, 345-7, 349, 379; National Tribal Council, 350; of Gove, 351, 387, 392-3, 394, 395, 396, 397; of Groote Eylandt, 387, 389-90; of Tasmania, 262-3, 268, 269-70; place names of, 103; population statistics, 262-3, 304, 345, 376, 377; reserves and settlements, 27-8, 333, 340, 345, 347, 349, 350, 352, 376, 378, 379, 380, 387, 390, 421 (*see also* Missions); sealers and, 430; social services payments to, 348, 376; trust funds for, 386, 389, 390; voting rights, 345
Abortion, 403
Adaminaby (N.S.W.), 169, 173
Adelaide (S.A.), 403-8; Art Gallery, 406; Bonython Hall, 406; Botanic Gardens, 406; churches of, 403; Conservatorium of Music, 404; Festival of Arts, 404-5, 406-7; Government House, 406; Light's plan for, 405; museum, 406; North Terrace, 406; population, 404; public library, 406; restaurants, 407-8; university, 406
Adelaide River (N.T.), 370
Admiralty Gulf (W.A.), 7, 456, 575
Advertising billboards, 436
Agnew (W.A.), 564
Agnew, Garrick, 499
Air Beef scheme, 460
Airline services, 18, 66, 129, 155, 305, 330, 331, 340. *See also* names of airlines
Airlines of N.S.W., 129, 155
Airlines of S.A., 426
Albany (W.A.), 543-5
Albatross Bay (Qld), 23
Albrecht, Rev. F. W., 353

Albury (N.S.W.), 181-2, 183
Alcan of Canada, 71
Alcoa of Australia (W.A.), 534-5, 537
Alectown (N.S.W.), 140
Alexandra Bay (Qld), 40
Alexandra Headland (Qld), 96, 97
Alexandria station (N.T.), 361
Alice Springs (N.T.), 303, 304, 305, 307-10, 330, 331, 336, 351
Allendale (S.A.), 445
Alligator Rivers (N.T.), 361, 365, 366, 367, 370, 384
Almond-growing, 411
Alumina/aluminium: N.T., 392, 393; Qld, 4-5, 7, 24, 27, 71; Tas., 27, 262, 266, 300; W.A., 7, 456, 534-5, 537, 574. *See also* Bauxite
Aluminum Company of America, 535
Alwest Ltd, 537
Amagula, Nandjiwara, 353, 389
Amax Mining (Aust.) Inc., 456, 485, 508
American River (S.A.), 431
Ampol Exploration Ltd, 513
Ampol Petroleum Ltd, 297, 512, 513, 515
Anaconda Mining Co., 555
Andamooka (S.A.), 154, 155
Andrews, Ossie, 317-18
Angas Downs station (N.T.), 312
Angelas iron deposits (W.A.), 478, 508
Anglesea (Vic.), 237
Animal and bird sanctuaries: Qld, 85-8, 95, 96; S.A., 409, 418-19, 428, 432, 433, 440; Tas., 270; Vic., 207, 208. *See also* National parks and nature reserves; Wildlife protection bodies
Ansett (airlines and transport), 18, 19, 25, 55, 60, 335, 338, 442, 450
Anti-Slavery Society for Protection of Human Rights, 345, 346-7
Antimony, 8, 151
Apollo Bay (Vic.), 237
Apple-growing, 282-3
Arafura Sea, 399, 400, 401
Archer River (Qld), 25
Argyle station (W.A.), 450, 453
Arkaroola (S.A.), 415-21
Armco Steel Corporation, 178, 478
Armidale (N.S.W.), 149-51
Arnhem Land (N.T.), 306, 358-68, 380-400; expedition to (1948), 313, 358-9
Arup, Ove, 109